CW01024499

ARAB MEDIA IN THE

INFORMATION AGE

ARAB MEDIA IN THE INFORMATION AGE

THE EMIRATES CENTER FOR STRATEGIC
STUDIES AND RESEARCH

THE EMIRATES CENTER FOR STRATEGIC STUDIES AND RESEARCH

The Emirates Center for Strategic Studies and Research (ECSSR) is an independent research institution dedicated to the promotion of professional studies and educational excellence in the UAE, the Gulf and the Arab world. Since its establishment in Abu Dhabi in 1994, ECSSR has served as a focal point for scholarship on political, economic and social matters. Indeed, ECSSR is at the forefront of analysis and commentary on Arab affairs.

The Center seeks to provide a forum for the scholarly exchange of ideas by hosting conferences and symposia, organizing workshops, sponsoring a lecture series and publishing original and translated books and research papers. ECSSR also has an active fellowship and grant program for the writing of scholarly books and for the translation into Arabic of work relevant to the Center's mission. Moreover, ECSSR has a large library including rare and specialized holdings, and a state-of-the-art technology center, which has developed an award-winning website that is a unique and comprehensive source of information on the Gulf.

Through these and other activities, ECSSR aspires to engage in mutually beneficial professional endeavors with comparable institutions worldwide, and to contribute to the general educational and scientific development of the UAE.

The views expressed in this book do not necessarily reflect those of the ECSSR.

First published in 2006 by
The Emirates Center for Strategic Studies and Research
PO Box 4567, Abu Dhabi, United Arab Emirates

E-mail: pubdis@ecssr.ae
Website: http://www.ecssr.ae

ISBN 9948-00-819-7 hardback edition
ISBN 9948-00-818-9 paperback edition

CONTENTS

[vii]

[ix]

SECTION 9: INFLUENCE OF ARAB GOVERNMENTS ON THE MEDIA

[x]

ABBREVIATIONS AND ACRONYMS

AAI	Arab American Institute
ADL	Anti-Defamation League
ADSL	Asymmetric Digital Subscriber Line
AEI	American Enterprise Institute
AIDS	Acquired Immune Deficiency Syndrome
AIPAC	American Israel Public Affairs Committee
ALECSO	Arab League Educational, Cultural and Scientific Organization
BBG	Broadcasting Board of Governors
BMENA	Broader Middle East and North Africa
BSE	Bovine Spongiform Encephalopathy
CAIR	Council on American-Islamic Relations
CIA	Central Intelligence Agency
CPJ	Committee to Protect Journalists
ART	Arab Radio and Television
BBC	British Broadcasting Corporation
CNE	Cable Network Egypt
CNN	Cable News Network
CPA	Coalition Provisional Authority
CRS	Congressional Research Service
CSIS	Center for Strategic and International Studies
DMC	Dubai Media City
DIC	Dubai Internet City
DoD	Department of Defense
ERTU	Egyptian Radio and Television Union
EPW	enemy prisoner of war
FAIR	Fairness and Accuracy in Reporting
FBI	Federal Bureau of Investigation

ICT	information and communication technologies
ICTDAR	Information and Communication Technology for Development in Arab Region
ICMC	Iraq Communications and Media Commission
IFA	Institut für Auslandsbeziehungen
IGC	Iraqi Governing Council
IIG	Interim Iraqi Government
IIP	International Information Programs
IMN	Iraqi Media Network
IOWG	Information Operations Working Groups
IT	information technology
ITU	International Telecommunications Union
JINSA	Jewish Institute for National Security Affairs
LD	line of departure
MBC	Middle East Broadcasting Centre
MEMRI	Middle East Media Research Institute
MEPI	Middle East Partnership Initiative
METN	Middle East Television Network
LBC	Lebanese Broadcasting Corporation
MPC	Media Production City
MTV	Music Television
NAACP	National Association for the Advancement of Colored People
NATO	North Atlantic Treaty Organization
NBC	National Broadcasting Company
NGO	non-governmental organization
NLP	natural language processing
PAG	Public Affairs Guidance
PARC	Pan-Arab Research Centre
PCC	Policy Coordinating Committee

RFE	Radio Free Europe
RL	Radio Liberty
SAIC	Scientific Applications International Corporation
SCIRI	Supreme Council for the Islamic Revolution in Iraq
TBS	Transnational Broadcasting Studies
UAE	United Arab Emirates
UAEnic	United Arab Emirates Network Information Centre
UNDP	United Nations Development Program
UNESCO	United Nations Educational, Scientific and Cultural Organization
UNRWA	United Nations Relief and Works Agency
USIP	United States Institute of Peace
VOA	Voice of America
WINEP	Washington Institute for Near East Policy
WMD	weapons of mass destruction

FOREWORD

During the past few years, the Arab media environment has witnessed many qualitative changes stemming from the requirements of media operations conducted in an open arena, which is flooded with a massive, round-the-clock flow of news, data and information from all over the world, transcending geographical barriers and national borders.

A glance at the current Arab media scene will reveal that the achievements thus far, though difficult to ignore in qualitative and quantitative terms, have been insufficient to satisfy the aspirations of the Arab peoples, considering the historical situation of the Arab world and its current challenges. Hence, there is an urgent need to introduce substantial changes in the Arab media's structure and discourse: liberating it from intrusive state control; reforming existing legislation and policies; unleashing freedom of opinion and expression, strengthening the culture of plurality, dialogue and respect for differing and opposing viewpoints; and developing the media's professional and technological potential.

Recognizing the media's primary role in improving current conditions in the Arab world and in advancing Arab societies, and acknowledging the importance of developing the Arab media in harmony with the values of the era, thus enabling it to respond to global transformations and to cope with the information and communications revolution in the first decade of the 21st century, the Emirates Center for Strategic Studies and Research (ECSSR) held its Tenth Annual Conference in Abu Dhabi from January 9–11, 2005 to address the theme of *Arab Media in the Information Age.*

The conference aimed to examine the realities of the Arab media, assess its performance, discourse and content and investigate its societal functions. It also sought to measure the Arab media's influence in forming Arab public opinion, and its role in shaping western perceptions about Arabs.

Since media organizations remain concerned about the problems of dependency, credibility and relations between the media on the one hand, and commercial interests and political influences on the other, the conference exerted serious efforts to study these significant issues while drawing comparisons with the experience of the western media. Moreover, the conference discussed the media's role during wartime, the impact of occupation on the media, the growing influence of the Internet in Arab societies and other vital topics.

With a view to achieving its aims and enriching its discussions, the conference assembled a group of elite, renowned experts, academics and media professionals from within and beyond the Arab world, to present their research findings and participate in the conference deliberations and activities.

It cannot be claimed that the conference produced decisive answers and solutions to Arab media problems and shortcomings. Yet it did highlight some of its structural flaws and weaknesses and offered the participants complete freedom to suggest their own approaches to tackle these imbalances. It may be argued that the conference raised many questions, predicaments and challenges that call for responses in order to promote the Arab media network's efforts to adapt to the Information Age.

In conclusion, I would like to express my sincere thanks and appreciation to the researchers and media experts who generously contributed their ideas, viewpoints, vital experiences and expertise. My thanks are also due to the team of editors, translators, proofreaders and typesetters of the ECSSR Department of Publications for their painstaking effort to compile and publish the conference papers in this volume.

Jamal S. Al-Suwaidi, Ph.D.
Director General
ECSSR

INTRODUCTION

Arab Media in the Information Age: An Overview

The revolution in communications and information technology has helped to usher in the sweeping changes that the Arab media has witnessed during the last decade of the 20th century. The Arab media has responded positively to these far-reaching effects by improving its existing capabilities in order to take advantage of the opportunities offered by this revolution. The so-called "new wave" media has emerged, represented by Arab satellite channels, on-line newspapers and magazines, and the news websites on the Internet.

The current media situation in the Arab world appears quite different from the past, when it was characterized by local state-run TV and radio stations and newspapers, which were used as instruments for fostering domestic policies, strengthening stability and national identity and consolidating the national government's domination.

Media activities in the Arab world have gained greater momentum in the past years with an unprecedented increase in all its component elements. For example, the emerging satellite channels, with their influence transcending national borders, have widened the margins of freedom and plurality, offered an alternative perspective from that of the state, ended the monopoly of news reporting by the western media, and placed the Arab media under the spotlight in the global arena.

Editorial Note: This volume contains several chapters translated from Arabic papers. Hence the quotations in these chapters represent a translated version rather than the exact wording of the original text.

[3]

Nevertheless, the Arab media is still suffering from some structural shortcomings and flaws, both in terms of the media domain itself and the socio-political conditions prevailing in Arab societies. Thus, issues relating to the Arab media cannot be addressed in isolation from the broader environment in which it functions, derives its inputs and generates its outputs. Such an approach, however, does not imply that the relationship between the media and society is a static one. Rather, the two parts are inextricably linked and exert mutual influence on each other.

The current situation necessitates a comprehensive review of the Arab media's performance, problems and weaknesses with a view to rationalizing its course of action and enabling it to fulfill the roles expected by Arab societies. In this context, freedom is viewed as the most vital prerequisite for the advancement of the Arab media, the absence of which represents the main obstacle that impedes its progress. Regardless of the extent to which the Arab media is empowered with the resources and the ability to use information technologies, it cannot move towards new horizons unless it is released from the government laws and restrictions that curtail its independence and freedom.

Yet, how can media freedom become a reality in societies inherently lacking basic freedoms? Freedom is indivisible, and any demand for media freedom cannot be achieved unless it forms part of a broader bid to pursue other freedoms. Similarly, is it possible to talk about media freedom when the instruments of the media are under the control of ruling regimes?

The modern media is playing the role of a catalyst, a mechanism that creates a favorable climate for developing civil society and introducing social changes in the Arab world by widening the base of participation in general debates and creating the "public space" required by civil society organizations to voice their stances, viewpoints and interests.

On the other hand, the UNDP Arab Human Development Report of 2003 has noted the weak role the media network plays in motivating Arab societies to acquire knowledge. For example, it is obvious that meaningful, educative and knowledge-oriented programs are often absent from the Arab satellite channels. Rather, the Arab media content is laden with sleazy, worthless and mostly sensational forms of amusement that have grave negative effects on the perceptions and values of Arab audiences, especially in view of the increasing influence of media on educational and social institutions and other entities.

Given the deterioration in the efficacy of traditional education, the Arab region will have to employ the mass media – the visual media in particular – as a means to achieve its desired developmental goals, without relinquishing its entertainment function by presenting programs that offer aesthetic delights and refined enjoyment.

In addition, the growing impact of commercial interests on the Arab media content is also felt, particularly with the establishment of satellite TV stations in recent years. The greater the revenue intake that the media outlet commands, the bigger is the impact of commercial considerations in shaping both the kind of programs it broadcasts and the content thereof. Producers of these stations are now facing the challenge of injecting new content on a daily basis. The dilemma surfaces when these producers encounter the sort of pressures that oblige them to opt for "short cuts" by importing or imitating selected western media works that have proved successful elsewhere instead of developing their own creative talents in this field.

The media has been one of the key factors affecting international relations. Through the creation of exclusive news satellite channels, *Al Jazeera* in particular, the Arab media has played an effective role in influencing regional and perhaps international policies. While the debate after the 1991 Gulf War concentrated on the "CNN effect," the focus after September 11 and during the Afghanistan and Iraq wars was on the "*Al Jazeera* effect." No evidence better demonstrates the strength of this factor than the US being forced to launch the Arabic-speaking *Al Hurra* satellite channel in response to *Al Jazeera* in particular, and other Arab news channels, in general.

[5]

On the other hand, since the events of September 11, it is difficult to find positive reporting about Arabs in the western and the American press, which are now concentrating on the negative aspects in the Arab world. The question is: In what way has the Arab media contributed to such a situation?

It appears that Arab media institutions design their programs and outputs primarily to suit their respective audiences—the Arab recipients who possess access to communication technologies. Moreover, there has been no interaction between Arab and western media outlets. The Arab media, for instance, has no access to American viewers, and the US media are only supplied with negative images and stereotypes that are conveyed to the American spectators who tend to shape their perspectives about the Arab world accordingly.

Until the Arab media starts presenting the US public with more positive images about Arabs, it would be impossible to alter their negative perspectives. The Arab media, moreover, will have to face the challenge of openness and interaction with the western media so as to rectify the distorted picture of Arabs and Muslims now prevailing in the West and the entire world.

The Arab media also faces the challenge of credibility. Although it has taken huge strides towards progress in the last few years, its practical experience is still in its infancy. In this connection, the television media in the Arab world seems to be much poorer than print journalism in terms of ethical parameters, professionalism and credibility, due to the speed at which the former needs to act in pursuing news stories. That is why its presentations often tend to be superficial and lacking in objectivity. Therefore, certain rules and norms have to be drawn up for the mass media. These parameters, however, must stem from the very core of media experiences in the form of codes of ethics to which media organizations and professionals should commit themselves.

Historically, Arab states and governments have sought to impose their domination over their respective mass media and to control the different media organizations with a view to serving their own goals and the interests of influential elites. Some have even considered the Ministry of Information as an integral component of their sovereignty.

Even though Arab governments have managed in the past to curb, even if only partially, the flow of information and media reports from outside, such control will largely disappear in the era of open information and the knowledge revolution. Therefore, it is very likely that the government's grip on the mass media will gradually wane.

However, the truth of the situation in the Arab world is that the communications domain is still far from being open and dissemination of information still remains under Arab governmental control and only a handful of Arab mass media outlets enjoy public popularity and credibility. The main question is: Will the next stage witness greater media openness, freer flow of information, and the emergence of more diverse, healthy Arab media alternatives and options?

KEYNOTE ADDRESS

The Gulf Media and Global Developments

H.H. Sheikh Mohammed bin Rashid Al Maktoum

I am pleased to meet with this distinguished group of Arab media professionals to discuss ways to liberate the Arab World from the shackles that curb its desire to progress and participate actively in the growth of human civilization.

Naturally, this is not the first conference to address the challenges facing the Arab world, particularly its media-related challenges. We need more conferences in order to assess the truth of the situation and to share knowledge. The media is a key issue of our time. It has penetrated the very fabric of life – the heart of economic, political and social activities – at both national and international levels. In the Emirates, this has prompted us to accord the media the importance it deserves by holding this and other such conferences; by the establishment of the Dubai Media City, the Arab Journalism Award and the Arab Media Forum; by the development of media instruments in the United Arab Emirates and by increasing the margin of permitted freedom.

Certainly, we need more conferences, but we also need more work and greater efforts to train personnel and improve performance and to be more serious and fearless when it comes to communicating the news.

Before I reveal my vision of the challenges that the Arab media faces in the Information Age, I would like to point out that I am not among those who put more weight on the media than it can handle or demand what it cannot supply. The media does not exist in a vacuum, nor does it operate in isolation from the active forces in state and society. It is part of an integrated whole—a part that greatly influences the other parts. If we compare society to a ship, then the media sits in the pilothouse. It helps to steer the ship, control its speed and bring it safely back to port on schedule, whether the sea is calm or rough.

In fact, the Arab media has played this role since the early stages of the Arab awakening and modernization. Media professionals have always been among the pioneers of enlightenment and progress. They were the heralds of both good and bad news. Among them were champions unafraid to speak the truth because conscience was their only censor. For them, the public good took priority over the private, the community over the individual, the homeland over everything.

However, this pioneering role suffered a setback when the Arab world was plagued by totalitarian thought and rule. When the leaders of these totalitarian regimes discovered the magic of the media, they rushed to clamp down on it and divert it from its real task, changing its focus so that it served those in control of the country rather than the country itself. Thus, instead of exposing mistakes the media was used to cover them up, and instead of creating a forum for dialogue among vital forces in society the media became a weapon to denounce rivals and criticize the viewpoints of others.

With the increasing number of defeats and the failure of development oppressing society, it became impossible to suppress the facts and those who failed to do so pointed the finger at others, blaming either internal or external conspiracies. The media was quick to justify failure rather than explain it, to portray the ones who had failed as victims so that they did not have to face any consequences. It also created sympathy and appreciation for them instead of subjecting them to interrogation or allowing them to be called to account.

Fortunately, this period of Arab history has ended or is nearly at an end. It is no longer possible to sell illusions, to justify failure with manufactured excuses or to re-label defeats as victories. Technology has increased people's access to information and has forced the Arab world with all its states, governments and societies to face the realities and challenges of the new age.

The first challenge for the media was that of credibility as people discovered that their national media had been presenting them with untrue images of themselves, their countries and the world they live in.

The media also had to face a challenge in the form of competition, but how could it compete when it was bound by the modes of work that it had used for decades? How could it face this invasion from space when it was bound by laws designed to control the media and suppress opinions?

The truth of the matter is that the media responded to this challenge very slowly. The foreign media remained the main source of news and information. There was a vacuum. And a vacuum waits for none—it yields to whoever steps in and takes the initiative. The vacuum was apparent to everyone and while there were attempts to fill it, these attempts were limited to switching from radio transmission to satellite transmission and repackaging the old. Then some of our brothers in Qatar launched the *Al Jazeera* satellite channel which, despite various opinions, had the effect of a huge rock being dropped into the stagnant pool of the media. The ripples created numerous media projects and new satellite channels in an attempt to respond to issues of credibility and competition.

It is natural for a transition from one state to another to involve mistakes and shortcomings. Change causes friction between the old and the new, the customary and the unfamiliar, and it creates disagreement about work styles and how to handle things. This disagreement is really about basic concepts such as development, modernization, reform, managing the state and the right to express one's opinions and defend one's interests. This disagreement is always on the verge of boiling over as a result of heated issues such as Palestine, Iraq and anti-terrorism measures. All of this is typically related to international policies – especially American policies – that involve the region and play a large role in its affairs.

[13]

This introduction was meant to illustrate that you carry a heavy inheritance on your shoulders and that your role is vital at this critical stage in the Arab world's history. There are many questions, a lack of priorities as well as increasing confusion and doubts that plague most ideas and projects now and perhaps, in the future.

I know that your job is not easy, because the issues that you deal with are not easy. So I shall focus on the most important issue that the Arab world faces today – change and reform – because information, like anything else, must be reformed and changed. It also plays a major role in reform and change.

Change and reform involves both critical and heated issues. The critical issue results from the conflict between a national demand for reform and the demands that are thrust upon us by outside forces. This embarrasses the reformers, forcing them to prove the originality of their reform-related ideas so that they are not accused of colluding with foreigners, because people reject foreign-imposed ideas regardless of goal or place of origin.

The heat generated by the issue stems from the dubious relationship between reforms and national identity with both its variable and fixed factors, particularly Arabism and Islam.

Any reform or change must make use of the achievements of the age and its best models by drawing on the methods that led to that success. As the achievements of this age belong to others, reform has a strong impact on the elements of national identity, which causes people to resist reform and change.

This problem has not been resolved, although it has existed since Napoleon's Egyptian campaign in 1798 marked the first point of friction between the Arab and Islamic world and contemporary Western civilization. This problem has surfaced at every significant turning point in Arab and Islamic history. It would eventually disappear beneath the surface again, ignored except by the intellectual elite who isolated themselves from changes in society while the problem was fermenting in

[14]

cellars and labyrinths. Groups formed around it – some dealt with the problem by violence and terror, some by estrangement and alienation and some by withdrawal from society and the world. For most people, this fermenting problem led to confusion, mental anguish and questions on how to reconcile heritage with modernity, and tradition with innovation.

In the Information Age, it is no longer possible for this issue to stay underground. It lies dormant at the core of conflicts and tensions and at the heart of efforts to develop, modernize and change. This forces leaders, intellectuals and media professionals to handle the issue with originality, rationality and courage in order to rid the components of the issue of its impurities, so as to be able to crystallize its essence as an incentive to reform and change.

As media professionals, you have a great responsibility with regard to this issue, either by not ignoring it or by sensibly guiding the debate about it. However, the greater responsibility lies with Arab leaders and their duty to encourage intellectual freedom, protect intellectuals, accept other opinions and sponsor hard work, initiatives and excellence.

The issue of identity is related to many other issues connected with your work and your role. I will discuss only one of these issues—your message to young people. As you know, Arab societies are young and our societies in the Gulf are younger still. Half of the people living in the Arab world are less than 20 years of age. They represent the future, and the future depends on what the young people are like. What messages does the media want to send them? How does the media decide its priorities and choose its programs? How does the media measure the effect that it has on values and conduct? Does it listen to young people? Does it know their opinions? Does it have a vision and strategy or is all this left to the entertainment channels?

These questions also apply to the media's attitude to women and their causes, to children and their needs, to education and its methods and programs.

Do you have the answers to these questions?

[15]

Perhaps you do. However, satisfactory answers must be based on experience, research and plans. Without these, the progress of the media will be random, controlled by improvisation and blind imitation and this will drive highly qualified people away. As a result, the media will lose its power to compete and reach out to people's consciences and minds. Consequently, we will fail completely in confronting the challenges of the Information Age or any other age.

You would have noticed that I have been talking about the Arab media in general and not about the Gulf media in particular, as the conference organizers suggested that I do. This is intentional. In the Information Age, it is difficult to draw a line between the Gulf media and the Arab media. In fact, even the line separating the Arab and the foreign media has almost disappeared. Furthermore, the Gulf media has a larger and more effective presence in the Arab world today. The Arab world's most important news channels are Gulf channels. The general channels that attract the most viewers are also Gulf channels. The most important newspapers and magazines that address the Arab world are Gulf publications. But the freely available entertainment channels are only Gulf-owned. The Gulf media sector attracts renowned Arab intellectuals, authors and media professionals to produce the finest Arab intellectual and artistic output.

This situation doubles the responsibilities of the Gulf media. Its success over the past few years has meant that it is a strong competitor in terms of satellite activities and that it is making its voice heard in various international forums. There are those who are keeping an eye on the Gulf media with negative intentions, waiting for a chance to discredit Gulf countries, their values and traditions.

The media can use its success to correct distorted images of the region, Arabs and Muslims by interacting with the international media and by opening channels of dialogue with intellectuals, politicians, economists, research centers and NGOs.

I can also see the Gulf media playing a role in the Arab world and presenting a 'Gulf message' – a message of enlightenment – to encourage development, to refine the human personality, and to call for moderation, dialogue, openness and modernization at economic, political and administrative levels.

Naturally, this message will not be successful without real openness about the actual situation in the Gulf with all its achievements, aspirations, problems and defects. If our media does not take the initiative to deal with local issues with courage, responsibility and reason, then the foreign media will, but with their own point of view and to serve their own interests.

Our media in the Gulf needs to take the initiative and to take a good look at the region. We must not be ashamed of problems or shortcomings. Only God is perfect. Our experience with development and administration is limited in comparison to other countries. We are proud of what we have achieved but we know that we have to do much more. The important thing is to work to solve problems, address shortcomings and always look ahead.

In my address I have touched upon some of the challenges, but I know that you are concerned about others, including preparation and training policies, the safety and living conditions of media people and the resources needed for large projects.

I am, by nature, optimistic about the future. With the progress of political and economic reforms in the Arab world, situations will improve, and there will be more transparency and increasing growth, the market will expand, the advertising industry will flourish, there will be an increasing demand for the media, and only that which is beneficial to people will remain on earth.

I have great faith in you and in the Arab media personnel. I have no doubt that you are worthy of the messages that you convey, enthusiastic to play your role in change and reform, and to face challenges. In the United Arab Emirates, you will always find brothers who work for the good of Arabs—for their awakening and progress.

[17]

MINISTRY OF INFORMATION AND CULTURE ADDRESS

The Arab Media: Challenges and Responses

H.H. Sheikh Abdullah bin Zayed Al Nahyan

At the outset, I have the honor to welcome His Highness Sheikh Mohammed bin Rashid Al Maktoum, the Vice President and Prime Minister of the UAE and Ruler of Dubai.

The important keynote address we have just heard gives us a lot to think about. H.H. Sheikh Mohammed's forthright style and comments brings us face-to-face with the major issues confronting the Arab world—those of reform and change. We greatly value H.H. Sheikh Mohammed's role and contribution to the overall advancement of the United Arab Emirates, including his support for the development of the information media.

The era of change in which we live makes it imperative to conduct a re-assessment of the field of Arab information as a whole, both internally and externally. We believe that the first step in this re-assessment must involve a complete and comprehensive review of the laws governing press and publications in the Arab world.

I am not talking about mere amendments or cosmetic changes but about a complete re-assessment that takes into account the developments in information technology (IT) and the changes in the speed and ease of information flow. If there *has* to be a law, what is required is legislation that guarantees free access to information and prohibits any denial of access, except what is clearly stipulated by the law and the judiciary.

[21]

Within the internal reform of the media that is required, attention should be paid to the development of personnel so that they are equipped to deal with information technology and can work efficiently in the new Information Age.

The emancipation of the media from laws that confine it is the first step towards the revitalization of the Arab media. The other, more difficult task is the responsibility of the people working in the media themselves—how they can strike a balance between professional needs and media responsibilities in terms of the way they deliver their message.

I am aware of the difficulties of this task. However, I am sure it can be achieved successfully if it is addressed within the framework of a proper understanding of the media's role in the projection of information, in a sincere and honest way, based on a commitment to seek the truth.

There is a need to change the way that our media and our journalists work. We need an environment that encourages innovative thinking and dialogue, even if this means that governments are embarrassed. The media *should* be able to question governments, and to criticize their policies—if there is something to be criticized. Otherwise, how can the media serve as the conscience, the eyes and the voice of public opinion? How else, indeed, can the Arab media earn the confidence of the Arab public?

Over the past few years, the Arab media has passed through a difficult period, one in which Islam and Muslims have become the targets of campaigns of distortion and misrepresentation, whether intended or otherwise.

We have opened our media institutions to allow justifications of the mistakes of those who use our religion as a cover for crimes that are unacceptable, both to our faith, and to our Shari'a. Thereby, we have contributed unconsciously – and sometimes irresponsibly – to the promotion of the stereotyped images that have dominated the Western media, by transmitting pictures and tapes that cannot serve Islam in any way, and which are at complete variance with the tolerance it teaches.

We have justified this by talking about the freedom of the press and competition, or the search for a "scoop" or for audience share.

We have failed to handle tapes of murder as we should have done—if we compare this with the way in which some of the Western media handled the tapes from the Abu Ghraib prison in Iraq. We were overwhelmed by a desire for professional achievement in a spirit that lacked objectivity, analysis and any concern for the real interests and security of the nation.

I do not mean to ignore or belittle the significant achievements and healthy developments that have occurred in the Arab media, whether these relate to information technology, putting forward different viewpoints, or discussing issues of concern to our societies, thereby shedding light on the deficiencies and negative aspects of society.

At the same time, I do not forget, nor do I wish to overlook the fact that some Western governments are now imposing restrictions, both direct and indirect, on some Arab and non-Arab media.

Some of the Arab satellite stations showed their ability to gain new audiences during the war in Iraq. Their coverage was even used by the international channels—which lacked their own footage. However, our channels were broadcasting only in Arabic. It is high time that we started addressing the world in a language it will understand.

This is not only the responsibility of Government, but also of the media organizations themselves and of the private sector.

My question is: Why do we not see a proper partnership between the Arab media organizations and the private sector, to establish strong and effective satellite stations that broadcast programs on the Arab World and on Islam in languages that the world knows, and in styles that it understands?

Why have we not yet succeeded in establishing a center that monitors what is said daily in the global media about Islam and Arabs, putting forward false information or distorted analysis? With such a center, the Arab media would be in a position to deal with such data, correct it, and transmit accurate and balanced programs that would help to enlighten international, and especially Western, opinion about Islam and Arabs.

[23]

This is an open invitation to everyone, in the government as well as the private sector, so that we do not remain hostages to a situation in which we talk to ourselves—but blame others.

We should make use of the opportunities presented by the Information Age and of the qualified personnel present in our media and academic institutions.

Any discussion about the Arab Media in the Information Age cannot take place in isolation, without talking about the painful situation in the Arab world. Any attempt to develop the Arab media, make it more effective, and raise it to new levels, will continue to be fruitless when the situation in the Arab world leaves a bitter taste, at all political, educational, cultural and social levels—a situation in which repugnant views are promoted that describe people as atheists with whom there should be no exchange of views, whether such people are Muslims or non-Muslims.

Finally, the Arab media, however much it is empowered with resources and the ability to use information technology, cannot perform as expected unless there is a comprehensive process of radical reform throughout the Arab world. Our Arab media cannot portray a beautiful image of an ugly situation. It cannot talk about principles, values and ideals while people see that things are moving in the other direction, and when the media itself reports on events that show an entirely different approach.

There is an Arab proverb that "a container can only spill the contents within it." The Arab media should be a means for enlightenment and change—*not* a way of ignoring, suppressing or distorting the truth.

CHANGES IN THE ARAB MEDIA SCENE

1

New Trends and Forces
in the Arab Media Arena

Mohammed Al-Sayyed Saeed

During the past decade, the Arab media arena has undergone important, but rather contradictory developments. The current scene seems rather unsettled because of a number of variables that have affected both the structure and content of the media. All these developments are not moving in a single definite direction, and some of these are highly artificial as they reflect political intervention.

This chapter seeks to examine the current trends in the development of the Arab media, identify the general course and principles governing this development, and explore the prospects for its future, with a view to suggesting genuine remedies for its ills and problems.

The chapter is divided into three sections. The first monitors the important historical and emerging factors that determine the media's diverse courses in different Arab countries. The second tries to outline a general code for tracking the future paths of the media based on a specific model that may be useful to predict developments. The third is devoted to clarifying the impact of factors that affect the media market in several Arab countries.

Factors Affecting the Development of Arab Media

The Arab media was, and is still, influenced by both historical and emerging factors, some of which stem from global developments – especially in the fields of communication technologies, expansion of capital and investment and modern social organization – as well as those taking place in the ideological and political arenas. Others are associated with the Arab region's social, political, economic and cultural formation and driving forces.

In its broader sense, the mass media organizations represent a relatively genuine, independent venue of societal activities, a fact that has always been behind the developments witnessed by both the global and Arab media, particularly in their early formative stages. In terms of tools and mechanisms, the modern mass media is linked to the development of the printing and communication industries. However, in terms of content, it is linked to the historical process of nationalistic crystallization and social organization. This was illustrated by the emergence of new ideologies and growth of political parties and their influence; the formation of a central state and the diminishing of regional fragmentation; the striking expansion of cities and urban areas; the establishment of modern educational systems; and the considerable increase in investments in this industry to satisfy a growing demand for information and other media products.

The two crucial factors, which have produced distinctive media features in developed countries and the world at large, were the growing levels of investments and the intensified struggle for power. However, imbalance was the predominant feature that marked the expansion of the media sphere. This meant the subordination of the less developed to the developed players at the economic and media levels, and the emergence of two relatively contradictory political systems, which follow the two political models that the new societies have produced—the authoritarian and democratic systems. In addition, big differences remain in the form and content of media institutions owing to the different educational, cultural, economic and social levels of the public segments they are addressing, as well as their grassroots cultural traditions.

In reality, the situation did not differ much in the case of Arab societies. The long-standing stagnation affecting these societies deprived them of the opportunities to move automatically towards capitalism and to achieve technological progress in the printing industry, among other things. The beginnings of the Arab mass media coincided with the western colonial expeditions that stormed the Arab world, including the Napoleonic expedition to Egypt in 1798. This led some central Arab states, like Egypt and Syria, to stand up to that challenge in the 19th century.

At that time, the processes of nation-building and modernization were underway and coincided with the adoption of capitalism, which involved the expansion of investments to include the field of the print media. Imbalance, however, remained the dominant feature of this development, as a limited number of Arab states – particularly Egypt, Syria, Iraq and Tunisia – had monopolized the Arabic-language mass media until the 1960s. However, at the beginning of the 1970s, mass media organizations became widespread in the Arab world.

Despite the modest capabilities and resources available to news organizations and agencies in the above-mentioned countries, their impact on other countries was remarkable owing to the emergence of strong nationalist movements and the rise of general political activity in the liberal era. However, the emergence of authoritarian regimes after independence put an end to the development of journalism and subordinated all mass media to government hegemony.

During the last few decades, the most effective forces in the Arab media developmental process have crystallized, producing diverse media structures. The most important of these forces will be discussed in the following section.

1-The Emergence of the "Restricted Plurality" Model

As noted earlier, the print media was introduced with the Napoleonic invasion of Egypt, but was rapidly turned into a means to construct the new, authoritarian state as illustrated by the Mohammed Ali regime in Egypt. The first intellectual concept of modern journalism started to

[29]

appear during the 1860s and 1870s amid the political and ideological upheavals that sought a means to confront western colonialism and revive Arab civilization. As a result, the educated classes or "intelligentsia" became a new social faction. Indeed, the relative freedom that Egypt enjoyed prior to and during the British occupation was the decisive factor behind the flourishing of journalism there, when Lebanon became the target of a severe wave of oppression by the Ottomans.

However, the relatively liberal experience that accompanied the British–French mandate rule over large parts of the Arab world, the emergence of many patriotic and nationalistic movements, the promotion of trade, progress in economic and educational fields, all contributed towards the concrete development of journalism in several Arab countries, such as Lebanon, Syria, Palestine, Iraq, Bahrain, Tunisia and Morocco. Nevertheless, the independence experience fundamentally altered the basic prerequisites of media performance, particularly in cases where radical regimes were established.

Although the media industry has witnessed significant progress, technically and institutionally, it had to abandon its function as a tool of free ideological expression and political plurality and as a means to seek and present truth in the best forms possible. Instead, it was forced to assume the function of "mobilization."

> It can be said that until the June 1967 defeat, journalism was under the subordination of the state's general policies, supporting all actions taken by the regime, and opposition forces were absent during the last two years (1965–1967) even from the details of these policies and implementation mechanisms.[1]

The levels of press freedom and plurality differed from one Arab country to another. While the Lebanese and Egyptian press enjoyed a wider margin of freedom, it was under strict, almost absolute dominance of the governments and political regimes in countries like Syria, Iraq, Algeria and Libya. Hence, it is assumed that the current form of Arab journalism was shaped under this "mobilization" model, and it still retains those features rather than those of the "democratic" model.

However, the rise of the "restricted political plurality" model has altered some of those earlier features and it has become one of the most important factors that have determined the direction of the current and future development of Arab journalism. It has codified the plurality of political parties and offered greater tolerance towards non-governmental organizations and associations, though it has guaranteed the total monopoly of power by bureaucratic, police regimes, sometimes ideological in character, which seized the state and proceeded to rule it with an iron grip.[2]

Under this model, the old, direct forms of administrative, political and legal hegemony over media performance – such as government ownership, daily and prior censorship, direct threats and suppression and intimidation campaigns – have been abolished. At the same time, various new indirect methods are employed to ensure that the press undertakes its "mobilization" role as effectively as possible with a palpable degree of diversity and freedom of expression.[3] This model, which first emerged in Egypt and later spread into countries such as Morocco, Algeria, Tunisia, Kuwait, Yemen and Sudan, has resulted in considerable improvement of professional performance and asserted the plurality and diversity of political and professional tenets, even though a substantial segment of the press remained under public ownership and hence government dominance.

The new element in this scene is that some Arab Gulf states have apparently distanced themselves from the political and governance aspects of the "restricted political plurality" model, and have increasingly opted for the media and journalistic aspects thereof. Indeed, press organizations in the Gulf have embarked upon significant new initiatives related to the art of journalism and relative freedom, especially in countries like the UAE and Kuwait, and to a lesser degree in the Kingdom of Bahrain and the State of Qatar.

The qualitative transformations that took place in Arab journalism under the "restricted plurality" model should not be ignored, but the big strides already made have not yet ensured the minimum level of press and media freedom. The print media is still suffering from censorship and punitive legislation in the majority of Arab states. The report of the Ninth Conference of the Federation of Arab Journalists expressed the hope that "Arabs would enter the 21st century under true democratic progress bringing about robust changes and systematic plurality." However, the report stated that "no serious steps have been taken in this respect which raises our concerns over both the present and the future."[4] However, the Arab media, under the said legal restrictions, could have ended up in a state of almost total stagnation had it not been for the second and the most effective factor in the Arab media development process.

2-Advances in Information and Communication Technology

The Arab media gained only extremely limited momentum by moving from the one-party system towards restricted plurality in some Arab countries. In reality, radical development was wrought by staggering advances in information and communications technologies and not through the Arab socio-political development process. Some argue that the initiative to employ these revolutionary advances, the Internet in particular, was taken by print media organizations set up by the Arab diaspora, who hastened to move their assets from western capitals, such as London and Paris, to certain Arab countries. Nevertheless, real progress has been made in the sphere of electronic and satellite television journalism. As Marc Lynch describes it:

> These new information media are increasingly creating the fundamental narrative frameworks through which the audiences understand news events. In a sense, the absence of real democracy in the region makes the basic outlets of modern media more powerful since they face only few competitors in forging the general agenda.[5]

As a result, Arabs have entered the era of satellite channels that address the Arab nation as a whole, and that of the Internet, which allows direct global dialogue between groups and individuals through hundreds of online news forums. The Arab Press Freedom Watch organization asserts:

> [This era] imposes a great challenge on the Arab media. Communications are now breaking through national barriers in unpredictable ways, and governments are facing growing difficulties in their attempts to control what their peoples are permitted to know.[6]

It can be said that these new media institutions present the most significant achievement since the introduction of the printing press to the Arab world and the emergence of print journalism. The new media not only enjoys greater freedom and striking knowledge potential, but they are also of higher professional quality than the old print media. Moreover, the importance of this development is intensified as it would cause deeper institutional changes, some of which might destroy the present improvements in the satellite broadcast system, while others would impose new constructive responses. According to the predictions of some experts:

> The mixture of media and information /communications technologies is increasingly motivating prominent players in these three sectors to work coherently together. Even if this would lead to loss of business and revenues, it could create new patterns of opportunities.[7]

The Arabs have not been true partners in the process of advancing satellite broadcasting technologies, nor are they prepared to undertake the necessary institutional changes that could rapidly adapt to the intensity and depth of information technology (IT) advancements.

> In addition to improving communications networks and developing new services, communications firms are facing the greater challenge of redefining the scope of their projects. Owing to the fact that telephone and cable companies are planning to move into the info media services sector, the nature of their activities will inevitably undergo radical changes...[8]

This will cause deep effects on the economies and operational methods of TV satellite channels. Nevertheless, it is certain that there will be greater opportunities for successful adaptation by communications companies and businesses compared to those available to the government departments.

3-The Adoption of Market Economy

The Arab world is not yet fully engaged in the historical process of democratic transformation, since it is only "borrowing" those means that secure authoritarian, bureaucratic regimes and hereditary systems of rule. This is not the case with regard to the adoption of the free market economy. Most Arab states have already laid the foundations of this type of economy within the limits available to those countries, which are heavily dependent on oil revenues. Others have, in fact, witnessed radical economic and developmental experiences during the 1960s that had resulted in suppressing private initiative and capital. Yet, these very countries are today exerting strenuous efforts to adapt to the market economy. A combination of oil resources and noteworthy encouragement has prompted the private sector to enter the field of the mass media, or at least expand its share thereof.

Within this context, it seems extremely difficult today to cite a common history of ownership patterns of institutions operating in this field. Whereas print media organizations were privately owned from the beginning in countries such as Lebanon, Kuwait and other Gulf states, it was only in the last few years that private ownership has been legalized once again in Egypt, though partially and discriminately. Despite the fact that a large number of newspapers and magazines were privatized, the overwhelming number of major publishing organizations are run and owned by the state. Indeed, private ownership of newspapers is totally banned in Syria and Libya.

At the level of the television media, the ending of state monopoly over the ownership of television stations in Egypt has only materialized very recently, while such a step is still prohibited in most other Arab countries. The biggest exceptions are the organizations set up by the diaspora, particularly in Britain, France, Italy and the United States. The two factors are inseparable—the prohibition had resulted in the migration of Arab media organizations and encouraged them to address all Arab societies. Hence these organizations were regarded as the true nationalist Arab media at a time when the media message was monopolized by the state. Once individuals and private institutions gained the right to set up and own TV stations, a counter migration started to the Arab countries for reasons related to costs, marketing plans and production economics.[9]

Despite the importance of this partial shift in the position of the Arab states concerning private ownership of TV and print media, the Arab media market remains under the control of these states, reflecting the active presence of what may be termed "political capital." The term implies that the central purpose of creating media organizations is political rather than commercial. It also suggests that the majority of satellite TV outlets cannot survive by depending only on market economics in the absence of the financial support by the state or other political bodies, particularly with regard to paid-up capital, type of ownership, basic guarantees of capital turnover, and distribution and advertising revenues.

This means that the electronic media remains the only democratic mass media in the Arab world and the only available venue for individuals and small capitalists, as it imposes no restrictions on the media message.[10]

The other pattern of freer, critical and more independent mass media is the so-called "civil media" which is run by non-governmental organizations (NGOs) in the forms of printed leaflets and releases addressing limited, intellectual elite audiences. It is normally dedicated to causes such as promoting the development process; protecting women's rights, human rights, and national culture; or politically-oriented issues, such as resisting the normalization of relations with Israel.

4-The Relative Shift in Audience Behavior

It is widely agreed that the audience behavior is strongly linked to the positive though slow developments taking place in the Arab media

[35]

domain in terms of quality and content. In the past, governments used to deal comfortably with an audience accustomed to absorbing the state's propaganda campaigns. In reality, this audience has changed and is no longer content with passive reception. Rather, it demands direct participation and interaction, and seeks to express both satisfaction and resentment through concrete means—albeit very simple. The first manifestation is the wide political isolation resulting from shocking ignorance of important events that the audience comes to know only through rumors—which seems to be the most important source of information in the current Arab culture.

The second is the tendency of Arab audiences to resort to western outlets (notably the BBC and Radio Monte Carlo), which show greater concern about Arab causes while the third is associated with the grave crises that hit different Arab countries as a result of wars, defeats and civil conflicts. In fact, Arab satellite channels were one of the outcomes of the first and second Gulf crises (of 1990–91 and 2003 respectively), which prompted large numbers of Arabs to seek information either through western media outlets or those offered by other Arab countries.

The setting up of state-run mass media represented an attempt by some Arab states to win this battle by diverting a segment of this audience towards information sources that disseminated the messages of these governments. It is not a coincidence that the most important development in the Arab nationalist media, both in print and in satellite TV broadcasting – as represented by the *Al Hayat* newspaper and the Egyptian Satellite Channel respectively – were linked with the military campaign in Iraq following the 1990 Iraqi invasion of Kuwait.

Lastly, this revolutionary development is represented in the mushrooming of satellite TV and print media outlets. The former has enabled the viewers to express their attitudes and moods, by simply pressing a button to select another channel or more actively, through contributions to TV "talk shows" and opinion polls conducted by the channels on the screen and/or their web sites.[11]

5-Rise of the Islamist Movement and Growing Anger with US Hegemony

Undoubtedly, the extraordinary rise of the Islamist movement – at a time when the mobilization potential and performance of Arab political regimes started to deteriorate – has brought about extremely strong repercussions in the Arab media. This coincides with growing tensions in relations between the Arab world and the United States, in particular, and the West in general, especially after the events of September 11, 2001 and the subsequent arguments about the "conflict of cultures" and the "clash of civilizations."

The rise of the Islamist movement, in parallel with the second Palestinian *intifada* (uprising) and the invasion and occupation of Iraq, have created a climate where fears and hatreds are heightened, as reflected in the Arab–US satellite media war during the war in Iraq, the last phase of the Arab-Israeli conflict and the so-called the "war on terrorism."[12]

Nevertheless, some argue that this media war was nothing more than a huge new upsurge aimed at reviving Arab nationalist political culture. This culture enjoys a strong presence in Arab media and journalistic circles, as well as in political and cultural public opinion, as clearly manifested in the attitudes of the Arab channels towards the *intifada*.

6-International Intervention

It appears that foreign pressures and interventions have tangibly influenced the Arab media performance, particularly after the US invasion of Iraq and during the media war between the Arabs and the Americans. The Arab media tended to depict the US actions and attitudes as another "crusade" against the Arab and Islamic world, [13] while the Americans were accusing the Arab media (notably *Al Jazeera* and *Abu Dhabi Television* channels) as unprofessional, claiming that "Arabs understand the news in different ways. And for several cultural reasons, demagoguism and sensationalism have been the rule in the Arab media."[14] The former US Secretary of State, Colin Powell, backed by some Arab commentators closely linked to certain US and western circles, echoed these allegations, especially those against *Al Jazeera.*[15]

Proceeding from the assertion that the Arab media coverage of the war in Iraq was unfair and provocative, some US officials have themselves goaded a number of Arab governments to suppress the TV outlets that enraged them. It appears that somehow, these pressures do not contradict their demands for democratic reforms in the Arab countries! In fact, a number of western governments have parroted the American positions taken against the Arab media, including the French government which has taken the strangest suppressive measure in its history by banning *Al Manar* satellite channel under the pretext of anti-Semitism.[16]

Though the importance of American pressures should not be exaggerated, they have further weakened the political foundations of the relative independence of Arab media. Thus, they constituted one of the factors that determine its future courses.

Tracking the Basic Paths of Future Media Development

While it is possible to trace the effect of each of these factors on the Arab media environment, the difficulty lies in tracing the interaction between them and their collective impact.

Media research and studies are addressing these complex interactions through various approaches. For example, the possible future paths of media development can be examined through a number of dualities involving different contradictions. There is the implied contradiction in media dependency, which makes us wonder about the extent of Arab media independence. In addition, there is the inconsistency between media freedom and the systematic violation of freedom of expression that prompts us to assess the level of freedom that Arab media effectively enjoys.

In general, the possible directions that the Arab media might follow can be monitored and traced through the following basic dualities:

1-Independence and Subordination

The dilemma of media independence assumes different forms in print and on-line journalism, as well as in television (ground and satellite) and radio broadcasts.

[38]

The establishment of Arab channels has created the broadest opening for the relative independency of the Arab media message owing to the growing percentage of television watchers in the Arab world and among Arab emigrants abroad. This fact, however, does not mean true independence because these channels are still under the ownership of governments that are willing to tolerate greater media freedom when addressing other Arab countries and Arab audiences in other parts of the world than that allowed to their own local viewers. In other words, these outlets enjoy discriminatory independence that differs from one country to another and indeed, from one channel to another within the same Arab country.

While it is expected that Egyptian state-run and private satellite channels, for example, may ignore news and comments dealing with certain aspects of Egyptian policies and conditions, they perhaps would impose lesser restrictions on journalistic content concerning other Arab states. This is true to a greater degree for the Qatari, Saudi and UAE satellite channels, as well as those directed to Arab audiences outside the Arab world. Eventually, it should always be borne in mind that the relative, discriminatory freedom these channels enjoy is totally contingent upon the will of high-ranking authorities. To a certain degree, such a discriminatory freedom can be viewed and defined as a gift rather than a state obligation or a genuine, constitutional right. Apart from exceptional circumstances, Arab states are currently not yet convinced of the importance of granting their satellite channels a higher degree of independence under the protection of the law—an independence that is not subject to the will of the ruling power.

Ironically, the national newspapers enjoy a lesser degree of independence than the satellite outlets enjoy, as most of the big Arab media organizations are still owned by the states. Hence, web journalism is the most independent amongst all media mechanisms and means in the Arab region.

[39]

The second consideration that governs the independence of the Arab media is the legal factor. The Arab media, particularly print journalism, is shackled by several legislations that curb freedom of expression. It is a feature that is apparently quite common in almost all Arab countries where journalists suffer from severe punitive measures—including detention, imprisonment and whipping. In other countries, the industry suffers from the presence of media organizations staffed with corrupt, non-professional personnel whose only concern is adulation and paying lip service to high-ranking government officials to attain higher positions and privileges. Unfortunately, this aspect of corruption and professional degradation has not been adequately dealt with in Arab media studies and research despite its highly negative repercussions on the integrity and independence of journalism.

Last, but not the least, is the media economics factor. Today, no satellite television network or leading newspaper can survive without massive advertising revenues. Although a strong advertising market is available in the Arab world for a limited number of newspapers and local TV outlets, it remains incapable of supporting large media establishments in smaller Arab countries without the backing of certain governments and/or major private businesses. In 1994, Jihad Al-Khazen estimated the size of this advertising market at US$900 million. Throughout 1997, the overall advertising expenditures rose by 96%, and for magazines and newspapers by 36% and 14% respectively.[17] According to him, such an advertising market can hardly support a handful of big media organizations in the Arab world. As a result, their economies have been heavily dependent on other Arab governments. Under such circumstances, it is not surprisingly that the financial conditions of these organizations will lack transparency, reflecting the fragility of their independence even in the case of privately-owned newspapers. Moreover, as they move towards a market economy, these large organizations are expected to suffer from increasing restrictions that would further deepen their dependency.

2-Professionalism vs. Manipulation

Relative independence does not necessarily mean that the Arab media will ascend to a higher level of professionalism that would enable it to satisfy the Arab audience's need for credible information, to expand the scope of their choices, to shed real light on prevailing policies and situations and to provide them with the necessary tools to understand events taking place in their respective countries, the greater Arab homeland and the entire world.

The level of professionalism attained by the Arab media has become an international political question owing to the hostile US position towards Arab satellite TV networks, at the forefront of which is *Al Jazeera* channel. The US accusations, in fact, also involve the issue of Arab media independency claiming that the Arab governments seek to divert media attention away from their poor performance by focusing on the "external enemy" – namely, Israel and the United States – thereby creating a favorable climate for extremism and violence.

However, such US accusations based on obvious ideological and political bias are not acceptable, and hostile Arab public attitudes towards US policies in the region cannot be blamed on the Arab media, even though some of these attitudes may have been voiced through this media. James Zogby dismissed the US accusations against the Arab media as being unfounded. Indeed, new studies have shown that the media – no matter what form it takes – only plays a limited role in shaping Arab attitudes toward the United States. A study by Zogby International found that it is US policies that are to blame for the negative image that Arabs have regarding American values and products.[18]

A large number of US experts suggest that the country's political stance toward the Arab media is erroneous, and that the media freedom earned should be the focus of attention rather called into question. In this respect, Daoud Kuttab stressed that "the challenge of US seriousness in seeking reforms starts with acknowledging the existing improvement, though slow and vague."[19] According to the Federation of Arab Journalists:

The US and Israel have aligned to pressure Arab governments in order to suppress the freedom of press…in flagrant contradiction of Washington's calls for democratic reforms and pressures directed at silencing voices protesting against their policies.[20]

From our perspective, it should be stressed that the Arab media performance has witnessed a real revolution, particularly with the establishment of *Al Jazeera*, and this was especially evident during the coverage of the US-led War in Iraq.

During the 1991 Gulf War, CNN was the dominant source, while the situation was completely different during the Gulf crisis of 2003 when reports came from Arab channels such as *Abu Dhabi Television*, *Al Arabiya* and *MBC* channels.[21]

The fundamental factor behind the unprecedented coverage of an international war fought on Arab soil is the emergence of a professional generation of Arab journalists who insisted on covering the events on the ground. The second important indication is the exceptional capability of the Arab media – particularly the satellite channels – to fulfill the tasks of planning and transporting the basic equipment needed for live reporting. Moreover, Arab reporters and journalists covering the 2003 Iraq War were willing to sacrifice their comfort – indeed their very lives – in order to report information as accurately as possible about a war that posed a grave threat to the lives of both local citizens and foreigners, particularly the reporters.

Nevertheless, some other professional factors and considerations were absent, including the implicit and uncritical acceptance of statements made by Iraqi officials during the first three weeks of the war. Consequently, the result was a total surprise for the Arabs who had been encouraged by the media to believe that the final outcome would be totally different. Still, Abdul Rahman Al-Rashid argues that the coverage of the Iraq War was similar to that of the June 1967 War.[22]

As a matter of fact, the Arab media lack their own tools that would enable them to assess the Iraqi statements and to place them in their real context. The accusations, therefore, ought to be leveled at the Iraqi media

[42]

management and not at the Arab media itself. Besides, there has been greater concentration on the physical requirements of coverage rather than on intellectual and scientific arrangements. That is why the Arab satellite channels and newspapers became victims of the media war conducted by the two warring parties. For their part, the American media were keen on airing political messages rather than seeking the truth.

> The new rules of the game are now being explained through the televised display of events in Baghdad...the sacking of Baghdad is designed to send signals to all other Middle Eastern and Asian regimes that the US finds annoying, threatening, distasteful, worrisome or even just a little strange.[23]

Arab satellite outlets were not any more biased then their American counterparts. "Both sides have provided biased reporting and slanted coverage," especially after the emergence of news networks known for both their hostile stances toward the Arabs and human, progressive values, as well as disdain for professional standards and considerations. Heading these is *Fox News* channel, which has become a leading inflammatory platform for stirring conflict between cultures and war against Arab peoples.[24]

In any case, since then, Arab satellite networks have sought to cover events through different perspectives in their "talk shows" and diverse methods of providing news services and reports. It appears that these channels have become aware of the need to promote the principles of institutional professionalism. For example, *Al Jazeera,* has adopted a new code of ethics to ensure accuracy and good taste in its news coverage.[25]

In contrast, Arab newspapers are still guilty of grave professional and ethical "slips." Evidence of this may be found in the reports by the Supreme Council on Journalism concerning the performance of the Eygptian press. In this connection, Mohammad Fahd Al-Harithy asserts:

> If the Arab media want to play their rightful role in the region, they will have to put their house in order first...The Arab media need to become more professional too instead of merely dancing to the tune the public want to hear.[26]

[43]

On the whole, there seems to be a growing tendency to abide by the rules of professionalism, despite the substantial differences between satellite networks and print organizations, and among the latter as well, depending on their policies, audiences, sizes, as well as their respective countries.

3-Balance and Diversity vs. Bias and Monopolization

Balance constitutes another criterion for assessing the Arab media which is generally accused of being an elite media and of being partial at the political, cultural and social levels. Historically, the print media (the press) has been the voice of political regimes and high-ranking elites in society. However, the liberal experiences that some Arab countries witnessed during different stages of their political history were characterized by the emergence of media and political forums that conveyed dissenting opinions and ideologies whether voiced by progressive or political Islam movements. Indeed, these liberal experiences have also witnessed concrete diversity in the political and cultural press as no single major newspaper in Egypt could have monopolized the media market during the liberalization stage.

Naturally, "political monopolization" is still dominating the Arab satellite channels market, a situation that is encouraged intentionally or at least acknowledged, by the state in most cases. More surprisingly, even the state-owned Arab satellite networks have moved gradually towards abandoning the state oratory and are choosing to adopt more of the mainstream political and cultural discourse.

Even when the state's grip over the print, audio and visual media was somewhat loosened, complaints continued about the lack of diversity in expressing political and social thoughts. Also, the approaches of different social forces and movements to the mass media were not identical. For example, there has been clear bias against the women's movement for equality. Dr. Naomi Sakr says that she realized while researching a report on women in the Arab media that "the challenge facing women has

[44]

become more daunting as the number of Arabic-language media outlets have increased." She questioned:

> What is the point of drawing up policies to make women's rights central to national development when, at the same time, negative stereotyping of women goes on daily in the national press and on television?[27]

It is likely that the current era of Arab cultural-political development will produce a counter-bias against progressive, liberal cultural-political voices. Although it is likely that the initial stage of media openness would reflect existing social bias, the media will probably witness a later stage of balance and diversity, which will coincide with the entire political environment moving in this direction. In reality, such a shift is already underway. Indeed, the most notable irony is that calls for liberalization are being voiced by Gulf newspapers, radio and TV stations or are supported by Gulf "political capital." This is despite the obvious incompatibility with prevailing ideologies in countries like Saudi Arabia. The Saudi role in financing and running the two major newspapers, *Ash-Sharq Al-Awsat* and *Al-Hayat,* is no secret and these papers enthusiastically advocate the liberalization process.

In general, it may be said that the future promises more decentralization in the ownership of media assets, with the entry of more newspapers, periodicals and satellite outlets in the market. While the Internet plays an obvious role in mitigating the effects of centralization, it does not eliminate it completely as might have been expected. Nevertheless, Timothy Balding underscores the fact that "the introduction of the Internet had changed the scenario of the world media." Mervat Al-Tallawy believes that "at least 6 million Arabs have access to the Internet," whereas Naomi Sakr stresses the importance of the satellite channels.[28]

Generally speaking, the steady growth and expansion of Arab satellite stations, as well as the involvement of the private sector in this significant industry, will inevitably reduce the levels of centralization and bias.

[45]

4-Development vs. Degradation

Many Arabs are voicing their concern that the cultural level of the Arab media has further deteriorated. An Arab citizen expressed his opinion that the media has lost its identity and its sense of direction:

> The Arab media has no place on the map at all...the media's original task is to gather, verify and disseminate news to the audience with the highest degree of credibility possible. The media myth that we call "the Arab media" is a media which has lost its identity and lost its way in mazes...[29]

Such feelings of disappointment reveal the huge cultural gap existing between the expectations of educated and well-informed audiences and the performance of the Arab media. It is believed that the expansion of the satellite media and growing openness will widen the competition to win more Arab viewers and almost certainly downgrade the cultural content of the media message. Historically, many developed countries have witnessed a vigorous tendency by sub-standard radio and TV broadcasters and press to control the media market, particularly in the United States. Thousands of radio stations woo ordinary citizens to participate in a media discourse that is very inferior in professional, cultural and religious terms.

The possibility that the impact of such a development would extend to the Arab world cannot be ruled out, especially in terms of the print media as the expansion of popular "tabloid" papers has shown. The reports they publish – including erotic photos, rumors, and unconfirmed stories of corruption – are meant to excite sexual feelings, stir violence and sectarian turmoil, and defame certain prominent personalities. The best example that can be cited here is the so-called "Cyprus newspapers" (those which are circulated in Egypt although established and licensed in Cyprus to circumvent Egyptian publication and distribution regulations).

For their part, the privately-owned television networks have created such a trivial and worthless entertainment culture that a highly pious occasion, like the Holy Month of Ramadan, is turned into a profit-making marketplace for the most trifling kind of entertainment. Walter Armbrust asserts that this bizarre combination of such frivolous entertainment and cheap advertising, which are associated with this month, is one of the many faces of the consumer-commercial culture, aimed at inventing a parallel model for the globalization of Christmas in the Anglo–American tradition. This is also associated with the irresistible driving force for the commercialization of culture and to present it in the form of practices – such as the "Riddles of Ramadan" show – that ridicule the solemnity expected of such a religious occasion.[30]

Nevertheless, TV and radio stations have historically served as an important medium of enlightenment and education. The increasing commercialization of the media does not necessarily imply the degradation of cultural structures. Rather, it would play some role – though in complex institutional ways – in assisting those who seek to acquire various types of knowledge. Of course, these contradictions in the different dimensions of the media sphere would render the task of reaching a general understanding and sound assumptions more difficult. And this study is not meant to advocate the "single factor" theory in order to understand the potential paths of the development of Arab media. The researcher, however, will have to forge a comprehensive theory based on what is believed to be the strongest and most fundamental factor behind the development of the Arab media.

Potential Direction of Arab Media: An Analytical Model

This model presumes the necessity of bringing the Arab recipient back to the core of media-oriented communication interactions. By adopting the "mobilization" pattern in their media policies, the Arab state presumed that it could tailor Arab citizens according to its own media rules or exclude them from the media realm, on the assumption that they are "creatures" of the media rather than human beings who are mentally capable of accepting, rejecting or altering the media message.

For some time, this assumption was not mere illusion. The so-called "inclusive" media starts with monopolization, following the courses that other loyal societal establishments have followed in supporting political regimes (for example, the educational system, the single ruling party, supreme religious bodies and others).

Indeed, the modern Arab state had only followed this pattern in totality in exceptional cases – in a limited number of Arab states – and for short periods of time compared with similar experiences in central and east Europe. Most of the current Arab political regimes fall within the authoritarian category, resorting to force and oppression to ensure monopoly of power by a certain elite establishment. The difference between these and totalitarian regimes is that they lack a concerted ideology and a popular party, and are unable to instill universal political ideals that we have seen in the Soviet-communist, the German nationalist and Italian fascist experiences. Hence, the media establishments of Arab political regimes have allowed the bureaucracy that runs these media systems a certain margin of professionalism, freedom and independence.

In principle, these media patterns do not fundamentally differ from those followed in the developed industrialized societies during the state-formation and nation-building stage, when the media played a prominent part in this process. Jon B. Alterman has developed the example designed by Benedict Anderson on the emergence of great nationalist movements. In Anderson's opinion, two factors have contributed to the motivation and development of nationalist awareness—commercial activities and language standardization. The press has played a significant role in realizing the second factor from one European state to another, since the rise of the religious Reformation movement in Europe.

However, Alterman is of the opinion that the introduction of the print media to the Arab region did not generate the same outcome. Rather, it consolidated national frontiers. At the present time, the Arab satellite networks are playing the part that the Arab print media should have played in Western Europe and Northern America. The Arab satellite media pursues viewers who possess the freedom of selection and strengthen their involvement in the general causes of the entire Arab Nation. Alterman, however, also believes that these developments have led to the creation of what he describes a "chaotic media system,"[31] a notion that will be discussed later.

It is adequate at this point to assert that the media has played an important role in the building up of big nations and nationalist movements in today's world with different economic and cultural prerequisites but with almost identical political preconditions. The individuality of the citizen was absent in most cases, and that is why the term "mass media" was introduced. This task has been repeated in the building up of the independent Arab state in which its mass media has become a symbol of sovereignty, along with the flag, the national airlines and others. Above all, the mass media served as a tool for forging a perception associated with its geography, history, and perhaps, its legitimacy.

The Arab world today is witnessing the long-term process of the gradual decline of authoritarian, bureaucratic regimes, accompanied by reduced media hegemony, even before these regimes fulfill their promises to introduce modernization, economic recovery and social changes. The nation-building task has not been accomplished either at the local or the Arab-nationalist levels.

What this process of decline means is that such authoritarian regimes are increasingly losing their hold over all fields of social life, and are launching political and ideological moves, certain behavior patterns, and economic, social and cultural operations that are alien to their thinking and logic. Yet, this does not mean that these regimes are collapsing and that societies are moving towards a more participatory political model. These regimes remain capable of granting the greatest resources and opportunities discriminately to its social, political and business allies, and to a lesser degree to those in the cultural field. The process gives rise to two sectors, each with its own, exclusive laws. The first includes elements capable of dealing positively with sources of knowledge and the modern media, who are hoping for the rise of a new Arab professional media discourse. The other, larger sector comprises the unofficial masses, who have been the victims of a long process of isolation and marginalization. This sector usually opts for the verbal media and direct communication, though the official government media boasts of its ability to address and satisfy the needs of this sector, unaware of the fact that the latter only deals selectively with the official and semi-official media and boycotts all modern media outlets. A third, median group is undoubtedly swinging between the authoritarian media forums (owing to its deep-rooted need for national affiliation) and the professional, more advanced ones (to satisfy its need to be aware of other points of view, even though selectively).

Although the government media officials are aware that the state's discourse is losing its acceptability and ability to attract local audiences, they insist on embracing the authoritarian media theory, due to the importance they attach to it during extraordinary situations and crises, which make it easy to invoke patriotic loyalties and national demagoguism. Nevertheless, they have started to absorb the notion of independent media, though marginally, in a process of careful selection.

As a result, unequal opportunities and margins of freedom and relative independence have been granted to new players depending on how close or remote they are from the core of the ruling elites. Thus, the national media market has gained a certain amount of independence and importance, both on the supply and demand sides, without being a real "free market" in the legal sense of the term.

While leading businessmen and wealthy families (who enjoy strong connections with the state authorities, particularly the security services) exercise the right of publishing or broadcasting – whether through the print media, TV, radio outlets and even the Internet – they are actually performing a controlled political function. This is so, not because their media outlets convey the traditional values and concepts repeatedly disseminated by the official channels and outlets, but because they fill the vacuum resulting from tedious repetition, either through supplementary productions (soap operas, cheap songs, other forms of entertainment that cloud awareness and encourage public apathy towards involvement in the political arena) or through launching "shadow" messages of the state's original message.

The special nature of this market is attributed to two factors. First, it is set up against a background of severe social and economic deterioration – though amidst the relative richness generated by oil wealth; second, it exists in an environment of disintegrating authoritarian regimes and not of democratic transformations. The result would be the diversity rather than the freedom or independence of media flows.

At this point, the conditions and outcomes of disintegrating authoritarian regimes should be carefully considered in terms of their impact on the media evolution and the resulting societal relationships, both local and national.

The "chaotic media system," referred to by Alterman, is in fact a fragmented system that will inevitably lead the Arab audience towards a deeper cultural fragmentation, which in turn would restrict – if not distort – the process of building the Arab nation.

At this stage, this chapter will closely focus on the various elements involved this analysis.

1-The Arab Recipient

The first fundamental fact to be taken into consideration is that recipients, by virtue of their intelligence and conscience, are capable of making their own choices, satisfying their needs, and pursuing sources of knowledge and entertainment that are in harmony with their moods, experiences and attitudes. It is assumed that, under media monopolization, the recipients would either opt to believe "unilateral" media sources or resort to the original source of information through verbal, direct communications. Naturally, repetition, pressure and concentration could lead to a certain level of consent. However, if the gap between mass media allegations and information derived from direct experiences was widening, recipients would opt to obtain the necessary information from verbal sources. Thus alternative ideas and assessments might be derived from others, such as colleagues and civil or religious leaderships. As Jon Anderson explains it:

> Citizens do not necessarily cooperate with this program…they also experience social distance from them, a disconnect between the rituals of state and everyday life. The typical response is to develop practical senses of distance, irony, deconstructionist skills, cynicism, and conspiracy theories of politics as 'hidden.' [32]

Perhaps the most interesting media experience is the way the audience uses the widespread "audio-cassette technology" to invent popular ways to disseminate information, opinions and speeches. As a result, an environment is created where banned ideologies, popular arts and entertainments are beyond the control of government authorities. Huge leaps were witnessed in this technology when *salafi* movements and political Islam groups succeeded in employing this technique for their own benefit.

Undoubtedly, the expansion and diversity of the media realm have granted the recipient an exceptional power to choose that obliged media outlets to compete fiercely in order to attract viewers for the longest time possible. However, this power, which is generated by technological progress, should not be exaggerated. Indeed, the most important element of the authoritarian media experience in dealing with the viewers is the amazing diversity of the audience itself in terms of education, level of interest in political affairs, financial and technical capabilities of dealing with modern inventions. For example, those who have obtained any educational diploma represent 38.5% in Yemen, 48.4% in Egypt, 62.4% in Saudi Arabia (in 1990) and 86% in Jordan (in 1994). The considerable differences in levels of education, incomes and skills needed to deal with this media domain are strongly restricting its role in the Arab region. Consequently, the Arab region is considered the lowest in the world in terms of benefiting from the use of media technology (1% compared to 22% and 58% in Europe and North America, respectively, according to

1998 figures). In the Arab world, Internet penetration rates differ greatly between countries. In the UAE, the penetration rate was 3% whereas it did not exceed 0.2% in Egypt.[33]

Traditionally, a high percentage of spectators prefer watching local channels, leaving a smaller portion of the population who are willing to, and capable of, utilizing the astonishing diversity of this media, especially 24-hour satellite news channels.

The conclusion reached is that media liberalization would not necessarily generate the revolutionary developments long awaited by those urging the elimination of the dominant government discourse. More importantly, the tendency of liberalized media to satisfy the needs of different sectors of Arab audiences – as dictated by market forces and earned freedom – would imply greater degrees of division and/or integration among these sectors depending on their tastes (non-political and entertainment media), religious fanaticism, traditional political and ideological trends. In this context, one should not ignore the small numbers of educated and political activists who are more isolated from their respective societies and practice what Taggart calls "the secret world of digital technology," or the "electronic arena militants."[34]

2-Media Organizations

It is widely agreed that the "authoritarian" oratory is still dominating the Arab media arena. However, the expansion and diversity of broadcasting networks have necessitated a tough, exacting process of accommodation and reconciliation. In this context, it seems that the Saudi experience has been more dynamic than the earlier Egyptian experience, as indicated by the competition between the Saudi Arabia's *Arabsat* and Egypt's *Nilesat* systems.[35] No doubt the capital made available to media networks is a basic factor that enables them to reach and influence a larger audience. This factor seems more favorable for Arab Gulf states in general which enjoy the needed financial potential and vast advertising market. Hence, Egypt would lose the competition due to its smaller advertising market, and the distribution of advertising revenues over a larger number of organizations.

Though quite important, the financial resources are not the only effective factor in this process. Factors such as social capital, dynamic management, level of technical performance, expanded field of coverage, diversity of programs, and the employment of the best expertise, all represent important elements in attracting the audience, and in achieving and maintaining the desired level of success.

From this perspective, the *Al Jazeera* channel remains the most successful compared to all other Arab satellite news channels, though it is neither the oldest nor the biggest. A fact that surprised Egyptian President Hosni Mubarak when he toured the *Al Jazeera* station compound was how such a tiny building could cause such a headache (to Arab regimes?!) No doubt, the President was mentally comparing this with the huge tower that hosts different Egyptian TV networks! From the same perspective, it is very likely that Dubai, not Egypt or Saudi Arabia, will assume the actual leadership of the Arab media market—by becoming the generator and the mastermind of an integrated media system that addresses the most advanced Arab minds who are highly influential in formulating ideologies capable of coping with cultural and political realities.[36]

As for the influence on socio-political thinking and on cultural life in general, the real competition would depend on the content, institutional and planning potential, technical performance, level of professionalism, and the ability to adapt to the needs of the "transnational" audience.

However, professionalism and other institutional factors should not overshadow the fundamental element that brought about such a tremendous revolution in the Arab mass media—the accumulation of professional media personnel with political messages that have readily satisfied an eager audience. It was the accumulated professional capabilities that *Al Jazeera* station acquired from the BBC that created the *Al Jazeera* legend and the other Arab satellite channels that followed. Accordingly, this development, stemming from the emergence of such professionals who managed to free themselves from the Arab authoritarian media system, represents the most powerful factor strengthening the Arab media market.

3- Interactions of the Arab Media Market

Among all the above-mentioned factors, the most fundamental factor is the strong and deep-rooted association between media and politics—which can be examined at different levels and areas.

At the top level are the transformations that the Arab states are undergoing while facing huge internal and external challenges. Still, these pressures have not weakened the will and ability of the ruling elites to maintain power (Iraq being the exception). They have, nevertheless, imposed more complex and flexible patterns of accommodation in many cases, particularly when internal and external pressures have combined. The media has been one of the areas where such an accommodation becomes inevitable, as the experience of *Al Jazeera* channel in Qatar has shown. The channel reflects a mixed nationalist, pan-Arab and Islamic discourse that is inconsistent in crucial aspects with the policies of the state. In other words, the granting of relative media freedom has become a goal by itself for a limited number of Arab countries.

With the exception of those Arab states that still represent the negative pole in the Arab media realm, accommodation strategies have become more complex. The Internet is only controlled in limited cases. However, no single Arab state has sanctioned the establishment of privately owned radio stations. Moreover, considerable differences exist between terrestrial and satellite channels with the latter having greater margins of freedom and independence. As for the print media, extremely complex and aggressive policies are employed. For example, many Arab states took the initiative to set up major newspapers – some transnational in character – or indirectly finance and empower these papers with the best Arab minds to become substitutes or even competitors to the newspapers of opposition forces. These aggressive strategies have proved highly effective, as shown by the respect they have earned. On the other hand, the same Arab and other states have urged elements strongly connected to the security apparatus – though seemingly adopting a critical discourse, particularly the most popular radical nationalist trend – to establish newspapers that disseminate such an ostensibly critical discourse but in association with the interests and policies of the highest levels of leadership.

Nevertheless, once the field of relative independence of the media has expanded, it becomes quite difficult to forcefully restrain the media without creating drastic tensions. Inevitably, the more advanced groups – both in the professional or political communities – would struggle to restore and expand the earned media freedom, as well as impart a broader political objective to it. In other words, in the absence of totalitarian revolutions in a country (as was the case in Sudan in 1989), the path will lead inexorably to steady expansion of media freedom, depending not only on internal changes within the state, but also on political transformations in their broader sense.

Political conditions represent an extremely important factor, which sooner or later, would automatically affect a society's media map. Thus political balance will boost media freedom, a situation that enabled Lebanon, for example, to maintain a reasonable degree of media independence and freedom compared to other Arab countries.

In contrast, in countries with unipolar political regimes like Libya and Saudi Arabia, media freedom is contingent upon government initiatives, while the political categorization process in the majority of Arab countries is increasingly heading towards bi-polarization between the authoritative state supported by the ruling elites on the one hand, and political Islam movements on the other. Religious-political groups and establishments have been capitalizing on their influence, over the public and over some state institutions, either to impose their discourse through different mass media – especially those not under continuous government control, such as the Internet – or to curb freedom of expression and encourage intellectual confiscation measures. No doubt, the content of the media message is modified in accordance with restrictions and determinants imposed by the current of political-cultural Islam. It is very likely that the political Islam movement, which is now the dominating force in a number of Arab states, would seek to spread this sort of media and political oppression. Once in power, it would not hesitate to impose its own media policies through diverse methods, mostly totalitarian and partly more sophisticated societal and cultural ones.

The rise of political Islam movements, and the hard-line attitudes they adopt towards media causes and ways of life in general reflect the turmoil that hit ideological and cultural fields in a number of Arab countries. The basic Arab media models – especially in Lebanon and Egypt – have been molded during the Arab Enlightenment Project which emerged during the second half of the 20th century. Indeed, the most efficient media men of political Islam movements follow the project's guidelines in shaping their professional performance, though in differing degrees of awareness and struggle. In the fields of media and cultural activities, the leftist, liberal and democratic movements now enjoy a wider sphere of influence than in the political arena. Such a paradox is revealing in itself, when the Arab Enlightenment Project has long been on the defensive against sweeping offensives launched by political Islam groups.

However, some Arab states have "usurped" the form of the slogans that these groups used to project and placed them at the top of their media agenda. Others seek to assert the old, eroded stances of "official" Islam, while some are in conflict with this movement and persecute its forces and symbols, thereby losing their ethical platform, along with the cultural initiative at the public level.

The most important manifestations of the vitality and strength of civil society organizations have taken various other forms. There is the so-called "community media" which is highly professional and is characterized by refined cultural content, though limited in terms of circulation and influence. It offers ample opportunities for contributions by civil and communal leaderships to appear in both the official and independent press, particularly the "opinion" articles in major newspapers (the nationalist one in the case of Egypt). Sometimes, civil society organizations launch robust campaigns to prevent certain violations or to stand up to challenges of fanaticism and partiality invoked by big media outlets, especially with regard to women's causes.

However, the true impact of this type of media has not yet materialized, owing to the relatively limited margins of freedom offered, and not forgetting the legal, political and economic restrictions imposed on it. Any future development of such media outlets will remain dependent on the level of the already strained economic and social development process in the majority of Arab countries.

It would seem that all these factors affecting the media sphere could lead to the creation of a climate of chaos and fragmentation until the implementation of radical democratic transformations or the outbreak of major economic revolutions.

Conclusions

Despite the fact that the concrete mobility, which is taking place in the mass media sphere, is generated by various emerging factors, this mobility remains heavily restricted for many reasons, leading to greater tensions and a more diverse and fragmented market at the same time. A more sophisticated professional performance than was permitted earlier to the Arab media during the past half century, has created a higher level of manipulation and an increased sense of alienation from advanced knowledge and more balanced worldviews.

In this context, it is quite likely that the pace of media fragmentation will escalate with the expansion of the margins of freedom and independence and lead increasingly to the disintegration of Arab audiences at the local and national levels.

As a result, a smaller segment will tend to acquire necessary information from pan-Arab media sources, while attempting to obtain advanced political knowledge through developed professional performance and a broader but less diverse coverage area. The larger segment would be content with the respective local media outlets which offer programs with greater diversity, simpler language, lower performance, which are less complex in terms of ideological content and more entertainment-oriented.

The Impact of Commercial Interests on Arab Media Content

Naomi Sakr

Media content as a product is very different from other products that are bought and sold. Most people consider it as being unique because of the meanings conveyed by media products. Others, however, point to more subtle differences that stem from the peculiar economic characteristics of symbolic goods. Although the meanings conveyed by the press and audiovisual media are "consumed" in a certain sense, they are not destroyed by the act of consumption and are thus never used up. Unlike tangible goods such as a sack of rice or a loaf of bread, the same film, television program or feature article can be enjoyed by any number of people, many times over. This simple fact has major implications for the operation of media markets. An understanding of these implications provides an appropriate entry point for a discussion on the commercial interests operating in the media field and their impact on media content.

The following introductory section deals briefly with the phenomenon of "market failure" as it relates to commercial broadcast media in particular. "Commercial" in this context refers to all editorial content that is broadcast along with advertisements and has business backing of some kind. In the light of this introduction, the chapter proceeds to consider three privately-owned commercial media organizations operating in the Arab world. It explores the commercial interests operating in these organizations and the various pressures to which they are subject in making choices about television content. The chapter concludes by weighing up the impact of commercial and corporate interests on Arab television programming.

Media Market Challenges and Commercial Responses

As noted in the introduction, the basic fact that a television or radio program can be watched by any number of people means that the market for such programs operates differently from that for tangible goods. Consumers of broadcast material are not potential rivals with each other in the same way that they might be for a coat or a house.[1] Consequently price mechanisms cannot reconcile the supply and demand of broadcast material as they can with other goods. Neither can viewers who have the necessary receiving equipment be excluded from hearing or watching free-to-air broadcasts. Whereas with tangible goods there is a moment of exchange at which consumers register their preferences through payment, no such transaction occurs when a radio or television program is switched on. Moreover, the cost to the producer of serving additional members of the broadcast audience is quite unlike the cost of meeting additional demand for tangible goods. Once a program has been made it can be beamed to an ever increasing number of people without any extra input required for the program itself. While the "non-rival" and "non-excludable" characteristics of broadcast media bring about a failure of normal market mechanisms, the virtually continuous potential for expanding the audience at no extra cost creates a further conundrum. As Nicholas Garnham and others pointed out in the 1980s, no natural market mechanism will stand in the way of a commercial broadcaster who seeks to "expand audience share to the point of monopoly saturation."[2]

At the same time, however, commercial broadcasters face unusual challenges. Watching a news bulletin or a soap opera episode does not destroy it, but neither do viewers want to watch the same bulletin or episode over and over again. Thus each weekly, daily or even hourly program has to offer something new.[3] Yet newness brings with it the risk of failure, because consumers' preferences are unpredictable. In the music and film industries this risk can be offset by increasing and diversifying output to ensure that at least some of it proves popular enough to make a profit. In broadcasting, where schedules are fixed by time and other constraints, the risk associated with novelty is more likely to be offset by a tendency to base new broadcasts on what has proved popular with audiences in the past. That is to say, the commercial motivation to maximize audience share for greater profit is likely to deter free-to-air broadcasters from risking the introduction of an untried program genre, a new presenter or any other form of innovation. Commercial broadcasters also face less risk when they are few in number and the audiences have limited choices. The trend towards mergers and acquisitions in the field is amply exposed by statistics. When Ben H. Bagdikian published the first edition of his book *The Media Monopoly* in 1983, some fifty corporations dominated the US media market. Under deregulation this number had shrunk to twenty nine by 1987, to ten by 1997 and to six by the time his book had reached its sixth edition.[4] On the pan-Arab scene, collaboration between MBC and Future TV reflects a similar trend.

It has thus far been established that commercial interests will push those in the free-to-air television business to produce content that pleases the widest possible audience with the least possible risk. Since companies in this business cannot compete with each other by means of price, any competition that does take place will be restricted to the realm of content. However, here there are other commercial factors restraining program diversity and competition. These include advertisers' interests and program costs. Advertisers address people in their capacity as consumers, not as citizens, whereas audiences need content that serves them as citizens, not only as consumers. Advertisers' preference for their products to be associated with certain types of programming is evident from statistics. During the first half of 2002, for example, political programs attracted the lowest level of advertising on pan-Arab satellite television. Drama serials, movies and quiz shows attracted 17 per cent, 13 per cent and 12 per cent of advertising respectively. News programs also attracted a relatively high figure of 14 per cent, but advertising slots booked with political programs accounted for only 4 per cent of total advertising spend.[5] Since these figures are believed to mask the effect of concealed discounts, the real discrepancies between spending on advertising by program type may actually be more pronounced. The obvious implication is that commercial interests favor certain types of content over others.

Advertisers are under no obligation to explain or justify their editorial preferences in public, but they are revealed in practice. For example, Procter and Gamble, McDonald's, Ford Motors, Sears Roebuck and American Express were among those withdrawing their advertisements from war-related news on US television networks during the 1991 Gulf War. It has been suggested that reasons for such action did not lie with any fall-off in the number of viewers but rather with dissatisfaction at the disturbing nature of some war reporting.[6] Al Jazeera, the Doha-based satellite channel, increased its worldwide audience to around 35 million during the US military attack on Afghanistan in late 2001, but advertisers such as General Electric and Pepsi Cola pulled out despite the increase.[7] Commercial influences like this are compounded by the fact that different types of programming cost different amounts to make. In the cost hierarchy, a newly-commissioned drama ranks as the most expensive, requiring approximately twice the investment involved in news and – at the very least – four times the cost of a game show. If guided solely by commercial considerations, television companies may seek to satisfy the demand for drama through cheap ready-made imports and save their budgets for contingencies, like the right to broadcast sporting events.

An awareness of these influences should inject a salutary note of caution into arguments for marketization of the broadcast media. As has been pointed out, the choice is not between "state licensing and control on the one side and minimally regulated market mechanisms on the other."[8] Instead, as Graham Murdock and other like-minded analysts have argued, the opposition is between policies designed to reinvigorate independent public communications systems and policies (including marketization) that are liable to marginalize or eradicate them.[9] Reinvigoration means, among other things, countering monopolistic tendencies and providing incentives for diversity and innovation in programming. Specifically, in the case of Arab broadcasting, it also means ensuring that some potentially benign effects of commercial media are not undermined. Thus, for example, the entry of commercial interests into what has hitherto been a state monopoly may enliven and increase program choices and thus provide audiences with a means of registering their preferences.

To some degree, this is what has happened with the growth in satellite broadcasting over the past decade. However, what has not yet happened is for advertising revenues to follow faithfully where audiences lead. Instead, it is customary for broadcasters to obstruct or undermine the collection of viewership statistics, to the point where one industry source recently drew a stark contrast between what he described as "a surplus in satellite channels and a deficit in audience research."[10] Given this deficit, advertisers make essentially political rather than commercial decisions about where to place advertisements, with a resulting mismatch between the level of advertising revenue a channel may enjoy and its actual audience share. Advertising executives regularly deplore the resistance shown by Arab broadcasters and their supporters in government to the particular market dynamics that can have a reinvigorating effect on content. One publicly urged the satellite stations to turn themselves into "viable and transparent institutions that answer only to the viewer, take the dynamics of the market into consideration and feel the pulse of the [Arab] nation through professional research."[11]

Therefore, in discussing the impact of commercial interests on Arab television content, the precise nature of these interests needs to be deconstructed to ascertain whether perceived influences on programming stem from the range of factors identified above – and, if so, how – or whether they stem from other factors. In the remainder of this chapter, the business motives and program choices of three contrasting commercial

Arab satellite television channels are studied. The first is the privately-owned Egyptian broadcaster Dream TV, selected because it was launched specifically as a "business project" in a country that only recently opened to private broadcasters on rather restricted terms. The second is the 24-hour news and current affairs channel *Al Arabiya*, launched from Dubai in 2003 with an explicit remit to compete with *Al Jazeera*, the previous 24-hour Arabic-language television news market leader. The third is Future TV. Here the rationale for selection lies in the fact that the Lebanese television market is dominated by privately-owned players and, as will be shown, Future's TV's President, Nadim Munla, has repeatedly stressed his preoccupation with sound financial management.

This study is based on a particular set of questions. One relates to the commercial and regulatory context in which each channel emerged and in which it now functions. Others relate to the channel owner's declared and undeclared motives and to the degree to which audiences have indicated satisfaction with the channels' program content. Equally, it is relevant to establish how the channels in question have differentiated themselves from others and how they have faced up to the challenge of balancing the conflicting commercial pressures already discussed. These imperatives call, on the one hand, for maximizing market share through creativity and distinguishing features. On the other hand, they call for minimizing risk. Finally the studies consider whether commercial interests ultimately constitute the primary influence on content, or whether other factors dilute these interests or counteract them.

Dream TV: A Business Project

The launch of Dream TV in November 2001 was made possible by an Egyptian government decision in 2000 to allow broadcasters other than the state-controlled Egyptian Radio and Television Union (ERTU) to transmit television programming by satellite from within a special "free zone" set aside for media activities. The free zone was located in Media Production City (MPC), near Cairo. MPC, managed by the majority state-controlled Egyptian Media Production City Company, houses outdoor film sets, production studios, editing suites and the technical centre for control of Nilesat, Egypt's own national satellite network. Equipped from the outset with digital technology, Nilesat offered possibilities for major expansion in broadcasting, especially after the second satellite in its fleet was launched in August 2000, bringing the total capacity of Nilesat 101 and 102 to 229 digital channels.[12] Several privately-owned Egyptian satellite television stations subsequently arrived on the scene. By late 2004, there were five private Egyptian networks transmitting from Nilesat, including Dream TV. Of the other four, one was Mehwar, a general channel offering entertainment and current affairs, two offered music television (Mazzika and Melody), and the fourth was the Egyptian tourism channel MTC. Dream and Melody occupied two channels each.

The launching of these channels on Nilesat was the culmination of a lengthy process. Egypt's private entrepreneurs had pressed throughout the 1990s for a relaxation of the country's media regulation to allow them to speak for themselves through the media to overcome a Nasserist legacy of popular suspicion towards private capitalists. Shafiq Gabr, as Chairman of the Artoc Group, chose a strategically important moment ahead of the Middle East and North Africa Economic Conference in Cairo in 1996 to call for private television stations. This was the same year that Ahmad Bahgat, one of Egypt's leading industrialists, launched his ambitious US$ 2.6 billion residential and leisure complex, under the name "Dreamland," on the road from Giza to Sixth October City. By 2000, at the time when the Egyptian government announced that private Egyptian companies would be allowed to broadcast from MPC, the Dreamland theme park had opened and its hotel was close to completion.[13] Its owner's other business interests were large and relatively diverse, with a substantial output of consumer electronics. Ahmad Bahgat consequently had an interest in vertical integration, realizing that he could sell more televisions and video recorders if potential purchasers had more compelling television programs to watch.

This background may provide insights into why Bahgat was one of the first private entrepreneurs to take advantage of the new regulations. With these new rules restricting private broadcasters to satellite transmission only, and with satellite penetration still very limited in Egypt at that point,[14] the potential audience for any new private station was widely regarded as too small to attract enough advertising to make the station viable.[15] Nevertheless, Bahgat took a chance. He established Dream TV with an initial investment reported at just £E30 million, equivalent to three quarters of the total sum he was then spending annually on advertising in all outlets.[16] In other words, he decided that advertising via a media outlet he owned himself would be potentially more profitable than continuing to let existing media organizations benefit from his advertising budgets. Dream TV's first Vice President stressed to an interviewer in 2002 that the company was a "business project." For example, she said, it had demonstrated that companies that advertised real estate on television could profit from the exercise, so long as they chose a suitably targeted medium, such as Dream TV.[17] As initially conceived, the project was to build up gradually to three digital channels offering entertainment and talk shows aimed primarily at young people. This made good business sense in a society where an overwhelming majority of the population is below 40 years of age. It steered the company's choice of content towards an emphasis on music, drama series, sport and talk shows about issues relevant to Egyptian households having satellite reception and a decoder for digital transmission.

In other words, Dream TV's target audience consisted essentially of those deemed to be potential buyers of products from the Bahgat Group's 28 factories, including furniture, marble and refrigerators as well as televisions. Younger people in this target group had already, during the second half of the 1990s, shown their fondness for music television. Back in 1993, Cable Network Egypt (CNE) had increased its subscriber base by adding Viacom's MTV to its offering, which prompted others to follow suit.[18] Thus Dream 1, the first channel to go on air, featured video clips, live concerts and interviews with celebrities such as singers and movie stars. Dream 2, launched a few months later, introduced a mixture of entertainment and information, with well-known figures pushing at censorship boundaries in a way designed to attract public attention. Bahgat had apparently decided that viewership would be boosted by screening bold content, which in turn would encourage other companies outside his own business empire to advertise their wares on Dream TV.

Bahgat's commercial calculations may also have taken account of the considerable growth potential for satellite penetration within Egypt. As noted earlier, measurement of audiences for actual programs has to be hedged with caveats in Arab countries, because broadcasters decline to buy research findings if these do not trumpet their success. However, there is more certainty in quantifying satellite reception and these figures show that the number of Egyptian viewers able to receive Dream 1 and Dream 2 increased substantially after their launch. A data-gathering exercise commissioned by Nilesat in 2004 revealed that 24 per cent of Egyptian households could receive Nilesat channels in 2003 and this rose to 32 per cent in 2004.[19] This was in comparison with an estimated 7 per cent in 2002.[20] Nevertheless, Dream TV, being a satellite channel, also targeted Arabic-speaking audiences beyond Egypt, while seeking to retain its Egyptian perspective. This was feasible from a business point of view, since Gulf viewers with high purchasing power are prospective customers for Egyptian real estate and also buy other goods and services during visits to Egypt.

As a business venture aimed at maximizing both audiences and advertising revenues, Dream TV started out with multiple incentives for showing eye-catching content. In the field of music TV, this was achieved by often managing to be the first of the pan-Arab satellite channels to air new songs and by offering music producers more favorable terms than those available on Egypt's state TV channels.[21] Programs like *Al-Hawa Hawana* proved popular with audiences because they offered new live music and suited Dream TV commercially because they boosted its library of recorded songs. For talk shows and political analysis, Dream TV chose high-profile presenters whose approach to challenging or sensitive content was guaranteed to attract the attention of other media. This policy was commercially sensible, since television series have only a short lifespan in which they can be publicized. However, it also compensated for the fact that independent newscasts were ruled out for Dream TV. According to company sources, cost was one reason for this decision.[22] Yet, it is also assumed that Dream TV received a licence to broadcast on the basis that it would not gather news. Under the terms of that licence, Bahgat had to accept that the ERTU would own 10 per cent of Dream TV.[23] Since the ERTU has its own news departments for its terrestrial and satellite channels, it has little appetite for promoting competition. In addition, its news-gathering operations are so strictly controlled that Egyptians have learned not to rely on them for breaking news. For example, when bombs killed 34 people at three Sinai resorts in October 2004, none of the government-owned Egyptian television stations reported the bombings until almost 24 hours later because they were waiting for official permission to do so from the Ministry of Interior.[24] Instead of filling this particular gap in the market, Dream TV's policy was to attract attention by engaging high-profile presenters.

This approach became obvious when Bahgat appointed Hala Sirhan as both Vice President of Dream TV and the company's leading talk show host. Sirhan's reputation when she joined Dream TV rested on her background in journalism and her previous performance as a popular and controversial talk show presenter with the Saudi-owned pay-TV network, Arab Radio and Television (ART). Sirhan herself told an interviewer soon after she joined Dream TV that the company's mission was first, to achieve "credibility" and second, to be entertaining.[25] She indicated that one way to acquire credibility would be through broadcasting programs that analyze news events. "We want to talk more about the future," she said, noting a plan to devote four hours a day of prime viewing time to analysis of politics, economics and sport.[26] Sirhan's ideas about relevance

[70]

and credibility were shared by Osama Al-Sheikh, appointed as General Manager of Dream TV. He joined with Sirhan in efforts to get the veteran political commentator, Mohammad Hassanein Heikal, to join the channel in a series entitled *Al-Ustaz* (The Professor), in which Heikal addressed the audience directly without a presenter. The prestige accorded to the channel by such well-known names helped it to attract others. Hamdi Qandil, host of the popular ERTU series, *Rais al-Tahrir* (Editor-in-Chief), also hosted a show for Dream TV. Another program in the same vein was *Ala al-Qahwa* (In the Café), in which Ibrahim Eissa criticized government failings, albeit often indirectly. According to Eissa, his contract with Dream contained guarantees that he would be allowed to express himself freely and "present what people are feeling."[27]

It is clear from this that Dream TV's commercial rationale pushed it to air content that would, in Hala Sirhan's words, "get people to watch." At ART, Hala Sirhan had advised her previous employer, Sheikh Saleh Kamel, that the best way to attract viewers to his pay-TV channels was to promote interactivity, whereby audiences would themselves take an active part in programs, through live interviews and phone-ins.[28] The subjects, according to her, ought to be ones that had "never been touched before," and, while maintaining standards of taste and decency, should "cross red lines."[29] Sirhan pursued this approach on Dream TV. When some 400 people died in a train fire in Egypt in February 2002, guests on her talk show openly accused the government of corruption and incompetence.[30] However, what also becomes apparent from analyzing Dream TV's content is that it has ultimately been influenced more by non-commercial interests than commercial ones. This is because the vision for bold, credible, "must-see" viewing was undermined by a mixture of administrative and editorial interference. An early external intervention to pre-empt certain material from being shown occurred in October 2002, just under a year after the channel started.

The intervention came from the General Authority for Free Zones, which warned that strict measures would be taken against Dream TV as an

MPC tenant if it ever again tackled sensitive subjects in a sensational manner. The warning was ostensibly issued in response to a talk show in which Hala Sirhan, along with her panel of speakers and callers to the program, had focused on divorce among young Egyptians. Discussion of marital relations had led to discussion of sex.[31] Skeptics, however, believed that the warning was actually triggered by one of Hassanein Heikal's political commentaries, aired during the same week. In this commentary, delivered as a lecture at the American University in Cairo, Heikal noted that Egypt, as a republic, is not under a dynastic form of rule in which power passes from father to son. This lecture, although scheduled to appear three times on Dream TV, was shown only twice, reportedly because of "advice" received behind the scenes.[32] Meanwhile the opposition newspaper, *Al-Wafd*, drew public attention to Ahmad Bahgat's indebtedness to Egyptian banks and suggested that these bank loans were paying for "offensive" material such as that covered in Hala Sirhan's show. Bahgat then appeared on his own channel to deny the accusation. Over the following two years, however, a link seemed to emerge between Bahgat's position with his state-owned bank creditors and his increasing unwillingness to broadcast controversial content. Sirhan left Dream TV in mid-2003, Eissa followed in December that year, and Qandil's weekly show was cancelled in March 2004. A scheduled appearance by Heikal in September 2003 to mark his formal retirement was withdrawn at short notice, after he had already arrived at the studio.[33]

Al Arabiya: Seeking Market Share

In early 2003, when the 24-hour news and current affairs channel *Al Arabiya* arrived on the satellite scene, audiences were already glued to *Al Jazeera*, another 24-hour news channel in Arabic. Paradoxically, despite its large audiences, *Al Jazeera* had few advertisers. Its controversial programming had provoked Gulf information ministers into urging advertisers to boycott it.[34] So *Al Arabiya*, by providing an outlet for advertising that was being denied to its closest rival, enjoyed an instant commercial advantage in terms of revenue. It also appeared to enjoy an advantage over *Al Jazeera* in terms of its access to highly-placed news sources in the Gulf. This was because *Al Jazeera's* uncompromising coverage of Gulf affairs had resulted in its crews being barred from important regional events, such as ministerial meetings and the 2002 *hajj* (Muslim pilgrimage).[35] In addition, Kuwait had ordered Al Jazeera to close its Kuwaiti office in November 2002 for allegedly taking a "hostile stand" against the country.[36] *Al Arabiya* gained a possible further commercial advantage in the amount of publicity it generated by starting up. Other satellite channels such as Arab News Network (ANN), Nile News, Abu Dhabi TV and *Al-Manar* had already added to regional sources of television news, but *Al Arabiya's* launch shortly before the US-led invasion of Iraq in March 2003 ensured unprecedented news coverage of the new channel in the international press.[37]

Al Arabiya, backed with initial capital of $300m, was the project of an influential group of existing media investors behind a Dubai-based company called Middle East News. Ownership of Middle East News lay predominantly with MBC's parent company, the ARA Group International Holding Company, headed in turn by Sheikh Walid Al-Ibrahim, a brother-in-law of Saudi Arabia's late ruler, King Fahd bin Abdel Aziz Al-Saud. Joining MBC in Middle East News was its business ally, Future TV.[38] MBC and Future had already forged an alliance in late 2001 to cooperate in the fields of newsgathering and selling advertising space. The precedents set by MBC's news coverage seemed to indicate the editorial line that *Al Arabiya* would take. That is to say it would be technically adept and proactive, but also cautious in its treatment of Gulf affairs.[39] For example, Ali Al-Hedeithy, head of Middle East News, declared that *Al Arabiya* would offer a "wise and balanced alternative to *Al Jazeera*."[40] Saleh Qallab, *Al Arabiya's* first Editorial Director, was a former Information Minister of Jordan, whose government had closed the offices of *Al Jazeera* in 1998, and again in 2002, in protest at views expressed by talk show guests.[41] Ali Al-Hedeithy confirmed in an early press interview that Kuwait was also involved in the channel.[42] However, Kuwait soon withdrew in protest at *Al Arabiya's* reporting of the invasion of Iraq.[43] As this decision demonstrated, the war on Iraq heightened sensitivities regarding every detail of editorial content on pan-Arab channels. Given the financial and newsgathering hurdles experienced by *Al Jazeera*, satellite broadcasters' commercial interests dictated that they balance the need for credibility among an Arab public overwhelmingly opposed to the US invasion with sensitivity to the dilemmas faced by US-backed governments in the Gulf.

Al Arabiya's evolving content testified to just such a balancing act. Walid Al-Ibrahim indicated to a *Washington Times* correspondent that the motivation underlying his media business was not primarily commercial but to "get rid of the Taliban mentality."[44] He also confirmed in the same interview that *Al Arabiya* had altered its policy on the use of politically sensitive words. For example, he said, it had stopped describing US forces in Iraq as "invaders." Others in the chain of command confirmed that the channel did not intend to take editorial risks. Salah Negm, who switched from being Editor-in-Chief at *Al Jazeera* to occupying a similar post at *Al Arabiya*, said the aim was steady and solid expansion. According to him, the channel was not seeking to boost its market share at any price, but wanted to achieve this through "accuracy and facts."[45] The balancing act seemed to involve partly emulating *Al Jazeera* in certain respects but not in others. A number of *Al Jazeera* staff members were enticed to join Al Arabiya for higher salaries.[46] Having positioned themselves vis-à-vis CNN and the BBC when they worked at *Al Jazeera*, the core team that launched *Al Arabiya* carried the same models with them to their new posts. Negm summarized the challenge as that of broadcasting news that would be "appealing instead of being boring and at the same time informative rather than didactic."[47] His team seems to have hit on a way of facing facts, while avoiding political sensitivities by leading on news coverage and deliberately downplaying analysis.[48]

This editorial approach, meanwhile, succeeded in pleasing some viewers but not others. When the US State Department polled viewers in seven Iraqi cities in October 2003, it found that 37 per cent of Iraqis with satellite access preferred to watch the news on *Al Arabiya*, compared with 26 per cent for *Al Jazeera*.[49] On the other hand, reports of *Al Arabiya* crews failing to obtain Qatari accreditation to attend Iraq War briefings at US Central Command in Doha, or being denied passage via Kuwait into Iraq, revealed that the channel's staff members were subject to the same politically-motivated obstructions that most journalists in the region are liable to face. Prior to its collapse, Saddam Hussein's regime confiscated one of *Al Arabiya's* two satellite uplinks in Baghdad. Yet Ali Al-Hedeithy let it be known soon afterwards that he would welcome Saddam Hussein's Information Minister, Mohammed Saeed al-Sahaf, as a commentator and analyst on *Al Arabiya*.[50] Meanwhile *Al Arabiya's* choice of Peter Arnett to boost its coverage of the Iraq War might have seemed at the time like an inspired step in the ongoing editorial balancing act. For one thing, Arab viewers of CNN in the 1991 Gulf War would have remembered Arnett's reports from Baghdad. For another, Arnett came to *Al Arabiya* after having been dropped by National Geographic for remarks he had made to Iraqi Television about the war. Even so, the initiative was criticized on technical and editorial grounds.[51] However, perceptions of the channel's editorial position appeared to crystallize somewhat when US President George Bush chose *Al Arabiya*, alongside the US-funded channel *Al Hurra*, to apologize to the Arab people for the torture of prisoners by Americans in Iraq.

In early 2004 it emerged that *Al Arabiya* had apparently accepted rules laid down by the US-backed Iraqi authorities for coverage of the conflict in Iraq. The channel had been pressured to do so by being banned from the country for two months. In August 2003, it had broadcast pictures of masked men who threatened to kill members of the US-appointed Iraqi Governing Council (IGC). The decision to screen this footage had provoked strong condemnation from US officials, who described the broadcast as irresponsible.[52] Then, in November 2003, *Al Arabiya* broadcast an audiotape in which the ousted Iraqi President, Saddam Hussein, called for attacks on IGC members. On this occasion the IGC banned *Al Arabiya* from Iraq on the grounds that airing the tape was tantamount to inciting murder. However, the IGC lifted the ban in January 2004 amid reports that *Al Arabiya* had changed its editorial policy for dealing with statements from Saddam Hussein. It reportedly received a handwritten message from Saddam in early December 2003, but refrained from reporting if for fear of triggering an extension of the IGC ban.[53]

The appointment of Saleh Qallab to a Jordanian government post resulted in Abdul Rahman Al-Rashid taking charge of editorial direction at *Al Arabiya* in 2004. Al-Rashid brought with him a reputation built up as Editor-in-Chief of the widely circulated, Saudi-owned, London-based daily newspaper *Asharq al-Awsat*. He endorsed the view expressed previously by Salah Negm, that *Al Arabiya's* aim was not to broadcast news at any cost. He told one interviewer that the aim was to "go after politics in the region" while taking a "popular but not demagogic approach" to news reports.[54] Senior staff members say privately that decisions about coverage were often taken for financial reasons, as they would in any commercial newsgathering organization. For example, resources were not allowed to remain temporarily idle in one location if they could be put to use elsewhere. *Al Arabiya's* own location in Dubai can be explained in similar financial terms. MBC, originally headquartered in London, moved to Dubai during 2001 to benefit from cost-savings, better technical facilities and closer proximity between its staff and their audience. With aspects of Dubai Media City tailored to the needs of MBC and *Al Arabiya*, the latter returned the compliment in April 2003 by signing a formal agreement to make a television documentary about a typical day in Dubai. The agreed film was the kind that would also yield still photographs suitable for a coffee table book.[55]

Yet, whatever its finances, *Al Arabiya* has paid a tragic price in human terms for its Iraq coverage. Its staff in the country suffered at the hands of

[76]

both Americans and Arabs. A cameraman, Ali Abdel-Aziz, and a correspondent, Ali Al-Khatib, died in March 2004, after being shot by US troops as they covered a rocket attack on a Baghdad hotel at night.[56] A lawyer for the station later complained that a US military report on the killing was "full of inconsistencies and mistakes."[57] The day the report was issued, more than 20 Arab journalists attending a press conference by Colin Powell registered their protest by walking out. Additionally, five employees of *Al Arabiya* were killed and 14 injured in Baghdad at the end of October 2004. On this occasion the cause was a car bomb specifically targeted at *Al Arabiya's* bureau in the Mansour district.[58] *Al Arabiya's* own website reported that a previously unknown group calling itself the "Jihad Martyrs Brigades" had posted a statement on the Internet claiming responsibility for the attack and threatening that it would attack again in future. In other words, the bombing was clearly targeted at the channel's economic viability and its content.

Future TV: Innovation of a Certain Kind

There can be no doubt about Future TV's status as a commercial operation, being run as part of the business empire of Rafiq Hariri, Lebanon's late Prime Minister who held office for all but two years between 1990 and 2004. Hariri's dual role as both a political and business leader makes Future TV an interesting case for discussing the impact of commercial interests on television content. The discussion here acknowledges that the company has a national and a pan-Arab arm, the latter having been launched as Future International in 1996. During its first six years, according to data collected by the Pan-Arab Research Centre (PARC) in Dubai, Future International consistently held one of the top three places among pan-Arab satellite channels in terms of advertising revenues.[59] During that period, it also attracted a sizeable share of the Gulf market, where the buoyant purchasing power of viewers makes them appealing to advertisers. PARC statistics indicate that in the late 1990s, it was watched by 26 per cent of satellite viewers in Kuwait, 19 per cent in

Saudi Arabia and 13 per cent in the UAE.[60] A further proliferation of channels since 2002 has affected the viewership figures of the three leading pan-Arab generalist channels—Middle East Broadcasting Centre TV Network (MBC), Lebanese Broadcasting Corporation TV (LBC) and Future TV. This in turn, has put increased pressure on them to retain their market share. Future TV's efforts in this direction have had particular implications for its approach to content, as will be shown.

First, however, it is necessary to establish that describing Future TV as a commercial channel is not the same as saying that it was created primarily for reasons of profit. The precise nature of the commercial interests behind it has to be understood in the context of Lebanon's reconstruction after the 1975–90 Civil War. As head of the Oger Company, built up through construction work in Saudi Arabia and elsewhere, Hariri did not retire from business after becoming Prime Minister in 1990. He took a 7 per cent stake in Solidère, the private real estate company contracted to rebuild downtown Beirut, which meant he also had a strong personal incentive to promote the reconstruction process and encourage other financiers from the region to support it.[61] Hariri's involvement in media predated the official licensing of Future TV under Lebanon's post-war media laws. Starting in 1993, his Luxembourg-based company Techniques Audiovisuelles, began to acquire the Paris-based Radio Orient, based on negotiations that probably started many years previously.[62]

Not surprisingly, Future TV was one of only four (later six) terrestrial television stations initially granted a license under Lebanon's Audiovisual Media Law (Law No 382 of 1994). The 1990 Taif Agreement that ended the civil war had declared broadcast regulation to be a priority for the post-war government, because chaotic use of the country's radio spectrum constituted not only a reminder of wartime anarchy but a threat to air traffic control.[63] Law No 382 revoked the broadcasting monopoly granted in 1977 to the state broadcaster, Télé-Liban, and transformed Lebanon into the first Arab state to formally authorize privately-owned terrestrial broadcasting within its borders. Yet it also drastically reduced the number of broadcasters in operation, from 60 private TV stations to four and from 150 radio stations to ten.[64] In effect, licenses were granted to representatives of the country's biggest confessional (religiously-affiliated) groups. Thus Future TV, associated with the Sunni Prime Minister, could be seen as an organ for the Sunni Muslim community, while other stations catered to the needs of Shia Muslims, Maronite Christians and Orthodox Christians. A separate law allowed holders of terrestrial licenses to transmit by satellite but gave government ministers the right to decide whether or not satellite programming could include news and political reports.[65] It was under this law that Future International began operations in late 1996.

A dominant confessional (as distinct from commercial) aspect of Future TV becomes apparent from a breakdown of the company's equity compared with that of other licensees. The National Audiovisual Council appointed to oversee the licensing process recommended that no more than 50% of the shareholdings in any broadcaster should be held by the same political party or religious grouping. However, virtually no television licensee complied with this ruling, with the result that public perceptions of confessionalism or religious affiliation in the allocation of licences corresponded in most cases to the actual ownership situation. In the case of Future TV, Rafiq Hariri himself was not a direct shareholder. Instead, his brother, sister and wife together held 30 per cent of the shares.[66] Additional shares held by his employees and advisors brought the total for his family and immediate associates to 56 per cent.[67] Besides its confessional affiliation, Future TV was also well-placed in political terms. This was due partly to Hariri's position as head of the government that allocated the first round of broadcast licenses under the 1994 law. Yet, evidence of strategic backing from Lebanon's wider political elite could be found in the Future TV shares held by three sons of Issam Fares, an MP with high-level Saudi and Syrian connections comparable to those of Hariri himself.[68] All these connections helped Future TV to gain access to audiences, advertising and resources outside

Lebanon. For example, Future's sister company, Radio Orient, was permitted to sell television airtime directly to advertisers in Syria, a move which indicated Syrian government approval.[69] In November 2001, Future TV announced that it would join forces with the Saudi-owned MBC for newsgathering and marketing operations. Under the agreement, ARA Media Services, a sister company of MBC, would represent both Future TV and its youth channel, Zen TV.

Future TV's President, Nadim Munla, cited the agreement with MBC as proof that the two outlets were "commercial institutions," interested in preserving a "healthy financial situation" by reducing production costs and increasing advertising income.[70] It was noted that the two companies had already exchanged programs and shared coverage of the war against Afghanistan. In fact some key programming decisions taken by Future TV during this period demonstrate how the desire to shore up the company's finances had an impact on content. Two examples are the development of youth programming and a foray into reality TV formats purchased from Western sources. These decisions, however, should also be seen against the background of existing characteristics of Future's program schedules. Indeed, one way to analyze these programming decisions is to consider whether they were truly innovative or were actually a shrewd move to minimize risk by opting for program styles and genres that had already proved successful elsewhere.

For example, it was often said of Future International in its early days that, like LBC, it relied on attractive female presenters to lure Gulf audiences unused to a relaxed female presence on TV. This presence was not limited to the studio, as demonstrated by the case of Diana Moukalled, who rose through the ranks as a general assignment reporter, producer, editor and presenter of documentaries.[71] Moukalled, who also worked briefly on Future's youth channel, Zen TV, made her mark with the documentary series *Bi'l-Ain Al-Mujarrada* (With the Naked Eye), for which she had filmed a program inside Iraq before returning there to cover the US-led invasion in March 2003.[72] As much of the commentary on

[80]

Arab women war correspondents has suggested, their role in reporting the invasion appeared to mark a breakthrough for pan-Arab television news. However, this was a development that had already been tried and tested by Western broadcasters in the 1991 Gulf War, where it seemed that female reporters in war zones heightened the sense of drama while distracting from the horror of events.[73] Future TV could also have been said to play safe with its series *Above the Siege*, aired during the Israeli offensive against Palestinian towns and refugee camps in April 2002. Although the program gave vent to outspoken opinions, it had much in common with highly popular slots already carried on other channels, most notably Al Jazeera's *Under Siege*.[74]

Commercial calculations can also account for the launch of Zen TV in January 2001. Given widespread neglect of the youth audience by other broadcasters, Zen promised to fill a glaring gap in the market and tap into related advertising budgets. It opted to provide what has been described as a "mix of MTV and Disney," albeit conducted entirely in Arabic against a backdrop in which Arab traditions and values centred on family and tradition loom large.[75] By 2002, Future TV was telling advertisers that Zen had acquired a viewer base of 2.6m, with a quarter of this number in Saudi Arabia and a fifth in Jordan, followed by Egypt, the UAE and Lebanon.[76] In fact, Future TV had already recognised the opportunities for pan-Arab youth programming in the late 1990s, when it introduced a pan-Arab children's quiz show.[77] The game show format, which locks audiences into a relationship with a specific channel so as to follow contestants' fortunes from week to week, made a striking appearance in Future's program plans in December 2002, when the company announced that it had agreed a deal with FremantleMedia (part of the Luxembourg-based European broadcasting group RTL) to show an Arabic version of Fremantle's format, *Pop Idol*.

In some ways, Pop Idol's Arabic version, called *Superstar*, may merit the title of the first reality format to arrive on pan-Arab TV.[78] However, it can also be argued that the level of risk-taking and innovation involved on

Future's part was tempered by at least two factors. For one thing the format bore interesting similarities to another programme already tested on Arab satellite channels, namely *Man sa yarba al-malyoon?*—the Arabic version of *Who Wants to be a Millionaire?* MBC bought this format from its western owner, Celador, in November 2000, after negotiations for the sale had apparently been conducted while MBC was still under a British Chief Executive, Ian Ritchie. Cooperation between MBC and Future allowed the latter to air this program[79] and discover how lucrative it could be, not only in attracting audiences and advertising but also in generating revenue from telephone interactivity between the channel and would-be contestants. The idea is for revenue to be shared between the broadcaster and telephone companies. The *Pop Idol/Superstar* phenomenon was designed to achieve even greater income from interactivity, since the program encourages viewers to vote by telephone week after week for the singer they wish to win the contest. Moreover, *Pop Idol* had already proved its commercial potential elsewhere. By the time Future bought the format, it had already become a star performer for Fox TV in the US, bringing it the highest ratings in its history and more than US$50 million in advertising revenue for just one series.[80]

There was one aspect of *Superstar* that earned praise for Future TV from unexpected quarters, in addition to the apparent appreciation of viewers who cast 4.8 million votes when it came to the last competition of the first 21-week contest in 2003, and around 10 million votes in the second, in 2004.[81] This was the fact that voting, although enthusiastically encouraged by cell phone companies that stood to benefit from the surge in calls, was not obviously rigged. The veteran columnist Rami Khouri described the 2003 result, whereby Jordan's Diana Karazon won 52 per cent of the votes and ceded 48 per cent to the runner up, as the first local vote he could remember that did not end in a victory of around 99 per cent. Khouri publicly thanked Future TV for what he called an "entertaining confirmation" of the "normalcy" of "ordinary Arabs," and a chance to show how they do vote when left to themselves.[82]

Superstar's success marked an important point in the development of content on pan-Arab television. It demonstrated the profitability of Western formats and encouraged other channels, notably MBC and LBC, to venture further down the route of importing program ideas from outside the region, thereby provoking mounting criticism from those opposed to the perceived westernization of Arab society. LBC's *Star Academy* and MBC's aborted attempt to screen *Al-Rais*, an Arabic version of *Big Brother*, are prime examples. However the trend towards programming which flouts social taboos cannot be separated from the imposition of boundaries to political coverage. *Superstar* simply proved, yet again, that viewers love locally-made content, even if it is based on an imported idea. If local program makers were permitted to produce material, such as soap operas, documentaries or political talk shows that challenged local censorship, this might also bring commercial success.

In Future's case, however, political considerations repeatedly put such material off limits. In late 1997, Hariri himself invoked the Lebanese government's power to ban news and political coverage on both Future and LBC.[83] At the beginning of 2003, a Lebanese channel was officially denied satellite access when it announced plans to screen a frank talk show involving Saudi dissidents. Officials later admitted the program had been censored to protect good relations between the Lebanese and Saudi governments.[84] When such limits are there for all to see, credibility becomes an elusive commodity for channel managers. Future's own commitment to a certain model of post-war reconstruction of Lebanon was evident from the time when its morning programs were introduced with a clip that ran "al-balad mashi wa'l-shughl mashi" (the country's up and running and work is up and running). To those who regarded the Hariri government's reconstruction efforts as less than equitable or successful, this approach dented the channel's credibility.[85] Hence there emerged a need to compensate by means of outright commercial programming.

[83]

Conclusion

Evidence in these case studies shows a pattern of commercial decision-making about media content. That pattern conforms to some degree with what might be expected in light of the particular characteristics of media markets and conventional corporate responses to them. In particular, it emerged from the analysis that content was chosen to appeal to the widest possible audience. For Dream TV this was a simple question of demographics. It targeted young people, who are in the majority in Egypt and the wider Arab region, and also sought to reach viewers in countries within the footprint of Nilesat. For *Al Arabiya*, the process of maximizing the audience was, at least in part, a question of adjusting content to meet the sometimes conflicting demands of different groups caught up in the US military action against Iraq. Future TV meanwhile created content that was pan-Arab by its very nature, in the sense that *Superstar* pitted contestants from different Arab countries against each other. Indeed, information about the repercussions of the contest (which was not included in the case study) suggests that sections of the audience came to regard contestants as their national representatives. Based on the increase in votes cast for the contestants between the first and second series, Future's audience maximization strategy appears to have succeeded.

Editorial decisions by the three companies also accord with what might be expected from broadcasters linked to larger business conglomerates whose general aim is to minimize both risks and costs. Thus content selection on Dream TV had to be understood in light of the venture's place in the Bahgat Group, and the Bahgat Group owner's indebtedness to Egyptian banks. In *Al Arabiya's* case, policy was determined within the framework of ARA Group as a whole and its connections to the Saudi polity. The same could be said of Future TV and Rafiq Hariri's political and business leadership positions. Although government–business relations are perhaps more easily seen in these instances than is the case with some other corporations around the world, they are by no means unusual when compared, for example, with the positions adopted by

[84]

subsidiaries of Rupert Murdoch's News International. It was in line with its commercial interests that Dream TV modified content on its second channel in response to warnings. A similar point could be made about *Al Arabiya's* change of heart regarding broadcasts of Saddam Hussein or masked men threatening the IGC. In Future's case, a positive portrayal of Lebanese post-war reconstruction served a wider set of business interests.

However, there is one area at least in which the editorial policies of these channels appeared to differ from what might be expected on purely commercial grounds. That is the way the audience was addressed. Reliance on advertising revenue in some other parts of the world has led to scheduling choices (such as make-over programs and game shows with cash prizes) which persistently forefront viewers' role as consumers rather than citizens. However, in a region afflicted by violence and insecurity and where citizenship rights are still contested, broadcasters who seek to maximize their audience appear to have understood that one way to do so is through content that does not shy away from political events.

Role of Media
in Social Change

3

Satellite Media and Social Change in the Arab World

Khaled Al-Hroub

The twentieth century drew to a close with Arab societies still seeking to extricate themselves from the predicament of the historical backwardness perpetuated during the preceding century or two. These societies are caught between their yearning for the past and loyalty to their heritage, and their constant effort to move towards political and social modernity. In addition, as these societies are subjected to the disquieting pressures of foreign intervention and sustained internal despotism, they are poorly equipped to develop their own unique systems and methods. Several successful ideas, ideologies and beliefs dominated the Arab social and cultural fields over the past century. This has ultimately resulted in a situation where these societies are divided by sensitivities, confusion, uncertainties, resentment and contradictions. The dilemma of choice between the "traditional" and the "modern" has been more or less a standard feature of the process of social change.

Structurally, there has been no real success in building a solid foundation based on "commonalities" so as to form the legal, social and cultural frame of reference according to which normal cumulative social progress occurs and differences are sorted out. Still there are questions which cast their shadow over all segments of society, from the highest level of authority, whose legitimacy is uncertain, to the lowest social groups, which have diverse orientations. These questions revolve round social reconciliation based on concepts of citizenry and equality, the relation between the ruler and foreigners, the legal and political status of women, distribution of wealth, social justice, the role of religion in the political system, political and cultural diversity, cultural, ethnic and religious tolerance, the relations with the "other," and other fundamental issues.

The absence of definite answers to these questions has created vacuums and deep fissures in Arab societies. Despite their apparent coherence and stability, these vacuums and fissures have not allowed the formation of any organic structure that can provide a solid foundation for these Arab societies. Therefore, the outer layer of stability tends to disintegrate rapidly when put to the real test—such as war with an external power, domestic tension leading to civil war, struggle between the opposition and the authorities, exacerbation of economic hardships or explosion of poverty. All this is subsumed by the ongoing and incessant struggle between the "traditional" and the "modern."

Returning to the multiplicity of difficult questions faced by Arab societies, it may be concluded that what was more destructive than the absence of definite answers in past decades was, and still remains, the inability to seek these answers—by publicly addressing these difficult questions in the widest possible terms, and by discussing them in depth and without evasion. In this regard, domestic political despotism bears the greatest responsibility since it banned the discussion of such questions or the search for answers in one form or another. Arab societies had to wait till the 1990s, with the launch of Arab satellite channels, to obtain a reasonable degree of freedom to discuss their realities and their destinies, which are enveloped in uncertainty and confusion. Satellite channels have given Arabs the opportunity to discuss hardships and exchange answers, but not to offer solutions.

In an attempt to document the chasm between the "traditional" and the "modern" in the Middle East societies, Daniel Lerner wrote his famous book *The Passing of Traditional Society: Modernizing the Middle East.*[1] In this book he proposed a "work program" to achieve complete transition from the traditional to the modern society. Lerner's thesis received harsh criticism. However, what is noteworthy, insofar as the subject of this chapter is concerned, is its emphasis on the media's role in achieving modernization. In Lerner's view, the media is the unifying link, a mechanism that creates social harmony between the different classes of the same society. Yet the current role of the Arab satellite media in the process of social change is more complex than Lerner's thesis and even contradicts his arguments in some instances. For one thing, media has a dual effect as we will discuss later—it creates social harmony and symmetry on the one hand, and helps to sustain social divisions and differences on the other.

This chapter seeks neither to amplify nor grossly undervalue the role played by the Arab satellite media in developing and advancing Arab societies and enhancing mechanisms of civil and social change. Rather, it posits that this role is almost restricted to enabling satellite media to encourage widespread discussion of the options of change and its mechanisms and to establish a credible platform. The mission of this platform is to moderate discussions on controversial ideas and topics so that it is no longer possible to claim that Arab governments and societies are in a perfect state, as the official Arab media regularly claimed in the post-independence era. Many problems have accompanied the flurry of satellite media platforms. However, this does not, by any means, belittle their important and tangible impact on the Arab socio-political landscape. Since these satellite channels provide platforms for discussion and dialogue as well as facilitate free airing of controversies, they are involved in the process of social change. However, as this chapter argues, the impact of satellite channels on the process of social change is superficial rather than deep-rooted. This stems partly from the nature of media operations and partly from the lack of far-sighted vision on the part of Arab media leaders.

In sociological and historical terms, the central role of the Arab satellite media will be documented as a "catalyst" in activating socio-political change and not actually causing it. Those who expect Arab satellite channels to play a substantive role in effecting change overestimate what the media can do in its current form. The satellite media is neither capable of ensuring change, nor does it possess the social tools necessary to translate what is publicly posited and broadcast over the ether into social action. Those who underestimate the importance of satellite channels by maintaining that they are just forums for loud debaters and sustain a culture of instigation and superficial thought, overlook the role of catalysts in a widespread process of social change.

When considering deep and widespread socio-political changes, it is not easy to document the role of different elements within a short period of time—such as the life of Arab satellite channels. The substantial issue here is the process of cumulative change. However, what is more important than accumulation of change and the role of Arab satellite channels is the degree of development of civil structures, civil and political awareness, networks, cultural multiplicity, forms of governance, and healthy foreign relations to unite different Arab social classes. All these together form the lowest common socio-cultural denominator which is indispensable for the creation of any society. The role of Arab satellite channels and of Arab media in general, is to continuously shed light on the absence of this denominator, and to deal with theses, ideas and approaches that claim to seek this denominator, discussing them with absolute transparency and testing their popularity, rationality and realism. However, it may be observed that the role of satellite media, in terms of contributing to the establishment of those collective civil structures and denominators, is weak and non-existent. This absence can partly be explained by a widespread argument—the objective of media is not to create change, but to transmit information. This may be an ideal argument in abstract terms but it is inappropriate for underdeveloped societies where the media lies at the heart of development and prosperity.

This chapter presents three main arguments. The first maintains that there are two levels where social change and the development of civil society take place. The first level is the visible surface level where the theses and visions of social and intellectual currents in society are reconciled. The second is at a substantially deeper level where the theses of these various currents differ. At the surface level of reconciliation, socio-cultural backwardness interacts with despotism and the total loss of independent control owing to external interventions. In response to these phenomena, public demands emerge, calling for human rights, indispensability of freedom, independent sovereign decision-making, general development, orientation towards knowledge-based production, harsh criticism of political repression often coupled with a weaker criticism of socio-political repression. On this level an apparent reconciliation emerges, which is sometimes illusive. This reconciliation gravitates towards social change in such a way that this process of change seems crystal clear in terms of action and outcomes. It becomes a public demand because all, or most classes within a country are pro-freedom and opposed to despotism. They favor improving and developing society and stopping state interference in society.[2]

The second level where social change occurs is more complex, being the substantive level. On this level "social change" splits into differing theses related to particular ideological visions – either Islamic or secularist – mainly in the Arab world. Here the argument of "social change" becomes obscure and its interpretation becomes subjective, based on personal perspective. In almost every Arab country, there is consensus regarding the necessity of social change on the surface. However, there are differences and a deep chasm that separates the two visions of social change—the "Islamic" and the "secularist." This shapes the discussion on the role of media in bringing about social change, and the course of action of such change.

The second argument posited by this chapter is that the Arab satellite news media is stimulating wide interest in theses advocating social change on the surface, or at the first level. This is evidenced by a number of facts: challenging of despotism, advocating calls for political freedom, providing

[93]

unprecedented platforms to demand human rights, enhancing social and political activities (if only at the level of speech and expression). Moreover, the Arab satellite entertainment media is trying to break social and artistic taboos. This is creating a controversy regarding social and behavioral freedom in Arab societies, which runs parallel to the controversy on political freedom created by the Arab news media. However, the efficacy of the media, which helps to stimulate interest in the theses of social change on the surface level, does not penetrate to the second level—the substantive level. Here, it is undermined by the splintering of the temporary consensus forged at the surface level between the advocates of social change across the political spectrum. Both news and entertainment media find themselves at the crossroads, where advocates of Islamic social change and advocates of modern, secularist social change part company. Satellite news media, either directly or indirectly, enhances the Islamic faction at the expense of the modernist faction for several reasons—including regional tension, foreign interventions that breed radical reactions, the power of Islamic factions among the Arab public and the national and Islamic orientation of the most important Arab news channel, *Al Jazeera*. Entertainment satellite media reinforces the modernist vision, but only in the domain of art, singing and behavior, not in the domain of thought, which is the deeper domain.

Thus the satellite media in general provokes discussion and unprecedented interest in social change, but on a large but superficial scale. Yet, at the same time, it reinforces the vertical social split between a religious vision of social change, which maintains that societies must embrace this particular mode of change and a competing secularist vision, which thinks that social change must be in accordance with its own conception of change.

The third argument stems from the fact that if the Arab satellite media should contribute towards social renaissance and help to develop Arab society in a substantive way, not merely on the surface, it must be restructured totally in accordance with a new and programmed vision.

However, in doing this, we must preserve the diversity of Arab media and its maximum limits of expression. This does not mean creating a controlled media whether partisan, ideological or official media. It is much deeper than this. Arab societies are passing through an historical epoch of a certain nature—one with deep social, intellectual and political divisions. As such, the required restructuring must move towards building bridges and widening accepted bases to cement the layer of "commonalities," which is a fragile layer prone to disintegrate at any turning point or change of political regime. In its current situation, the Arab satellite media helps to destroy this already weak layer, rather than reinforce it. This is so because it relies on sensationalism, polarization and heated discussions between representatives of social and intellectual groups. Instead of relying on the thought and voices of the conciliatory moderates represented in every group or faction, it relies on the thought and voices of extremists represented in each group. This leads to the deepening of divisions and shattering of consensus. It is not conducive to the process of social change by collective agreement.

Social Change and the Media Position

What is meant by social change? What does it mean to "develop civil society," which is imperative for any efficacious, contemporary process of social change? What is the position and role of media? It is necessary to pause for a while and seek to define these high sounding terms to prepare the ground for the subsequent discussion on the role of the media and to place it in an appropriate context.

Perhaps the term "social change" is the most complex term to define, especially in the framework of the Arab (Islamic) controversy on progress and development and the debate over modernity and commitment to heritage. In fact this is our major concern. Social change is open to differing interpretations: its nature, the way it is perceived, its course of action and outcomes. The desire to influence these courses of action and outcomes is the most effective driving force for contesting ideologies, ideas and beliefs. For the wide Islamic segment in the Arab states, with its different factions, both extremist and moderate, social change means the "Islamization of society," with respect to the rulers and the ruled. It also means molding society after the "Islamic model of society." According to this vision, Arab societies in general live in a state of deviation from this model, a deviation which is reduced or magnified according to each society and faction assessing the case. Hence the task of socio-cultural change is to correct this deviation. In the continuum of social change targeted by the perspective of Islamic factions, other advocates of the "vision" of social change who have non-religious points of departure are viewed in a completely different light.

The vision of the Islamic faction almost completely contradicts the secularist vision of social change. The secularist vision of social change is at the heart of the outlook of liberal, Marxist and national factions in the Arab arena. There is a prevailing viewpoint, which has a completely different point of departure from the religious vision. According to the secularist vision, Arab societies suffer from a widespread state of backwardness not because they are estranged from religion, but because they have not adopted social, political and cultural modernity. These societies do not follow rational, modern methods of thought and are constrained by religion in assessing matters and understanding people and in formulating a general outlook on life, history and the future. The absence of a secularist, modernist stance in society leads to the continuity and perpetuity of traditional and obsolete customs. The traditional outlook includes aspects such as social relations based on ties of kinship and the tribe; concepts that stifle equality and merit-based competition, inferior and subordinate status of women, lack of ethno-religious plurality and denial of equality on the basis of citizenship and the dominance of the religious, tribal and sectarian hierarchy. All these norms are not uniformly followed, but vary from one society to the other.

Two Visions of Change: The Destructive Vertical Division

Essentially, the Arab world is confronted by two visions of social change that are wholly contradictory, and which are tearing society apart. As Ilya Hariq explains, it seems that "the thesis in secularist thinking for conformity in terms of a modernist formula, when this formula is a carbon copy of the dominant model in industrially advanced countries, has attested unequivocally to the divide between Arab-Islamic heritage and western civilization." The western model, as envisaged by modernists, links "the prevalence of the role of religion in society with backwardness.[3]

Mindful of the heated or quiet intellectual struggle which is manifested in various forms in the Arab states, it must be admitted that it is difficult to imagine a true reconciliation on a substantive level between these two visions. It is possible to conduct negotiations and strike occasional political deals, which are dictated on both sides by collective spatio-temporal pressures. However, this does not impact on the central vision itself. At the core there is a sharp vertical contradiction between the two positions. Ignoring this contradiction or unrealistically underestimating its acuity amounts to self-deception. Arab societies have lost two centuries in the collision between these two positions in their failed attempt to find a conciliatory formula that reconciles heritage with modernity.[4] The predicament centers round the fact that each faction pulls in the opposite direction. If one faction succeeds in seizing power, or dominating the socio-cultural landscape, it thrusts others in the same direction of its own "vision" of social change on the substantive level. This pressure has caused, and is still causing, a vertical rift dividing Arab societies from the top of the political hierarchy to the lowest point in the social setup.

In an approach similar to the present analysis, twenty questions were posed to a group of Arab writers and intellectuals, along with some specialists and employees working in the Arab satellite media. The occasion was a symposium organized by the Pan-Arab Center in Beirut in October 2003 under the title *Arab Satellite Channels and National Causes.* One question read: "What is the role of the Arab satellite

[97]

channels in the realm of the relationship between secularist and Islamic movements in the Arab World? Are they building bridges of understanding and common awareness of the challenges, of mutual cooperation, or has the dialogue between the two currents been transformed into a competitive controversy—one which deepens the rift and shatters commonalities and consensus?" The answers to this question were generally negative, with the exception of the answers given by those in the media sector which were defensive in nature. Nabil Dijani, a lecturer in media at the American University in Beirut, said:

> As far as bringing the secularist and Islamic currents closer, I think that generally the interest of satellite channels is not dialogue or public service, but agitation…the concept of social and national responsibility is still very narrow in satellite channels.

In a similar way, Gamil Matar, Director of the Arab Center for Development and Futuristic Research in Cairo, responded:

> Satellite channels give the louder voice an advantage over sensible, wise and expert voices…they have helped in glorifying Islamic movements; I mean here the religious sense of excitement after the attacks of 9/11 which suggested to simple people that religious heroism was not a myth but a fact.

Amr Nasif, from the Lebanese Al Manar TV, speaks of a related point—the way satellite channels evade "addressing intellectual or research questions which involve discussion in depth, the pretext being audience preferences…and the fact that they resort to extremely coarse personalities whose discourse is radical and see things in terms of black and white."[5]

To turn to non-theoretical aspects, it would be beneficial to mention some examples from and comparisons with other societies, especially western societies which have achieved a certain degree of social stability and welfare and are much ahead of the rest of the world. Let us consider, for instance, the question of citizenship and total equality before the law. This is still a thorny issue when addressed by many of the advocates of Islamic factions and their theoreticians. Also, there is great hesitation with respect to the full rights of citizens, including their right to occupy high positions of authority, like the presidency, irrespective of the citizen's religion. In this respect, Sa'ad Al Faqih (the traditionalist Saudi dissident) says:

> Traditional schools of thought agree on rejecting 'the idea that the citizens of the state are inherently equal with respect to rights and duties irrespective of religious faith.' Traditionalists of all currents insist that the status of the Muslim in the state differs radically, in terms of rights and duties, from the non-Muslim; they reject absolutely the principle of equality between them.[6]

The question of women, their participation in politics and complete equality with men remains hazy and undetermined. This means that any "Islamic social change," which is consistent with this specific Islamic vision, will preserve "inequality," sustain it one way or the other, and regenerate or re-legitimize it.

Needless to say, the above view does not represent the dominant opinion in the moderate Islamic faction. However, the point of reference here is the difficulty of the issue we are addressing and its complexities— what is the nature of social change? What form of civil society will the media help to shape? Is it change according to the vision of the Islamic or the secular faction? Similar questions arise in the case of the development of civil society. What is the civil society envisaged by both the religious and secularist visions? What are the pillars of each one of the two visions? With respect to the view of civil society and its institutions, for instance, the Islamic faction wants to consolidate the role of mosques in social and public life in a way that transcends their ritual worship function. On the other hand, the secularist vision urges regulating mosques to ensure that their role does not extend beyond religious worship, social and charitable work. This divergence in perceiving civil society applies to a broad spectrum of social, political, artistic and other activities and functions. In terms of modern secularism, the characteristics of the secularist, modern

[99]

vision are reflected in the form and mechanisms of national consensus and the civil means of achieving it through "social change." These features include, for instance, the focus on individuality, freedom, absolute personal equality, softening or resisting relationships founded on blood ties, tribe and creed, encouraging loyalty to the state and community at the expense of narrow, parochial loyalties. From an Islamic standpoint, the characteristics of the Islamic vision of social change are reflected in the form and mechanisms of national consensus and the methods used by civil society to achieve that social change. These include the idea of supporting *Jama'a* (Islamic society) at the expense of the individual, heeding the call [*da'wa*] to adhere to religion in individual behavior and norms, according religion a central position in politics, prioritizing commitment to the creed even at the expense of the state, among other things.

In viewing the contribution of the Arab satellite media to the issue of social change and developing civil society, what must be considered is its impact on this process—which is bifurcated into two categories, represented by the modern secularist and Islamic factions. Measuring this media contribution is determined by the individual perspective of the observer. A subscriber to the modernist vision will consider any media contribution that drives society in the direction of this particular vision as being positive. The reverse is true of an observer who is closer to the Islamic vision—whether traditionalist or contemporaneous.

If the analysis is confined to the first level, the level of apparent consensus, the conclusion is quick and simple—the contribution of the Arab satellite news media is positive and excellent. This may be attributed to two facts. First, it has provided unprecedented platforms for discussion and dialogue on acute crises and economic straitjackets suffered by Arab states and societies. Second, it has encouraged the culture of dialogue and acceptance of contrary points of view, in addition to making audiences aware of alternative viewpoints that were either difficult to know about or even banned.

[100]

News and Entertainment Media: Conflicting Contributions

In the light of the above-mentioned differences between the two modes of social change supported by the two largest Arab social groups, it is possible to consider the performance of the Arab satellite media, record its contributions and determine its location in terms of influencing social change. Contributions from different angles will be recorded so that it not only clarifies the idea of consolidating the "vertical rift" (which is the most important media effect of both genres), but also other horizontal divisions based on multiple orientations. However, this should be viewed as objective criticism of this phenomenon without passing value judgments. Moreover, the positive effect of this satellite media must be acknowledged unequivocally, as already indicated.

Remote Control Protest: Freezing Social and Political Public Action

Satellite news media has sought to achieve a strange and dual paradox. The first dimension of this paradox is its ability to increase political, social and cultural consciousness in the Arab states to a certain extent as universally acknowledged. By increasing the limits of the freedom of expression and overcoming taboos, especially political ones, the individual Arab can acquaint himself with a spectrum of sensitive issues, which were previously either beyond his reach or not permissible. In this respect this media has revived trans-border Arab consciousness, which is of vital importance. Individuals in the states of *Al Magharib Al 'Arabi* (the Occidental Arab World) can watch live what is happening in Palestine and Iraq. Individuals in Lebanon and Egypt have become informed about Algerian and Moroccan issues in an unprecedented manner. Wherever a crisis occurs and intensifies, such as the Darfur crisis in the Sudan, individuals in the Kingdom of Bahrain and the United Arab Emirates can easily learn about it and follow its ramifications.

The other dimension of the dual paradox consists in the important cumulative individual consciousness of people in the Arab states. This consciousness stems from the impact of the satellite media, especially in matters that directly affect the individual—such as corruption in his country, despotism, or loss of the country's independence in the face of foreign intervention. However, this kind of dormant consciousness has not developed to a degree that spurs positive political action and has remained incapable of propelling people to take positive action. For example, anger and indignation on a particular issue have never accumulated to the level of people taking to the streets to express these sentiments in a direct manner. It appears that in the Arab world, at the level of the "collective unconscious" people increasingly consider that following up dramatic events and releasing pent-up tensions amounts to actual protest or resistance. Thus a negative sort of participation has developed, which may be termed "remote control protest"— a resistance staged at home, either by surfing different channels to follow more details about a hot or sensitive issue, hurling more abuses at the general situation, or, in extreme cases, phoning in to participate in a particular talk show. Hence, it may be said that "the Arab street has withdrawn into their houses," instead of residents taking to the streets to participate in public affairs or protest against matters they find unacceptable.

Some recent events may be cited in support of this phenomenon. For instance, no large demonstrations took place in the Arab streets in protest against the war on Iraq and its occupation by the American–British coalition. The small, symbolic demonstrations that took place in some Arab capitals are incomparable to the demonstrations of millions in the streets of Paris, Madrid, London and even Washington itself. Millions of Arabs participated in a strange, negative flight into their own homes and were glued to Arab satellite channels to watch the build-up for the war by the minute. Later, they watched the war itself without staging any protests against it. This applies to many other cases such as the siege and invasion of the Jenin camp during the second *intifada* in April 2002. On that occasion also, no major demonstration took place in the streets of Arab capitals to express anger or attempt any protest.

[102]

For more clarification on this issue of negative participation, it is helpful to compare the present situation, an aberrant situation in which people are remaining silent, with the era of 1980s, which was the pre-satellite media era. During those years, especially towards the end of that decade, many Arab states witnessed small scale public uprisings propelled by protest or indignation. Instances include the April 1989 uprising in Jordan, the bread uprising in Tunisia in 1984, and a similar uprising in Morocco during the same year, and also the events in Algeria in 1988, which is well-known. At that time there were no satellite channels to cover events minute by minute. However, social action was more vital and self-expressive. The people were not captive to the television screens, which have robbed them of their ability to act.

It would not be fair to hold only Arab satellite channels responsible for freezing socio-political action, which has occurred as a partial and indirect result of intensive satellite news broadcasting. The problem lies in the lack of social institutions that can promote collective awareness of issues raised by the media. There is a vacuum in terms of politics and mechanisms in the Arab society, which is not conducive to bridging gaps in awareness and theorization and developing them into tangible reality. However, this is a different issue. A significant point remains—the position of the media vis-à-vis social action and its impact on such public action.

Spectacular TV Performances and Consolidation of the Vertical Rift

Spectacular television performances dominate the satellite news media (as well the satellite entertainment media). This is derived from the fact that television itself is a spectacular tool. This orientation is based directly on the perception that the focus must be on appearance, eye-catching performance and elements that attract the greatest number of viewers. In this formulation, content is relegated to a secondary position. This argument is advanced in response to the criticism that the content of talk shows on Arab satellite channels is weak. Also, it is used to counter

[103]

criticism that the discussion is superficial and the aim is sensationalism, rather than a fuller understanding of the subject of the discussion. This entails selecting topics and program guests who are best suited to the goal of putting up a "show" or spectacle. This inevitably leads to the choice of trivial topics. In his analysis of this point, 'Azmi Bushara discusses how television controversies change into "shrieking and screaming" matches where one participant flattens the other completely.

> Hence the intellectual is not supposed to posit a point of view and then analyze it scientifically; but rather to put on a show by raising his voice to its highest pitch in order to stand his ground before his political opponents...what is required is shrieking, arguing and alleging regardless of the logical coherence of these words, the power of the other party's argument, and the degree of damage caused by a speech which is divorced from reality.[7]

It may be recalled that Faisal Al Qasim, the presenter of the famous program "The Opposite Direction" on Al Jazeera channel confirmed the point that television as well as his own program are intended to be sheer spectacle, and that those who wanted more profound coverage should turn elsewhere. This comment was made at a conference on Arab satellite media in Cambridge University in September 2004. The American academic and researcher, Jon Alterman, cited Al Qasim's comment and observed:

> In a recently held conference on the political effects of Arab satellite television broadcasting, the presenter of a famous talk show said the following: 'I will tell you the secret of television—it revolves round spectacle. Spectacles come first, second and third...' [Alterman continues] By using these words the presenter, inadvertently, put his finger on the reason why the spread of the freedom of expression in the Arab World [via satellite channels] has produced little political change.[8]

In practice, creating a "spectacle" means hunting for flamboyant personalities who ensure the success of the program at the expense of content or any other objectives. Hence the guests who are fortunate

[104]

enough to appear in talk shows are those who have definitive, strict and extreme views—opinions that are either black or white. Guests who present middle-of-the-road, grey views are boring.

In summary, proponents of extreme views in their dialogue, or rather their "screams" tend mostly to consolidate vertical rifts. They do not contribute to shared viewpoints that can bridge the intellectual, political and social gaps confronted by Arab societies. In their defense of their program style, the producers and presenters of talk shows say that western media is full of rambling models of "scream" programs. This is a weak defense as the western media has the luxury of producing such programs because their societies are built on a solid base of social cohesion, and are not likely to split asunder as is the case with Arab societies. Of course, there are many divisions in every western society but these are more superficial and do not extend deep into the very foundation of society.

Widening the Gap between Generations

Arab satellite channel audiences are divided into two major categories: the youth segment of those under twenty or twenty-five years, and the older segment of those thirty years and above. This is not a clear-cut division but rather an approximate categorization. The youth category watches entertainment media—including variety shows such as those presented by Future TV and LBC, quiz programs and others. This category also watches channels devoted to entertainment and music such as Rotana and Tarab channels and the channels of the Arab Radio and Television Network (ART), as well as other channels. The older category in general watches major news channels such as *Al Jazeera*, *Al Arabiya*, *Abu Dhabi Television* and *Al Manar*. Certainly, there is some overlapping between these two categories in any media survey. However, the overall picture is one that is quite divisive. To add to the complexity of the situation, there is a youth category that watches *Iqra* and *Al Majd* the two religious channels, in contrast to the youth category that watches entertainment channels. This means that there is a fractured landscape on the fringes of which social and cultural changes interact in a contradictory manner, and groups pull in different directions according to age and outlook. This situation is an inseparable part of what the satellite channels broadcast and this aspect will be dealt with the next section.

Condemning Art and Entertainment Channels

Arab satellite channels are promoting the spread of Arab art and entertainment in their various forms such as literature, drawing, songs and dancing, in an unprecedented way within the Arab world. Um Kalthoum transcended borders within the Arab world at the zenith of the era of nationalism, when the Arabs of the Occident and the Orient used to sing her songs. Today, thanks to the Arab satellite channels, singers like Kazim Al Sahir and Nancy 'Ajram from the Orient and Al Shab Khalid and Abdul Wahab Al Doukali from the Occident do not have to depend on a Nasserite and unionist atmosphere to transcend Arab borders and make millions of Arabs echo their songs disregarding the barriers represented by varying geography and diverse nationality. This is a process whereby voluntary assimilation of artistic and cultural tastes in a language framework mingles with the democracy of diversity and there is a country-wise artistic multiplicity (art in the Gulf, Egypt, Lebanon, Morocco) which imbues the artistic scene with special aesthetics. Moreover, in this scenario, there is stiff competition to attract the greatest number of Arab viewers. The prerequisite for this competition is simplicity and language comprehension, in addition to its proximity to middle linguistic variations which are widely understood in the Arab streets among the members of the public as a means of communication.

The impact of satellite broadcasting goes beyond the question of singing and delves into interesting issues and geographical locations. There are some noteworthy instances here. Suffice it to cite the Moroccan novelist and sociologist Fatema Mernissi in the remote locales of

[106]

Morocco. In the heart of the central Moroccan countryside during her journeys to the local villages, she met Moroccans who used to follow Arab satellite channels in a manner that surprised and attracted her attention. She referred to an artist named Banour and the way he used to follow satellite channels closely and benefit from this. As the artist comments:

> As a fresh artist I have benefited a great deal from the 'dish.' It has shortened the distance between me and the artistic and cultural space; a space I am far removed from because I live in a place too remote from the art's location. But the television gave me the chance to see cultural programs and art exhibitions on the screen. I also knew about artists and innovative individuals whether in plastic art, writing, poetry, acting and music…I draw my strength and morale, both prerequisites of innovation, from this source.[9]

On the other hand, there is a critical evaluation and condemnation of the satellite media from the angle of the aforementioned "vertical rift." The satellite entertainment media is accused of "spoiling and corrupting youth" and spreading the culture of "Arab pop" and "vulgar songs," and similar forms of entertainment. There is a harsh exchange of charges between both sides of the modernist/Islamic "divide" even amounting to *takfir* [charging one with apostasy] because of the popularity of "video clips" and the way they have attracted a wide audience both from among the youth and older groups. There is a need to pause and discuss these charges to try to identify a multiple, broad and underlying denominator. Without passing value judgments, what the people who level these charges fail to see is that, in the era of open skies for trans-national television broadcasting, young males and females are provided with greater freedom in their interests to choose "Arab pop" or "western pop," Nancy 'Ajram or Britney Spears, Amr Diyab or Michael Jackson. Given these options, it is correct to say that it is culturally more beneficial to "spoil" this generation of Arab youth within the framework of Arab civilization and culture rather than beyond it, since the latter will amount to civilizational alienation and not merely "effeminization." The Arab-

Islamic civilization has always encompassed "effeminized" as well "serious" categories. Moreover, there is some contradiction in the social acceptance accorded to TV entertainment, which is branded as decadent and amoral when it originates from outside, and is rejected even when broadcast by Arab satellite channels with a very different content from what is broadcast, viewed and accepted in the western channels which penetrate every Arab house.

Some will object on the basis that confining options to only two, both of which fall within the circle of artistic "effeminacy" (Arab or western) is tantamount to manipulating the discussion. This is so because there are other serious options for youth on which Arab satellite broadcasting can focus its attention. However, this is only partially true because many Arab youth categories will continue to be inclined towards the most recent hits in singing, art and dancing regardless of approval. Hence they will turn on Arab satellite channels and global western ones till they find what they like, especially in the age of a globalized media, which does not recognize national boundaries. In other words, if we close down the Rotana or any other music channel, and ban Nancy 'Ajram, Elisa and Ruby from singing so that Arab youth are not affected, this does not mean that they will promptly turn to the *Iqra* and *Al Majd* channels.

Thus if strictness and seriousness are the only assets of entertainment broadcasting in the Arab satellite channels, there will be an automatic repulsion of millions of Arab male and female teenagers who will be driven to reorient their TV dishes to receive western entertainment broadcasts. Hence they will become westernized, despite the fact that their guardians want to Arabize them. In short, it is not possible to counter the influence of Michael Jackson by promoting Saiyd Darwish. From a relative perspective, "Arab effeminacy" (and not "Arab strictness") is the only thing which can combat "western effeminacy." Large numbers of youth can be stopped from slipping into distorted and ostensible westernization, by keeping them within the kind of broad framework of tolerance associated with their nation and countries.

In this regard, it is worth considering the success of light entertainment programs such as "Star Academy" and "Super Star" and others which are described by many as effeminizing and diverting the interests of youth groups away from important causes. Such programs surpassed the popularity in the Arab countries of the most popular talk shows such as "The Opposite Direction" program in *Al Jazeera*. Sai'da Killani says that the viewers of "Super Star" in Jordan who voted for the Jordanian singer who competed with other contestants exceeded in number the voters in any Jordanian parliamentary elections.[10] In a sense, the level of support and the astonishing categories of Arab viewers of these programs, ranging from Morocco to the Arabian Gulf, have deep socio-cultural implications.

Indirect Dissemination of the Culture of Extremism

In accordance with the idea of the vertical social rift—the modernist/religious divide caused by both entertainment and news satellite media, and contrary to the previously mentioned popularity of the artistic culture which shocks conservative societies, there is a dissemination of certain aspects of an extremist, exclusive culture to which the satellite news media has contributed. These aspects can be traced back to the immediate aftermath of the events of September 11, the emergence of Al Qaeda and the outbreak of wars in Afghanistan and Iraq. This phenomenon reached its zenith in the period 2002–2004 and then began to ebb at a later stage. At its peak, in the context of the race for scoops, the satellite news media, or at least some of these outlets, were poised to indirectly market those terrorist groups that relish shedding blood before the cameras under the label of *jihad* and other forms of resistance. This was done by receiving video cassettes showing killings and beheadings, and masked men threatening to kill abducted victims and hostages. Such video cassettes were broadcast so regularly that viewing them became a routine, daily occurrence on satellite TV screens. The negative effect of broadcasting such video cassettes is that blood spilt so easily and routinely helps to establish a violent culture that tends to encourage and relish such killing and slaughtering. It must be admitted that the satellite channels bear some of the responsibility, at least indirectly, of encouraging and accepting such a culture as normal.

During the aforementioned years, some Arab satellite channels fell into the trap of extremists who used such channels to transmit their message after they discovered the power of the image and the efficacy of the video age. These satellite channels, driven by competition in the search for exclusive news and pictures, adopted an "open" policy with respect to receiving the "*mujahideen* videos" and initially broadcasting them in full, especially during and immediately after the war on Afghanistan. Moreover, Osama bin Laden successfully made use of the satellite channels as a platform to voice his blunt, hostile and disastrous rhetoric to the whole Islamic world as if he were the Caliph of all Muslims. He formulated the language of "Al-Fustatain" [the two tents or camps] which is devoted to the clash of religions and civilizations—words that correspond to Samuel Huntington's arrogant language, which is a precursor of hatred and war.

In parallel with the increasingly intense satellite competition, groups affiliated to Al Qaeda emerged, together with *jihadistic* splinter groups in Iraq which killed many times the number of Iraqis as they killed occupying US troops. Amid this competition and the obscure nature of the Iraqi "resistance," the flow of *jihadistic* video cassettes sent to the satellite channels increased. These channels were surprisingly ready and willing to receive and broadcast any video cassette. Of course, some satellite channels fell into traps—including fabricated videos and old videos sold as new ones. In the multiple incidents of bloodshed and chaos, a black market sprung up, together with widespread corruption linked to the aforementioned videos. On many occasions, the "brokers," who were supposed to take those videos to eagerly anticipating satellite channels, would refuse to hand over the videos without receiving large amounts of money that went into their pockets.

[110]

The dissemination of those videos and broadcasting them to the Arab audience led to difficulty in following-up the emergence of the *mujahideen*, who were divergent in their inclinations but agreed upon the horrific means of killing civilians—whether Iraqis, Saudis, Shī'ites, Sunnis, UN personnel or members of western charitable organizations who were helping destitute Iraqis. The mixed signals that were repeatedly sent confuses what is right with what is false, the means with the end, and thus provide us with the most macabre representations of political Machiavellianism to which is added a bloody brutality which is alien even to the ethics of *Jahīlīyah* Arabs. (The term *Jahīlīyah* means "ignorance" or "barbarism" in Arabic and refers to the period preceding the revelation of the Holy Quran). Such brutality cannot possibly be related to Islamic ethics and Islamic teachings on the subject of fighting wars and battles.

The important thing is the socio-cultural effect of broadcasting such videos. It was destructive and sustained the culture of violence, especially in a tense atmosphere which was deepened by a long struggle against Israel and resentment towards the West for its support of Israel. In the reality of narrowing political horizons in most Arab states with respect to peaceful change and liberation from western hegemony, these extremists pose an instant formula for dealing with the "other"— giving vent to cumulative hate whose ultimate outcome is self-defeat. What is more, violence and extremism extend beyond the occupying forces and its allies and in the lexicon of these extremists is applied to anyone holding a different opinion from the society which they claim to defend. Thus it has been witnessed how they target sects and social groups which disagree with them either ideologically or politically. The media, whether one likes it or not, provides these extremists with platforms to justify and defend their theories and thereby renders them a great service.

Creating Patriarchal Idols in Thought and Theory

The Arab satellite news media has created a group of commentators and moderators who are concerned about the popularity of their opinions.

These commentators and moderators tend to express their views on every public affair. They are not intellectuals and thinkers whose hallmark is profound reflection and foresight, rather than seeking public approval. In an atmosphere of surging populism, this group tends to beg for audience admiration and stir up their emotions by saying whatever the listeners want to hear. In the context of intensive news events and a need for commentators and analysts, the real intellectuals are few and are sometimes excluded because they avoid sensationalism. Thus the demand arises for superficial thinkers, whose goal is to activate people. What is worse is that these commentators and moderators have acquired grand titles bestowed on them by the news anchors and program presenters.

During the few past years, the Arab television screen has become crowded by numerous "experts," "thinkers" and "respected pundits," and others like them. If such people were truly experts, the backward situation of Arab societies and states would have been transformed. There is a cultural, social and sociological problem in glorifying such people by describing them as distinguished experts. The problem lies in the indirect message conveyed to the recipients—to listen respectfully to what is said on the screen without any argument. In societies permeated by traditional and cultural illiteracy, the position attained by the speaker on the screen, who is credited with great expertise becomes risky and exerts a negative influence.

A good number of the aforementioned group engages in deliberate over-elaboration to compensate for their paucity of ideas or to avoid telling the real truth. Therefore, much of what is said on the screen does not help to create a critical mentality in the audience. A prominent phenomenon here is the "cowardice of the intellectual or the expert." This is evidenced by the fact that usually the intellectual or expert is objectively very much aware of the subtleties of the event or its details but does not dare to voice the truth. Doing so will contradict dominant illusions or anger the audience, which relies on false perceptions. What emerges is the pursuit of public approval by reiterating extremist slogans. In such a situation, nations cannot achieve even their minimum requirements and their rights and demands are lost amid such acts of exaggeration.

Loud statements on the screen help to falsify consciousness, override the public intellect and encourage receptiveness and acceptance of instructions. When so many persons are described as great philosophers, thinkers, strategic experts, pioneering scholars or similar titles, there is no margin for questioning their ideas. The titles used are intimidating, and if only indirectly, tend to suppress contrary ideas, especially in societies with diffident cultures.

What is mentioned above is inseparable from a more dangerous phenomenon—a prominent display of "patriarchalism" in screen performances, which seeks to monopolize and support the truth. The prevailing belief is that everyone claims to be the "guardian of truth," defending it and exhibiting concern with the nation when others jeopardize it. The aspects and signs of this patriarchalism can be observed in the program guests and presenters who appear on the screen and even those who phone in to participate in any program. Leading this trend towards pervasive patriarchalism are clergymen who enjoy distinguished positions in vitally important and influential satellite media outlets. Millions of viewers are addressed through these media outlets and all of their opinions are shaped by the orientation of the clergyman. Here, the danger lies in the mode of forming and formulating public opinion.

Judging from a broader socio-cultural perspective, it may be said that this patriarchalism has easily infiltrated the satellite media. It is nothing more than a reflection of the traditional patriarchalism that is dominant in Arab societies. However, it is very dangerous because it reaches out to the largest and most influential social groups and as the distance between the orator and his audience is great, it gives the orator a free hand to state whatever he wants without being challenged by his listeners.

Impact on Arab Communities in the West

Arab satellite media has another impact on Arab communities abroad, especially those in the West. This impact is of paramount importance. The "globalization of the media," by which the Arab satellite media has reached every corner of the world, has enabled it to address Arab communities abroad and create communication channels with them everywhere. Undoubtedly, this communication is a radical and historic change insofar as it concerns the relations between emigrant communities, their homelands and original societies. This is true of all communities and minorities in the world since they have established permanent links with their homelands via local trans-national satellite television stations which span the globe via the ether.

However, this communication between Arab communities abroad and their societies occurs against an unhealthy backdrop. This arises because these communities exist in a state of voluntary isolation from the western societies they live in. Generally, emigrant Arabs are not adequately and effectively assimilated into the western societies but live in a state that may called an "optional ghetto." These "Arab ghettos" in the West are not material and spatial ghettos, because Arabs are not confined to a particular place or denied access to others. These are moral ghettos in communicative and cultural terms. This is so because communication, acculturation and relations occur between members of Arab communities despite the distances between their residences through societies, schools or mosques. The same communication is achieved with their homelands through satellite channels or trans-national Arab media. At the same time, communication and interaction are at a minimal level with their surrounding western communities and almost verges on estrangement. This deprives Arab communities of the opportunity to project a good image of Arabs among westerners and to explain important Arab issues to them. This isolation also perpetuates the dominant negative image of Arabs—whether in relation to Arab countries, people or communities. In fact, these Arab communities were not really responsible for the emergence of this negative image.

The degree of communication within Arab communities intensifies in various forms until it borders on negativity, or becomes an anti-climax.

The intensive interaction among Arabs for social, cultural, religious, festive and educational reasons leaves no room for communication with the western milieu in which these communities live. Such intensive interaction has been boosted in recent years by the spread of services suitable for Arabs in western cities, such as restaurants, groceries, libraries, mosques and clubs. Undoubtedly the provision of such services has many positive aspects, but it has begun to have some negative effects. This negative aspect is manifested in the isolation of Arab communities, which in turn reduces their chances of communicating with others and minimizes their knowledge of what goes on within their social milieu. Moreover, Arab satellite channels services help to sustain this Arab interdependence and estrangement from milieus and thus consolidates the peculiarities of "ghetto-type" isolationism. As a matter of fact, Arab communities in the West live vicariously in their native lands through their sentiments and close monitoring of homeland news. They have hardly any links with their host community and do not participate in local politics. Accordingly, only a small percentage of typical emigrant Arabs follow happenings in their host country, exercise electoral rights, or interact either negatively or positively with developments occurring in their country of residence.

In reality, global satellite broadcasting and the communications revolution have contributed to the spread of this phenomenon—that of ethnic, national and religious compartmentalization. This phenomenon has become more globalized recently—it goes beyond Arab and Muslim communities and extends to all minorities in the world. The reason for this is the abundance of trans-national satellite media channels and communication which can convey the problems of the homeland in the listener's mother tongue. (For instance, the Kurds all over the world are united by satellite broadcasting, just as the Chinese, Mexican and Latino communities are in the United States). However, the problem in the case of Arabs is that great aspirations are attached to emigrant Arab communities. These relate to collective issues on which homeland Arabs and emigrant Arabs trade accusations for their respective failure to shoulder responsibility.

Is the Arab Media Required to Play Non-Media Roles?

In the light of the foregoing discussion, the central question is whether the media is required to undertake other unconventional tasks such as news coverage, conveying information and defending individual rights in the face of news monopolies whether by governments or other centers of power? Will the media process expand to include direct or indirect influence on the process of socio-political change and its general atmosphere, thus widening its context, redefining its elements or introducing new elements? Many answers and viewpoints may be forthcoming, especially if they rely on pure theoretical and academic frames of reference which restrict the media role to one of classic instrumentality as taught in university courses on the subject. An important approach to answering this question is to consider the temporality and spatiality of the political, economic and evolutionary atmosphere in which the media in question operates. In other words, there is no definitive theory or answer to be given which applies equally to all cases without taking into account the temporal and spatial elements of every case. Consequently, it becomes illogical or impractical to insist on quoting the experience of the western media when discussing the reality of the Arab media and its performance. The fundamental difference is that the point of departure of the western media encompasses historical, political, economic, cultural and strategic circumstances that completely differ from those of the Arab media. The Western media has special circumstantial preconditions, which impose on it a mode of performance, a certain agenda with respect to concerns and specially allocated tasks of coverage. The Arab media also has preconditions that emanate from the circumstances of historical evolution through which Arabs are passing now. In the case of the latter, the circumstances are not cultural or integral but merely political, economic and social, with parallels reflected in other locales whether in Africa, or Latin America or Asia.

The western media has the "luxury" of reducing its political and national responsibilities because of certain elements. These relate to certain preconditions and circumstances in the countries in which the western media operates: the good standards of living, the lack of existential threats to these countries and their independence, sustained concord on a national democratic equation and the high level of general consensus. In addition, the western media forms temporary alliances with governments when the official establishment engages in battles and conflicts beyond the borders as was the case in Iraq.

In contrast, the general atmosphere in the Arabic countries has few similarities with the convenient situation in which the western media operates. This difference breeds different preconditions for the Arab media, which in turn create predictable media roles. The Arab media operates in a reality which is historically backward-looking. This reality is disintegrative, politically closed, culturally frozen, socially and economically frustrated. The Arab media is unable to overcome these realities and reduces its responsibility to confront them. It is also a reality that presents many challenges, harbors ambitions of changing for the better and where slogans and attempts at democratic transformation, reform and liberation from despotism abound. Hence these circumstances impose themselves on the Arab media even if it seeks to escape and hide behind slogans of objectivity, neutrality and composure in tackling issues. Any media approach to any Arab issue will quickly come into conflict with one of these problems. The question that arises is how can the media deal with this predicament?

For the discussion to move from the abstract to the concrete, it is useful to discuss some examples of these predicaments to grasp the depth of the problem and suggest a suitable approach. If the issue under discussion is associated with human rights or concerns one Arab government suppressing the political opposition or a group, how can the media deal with this? Can the media entrench itself behind a shield of neutrality and deal in equal terms with the oppressor and the oppressed? Can the media refuse to take sides in the tussle between pervasive despotism in the region and desired freedom, or remain detached with regard to the question of democracy? The dilemma that media neutrality will face with regard to these questions will force it to adopt binding positions. Neutrality vis-à-vis democracy and despotism often means flattering the latter, whereas neutrality vis-à-vis the oppressor and the oppressed generally means siding with the oppressor. Such questions and paradoxes do not confront the western media and do not shape its domestic role in determining the national direction in which its societies are headed.

Under the present circumstances, Arab media is viewed by millions of its audiences as a role model and not merely as a means of conveying news and information. It is judged by its audience on the basis of its orientation and internal and external biases. New Arab media, as represented by satellite channels, is different from state media in that it has provided an outlet for many people excluded by the official media, as well as many issues which were taboo or considered off-limits to some extent by the state media. Despite obstacles and restrictions, the Arab media has made a meritorious contribution in creating a unique "political space" for the general public in the last few years insofar as the exchange of information and ideas is concerned. Thus the new media's unique contribution is derived from the distinctively political role it plays. As mentioned earlier, all this has taken place on the superficial level of social change.

On the basis of this media role, the more important thing is the initiation of a deepening dialogue between the existing polarities in Arab societies about changing the core of the social structure. Deepening the dialogue and expanding consensus involves two major schools of thought: the modernist and the Islamic currents. The aim of deepening the dialogue between the two sides is to expand and sustain commonalities, not as the outcome of bargaining between ideological currents that are detached from social change, but as a structural necessity for societies afflicted by tension which are being pushed and pulled in all directions.

The Arab satellite media – comprising both news and entertainment segments – is at the crossroads. It must choose between creating commonalities that reinforce the consensus upon which Arab societies are built, or strengthening ideological polarizations and bias in a historical epoch in which these societies cannot withstand more tensions.

4

Contribution of Arab Media to Creating Social Change and Developing Civil Society in the Arab World

Musa Shteiwi

During the past few decades, mass media and communication organizations have witnessed considerable progress in the Arab world. Although the development of the print media can be traced back to the 19th century, real progress began after World War II, when journalism was boosted by the introduction of radio and television technologies. Moreover, the advent of mass media and communication organizations coincided with the emergence of new states and the decolonization process. During the 1950s and 1960s, radio stations became the primary media tool playing a significant role in nation-building activities both at the local and national levels, as well as in the development process. By the end of the 1960s, television was introduced in the Arab world and along with radio stations and print journalism, became a vital pillar of mass communication across the Arab world.

Early in the 1980s, many Arab states began to use satellite technology and Arab satellite channels gradually come into existence. In responding to the effects of globalization and the Information Revolution of the mid-1990s, the new Arab media has witnessed such qualitative improvement that it is now described as the "modern Arab media," in contrast to the older "traditional" media.

The most important tool of the "modern Arab media" are satellite channels (especially those which are not identified with particular Arab states), the Internet, on-line and transnational newspapers. Undoubtedly, the information and communications revolution has had important effects on different dimensions of social change in the Arab world. Thus, the relationship between this social change and mass media institutions has to be examined through the perspective of interaction as the latter are influenced by any technological, economic and social transformations.

This chapter will discuss briefly the progress witnessed by the Arab media, focusing on the characteristics of different media outlets, the concept of social change and the role and contribution of the media towards this process as well as the prospect, dimensions and development of civil society in the Arab world.

Traditional and Modern Arab Media

Traditional Mass Media

Traditional Arab media was "institutionalized" along with the creation of new Arab states in order to reflect state needs. This is particularly true of mass media such as radio and television. Despite similarities in the mission of the mass media networks in all Arab countries, there were differences arising from the nature of the relationship between the media and the respective state. As a result, the so-called "mobilization media," emerged, which is almost completely subject to state dominance, both socially and politically. This is the case in Egypt, Algeria, Syria, Iraq, Yemen and Libya. The second category is the non-ideological, non-revolutionary "partisan media," which is fully supportive of the ruling regimes. The third category is the more diverse media that enjoys a greater margin of freedom, independence and openness to other viewpoints.[1]

The traditional type has taken the form of print (newspapers and magazines) and broadcast media (terrestrial). Despite the differences already mentioned, the most important common features of such traditional media can be summarized as follows:

- Its discourse was generally confined to the geographic and socio-demographic borders of the respective state, although it has also addressed outside audiences. In particular, ideological and revolutionary regimes have sought to influence political conditions in other Arab states. However, in the final analysis, the influence of such media on the political development of these states was limited.[2]

- Most of the traditional mass media organizations have been state-run, except in rare cases where some media institutions (especially print media) were owned by the private sector.

- The traditional media in Arab states was almost completely subjected to government censorship, thus denying freedom of expression to the opposition, which had to resort to publishing underground leaflets and publications as dissenting political parties were prohibited from any political activities.[3]

The 2003 Arab Human Development Report characterizes the common features of the traditional Arab media as follows: [4]

- *Authoritarian*: Authority heavily controls the media discourse, imposing its own topics, directives, values, details, preferences and timing.

- *Uni-dimensional*: The discourse mostly excludes the other point of view, keeping it away from the public mind.

- *Official*: The majority of Arab media institutions are incapable of taking action or reporting on events until they receive official direction, even if this entails ignoring an important event for a certain period of time. This of course discredits the media in the eyes of its audience.

- *Sacred*: In many cases, a sacred aura is bestowed on the discourse, one that might not exist in other regions. This aura is not necessarily religious, but reflects the determination with which the objective of a particular discourse is being pushed.

[123]

Modern Mass Media

The past decade has witnessed radical changes in the field of the Arab media, through the introduction of modern media technologies and the changes that have occurred in the political and economic environments. The following are the most important features of the modern mass media compared to those of the conventional media:

- Modern media is transnational in character, and as such, it has resulted in the collapse of geographical and political borders between societies and states, which, despite all their efforts, are no longer able to control the flow of information to their citizens. This has led most Arab countries to ease or totally abolish censorship measures. Barring hurdles relating to costs and availability of the required technologies, Arab citizens are now able to obtain all the necessary information regarding local or public issues in an unprecedented manner.[5]

- Modern media is known for its abundant choice and wide diversity, which includes satellite channels, the Internet, electronic journalism, transnational (including Arab) newspapers and magazines. Satellite channels have grown so rapidly that the Arab domain is currently crowded with around 200 channels. The Internet, an equally important medium, offers different frameworks and contexts. Even though Internet penetration in the Arab world is still low, the recorded number of users is relatively higher, while electronic journalism is spreading at a slower pace.[6]

- In terms of programming, some modern media outlets opt for specialization (news, music or entertainment), while others tend to offer diversity. They also differ in terms of ideological and social orientation (liberal, conservative, nationalistic or Islamist). Thus, they reflect the diverse realities of the Arab world, at both the official and public levels. Most importantly, at the ideological and content levels, modern media has become relatively pluralistic.[7]

- Modern media also differs in terms of ownership, as some are either directly or indirectly owned by the governments (although ostensibly independent), while others are wholly owned by the private sector.[8]

[124]

The Impact of Media on Social Change and the Development of Civil Society

Historically, the complex process of social change has been influenced mainly by demographic, economic, technological and media factors. Similarly, many internal and external factors are affecting the development of civil society, with the political system playing a crucial role. Hence, there is systemic difficulty in determining the causal relationship between media, social change and the development of civil society. However, there appears to be a general consensus on the important role that the media can play in bringing about social change, developing civil society and ushering in modernization.

A strong and mutual relationship has already been established between the media and civil society organizations, thanks to the media's role in creating the venues and opportunities for these organizations to express their stances, ideas and interests.

For the media to be an active and influential factor in the process of democratic transformation, it should enjoy a reasonable degree of freedom, independence and plurality.

Lastly, the role of media in the process of social change is fundamentally associated with the overall political situation and the general development of state and society. In this context, the media can contribute, among other things, to the enhancement of knowledge, transfer of information, promotion of public awareness and creation of a culture of accountability.

The Impact of Traditional Media

The influence of the traditional media on the process of social change has varied in form and degree during five decades of its domination over political and social life in the Arab world. In general, the impact of the traditional media is evident in the following aspects:

- The developmental aspects covered in the radio and TV programs, which are directed towards different sectors, especially the fields of agriculture, health and education.
- On account of the high illiteracy rate and weak education systems prevalent during the early stages of the formation of Arab states, the traditional media became an important means for disseminating information, raising the level of knowledge and enhancing general awareness in Arab societies, despite the setting up of educational institutions at all levels.
- The traditional media has also played a significant role in strengthening prevalent traditional cultural values, at both the social and religious levels. Indeed, the Arab media often tended to embrace conservative trends with a view to winning the political support of influential classes and factions in society.
- Politically, the traditional media in its role as the voice of the state and the ruling powers has been highly supportive of Arab central governments both in their pursuit of political legitimacy, as well as in strengthening their authority over peripheral regions.

On the other hand, the traditional Arab media, by functioning typically as an arm of the government, has failed to fulfill its role in monitoring ruling regimes, or giving different political, intellectual and social organizations the opportunity to voice their viewpoints freely. Hence, the traditional media has been unable to achieve the desired social and political changes, while its role in developing civil society institutions has been severely limited, if not unfavorable.

The Impact of Modern Media on Women

1-Satellite Channels

Television is widely watched in the Arab societies, recording the highest rate in the world in terms of time spent viewing programs. Thus, television has had an enormous impact on Arab households in general and on women in particular. The possible effects of satellite television on Arab women may be summarized as follows:

- Arab women enjoy a remarkably strong presence in the satellite TV channels whether as writers, scientists, anchors, producers and even war reporters (in Iraq and Palestine, for example). Thus, they are actively involved in professions that were previously monopolized by males. The new, unconventional roles and opportunities that the satellite media is offering to women will enhance their status in society and inspire younger generations to pursue more positive and important positions in the public life.[9]

- Special programs are designed by satellite channels to address women's issues (political participation, education, marriage) more actively and freely compared to the traditional media. Female viewers interact by voicing and exchanging their points of view, thereby turning such programs into a satellite "forum" to discuss their causes and positions, as well as a means to improve their levels of knowledge and awareness.

- Satellite channels present a broad and diverse range of Arab women holding different positions in societies, whether liberal, conservative or radical, thus erasing the traditional stereotyped image of Arab women.

Yet, the positive and favorable effects of satellite media must not be overestimated or exaggerated in conservative Arab societies that are still embracing traditional, paternalistic values. Indeed, the same satellite channels could be used to reinforce the traditional conservative stereotype of Arab women, who have become the theme of a host of programs seeking to highlight and promote their traditional role in society. In contrast, since the viewers of the Arab satellite channels are seen as "consumers," women can also be commercially exploited for propaganda and advertising purposes.

2-Internet Impact on Women:

The Internet is viewed as a unique means of communication, which is characterized, according to the expert Sola Pool, by five distinctive features:[10]

[127]

- the removal of distance as an obstacle to communications
- the merger of sounds, images and words in a digital form
- the integration of computerization and communications
- the amalgamation of work and entertainment activities
- the manifestation of the mass communication revolution

Although the rate of Internet penetration remains modest in the Arab world, it is spreading at a greater pace through the Internet cafés now being set up in large numbers in major cities all over the Arab world. Thus, they help users, including women, by providing a suitable solution to the problem of expensive personal computers and Internet connections, besides allowing them an opportunity to meet and communicate with others without the family's control.

Today, almost all Arab countries allow public access to the Internet, which is being introduced in schools, universities and government institutions.

The Internet has the potential to become a modernizing force in the Arab world. It can provide many benefits, such as leveraging scarce educational resources, providing forms of entertainment, and serving as a tool to communicate with people who are far away, separated by geography, culture, politics or gender. Additionally, the Internet has the potential to empower Arab women in the exercise of their rights, to allow them to seek and receive information and ideas, and provide them with a new public space—albeit of the "cyber" variety.

What is unique about the Internet and its potential influence as a medium of communication is the individual aspect of its use. Unlike most modern communication methods that are family-oriented, the Internet is individual-oriented. This is even more important in Arab society for young people, particularly women. Women's behavior and social interaction in a conservative Arab culture is largely subjected to the scrutiny and control of the family, the community and the society. The Internet makes the traditional social mechanisms controlling women's behavior quite useless and ineffective. Women can thus use the medium independently, without the family's control and they can remain anonymous. This anonymity facilitates individualized and free interaction.

The Internet's impact on women varies depending on age, educational status, place of residence, marital status and social position. The new "public space" generated by the Internet affects women in the following ways: [11]

- Generally, the Internet has provided the opportunity for feminist groups and activists to use the Internet as a forum for discussion and as a valuable source of information, thus reaching out to many women who would be very difficult to contact otherwise. There are many sites on the Internet that provide information about women's issues that are still considered taboo and are difficult to discuss in the traditional media. These and other sites provide access to information for women, and therefore help to empower and link them with other women activists and organizations.

- The Internet has responded to the demands of Arab women to portray a more balanced image and role in society to counteract the prevalent stereotypes of Arab women who are usually portrayed only as daughters, wives and mothers.

- Traditionally, Arab women are controlled by the men in the family and are not allowed to communicate with other men outside the family circle. However, through chatting and e-mail communication, women are able to meet and convey ideas and feelings to other women and men.

- Women can access information about various topics in the political, social, economic, cultural and other fields. In other words, women can enhance their general knowledge about many issues, which can contribute to their intellectual enrichment and increase their self-esteem.

- More importantly, and because of the high costs of owning a PC with Internet access, Internet cafés are spreading rapidly in Arab cities and around universities, schools and other institutions. In the city of Irbid in Jordan, for example, there are more that 100 Internet cafés in a one-kilometer stretch. Internet cafés have an added value for women who frequent them. Not only do they provide Internet access for women who do not enjoy such access at home, but also allow them to meet and interact with other women and men in public places. Thus, they enhance women's personal freedom to engage in social relations and liberate them from several family and social restrictions.

Although the impact of the Internet on women in general could be limited due to low penetration rates and barriers of illiteracy and language, its effects on the younger generation are expected to be greater.

The Internet and Civil Society

The impact of the Internet on society is growing steadily as it provides a vital means for civil society groups and organizations to exchange, receive and distribute information quickly and effectively. Thus it enables such organizations to overcome obstacles created by censorship and high expenses.

Some rightfully argue that the Internet is an autonomous technology that serves to bolster democratic political practices based on the principle of public participation, particularly in those Arab states lacking democratic institutions and structures.

Most Arab governments have found themselves in a sensitive and problematic situation in their endeavor to benefit from revolutionary advances in communications and information technology, and to reconcile these advances with traditional religious and cultural values while maintaining political dominance over their societies. However, the course has been set, and it is no longer possible for these governments to effectively control and check the free flow of information through modern means of communication like the Internet and satellite outlets. As a result, these governments will inevitably be obliged to increase – albeit gradually – the level of transparency in dealing with the users, information and events, thus enabling civil society organizations and their members to further strengthen democratic practices in the Arab region.

[130]

A large number of studies have highlighted the role that economic, political and cultural factors could play in the process of democratic transformation. Despite the differences in the role and importance of civil society from one Arab state to another, there is a general consensus that civil society – which represents a network of economic, social and cultural relations and practices – could play an important and decisive role in transforming authoritative regimes into democratic ones. Thus, it can make significant contributions towards activating the political process and strengthening institutional representation in all fields.[12]

Civil society organizations are generally set up in response to the unsatisfactory performance of governments, seeking to promote human rights, protect the environment, assist the poor, combat illiteracy, or provide religious education and health care. In the case of the Arab world, these organizations also appear when the public dismisses the state-run and independent entities as untrustworthy. Under such circumstances, people search for alternative outlets for expression, participation and political organization. Thanks to modern means of communications and information resources, civil society organizations will be able to directly defy state interests and legitimacy and undermine the state's ability to exert control over society.

Modern Media, Social Change and Civil Society

The political effects of modern mass media are not yet obvious for more than one reason. First, the transfer of media ownership from the state to the private sector does not constitute a qualitative stride. Most private, unofficial satellite stations are still indirectly financed by several states (except for the Lebanese channels). Hence they are not completely independent. Second, most Arab satellite media are transnational, and therefore their impact is more obvious on the regional rather than the local political environment, especially since the national media is still under the state's dominance, except in Lebanon, Palestine and Iraq (under occupation).

Satellite channels play a significant role in the general development of civil society institutions through the bold and unrestrained debates they conduct on various civil society-oriented issues, some of which are highly sensitive and controversial. Thus the satellite media has contributed to the promotion and spreading of the civil culture badly needed in the social system. Furthermore, the democratic style of these dialogues and discussions will certainly strengthen such a spirit among the viewers. In this way, satellite television has played the kind of role that conventional media has failed to fulfill for decades.

Moreover, the transnational Arab satellite channels have helped to foster a pan-Arab identity and by undermining geographical and political boundaries have enabled Arabs to deepen their loyalty to a common Arab culture with a single identity.[13] For the first time, Arab nationals have the opportunity to examine and discuss different political, ideological, social and cultural issues closely related to the Arab world.

The development and consolidation of a common Arab identity by the satellite media represents an accomplishment more significant than what Arab ideologies and nationalist regimes have vainly sought to achieve over past decades. Paradoxically, the consolidation of a common Arab identity has indirectly created more awareness among the respective Arab states of their own distinctive political identity, because the satellite media has also exposed their political dissimilarities and variations.

In addition, by offering the means and opportunities for communication between Muslims all over the world, satellite television channels have also helped to develop and promote a political and cultural Islamic identity and have facilitated the formation of a "virtual Islamic community" at the Arab and international levels.

The satellite media has also been highly successful in being a significant source of information on social, economic, political and other fields,[14] thus compensating for a major shortcoming suffered by the audience, and thereby enhancing the general development process in the Arab world.

Furthermore, satellite channels have had positive, though indirect effects on bringing about political change in the Arab world (whether of internal or external origin) through peaceful, non-violent means, the most recent example of which is the so-called "the independence uprising" in Lebanon. This would motivate some political movements and groups to break the barrier of fear and stage similar peaceful political activities.

Conclusions

Along with the fundamental transformation that the Arab world is witnessing at the economic, political and social levels, the Arab mass media has also undergone important changes, entering the Information Age through satellite channels and the Internet. For decades, the traditional audio and visual media have been under the state's ownership and dominance and have reflected the visions, positions and interests of Arab governments and the social factions they represent. Therefore, the overall contribution of such traditional media to furthering social change and developing civil society remained weak and limited at best. Indeed, the media's effects on the development of civil society were sometimes extremely adverse (even leading to marginalization and exclusion). Owing to its strong linkage with the state, the traditional media has failed to present an alternative discourse to compete with civil society.

At the social level, the conventional media has been unable to overcome prevailing traditional social realities because of political considerations that are related more to the legitimacy and survival of ruling regimes than the media's tendency to reflect its own convictions or mainstream requirements.

As an outcome of information technology, globalization and other developments taking place in the Arab world, modern media outlets, mostly transnational in character (satellite channels, cross-border newspapers and the Internet) have started to "conquer" the Arab domain. The type of ownership (private, directly or indirectly state-owned) of these outlets and their main focus (news, entertainment, educational) often differ from one Arab state to another.

In spite of its slow start, Internet penetration has grown rapidly in most Arab countries, despite attempts by some Arab governments to ban, control and regulate its use.

These developments have laid the foundations for a free Arab media that would pave the way for political openness and a new media–society relationship. Due to the fact that the satellite media enjoys greater degree of freedom, independence and professionalism than the conventional media, it is expected that the former will have promising effects on the processes of social change and development of civil society, notably in disseminating civil society values and culture, providing information and advancing the general development process.

The modern media has also contributed to the creation of a new media domain for civil society entities enabling them to use the Internet and satellite channels to present their perspectives and debate issues of interest. These outlets have played an important role in crystallizing and promoting a common Arab identity at both political and social levels, strengthening the presence of women by allowing them the opportunity to take part in the discussions concerning their own causes, and creating new jobs for them as presenters, anchors, reporters etc.

The Internet has made it possible for civil society organizations, as well as other associations and groups, to communicate with their members and exchange information other than those disseminated by government sources. It has also made a significant contribution to the empowerment of Arab women by liberating them from repressive social restrictions.

However, the role of transnational satellite media in enhancing the democratic transformation process remains limited for two reasons:

* the continued state control over these channels, which curbs their impact and subordinates their policies to those advocated by the respective governments.

- the inability of these channels to participate in the dynamics of political and civil society in any particular Arab country. Therefore, the best and only means for the satellite media to be effective and influential in this context, is to remain free of state control.

Lastly, despite the modest rate of penetration and use of the Internet, its impact on the social and political change process is expected to be greater than that of the audio and visual media.

MEDIA FUNCTIONS: EDUCATION AND ENTERTAINMENT

5

Impact of Media on Education: Reality and Ambitions

Ali Mohammed Fakhro

At the present time the world is no longer governed by a militarist, ideological partisanship, or even an economic dictatorship as much as it is governed by a media dictatorship exercised via visible and hidden instruments involving symbols. Through its theses and suggestions it has been able to program the mind, soul, emotions and trends of people everywhere. In this age capital has shifted from classic hegemony, whether militarist, political or economic, to control of symbols. Media dictatorship has succeeded in replacing state dictatorship and substituted itself for the human conscience. Media authority is exercised in devious and multiple ways, which fosters a consumer culture that serves the industrial-technological machine. There are also other tranquilizing, sensual and simplistic ways in which the media contributes to justifying unwarranted societal relationships and to discouraging young generations from getting involved in public life.

Thus the great importance of the influential links between the fields of the media and education becomes apparent. Education, like other fields, is no longer capable of remaining detached from the sweeping flow of ideas, attitudes, analyses and behavioral traits dispersed incessantly, at any given moment by the media all over the world. However, the Arab world has its own particular characteristics, which warrants attention. Though the media in advanced societies forms a dictatorial force complete unto itself and capable of competing with all other forms of dictatorships, including

[139]

the state, the situation in Arab countries differs a great deal. In Arab countries the ruling regimes use the power of the media and its great potential to condition minds and souls in order to enforce domination by the different, narrow class interests which they represent in society.

Future Challenges

It is necessary to sketch very briefly a picture of future challenges in order to show the urgent need to integrate the efforts in the two most important fields of human development—education and the media. This must be done as a step towards meeting those challenges. Any tension between these two fields will doubly weaken the efforts of this necessary confrontation.

There are common challenges that confront both the Arab world and the rest of the world. These include, first, environmental pollution, which does not recognize geographical or human borders. Second, there is the challenge of confronting new diseases that humankind has never known before such as AIDS and BSE (Bovine Spongiform Encephalopathy or Mad Cow Disease). Third, there is the drying up of water sources necessary for life and civilization and the approaching depletion of oil resources. Fourth, there are the increasingly negative side effects stemming from the rapid pace and phenomenal advances of science and technology. Fourth, there is the challenge of cultural fundamentalism which heralds the end of history and the hegemony of one ideology—that of western liberal capitalism. Fifth, there are the economic, political and cultural problems stemming from the phenomenon of globalization. Finally, there is the shocking breakdown of values and ethics as a part of the post-modernism phenomenon which is sweeping western societies in particular.

These challenges alone are sufficient to encumber the future of the Arabs with excessively heavy burdens and complications that require extensive and diverse human development. However, the Arab world, divided, backward and targeted as it is, faces its own special challenges.

In my view, these challenges can be summarized in the six elements of the Arab Renaissance Project. These include achieving Arab unity, the shift to democracy, building independent development, enhancing social justice, overcoming subordination in favor of national independence and embarking on civilizational renewal, which is represented essentially in reviving Arab heritage and its concept of modernity.

A nation that faces all these huge future challenges cannot afford to allow any contradictions to emerge between the fields of development. The fields of development must grow harmoniously and symmetrically or else the negative aspects in any field will neutralize the positive aspects in the other fields.

Media and Education: Common Factors

If educational responsibility, especially at the university level, involves generating and producing knowledge, then the fields of education and the media are concerned with disseminating, analyzing and criticizing knowledge in order to integrate it into the cultural fabric of society. To carry out their knowledge responsibilities, these two fields require a large margin of freedom to gather information, conduct research, make presentations and express opinions. Neither field can deal innovatively and effectively with knowledge if information and statistics are regarded as official secrets and the divulgence of these is subject to the whims of officials in governmental agencies; or if expressing what this information means is controlled by inflexible, authoritarian laws or strict administrative directives, or if it is governed by perceived social and religious sanctities.

Such legal and administrative controls abound in Arab societies, causing both these fields to suffer in their pursuit of knowledge and culture. As a result of these controls, both fields suffer from the same pattern, by repetition and reproduction of the same social culture through the years, despite changing circumstances. Those who work in both these fields feel frustrated and powerless, apart from enduring mental and

[141]

psychological pressures due to the fear of crossing the red lines drawn by the controlling authorities at the state and society levels. The relationships between departments and directorates and also between officials and their subordinates are authoritative and undemocratic. Selecting personnel in both fields is subject to strict criteria, topping which is loyalty to the political regime and defending its methodology in administration and rule, and its system of values. Arab authorities are obsessed with controlling the ideas and beliefs of children and youth in schools and universities as much as they are obsessed with controlling trends in public opinion and sentiment.

It is important to highlight these common factors which govern the course of action in the two fields because they constitute one reason for Arab failure in both fields. Also, it is difficult to conceive that either field can help the other, being under the repression of the same forces which dominate the content and instruments of education and media in Arab countries.

The Media versus Education

Although educational and media institutions are controlled by the same powers, the contradiction between the two is a phenomenon that disturbs those managing them. Through past decades, voices in different Arab institutions, such as Arab League Educational, Cultural and Scientific Organization (ALECSO), or the Bureau of Education for the Gulf States, called for coordination and integration between media and educational institutions. Several conferences were held to explain what educators expected from the journalists and vice versa. However, those conferences did not yield executive mechanisms that would lead to the creation of real coordination and constant integration between the two fields. The Arab world still lives in a state of collision or disconnection between the educational and media discourses.

Since the fields of media, information and communication grow successively stronger, increasingly attracting and gaining direct and indirect influence on all social classes, and allowing them to impose semi-total hegemony on the home and family life, the issue of confrontation between the media and education increases in complexity and acuteness compared to the situation some decades ago. Where do the major contradictions lie between the two fields? Is there a possibility of reducing them to the minimum level?

First, there is the greatest goal towards which humans have sought to direct their efforts—arriving at the truth regarding all things including the phenomena of life and the universe and all human activities. The search for truth has primarily been via the mind, thought and imagination. Thus, the educational institution set itself the task of educating human beings who are capable of analysis, criticism, structuring, experimenting and creative innovation to enable them to seek the truth and give them the ability to differentiate between fabricated "truth" and genuine truth. Since arriving at the truth is difficult, it is necessary to familiarize man with the virtues of patience, taking time to reach judgments, spending sufficient time in reflection, and not allowing emotional desires to interfere with strict intellectual requirements.

Yet in the world of today – the world of globalization – there is no place for employing pure mind, soul and emotion. Our world is governed by the hegemony of the present moment—everything must happen immediately and with utmost speed. The motto of the age is constant haste in doing everything. The motto of speed leads to the phenomenon of reduction: in the news, in intellectual discussions, in advertisements and in images. This is practiced particularly in the audio-visual media channels. The result is greater simplification of complex issues by reducing them to mere titles and headlines as well as developing negative qualities, the most important being the lack of patience required in the process of acquiring knowledge, and not practicing the necessary reflection to reach the profound truth. Reflection is not boosted when the media seeks to attract the viewer to all its programs and does not allow even a moment for rest or relaxation by the constant introduction of new shows, materials, words and suggestions to achieve the greatest degree of direct and indirect influence through such programming. This process creates an audience incapable of practicing quiet reflection and sound thinking. What is strange is that neither reduction, nor haste is practiced during the simplistic and unintelligent interviews conducted with singers and comedians whereas this is invariably practiced in the case of interviews with thinkers and serious politicians.

The pupil who spends more time per day watching television than he spends in the classroom will not practice the methods that the school teaches him in order to ascertain the truth. He will practice the superficial and hasty methods that the audio-visual media teaches him and arrive at a false or distorted truth. This is exactly what the owners of media outlets want to achieve. The truth that is projected to convince people is that of globalized capitalism with all its requirements and manifestations—the voracious consumption of all material goods and intangible services and an immersion in sheer sensual pleasures.

Second, the school seeks to convince pupils to identify themselves with the great heroes of humanity who have enriched human life with their inventions and discoveries in the different fields of knowledge, and with their heroic deeds and unforgettable achievements. The aim is to encourage the pupil to find a human model worthy of emulation among such great heroes.

As for the media, it has created heroes of a new kind who are suitable advocates of the consumer culture produced by the industrial/technological/financial machine, owned by the great multi-national companies. These are the celebrity heroes in the world of popular art and sports. Since the majority of such celebrities are addicted to consumer goods such as fancy dresses, posh cars and a constant stream of new models of luxury goods produced by the machinery of the market economy, it is not difficult to see why they have become the heroes of the age with whom boys and girls try to identify themselves. All this is presented in the form of strident programs in which words mix with deafening music, or the uproar of game spectators, with a strong focus on the symbols of sex and stardom.

In such atmosphere, chastity becomes an obsolete value and the scene is dominated by irrationality, which successfully induces people to buy new goods and associate themselves pathologically with fashions that appear and fade with the speed of lightning. Certainly, the kind of identification that the school wants to promote recedes and disappears from the pupil's mind. Instead, it becomes identification without commitment to the pupil's daily reality, or to the talk he engages in with his friends inside and outside the school. Thus what the teacher says becomes sheer nonsense and what the television presenter says is perceived as pure truth.

Third, the Arabic school system – if only indirectly most of the time – seeks to reinforce the idea of citizenship with its attendant rights and responsibilities and its reliance on law and human decency, in the minds and emotions of the pupil. Even under despotic or class-dominated systems of rule, no educational institution places hurdles in this attempt, especially at a time when the Arab landscape has been witnessing the tide of democracy for some years.

However, most media channels – especially the print and visual media, either consciously or unconsciously – reinforce the kind of loyalty which personifies some leader or official. Regardless of the triviality of the news relating to him, it appears on the front page and is the main focus of the newscasts. When he appears on television, his nose, shoulder or hand is kissed in monotonous repetition by a number of people. When his motorcade passes in the streets, the focus is on people who applaud and dance in a hysterical, crazy way.

When the leader holds a council with people and other officials, the focus is on the lightly bent backs or lowered heads, or any bodily gesture indicating submission. When he makes a decision it is broadcast and published as a deed of benevolence, or as an order or directive so that the decision is based on a relationship of subjugation. All this has nothing to do with respect for public personalities but is strongly associated with the personification of authority and representation of the state through this leader or official. This is also not limited to political characters. It extends

[145]

to religious, tribal, military or financial personalities even if the gestures expressing subservience and shocking displays of human indignities differ. Although the educational institution complains about the same phenomenon between the pupil and his teacher or headmaster, there is a vast difference between a phenomenon restricted to an institution and a phenomenon that is marketed in the entire society. It is a phenomenon which hurts the principles of democracy and Islamic values, and subsequently neutralizes the educational institution's attempt to train what it terms the "good" citizen.

Fourth, we live in an age of exploding knowledge in the fields of science and scientific applications. From the primary stage, the school seeks to raise the pupil to become a human being equipped with the cultures of both the humanities and natural sciences as advocated by the English scholar C.P. Snow in 1950s when he realized the dangers of the imbalance between the two cultures in the modern human being. Moreover, the school realizes the constant mobility in the world of work, which could lead the worker of the future to change his job many times. However, the media institution – which is preoccupied with sex symbols and themes and obsessed by the constant shift from the real to the imaginary, and from seriousness to humor – neglects the field of science, especially that of the natural sciences in a bewildering way. Even when it shows scientific programs, these are usually translated from different milieus and societies. There is constant discussion of animals, plants and insects that are non-existent in the Arab environment, as well as diseases that are not a priority for Arab health. Though there is enough money to produce outrageous and lewd artistic programs, money is scarce for producing programs that promote scientific development and ushers the Arab human people into the dual age of science and technology. Hence Arab youth know the minutest details about Arab entertainers and sportsmen and their activities but know nothing about Arab scholars and researchers, who are not welcomed by most Arab media channels.

The matter is exacerbated when the Arab media focuses on marginal religious issues and abstract matters that have no relation to the rationality

[146]

of the Holy Quran and its strict methodology. This often happens at the expense of rationality which can be enhanced by focusing on the different fields of science.

The Arab media is urged to give scientific programs their due importance provided that these are not just translated foreign programs revolving round scientific issues that are remote from Arab realities. They must be programs prepared by Arab scholars and deal with sciences directly related to Arab societies and milieus. The situation is particularly painful because the audio-visual media can truly create qualitative shifts that support school programs and make the Arab students more interested in modern sciences. At present, they are not much inclined towards these fields because science does not appear to have an obvious and tangible impact on the Arab world.

Fifth, the school, with its role and function as the point of departure, seeks to enrich human emotions by inculcating in the pupil a greater sensitivity towards injustice, crime, cruelty and other horrible acts committed by people. In doing so, it depends on stories, poetry, religious education and other aspects of school subjects that express rejection of such brutal practices.

Yet the media engages in a competition to have the most direct, instantaneous and dazzling impact and in the process makes it a routine pastime to show scenes of bizarre death, banal sex, or crimes of insanity, and make all this an ordinary part of the lives of pupils. It is not considered absolutely important to give these scenes an understandable and justifiable context within the plot of a story or a television event. It is important for these to appear on the screen primarily to heighten the excitement of what is being presented.

The media does not treat the viewer as an independent individual capable of practicing freedom of thought and respecting his own judgment. Rather, it treats him as a client with wild desires irrational demands and value preferences which need to be satiated. The media has to provide instant gratification without consideration for the long-term harm it causes. When these scenes become a daily routine it gradually

[147]

becomes a consumer good like other commodities—it can be enjoyed without prohibition, without any pause or disruption all day and night. The vulgarization of human emotions will turn a person into a machine, devoid of feelings, and once this happens, no school can raise the level of his humanity.

After all, it is not necessary to narrate all the contradictions between the discourse of education and the discourse of the media—these are both stark and abundant. There is a focus on the negative aspects of the relationship to reveal the importance of coordinating the two fields through a permanent mechanism. This is so because the positive effects which support the mission of education and educational activities have become clear to some media channels. The computer and the Internet, for example, play a significant scientific and cultural role, as well as a role in acquiring knowledge. With the passage of time they will become two of the most important educational tools for collecting information, educational interaction, self-learning and adult teaching. Television has acquired great importance in the system of open universities, distance education, continuous and life-long learning, eradication of illiteracy and other things. Yet the issue is not regarding the availability of media and means of information. Rather, it is an issue concerning the content of the discourse conducted via these means. This discourse must modify its content and objectives. It must also liberate itself from attempts to use it as a means of spreading and reinforcing the worst in the civilization of the age and manipulating the worst instincts of humankind. The co-existence between education and the media in Arab societies is necessary in order to lift the Arab nation out of its civilizational predicament.

6

The Media as a Component of National Culture

Daood Al-Shiryan

According to Anthony Smith, author of the 1980 book *Geopolitics of Information: How Western Culture Dominates the World*, information is the pillar of sovereignty and cultural products are more devastating to nations' identities than fizzy drinks and hamburgers. Smith goes on to state that undoubtedly national independence rests now – more than at any time in the past – on the ability to make independent decisions relating to information or ideas exchange. Hence, many nations have now discovered that sovereignty, national identity and independence stem not only from official decisions but also from cultural conditions and economic life.

This is not an amplification of the media's role in conveying the currents and thoughts of globalization if we consider that "culture is the social and intellectual environment where the thought of a particular nation is shaped, as well as its lifestyle, values and behavior." If we recognize that the media has become the most important means in forming this environment, and that what is broadcast today via the media is merely an aspect of behavior and norms that are acceptable in the society that has produced these media outputs. On this basis, the societies that fail to produce their own cultural and media materials will find their culture disappearing over time, or becoming a hybrid incapable of enduring against other cultures or of influencing them.

This is not a call for isolation and rejection of other cultural currents. Neither is it a call to oppose freedom under the slogan of nationalism.

Absolute freedom in absorbing modern ideas and knowledge given the prevailing imbalances in power, influence, technological progress and economic and military hegemony means one outcome—the dominance of the currents of western culture through cultural and informational invasion. Moreover, it should not be forgotten that "free beliefs and knowledge currents of the dominant nation are not necessarily in favor of the dominated nations."

The protection of national culture does not mean isolationism, suppressing other opinions and prohibiting freedom of choice and expression. It also does not mean suppressing innovation under the pretext of combating cultural estrangement. However, it does not mean that in the pursuit of progress, we should commandeer modern means of communication to disseminate other cultural currents and values indiscriminately. Nor does it mean employing Arab cultural movements and values as a means to market the cultural and informational products of others regardless of the nature and content of these products. The protection of national culture requires the following steps:

- an awareness of the influence of imported cultural currents either in the absence of a local counterpart or its weakness or defeat.
- a consensus on the fact that freedom is a vital matter, an essential means of cultural cohesion without which cultural standing is weakened and the public is impelled to question its own culture and the symbols of this culture.
- a consensus on the fact that wholesale rejection, in the absence of dialogue, transparency and conviction, is no longer tenable in view of the collapse of the wall of isolationism that separates nations and the profusion in the means of communication and their impact.
- refraining from countering our ineffectiveness against the cultural currents and thoughts of others by seclusion, repression or rejection, sometimes under the pretext of preserving values, customs and traditions or at other times, by slogans of national pride.
- realizing that the protection of national culture should not become a political slogan and a means of instigating people against their

governments, leveling the charge of betrayal against elites, and achieving political and partisan gains, because it is a question relating to the existence of the entire nation; and addressing this question is not solely vested in a particular institution, government or group but is the task of the whole society with all its institutions and individuals.

- believing that the absence of civil society institutions renders the role of nations in this vital issue void and weakens the position of regimes in addressing this problem.

Certainly, the role of the mass media has expanded tremendously in the last few years. Modern studies on the role of the US media in society have provided evidence that the mass media, in its totality, is the most important means of conveying and spreading culture, and that it has replaced the school, church and family in influencing people, teaching them modes of behavior and the norms that support or justify this behavior. The significant role of the media in forming the values and behavior of people has become a subject of research in the United States. However, as television belongs to a dominant culture in this instance, it does not give room for importing other cultures. This being the case, what is a nation's position if its television stations continue to feed on the materials and ideas of others?

In this regard, the television media adopts one of two positions, as maintained by Dr. Victor Sahhab. The first position is that "the audience knows more than we presume and we should not claim that we inform people. This position consists in false modesty that exonerates us in effect from setting ourselves a necessary task—that of informing people. Or we say people are generally ignorant and the media must cope with this fact and this betrays a veiled arrogance. In both cases there is solace for the incompetent. However these views are widespread among us media personnel, and may be a source of complacency for us. Yet they are false views at best and destructive at worst."

Our political independence remains incomplete in view of our economic and cultural independence. We must realize that the preservation of our existence, the components of our culture demands a review of our cultural, economic and political situations, and the finding of a new affinity between culture and economics that annuls the presumed misunderstanding between the two fields. Culture that is not backed by money and economic influence does not cross borders. On the contrary, it will be defeated on its own platforms. In the Arab world, companies have not availed of an opportunity to develop culture for several reasons. The most important of these reasons is that culture remains a part of the governmental-administrative system. Also, the conceptual differences between the intellectuals and the businessmen lead to mutual suspicion. For evidence of this, it would suffice to review literary texts, films and television series to gauge the image of Arab businessmen as perceived by Arab journalists and men of letters. This image is often reduced to that of an ugly merchant characterized by ignorance and coarseness, who is only concerned about his personal interests. In addition, he is shown as having made his fortune through deceit, fraud and stealing citizens, not to mention trafficking in drugs and out-of-date foodstuff.

There is no magical solution for preserving our national culture in its confrontation with the currents of globalization. However, there are some concepts and general principles that point towards the solution. The most important of these are listed below:

- Our need for defending our cultural uniqueness is not lesser than our need for modernization and for delving into the age of science and technology effectively and independently.
- Resisting the penetration of our cultural identity does not mean isolationism and rejection of the new. Moreover, the preservation of cultural identity is preconditioned by significant modernization and changes in our modes of thinking.

A closed culture that loves to shelter behind a dam of pretexts, and lacks internal freedom will find it difficult to confront others or engage in dialogue. Moreover, it will fall short of influencing others in a world dominated by political participation, the freedom of imaginative enterprise and expression, as well as differences and the freedom of choice.

7

The Role of Media: Between Education and Entertainment

Ali Q. Al-Shuaibi

The essential role of the Arab media both today and in the future is to take the initiative to counter effectively the fierce and organized attack to which Arabs are currently being subjected. Those responsible for this attack are the very people who have been assigned the task of overseeing the media. This initiative must be taken in order to promote the cultural sector and develop its ability as well as the capabilities of those who work in this sector to ensure positive choices in the future. At present, these choices are being scattered by the winds of cultural globalization and swayed by the clout of media channels and entertainment companies, as well as the hegemony of advertising, given that most Arab media outlets favor advertisements at the expense of the recipient's interests and the cultural output as a whole.

Studies confirm that television has become the undisputed school for public education, which remains open round the clock. It conveys a great deal of knowledge, information and trends, which can help either to support existing value systems or to shatter cultural and value barriers. This fact imposes a massive responsibility on the media, not only in educating children and youngsters, but in educating society as a whole.

Regretfully enough, against this random and uncontrolled multiplication of Arab government and commercial satellite channels, an obvious imbalance has emerged between different television functions—those of spreading culture, education and entertainment. Entertainment has always gained the upper hand. It is necessary to acknowledge the importance of entertainment to human life, and its ability to relieve psychological stress, depression and social anger. However, negative entertainment takes the form of deliberate violence, which is often broadcast at the expense of cultural content, which is shown only in off-peak television time. Even this limited programming is done with reservations and even aversion and resentment by program managers and chairmen of television stations. This is true to such an extent that programming and coordination departments in these television stations often seek off-peak hours to broadcast cultural programs because they are considered too dry and elitist. It is true that many of the Arabic cultural programs on television suffer from dryness and elitism. This defect stems from the inability or the lack of motivation to present cultural programs acceptable to viewers, especially when televised programs are turned into radio-type programs or into a frigid block of elitist discussions that fail to blend sound, image and motion in a manner typical of television productions.

The Arab media machine is making coordinated attempts to eclipse its cultural programming and contribute to the deterioration of public taste by showing mindless plays, distasteful songs and trivial talk shows. Moreover, there is a lack of political content, few artistic productions and high reliance on imported foreign programs.

The television message may reap positive effects if formulated according to a correct educational methodology that is scientific and media-oriented. In contrast, the outcome may be destructive when the media message is distorted by comedians, hardware merchants and other destructive elements.

In the late 1950s, the scholar Alberta E. Siegel introduced the first glimpse of what was later known as Cultivation Theory. This media theory is concerned with studying the effect of television programs on the audience—especially children. The theory proved that viewers who continuously watch television programs, especially dramatic ones, begin to see social realities from the perspective presented on television. It has also proven that media channels, especially television, affects the perception of viewers and their understanding of the real world, and that most of the information they gain regarding the world is derived from the media message, which is conveyed through image, sound, color and motion. Watching the world portrayed in drama affects their system of values to a great extent and may even destroy it.

I do not know – and neither do most Arab viewers – the social, political, educational and entertainment objectives of Arab TV stations, especially the Gulf terrestrial and satellite stations. They present programs that mislead recipients, play with their emotions and transport them to the world of buffoonery and negative entertainment.

Several Arab researchers and media personnel are concerned about diagnosing the state of the Arab media and the depths of triviality to which it has descended. They blame political decisions, which have had great impact on the constant shrinking of media content, and its failure to perform its role in terms of raising awareness and furthering development. Many social studies confirm that the deterioration of the Arab media is a reflection of Arab society and its successive failures after the collapse of the Arab Renaissance Project, the reduction or lack of liberties and the crushing of personal and differing opinions. The media's concept of falsifying awareness began in Arab radio stations, which relied on hoarse rhetoric. After this the traditional newspapers, columnists and opinion leaders emerged, who betrayed the trust conferred on them and became the scribes of the Sultan. Having got rid of the Arabic discourse that created such false awareness, we are now under attack by new Arab media armies and a trend that may be described as the "tumultuous" media.

Dr. Khalid Al Karki, the former Jordanian Minister of Culture, in a lecture at Bahrain University in May 2000 identified five basic cultural criteria that are considered crucial to understanding the problems of the Arab media. These are:

- *Attitude towards freedom:* No two persons differ on the fact that culture and democracy are the best mottos for the future.

[155]

- *Reality:* This reality should be understood by time-tested scientific analysis because the link between the media and science must be strengthened.
- *Understanding the world:* This understanding cannot be based on rejecting the world or claiming that it is on the verge of collapse.
- *Dialogue:* This should be the basis of the Arab stance on media and culture.
- *Vision:* This vision must be specified through an in-depth assessment of the link between culture and the media.

Some researchers maintain that media channels perpetuate some kind of cultural consumption of simplified information, which limits the span of thinking. The scientific evaluation of the relationship between culture and the media requires accurate data which study systematically and quantitatively the following aspects:

- the impact of media channels on patterns of living and audience behavior
- the extent and quality of information with cultural dimension in media channels
- the role of the media in marketing and promoting cultural activity
- the role of the media in eradicating illiteracy and on-the-air learning.

In my view, the Arab media, encompassing both government and private institutions, bears great responsibility for Arabic cultural stagnation, manifested in the following aspects:

- *Falling book circulation:* There is an absence of Arabic books among the general public and its circulation is falling even within the community of educated elites. No more than three thousand copies are printed of even the most successful book. The only exceptions are religious, heritage and educational books.
- *Deterioration in cinematic production:* Arabic cinematic production has deteriorated. Even in Egypt (the Arab Hollywood) cinematic production has dropped to a few films a year, most of them of poor standard. In contrast, India's film production has jumped to one

[156]

thousand films annually. In Syria, Tunisia, Morocco, Algeria and other film-producing countries, the production of each country is not more than four or five films annually despite the correlation between the increase in television channels and the number of films produced to satisfy broadcasting needs. In this context, we may mention a number of factors behind the deterioration of the Arabic cinema. These include the shocking technological backwardness of the cinema industry; the industry's acceptance of the argument that "the audience wants it this way;" stereotypical and traditional cinematic ideas; the emergence of new players in cinema production such as the hardware merchants; and the fact that the state has abandoned cinema production and left it to the mercy of the winds, stranded between an audience which is turning its back on it, the modest gains of the industry itself, and an sweeping invasion of American films, which are skillfully made, exciting and inexpensive.

- *Receding theatrical activity:* There is also the general inactivity of Arabic theatre and the receding activities of national theatres in comparison with commercial ones. However, we can still witness the efforts of Arab theatre artists who try to preserve the existence of Arabic theatre through annual festivals, such as the experimental theater in Egypt.

If literature – poetry, novels, articles – form the subject matter of the press as a media channel, it provides the visual arts with only limited material, notably the Arabic novel, which is often used as raw material by the television and radio drama industry. While the media role in the retreat of Arab culture is undeniable, it must be pointed out that television has diverted the reader's attention away from reading, and via the art of serials has competed with the cinema and theatre, promoting a consumer culture and becoming directly responsible for the triviality and vulgarization associated with the promotion of distasteful music and decadent songs.

It seems that culture in the Arab media – both written and audio-visual forms – is retreating to a marginal position. Actually, it is insufficient for some newspapers to publish literary supplements, or for some magazines to allocate a few pages for cultural content, such as reserving space for folk poetry.

The reality of the deterioration in the Arab media coincides with the machinery of the American media – represented by Radio Sawa, Al Hurra channel and *Hi* magazine – being directed towards Arab audiences. The American media is eager, via this integrated chain of printed and audio-visual outlets, to establish firmly a new culture in the mindset of the young Arab generation. The requirements of globalization and the idea of shaping individuals and creating global consumers who are in tune with market trends are all harmonized.

Radio Sawa, which targets the younger generation of boys and girls, and has attracted a huge audience in a record time, aims to penetrate their minds, mentality and the thought processes by means of intelligent programming and skillful formulation of news. Through the news, it conveys the media ideas and message, and this helps to penetrate their creed and ideological education.

In addition, *Hi* magazine, with its brilliant layout and skillful editing, is directed towards Arab youth. Its objective is to bridge the gap in the relationship between Arab and American youth, familiarizing Arab youngsters with the vocabulary of American life and creating a culture which calls for improving the American image. As for *Al Hurra* channel, it is a satellite television channel targeting the Arab world. It is a miniature copy of Radio Sawa insofar as orientation, goals and the targeted audience and the expected effect are concerned.

In contrast, the most important objectives behind the establishment of the Arab Satellite Communication Organization known as Arabsat, are as follows:

* Connecting the Arab World with the outside world and providing more opportunities for exchange in the fields of culture, science and programming, as well as conveying information and modern technology and achieving cultural openness.

[158]

- Contributing to the development of remote areas and providing them with education, culture, training, guidance and strengthening the ties of civilization between them.
- Connecting educational and scientific institutions, research and documentation centers and libraries by a means of fast communication, and achieving national integration intellectually and culturally.
- Upgrading the level of educational services based on scientific methodology and learners' competence, and contributing effectively in the field of eradicating illiteracy and adult education.
- Upgrading the cultural level of Arab audiences and the level of their artistic taste.

No doubt these grand and illuminating aims, which are considered a constitution and mission for Arabsat could have occasioned a revolution in the ways of thinking and the domains of Arab inventiveness, at the very least. The optimal use of satellite broadcasting technology could have played a real role in achieving comprehensive development across the Arab World. However, the reality is quite different from the dreams. The actual launching of the Arab satellite media began after the liberation of Kuwait in 1991 and the emergence of the CNN channel as an important media player and a source of news that has attracted audiences. Since then, the fashion of launching Arab satellite channels has spread, and most satellite channels have turned into local stations that broadcast repetitive programs and reruns.

As for so-called family magazines or women's magazines, most of their interests are focused on matters such as décor, cooking, the latest fashions and make-up techniques, beautiful looks, and news about male and female artistes and singers. They are not oriented towards discussing heated issues and serious problems which affect Arab women—from education to the civil and other rights of women and their rights of political participation. Some subjects are cordoned off by red lines, which are drawn by publishers and chief editors and not by media censors. Such topics are not approached, being considered taboo, especially when they relate to women learning about motherhood, nurturing and other vital matters.

The real deterioration in the Arab media reflects the general deterioration in the Arab World. It is a reality which will not change without a real change in Arab political reality, ways of thinking, eradication of illiteracy, transformation into a state with institutions, and efforts to achieve a comprehensive economic and social development.

There is one final question that ought to be posed: Is there any hope of reforming both government and private Arab media to make it express Arab aspirations, defend the values of goodness, beauty, rights and justice and expose all aspects that lead to the subjugation, humiliation and marginalization of the Arab people?

8

Satellite Channels and the Entertainment Debate

Abdul Rahman Al-Rashid

There is a heated debate today in the Arab world over which television station can be watched, which film is suitable and which song is appropriate. The question often posed is: Does the content of entertainment channels promote vulgar pleasures and contain messages that stir dangerous emotions? This current debate has reached such an acute level that any question of whether something is permissible or prohibited is turned into a subject of controversy. Some demand that broadcasting by certain television channels should be stopped and that these TV outlets must be punished. Is it true that the channels have reached such a level of vulgarity? How far does their content really constitute obscenity?

It is true that we live in a new age, the like of which we have never experienced before—under an open sky which bombards us with television broadcasts from anywhere to anywhere. Television broadcasts present news, songs, dances, religious exhortations, cooking demonstrations and matches. All these raise questions about their identity and subject matter. The social content of these programs sparks big protests, which emanate from inherited traditions that allow limited choices. Music stations in particular, have come under scrutiny and anger some people because they are perceived as challenging our conservative societies. In my view, these conservative societies will have to learn to cope with this challenge because they are living in a "time capsule" which is rapidly undergoing transformation. Definitely, the pace at which this "time capsule" is changing is faster than the ability of the people to adapt and become acclimatized.

We are victims of fear and religio-political polarization, which leads to confusion about what is new and acceptable within reason, and what is strange, absurd and worthy of rejection. What is certain is that even if what is new is rejected, it is impossible to stop water pouring through the cracks in the dyke by plugging it with a finger. Moreover, we cannot resolve the cultural conflict without understanding the problem and differentiating between what is tolerable and intolerable while giving the utmost consideration and tolerance for the expectations of the young generation. Even what is worthy of rejection cannot be easily prohibited. It is almost impossible to ban everything that deserves to be rejected in the context of technological developments. With mounting challenges and the inability to ban the objectionable broadcasts of satellite channels, there is a confused situation in which attempts are made to rapidly build barriers without taking the opportunity to review and understand the challenges and adopt a course of action that will remedy this state of isolation.

The problem is multi-faceted. Some aspects are clear, such as having satellite channels agree on what is permissible—the essentials over which there is no controversy. However, some facets spark differences and these form the subject matter of our discussion. In other words, satellite channels present certain songs that some consider obscene and want to stop while others consider this to be a matter of taste. In such cases, we should respect them despite the conflicting opinions they arouse. There is no disagreement, however, over what is absolutely objectionable.

The problem lies in the conflict between generations and their related cultural differences. It is inconceivable that a man in his fifties should determine the appropriate song for a young man in his twenties. This is inconceivable at any time, more so when young men have the means to reach out to any kind of art form they want and can make their personal choice in a much easier way than before.

[162]

My colleagues who have already made their presentations have been voicing protests that primarily reflect differences in taste and age, and which have nothing to do with the decadence that they urge should be combated. The greatest difference is over the words of certain songs which are described as uninhibited. To my thinking, these songs are less scandalous than some Arabic poetry in the Arab renaissance eras–the Arabic poetry which boosts our pride and which we seek to revive. The words of the Andalusian poetess Wallada bint al Mustakfi cannot be found in the album of cheap songs which conservatives are fighting against today:

> *I generously offer my cheek to my lover*
> *And amorously kiss anyone who desires my lips.*

In those days there were no satellite channels and no concerts. Yet the Arab nightly entertainment gatherings of old included all the traditional arts and these gatherings were somewhat similar to the "video clip" entertainment of today. These gatherings were a feature that lasted for one thousand years without objections from contemporaries. The total rejection of the content of some satellite channels and the call for their closure because of some flirtatious lines exchanged by the young that appear across the bottom of the screen represent an exaggerated reaction and only express a state of hysteria that has afflicted the conservatives in our society. As for me, I know that it is not possible to force the young people to love the songs and music that we appreciate and we must learn to accept their tastes.

We tend to forget that we are embarking the same route as our forefathers who disagreed on the same issue. In the 1970s when audio cassettes appeared for the first time, a fight ensued over what the conservatives viewed as "uninhibited songs." The combat was sparked by the words of a song which says:

> *The washtub said to me: Oh beauty!*
> *Get up and have a bath*

[163]

Critics urged banning the song on the ground that it represented uninhibited, tasteless words, and called for punishing its promoters. The audio cassette spread among the public because no one had control over its distribution. The song got a high public rating and even shook the pillars of classic Arabic singing represented by singers such as Umm Kulthum and Abdul Halim Hafiz. The voices of the critics who urged the banning of the songs got shriller in the Arab press. Yet the cassette was a new source of songs, which escaped the fetters imposed by "good taste" censorship and gave people the freedom to make their personal choice of songs.

The story of song selection deserves telling because this phase is on the verge of extinction. In the past, the radio was the major source of songs, along with some record companies and there were official committees established to approve the songs. A committee in the radio station would decide which singer was suitable, what words were appropriate, and which music was acceptable. If the song was approved in terms of taste and morals, it would be repeatedly played for years but if it was not approved, it would perish, so to speak. A handful of people, not more than ten in every Arab radio station used to decide what public taste should be and specify the traits of appropriate singing. With the appearance of the cassette, which was cheap and easy to copy at home, the authority of such committees started to fade. The cassette was the reason for the ascendance of most independent singers. Most cassette singers expressed prevailing public taste, which was "held hostage" to the approval of the song committees, which often despised such common taste. Cassettes sold in millions, defeating the committees, big singers became extinct, and the general public won the battle. With the appearance of satellite channels this experience was replicated. Popularity used be dependent on the "stereo" system alone. Satellite channels are a bigger shock to these approval committees whose current members are conservative parents, who think that the new television stations have crossed all the red lines, and therefore they must be confronted and banned and those in charge must be punished.

Although I do appreciate the predicament of the protestors and the sincerity of their feelings, I would advise them to first understand the power of the new, unstoppable technology because the new media penetrates deep, like the Internet, which has become the best companion of young people. It is worth noting that grown-ups complain about satellite channels but say nothing about the Internet. This reflects a lack of understanding of their surroundings because electronic technology is more influential than satellite communication but they are not yet aware of this fact. Closing local satellite channels will not stop the reach of distant satellite channels that broadcast via neighboring satellites. Even if all satellite channels are closed, conservatives will still have to deal with the Internet which knows no limits, regardless of screening procedures. Also, the closure of satellite channels will not stop those who broadcast via the Internet. It is worth mentioning that most songs and films can be downloaded electronically, cheaply and sometimes free of charge—and they do not have to pass through any customs or control checkpoints.

In my view, the solution is a return to our origins: education, acculturation, constant enhancement of awareness and placing trust in our sons and daughters. Aside from this, there is little that can be done. Waging war against the satellite channels is a fruitless exercise—rather like Don Quixote's fight.

THE MEDIA AND INTERNET IMPACT

9

The Impact of the Electronic Media on Arab Socio-Political Development

Mohammad Al-Jassem

At the outset, it is necessary to pause and consider the meaning of three words in the title of this chapter: the first is "media," the second is "development," and the third is "Arab." The word "media" has both a general meaning and a particular one. The general meaning is connected with conveying knowledge regardless of the means, whether it is a printed newspaper or an electronic version, a television or radio station, a website on the Internet or any other medium for conveying information, news, analysis and opinion. Hence a research study on the impact of the electronic media on socio-political development encompasses the general impact of the Internet in its totality as a medium of the electronic media. The special meaning of the word "media" is associated with the press. Therefore, the term "electronic media" in this context denotes that the discussion is focused on the electronic press and not the Internet.

In fact, in the context of this research study, it is difficult to determine the impact of the electronic press in particular on the socio-political development of Arabs. Investigating such an impact requires detailed studies which are based on credible data and accurate information. This is something that goes beyond my personal endeavor. Whatever credible information is available relates to the Internet as a means of communication and a conduit for information. Hence this study will not investigate the impact of the electronic press as much as it traces the impact of the Internet as a means of communication.

The second word to consider is the word "development." The commonly accepted meaning of this word is "improvement" and "change for the better." This word conjures up a dull image of the past and a bright new one representing the present or the future. However, the word "development" in Arabic is derived linguistically from "phase" or "phases." The nearest general meaning to this Arabic word is "stage" or "stages." This meaning is not qualitatively specific in the sense that when we say something has "developed" this means that only that it has moved from one stage to another. However, this other stage could be either negative or positive depending on one's vision.

The third word under consideration is the word "Arab." Here it must be pointed out that Arabs certainly have a common culture and share somewhat similar political and social situations. Moreover, they definitely have common concerns as well as extensive familial and tribal ties. Nevertheless, all these shared aspects do not eclipse the importance of the local culture of every Arab state—whether small or big, rich or poor.

The influence of local cultures on society surpasses the impact of the general common culture and thus controls the direction in which that society moves. In every Arab state there are factors specific to that state— the type of governance, the nature of the ruler and the security system, economic policies, the standard of living, the percentage of foreign residents, and other domestic factors which control development – whatever the term means – in each individual state. Hence the assessment of any case – such as the impact of electronic media on the Arab socio-political development – must rely on "local" standards of measurement that are specific to each state, without generalizing these findings as including all "Arabs."

A specific example will help to clarify this point. A specialized source says that by the end of 2004, the number of Internet users in the State of Kuwait had reached 567,000 users, amounting to nearly 24% of the population, which is approximately 2,430,000.[1] This percentage reflects the reality of Internet usage in the State of Kuwait. However, taking into account the fact that the Kuwaitis represent 37% of the total population, it

[170]

is clear that the indicators associated with Internet usage in the State of Kuwait cannot be viewed as necessarily reflecting the Kuwaiti or Arab situation. The same is true of the United Arab Emirates and other states with a high proportion of non-Arabs in the population. Hence I think that conducting research studies in Arab countries and presenting overall findings that claim to represent the general Arabic situation, regardless of whether this situation is negative or positive, is rather misleading.

In view of the unavailability of credible information about the percentage of non-Arabs using the Internet in the Arab States, this chapter will attempt to document the impact of electronic media on Arab socio-political development in the light of the general indicators available.

This chapter is divided into three parts. The first part deals briefly with the stages through which the Arab media passed till it reached the stage of the electronic media. The second part is devoted to discussing Arab electronic media. In the third part the impact of the electronic media on Arab socio-political development will be discussed. In the conclusion, the research findings are summed up.

Arab Media: The Sultan's Media and the Revolution's Media

The major instruments of the media in the period preceding the use of the Internet were restricted to three: the press (print media), the radio and the television. The Arabs were familiar with the press from the nineteenth century when the first Arabic newspaper appeared in 1800. It was issued by Napoleon Bonaparte under the title *al Tanbih*. In 1828, the Egyptian Ruler Muhammad 'Ali Pasha issued *al Waqai' al Masriyyah*. The third Arabic newspaper was the Algerian newspaper *al Mubashir* issued in 1847. Some say that *al Tanbih* was not issued in Arabic and that *The Khedive Journal,* issued in 1827, was the first newspaper that marked the start of the formal Arabic press.

Despite disagreement on which Arabic country was the first to know the art of printing, the Arab world generally did not know this art till after the printing press was introduced in some Arab countries. Lebanon and

Syria were the first Arab countries in which printing presses were established around 1730. Despite this, the press in the Arab world emerged rather late. This was due to the policy of the Ottoman State which was intent on sealing off the Arab world and isolating it from aspects of European civilization for four centuries.

> Yet the Arabs soon began to enter the field of journalism by themselves, imprinting it with their own private style without imitating westerners. The Arabs understood that the press was a tool of *Jihad*, a means of war and struggle, and a path towards revolution and liberation from the shackles of the foreigners and obsolete traditions and customs. The Arab press was trying to liberate the nation from the Ottoman Sultanate and thus it devoted its efforts to incite people and awaken their determination. The Arab Press was carrying a sword not a pen; it played the role of a *Mujahid* [fighter] not that of the organizer or reformer…it fought against ignorance, poverty and the *hijab* [veil]. Then it struggled to liberate women and the nations…Then it fought against tyranny, aggression, feudalism and tyrannical rulers, considering itself a national school not a commercial enterprise.[2]

At the outset, we must differentiate between the beginnings of journalism in the Arab world and the emergence of the Arab press itself. Within this last specification, we must also differentiate between the emergence of the official and the popular Arabic press. If the introduction of the mass media in the Arab World came through the Europeans or the Ottomans, the Arab press originated with the rulers. Although this historical feature had both positive and negative results, what remains are only the negative aspects in all its intellectual, political and media dimensions. This feature was destined to create its exact opposite—the popular press, which represents the thoughts and interests of the Arabic social forces that have led the national struggle against the Ottomans throughout the nineteenth century and the early twentieth century, and later against the Europeans since the end of the First World War and until the achievement of national independence.[3]

Popular Arabic newspapers started to appear in 1908 in reaction to the newly promulgated Ottoman constitution. The Arab press contributed significantly to combating the Ottoman Rule:

It kept on record its own history as a part of the Arab liberation movement against Ottoman dominance. National Arabic newspapers endured Ottoman harassment and different forms of persecution, which reached a peak when 17 Arab journalists were executed in the infamous massacres committed by the Turkish Ruler Jamal Pasha against Arab nationalists in 1916.[4]

In the Aftermath of the First World War and the demise of the Ottoman State and the advent of the European colonization, "the process of publishing newspapers and the quality of the social, intellectual and political issues in hand was affected by the modes of struggle between Arab national forces and the colonial authorities."[5] During that stage, Arabic newspapers used to represent the colonial authorities, governments or national forces. The newspapers affiliated to the national forces "were engaged in a dual fight in the process of confronting official newspapers and those newspapers which were aligned with the colonial powers."[6]

By the end of the colonial era, the Arab Press entered a dark tunnel. Its mission was restricted to the glorification of the revolution and the leader. The margins of freedom available prior to the fall of the Ottoman State and the stage preceding the end of European colonization, faded away. The task before the Arab Press consisted of three major issues: the first and most urgent was the question of Arab unity and the liberation of Palestine; the second was development and social justice; and the third related to freedom and democracy.[7]

However, Arab regimes which dominated the 1950s and 1960s were repressive regimes. The task of the press was represented in consolidating the status quo and practicing propaganda in the interest of the ruling regime. The Arab press never parted company with its planned role— being the megaphone of the "Sultan." Generally, the Arab press continued to enhance the image of the ruler in varying degrees till the end of the 1980s.

That was the state of the Arab press. As for other means of information—the radio and television, they were, in terms of liberties, in a bad position. This was so because there were only state radios and television stations.

> After the defeat of June 1967 the television and the cinema moved forward and occupied the position of an anesthetic force without parallel in the Arab world; not only did they benumb feelings, but also minds, hearts and visions.[8]

Despite the technological progress witnessed by means of information during that period, the Arab media was suffering from a "complex crisis." It was a media which flowed in "a vertical direction: from the rulers to the ruled," performing a basic role in "the processes of social pressure and protecting the socio-political status quo." Its aim was also to "convince the public and keep them in a state of compliance in favor of official and governmental policies."[9]

This was the environment of the Arab media till August 1990, when Iraq invaded the State of Kuwait. That invasion was a turning point in the march of the Arab media in general and television in particular. A sharp division occurred between Arabic public opinion and Arab governments. While most Arab governments supported the liberation of the State of Kuwait from the clutches of the Iraqi army through a war led by the United States, Arabic public opinion opposed the deployment of American and British troops in the region. Popular Arabic tension represented a danger to some Arab regimes and so pent-up tensions were allowed to be vented to some extent via the press, which voiced views opposing the "foreign presence in the region."

However, the television played an important role during that phase. The American CNN station played the role of information "provider." Some official Arab television stations linked their broadcasting to the CNN prior to and during the outbreak of the war for the liberation of Kuwait. This paved the way for the major transformation which dawned on the Arab media afterwards when the first Arab satellite television channel appeared—the Middle East Broadcasting Center (MBC). Although the margin of freedom in that stage was not distinctive, the style of presentation and the shift from direct to implicit political propaganda, in addition to the diversity of programming and a shift from the traditional pattern in presenting news in particular, as well as the absence of competitors, made this station a significant landmark in the march of the Arab media.

As it was easy to receive and view the programs broadcast by satellite channels, Arab regimes confronted an unprecedented challenge. Arab people began to have open access to information. Ways of dealing with this accessibility differed among those regimes. While some states – such as Kuwait and the UAE – turned their eyes away from satellite media and did not prohibit their people from owning satellite dishes, other states – such as the Kingdom of Saudi Arabia and Iraq (during the rule of Saddam Hussein) – deliberately prohibited the use of the satellite dishes. This represented the first major confrontation with the "technology of freedom." With further technological advances, the Arab regimes despaired of achieving results in their favor. Thus they founded satellite television stations to undertake the task of political promotion by unconventional modes—such as the style adopted by *Al Jazeera* channel to promote Qatari politics. Regardless of the content of the Arabic satellite television channels and their standards – including that of music television stations – they have reinforced the right to choose.

Jon Alterman writes about the impact of the emergence of Arab satellite television stations. When such programs started in the mid-1990s, some hoped they would become a pillar for democratic openness because censorship was the prop of despotic regimes in the Middle East in the past. Satellite television began to destroy censorship. Yet a decade later, not a single Arab regime was brought down by its people and few regimes took limited steps towards democratic reformation. According to Alterman, Arab satellite television succeeded in bringing a more frank political discourse into the studios, but it did not bring more open policies on the ground. [10]

Although newspapers, magazines and state television stations existed for a long period without competitors, Arab satellite television stations do not enjoy this stability. In addition to the multiplicity of such channels, the Internet was introduced in the Arab states in the beginning of 1990s. Most Arab states got connected to the Internet during the period from 1992 to

1999. Though Internet usage is not widespread, some Arabic newspapers founded their own websites on the Internet in the mid-1990s. Since then the electronic media phase has started. It emerged as a tool of the media alongside the press, the radio and the television.

The Electronic Media

The electronic media is but one option provided by the Internet for the user. It is not logical to speak of the electronic media and its impact without speaking first of the Internet itself. This is particularly so because documenting the electronic media is linked to knowing the extent of Internet usage in Arab countries or the number of Internet users in the Arab countries. It must be acknowledged in the first place, before relying on any of the reports showing the number of Internet users in the Arab countries, that knowing the actual number of users is very difficult. While counting the number of subscriptions to the World Wide Web is possible, knowing the number of those who make use of one subscription or "account" depends on approximation. For example, the number of subscriptions to the Internet in the state of Kuwait is nearly 120,000[11] as we have already mentioned, credible estimations indicate that the number of the Internet users in the same state has reached 567,000 users. This means that the same subscription is used by 5 persons. The average number of users per subscription in the State of Kuwait cannot be generalized for the other Arab countries. This matter is subject to socio-economic considerations because this average may rise or fall.

The total number of the Internet users in the Arab countries till December 2004 reached about 13,625,000 distributed as shown in Table 9.1. The table itself makes it clear that the ratio of the Internet users in the Arab countries – both Arabs and non-Arabs – to the total number of the population is small. This ratio is very low in itself without comparing it with corresponding figures in the European countries and the United States.

[176]

Table 9.1

Internet Users in the Arab States

(upto December 2004)

Country	Population	No. of Internet Users
Egypt	68,648,500	2,700,000
Kingdom of Saudi Arabia	22,287,100	1,500,000
UAE	3,341,900	1,110,200
Morocco	30,552,000	800,000
Tunisia	10,001,400	630,000
Kuwait	2,429,200	567,000
Algeria	32,080,000	500,000
Jordan	5,642,200	457,000
Lebanon	4,432,000	400,000
Sudan	34,222,000	300,000
Syria	19,229,200	220,000
Kingdom of Bahrain	6,99,400	195,700
Sultanate of Oman	3,234,500	18,000
Libya	5,681,000	16,000
Palestine	3,827,900	145,000
(The West Bank [and Gaza Strip])		
Qatar	649,600	126,000
Yemen	16,677,800	10,000
Iraq	27,139,200	25,000

Source: Internet World Stats (http://www.internetworldstats.com/stats5.htm#me).

It can be said that the most important reason for the low number of the Internet users in the Arab countries is the high price of the service, in addition to the high cost of acquiring computers. As the Arab Human Development Report for 2003 stated:

> The mass media are the most important agents for the public diffusion of knowledge yet Arab countries have lower information media to population ratios...There are just 18 computers per 1000 people in the region, compared to the global average of 78.3 computers per 1000 persons and

[177]

only 1.6 per cent of the population has Internet access. These indicators scarcely reflect a sufficient level of preparedness for applying information technology for knowledge diffusion.[12]

The same report mentions that the low number of Internet users in Arab countries may be attributed to a number of factors. The most important of these are "computer and Internet illiteracy, the high cost of the lines used and high personal computer prices and access fees."[13] Although the present indicators point to the low number of Arabs using the Internet, the expectations are that, in all likelihood, the number of Arab users will reach 52 million by the end of 2008.[14]

The number of the Internet users in the Arab countries is very low. Moreover, there is censorship of some World Wide Web content (for instance, one Arab government sought to block 400,000 websites on the Internet).[15] In addition, Internet communication lines are weak, and generally there are obstacles to the spread of Internet use in these countries. All these factors do not significantly reduce the importance of the Internet and its impacts.

As the content of the Internet is diversified, the content with socio-political impact multiplies. Perhaps the electronic media is one option available on the Internet. Electronic newspapers are not the only means of electronic media on the Internet. There are several websites which provide the user with news and information. Apart from this, there are websites which engage in political mobilization. It has become common to use terms like "e-Islam" and "e-jihad." Also, there are other political and terrorist organizations which have websites. These websites transmit information ranging from ideological propaganda to showing scenes of hostages being slaughtered.

In addition to Arab and foreign television and radio stations that have websites, there are Israeli newspapers publishing their news on the Internet in Arabic too. Moreover, there are Arab governmental institutions which engage in political propaganda for the regimes and websites in Arabic for foreign governmental institutions engaging in a similar task. Also, there are other websites supported by intelligence agencies. One cannot ignore the importance of the e-mail which is also used by several bodies to publish news and rumors as is the case in "chat rooms."

A crowded environment like the Internet must have an impact on Arab socio-political development. However, the attempt to determine this impact also requires knowledge of the age groups which deal with the Internet. Although pursuing such information is beyond the scope of this research study, available indicators confirm that more than 60% of Arab Internet users are below 35.[16] This age group is easily susceptible to influence, but in my view, it is not the group that leads or imposes political or social change in Arab countries.

In the light of the above, the next section will attempt to determine the impact of electronic media on Arab socio-political development.

The Loss of Control Stage

This section of the research study presents a concept regarding the impact of the electronic media on Arab socio-political development. At the outset, it must be admitted that I have not observed a special impact of the electronic media which is distinct from the impact achieved by the Internet generally with all its contents. This does not indicate the inefficacy or futility of the electronic media. However, it means that the overall impact of the Internet superimposes itself on the impact of its individual sectors.

Whether in the Arab world or elsewhere, the Internet has created and enhanced the user's right to choose. The Internet user always has an endless list of choices. Any person who regularly logs on to the Internet, gets accustomed to exercising the right to choose. The user chooses the information that he wants to read, instead of reading whatever is imposed on him. The user makes a personal choice regarding the opinion and the analysis presented. The more a person exercises the right to choose, the more his or her will be reinforced and hence will be very difficult to control or direct. This means the loss of the most important traditional weapon used by totalitarian regimes, including several Arab regimes—the weapon of selective information feeding. The loss of this weapon spells the end of the patronage phase. Though "imposing censorship on the Internet is commonplace in Arab countries,"[17] in my view, it is no longer possible for any Arab regime to block the Internet. The use of the Internet has become an integral part of daily activities.

However, I do not think that the electronic media or the Internet in general, is capable of creating a revolution or political change in the Arab region by making a thrust towards imposing the values of freedom and democracy in direct proportion to the political pressure from the United States and the West. For example, Tunisia was the first Arab country to get connected to the Internet in 1992. However, in June 2002, the Tunisian authorities prosecuted a number of Internet users (who became known as the Internet dissidents) on charges relating to state security and closed a number of Internet cafes.[18] Nevertheless, the multiplicity of knowledge sources and the reinforced contact with other cultures make it a difficult task for Arab regimes to maintain policies of repression, authoritarianism and seclusion, even if these regimes make use of the same technological systems to block information.

The important impact of Internet usage is to change the character of the Arab personality. Arab citizens are employing the Internet not only for the opportunity to obtain information, but also for expressing views and ideas. This adds a new element to the personality of the Arab individual, who was not allowed to express opinions earlier. Through forums, chat rooms, e-mail and opinion polls, Arab citizens, or the Internet users among them, have been given an opportunity for free expression—an opportunity which was unavailable for decades.

Freedom of expression and freedom of information mobility do not mean that Arab citizens have started to experience democracy. However, they definitely enjoy the taste of what can be called "electronic freedom." This will undoubtedly lead, along with the spread of Internet usage, to a shift towards freedom not inside personal computers, but in the streets and public squares. The Internet connectivity of some Arab countries, like Jordan, Qatar, Morocco and the Kingdom of Bahrain coincided with the ascension of young rulers to power in those countries. Among other factors, this change has also facilitated progress in their countries and the opening of the gates of freedom, albeit partially.

It may be mentioned that among the positive effects of the Internet is the creation of a new class of intellectuals. Traditional research methodology is no longer appropriate. It may be said that groups which rely on the Internet to conduct its research present a greater amount of information. Researchers who are unable to use the Internet will face a great challenge in retaining their position among intellectuals.

If the above aspects are considered part of the positive developments, there are negative developments that cannot be overlooked. These include the way terrorist groups exploit the Internet as a media tool to spread the ideas of extremism, transmit scenes of killing, and stir sectarian conflict between Sunnis and Shi'ites. Moreover, there is pornography and lack of checks and controls on electronic media in this connection.

In speaking of the electronic media in particular, it should be noted that this kind of media tends to turn rumors into credible news. Also, the anonymity of the electronic source has contributed to the practice of deliberately misleading the media. Hence the truth has drowned in a sea of rumors, lies, misguidance and deception. In addition to this, the negative impact of the electronic media has started to trickle into the traditional press. For the traditional press, some unidentified websites have become a source of news. Traditional newspapers often reprint the news, contenting themselves with references to the particular website without verifying its authenticity.

The first Arab country was connected to the Internet twelve years ago. This means that there is a generation that has practiced the "right to choose" since their early consciousness. This generation has not yet come of age. Hence it is expected that the effective change will occur ten years from now—when twenty years would have lapsed since the beginning of the Internet usage in the region. In my view, this generation will be qualified to lead the change that will, by necessity, be positive.

A realistic example summarizes what this research study has attempted to infer. When I was the Editor-in-Chief of *Al Watan* newspaper, I asked a number of young employees what would be their reaction if I decided to prohibit using the Internet at work. They answered by saying that they would be looking for other jobs.

Conclusions

This chapter traced briefly the development of the Arab media from the emergence of the Arab press (print media) to terrestrial radio and television stations, through satellite stations, and finally to the electronic media. It may be observed that the political environment in which the Arab media – in all its forms – practices its task is a closed environment controlled by laws restricting freedom and a security system which is unchallengeable. This is the dominant environment in most Arab countries with one or two exceptions.

No doubt, practicing journalism in such an environment will not reinforce freedoms regardless of the wide margin of existing freedom that enhances the scene. Neither the political dialogues broadcast by *Al Jazeera* channel, nor the websites of Islamists, are capable of spreading the culture of democracy. Hence I believe that the assured impact of "electronic freedom" is manifested by bringing about an important change in the character of the user's personality, and in reinforcing his right to choose, and his right to receive varied information from multiple sources. However, the low number of Internet users in the Arab countries remains a hurdle in the way of achieving respectable results at the level of Arabic public opinion. Ten years after the first Arab country was connected to the Internet, the media laws in Arab countries still date from a period of political repression. It is not surprising that Arab countries are ranked low down on the list with regard to the freedom of the press, as indicated by the annual report on the *Freedom of the Press* in the world for 2004, released by the Reporters Sans Frontiers organization.[19]

10

Empowering the Arab Media through the Internet

Ahmad Abdulkarim Julfar

In an era of globalization, the Internet has become a strategic weapon for most countries. Just as oil played a key role in the Industrial Revolution, so the Internet has become an essential pillar of the Information Age and the knowledge economy. The Internet has evolved to the extent that it can provide almost any service or information literally at our fingertips—sending e-mail, searching for information, downloading music, getting driving directions, paying bills or buying groceries. The medium has transformed modes of governance, political processes and means of media reportage.

The Internet is crucial for nations seeking to move towards the service and knowledge economy. By facilitating all kinds of services and providing all sorts of information, it drives efficiency, customer orientation and information dissemination. With the advent of ICT (information and communication technologies), the economic vision of perfect competition is becoming a reality. Consumers are in a position to check and compare the prices offered by all vendors for any product. New markets have opened up, and consequently, prices have dropped. When businesses can deliver their products through a phone line anywhere in the world, twenty-four hours a day, the advantage goes to the firm that provides the greatest value addition or the best known brand. Software provides the best example. It represents huge added value through its computer code and is a product that can be delivered anywhere at any time. Competition is fostered by the expanding market opened up by these technologies. Products with a high knowledge component can generate higher returns and attract a greater growth potential.

The Internet in itself is just a delivery mechanism for content and as most Internet surfers would affirm, content is indeed king in the online world. In a scenario of technological parity, it is the content that drives customer acquisition. What you present on your site is at least as important as how you present it (and how often you do so), if you expect to give your visitors a reason to keep coming back.

The Media and the Internet

The Internet offers media outlets in the Middle East a powerful medium to reach their audiences as more and more people stay online for longer periods of time. Many examples may be cited such as: aljazira.net, emi.ae, dubaitv.gov.ae, alarabiya.net and bbcarabic.com. The bbcarabic.com website has been actively trying to find ways to generate debate based on the views exchanged by people with different perspectives. It is also actively encouraging its radio and online audience to interact with the site in response to its coverage of news and current affairs.

At the global level, the Internet has impacted upon the media in many ways, helping this sector to be more productive and reach wider audiences. Cable News Network (CNN) for example, has digitized its vast videotape library to put it online, thereby providing better protection for its footage, and making it more easily accessible to CNN journalists worldwide. Through the Internet, CNN staff and correspondents can log on to the CNN network and access video and other content directly from a laptop anywhere in the world. Previously, to provide the same content, a production assistant would have had to search, log and then ship the relevant video from CNN headquarters.

However, as the media merges from newspaper websites to interactive TV, along with multimedia advertising formats and promotional campaigns, it attracts a global audience. The profession of journalism is being totally transformed by media technologies, and online journalism has been spawned by the latest technological developments.

In the past ten years, the World Wide Web has become a successful platform for innovative, critical and creative journalism. Web-based magazines, have in fact become an important voice for minority groups, grassroots journalists, and those with alternative views. Thus, the Internet has provided the technological base for new and often surprising ranges of diversity on the part of both producers and audiences.

The media must tell the truth. If the media were to remain free and diverse, then the truth is bound to emerge eventually. Thus the key is to allow sufficient media diversity, to ensure that different voices are heard. In recent decades, media mergers have reduced previously diverse voices by restricting ownership to fewer companies. With the Internet, however, there is still a medium in which true diversity is both more likely and readily available.

However, all too often, the popular news websites are largely online facsimiles of conventional newspapers and magazines or digitized versions of analogue editions repackaged for broadcast. The really successful news websites tend to provide interactive features, such as online polls, searches of news archives, and links to related stories, which provide a historical context and analysis to a particular news story.

The Broadband Impact

Consumers are also increasingly turning to the World Wide Web for richer content and enhanced entertainment and communication capabilities without abandoning other conventional media. This trend has been confirmed by a study commissioned by Yahoo and Mediaedge:cia in the United States, the findings of which are broadly summarized in this section.

According to the Yahoo/Mediaedge:cia study, broadband users view double the number of pages per month as dial-up users. The Internet is being interlinked to all aspects of people's lives in unexpected new ways. The study also revealed that over half of broadband users are relying on both online and offline media concurrently, often turning to the Internet to supplement their usage of more conventional media such as radio, newspapers and television.

The "always on" facility provided by broadband access has completely altered the way in which consumers are now able to obtain information, communicate and live their lives. However, just as television did not fully substitute radio services, and the radio did not completely substitute printed newspapers, the Internet has taken its place in consumers lives' not by supplanting but by supplementing existing media forms.

Broadband access permits consumers to obtain available information on different aspects of the story from multiple media forms and sources. It thus plays a crucial role in facilitating the integration of information and entertainment experiences. Broadband consumers are twice or thrice as likely as dial-up consumers to download video content such as movie clips, trailers, news videos, short movies, sports events and cartoons.

Moreover, the study indicated that 64 percent of broadband users also make use of some form of traditional media (TV, magazine, newspaper, or radio) while actively online, compared to 57 percent of dial-up users. This number rises to 71 percent for wireless broadband users.

Richer Content

According to the study, offline media experiences are being supplemented by broadband-accessed Internet to provide richer information or different points of view on subjects first brought to consumers' attention by other media. The desire and ability to find more detailed or in-depth content online has increased dramatically, as people refer to the Internet to obtain photos, videos, stream music, games and more. For example, broadband users are nearly four times more likely to download or stream video or audio and over two times more likely to use the Web to decide what movie to see over the weekend.

[186]

Wireless Capabilities

Broadband wireless is able to provide "instant gratification" to consumers who rely on the Internet as a constant resource. Wireless capabilities delivered via users' home networks are altering consumption patterns in a novel way. The fact that online access is possible virtually everywhere, is erasing technological boundaries and making the all pervasive Internet an integral aspect of daily life.

By altering daily routines, broadband access is having an impact on marketing strategies as well. The survey findings offer additional insights to marketers, suggesting that the bandwidth capabilities of broadband are promoting greater reliance on the Internet as a complementary resource to the more traditional media forms.

While the above mentioned study is based on broadband usage in the United States, its findings can be generalized to a certain extent. It may be concluded that similar experiences are likely to be witnessed here in the Middle East as broadband usage rises. From Etisalat's perspective, the expectation is to have an exponential growth of 100% per year in the UAE, in terms of broadband users over the next few years, with a target of 100,000 connections by the end of 2005. Etisalat is committed to promoting the benefits of broadband access to homes and businesses across the UAE and is therefore set to pursue an aggressive mass market deployment for broadband.

The Blogging Phenomenon

Web logging, commonly known as "blogging," is a publishing format that allows users to write and publish online in diary form, often focusing on a specialist subject. Blogging is becoming an increasingly significant publishing tool, with several major news sites such as *The Guardian* in the United Kingdom adopting this format.

The demand for independent comment has been crucial to the success of blogs. Blogs liberate journalists from the political and economic restraints

[187]

of global media organizations. Blogs are keeping the Internet's first promise—to give publishing power to whoever wants it. Salam Pax is an Iraqi blogger who wrote about his experiences during the Iraq War. He became a cyber celebrity after his sharp and often humorous accounts of everyday life in Baghdad began circulating on the Internet. Indeed, the distrust of traditional journalism means that a lot of people gravitate towards bloggers like Salam Pax. However, blogs can also be used as a research tool, allowing journalists to float ideas and gauge general interest and public opinion.

In general, the failure of media outlets and publications that have not adapted quickly to the Internet is not because they have failed to adopt technology. Instead, it is a failure to appreciate the fact that the readers have moved on. Consumers, especially younger consumers, now have a multiplicity of information sources. Moreover, easy-to-use web publishing tools, broadband connection and cheap mobile devices have given people the ability to create their own media spaces. Consequently, people are no longer content to be merely passive consumers of mainstream media output. This explains the wide popularity of weblogs and weblogging.

Reporters want to reach out to their audience, and they realize that their audience is increasingly accessible online. They want to break their stories before the competition does, and they realize that the web is the quickest medium to achieve this purpose. Blogs provide a way to publish material that may not have an appropriate place in the traditional media. These are some of the very aspects that make online journalism particularly exciting—the immediacy, the ability to make it interactive and to get readers involved in dynamic ways.

Internet Usage in the Middle East

According to the Arab Advisors Group, the penetration level of the Internet is only 2% in the Arab world as compared to almost 76 % in the United States.

Figure 10.1
Internet Penetration in the United States and the Arab World

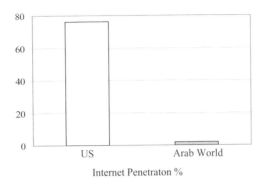

Internet Penetraton %

Source: Arab Advisors Group (http://www.arabadvisors.com)

In comparison to the rest of the region, the UAE has the highest Internet penetration in the region, with 40 percent of the population having access to the Internet, according to the Arab Advisors Group.

The UAE's vision is to be the regional media leader and the country has been at the forefront in providing a suitable environment and infrastructure for knowledge industries to flourish. The Dubai Media City (DMC) and the Dubai Internet City (DIC) are cases in point. The Dubai Internet City provides a Knowledge Economy Ecosystem that is designed to support the business development of Information and Communications Technology (ICT) companies. It is the Middle East's biggest IT infrastructure, built inside a free trade zone. The DMC offers state-of the-art infrastructure that enables media-related enterprises to operate globally out of Dubai.

Dynamic Media Scenario

Looking at the general media scenario in the Middle East, there is evidence of a dynamic and growing media presence. Consider the following numbers provided by the Middle East Media Guide: there are about 128 TV channels (with 13 of these being 24-hour news channels in

Arabic), 500 newspapers, 215 consumer magazines, 189 trade magazines, 500 radio stations, 44 news agencies and 68 news portals in the region.

The media in the UAE is also unique in the Arab world for its relative press freedom. The country has a plethora of publications, television and radio stations with a mushrooming Internet development and content creation sector.

Issues affecting Media Institutions in the Middle East

However, there are several issues affecting Arabic media content. Censorship is the biggest of these factors. Print and broadcast media are predominantly controlled by governments in the region. Censorship raises doubts about the reliability of regional news media and their output. This is the most important challenge. The rapid development of the Arab news media over the past decade has meant that journalistic standards and above all, public expectations, have risen. New satellite television channels have emerged, challenging old taboos and introducing public debate and greater openness. The Internet has also opened spaces for alternative news and views, but despite these developments, few Arab governments have actually loosened controls over the media.

Increased Internet usage has meant that consumer preferences have shifted to international networks and Internet sources, since viewpoints that are restricted locally are readily available online. In fact, uncensored news is available in the Middle East as never before. People in the Middle East are already using the Internet to undermine controls on information and to counter censorship. Local human rights organizations are disseminating news more effectively than ever before and newspapers can easily post the stories censored from their print editions in their online editions.

Satellite stations have also proved resilient in reporting under difficult circumstances, even in countries where they are banned. Despite the existing ban in Iraq, *Al Jazeera's* Baghdad staffers, relocated to Doha, continue to report on events. A network of stringers and volunteers on the ground help to provide information and video footage.

Al Jazeera has been able to circumvent bans in other countries as well. Three years ago, Bahrain prohibited *Al Jazeera* from covering its 2002 local elections, but the station was able to provide limited coverage. When the Bahraini opposition decided to boycott the election and held a conference in Manama to announce it, *Al Jazeera* got the picture the same day from Bahrain from three sources. Technology such as cell phones, text messaging, video transmission, and the Internet have greatly aided news gathering.

Regaining Credibility

Dispassionate, knowledgeable reporting and fairness are essential for the Arab media to gain credibility in today's world. Sensational and spectacular reports may excite readers and viewers but cannot hold their attention. The media needs to move beyond spectacle and become more relevant in order to regain its credibility and audiences. A case in point is *Al Jazeera* Television. Today, 82% of Saudi households watch the *Al Jazeera* channel and 69% of them believe it to be either trustworthy or very trustworthy according to a study by the Arab Advisors Group.

Limitations of the Arabic language

The Arabic language also faces certain limitations when seeking to increase the penetration of Arabic content on the Internet. Arabic content needs to evolve to encompass new business, financial and technology terms that are becoming commonplace. Improper translation is a sure way to lose the true meaning of a certain text. Typical pitfalls of literal translation in technological terms of technology usage could include "Mouse" becoming (فأرة), "Hard Disk Drive" (سواقة أقراص صلبة), and "Monitor" (مرقاب)

Low Technology Adoption

The United Arab Emirates has the highest penetration in the Middle East with 40 percent of the population having access to the Internet. While the

[191]

Gulf States of Qatar, Kuwait and Oman possess the financial strength and state-of-the-art technological capacity to promote their Internet infrastructure, the number of Internet users is growing more slowly in these states than in other countries with far weaker economic capacities such as in Egypt and Jordan. Middle Eastern Internet analysts have determined that low Internet penetration in the Middle East is due to a number of factors: weak infrastructure, poor economic growth, high illiteracy levels, lack of relevant language skills, content and applications as well as cultural factors.

Firstly, a relatively weak telecommunications infrastructure hinders the wider adoption of the Internet. Though some Middle Eastern telecommunication indicators can be compared with those of developed countries, overall network capacity in the region is poor, leading to low usage and high Internet costs. In most cases, this infrastructural dilemma is the responsibility of state-run telecommunication companies, with the capacity and quality of the different networks varying from country to country. Progressive and growth-stimulating initiatives from the government and private sector are needed to fill this gap.

One issue that also affects people's attitudes in accessing the Internet is the problem of finding suitable Arabic content on the Net. Arabic content has generally been of lower quality and often lacks the originality needed to attract users. Content development has been largely restricted to government efforts in the Middle East with a limited role for the private sector. Financial incentives and encouragement for private players is lacking and a serious effort needs to be made to encourage the growth and publishing of quality Arabic content.

Directions for the Future

Changing mindsets will be a key element in propagating the spread of the Internet. A technologically "enlightened" attitude also needs to be adopted by governments. The UAE has emerged as the forerunner in the Arab region in this regard. The progress made here offers valuable lessons in

[192]

how such initiatives can be undertaken to move the country steadily in the direction of an information and knowledge-based society.

In terms of infrastructure, the UAE has been successful in expanding the telecommunication infrastructure and penetration of the Internet. The UAE has undertaken a number of projects and initiatives to improve the information/knowledge capacity of the economy with the help of incubation programs, technology parks, e-government programs both at the Federal and the state levels, and e-commerce initiatives both in the private and the public sectors. The Steering Committee of the UAE federal e-Government and Dubai e-Government has been very supportive in the quest for the creation of an information/knowledge based economy. All the initiatives undertaken were initiated by the government and supported both politically and financially by the top political leaders of the Emirates.

The distrust in new technology needs to be reduced and the government can and should play a key role in boosting efforts to expand the use of Internet. The low penetration rate of personal computers in the Arab world is also one of the biggest obstacles in widespread PC literacy and Internet penetration. While fixed telephone lines have a much higher penetration and Internet access is becoming affordable to larger segments of Arab societies, PCs still remain beyond the financial means of millions of Arab families.

From a language perspective, there seems a clear role for the establishment of a regional body to deal with the issue of Arabic language development for the Internet. This would help in incorporating new business and scientific terms into the Arabic language. The cooperation of international partners, private sector as well as non-governmental organizations (NGOs) needs to be enhanced to develop content that can be aggregated by various websites.

Arabization of the Internet

The effort towards Arabizing the Internet needs to happen at multiple levels. One of the significant initiatives in this regard is the process of Arabizing domain names. The initiative has gained ground in order to help

Arabic users unfamiliar with the Latin script to use the Internet in Arabic alone. Under the present system, all the addresses on websites must be written in English or other languages using exactly the same characters.

Such initiatives are necessary in order to preserve the Arabic identity and encourage Arab users to use the Internet widely. The English language is incapable of representing Arabic characters. Well-known entities would like to maintain their Arabic names in all media including the Internet.

Arabization of domain names is expected to become a reality soon, with Etisalat taking a leading role alongside counterparts from other countries like Saudi Arabia and Qatar. The United Arab Emirates Network Information Centre (UAEnic) is working with counterparts in Saudi Arabia and Qatar to develop domain names in the Arabic language. Technical trials are under way to launch full Arabic domain name capability in the UAE by mid-2005.

Content management systems also need to be put in place to Arabize international content in real time. The implementation of e-Government services will also play a key role in Arabizing the Internet. There is evidence of committed efforts throughout the region to capitalize on IT advances to enhance the services that governments provide to their people. Understandably, such efforts have varied in size and intensity across the region. The UAE has been a forerunner in the field of e-Government in the region. A Dubai Media City-based company, Madar Research, cites Dubai as a good example because it is now on equal terms with leading European Union states in the delivery of basic online services on offer to individuals and businesses. It may be noted here that the Internet represents more than just a new channel for service delivery. Fundamentally it acts as a catalyst by challenging age-old assumptions about how governments operate.

Regional Successes

On the technological side, the example of the Sakhr Software Company shows how a determined effort can pave the way for using ICT to serve the unique needs of the Arabic language. The company's effort in basic research on the core linguistic characteristics of the Arabic language, and natural language processing (NLP)[1] has led it to produce Arabic linguistic components[2] that perfectly understand the language, thus allowing organizations to increase the usage of Arabic.

Naseej.com pioneered such services as Arabic instant messaging and personalization. It also was the first Arabic site to publish on the Internet using Arabic text characters, and it was also the first to develop an Arabic webmail service. Aside from the technical capabilities, Arabic Internet users are attracted to Naseej.com due to its original content. Unlike other Arabic portals which depend on foreign news agencies to provide the bulk of their content, Naseej.com's content is produced by a large content development team spanning the entire region.

Founded in November 1998, Maktoob.com (www.maktoob.com) has revolutionized Internet culture in the Middle East by pushing the creative boundaries in which the Web can be applied for communications. Since its launch, Maktoob.com has played a crucial role in uniting Arabs worldwide by providing sophisticated and reliable web-based communications and community development tools, including the Arab world's first free bilingual (Arabic/English) Web-based e-mail service.

Promotion of the Internet

Access to computers and the Internet and the ability to effectively use this technology are becoming increasingly important for full participation in a nation's economic, political and social life. People are using the Internet to find lower prices for goods and services, work from home or start their own business, acquire new skills using distance learning, and make better informed decisions about their healthcare needs. The ability to use technology is thus becoming indispensable in the workplace.

Countries in the Middle East should do their utmost to allow the Internet to flourish and create greater public awareness. Supporting infrastructure should be put in place to increase Internet penetration. At the same time, affordability should also be considered a factor in

[195]

increasing Internet penetration. Such efforts are already being made but the process needs to be accelerated. Looking at the regional efforts to promote broadband Internet, it is heartening to note that such activity is picking up. More competition is also expected to bring down broadband prices. Today, the UAE offers the lowest price per minute for Asymmetric Digital Subscriber Line (ADSL) broadband access in the region.

Tax incentives should also be offered to content companies in order to encourage the spread of Arabic content. Organizations like the ITU (International Telecommunications Union) are also doing their bit and are exploring the prospect of creating an Arabic content aggregation platform to be hosted within the Arab countries including search engines and a database with Arabic characters. One initiative that should be undertaken involves the establishment of conditions for development of digital content and local multimedia industries including intellectual property right provisions.

Censorship reform also needs to be implemented. Regional governments should consider relaxing excessive censorship of Web content to allow the Internet to flourish and function effectively. The use of local publishing, content management and translation technologies is imperative to boost the spread of Arabic on the Internet. This is borne out by companies such as the Sakhr Software Company, which is a globally recognized leader in developing technologies for the Arab world. At the heart of these solutions lie Sakhr's Arabic NLP technologies. Sakhr Software has created specific market offerings focused on customer needs, namely in the areas of content management, machine translation, speech technologies and education

The concept of a global marketplace has established itself on the Internet, highlighting the growing need for a multilingual Internet presence. Sakhr Software's Arabic NLP research has positioned the company as the leading player in the machine translation market. Its offerings in this field include "Tarjim" which is a Web-based online translation service that translates "on-the-fly"[3] any English Web page to Arabic and vice versa, while preserving the original Web page layout and adjusting the language direction. The service also allows for the translation of text.

Digital Journalism: The Way of the Future

Online and wireless reading of news will become more common than reading printed newspapers. The latter will not disappear altogether, but it will no longer have the dominance that it enjoys today. A newspaper's digital offerings will be as important as printed editions—both in terms of audience size and revenue.

Portable reading devices will make great strides. Many people will have a tablet device that is always connected to the broadband Internet and serves as their portal to the media world. It will replace printed magazines for many people, who will get their news on it—from a range of sources. The content will be a combination of text, static images, audio, video and interactive features.

Conclusion

The empowerment of the Arabic media through Internet usage can be realized through active government support in Internet promotion and content development. A strong focus is needed developing the Arabic language to include new business and technology terms. There is also a need to offer incentives to the private sector so that its entrepreneurial drive and energy can be harnessed to promote the Internet with a special focus on content providers.

A free and empowered media that is unrestrained by censorship laws is also vital in helping the sector to move towards excellent reporting standards and high quality journalism. Indeed, it will take the collective effort of all concerned players such as the government, media and technology providers to effectively empower the Arabic media on the Internet and thereby bridge the digital divide.

[197]

11

Enriching the Arabic Content on the Internet

Fahd Al-Othman

The Internet is viewed as a gigantic network that facilitates the spread of knowledge. In this regard, it presents an historic, unprecedented opportunity for developing societies to employ it for developmental purposes. However, in order to enrich the Arabic content on the Internet, the Arab world will have to identify its own concepts of knowledge, establish its own goals, and determine the role that knowledge could play in achieving these goals. In this way, it will be able to create a vision for the future.

It will also be necessary to specify the ways in which the Arab world can use the Internet's tremendous potential to spread and enhance knowledge, and to promote development projects in Arab countries.

In discussing this topic, the question that arises is: What sort of content needs to be enriched? Data, information and knowledge are the terms generally used as synonyms to define content. However, it must be clarified that data is not information, and the latter is not knowledge, and although these three terms seem correlated, they do not mean the same thing. Indeed, data are "unprocessed" and pointless numbers, letters and names, which become information only when they are rendered meaningful, such as the share prices of a certain firm. Hence, information is meaningful data with certain connotations but such information alone does not denote knowledge.

In their 1997 book *Working Knowledge: How Organizations Manage What they Know,* Thomas Davenport and Laurence Prusak suggested that the useful and utilizable information that human beings can amass will become knowledge. In other words, knowledge is information that is combined with expertise, experience, intelligence, insight, sentiment and conscience in a specific context and milieu. Accordingly, knowledge does not exist in books or on the Internet, but rather in the human heart. People grasp some information, and they amalgamate and reshape it according to their talents, skills, loyalties and creative abilities. Therefore, for information to become knowledge, it must be useful and usable.

Given the fact that approximately 60 per cent of the total population of Arab societies are less than 21 years old – mainly students – and that the curricula applied in most, if not all, the Arab educational institutions are based on the dictation method, it can be said that 60 per cent of education and knowledge development plans in the Arab world do not function effectively.

On the other hand, knowledge development programs designed for the Arab workforce are often set up and conducted by the government sector, the biggest employer in the Arab world. And since a large portion of this force falls within the "hidden unemployment" category, therefore it is also excluded from these programs. The already limited Arab private sector also lacks the necessary institutional culture and structures as well as knowledge development process.

The present situation in the Arab world features distorted knowledge management and imbalanced, disorganized knowledge accumulations that impede the entire development process. Moreover, the Arab world as a whole lacks a clearly defined project for knowledge development.

At any rate, such a project should be based on three elements: incentives for innovative, daring businessmen (or entrepreneurs), the provision of finance, and the promotion of the culture of success and achievement to replace the culture of failure.

For this project, finance represents the blood, while these innovative and daring entrepreneurs represent the soul, which is the most important component of any national resource. In order to grow and flourish, this group of businessmen must be provided with financial support. As for the promotion of the culture of success, they should focus less on justifying failure than on shouldering their obligations and attaining success.

Everyone must pursue knowledge as the highest priority in order to achieve development.

THE ARAB MEDIA VS. THE US MEDIA

Symptoms of Alienation: How the Arab and American Media View Each Other

Hussein Ibish

O ver the first four years of the new millennium, certain trends have been emerging in the field of media and cross-cultural communication. While focusing generally on these trends, this chapter examines particularly how the Arab and American press view each other. In this context, the media is being considered as an active player in cross-cultural communication, rather than a merely passive medium. Certainly, the media and media professionals are shaped by and reflect attitudes already prevailing in their broader cultural milieu. However, they in turn help to shape the discourses within which they work and in which they intervene. In this formulation, media organizations and journalists, in the course of their mutual interaction become both subject and object, and when Arab and American journalists try to describe and analyze each other, they unwittingly reveal much more about themselves than they do about their counterparts.

It has become almost a cliché to observe that increased hostility and negative sentiment in the media reflects a broader alienation between Arab and American societies. Nowhere is the divide between the mainstreams of these two societies more evident than in the news media, especially the way in which journalists talk about and at, but rarely to, each other. For example, in an otherwise quite reasonable article in late 2001 responding to a silly attack on National Security Advisor

Condoleezza Rice in the Arabic language daily *Al Quds Al Arabi*, Deputy Editorial Page Editor Colbert King of the *Washington Post* wrote in his column: "The newspaper's Editor-in-Chief, Abdel-Bari Atwan, is an Osama bin Laden groupie and ardent critic of the United States."[1] The casual, almost flippant manner in which a well-known Arab journalist, who is indeed a critic of many US policies but from the left, is transformed somehow into a "bin Laden groupie" is symptomatic of a bitter war of words between American and Arab journalists that has not only become increasingly unfair on both sides, but also irrational and dangerous.

1-How the US Media sees the new Arab Media

Based on traditional state ownership and strict control over journalism in the Arab world, the traditional US view of the Arab news media has been to impute to it all the qualities traditionally associated in the American mind with the press in the countries of the Warsaw Pact and the former Soviet Union: media as pure propaganda, completely in the service of state policies, and designed primarily to divert attention away from domestic political failures onto foreign enemies, most notably Israel and the West. Additionally, the assumption is that the Arab individual is left with no information choices and is therefore completely at the mercy of these brainwashing media tools. The result is either a society completely misinformed about basic political realities or individuals who may resist manipulation by the state-controlled press but who are then left with no real source of information. To a very large extent, this model explains why Arab public opinion has never been taken seriously by either the US government or the US media. Since Arabs are supposedly informed by a media with a total information monopoly, which seeks to manipulate the public and propagandize information in the interests of the narrowest forms of state power, there has been a general assumption in the United States that this opinion simply reflects the distorted effects of such shameless deception and that Arab public opinion can therefore be easily

[206]

transformed by the introduction of hitherto withheld information and perspectives. In particular, this accounts for a persistent refusal by the United States to credit Arab public opinion on issues such as the Palestinian-Israeli conflict and the US role in the Arabian Gulf region. Such a perception remains central to the way in which many Americans, including journalists, view the role of the media in the Arab world. However, the rise of the new Arab media, including various satellite news channels, Internet sites and pan-Arab daily newspapers has created much greater interest in the Arab media, and a much more developed, although still deeply flawed discourse about it in the US press.

Given the way discourse has developed since September 11, 2001, it is easy to forget how much the mainstream US journalists and news organizations loved the Qatar-based *Al Jazeera* when it first emerged in the late 1990s. It was frequently cited as an unprecedented casting-off of censorship and a radical break with the imagined Stalinist or totalitarian tradition described in the caricature outlined above. Thomas Friedman, *The New York Times* reporter who turned columnist, an influential commentator who is shaping the way other American journalists view the Middle East, described *Al Jazeera* as "a flower" and observed:

> Al-Jazeera owes its success to the fact that, more than any other TV station in the Arab world, it airs free and lively debates, offers timely news, even interviews Israeli leaders, and allows anyone to criticize Arab regimes.[2]

Friedman described the creation of *Al Jazeera* as "Glasnost in the Gulf," underscoring the sense that an Arab media system analogous to that of the former Soviet Union was being threatened by principles of democratization embodied in the new Arab media and *Al Jazeera* in particular.

In the same paper, John F. Burns, the Middle East correspondent of the *New York Times* in his front-page story on *Al Jazeera* described the sensation it was causing in the Arab world:

> In millions of homes and offices across the Arab world, television sets are regularly tuned these days to Al Jazeera, a hard-hitting Arabic-language

news channel that explores issues long suppressed by the region's rulers, including the lack of democracy, the persecution of political dissidents and the repression of women. From studios in this tiny emirate...Al Jazeera offers round-the-clock programming based on a principle revolutionary by the traditional standards of Middle East broadcasting, that all coverage should be free of censorship or bias. In another innovation for the Arab world, ordinary Arabs can air their views on an array of freewheeling phone-in shows. The result has been a sensation in the 22 Arab countries where Al Jazeera's broadcasts can be seen. In Algiers's Casbah, in Cairo's slums, in the suburbs of Damascus, even in the desert tents of Bedouins with satellite dishes, the channel has become a way of life. In its 30 months on air, it has drawn viewers in droves from the mind-numbing fare offered by the region's state-run networks, whose news coverage often amounts to little more than a reverential chronicle of government affairs.[3]

In short, there was a time, not so long ago, when major American journalists writing about *Al Jazeera* sounded rather like publicists for the station, or at least ardent admirers.

Moreover, this celebration of the new Arab media was not restricted to *Al Jazeera*, but was widely regarded as a development that combined political involution with technological innovation, and saw the two as inextricably intertwined. As the influential commentator Jon B. Alterman of the United States Institute of Peace (USIP) wrote in the *Washington Post* in March 2001:

> It is true that the Arab press has a collection of hack writers who mindlessly repeat the tired slogans of the 1960s. But their tendentiousness and mediocrity represent the exception rather than the rule. The Arab press in the past decade has become far more accurate, objective and open to new ideas than it was before the Gulf War. The main engine driving this change is competition. Whereas state-run dailies and state-run television used to have a near monopoly of distribution in their own countries, they now must compete with international newspapers and a broad array of satellite television channels. Arab audiences are seeking authoritative news, and the tabloid sensationalism of the past is pushing them to other outlets. CNN's coverage of the Gulf War turned Arab news organizations on their ear. The meteoric rise of the Qatari satellite news channel al-Jazeera since 1996 has proved to audiences that Arab news need not be mendacious drivel.[4]

The dominant narrative during the year and a half preceding the attacks by Al Qaeda on the United States was that traditional Arab media, supposedly the source of so much tension between Arab public opinion and American perceptions and policies, was being supplanted by a new discourse derived from those two panaceas of capitalist ideology, technology and competition, and best exemplified by *Al Jazeera*. The implied expectation was that, given time, this new media and new discourse would give rise to new public opinions (more consistent with American world-views) and possibly even new and more democratic political structures.

As already implied, the attacks against the United States of September 11, 2001, overturned this narrative completely. In rapid succession, three developments cast both traditional and new Arab media in a new and more sinister light in American discourse. First came completely divergent interpretations and receptions of the Al Qaeda attacks in the American and Arab media, with widespread outrage at every level in the United States over the skepticism in the Arab press that the Al Qaeda was responsible for the attacks, and with an exaggerated sense that the entire Arab media was peddling extreme conspiracy theories blaming Israel and/or the CIA for the attacks. Second, images of Osama bin Laden and other leaders of Al Qaeda in videotapes on *Al Jazeera* and other Arab satellite channels, heightened the sense that the new Arab media was either supportive of, or had an unsavory relationship with, the terrorists who attacked the United States. Finally, heightened tensions produced by the invasion of Afghanistan, which was almost universally regarded as necessary and justified in the United States but which was widely criticized in the Arab media, seem to cement the perception among American journalists that their Arab counterparts were essentially hostile and in a position of antagonism to American interests and sensibilities.

Now the Arab media generally, and the new media in particular, were perceived not as being in an antagonistic relationship with Arab governments and a force for democratization, but in an antagonistic relationship with the US government and having, in effect, a tacit alliance with the terrorists. US journalists' condemnation of Arab media became extremely heated and emotional at this stage. It was in this context that Colby King called Abdel-Bari Atwan, "an Osama bin Laden groupie," which, judged by the standards of the moment, was perhaps not a particularly extreme attack. The most vociferous American commentators actually urged attacking and destroying Arab media institutions. In October, 2001, New York *Daily News* columnist Zev Chafets demanded the physical destruction of *Al Jazeera*, declaring: "Dealing with Al Jazeera is a job for the military. Shutting it down should be an immediate priority..."[5] Shortly thereafter, the US military attacked and destroyed *Al Jazeera's* Kabul bureau, although not its Qatar headquarters, in the hours before the Northern Alliance took the city, on the completely unconvincing pretext that Al Qaeda forces were present in another part of the building. The station's Baghdad offices met a similar fate during the invasion of Iraq and a number of its journalists and cameramen have been killed by US forces.

Journalistic anger in the United States against the new Arab media was powerfully encouraged by official US government complaints and criticisms against various Arab satellite channels which has been a continuous feature of Bush Administration rhetoric until the present day. These complaints were at their most heated in the immediate build up to and during the invasion of Iraq. Some commentators who had either remained silent or, like Thomas Friedman, had continued to defend the idea that the new Arab media might be a source of democratization in 2002 turned on them when it came to conflict over the invasion of Iraq. In April, 2003, echoing official US military commentary, Friedman complained: "Throughout this war, Saddamism was peddled by Al Jazeera television, Arab intellectuals and the Arab League."[6] He complained that although the Iraq war was popular and widely viewed by Iraqis as a war of liberation, this viewpoint could not be gauged from the *Al Jazeera* channel:

> You'd never know this from watching Arab satellite television like Al Jazeera. Because although these stations have 21st-century graphics, they're still dominated by 1950s Nasserite political correctness—which insists that dignity comes from how you resist the foreigner, even if he's come as a liberator, not by what you build yourself.[7]

Again, this complaint, and the radical change of heart it expresses towards the new Arab media mirrors that of the US government. The glee that Friedman and others had expressed when the channel was drawing the ire of many Arab regimes had vanished completely. By January 2004, Friedman, once the station's leading proponent in the American media, began to describe the new Arab media in general and *Al Jazeera* in particular, as a positive danger:

> Three dangerous trends are converging around Israel. One is a massive population explosion across the Arab world. The second is the worst interpersonal violence ever between Israelis and Palestinians. And the third is an explosion of Arab multimedia—from Al Jazeera to the Internet. What's happening is that this Arab media explosion is feeding the images of this Israeli-Palestinian violence to this Arab population explosion—radicalizing it and melding in the heads of young Arabs and Muslims the notion that the biggest threat to their future is J.I.A.—"Jews, Israel and America."[8]

Thus, in the space of less than three years, in the evaluation of Thomas Friedman, *Al Jazeera* had gone from being a beacon of hope representing "Glasnost in the Gulf" to being a source of danger and radicalization.

In fact, Friedman was a relative latecomer to this viewpoint. Much of the mainstream American media had developed an essentially hostile attitude towards the new Arab media shortly after September 11, 2001, concurring with the government and other sectors of US society, that the new media, along with the traditional media had laid the groundwork for the terrorist attacks and for a more generalized sentiment that opposed decades-long American regional aims and policies. Although expressed in many ways, nothing reflected the seriousness of the critique that held both new and traditional Arab media to be irredeemable as dramatically as the establishment of Radio Sawa and *Al Hurra* TV. The objection may be raised that since these are government-funded entities, their interventions and even their existence, reflect official US government views and not those of the US media. The Board of Broadcasting Governors which oversees both Radio Sawa and *Al Hurra* includes many media professionals, although mostly drawn from administrative positions. Moreover, there has been almost no debate in the United States about the wisdom of creating such US-government-sponsored broadcast media in Arabic directed towards the Middle East, only discussion about its efficacy.

The creation of Radio Sawa and *Al Hurra* reflects the heightened importance that Arab public opinion currently holds in the United States, mainly as a result of fears about future violent actions by disgruntled Arabs, and a consequent desire to influence those perceptions. Americans, including the government, media and other segments of society are well aware of the growing distrust of the United States and outrage over its foreign policy, particularly with regard to Palestine and Iraq, in much of the Arab world. However, few US commentators and journalists have been willing to seriously examine whether these negative attitudes are based on fundamental realities or reflect a reasonable critique of American policies and behavior. The ubiquitous and almost unchallenged assumption is that Arab public opinion need not be taken seriously on its own terms, but that it is symptomatic of the relentless distortions of Arab media—the new media in particular. Since Arab public opinion is perceived as symptomatic of what is wrong with the Arab media, and not reflective of what ails US foreign policy or US attitudes, the conclusion drawn is that it is the Arab media, not US policies that need to be changed. Thus Radio Sawa and *Al Hurra* represent a confrontation with and a challenge to the new Arab media, which under the new post 9/11 diagnosis is no longer viewed as part of the cure but rather as part of the malaise afflicting the Arab world.

The creation of Radio Sawa and *Al Hurra* also reflects a reversion to the Cold War model of public relations and information warfare conducted against the former Soviet bloc. The idea here, partially abandoned prior to 9/11, is that the Arab media is analogous to Stalinist media and the public is held hostage to a totalitarian discourse, which can only be broken by external intervention. Accordingly, there should be no more talk of *glasnost*, only of Radio Free Europe. The Arab media would thus be confronted by these US-controlled media organizations in its own language and on its own terms. Consequently, the benighted and information-starved Arab peoples would supposedly have access to "the truth," and a taste of responsible, respectable journalism for the first time in their lives. As the chairman of the Board of Broadcasting Governors, Kenneth Tomlinson, told a congressional committee hearing on funding this Made in America "new-new Arab media," as reported in a newspaper column:

> The knowledge base for the people in the Arab world is further limited by the indisputable fact that the news and information they receive from several popular satellite television outlets like Al Jazeera have given them a picture of the world which is frequently distorted by institutional prejudices and sensationalism.[9]

Al Hurra gallops in to the rescue. This is a familiar and comfortable position for Americans, even if the analogy is strained beyond recognition. Indeed, it should be acknowledged by everyone that Radio Sawa and *Al Hurra* represent an extension and an amplification of an ongoing effort since at least the early 1950s to somehow get the Arab peoples to shift their attention away from the plight of the Palestinians and US foreign policy in the Middle East, and focus on what the US perceives as problems of development and the lack of democracy and good government in the Arab states. The effort, during the same time frame, to convince the Soviet Union to renounce communism and dissolve itself proved more successful. Among the many crucial differences between the *Al Hurra* and Radio Free Europe is the propensity of its leaders to reflect outright sentiments of cultural, not to say racial superiority over the Arabs. Normally this sentiment is implicitly expressed in its formulations.

[213]

However, Tomlinson told a Canadian Broadcasting Company radio documentary:

> I would argue that in their [Arab] countries that their rules and traditions are holding them back, so they have to be freed of the chains of prejudice that is keeping them from the fruits of education that they need to develop as civilized people.[10]

The kindest response that could be made to this very revealing statement is that this betrays a colonial attitude.

News that so far at least the US Arabic-language news channel has been a colossal failure at affecting discourse or public opinion in the Arab world seems to have left many Americans in media and the government without a strong sense of what to do next (for complex political reasons, actually debating the policies in question remains completely unacceptable). This failure, which was outlined in grim detail in a recent Department of Defense (DoD) report, is not disputed by anyone who is not either a member of the Broadcasting Board of Governors or an employee of one of their enterprises. However, the reasons for this failure have not been the subject of much commentary, perhaps because people fear, as the DoD report makes clear, until policy is reviewed and revised there is little that public relations can actually accomplish. On the other hand, a more credible effort could surely have been made. For one thing, *Al Hurra* is frequently charged, apparently with some justification, of being dominated by Lebanese Christian immigrants to the United States, some of whom have a political agenda reflecting what Tariq Al-Humayd in *Ash-Sharq Al-Awsat* diplomatically called "an approach similar to that prevailing during the civil war in Lebanon" and observed that "the administration [of the station] is in the hands of people who want to settle accounts in the Arab world." Less diplomatically, his commentary concluded:

> A situation where such large media institutions are in the hands of Arabs of this type resembles a situation where a modern plane is under the control of Muhammad Ata the leader of the 11 September hijackers, who would only seek to hit it against the nearest skyscraper.[11]

[214]

Here there is a perfect inversion of the basic accusation that the harshest US media critics have leveled at the new Arab media—that, because of ideology, its effect is either literally or figuratively equivalent to terrorism.

2-How the Arab Media sees the US Media

The Arab media, for its part, takes a largely negative view of the Western press in general and the US press in particular. This skepticism and condemnation is occasionally tempered with professions of admiration for the independence of the US media, its role as a watchdog against the government, or its institutional ability to engage in investigative reporting (which unfortunately remains quite rare in the Arab media for several reasons). However, the overall sense is that the US news media is biased against the Arabs, serves indefensible US government policies, and is possibly controlled by nefarious interests. The resulting image is of a set of institutions that are not worthy of respect, which cannot serve as a model for the developing Arab media, and which should be countered by an Arab media free from such constraints and biases.

Perhaps the strongest and most frequently voiced critique of US journalism and journalists by the Arab press is the notion that the US media suffers from a profound nationalist bias, and frequently puts patriotism before professionalism. For example, during the invasion of Iraq, *Al-Quds Al-Arabi* argued:

> In the battle for unbiased credible and reliable coverage of the Iraq war, the Arab media seems to have beaten its British and American counterpart. The US and British media has lost the battle for credibility in the case of the war on Iraq. They have often let national bias get the better of their professionalism.[12]

This reflects the understanding that, through the embedding of journalists with troops, and the strong deference given to statements by US military and political leaders, as well as a perceived failure to show the consequences and the professed motivations for US military action, that the American press was actually outstripped by its Arab counterparts as a source of information for readers and viewers. The argument advanced by many Arab journalists, including those representing channels such as Al Jazeera, was that there was a broader selection of perspectives available to Arab audiences, and that more opinions, assertions and allegations provided viewers with a fuller picture of the situation. US journalists, for their part, certainly felt that too much deference and seriousness was accorded by the Arab media to press conferences held by former Iraqi government representatives who made what were regarded as plainly preposterous allegations and that not all information or assertions should be treated as equally credible. These arguments seem to apply with greater force to the media's representation of the respective battlefield fortunes of the coalition and Iraqi troops during the invasion, than to coverage of Bush administration claims regarding the alleged Iraqi weapons of mass destruction (WMD).

Along these lines, another frequent allegation against US news media institutions by the Arab media is that the former are passive creatures playing along with the US government and policymakers, especially insofar as their intention is to attack and humiliate the Arabs. This is often linked to a corporate agenda, vaguely ascribed to large business interests that are usually not defined. One columnist for the leading Arabic language daily *Al-Hayat* put it this way:

> Today we read commentators' articles [in the US press] that have no other objective but to humiliate Arab people and bring desperation to their political and cultural leaders. The truth is that media empires have tight relations with the political authorities, which prevented them from playing the role of watchdogs. These media empires became dependent on the financial entities financing them.[13]

In this formulation, the US media are dependent on the larger multinational corporations which control them and which are presumed to be in absolute agreement and cooperation with the government. The media thereby lacks independence and cannot be relied upon. Their role, as dictated by their financial masters, is simply to provide legitimacy to government policies. The subject of whether the Arab or American news media is more distant from financial or official meddling is a particularly contentious argument between many Arab and American journalists. Some Arab journalists argue that despite formal ties and more obvious restrictions in the Arab world, a greater range of opinions and more information is presented to the public by the new Arab media. Some US journalists find these arguments so outlandish that they profess amusement at the very idea of discussing the relative independence of Arab and American media from government or financial manipulation. The debate is exacerbated by the degree to which independence is largely a subjective quality reflecting the observer's satisfaction with the information or opinions put forward.

A traditional but still potent wrinkle on this broader critique is a specific link to biased coverage in the American media of the Israeli-Palestinian conflict, as well as US military actions in the Middle East. For many Arab media institutions, the sense that the US media is shamelessly biased in favor of Israel and against the Palestinians is the ultimate demonstration of the failings of the American press. In some cases, this is linked to allegations of "Jewish control" of the American media, but more typically the accusation rests simply on the idea of unjustifiable bias, as in the following example from a leading Jordanian daily:

> It is enough to observe how this 'objective and balanced' media presents news of the Palestinian intifada, or reports of Zionist crimes against Palestinian civilians to ascertain that what we have is a media whose bias and lack of objectivity and balance are shameful. It is also enough to compare the images and news sent by journalists to Arab satellite TV stations, and the images and reports sent by their Western counterparts, with what appeared on the American TV stations during the invasion of Iraq to ascertain how false the claims about Western – and especially US – objectivity and balance really are. If the Americans believe that even by spending billions of dollars on al-Hurra, they will be able to win Arab hearts and minds and influence Arab public opinion, while continuing to take part in the killing of Palestinians, occupying Iraq, and attacking Arabs and Muslims, they would be akin to someone trying to plough the sea. [14]

[217]

It may be noted that in this instance, the columnist is specifically citing US media failures as reasons why official public diplomacy by the United States through mass media outlets such as *Al Hurra* will not succeed among the Arabs. In other words, it is not just US policies that are responsible for Arab skepticism and public hostility towards the United States, but also representations of the Middle East in the US media itself that actively fuel Arab anger. While some exhortations urge the United States to take Arab perceptions about policy seriously and not worry too much about the issue of representation, this column contradicts such an assessment by suggesting that it is not Arab media representations of US policy or US representations in the Middle East but rather US media representations regarding the Middle East that contribute to the problem. It is an "adding insult to injury" argument that casts the media as an active player on the political scene and as usual, in a negative light.

In essence, the main argument against the US news media by its Arab counterparts is that it is untruthful and hence inferior to the Arab media, which is presented as being more truthful despite all its failings. The following comment, although it does not mention Zionism, sums up many of the strongest criticisms of the US press leveled by the Arab media: that it is a colonial tool that serves the government, that it is controlled by major corporations, and that it is generally untruthful.

> The US seems keener on suppressing the truth than promoting any real democracy in the area. American media organizations, driven by the giant military-industrial complex and big business, have been trying to justify Washington's military adventures and illegal wars against peace-loving peoples; wars whose aim has been to subjugate free nations, seize their resources, and try to reshape their futures to the advantage of big money that controls the decision-making process in advanced countries. The same does not hold true, however, for all media organizations. That was why US and British forces targeted Arab and other newsmen in Baghdad, killing three and wounding many others on a day that should be seen as a massacre of the press. The media, like Iraqi children and Iraqi civilians as a whole, were not spared the wrath of American bombs.[15]

This is also an interesting example of the traditional Arab media – a government-controlled Syrian newspaper – in its own formulation at least, coming to the defense of the new Arab media. In the version of reality presented to readers of *Al Baath*, the American media is a malevolent and despicable tool of imperialism and capitalism and the professional superiority of the Arab press demands US military action against them. (This is an odd reversal of Zev Chaffets' arguments that the Arab media, or at least *Al Jazeera*, is so unprofessional that it should be targeted by US military forces). Here, the US media is simply another weapon in the American arsenal, indistinguishable in its ultimate purpose from armored divisions and intelligence services.

In the midst of all of this powerful negative imagery about the US media in much of the Arab press, there is a growing body of opinion that grudgingly or at times glowingly, praises the Western media, especially US journalists. Some even go so far as to encourage their fellow Arab journalists to look to their US counterparts as role models. Grudging admiration could be noticed in the aftermath of the Iraq prisoner abuse scandal in 2004, which was revealed by Seymour Hersh of the *New Yorker* magazine and several other investigative journalists in the United States. One columnist in the Egyptian daily *Al Ahram*, in an article that mainly slammed the United States government and military for the torture scandal noted:

> We have to admit first of all that had it not been for the courage and diligence of the American press, we would never have known about the torture and abuse going on in Iraqi jails.[16]

This praise is openly framed as grudging, being an "admission," that the author and his readers are being forced to make but he does acknowledge "courage and diligence" on the part of the American media. The implication is not so much that the Arab media is incapable of similar "courage and diligence," as it is a recognition that the American media is independent, and willing to challenge the government when it is important for them to do so. A similar sentiment was expressed in a column in *Al Watan*, which argued:

[219]

> The American media – especially when fundamental issues are at stake –
> give priority to the exercise of their right of expression, publication, and
> criticism, and to informing the citizens of the true nature of what is
> happening, rather than pleasing American officials and the
> administration.[17]

Again, this is a defense of the independence of the American media,
and a call for it to be treated with respect on the basis of its work as a
watchdog against the government, and its willingness to reveal
information that is unflattering and inconvenient to the Administration.

Some Arab journalists and columnists go further, arguing that the
Western media in general and the American media in particular, reflect
the level of professionalism and independence largely unknown in the
Arab world and that they should be seen as role models for an improved
Arab news media. Some even include the Israeli press as well as the
American press, as did Salameh Nematt, Washington correspondent for
Al Hayat, in the following analysis:

> It is true that the policies of America and Israel deserve a lot of criticism
> and attack, which is what a lot of prominent American and Israeli writers
> do. Today, half of the American media seems to be in confrontation with
> the other half, in a struggle that reflects a sharp division between the
> supporters of the policies of the Republican administration and its
> opponents. The Israeli media also reflects a similar division in the Israeli
> political body, although more inclined to support the official position.
> What is striking in Arab media, the influence of which is almost
> nonexistent outside of the Arab world, is that it is incapable of addressing
> the issues of national priorities.[18]

In effect, this formulation is a reversal of the standard analysis and
moral and professional hierarchy reflected in the Arab media. Here, it is
the American and even the Israeli press which is being viewed as more
professional than the Arab journalists, and serving the public better.
Interestingly, for Nematt, it is the diversity of opinions that once again
seems to be the standard for measuring professionalism in the news
media. In this case, however, he argues that particularly in the United
States, the media is far more diverse than that in the Arab world. In
essence, *Al Jazeera's* argument is that there is a broader range of opinion

[220]

on its channel than there is on CNN, whereas Nematt argues that, when comparing a number of institutions, rather than the range of opinions and content in any single institution, the American press as a whole reflects a much broader and diverse political orientation than the Arab media. Nonetheless, the standard of diversity in political orientation remains consistent in both sympathetic and hostile assessments of the American news media's performance by Arab journalists, although this is a standard that many American journalists and media institutions would not accept as definitive, or in some cases as even particularly relevant.

In Arab media assessments, what we are left with is a strong sense of ambivalence towards the American press: suspicions of its motives and fear of its effects on the one hand along with admiration for its relative freedoms and its ability to effectively serve – to some extent at least – as a watchdog against the government. In particular, some Arab journalists seem to recognize that investigative reporters play a role in the US media and society that does not have an obvious analogue in the Arab world, and that this constitutes a social and professional deficit.

3-Where are we Going?

In spite of the ambivalence on both sides that we have outlined above, the primary attitude has been and remains one of mutual suspicion at best and sometimes even outright confrontation. The prevailing level of mutual vitriol between Arab and American journalists in recent years was encapsulated in a shouting match on-air in December 2001 between CNN morning anchor Paula Zahn and *Al Jazeera's* Washington bureau chief Hafez Al-Mirazi. Zahn accused *Al Jazeera* of "using anti-American language" and "glorify[ing] Osama bin Laden." Al-Mirazi accused CNN of "rubber stamping" whatever the US government does in foreign policy, and of "bashing the Arabs." Zahn called Al-Mirazi dishonest, and Al-Mirazi accused Zahn of defending Israeli Prime Minister Ariel Sharon. To cap it all, Zahn simply could not get Al-Mirazi's name right, in spite of his repeated corrections. For the purposes of this study, it is worth quoting a lengthy part of the transcript of this media encounter:

[221]

Paula Zahn (CNN): Mr. Al-Mirzari, I think we could all agree this morning we are products of our culture.

Hafez Al-Mirazi (Al-Jazeera): Al-Mirazi.

Zahn: But as you know, your station has been accused of using anti-American language, of running graphics that feature and glorify Osama bin Laden. Even Secretary of State Colin Powell denounced the station when you repeatedly aired Osama bin Laden's statement and Colin Powell said that that was vitriolic, irresponsible kinds of statements. What is your defense to his criticism?

Al-Mirazi: Well, Secretary Colin Powell gave interviews to Al Jazeera and later also said good words about Al Jazeera, as well as Dr. Condoleezza Rice and other US officials. They respected the credibility of Al Jazeera and the objectivity.

The problem actually is with the American media and the Western media, who instigated the government, and they always instigate against an independent media like Al Jazeera, because they do what the American media cannot do, which is not to mix patriotism with journalism.

We cover a war in Afghanistan by putting both sides of the story, the side coming from Kabul at that time and...

Zahn: Well, Mr. Al-Mirzari, I have to stop you there...

Al-Mirazi: It's Al-Mirazi.

Zahn: I think that charge is blatantly ridiculous.

Al-Mirazi: Well, I'll tell you what is ridiculous...

Zahn: I think if you watch the majority of the coverage in this country we do question the policies of our government.

I think we constantly put the leaders of our government on the spot when we question the progress of this campaign.

Al-Mirazi: Only on domestic policies. But in foreign policy, you are just rubber stamping whatever the government do.

Zahn: Oh, Mr. Al-Mirzari, you're not being honest at all.

Al-Mirazi: It's Al-Mirazi.

Zahn: Look at the debate in this country about the Israelis' retaliatory strikes in the Middle East. I mean, you have read the editorials in this country. You've seen the front page headlines.

Al-Mirazi: Let me just remind you of the CNN coverage of what happened Saturday night—last Saturday. For two hours, CNN was doing exactly what people were criticizing Al Jazeera of doing—footage of 10 minutes

[222]

coming out of Jerusalem, terrible footage, of course. Nobody would allow or accept the killing of civilians. But 10 minutes of footage have been kept repeating all over for more than two hours with commentators from your own reporters like Leon and others, and adopting the rhetoric and the argument of the Likud, not only the Israelis or the Labor, but the Likud, and giving a podium for Mr. Netanyahu and all the Israeli right to bash the Arabs.

Zahn: I have to tell you, I beg to differ with you.

Al-Mirazi: That is not creative reporting.

Zahn: I can't say that I watched every minute of our four hours of coverage that night, but I will tell you that, as with all news organizations, one would hope that you get on the phone and you try to find differing points of view. We, of course, had Palestinian representation on our air. That is absolutely absurd.

Al-Mirazi: But you give them a tough time the same way that you are giving me a tough time. Had you had an Israeli journalist with you, you have been pampering him or showering him with praise, very easy softballs. But only the problem with that—you get Arabs only to grill them. And this is the problem.

Zahn: No, sir, that is not true. I had the former Prime Minister of Israel on yesterday and we asked him the question, why is it Shimon Peres walked out of this meeting when the vote was taken to possibly try to in some way topple the government of Yasser Arafat?

Al-Mirazi: Exactly...

Zahn: Shimon Peres, we well reported the story that there is a rift within the Israeli government, that not all Israelis supported...

Al-Mirazi: OK. You are defending Sharon.

Zahn: That is absolutely not true.

Al-Mirazi: You were defending Sharon. You were criticizing the liberal, Paula.

Zahn: There are people, as you well know, within the Israeli government that do not support these retaliatory strikes. I think our coverage is fair and balanced.

Al-Mirazi: Wait...

Zahn: A final thought, sir, this morning on what the goal of Al Jazeera's coverage is.

Al-Mirazi: The goal is the motto of Al Jazeera, to cover both sides of the story, the view and the other point of view, to make sure that we would

[223]

have an Israeli journalist or an Israeli official with us in the interview, deal with him with respect the same way we would interview Arabs. And we would also remind people with that word that you called the ancient, Paula, yourself when you interviewed Hanan Ashrawi. The word is occupation. And this is the word that we should always remember.

Occupation is an ancient, I agree with you. That shouldn't have been, that shouldn't have stayed in the 21st century and it is the responsibility of credible journalists like you and journalists in the US to remind people that the occupation of the Palestinian land should be ended.

Al-Mirazi: Mr. Al-Mirzari, we're going to leave it there this morning. But I do once again need to remind you in our coverage with various guests we've had representing the Israeli government this week asked questions, as we have over the last couple of weeks, about the settlement issue, which is deeply important to the Palestinians, and also the whole issue of refugees and their potential return if a Palestinian state ends up being created.[19]

If the Zahn–Mirazi brouhaha encapsulates so much of the worst in relations and recriminations between Arab and American journalists in recent years, it is important to note that these suspicions, especially on the US side, do not persist in a vacuum. There are highly influential pro-Israel organizations that spend much, or in one case all, of their time trying to paint the Arab press in the worst possible light to US audiences, especially in government and media circles. Among these are the Anti-Defamation League (ADL), which produces regular reports on alleged anti-Semitism in the Arab media (usually a mixture of the genuinely offensive combined with run-of-the-mill discourse), almost always highly exaggerated. They have pushed Congress to adopt a law in 2004 mandating the State Department to issue annual reports on "global anti-Semitism," the first of which was issued in January 2005 and which focuses a great deal on the Arab media.

The Washington Institute for Near East Policy (WINEP), a think-tank that is an offshoot of the main pro-Israel Washington lobby group, the American Israel Public Affairs Committee (AIPAC), engages in similar tactics. It has recently spearheaded a successful campaign to get the US government to designate the Hezbollah TV station *Al Manar* as a terrorist organization and ensure that no satellite dish carrier will transmit its broadcasts in range of US territory. This was accomplished in part by the publication of a book called *Beacon of Hate* which included a DVD featuring damning clips from *Al Manar* broadcasts. The book and DVD were widely circulated free of charge in Washington. This banning of *Al Manar* is unprecedented in recent US history, as it is aimed specifically at preventing Americans from accessing views and information that the government does not approve of and in some instances may well be offensive.

Perhaps the most influential source casting the Arab media in a negative light is the shadowy Middle East Media Research Institute (MEMRI), which is quite plainly either a direct or indirect effort of the Israeli intelligence services and is headed by Yigal Carmon, a former Israeli intelligence officer. MEMRI's strategy is simple, but highly effective: they scour the Arabic language and Iranian media for anything that might cast Arabs, the Arab states and Iran, Islam or Muslims in a bad light. This typically consists of two kinds of expression: a speech that either is extreme or can be fairly or sometimes unfairly cast as such, and a speech that is self-critical (which also casts states and societies in general as negative). MEMRI's translations, bulletins and reports are distributed to the key government, media and think tank desks in Washington, DC and have had a profound effect in recent years in shaping the way the American establishment imagines the Arab media to be: an unending stream of violent incitement and hatred, punctuated by occasional *cris du coeur* (cries from the heart) from lone voices of sanity. No sane, sober, serious analysis that is not a self-criticism from the Arab press has ever been publicized by MEMRI, nor has the organization ever had any comment on incitement and racist speech in the Israeli media. The whole point of MEMRI is to cast the Arab discourse in the worst possible light, and it has been extraordinarily successful since it is the only source for Arab media translations that are free, timely, designed to interest and indeed outrage its Washington audience. And, it has to be said, some elements of the Arab media provide them with ample fodder for their mission.

In addition to all the factors elaborated already, these efforts help ensure that American media, especially its populist variety, remains deeply hostile to the new Arab media in general, and *Al Jazeera* in particular. "Al Jazeera is a terrorist outfit," thundered Fox News channel's top-rated talk show host Bill O'Reilly on October 25, 2004. Because *Al Jazeera* showed videos of hostages being held in Iraq, "By playing along with the terrorists, Al Jazeera has become a terror organization itself." He then falsely claimed that the station "actually broadcast the beheading of American Paul Johnson in Saudi Arabia." Needless to say, the station did not show any actual beheadings. "The US government should immediately brand Al Jazeera a terrorist organization, expel their employees and ban the network in America." O'Reilly continued, "The Bush administration should also put pressure on the Qatar government to close down Al Jazeera." He concluded, "Nobody should be playing that tape."[20] One can easily agree with that sentiment, without concluding that an editorial disagreement over news content is a reasonable ground for censorship and expulsion, let alone that such coverage constitutes collaboration with terrorists and murderers. Undoubtedly, had the subject been a western news source, O'Reilly's criticism would never have extended to calls for banning and expulsion. The antagonism is alive and well.

The most interesting effort to soften the American media discourse on Arab journalism is a cover story in the January 2, 2005, *New York Times* magazine. This lengthy cover story on *Al Arabiya* was entitled: "The war inside the Arab news room." The story paints *Al Arabiya*, which heretofore has been viewed in the United States as indistinguishable from *Al Jazeera*, as a "moderate" alternative, in language reminiscent of the pro-Jazeera pieces from the pre-9/11 era. The author, Samantha Shapiro, acknowledges that American military authorities in Iraq and the American-appointed Iraqi Governing Council certainly did not seem to distinguish between the two satellite channels—they considered both to be allied with the enemy. In September 2003, the Governing Council suspended *Al Arabiya* from reporting on official government activities for two weeks because, the council maintained, the channel was supporting resistance attacks. In November of the same year, the council ordered *Al Arabiya* to stop all of its Iraqi operations after the channel broadcast a taped message from Saddam Hussein in hiding. At a news conference that month, US Secretary of Defense Donald Rumsfeld called *Al Arabiya* "violently anti-coalition" and in a separate interview said:

> There are so many things that are untrue that are being reported by irresponsible journalists and irresponsible television stations, particularly like Al Jazeera and Al Arabiya, that are leaving the Iraqi people with a totally imbalanced picture of what is happening in their country.

However, Shapiro paints *Al Arabiya* as intentionally designed to create a distinction with *Al Jazeera*, one that Americans should be able to understand from the point of view of their own media:

> Sheik Walid [Ibrahim, its owner] started Al Arabiya in February 2003 to provide a more moderate alternative to Al Jazeera. His goal, as he told me last month, was to position Al Arabiya as the CNN to Al Jazeera's Fox News, as a calm, cool, professional media outlet that would be known for objective reporting rather than for shouted opinions.

While she does credit a number of people, including Sheikh Walid and several *Al Arabiya* journalists, with being important players in the station's mission, the story focuses almost entirely on Abdul Rahman Al-Rashid, the General Manager of *Al Arabiya*. He is cast as an (almost) lone figure, striving against terrible odds and not fully evolved colleagues to bring sense to a region awash with hysteria and delusion. She writes:

> His goal is to foster a new kind of dialogue among Arabs, to carve out space for moderate and liberal ideas to enter the conversation, and in the process to do nothing less than save the Arab world from itself."[21]

So we see hear one more familiar trope: the only hope of the Arabs is a TV station, one maverick organization set against all the others, and the lionization of a single, specific individual who will lead the salvation of an entire people. Thus the war inside the Arab newsroom, according to the American newsroom, turns out to be less *Al Arabiya* versus *Al Jazeera* than Abdul Rahman Al-Rashid versus everyone. If experience is any guide, this latest infatuation is likely to give way to cooler ardors towards both the station and its General Manager, given time. We have already seen how quickly some flowers can wilt.

[227]

13

Washington vs. Al Jazeera: Competing Constructions of Middle East Realities

*Michael C. Hudson**

This is a story about the collision of two forces, both of which, in their respective and contradictory ways, are reshaping the contemporary Arab world. These forces of change are first, the new information technologies, especially satellite television, and second, America's project to secure the region, a quest being carried out with new energy and determination since the attacks of September 11, 2001. On one level, both agents of change share the objective of transforming the region. An *Al Jazeera* staff member interviewed in Doha in 2002 viewed the channel as a "liberating force" in a stagnant and authoritarian Arab world while the American President himself has set a goal to bring freedom to this benighted region, by force if necessary, in order to terminate the threat of "Islamist terrorism" to the United States. However, the "Al Jazeera effect," while opening up new political space, has created an opportunity for anti-American sentiments to be voiced and perhaps, anti-American activities to be encouraged. Meanwhile, the "American effect," while supporting civil society and (limited) political participation, has inadvertently stimulated nationalist as well as religious resistance to what is widely seen as the neo-imperialist agenda of a superpower, many of whose regional policies are detested.

---

* The author wishes to thank Dr. Leila Hudson for her advice and assistance in the preparation of this paper. He would also like to acknowledge the valuable help of his student research assistant, Sara Sari Dajani.

This collision drama is being played out across the Arab and Islamic world. It influences the domestic politics of every country in the region by shaking up established structures and underlining sociopolitical contradictions. The twin transformations both weaken and strengthen authoritarian governments. They not only energize societies but also heighten societal cleavages at the same time. They accentuate the global but simultaneously stimulate the local. Most observers agree that fundamental changes are occurring, but have reached no consensus on the nature and direction of these changes.

Our story unfolds on a much smaller canvas. It takes place mostly in Washington, D.C. and involves only hundreds, not millions of people. It is the story of the relationship between an agent of social change (the Al Jazeera bureau) and an agent of political-military change (as represented by certain elements of the US government). Although not static, it would be simplistic to describe this as a "love-hate relationship." In the beginning, less than a decade ago, it appeared to be "love at first sight." Washington and "the chattering classes" that influence American policy welcomed the advent of an Arab media venture based on a Western model (the BBC) that was prepared to challenge existing political orthodoxies in the region—even to the point of including Israeli spokesmen in its programming. For their part, the creators of *Al Jazeera* and their backers – notably the ruling family of Qatar – were seeking to open the minds (if not the hearts) of Arabs everywhere to a global community and sought to bring international standards to their profession. To them, American policies toward Israel and Palestine were a problem but America's liberal values and the remarkable societal accomplishments that derived from them were qualities to be emulated. Pundits and professors – Americans and Arabs alike – celebrated the advent of Arabic satellite TV.

However, the honeymoon ended abruptly after 9/11 and the subsequent US invasion of Afghanistan. When *Al Jazeera* aired a videotape from Osama bin Laden (the first of many to come), Washington was outraged. With the US invasion of Iraq in 2003, the relationship soured even more.

[230]

While deep animosities remain, both sides have sought to smooth them over, and there has been introspection on both sides about the nature of the problem. Serious issues continue to persist: Can *Al Jazeera* ever appear "fair and balanced" in the eyes of the US government when its mission is to report candidly on American behavior in the Arab world, "warts and all"? Can Washington reconcile its principled commitment to a free press with its perceived security and other national interests? Many Americans nodded approval when *Al Jazeera* reported and commented critically about various Arab governments and criticized those governments when they sought to muzzle *Al Jazeera*. However, when the channel showed the United States in an unfavorable light, and when its commentators attacked America, the US government showed that it had little more tolerance than sensitive Arab regimes.

The "Al Jazeera Effect"

The remarkable story of *Al Jazeera* needs no recitation here. Suffice it to say that since its founding in 1996 it has become a household word wherever Arabs gather in front of a television set. The channel estimates it has 35-40 million viewers in the Arab and Muslim world, four million in Europe, and 200,000 subscribers in the United States. Even in the United States its fame – or notoriety – extends well beyond the Arab community. When late-night comedians on American TV joke about *Al Jazeera* there can be little doubt that it has become part of the mainstream. Journalists and academics alike have seized on the "Al Jazeera effect" as a phenomenon of huge importance. El-Nawawy and Iskandar's popular book, *Al Jazeera,* celebrates its accomplishments not only in terms of news coverage but also in airing issues that bind 300 million Arabs to each other.[1] The influential American columnist Thomas Friedman wrote that it was "not only the biggest media phenomenon to hit the Arab world since the advent of television, it also is the biggest political phenomenon."[2] Rami Khouri, the distinguished Arab columnist, who is not uncritical of *Al Jazeera*, nonetheless states:

[231]

I have a pretty good view of a broad range of American television, and then I watch European television. Every single day, I flip through the channels to see what they are reporting. I concluded that if you wanted to see the most comprehensive coverage of the Iraq war, you should watch al-Jazeera or al-Arabiyya, no doubt about it whatsoever. I challenge anyone who has done an empirical study, do go back and do a content analysis, to look at CNN or CBS or NBC, to look at European stations and at the Arab satellite stations. Far and away, the Arab satellite stations presented the most comprehensive coverage. They broadcast every single American official press conference with live simultaneous translation into Arabic, they aired the Iraqi government spokespersons, they put on Arab commentators and analysts from other Arab countries, they interviewed the American generals sitting at their control centers in Doha, and they interviewed the mothers whose children had just been killed by American bombs.[3]

Policy analysts also were quick to recognize that *Al Jazeera* was, as Jon Alterman put it, "a hot story."[4] However, it was not just the ability to provide "breaking news" that stirred interest; it was also the fact that "it intentionally seeks to be provocative in a region in which news reporting has often been the private fiefdom of government information ministries, and in which dissent has been tightly controlled." Indeed, for Arab regimes, it is the popular *Al Jazeera* talk shows that have been most intolerable, because of the often heated and intemperate utterances of the participants, who sometimes end up shouting at each other or even walking off the set. Thus, the *Al Jazeera* effect was combination of two elements: the dramatic on-the-ground uncensored reporting, particularly in conflict situations such as Palestine/Israel, Iraq and Afghanistan; and the heated airing of the most taboo sociopolitical issues such as religion vs. secularism, men vs. women, and rulers vs. ruled that captured and captivated a large and growing Arab audience.

Academics took an even more expansive view. For example, in 2002, I advanced the argument that "as a potential 'fourth estate' in Arab political systems the press has gained new power and dynamism through the internet and satellite television."[5] I ventured to suggest that the Information Revolution, including the "Al Jazeera effect," was loosening the grip of authoritarian regimes over their societies and "creating a new

[232]

transnational public space for Arabs to converse, debate, and inform one another." I also noted that Islamists were proving particularly adept at harnessing the new information technologies for their purposes. In all fairness it must be added that some social scientists specializing on the Middle East, including some of my valued colleagues, thought such views were exaggerated, or premature to say the least. Yet, I believe that these were, and still are, worth consideration.

US Attitudes and Actions towards Al Jazeera

It would be a mistake to assume that American attitudes toward *Al Jazeera* are or have been uniformly hostile. As already noted, initial assessments by influential opinion-makers were quite positive. On the face of it, the phenomenon of transnational satellite television in the Arab world seemed to represent a liberal step forward. It was also noted approvingly that *Al Jazeera* was giving Israeli spokesmen a platform and the channel's credibility in the United States was probably strengthened by the criticism in some Arab quarters that it was an Israeli tool.

Some government agencies and officials weighed in on the positive side. The State Department's annual Human Rights Report for 2000 commended *Al Jazeera* for "operating freely." Kenton Keith, a former US ambassador to Qatar, told *The Christian Science Monitor* (in 2002) that *Al Jazeera* has a slant, no more than other news organizations:

> Its slant happens to be one most Americans are not comfortable with.... But the fact is that Al Jazeera has revolutionized media in the Middle East....For the long-range importance of press freedom in the Middle East and the advantages that will ultimately have for the West, you have to be a supporter of Al Jazeera, even if you have to hold your nose sometimes.[6]

Christopher Ross, a former US ambassador to Syria and an official in the State Department's public diplomacy program, had a kind word for *Al Jazeera* even as he was criticizing it for airing a bin Laden tape: "You at Al Jazeera know that since Al Jazeera's inception, the US administration has been a great admirer of the channel."[7] *Al Jazeera* even got favorable treatment on *60 Minutes,* the widely viewed CBS-TV newsmagazine.[8]

However, the events of 9/11, the US-led attack on Afghanistan, and the airing of the Bin Laden tape certainly changed the mood. On October 3, 2001, US Secretary of State Colin Powell urged the visiting Ruler of Qatar, H.H. Shaikh Hamad bin Khalifa Al Thani, to rein in the channel because it was unbalanced, anti-American and airing vitriolic and irresponsible statements.[9] US Secretary of Defense Donald Rumsfeld criticized *Al Jazeera* for repeatedly playing images of Afghan children injured by American bombs, asserting that this amounted to propaganda for the Taliban.[10] The conservative, pro-Israeli wing of the US foreign policy establishment weighed in shortly thereafter with a slashing critique of *Al Jazeera*, written by Fouad Ajami in *The New York Times Magazine*.[11] When US planes bombed *Al Jazeera's* offices in Kabul on November 13, 2001, *Al Jazeera* officials accused the US Air Force of a deliberate attack, although the Pentagon firmly denied it. A year and a half later on April 8, 2003, when US planes bombed the *Al Jazeera* office in Baghdad, killing one of its correspondents, Tarek Ayyub, and wounding a cameraman, suspicions about American intentions toward the channel were rekindled.

The Pentagon's pressure on *Al Jazeera* has continued to the present day. In the summer of 2003, US Assistant Secretary of Defense Paul Wolfowitz attacked *Al Jazeera* claiming that it had broadcast false reports and endangered American troops. According to Robert Fisk, writing in the London-based newspaper, *The Independent*:

> Only a day after US Deputy Defense Secretary Paul Wolfowitz claimed that the Arabic Al-Jazeera television channel was "inciting violence" and "endangering the lives of American troops" in Iraq, the station's Baghdad bureau chief has written a scathing reply to the American administration, complaining that in the past month the station's offices and staff in Iraq "have been subject to strafing by gunfire, death threats, confiscation of news material, and multiple detentions and arrests, all carried out by US soldiers…"[12]

Another of Wolfowitz's claims involved the station's coverage of an incident in the Iraqi Shiite city of Najaf. "Al Jazeera ran a totally false report that American troops had gone and detained one of the key imams in this holy city of Najaf, Muqtad[a] Al-Sadr," he said. "It was a false report, but they were out broadcasting it instantly."[13]

Wadah Khanfar's detailed reply to this claim – and his sense of frustration – will be familiar to any Western newspaper editor. He wrote:

> Al-Jazeera never stated at any time that Muqtada As-Sadr was detained. Our correspondent Yasser Abu Hilala, a top reporter with thirteen years experience covering the Middle East, stated he had received phone calls from Muqtada As-Sadr's secretary and two of his top deputies saying the imam's house was surrounded by US forces after he called for the formation of an Islamic Army. The phone calls were not only made to our offices but to all the offices of As-Sadr's followers in Baghdad resulting in a massive demonstration in front of the Republic Palace within 45 minutes which we reported, along with the New York Times, CNN and a host of others.[14]

The US Secretary of Defense has continued the attacks. According to the Associated Press on November 26, 2003:

> Defense Secretary Donald Rumsfeld and his top military adviser said Tuesday they had evidence the Arab television news organizations Al-Jazeera and Al-Arabiya cooperated with Iraqi insurgents to witness and videotape attacks on American troops. Rumsfeld said the effort fit a pattern of psychological warfare used by remnants of the Baathist government, who want to create the impression that no amount of US firepower can end the insurgency. "They've called Al-Jazeera to come and watch them do it [attack American troops], and Al-Arabiya," he said at a Pentagon news conference. "Come and see us, watch us; here is what we're going to do." Pressed for details, Rumsfeld and Gen. Richard Myers, chairman of the Joint Chiefs of Staff, indicated that US forces in Iraq had collected more than just circumstantial evidence that one or both of the Arab news organizations might have cooperated with the attackers. "Yes, I've seen scraps of information over a sustained period of time," Rumsfeld said. "I'm not in a position to make a final judgment on it," but it needs to be examined in an "orderly way," he added.[15]

[235]

In March 2004, a high-ranking US officer in Iraq, General Mark Kimmitt, was quoted as follows:

> My solution is to change the channel to a legitimate, authoritative, honest news station. The stations that are showing Americans intentionally killing women and children are not legitimate news sources.[16]

In the same article, Secretary Rumsfeld is quoted as saying:

> I can definitely say that what al-Jazeera is doing is vicious, inaccurate and inexcusable. We know what our forces do. They don't go around killing hundreds of civilians. That's just outrageous nonsense! It's disgraceful what that station is doing.[17]

In April 2004, according to the *Los Angeles Times,* Secretary of State Colin Powell complained to the visiting Qatari Foreign Minister, H.E. Sheikh Hamad bin Jassim bin Jabr Al Thani, that *Al Jazeera's* broadcasts had "intruded" on relations between the United States and Qatar.[18] It may be recalled that Qatar hosts the largest American military base in the region.

On August 6, 2004 Secretary Rumsfeld spoke before the Chicago Council on Foreign Relations. According to the official account:

> Defense Secretary Donald Rumsfeld told the Council on Foreign Relations in Chicago August 6 that some of the reporting by Arab media such as al-Jazeera and al-Arabiyah has damaged U.S. initiatives in the Middle East.
>
> For example, he said, "they have persuaded an enormous fraction" of people that the United States is in Iraq as an occupying force, "which is a lie." Or, he added, they have persuaded people that U.S. soldiers "are randomly killing innocent civilians," which is a lie….Rumsfeld said some of the al-Jazeera reporters in Baghdad have been in the past on the payroll of the regime of Saddam Hussein. By conveying false or misleading information now, he said, it "makes everything harder" for the United States and even for countries that are neighbors to Iraq.[19]

How do *Al Jazeera* representatives in Washington view the situation? A staffer in the Washington Bureau (interviewed on September 30, 2004) disputed the notion that the US government is carrying out a "sustained" battle against *Al Jazeera*. The worst "enemies" are in the Pentagon: Donald Rumsfeld, Paul Wolfowitz, Peter Rodman and some others. At the National Security Council, Dr. Condoleezza Rice falls in that category, as does the official State Department spokesman Richard Boucher. The staffer observed that President Bush himself has been silent. In fact, the relationship "has its ups and downs." Secretary Rumsfeld and Dr. Rice have occasionally appeared on *Al Jazeera*, as have a number of other civilian and military officials. The staffer recalled that only a few days after Secretary of State Colin Powell reportedly called *Al Jazeera's* coverage "horrible," he was asking to do an interview on the channel. In the State Department in particular there is a viewpoint that the US government should take advantage of *Al Jazeera* and other Arabic channels, with their huge Arab audiences, and seize every opportunity to appear.

Some movers and shakers on the Washington political scene are friendlier than others. At the Democratic Party Convention in July 2004 the officials were quite nasty, tearing down the channel's banner from its location in the convention hall. Surprisingly, the Republicans, at their convention, were very hospitable. In its early years, *Al Jazeera* was praised by US liberals, mainly because of its readiness to present Israelis, but later the warmth diminished. For example, Norman Pattiz, the chief engineer of the US "public diplomacy" campaign to the Arab world (godfather of Radio Sawa and *Al Hurra* satellite channel) was initially complimentary but currently he is hostile. He disputes the idea of those in the State Department and academia who argue that the US government should engage the Arab media, "because it presupposes that the indigenous media is the solution, not the problem." Moreover, according to him:

> Al Jazeera and Al Arabiya transcend traditional media roles. They function, in effect, as quasi-political movements, reflecting two of the defining characteristics of the Middle East today. One is the lack of political and press freedom. The other is Arab nationalism. Arab networks manifest both.[20]

The US government is a massive establishment with many offices, communities and factions, apart from its formal separate divisions. Moreover, the influential "political circles" outside government itself represent a diversity of backgrounds and points of view. These include the political parties, the media, the lobbies, the think-tanks and academia. While neoconservative and strongly pro-Israel think-tanks echo the hostility towards *Al Jazeera*, the liberal and neutral organizations, even if they are not necessarily positive, take a more pragmatic stance.

In response to the unmistakable deterioration of the American image in the Arab and Muslim world, the US government went to work to create various boards and commissions to study the matter. The Congressional Research Service was assigned the task of producing a report on *Al Jazeera*. An Office of Global Communications was set up in the White House, which had a series of short-lived managers. The US Agency for International Development and the Department of Defense were mobilized. A Strategic Communications Policy Coordinating Committee (PCC), jointly managed by the National Security Council and the State Department, was established. In the State Department an Office of Policy Planning and Resources was created. An important body called the Broadcasting Board of Governors was established to undertake an American response to the challenge of *Al Jazeera* and the other Arabic channels.[21]

The Congressional Research Service (CRS), an arm of the US Congress produced a report on *Al Jazeera* in July 2003 which laid out, in neutral terms, the "opportunities" as well as the "challenges" presented by *Al Jazeera* to US foreign policy interests.[22] Its conclusions are worth stating at some length:

> Al-Jazeera's ability to cover breaking news, to promote its slick, entertaining format, and to project subtly its pan-Arab, pan-Islamist approach to covering the news has sparked some US officials and analysts to suggest ways of promoting a response to its distinctive influence. Others have dismissed calls for policy responses. Some experts warn that any overt US action could be viewed as heavy-handed in a region which has traditionally been sensitive to outside involvement in regional or local affairs. Al-Jazeera claims that US steps intended to promote a more balanced media in the Arab world will backfire, because Arabs will consider it a propaganda effort of the US government. A range of possible actions has been proposed. In one category are actions that actively promote US policy. They include:
>
> *Create an alternative Arabic Language Television Network*: In the Emergency Supplemental Appropriations Bill of April 16, 2003 (Public

Law 108–11), Congress designated $30.5 million for the Middle East Television Network (METN). According to Norman Pattiz, the founder and chairman of Westwood One Radio Network and a member of the US Broadcasting Board of Governors (BBG), "as most people in the region get their news and information from TV, we need to be on TV so we can explain America and its policies, its people, and its culture from our own lips rather than have it described by the indigenous media." The exact scope and style of METN has yet to be determined. The BBG already sponsors Radio Sawa, an Arabic radio station, which combines popular music with news headlines.

Tie foreign aid to media reform: Some analysts contend that this technique, which has worked for some human rights cases, might be applied to the media as well.

Buy commercial air time on Arab networks: During the last two years, the State Department Office of Public Diplomacy has been implementing the "Shared Values Program," a $15 million effort to promote positive images of Muslim life in America. TV advertisements depicting American Muslims ran for 5 weeks in late 2003 in Pakistan, Kuwait, Malaysia and on some pan-Arab channels but not Al-Jazeera. Although the overall campaign continues, the State Department stopped running the commercials after the governments of Jordan, Egypt and Lebanon refused to carry them on state-run television. Other policy experts have suggested more indirect ways of influencing the Arab media, including the following actions:

Get US officials to engage the Arab media more actively: As previously mentioned top United States cabinet officials have appeared on Al-Jazeera television for interviews. Proponents of this strategy believe that more appearances by US officials, particularly those fluent in Arabic, would convey confidence in US foreign policy. Skeptics of this strategy believe that Al-Jazeera and other channels could skew the pre and post-interview analysis against the US position.

Favor the more moderate Arab satellite networks: With almost a dozen different Arab satellite channels, some analysts believe that US interests would be better served if US officials appeared on less sensationalist Arab networks in order to foster competitors to Al-Jazeera. Some even suggest encouraging US companies to advertise on these types of stations.

Encourage more privatization of media: Under the auspices of the State Department's Middle East Partnership Initiative (MEPI), there have been plans to fund media reform programs in some Arab states. As MEPI is just starting to take shape, the initiative could fund media training for aspiring journalists, as well as programs that promote freedom of the press.[23]

[239]

One argument, which is widely circulated in Arab intellectual circles, is that the best way to combat the coverage of channels such as *Al Jazeera* would be to focus US foreign policy on solving the Arab-Israeli conflict. Others argue that biased coverage will continue no matter what direction the United States takes its policy in the Middle East. With the United States heavily engaged in Iraq, Afghanistan, and elsewhere, *Al Jazeera* will continue to play a role in reporting and interpreting US foreign policy to the Arab world.

In October 2003, the Advisory Group on the Arab and Muslim World, an offshoot of the Advisory Commission on Public Diplomacy, issued a report entitled "Changing Minds, Winning Peace: A New Strategic Direction for US Public Diplomacy in the Arab and Muslim World."[24] Chaired by former Ambassador Edward Djerejian and staffed with several Middle East experts, the report identified the problem the US faces:

> As one of many examples, we watched a program on al-Arabiyya satellite television titled "The Americanization of Islam," whose theme was that the United States had embarked on a sinister plot to change the 1,500-year-old religion. The true American position was nowhere represented. Our views were absent from the program, just as we are absent, despite the dedicated efforts of our public officials at home and abroad, from much of the intense daily discourse on US policy and values taking place throughout the Arab and Muslim world.[25]

The Group recommended various structural reforms that would reconnect the United States with the Arab and Muslim societies— reversing a decade-long tendency toward isolation and neglect of public affairs and cultural diplomacy. However, its concluding statement is notable for its recognition of the underlying causes of the growing gap between the United States and the people of the Arab and Muslim countries:

> Americans, on the one hand, and Arabs and Muslims, on the other, are trapped in a dangerously reinforcing cycle of animosity. Arabs and Muslims respond in anger to what they perceive as US denigration of their societies and cultures, and to this Arab and Muslim response Americans react with bewilderment and resentment, provoking a further negative

[240]

response from Arabs and Muslims. A transformed public diplomacy that is candid about differences but also stresses similarities – especially in values – can dampen the animosity and help end the cycle. Most changes will not occur overnight, but some steps, taken immediately, will produce short-term solutions. More importantly, however, the US Government needs to view public diplomacy – just as it views state-to-state diplomacy and national security – in a long-term perspective. Transformed public diplomacy can make America safer, but it must be sustained for decades, not stopped and started as moods change in the world. Public opinion in the Arab and Muslim world cannot be cavalierly dismissed. We must also confront the contradiction that troubles believers in democracy and liberalization. They see official US diplomacy as frequently buttressing governments hostile to freedom and prosperity. Public diplomacy gives the United States the opportunity to supplement the support of such regimes – often a policy necessity – with broader, long-term promotion of universal values and economic, political, and social reforms that directly support public aspirations, candor and confidence, not spin and sugar-coating. **Finally, we want to be clear: "Spin" and manipulative public relations and propaganda are not the answer. Foreign policy counts. In our trips to Egypt, Syria, Turkey, France, Morocco and Senegal, we were struck by the depth of opposition to many of our policies. Citizens in these countries are genuinely distressed at the plight of Palestinians and at the role they perceive the United States to be playing, and they are genuinely distressed by the situation in Iraq. Sugar-coating and fast talking are no solutions, nor is absenting ourselves. America can achieve dramatic results with a consistent, strategic, well-managed, and properly funded approach to public diplomacy, one that credibly reflects US values, promotes the positive thrust of US policies, and takes seriously the needs and aspirations of Arabs and Muslims for peace, prosperity, and social justice.** [Emphasis added.][26]

This report indicates a deeper and wiser recognition on the part of some influential Americans that "killing the messenger" is no solution for the problems faced by the United States.

Al Jazeera's Response to American Attacks

Situated just fifteen miles from the largest American base in the Middle East, *Al Jazeera* and its management must be unusually sensitive to the mood of the US Administration. The government of Qatar, a Middle East mini-state, lacks the ability to protect its prized if prickly asset from the wrath of the American military. Governments in the region – including Saudi Arabia, Jordan, the Palestine Authority, Egypt, Morocco, Algeria and the Iraqi interim government – may fume but they lack both the force and the influence that the United States can bring to bear. Moreover, the American pressure has been incessant. Qatari diplomats in Washington say that their chief headache is Washington's (and especially the Pentagon's) unhappiness with *Al Jazeera*. The Qatar government appears to be playing a particularly audacious strategic game with its neighbors large and small. On the one hand it has actively courted a US presence despite Washington's partiality to Israel but on the other, it has sustained and protected its famous media outlet (thus far at least) from the anger of Washington's neoconservatives.

At the local, tactical level, *Al Jazeera* has sought to mollify and engage its Washington community. The Bureau Chief, Hafez Al-Mirazi does not miss an opportunity to insist that he is "begging" Administration officials to appear on the channel, and in fact several of them have done so. He has also tapped into the think tank and academic community of Middle East specialists and commentators. Despite the hostile words from top level officials, the channel has good working relations at the middle levels of the Executive Branch. It reports frequently from the Pentagon, the State Department and the White House. "We have a lot of friends in town," remarked an *Al Jazeera* staffer. Al-Mirazi has also testified before the US House of Representatives Subcommittee on National Security, Emerging Threats and International Relations. In an August 2004 hearing on strengthening American "public diplomacy" in the region he forcefully defended his channel's work and urged American officials who routinely make the rounds of the Sunday morning news talk shows in the United States to appear on the Arabic channels as well. He criticized the idea of US government-run Arabic media outlets as inconsistent with American values about an independent press. And he endorsed the view of many

American Middle East and foreign policy specialists that the country's problem in the region is its policies, not its values. No amount of slick advertising could get around that fundamental reality.[27]

In an important sense, however, *Al Jazeera's* fate is beyond its control. Yet its management has hardly been oblivious to the storms the station has created. Saudi capital is underwriting a relatively new but very professional competitor, *Al Arabiya*, to try and clip the wings of a channel whose very name is considered a backhanded insult to the dynasty. Top management changes at *Al Jazeera* itself may have been influenced by US pressure on the Qatari authorities, and some regular viewers have recently noted a toning down in coverage and presentation. *Al Jazeera* organized its first "World Forum" in Doha in July 2004, a conference devoted both to self-criticism and exogenous evaluation of the channel's product. Out of the meeting emerged a new "Code of Ethics" (see Appendix at the end of this chapter). In it, the channel pledges, among other things, to adhere to journalistic standards of balance and validity; to treat audiences with respect and decorum; to present diverse points of view, and to distinguish between news and opinion. So worthy and well-understood are these principles in the journalistic profession that one wonders why it was necessary to state them at all. Perhaps the answer is that the channel felt a need to respond to American (and Arab governmental) pressures.

For its part, the current management of *Al Jazeera* professes optimism about its future.[28] Despite lackluster advertising revenues (mainly the result of Saudi pressure on would-be advertisers), the channel is expanding. Plans are well advanced for a sports channel and an English-language service. Its executives dismiss the "threat" of competition from *Al Arabiya* by insisting that their true competitors are global—BBC World and CNN International. While no outsider can fathom the relationships between the station and the Qatar authorities, it seems clear that it has been a huge political, strategic and public relations asset that has given a higher profile to that small country. It is no exaggeration to say that *Al Jazeera* has put Qatar on the global map in a way that huge gas reserves could never do. A careful combination of journalistic professionalism and principled pragmatism may be *Al Jazeera's* best protection against its many ill-wishers. And in the final analysis, as its managers like to argue, successful competition for audience share may preserve the project.

Whose "Reality" is Real? Al Jazeera and Alternative Models

If many philosophers and social scientists deny the possibility of a single, objective reality, ordinary people go about their lives acting as if there were one. Anthropologists and some political scientists argue that communities are "imagined" and realities are "constructed." The imagining, construction or reconstruction of sociopolitical identities in today's volatile Arab world is a huge issue, both for Arabs and for outsiders who believe, rightly or wrongly, that this region is too important – perhaps even dangerous – to be ignored. Many structures, institutions, ideas and processes affect identity construction and political legitimacy. The rapid implantation of new information technologies across the Arab region would seem to play a significant role in these formations. And the hegemonic presence of the United States also would seem to play an important part—with perhaps unintended consequences.

Some *Al Jazeera* employees, as well as hostile critics and friendly commentators, contend that the channel is the driving force behind a renewed sense of Arab identity across the region. Some would argue that it is building a new Arab nationalism and a new will to resist foreign encroachment. For many Arabs, this development, if true, is good news.[29] For many American officials, such as Norman Pattiz (quoted above), it is bad news because it impedes the construction of a new global reality that would be harmonious with American interests. There may be some truth to this proposition, but there are some caveats to bear in mind as well.

For one thing, few social scientists accept any longer the sweeping claims of 1960s modernization theory that new, liberal, "modern" identities and communities could be constructed by the new media and educational facilities, thus "shattering the glass" of "tradition." New

[244]

media and information technologies today may play a role, but it may not be transformative and may take much longer than naïve modernization theorists once thought. Moreover, there are other factors at work. That said, one can still argue that satellite television and the Internet are engendering a sense of commonality in a particularly powerful way. However, the new media are not just *Al Jazeera* or *Al Arabiya*. Entertainment and cultural programming is far more popular in the Arab world than 24-hour news— just as is the case in the United States and other countries. Professor Marwan Kraidy, who studies the effects of entertainment programming, argues that these programs are as important – maybe more so – in engendering a transnational sense of Arab community. This sense of community is in itself not "political" but it may stand as a cultural prerequisite for more ideological manifestations of Arabism.

Al Jazeera employees themselves almost certainly are not of one mind about their "mission" and their effect on Arab society. The staffer in Doha, cited earlier, articulated an ideological agenda. However, the staffer in Washington, also cited above, demurred at a characterization of *Al Jazeera* as framing a "nationalist-anti-imperialist" worldview. It should be recalled, the Washington staffer said, that *Al Jazeera* achieved its initial influence and fame not by bashing the United States but by providing a forum for criticizing authoritarian Arab governments. Its reputation was advanced by allowing Israelis air time on the channel—hardly a narrow "nationalist" policy. Moreover, if the channels current management is to be believed, *Al Jazeera* sees its future as a global media institution, not just a regional (or "nationalist") one. However, any regular viewer of *Al Jazeera* would definitely note the centrality of Palestine-Israel and the Iraq situation in its coverage. Is that concentration evidence of a nationalist agenda? Those associated with the channel deny this, saying that what it covers is news, and represents what viewers want and expect.

Official circles in Washington appear to have quite a different understanding of "reality" in the Arab world. To the Bush administration, and especially its neoconservative thinkers, the Arab region has mostly poor people whose highest priority is to be "free." They are supposedly thirsting for democracy, and clamoring to become part of the global economy. In Washington's view, their aspirations are perpetually thwarted by what are seen as authoritarian and inefficient governments. Unfortunately, people in the region are to some extent being brainwashed by "Islamist terrorism" organizations, which have hijacked what Washington policymakers know to be the true Islam. Stagnant economies and anachronistic educational systems are helping to create a breeding ground for Islamist terrorism, with its particularly anti-American and anti-Israeli character. According to this view, the new satellite channels, especially *Al Jazeera*, promote incitement, xenophobia and retrograde nationalism instead of facilitating the Arab quest for freedom, democracy, and global integration. It follows that a vigorous program of "public diplomacy" in the Arab world will somehow neutralize these impediments. Such a program would educate Arabs about the virtues of American values and deflect their misguided hostility to American policies.

Which reality is "real"? There may be kernels of truth in both. However, "real reality" is surely too complex to be compressed either into a "nationalist" frame or Washington's "liberal-global" frame. One thing is clear: *Al Jazeera* is hardly the sole player in this game of ongoing cultural construction. Serious competition has now arrived in the form of *Al Arabiya*, the Saudi-owned news channel based in Dubai. The channel was profiled recently in *The New York Times Magazine* as an antidote to *Al Jazeera*.[30] Shaikh Walid Al Ibrahim, the owner of *Al Arabiya*, declared that his intent was to provide a more moderate alternative to *Al Jazeera*. "After the events of Sept. 11, Afghanistan and Iraq, people want the truth. They don't want news from the Pentagon or from Al Jazeera." The free marketplace of ideas seems to have taken hold in the Gulf, at least, guaranteeing that no single outlet will have a monopoly on framing reality. What does *Al Jazeera* feel about the competition? At a recent conference on the Arab media held at Georgetown University, Hafez Al-Mirazi, the *Al Jazeera* Bureau Chief, remarked:

> There are positive ways to answer Al-Jazeera, and there are negative ways.
> Al-Arabiya is a good answer to Al-Jazeera, even if it is a Saudi-owned, all-

news network. The idea was to get some of the people who founded Al-Jazeera and try to construct the same model, with different red lines and different sensitivities, but not to do it as big as Al-Jazeera has. In order to compete with Al-Jazeera, you have to push the envelope, widen the margin of freedom. That is healthy competition, because it prevents Al-Jazeera from retreating and covering up something that happened in Qatar, like the car bombing of some of the Chechen leaders that took place there.[1] If Al-Jazeera does not broadcast that picture, Al-Arabiya will. Thus this dynamic really helps to prevent de-liberalization by Al-Jazeera. [But] when the leader of the free world is encouraging Arab people to be free, and is promoting democracy and non-government intervention in the media, it really sets a negative example to contribute to a government-run station like Al-Hurra. By creating Al-Hurra as the "answer" to Al-Jazeera, the US is telling the Arab world that to solve its problems, get government-controlled media to answer more independent media. The US is trying to diminish a non-government-controlled media outlet that is modeled on the BBC, a public corporation.[31]

Conclusion: Washington's Double Standard

The story of Washington's confrontation with *Al Jazeera* is not yet over. It would be a shame if it ends with the closure of the *Al Jazeera* office. "Killing the messenger" who brings bad news is no substitute for sound policy. Although, as noted earlier, the criticism from high administration officials has been fierce, it appears that there are some elements in Washington who appreciate the importance of *Al Jazeera* and other transnational Arabic channels operating there. The controversy over *Al Jazeera* itself has had a beneficial effect in initiating a debate about what America's true intentions in the region are and what they should be. An administration whose foreign policy mantra is "the transformational power of freedom" should practice what it preaches when it comes to dealing with the powerful new media forces that are shaping tomorrow's Arab world. The United States should remain true to its liberal principles and support rather than suppress "the free marketplace of ideas" in the Arab world and the Middle East.

Appendix

The Al Jazeera Code of Ethics

Being a globally oriented media service, Al Jazeera shall resolutely adopt the following code of ethics in pursuing the vision and mission it has set for itself:

1. Adhere to the journalistic values of honesty, courage, fairness, balance, independence, credibility and diversity giving no priority to commercial or political considerations over professionalism.

2. Endeavor to get to the truth and declare it in our dispatches, programs and news bulletins unequivocally in a manner which leaves no doubt about its validity and accuracy.

3. Treat our audiences with due respect and address every issue or story with due attention to present a clear, factual and accurate picture while giving full consideration to the feelings of victims of crime, war, persecution and disaster, their relatives, our viewers, and to individual privacies and public decorum.

4. Welcome fair and honest media competition without allowing it to adversely affect our standards of performance and thereby 'having a scoop' would not become an end in itself.

5. Present diverse points of view and opinions without bias and partiality.

6. Recognize diversity in human societies with all their races, cultures, beliefs, values, and intrinsic individualities so as to present an unbiased and faithful reflection of their societies.

7. Acknowledge a mistake when it occurs, promptly correct it and ensure it does not recur.

8. Observe transparency in dealing with the news and its sources while adhering to internationally established practices concerning the rights of these sources.

9. Distinguish between news material, opinion, and analysis to avoid the snares of speculation and propaganda.

10. Stand by colleagues in the profession and give them support when required, particularly in the light of the acts of aggression and harassment to which journalists are subjected at times. Cooperate with Arab and international journalistic unions and associations to defend freedom of the press.

Doha, 12th July 2004.

14

The Role of Political Influence
in the US Media

James J. Zogby

The role of political influence in the US media is a complex issue and therefore, some initial observations about aspects covered in this discussion are appropriate. First, the term "media" in this context refers to the collection of mass communication instruments, including but not limited to television, radio, newspapers and magazines. Conveyors of popular culture and entertainment are also considered part of this media definition, since the images and values that they project often play a decisive role in creating the lens through which we view and interpret the information received through news reports.

In the United States today, the mass media is a powerful and all-pervasive instrument that not only informs and entertains. It also shapes ideas and behavior, defines images and creates realities. The media is not an isolated entity that operates independently to achieve its own ends. Rather, the media is an instrument, or a collection of instruments that serves specific sectors of a society. Therefore, in order to be understood in its proper role, the media must be viewed in conjunction with the interests and entities it serves and those who use its power.

Second, my remarks are confined to the arena that I know best—the United States, and to media coverage of a topic that I know well, and which I assume elicits great concern here—US policy in the Middle East.

Finally, my analysis will be broadened to include cultural and commercial influences, as well as political influences, because of the rather intimate interrelationship that exists amongst these three influences in shaping what the media covers or does not cover and how the media covers events.

During the course of this discussion, it will be clear that I am not speaking about direct political influence or media control, as may exist in societies with a state-run media, but about the kind of influence that constantly "controls" coverage in ways that may be subtle, but are nevertheless pervasive and decisive.

Most US-based news organizations like to claim objectivity as their trademark, ranging from Fox News' "fair and balanced" coverage to the *New York Times'* "All the news that's fit to print." While critics from both the right and the left of the political spectrum argue that various television networks and newspapers report the news with either a liberal or conservative slant, the reality is that the forces that shape bias in media coverage run deeper and are more complex. Cultural, commercial and political influences have a profound impact on the editorial decisions made by media outlets, as well as on the content of the information they actually disseminate.

First, there are cultural influences, the importance of which cannot be overestimated. The media exists and functions within a culture and before it interprets or acts to inform or influence that culture, it is shaped by the cultural milieu in which it exists. News reporting, like any other form of information gathering and communication, is dependent on shared meanings and values and a shared sense of history that connects the dispensers of news with their publics.

Second, there are commercial influences. It is important to recognize the fact that the media is a business where commercial interests have become central to decision-making. With the ratings of television network programs and newspaper sales playing the key role in determining advertising rates, it is necessary to reframe the relationship between media and the public. Television viewers and newspaper readers are not just consumers of the product of the media outlets; they have themselves become the product which media outlets use to sell advertising to businesses. The higher the ratings of a TV show, and the greater the share of readership enjoyed by a local newspaper, the greater the revenue intake of that media outlet. These commercial considerations have had a major impact in shaping not only what programs are aired but also in deciding the content of these programs.

Finally, there are political influences. These stem from the role of government and government policies. In a media-saturated democratic society like the United States, the relationship between the media and government is both intimate and complex. If media has the ability to influence government policy, it is also influenced and shaped by government policy. Those in government realize that their ability to control their image and message, so central to the success of their electoral strategies, remains critically important if for successful governance. Hence, there is either an ongoing contest or partnership between media outlets and the government officials they cover.

These three factors will be discussed separately, while being mindful of their often intimate interrelationship.

Cultural Influences

Major reporters, editors, TV news presenters and commentators along with the government officials and other newsmakers they cover, form a very small circle in Washington DC and New York. The often close relationships that exist within this restricted circle are evident on occasions such as the annual series of black-tie correspondents' dinners and other exclusive social functions that bring these elites together.

They share the same class, come from the same neighborhoods, socialize in the same circles and live in worlds connected by a revolving door. While much has been made of the revolving door between government and business, the similar door that connects government and media should not be overlooked. Familiar media personalities like Tim Russert, George Stephanopolous, Chris Matthews and Bill Moyers, to name only a few, are among those who have gone from government to media or media to government and back again, over the years. Much the same is true of the commentators or analysts hired by the networks to interpret the news. This whole group, therefore, largely shares a similar worldview, the same sense of history or lack of it, and the same shared policy narrative and self-imposed limits and available options of the government officials whose portfolios and actions they cover.

The same applies to the guests invited by the media for interviews, and those on whom they rely as "sources." This can be seen in a series of detailed studies conducted by Fairness and Accuracy in Reporting (FAIR), a US media watchdog, which catalogues the guests and commentators invited by networks to appear on their interview programs or who are quoted by major newspapers as sources for their stories. Overwhelming percentages of these guests, commentators and analysts are government officials, former government officials, or former military officers.

In the first month of the Iraq War, for example, over one half of all guests invited to appear on network newscasts were either current or former US government officials, and a substantial majority of those who appeared on network programs were supportive of the war. A follow-up study in October 2003 found that over three fourths of all invited commentators on TV news programs were current or former US government officials, divided about evenly between civilian and military officials, and almost 80% of all these guests were supportive of the administration's policies.

News reporters operating in this culture, or near "tribal" world of Washington elites, understand the "rules of the road," shared values, shared meanings of words and shared narratives. They accept them and largely operate in accordance with them. In this shared world, pack journalism or "group think" becomes a problem. Describing this phenomenon, former Senator Eugene McCarthy once likened the

Washington press corps to "crows on an electric wire. When one lands, they all land and when one takes off, they all take off."

And Chris Matthews, former Capitol Hill and White House aide, once teasingly described the "social set" in question as a group with shared meanings, out of touch with average Americans. When they used the word "choice," they all understood it to mean "a woman's right to an abortion," when for most Americans, it describes the "cut of beefsteak they cannot afford to buy."

And in this "tribal" sort of culture, one learns not to challenge the rules of the tribe, because to do so, is to risk "losing face," or what's worse in this particular profession, "losing access."

Commercial Influences

The myth of the "good old days" of American journalism might be recalled, when small family-owned newspapers courageously battled with government and business establishments for the truth and when major and even minor US cities had three, four or more of these fiercely independent and competitive outlets. Stories of that period have often been based more on fiction than fact, but in any case, those "good old days" are definitely confined to the past.

Today, ownership of the media has been increasingly consolidated in fewer and fewer corporate hands and cuts across the spectrum—with one corporation owning multiple radio outlets, TV stations and newspapers, or a number of networks, movie studios, major newspapers and even websites and internet providers.

Most US cities now only have one newspaper and large cities have two, and only rarely do they host more than that number. As a result of this media consolidation, the sources of information have become fewer and less diverse. Most Americans, therefore, get their information from the same conglomerate sources: one of five major networks, a handful of national newspapers (*New York Times, Washington Post, Wall Street*

Journal, Los Angeles Times), or a few wire services (Associated Press, Reuters or Bloomberg)

It is inevitable, therefore, that in this new media world, corporate and commercial interests will supersede other considerations. Profits must be made, shareholders' demands must be met, market shares must be protected, government regulations must be followed and politicians must be courted.

A review of Federal election campaign contribution and expenditure filings, for example, shows that owners of these media empires are major donors to the candidates and political parties and, simultaneously, are also major recipients of hundreds of millions of dollars in the form of political advertising revenues.

Ratings are critical to revenues, with programs, program line-up and even program content feeling the impact of the quest for higher ratings. This affects not only entertainment but news programming as well, leading to phenomena such as the following:

- The "celebrity news anchor," who not only reports the news, but, who by his/her presence, makes an event newsworthy
- The use of young starlets or "target demographic" newsreaders to attract audiences
- The "dumbing down" of evening news to include more "soft" news at the expense of "hard" news items
- The need to fill the shrinking news cycle with sensationalism and "hype."

In this brave new world of commercial journalism where "audience share" is the key to survival, and higher ratings mean higher advertising revenue, the media, like politicians, follow the polls and hesitate to overstep the boundaries of "conventional wisdom."

This serves to explain why, in the lead-up to the war with Iraq, the media was shamelessly complicit in echoing the administration's drumbeat for war. Special logos with dramatic themes, such as "Countdown to War" were created. One network even put a clock in the lower corner of the screen ticking down the time until the start of the war.

The media monitoring group FAIR has suggested that the media behaved more like "stenographers" than journalists. They reported without question and, at times, even became conduits for the Pentagon's "disinformation campaigns." As a result, the extremely effective public relations effort of the White House could utilize a compliant media to build public support for the war. This issue will be discussed subsequently in greater detail.

Political Influences

In a media-saturated democratic society like the United States, the relationship between the media and those who govern it is both intimate and complex. Presidents cannot get elected if they do not know how to present their message in the media and how to manipulate and control media.

In many ways, elections have become media contests. There is still the effort to energize and organize voters on Election Day. However, a significant component of electoral politics has become the candidate's efforts to establish a media-driven message. In some instances, this involves tens of millions of dollars in evocative paid advertising. In others, it involves carefully constructed events, designed solely for their media impact. In all cases, the candidates seek to control how their image and message is projected, while at the same time positioning themselves so that they can define the image and message of their opponents.

In this era of all-pervasive media, examples of the above are plentiful. Jimmy Carter was no match for that master of the media, Ronald Reagan. George H.W. Bush devastated Michael Dukakis because he succeeded in defining him as a weak liberal. Similarly, while riding high with his popularity as victor of the First Gulf War—Democrats took advantage of Bush's delay in beginning his reelection campaign by defining him as a "failed president" who, while winning foreign wars, ignored domestic economic needs.

Bill Clinton, like Reagan, was a master at handling the media. Time and again, he used the media effectively to define himself and his message, and succeeded in overpowering and drowning out competing messages. In instances where Clinton could not overcome the preponderance of negative press instigated by the Republican-led House and Senate, harped on by ideologically motivated right-wing commentators and then echoed by more mainstream media, the White House would go around the national media and give local journalists who were starved for "exclusives," direct access to the President.

George W. Bush used the same tactics during his two campaigns for President. When plagued by reports of "not so youthful" indiscretions, or reporting on his failed policies, Bush provided access to local media outlets casting himself as "a regular guy," a man of character and resolve, fighting Washington politics and the "Washington media."

In contemporary times, US Presidents have learned that the media is to be mastered not only to be elected, but also to govern. Reagan largely escaped media criticism over a humiliating US withdrawal from Lebanon after the devastating attack on the Marine barracks in Beirut, because it was closely followed by a quick victory in Grenada. In contrast, Clinton had to face considerable criticism over his decision to launch retaliatory US attacks against Al-Qaida interests in Sudan and Afghanistan.

George H.W. Bush's conduct during the Gulf War is probably the most successful example of this point. For months after deploying a substantial force in the Arabian Gulf, the President and his spokespersons consistently maintained that the forces were there only to "defend and deter."

Meanwhile, the administration, working with Kuwait and a US public relations firm, slowly but steadily built public support for future action. In September 1990, the US public was not prepared for an assault on Iraq or a substantial effort to liberate Kuwait. Different messages were tried and tested daily, and the public's reactions to these messages were examined and evaluated. There was an observable shift in public attitudes during the next four months. This media-driven public relations campaign worked. By the time the war actually began, the public was ready and Congress proved supportive.

Similarly, in the lead-up to the invasion of Iraq, the second Bush administration used the power of the Presidency and the public's insecurity resulting from 9/11 to move a pliant national media to build the campaign for war. The media was, in all these instances, managed in the service of policy and governance, and did not play an independent role in examining the administration's campaign efforts. As noted earlier, media often merely "records and reports" what government officials say and does not actively seek the truth. In fact, only when major dissident voices were raised did the media cover "the other side" and even then, in a coventional "he said-she said" format.

Thus in the lead-up to the Iraq war, only after "quotables" like Brent Scowcroft (former National Security Advisor under President George H.W. Bush) spoke out, or when Howard Dean (the former Vermont Governor and Presidential candidate) built a bottom-up campaign in opposition to the war, did the mainstream media raise serious questions about the war. These challenges have been further fed by new questions that are being raised, now that stubborn Iraqi realities have defied the administration's fantasy scenario about the war's successes.

The administration's response to all of this has been vigorous and sustained. They have denigrated their opponents, preyed on fear and relied on patriotic fervor, and managed an effective counter media campaign effort to win the day with public opinion—at least for now.

In conclusion, allow me to quote two celebrities in the US media—news anchors Dan Rather of CBS News and Peter Jennings of ABC News. Speaking at a 2004 Harvard University forum on the media, both made rather revealing comments that illustrate both the linkages between the political, cultural and commercial factors noted earlier and the influence they exert on the US media. As Steve Rendell of FAIR cites them:

> *Rather:* Look, when a President of the United States, any President, Republican or Democrat, says these are the facts, there is heavy prejudice, including my own, to give him the benefit of any doubt, and for that I do not apologize.

> *Jennings:* I think there is this anxiety in the newsroom and I think it comes in part from the corporate suite. I think that the rise, not merely of conservative opinion in the country, but the related noise being made in the media by conservative voices these days, has an effect on the corporate suites...This wave of resentment rushes at our advertisers, rushes at the corporate suites and gets under the newsroom skin, if not completely into the decision-making process, to a great degree than it has before.

And so it is that while technically free of government influence, the US media is nevertheless profoundly influenced by political and governmental factors. The close links between political, cultural and commercial considerations combine to make the US media more responsive to these external pressures and consequently, less free and less inquisitive.

15

The US Media Approach: Right-Wing Campaign against the UN and the Oil-for-Food Program

Jihad B. Al-Khazen

This chapter will focus partly on the official US attitude towards the Arab media and partly on the performance of the US media in covering Arab news and causes and the criticisms leveled against it in this regard. It will also study the campaign launched by the right-wing press in the United States –the mouthpiece of the neo-conservatives – against the United Nations and its Secretary General Kofi Annan.

Some Arab media outlets have been subjected to pressure from the American administration since the terrorist attacks of September 11, 2001 on the United States. This pressure increased after the war began in Iraq on March 20, 2003. On April 27, 2004, Colin Powell, the then US Secretary of State, raised the issue of the *Al Jazeera* channel with H.E. Sheikh Hamad bin Jassim bin Jabr Al Thani, the Qatari Minister of Foreign Affairs. He claimed that the channel was guilty of incitement and misguided coverage of events in Iraq (there was also criticism of *Al Arabiya* channel but it was not as sharp). The meeting took place against the backdrop of the list of alleged mistakes or faults of *Al Jazeera,* as prepared by the Bush administration. However, it seemed that aside from those "mistakes," the Americans were exasperated by the channel's focus on the destruction and civilian casualties in Iraq, and the airing of news regarding Osama bin Laden and other terrorists.

Powell's views reflected the attitude of the US administration. Donald Rumsfeld, the US Secretary of Defense, condemned *Al Jazeera's* coverage of the Iraq War, describing it as "vicious, inaccurate and inexcusable." In addition, some American generals in Iraq said that the station incited Iraqis against US troops. A statement made by the former US State Department spokesman, Richard Boucher sums up the general American attitude:

> We are deeply worried by Al-Jazeera's news because time and again we find that it is inaccurate and false. The reports it airs aim at incitement …This can make the situation more dangerous for the Americans, Iraqis and Arabs.

If *Al Jazeera's* coverage is accused of being inaccurate, we should refer to December 21, 2004, when *The New York Times* published a story – that the Pentagon did not deny – which claimed that there was a high level controversy within the Pentagon on the issue of manipulating information to influence foreign public opinion. It may be argued that such manipulation would amount to misleading the public. In December 2002, Donald Rumsfeld was forced to close the Office of Strategic Influence, which was opened after the 9/11 attacks with the objective of providing foreign journalists with false news and misleading information.

This is a well-known communist technique. The fact that Rumsfeld accuses *Al Jazeera* of exaggeration, incitement and even lies, amounts to insolence. It may be mentioned that this channel had been issued a certificate of good conduct by Alastair Campell, former Director of Communications in the office of the British Prime Minister Tony Blair. He had previously criticized the channel repeatedly for its coverage of the War in Iraq. However, he admitted that he was mistaken in his view about the channel, after visiting its offices in the State of Qatar in September 2004. He anticipated that it would be a leading media player in the future, the importance of which would increase once its sister channel in English was launched. Campell urged the Americans to consider *Al Jazeera* as an opportunity to reach out to the Arabs.

Even after 2004, the US administration has continued to complain about *Al Jazeera's* coverage of events in Iraq despite the channel's efforts

[260]

to counter these criticisms by taking particular steps or giving specific promises.

Al Manar television is an easier target because it is the station of the Hezbollah party in Lebanon and consequently, from the US perspective, it is considered a terrorist organization along with the party itself. In 2004, France stopped the television channel from broadcasting within its borders via European satellites after accusing it of airing anti-Semitic material. The United States followed suit in mid-November 2004, by adding *Al Manar* television to its list of terrorist organizations. This goes well beyond stopping its broadcasts and involves tracking its television personnel, freezing their financial accounts and any accounts of the channel itself.

The campaign against *Al Manar* television is not new. It was spearheaded by the Washington Institute for Near East Policy, which published several studies on this subject. Among these is the 2004 book entitled *The Beacon of Hate: Inside Hezbollah Television*, written by Avi Jarish, a researcher at the institute.

In fact, the issue of the US dealings with *Al Jazeera* or *Al Manar* television could have been used as a case study. However, I preferred to use as a model the campaign led by the neo-conservatives, their media and their institutions against the United Nations and its Secretary General Kofi Annan. Before discussing this, however, I will attempt to evaluate the efforts of the American media in covering the issues relating to the 2003 War in Iraq.

The Relative Failure of the American Press

When I speak of the failure of the US media in the build-up to the War in Iraq and the coverage of the war itself, I must stress that the US media was generally expected to provide professional coverage. When I speak of the limited success of the Arab media, especially television, I must express amazement because I never expected Arab television to succeed where US television failed.

As for the press, I do not want to add anything more to the kind of criticism hurled at *The New York Times*. On May 26, 2004 this newspaper published a message from its senior editors in which it said that they were proud of its coverage both prior to and after the War in Iraq. However, they felt that there were some articles in the newspaper that were published from unknown sources and without adequate scrutiny (those who are interested in more information can refer to this particular message, which refers to certain articles and records the dates of their publication).

There were two books published in 2004 about the above-mentioned newspaper. One was written by Seth Mnookin entitled *Hard News: The Scandals at the New York Times and the Future of the American Media* in which he alleges that Howell Raines, the former Executive Editor of the newspaper, wanted to prove that his liberality would not obstruct balanced coverage. To do this he permitted the publication of news during the war which later proved false. The second book is *The Record of the Paper: How the New York Times Misreports US Foreign Policy* by Howard Friel and Richard Falk. They accuse the *New York Times* of ignoring international law and stress the necessity of compliance with international norms. Perhaps the only solace for the newspaper is that it was attacked by critics on both the Left and the Right.

I cannot add to what was gathered by Michael Massing – Contributing Editor of the *Columbia Journalism Review* – about the US media and the War in Iraq. He wrote a series of articles on the failings of the US media's coverage of the war. One article in the *New York Review of Books* on May 29, 2003 was entitled "The Unseen War." The gist of the article was that Arab and European journalists asked more questions than their American colleagues. Their questions were specific and bold in raising issues relating to the accuracy of missile targeting, civilian casualties and the use of depleted uranium in shells. This American silence was also the subject of an article by John Pilger published by the British magazine *New Statesman* on September 29, 2003. In the article he referred to Charles

Lewis, Executive Director of the Center for Public Integrity, as saying that the silence before, during and after the war was worse than the silence that reigned in the 1950s.

On February 26, 2003, the *New York Review of Books* published an article by Michael Massing entitled "Now They Tell Us" in which he explained accurately and with clear examples how major US newspapers published news that later proved false. On June 24, 2004 in his article "Unfit to Print," published in the same magazine, Massing said that Bob Woodward's refusal to reveal the suspicions expressed by some senior officials about the White House claims that Saddam Hussein owned weapons of mass destruction was another indication of the desire of *The Washington Post* and other newspapers not to challenge the US administration.

Interested readers will find good and accurate material in the articles by Massing, which draw an image of the American media. However, despite Massing's views on the failings of the US media, it must be remembered that US television did reveal the torture in Abu Ghraib prison. In any case, the talk about failure and success is relative in this chapter. I believe that in failure the US press is more successful than the Arab press in its success. A comparison is impossible, especially because the US media is based on major institutions. Suffice it to state that last year, the income of the whole Arab media, from the Atlantic Ocean to the Arabian Gulf, was about $1.8 billion whereas the income of the *New York Times* alone was $2.2 billion.

Faced with a weakening professional American press, the media outlets of the neo-conservatives have become more active and vicious—a good example being the campaign waged against UN Secretary General Kofi Annan by this media. If I were to describe this media in one word it would be audacity, as exemplified by Hugh Hewitt who wrote an article in the *Weekly Standard* magazine on December 28, 2004 in which he wrote the obituary of the "old press." He said had it been a city, it would have been comparable to Stalingrad in 1944. It is regrettable that he wrote this in a newspaper whose circulation is only 60,000 copies which is small in

[263]

comparison, for instance, with *The Nation* magazine, which circulates 180,000 copies, is renowned for its staidness and credibility, and is still much less influential.

Campaign of the Neo-Conservatives and their Media against the UN

The neo-conservatives play a prominent role in the ongoing vicious campaign against the United Nations. However, their enmity with this global organization is a long-standing one. There are signs of coordination with extremist Israelis in holding common debates, waging shared campaigns and issuing simultaneous articles.

In their 2004 book entitled *America Alone: The Neo-Conservatives and the Global Order*, Stefan Halper and Jonathan Clarke remind us:

> The question of the American-UN relationships has witnessed a clash between the realism of the neo-conservatives and the UN, before the appointment of Jeane Kirkpatrick as ambassador to the UN in the term of Ronald Reagan in 1980. The 1970s witnessed heated criticism of the efficiency of UN as an organization by the neo-conservatives.

In a chapter in the book titled "Israel, Non-Semitism and the UN," the authors point to the fact that neo-conservatives were preoccupied with the United Nations itself and Israel's relationship with it. They also wrote in the 1970s:

> The UN, communism and many third world countries are anti-Semitic, so too is a large sector of the American intellectual community. Therefore, neo-conservatives, the USA and Israel partake in one ideological struggle against the common interests (of the other party).

Halper and Clarke are of the view that as the United States has emerged as the only superpower, the neo-conservatives have created a crisis in the bilateral relationships within the western world and with the United Nations. While they say that the United Nations has failed in its major task of providing a rational mechanism to prevent wars, the belief of the neo-conservatives that the United States can act alone is obviously flawed.

[264]

The War in Iraq and UN Secretary General Kofi Annan's attitude towards it made the Bush administration pursue attempts to dominate the international organization and replace those officials who are opposed to US policies with those who support them. The campaign against Dr. Mohamed ElBaradei, Director General of the International Atomic Energy Agency (IAEA), was pursued because he exhibited the kind of independence that angered Washington. The *Washington Post*, in its December 12, 2004 issue, revealed that the American administration had bugged telephone conversations between ElBaradei and Iranian diplomats, hoping to find a pretext for forcing him out of his position. The US administration had opposed his election for a third term as head of the agency.

Kofi Annan is now paying the price for his lack of enthusiasm for the War in Iraq and for having publicly expressed his opinion – in a statement to the BBC on September 16, 2004 – that the War in Iraq was not legitimate. Of course it was neither legitimate nor popular. In mid-February 2003, some 15–20 million people participated in anti-war demonstrations organized in 600 cities around the world—including 150 American cities. The UN Security Council opened its doors on February 15, 2003 to non-members and for three days the world listened to 64 speakers from all parts of the globe who were opposed to the war.

An unholy alliance has apparently been formed by many parties against the United Nations and its Secretary General. Among these are Richard Perle, Dore Gold, William Safire, Ann Bayefsky and Claudia Rosett, as well as some well-known neo-conservative publications such as the *National Review* and *Weekly Standard* magazines, and affiliated think tanks such as the Hudson Foundation, American Enterprise Institute (AEI) and the Jewish Institute for National Security Affairs (JINSA). To this list may be added the "Jerusalem Summits" attended by Christians and Zionists. All this suggests that the campaign stems from a desire to settle old scores, linked perhaps, to the UN General Assembly resolution passed on November 10, 1975, which considered Zionism a racist movement. In any case, the above resolution was annulled on December 16, 1991 under pressure from the United States. The campaign may also be related to the fact that the General Assembly has often voted for resolutions against Israel by a great majority.

As I cannot present all the details of the neo-conservative campaign against the United Nations in a comprehensive manner in this chapter, I will restrict myself to sketching the profiles of some typical neo-conservative individuals, as well as highlighting their publications and foundations.

Richard Perle

Richard Perle, the "Godfather of the Neo-conservatives," wrote an article in *The Guardian*, which was published on March 21, 2003, coinciding with the beginning of the War in Iraq. Its title was "Thank God for the Death of the UN." Perle and others like him anticipate a hasty demise of the United Nations. Perle predicted that whenever Saddam Hussein fell, he would:

> ...take down the UN with him. Well, not the whole UN. The "good works" part will survive, the low-risk peacekeeping bureaucracies will remain ...What will die is the fantasy of the UN as the foundation of a new world order. As we sift through the debris, it will be important to preserve, the better to understand, the intellectual wreckage of the liberal conceit of safety through international law administered by international institutions.

Perle claimed that the idea that the UN Security Council alone can legitimize the use of force "is a dangerously wrong idea that leads inexorably to handling great moral and even existential...decisions to the likes of Syria, Cameroon, Angola, Russia, China and France." He added that history proves that the UN Security Council is not capable of "ensuring order and saving us from anarchy." He went on to state:

> This new century now challenges the hopes for a new world order in new ways. We will not defeat or even contain fanatical terror unless we can carry the war to the territories from which it is launched.

He pointed to the UN's failure in implementing its resolutions because in his view, it is not qualified to carry out this task.

[266]

When Perle wrote this article he held the position of Chairman of the Defense Policy Board, an advisory panel to the Pentagon. Shortly after it was published, he resigned as Chairman following issues and accusations relating to a conflict of interests. However, he remained a member of the board, and only resigned in February 2004 when these issues continued to be raised.

In the 2003 book that Perle co-authored with David Frum under the title *An End to Evil: How to Win the War on Terror*, there is a massive campaign against the United Nations with a call for amending its charter to allow abortive and pre-emptive strikes.

Dore Gold

Dore Gold works as an Advisor to the Government of Ariel Sharon. He was the Israeli ambassador to the United Nations in 1997–1999 when Benjamin Netanyahu was the Prime Minister of Israel. He has also written a book entitled *Tower of Babble: How the United Nations has Fuelled Global Chaos* (2004), in which he focuses on the Arab–Israeli conflict. *Publishers Weekly* magazine described him as a one-sided, ardent dialectician. On January 20, 2004 a party was held on the occasion of the publication of the book. It was hosted by the Wednesday Morning Club in Los Angeles, which is chaired and funded by David Horowitz, an old leftist turned neo-conservative. Horowitz helped to publish *The Front Page* magazine which supported the resignation of Kofi Annan.

William Safire

This extremist writer boasts of his friendship with Ariel Sharon, whom many in the Arab World think should be tried for possible war crimes. He wrote amicable articles about Sharon on January 3, 2005 in the *New York Times*. He considers him a man of peace with no crime on his record (I will not refer to the massacres at Sabra and Shatila to attest to the contrary. Rather, I will refer only to happenings in the south of the Gaza Strip where during the last three months of 2004 alone, 350 Palestinian civilians were killed, including 150 boys below the age of 15 years).

[267]

An article by Safire drew my attention to the campaign against Kofi Annan. The article was published in the same newspaper under the title "AnnanGate." In the article Safire insisted that there was a scandal. At the beginning of December 2004 he wrote an article in which he urged Annan to resign because he brought shame to the UN Secretariat-General first by failure, and second, by obstructing work.

In *Salon* magazine, Barry Landon described Safire as the "misguiding Minister of Information." The reason for this was Safire's claim in November 2003 that Saddam Hussein had established a relationship with Al Qaeda over a period of ten years. It transpired that the source of this information was Douglas Feith, who was at that time the third man in the US Department of Defense and a senior neo-conservative.

Norm Coleman

At the beginning of December 2004 (was it just similar thoughts or based on the same sources as Safire?) Senator Norm Coleman, a Republican who strongly supports Israel and chairs the Permanent Select Committee on Investigations in the US Senate, which investigated the Oil-for-Food "scandal," wrote an article in *Wall Street Journal*. In this article he stated that "it is time for Annan to resign." He added that if this "widespread corruption" had occurred in any professional global organization, its chairman would have resigned in shame a long time ago.

Ann Bayefsky

Professor Ann Bayefsky, who works as a Senior Fellow for the Hudson Foundation, a neo-conservative institution, is one of the fiercest opponents of the United Nations. She held the Lady Davis Chair at the Hebrew University in Jerusalem during the period 2002–2004. In January 2003 she created her own website on the Internet claiming that she wanted to enhance the standards for implementing human rights in the United Nations. In 2001 she was a delegate of the International Association of

Jewish Lawyers and Jurists to the NGO Forum and a delegate of UN Watch to the Durban World Conference against Racism held in South Africa. Bayefsky publishes her articles in the *Wall Street Journal* and *Jerusalem Post* newspapers, *Commentary* and *National Review* magazines, the Canadian *National Post* magazine, as well as the *Chicago Sun Times* and *New York Sun* newspapers. All these are right-wing publications.

Claudia Rosett

This journalist has persistently written negative articles about the United Nations for years. In some of her articles she has focused on Kojo, the son of Kofi Annan. Some of her articles published by the *New York Sun* were funded by Conrad Black, the Canadian media magnate. Rosett writes a column titled "The Real World" in the *Wall Street Journal*. Some of her articles were also published in the *New York Times* newspaper, and the *Commentary*, *American Spectator* and *Weekly Standard* magazines.

Instances of Rosett's anti-UN articles abound (although the publications in which they have appeared are not detailed here). There is an article titled "Kofi Annanderson: Accounts Enron Style in the Oil-for-Food Program," hinting at a failure similar to the Arthur Anderson company in auditing the accounts of the Enron company. Another is titled "The Process of Embezzlement in Oil-for-Food: What did Annan Know and When?" Yet another is entitled "Cotecna-Annan Relationship Becomes More Sensational" in which she focuses on Kojo's work with Cotecna Inspection SA, the Swiss company which monitored parts of the Oil-for-Food Program. She claims that this article relies on "new documents" that became available after investigating the work of Kojo in the company. There are many details provided about Kojo's dealings with the Deputy Director General of Cotecna company. However, she concludes by saying that she does not know how Cotecna has actually benefited from Kojo's work for the company.

[269]

National Review Magazine

For the purposes of this study, I would have liked to add part of what has been published by *Weekly Standard* magazine, to which I will repeatedly refer. I content myself with referring to the campaign by the rightist magazine *National Review* against Annan and its calls for his "resignation if he is honest and his dismissal from office if he isn't…whereas nice Annan may not be corrupt, he has been at the top of the greatest corruption scandal in the history of the world. The UN has never been as disrespectful and non-beneficial as it is now."

The First Jerusalem Summit

The First Jerusalem Summit was held between 12–14 October, 2003, at the King David Hotel in Jerusalem. On the final day Richard Perle was given the Senator Henry (Scoop) Jackson Award. Among the participants were neo-conservative American Jews such as Daniel Pipes, Frank Gaffney and Hillel Fradkin.

The title of the first session was "The Crisis in Morality and International Policy: How Israel May be the Solution." The title of the second session, which was chaired by Morris J. Amitay, Chairman of the Jewish Institute for National Security Affairs, was "Israel Endangered: A Threat to the Free World." As for the third session, which was chaired by Herbert Zweibon, Chairman of Americans for a Safe Israel, its title was "Alternatives for a Just and Durable Peace in the Middle East." The declaration issued by the First Jerusalem Summit reads:

> We have commenced this conference because we realize that our civilization has reached a turning point. While its basic security and fundamental humanistic values are challenged by a new form of totalitarianism called Radical Islam, our resolve to fight it is simultaneously undermined by the false philosophy of Moral Relativism.

The declaration goes on to state:

> We hold that the struggle against totalitarianism, previously manifested by Communism and Fascism, to be the contemporary history's greatest test and

challenge, Radical Islam is the third such attempt in 100 years to strangle the Free World—a very lethal attempt whose perpetrators cynically exploit the very openness of the democratic society they seek to destroy.

It is worth noting that the subject of the first five sections of the declaration focuses on substituting a "Council of Civilizations" for the United Nations. Benjamin Netanyahu addressed the conference on "The Failure of the UN in Dealing with the Global Moral Crisis."

The declaration has merely spread Israeli propaganda alleging that the United Nations has betrayed its principles and allowed a dictatorial confederacy from the Third World to help radical Islam by every possible means. The declaration adds that the United Nations in its present form "cannot ensure the life and continuity of our civilization." It then speaks of *jihad* and the danger that the establishment of a state for the Palestinian Liberation Organization poses to peace, in addition to other issues often echoed by the voices of Israeli extremism. The Declaration speaks of maintaining democracy while rejecting the democracy of the United Nations, which has issued a record number of statements condemning Israel for violating international law.

The Second Jerusalem Summit

More than 150 delegates from Israel, Europe and the United States participated in the Second Jerusalem Summit, which was held at the King David Hotel from November 27–30, 2004. Professor Bayefsky was one of the speakers at the summit, which witnessed ongoing hostility towards the United Nations. The participants continued exploring the establishment of a "Council of Civilizations" in place of the United Nations.

The first part of this summit focused on "Assessing the UN: The Search for Alternative Approaches." Bayefsky described the United Nations as the leader of the campaign of anti-Semitism around the world as demonstrated by the "shameful" Durban Conference. She added that 30% of all resolutions of the Human Rights Committee in the United Nations are against Israeli violations of human rights.

Among the speakers was Dore Gold, whose subject was "Why the UN Undermines International Peace and Security." The topic of the second session was "Enhancing the Status of Muslim Women as Means of Regime-Change." The session was chaired by Baroness Caroline Cox, a Member of the UK House of Lords (who is well known for her hostility to Muslims). The film *Submission* was screened. The film was scripted by Ayaan Hirsi Ali, a Dutch Parliamentary Deputy of Somalian Muslim origin and co-directed by her and Dutch director Theo van Gogh, who was killed because of his association with the film.

In another session, the conference proposed a humanitarian, not political solution to the Palestinian-Israeli conflict, indicating lack of support for any Palestinian state. However, the solution proposed by Daniel Pipes, Director of the Middle East Forum and a powerful American neo-conservative, was to terminate the work of the United Nations Relief and Works Agency (UNRWA) for Palestine Refugees in the Near East. In other words, his proposed solution was to halt essential aid to the Palestinians besides denying them a state. Isi Leibler, the Senior Vice-President of the World Jewish Congress, attacked the United Nations and described it as being a "burden to global tranquility." Shabtai Shavit, a former Mossad Director, urged the establishment of an international authority to replace the United Nations.

Hudson Institute

"It's Not the Problem of Israel Alone," reads the title of an article by Bayefsky, which appeared on December 17, 2004 in the *American Outlook* journal, published by the Hudson Institute. It was one of several articles, debates and sessions of the Hudson Institute, one of the neo-conservative institutions involved in the campaign against the United Nations. Bayefsky said that over the last four decades, the United Nations has turned into a "propaganda machine for the Palestinians…its goal is to weaken Israel, portray it as a devil and then annihilate this devil." The same writer also attacked the UNRWA. It seems that by such attacks, the

[272]

neo-conservatives and the Sharonites are seeking to force the Palestinians into making peace.

Heritage Foundation

The Heritage Foundation is another institution dominated by neo-conservatives. On December 15 2004, it highlighted an article written by Nile Gardiner, Fellow at the Margaret Thatcher Center for Freedom, in which he called on Annan to resign. This was a call which had been echoed by Senators Coleman and Stone of the American Congress. Gardiner said that it was in the interest of the White House to support the call for Annan's resignation. He said that history would accuse Annan of colossal failure since he has supervised an era that has witnessed massive erosion in the reputation of the international organization. Gardiner added that Annan is a "lame duck" as a Secretary General and an obstacle to the efficacy of the United Nations. He stated that real reform to make the organization efficient, transparent and accountable is impossible in the presence of Annan.

American Enterprise Institute

This institute is another example of political extremism. On December 8, 2004, it organized a debate in which the United Nations was sharply attacked. The participants included George Lopez from Notre Dame University, Edward Mortimer who is responsible for communications in Kofi Annan's office and Danielle Pletka, the Director of the Institute and journalist Claudia Rosett from the Foundation for the Defense of Democracy. The discussion was moderated by Joshua Muravchik.

Mortimer, a respectful and well-known journalist who has worked in London, said that Saddam Hussein exploited the Oil-for-Food Program in two ways: to receive bribes from importers first, and, second, to impose additional amounts of money on exporters who bought his oil. He added that people ask how the United Nations had overlooked this matter. In fact, the United Nations did not overlook this. Rather, it had provided the UN Security Council with information about the additional amounts of money imposed on Iraqi oil. Mortimer admitted that the program was not wholly correct and expected that the United Nations would have its share of the blame in several reports on the subject. One of these reports was by the US Congress, which condemned the United Nations right from the very start. The other was prepared by Paul Volcker as head of the independent inquiry into the United Nations Oil-for-Food Program.

Pletka violently attacked the United Nations saying that the mistakes of the Oil-for-Food Program reflected the problems within the organization. She considered that the UN's internal investigations were fabricated. Pletka thought Annan was linked to some of these affairs, as well as to corruption. As for Rosett, she said that the United Nations as an organization "is rotten and corrupt."

I do not claim to know all that has been written in the campaign against the United Nations. However, I must point out that Joseph Loconte wrote an investigative report in the *Weekly Standard* titled "The U.N. Sex Scandal," in January 2005. Also, the well known Canadian extremist David Frum, who co-authored *An End to Evil* with Richard Perle, claimed in a television interview that the United Nations "acted inadequately" in the relief operations after the tsunami catastrophe that hit the coastal areas of South Asia, and that this was why the United States hesitated to entrust the United Nations with managing the relief operations. In reality, only a few days had passed after the disaster, when the neo-conservatives and their supporters in the US Congress decided that the United Nations had failed to deal with the catastrophe.

Defending the United Nations

The international organization is not without friends and liberals have stepped in to defend the reputation of the United Nations. On its website, the Fairness & Accuracy in Reporting (FAIR) organization published a report in August 2004 entitled "A Timely Scandal: Oil-for-Food Charges

Conveniently Tarnish UN." In this report, Seth Ackerman wrote that as the Bush administration failed in Iraq, it transferred the responsibility for the country to the United Nations, so that the latter could be held accountable for the outcome. Some believe that this attitude on the part of the US administration amounts to apostasy. Thus with the completion of the transfer of authority, a "scandal" arose around the United Nations, which had been in charge of the humanitarian program in Iraq that has since been suspended. Ackerman said that the right-wing press exaggerated the subject, and that there was an obvious contradiction in news broadcasts to the extent that those who received the news were confused and failed to see any mistake committed by the United Nations.

Ackerman added cynically that decoding the campaign requires complete reliance on what Claudia Rosett wrote, especially in the *Wall Street Journal* and other publications. While Rosett herself could not be unbiased in the light of her writings, she was summoned to give testimony before the Congress which seemed equally biased. Ackerman insisted in his article that no convincing evidence was provided of the involvement of UN officials in the scandal, despite the thousands of words with which Rosett had embellished her articles. He added that the resolutions executed by the United Nations were those of the member states, especially those in the UN Security Council. Rosett was well aware of this fact, yet she accused the UN officials.

Jude Wanniski, a former Editor-in-Chief of the *Wall Street Journal* and the founder of Polyconomics, Inc. wrote an article entitled "The Neo-Cons Smear Annan: What Oil-for-Food Scandal?" which was published in the *Wall Street Journal* on December 11, 2004. In this article he argued that the campaign against the United Nations formed part of the neo-conservative goal of founding "an American empire with a permanent site in Baghdad." Since achieving this goal requires the removal of all potential obstacles in the way, the neo-conservatives were moving to target world organizations that have been established to prevent war through diplomacy and threats of sanctions. For this reason they insult the United Nations and the inspectors of banned weapons under the

[275]

chairmanship of Hans Blix and Mohamed ElBaradei. He added that when France, Germany, Russia and China opposed regime change in Baghdad, the neo-conservatives used their megaphones in the press to allege that these countries were behaving in a manner consistent with their own selfish interests. Wanniski documented that the charges against Kojo Annan were first published in the *New York Sun*, a small newspaper founded just four years earlier by Conrad Black, the Canadian media magnate. As Chairman of Hollinger International Inc., Conrad Black had appointed Richard Perle as a top executive of its media management and investment wing called Hollinger Digital Inc. Consequently, Perle was listed on the advisory boards of several US media corporations, including those with links to *Fox News* and *National Review* magazine.

The Nation Magazine

Joy Jordon wrote in the liberal magazine *The Nation* that the UN Security Council failed to stop trade between Iraq and Jordan and allowed smuggling under the eyes of the multinational interception force, which had the task of monitoring the international embargo imposed on Iraq. Later, it transpired that the force was wholly composed of US marines. Thus the failure to halt the oil smuggling operations managed by Saddam was in fact the failure of the American Navy. The writer stressed that the Oil-for-Food commissions were not given out in the way it was publicly reported by the media. The journalist concluded that the most important organization in the world was suffering damage owing to exaggerated smear charges, and that the world ought to fear the consequences.

As for Jim Lobe, who works for Inter-Press Service, he wrote on November 30, 2004 that the neo-conservatives were echoing the charges leveled by the extreme right against the international organization.

Brian Urquhart

Sir Brian Urquhart was Under Secretary General of the United Nations, from 1974 until 1986 and has occupied distinguished international positions for almost 40 years. He explained to Radio Free Europe and Radio Liberty in mid-December 2004 that the tense relations between the United States and the United Nations reflected the activity of a small circle in Washington that enjoys the support of the American administration. He said that those within this small circle reject the idea of the United Nations itself and that no one should underestimate the influence of this group.

James Dobbins

To my thinking, what James Dobbins has written is perhaps the best defense written about the United Nations. James Dobbins, a former US Assistant Secretary of State, served as the US ambassador to Afghanistan. He is now the Director of International Security and Defense Policy at RAND. On December 10, 2004, the *Washington Post* published an article in which he stated:

> The American anger over the transfer of the money of the Oil-for-Food Program has missed its goal. First, no US money has been stolen. Second, no United Nations money has been stolen. And third, the program has achieved its two goals: providing Iraqis with food and stopping Saddam Hussein from rebuilding weapons of mass destruction.

Dobbins thought that the Program was most successful in terms of applying sanctions for humanitarian purposes.

Diplomatic Support

On December 3, 2004 Sir Emyr Jones Parry, the UK ambassador to the United Nations, announced that Britain fully supported the multinational system of the United Nations and its Secretary General. At the same time Jack Straw, the Foreign and Commonwealth Secretary, said that "Kofi Annan is doing an excellent job as a Secretary General."

However, the United States hesitated in supporting Annan. A week later, John Danforth, the American ambassador to the UN at the time, said that it was important for the United States to clarify its position and added: "We don't ask for Kofi Annan's resignation, nor do we want that. Nobody suspects his personal impartiality." When Danforth was asked about Kojo Annan and his work with a Swiss company linked to monitoring the Oil-for-Food Program, he merely said, "Kojo is an adult person." Danforth thought that referring the Oil-for-Food Program to a federal jury eventually was not just a remote possibility and pointed out that there were six congressional investigations into the case. This seems rather strange considering that the money that was legally paid or stolen was not US money.

I read about a meeting in the flat of Richard Holbrooke, the American ambassador to the UN in Clinton's administration, at which a number of UN supporters discussed ways to save the international organization and its Secretary General. What emerged consistently and repeatedly in the details of the discussions was the need for the United Nations to reform its relationship with Washington.

Finally, the problem of the United Nations with the neo-conservatives is an issue affecting all. The neo-conservatives have virtually thrown a cordon around the Bush administration, which is difficult to break through. The administration listens to them and implements some of their extreme ideas. Even when the administration realizes that it has made a mistake, as in Iraq, its unwillingness to acknowledge this, drives it to commit further mistakes.

MEDIA AND THE IMAGE
OF THE OTHER

16

The Role of the Arab Media in Shaping the Western Perspective of Arabs

Jean AbiNader

The notion that the Arab media does have a role in shaping the Western perspective of Arabs is a novel concept that reflects the dramatic changes occurring in global communications over the past decade. It may be argued that there are two propositions involved in this topic. First, that the Arab media, utilizing contemporary technology, is able to reach Western audiences. Second, that Arab media coverage has a resulting impact on Western images of Arabs without specifying the type, depth, duration or audiences affected. Alternatively, it may be argued that the concept is a proposition that will generate data to inform us in a scientific way about the Arab media in its "role" as a shaper and influencer of public opinion on a certain topic or issue—in this case, "images" of Arabs held by Westerners. Stemming from this query, the answers may presumably provide the Arab media with information on which to build communication strategies and policies that can indeed give the Arab media a role in affecting the Western perspective of Arabs.

In any of the above constructs, the notion of a connection between media and public opinion or perceptions is the critical variable. This relationship has been examined by US social scientists and pollsters since the 1940s, and there is no concrete evidence establishing a causal relationship between media and public opinion in the absence of other environmental influences.[1] The key summary statement that can be made is that public opinion accelerates or deepens notions already held by the target public.[2] Whether or not that enhanced perception results in specific actions is subject to challenges. Notionally, then, there are four layers of inquiry that need to be addressed: What are the existing Western perspectives of Arabs that may or may not be influenced by the impact of Arab media? Which Arab media organizations have the capacity and desire to reach Western audiences? What are the priorities of the Arab media organizations that seek to impact Western audiences? Who and what are the mediators that facilitate or restrict the access of the Arab media to Western audiences?

Changing Environment and Key Propositions

In the past decade, there have been many articles and conference discussions on the changes in the Arab media, particularly since the advent of satellite video broadcasting in the mid-90s. Descriptions of the Arab media ranging from "the voice of terrorists" to "independent voices of change" can be found in both Western and Arab papers. Journals such as Transnational Broadcasting Studies (TBS) in Cairo, provide insightful articles and interviews on Arab media and how it is viewed within the Arab world and elsewhere. As with much else in the Arab world, media is undergoing a transition, from being state-owned and state-directed to becoming state-influenced. The level of self-censorship is most obvious in national newspapers and is also evident in the coverage policies of the so-called "independent" satellite stations. No one can honestly argue that their station management is not conscious of the reality that advertising revenues account for perhaps $150–180 million of the approximately $5 billion in annual production costs across the breadth of the Arab satellite television community.[3] Being the latest rendition of the "Voice of the Arabs" can be very lucrative with the right investors, who are expecting something other than currency as a return. The most independent but not necessarily objective media is to be found on the Internet when one moves beyond official websites and sanctioned news sources to blogs and publishers who do not rely on institutional financial backing.

[282]

A similar revolution is occurring in the West, where satellite and cable offerings have increased exponentially, and audiences of less than one million in a market of more than 220 million US viewers are considered significant! Tens of thousands of Internet blogs spew forth an abundance of critical and uncritical remarks, opinions and commentaries; thousands of chat rooms and list serves connect users globally; and special interests increasingly drive most political activities in capitals throughout the country. This media cornucopia means that identifying target audiences is another challenge given the backdrop of a self-conscious and expanding electronic Arab media and fragmented, highly segmented, bombarded viewing audiences in the United States. The current analysis, which confines itself to the United States, includes several propositions that ought to be explained at the outset:

- Given data from polling studies, it is difficult to define a single "Western [in this case, "US"] perspective" of Arabs.
- There are multiple audiences in the US market with varying levels of interest in international affairs and more specifically, the Arab world.
- There is no proprietary channel by which Arab media can address these multiple audiences. The dominant use of the Arabic language and the availability of Arab media primarily through satellite subscription limit access to US audiences.
- There may be only very limited, and possibly not neutral, audiences for English language news and features from the Arab world.
- A critical consideration is defining the role that intermediaries such as the US government and US media play in selectively presenting Arab media products in the US markets.

Sources of US Images of Arabs

Arab–US relations, and the images that are derivatives of those relations, are defined largely by the political contexts and environments that have emerged since World War II around three poles: energy/commerce, security/terrorism, and emerging national political identity/Islam. There

[283]

are sub-groupings within each vertical pole, and the resulting network of interests are dominated by US ties with Israel, US support for Arab regimes, the push and pull of oil policies, and since 9/11, an intrusive and somewhat ill-defined "global war on terrorism." US images of Arabs have become increasingly discrete as the general US population has learned that all Arabs are neither Saudis nor Egyptians, that Palestinians can be obstacles or partners for peace, and that oil continues to fuel governments that may or may not be "friends" of the United States. Again, there are crosscutting identifiers that reflect the contemporary fixation on terrorism and oil. These include the following, often mistaken perceptions: that all Arabs are Muslims, that the majority of terrorists are Muslims, and that Arabs sometimes use oil money and funds from Muslim organizations to support groups that are anti-American. There are few benign images of Arabs in contemporary US media whether the discussion is about Arab immigrants in the US or Arab students studying in *madrassas* wearing blue jeans and *hijabs*. Even the *Bedouin* and *fellah* have been transformed into the cultural icons of a supposedly backward and repressive culture, which it is claimed, denies opportunities to women, subjects children to a misguided and misanthropic education, is corrupt, and is invariably jealous of those benefits that accrue to the lucky millions who live in Western-style democracies.

It is in this context that the Arab media must weigh the proposition that they do have a role to play in influencing US perspectives of Arabs.[4] After all, "perspective" means to see data in relationship to one another. If Arab media is to create a perspective, then it must be able to define or redefine relationships among various phenomena, in this case, Arab behaviors.[5] This challenge has two main components:

- the content of the message itself
- the context that places the message in a setting familiar to the listener

Questions that need to be asked are: Who listens to Arab media? Who cares about the content of the messages? Analysts agree that Arab media lack a distinct identity in the US as a news source.[6] From the rapid emergence of Arab media on US channels after 9/11 and during the war against the Taliban government in Afghanistan, to images of Osama bin Laden and terrorist cadres announcing their victories and *fatwas,* culminating in the seamless and endless font of destruction and death pouring out of Iraq, Arab media are seen as sources of "images" not content, a means by which the "bad guys" communicate their intentions and messages to a misguided and ignorant American public.[7] Arabs are no longer the romantic figures of widescreen movies and picturesque tourist destinations. Arabs are people at war with themselves, with their leaders, with America, with the world at large. The conflation of Arab and Muslim identities extends this simplistic view into a template that views Islam as being adrift with its principles being distorted by fanatics who claim to speak in its name and kill its adherents as well as the infidels. Islam, as a non-centralized religion, lacking a single, distinct voice of authority is unable to compete effectively in projecting its image because so many claim to speak and act in its name without decisively countering its detractors across the spectrum.[8]

Who Watches? Who Cares?

Who watches Arab media? What does this tell us about US perspectives? It should be clear that Arab media, first and foremost, shape and direct their productions to their audiences—Arab people with access to satellite dishes, cable, Internet and similar communications technology. It is absurd to assert that it should be otherwise, given the somewhat narrow band of viewers in the West and the United States in particular. Moreover, there is the very Western concern with "market share" as Arab satellite television is very competitive.

Unfortunately, because of linguistic limitations and the general US lack of curiosity about "foreigners," the primary audiences for Arab media in the US are Arab watchers and Arabic speakers. These include immigrants, academics, analysts and language learners, all of whom bring their unique perspectives to their viewing experiences. Immigrants and

Arab Americans generally offer uncritical appraisals of Arab media unless they believe that finding anti-Americanisms in whatever Arabs are doing and saying separates them from the others. Academics, ranging from those informed by the Middle East Media Research Institute (MEMRI), Campus Watch, and pro-Israel think tanks, to those of the Noam Chomsky/Edward Said school of anti-colonialism and anti-imperialism, study the Arab media under microscopes that are sometimes concerned less about objective research as they try to fit data into preset molds rather than discovering new models or assaulting unproductive or biased paradigms.

Analysts, either in think tanks or government agencies, have their own difficulties in objectively assessing the performance of Arab media. Content analysis is often done by people who speak little or no Arabic and who rely on selective translations from MEMRI and US government sources. In other cases, the analysis is carried out by Arabic speakers with little or no comprehension of Arab culture and Islamic perspectives, who thereby lack the context in which to perform content analysis. When analysts are heard to say that the best source of information on Arab worldviews is *The Arab Mind* by Raphael Patai, then it becomes clear that there is a problem.

Similarly, think tanks that are committed to certain points of view ranging from neo-conservative to libertarian have a vested interest in describing the Arab media as an illustration of the gap between their performance and their Western counterparts. Comparative analyses reflect criteria based on the Western experience of journalism and news coverage, with little reflection on why and how Arab media is or is not an accurate reflection of or dominant influence on Arab public opinion. Arab analysts are also quick to make claims for the Arab media that generally feed this perception of a direct relationship between the Arab media and Arab behavior. Hussein Amin contends that "Arab transnational television coverage of the [Iraq] war has already been playing an important role in the [US-Iraq] conflict, increasing public anger towards America and Britain."[9] Accepting statements like this, devoid of any longitudinal measure of Arab public opinion towards the US and Britain before the war, feeds the impression that the role of Arab media is a negative one or that the public anger is somehow unjustified. The style of the Western media itself does not communicate effectively in Arab markets, and if the Arab media's primary audience is Arab, then the appeal to the Western audience is hardly a priority. In American-style news "dispassionate objectivity is contained so as not to weaken the validity of the facts. In the Arab world, emotional neutrality, in an emotionally charged context, can be perceived as deception. If one hides one's emotions, what else is being hidden?"[10]

The most significant in terms of the US audiences are those whose interests converge on the Arab and Muslim worlds and who are interested in understanding, and sometimes proclaiming, "Why do they hate us?" It is this very small yet significant chorus of voices that is the source of the multiple US perspectives on Arabs, and it is this stage that is the most difficult for the Arab media to penetrate effectively. This group is made up primarily of American media groups with various orientations, policy analysts and commentators with a particular view of US–Arab relations, and Members of Congress and the Administration who sense the value of Arab media but lack the confidence or comprehension to engage it in a long-term positive partnership to advance the many mutual interests of Arabs and Americans.

How the Arab Media Reaches the US Markets

The first problem to be addressed in examining the role of the Arab media in the West is to comprehend the latter's definition of the former. As has been pointed out, Arab media organizations are seen primarily as transmitters of images. Even *Al Jazeera*, the pioneer in Arab satellite broadcasting, is defined largely in these terms. As Marc Lynch points out, "While Al Jazeera's news coverage receives the most attention in the West the station's live political talk shows have had the most revolutionary impact."[11]

So we can conclude that the general public seldom sees the Arab media except as a source of generally unhappy images from the broader Middle East. *Fahrenheit 9/11* and *Control Room* are excellent examples of the bind in which the Arab media are placed in dealing with the West and the United States. Given their desire to "brand" themselves as "the" source of Arab news, and the narrow track of cooperation available in working with the US media, there are few options at present for Arab media organizations to become more clearly defined in the United States. It is very difficult to overcome the perception that the Arab media are first and foremost the sources of images unavailable to the US media for various reasons. Contrast the "embedded" Western (and some Arab) reporters during the war against Iraq with those whose access was neither sanctioned nor protected by the coalition military forces. For the embedded reporters, the war became a video game of night vision tableaus, bright continuous flares of artillery and bombings disassociated from the human and physical damage, strictly controlled briefings, and a continuous stream of advisories issued by the Department of Defense. The Arab media, exposed in the field, had the monopoly on pictures of the carnage, death, injuries and humanity on both sides that were absent from the Western/US media. Over time, as the stark differences in reporting became embarrassing to some editors and reporters, the Arab media again became the source of images that brought home to viewers the terrible cost of war. People were reminded that these media organizations carried messages from Osama Bin Laden and later Abu Musab Al Zarqawi, taunting the United States and condemning its intentions and actions.

During and after the war, members of the Bush Administration condemned *Al Jazeera* and others as anti-American and inciting negative public opinion:

> Tensions increased after the US intervention in Iraq, and Washington again complained to Qatar. Powell told the Qatari Foreign Minister in April 2004 that Al Jazeera was inciting Arab audiences to violence against American troops, and that its new coverage was undermining good US-Qatari relations. Secretary of Defense Donald Rumsfeld accused *Al Jazeera* of "vicious, inaccurate and inexcusable reporting," and other officials echoed these charges.[12]

In providing their viewers with Arab perspectives on the war and enabling Arabs to hear what "insurgents and terrorists" had to say directly, without the intervention of governments, Arab media organizations were testing the ground for defining their identities vis-à-vis the global media marketplace, with little concern for their acceptance by the Bush administration. Despite lapses in judgment regarding what constitutes a news story as opposed to editorializing and sensationalism, what is interesting from an analytical point of view is to observe the maturation process of the Arab media, which is torn between serving their audiences in their own way, and gaining acceptance from the world at large.

From a research perspective, it may be noted that there has not been a comparative study of how the Iraq war story was told, in words and pictures, in other countries and in other regions. It would be interesting and useful to compare any shifts in reporting content with public opinion polls taken throughout the buildup, invasion, collapse of the Baathist regime, and the post-war conflict. Looking at percentages of change would compensate for the differences in starting points in public opinion towards the US campaign and the pre-existing attitudes towards the United States in that part of the world.

Regardless of one's opinions on linkage claims, it is doubtful that there is any hard data that makes a defensible link between reporting by the Arab media and increases in anti-Americanism or a disposition to harm Americans. Anti-American sentiment has been growing in the Arab and Muslim worlds over the past decade. In fact, Arab public opinion has hardened against the United States since the beginning of the second *intifada* and the collapse of effective peace negotiations between Israel and Palestine. Coverage of these views and images made the Arab media quite unpopular with the US media and politicians who complained about the lack of balance in Arab reporting and commentary. Even the film industry has been assailed for its complicity in producing anti-American features, a statement challenged by Walter Armbrust, an expert on the Arab mass media.

> Egyptian cinema has sometimes attracted attention in the United States not for opposing political Islam, but for fomenting anti-Americanism or even anti-Semitism. Such charges are exaggerated, and a case of the pot calling the kettle black, given the anti-Arab bias prevalent in parts of the American media...But they [controversial Egyptian films] are not so much anti-American as they are nationalist.[13]

However, to accept this notion that the Arab media is conscious of its role as an expression of Arab public opinion puts it at odds with those in the US Administration and media who want to see political change along Western models take place throughout the region. The US media mostly plays its role in shaping images of Arabs both by defining "good" Arabs as exceptions to the usual stereotypes, and emphasizing the need for Arab society to forswear terrorism and become modern. The Iraq war is only the latest installment in this sad affair of US–Arab media relations.

> But neither the US nor the Arabs have taken any serious systematic approaches to learn why there is this gap of misunderstanding and mutual mistrust. The concern seems now more focused on how to set up media channels for reaching the other side, rather than about the content of the exchanged messages. Arabs have not been able to effectively use the existing mainstream US media. The common assumption is well known: their absenteeism is by the design of stronger lobbies in the US media. The less talked about reason is the chronic absence of media content that Arabs are able to convey to the US general public.[14]

It is clear that Arab media are at a threshold, building capability and working hard to be taken seriously without losing their primary audiences, and finding their integrity and credibility questioned while still being courted in some fashion by the US government.[15] It is worth examining what forces define Arab media in the United States and what is the impact of those intermediaries who largely control the access of Arab media to US audiences.

Exposing the Filters

Arab media reaches the United States largely through secondary sources although logos of major Arab stations are seen with more frequency as their footage is incorporated into mainstream US newscasts. Since the footage is in Arabic, audio tracks are provided by US stations; unless it is *Al Hurra*, where there is no disclaimer that this is a US-funded broadcasting station. Thus the two major vehicles for Arab media visibility in the US market are the US media and the US government. Arab media's relationship with US counterparts has shifted considerably since 9/11 and the war against Iraq.[16] As one frustrated Arab news anchor based in Washington, DC explained it, "They [US media] want us to become like them on Middle East news and forget that we are Arab stations. We don't want to follow their standards, which have failed miserably in all the issues surrounding the Middle East."[17] Jihad Fakhreddine points out this conflict:

> Each of the main US print media has taken its turn in giving the Arab states the recipe for political change, which will grant them good ratings under western political norms. The key Arab states that have been particularly targeted by this campaign insist that this is not the official US policy towards them. But in the Arab world there is very little differentiation between the official US policy towards the region and the mainstream US media. In anything, the US media is perceived to be even more critical than the US government on issues related to the Middle East conflict, Islam, and the Arab world. From the Arab perspective the current provocative role played by the mainstream US media can only contribute negatively to the US public diplomacy campaign towards the Arab world.
>
> For the Arabs, most puzzling is the timing and scale at which the negative media rhetoric is sustained against them in the US press…From the Arab perspective, the US media has never been considered friendly to Arab causes…This campaign in the US media has been a rude awakening to Arabs and Muslims at all levels…Thanks to the US media, the Arabs have realized the power of media in projecting images or even influencing foreign policies. The scale of the new profiling of Arabs and Muslims at world levels has, like never before, exposed the feeble media power Arabs and Muslims possess to fend off what is being projected about them.
>
> The agenda set by the mainstream US media does not seem to be geared towards reconciliation.[18]

When asked how Americans perceive the Arab media, a US policy analyst pointed out that the most common image is *Al Jazeera* and the charges that it incites violence.[19] Yet, the analyst continued, there is no real content analysis to measure the performance of the Arab satellite channels on these various indictments of anti-American broadcasting. The analyst felt that despite the recent inclusion of *Al Manar* on the US State Department's list of the supporters of terrorism, based in large part on a critical analysis provided by the pro-Israeli Washington Institute for Near East Policy (WINEP), the clear trend for Arab satellite channels is towards greater professionalism, a broad range of products that engage the Arab public, and genuine efforts to create programming that brings challenging information to the viewers. Yet the damage has been done. In general, Americans do not perceive the Arab media either as friendly or objective. The analyst also noted that US government bureaus in general lack the level of Arabic fluency or understanding of media as a service industry, to develop a strong contextual framework for their content analysis, relying instead on think tanks, MEMRI, and other analysts for guidance. The analyst commented that the great amount of attention given to *Al Jazeera* based on misperceptions and untested assumptions probably credit the satellite station with more influence than is warranted.

Furthermore, the analyst indicated that most studies on the Arab media do not look at programming other than newscasts or editorials. The vast majority of the programming is overlooked and it is assumed that it has no relevance for analysts. It is ironic, the analyst believes, that in the past decade, there is growing pressure for self-censorship in the United States while it is less so in the Arab world in many instances. Finally, the analyst calculated that the tense environment in the Broader Middle East and North Africa (BMENA) region, especially since 9/11, has created a heightened sensitivity to propaganda on all sides, and the Arab satellite channels are being swept up in the competition to make one's message dominant in the market.

A policy analyst at a major Washington-based think tank expressed similar opinions.[20] Given that Arab media programs are "foreign" broadcasts, they are reduced to a series of images selectively used by the

US media. There is limited and declining interest among US media in forming news sourcing agreements with Arab media organizations given domestic political pressures that are fluid and temperamental ["Some days we like them; some days we don't!"]. The key to stronger cooperation and less selectivity in integrating Arab media with American media is editorial agreement on the premises of issues and stories to be covered so that there is less need to "translate" a story for the American public. The most important untold story line, the analyst believes, is to look at the dynamics of change in the region and encouraging coverage of how Arabs are taking control of their daily lives and aspirations. The coverage of the Forum for the Future illustrates the gap between reporting good news about Arabs wanting to pursue reform and the bad news reflected in the US media that they do not want to do it the American way.

Such is the situation. The role of the Arab media is mediated in the United States by the US media and the US government. The US media is reluctant to accept Arab media organizations as qualified news sources. Arab media are filtered through a series of stereotypes, some of which stem from their perceived "unprofessional standards." Some images of the Arab media are based on their unique access to newsmakers, especially Al Qaeda, insurgents in Iraq, and other less-than-attractive images of Arabs and Muslims. The reporting of the statements and actions of such newsmakers has diminished Arab media credibility and made it difficult to establish long-term relations with the US media. The latter, fragmented and often driven by political interests, use simplistic images of the Arab media even though the US media does not have the capacity or willingness to analyze events in the region with the same thoroughness and exposure as the Arab media. The negative images of the Arab media expressed by the US government also impose a reality check on US media organizations that want to cooperate with Arab media. Neither the US media nor the government allocates sufficient resources to carry out accurate research to validate the assumed negative impact of the Arab media on public opinion and behavior in the Arab world and elsewhere.

[293]

Next Steps

So, perhaps the Arab media will have to make it a priority to influence US and Western perspectives of Arabs. The GCC information ministers "announced plans to launch a joint media campaign to promote Islamic moderation among their citizens and improve their countries' image abroad; Saudi Arabia launched *Al Fajr* television channel "to spread the message of the Holy Quran;" Morocco launched Muhammad VI Quranic Radio to tackle various religious issues, especially fanaticism; and new liberal papers were licensed in Egypt and Jordan.[21] Arab media must also decide whether changing Western perspectives is part of their mission. If so, they should look at the research that has been done on the relationship between media and public opinion in order to generate strategies that respect their audiences while crafting their roles as "centers of influence" towards the West. As Stuart Soroka notes, "Mass media content is the most likely source of over-time changes in individuals' foreign policy preferences."[22] He points to a number of criteria that may help define policy preferences and priorities among Americans that are relevant to the Arab media. He begins with research on "issue salience" and "issue opinions" as factors that indicate how citizens define their MIP (*most important problem* facing our country). *Issue salience* refers to the relative significance of an issue to people—what they pay attention to; and *issue opinion* has to do with their policy preferences.

Soroka finds that the more media attention given to a foreign policy issue, the greater the public concern about that issue. As one might assume, if the news is largely negative, it will have a significant and negative effect on the public's interest in that element of foreign policy. Additionally, when news articles emphasize the importance of an event to the home country, issue salience increases significantly. Soroka does not claim that the MIP measure tells us about the direction of public opinion, only that it is important to the public and needs to be correlated with policy preferences in order to have any utility over time. "Evidence suggests that the changing salience of foreign affairs for the public is in large part reflective of media content and that changes in issues salience can have both indirect and direct consequences for foreign policymaking."[23]

Another concept that is being developed to determine the relationship between public opinion and foreign policy is that of "international trust."[24] Analysis of this concept by Brewer et al., suggests the following:

> It may be that mass beliefs about the general trustworthiness of other nations are uninformed or misinformed—which, in turn, could lead citizens to form opinions about world affairs that they would not hold with full (or fuller) information. For example, one might argue that the low levels of international trust among the mass public lead citizens to form unrealistically cynical views...[25]

Regardless of what the various research results demonstrate, the challenge remains of how the Arab media, if it wants to, can gain direct access to the US market in order to influence "the Western perspective of Arabs." The first step is to understand how Americans define their interests in the region. The notion of "international trust" may have some utility in identifying the tendencies of various constituencies in the United States towards Arab world concerns. The study by Brewer, et al, argues "Citizens use generalized beliefs about how much their nation can trust other nations to form judgments about world affairs." They begin with the notion that people who believe that they can trust strangers[26] have a general preference for internationalism and favor international involvement. This concept of "social trust" combines with "political trust," which is based on people's normative expectations of government institutions, to form their opinions about other countries—international trust.

> We conceptualize international trust as a generalized belief about whether most foreign countries behave in accordance with normative expectations regarding the conduct of nations. Citizens with high levels of international trust see the realm of world affairs as a friendly environment where trust and cooperation among nations is the norm; in contrast, citizens with low levels of international trust see the same realm as a hostile environment where all nations strive against one another for advantage and readily defect from cooperative efforts.[27]

The study does not claim that international trust is the sole explanation for how people form beliefs about world affairs, "but rather to show that it plays an important role in shaping mass opinion that has previously gone unrecognized." They further point out "...the nature of international trust may differ from the American public to other nations—in fact, our theoretical account implies that is it likely to do so when those other nations face different international environments..."[28]

Given these insights into how Americans form their attitudes about foreign policy, it is not too much to assume that these same variables affect American perspectives about Arabs or any other nationality or ethnic group. Polling that asks respondents to match descriptors (trustworthy, friend of the US, unreliable, lacks credibility, etc.) with national groups (Saudis, Chinese, Russians, French, etc.) have been carried out for more than a decade. Analyzing this data over time and correlating it to political events may at least present some inferential relationships worth considering as a basis for further research. In addition, a great deal of polling has been done regarding various aspects of the threat of terrorism, supporters of terrorism, attitudes towards Muslims and Arabs[29] and similar studies that also present a wealth of data and correlations that may be very useful in determining if it is even possible to develop a set of targets in American public opinion that are likely to respond to Arab media efforts.

Once this has been determined, several strategic decisions must be made. First of all, is it worth the effort for the Arab media to have a long-term effort to affect US public opinion or will other parties continue to mediate their access to US audiences? Second, will the evolving and growing sophistication of the Arab media gradually develop sufficient credibility and weight to garner cooperative agreements for news sourcing with the American media? Is it the best hope of the Arab media to mature rapidly and enhance production quality across the board so that they will achieve a distinct professional identity regardless of relations with the Western media? Will political events in the next decade make this a moot point as terrorism is defeated, a two-state solution is achieved in Palestine, political, economic, and social reforms become sustainable priorities for Arab governments, and the West develops a sense of propriety in dealing with Islam in its many manifestations?

While none of these scenarios are mutually exclusive, it is illogical to encourage the Arab media to change merely to appeal to the West. As the status of Arab media has shifted with efforts such as the Dubai Press Club, the Al Jazeera Center for Media Training and Development, a multitude of bilateral and multilateral training initiatives, efforts to eliminate ministries of information, the loosening of restraints on professional journalists and their societies, the growth of media options, and the continuing struggle between governments and media about censorship and standards of journalism, the days of a docile, fawning, unfocused Arab media have passed. The role of the Arab media in shaping the Western perspective of Arabs begins with recognizing its role in shaping the national and regional perspectives of Arabs themselves.

17

Communicating with the Arab and Islamic World: US Public Diplomacy and German Diplomacy of Dialogue

*Mohammad Ibahrine**

After September 11, 2001, Americans sensed the urgent need to communicate with the world, particularly the Arab and Islamic world. Anti-Americanism seems to have become a new buzzword in today's world. For scholars of international politics and international political communication, 9/11 presented a pressing need not only to examine the root causes of this unprecedented expression of anti-Americanism but to solve America's image problems by explaining US policies and ideas to overseas audiences.

For many Americans, public diplomacy helped to win the Cold War. In the aftermath of the events of September 11, 2001, many Americans, including policy makers, journalists and academicians concluded that public diplomacy could help to overcome anti-Americanism, particularly in the Arab and Islamic world. The US political leadership responded to this anti-Americanism by a public diplomacy campaign to "win minds and hearts," and thus create a new resource for power in international relations.

Public diplomacy has become an almost invisible feature of contemporary global politics. International politics has been turned into an arena of competing news stories between media players. In recent years, it has been agued that the "means to success in world politics" is to know

_____

* The author would like to thank Dr. Kai Hafez, Chair for International and Comparative Communication Studies at the University of Erfurt, Germany for his valuable advice, continuous encouragement and immeasurable help along the way.

how to wield word politics or soft power effectively.[1] The media has become one of the central players in international politics. The rise of *Al Jazeera* demonstrates that the crucial resources of soft power are outside the control of governments. *Al Jazeera* has established credibility by developing a reputation for its comprehensive "on-the-ground" coverage of political and military events.

This chapter compares the functioning of two different approaches to public diplomacy. Relying on the works of Joseph Nye, the links between international relations and public diplomacy are discussed, with a particular focus on the role of international communication. The second section examines the main features of US public diplomacy. The third section will outline the approach of German public diplomacy, which is based on cultural and educational programs.

International Relations and Public Diplomacy

International relations are witnessing a shift in the way countries manage their foreign affairs. The success of a country's foreign policy relies on the success of its public diplomacy. Immediately after September 11, 2001 several policy makers, politicians and academics argued that in an age characterized by the limits of military power, public diplomacy should be made an integral part of US foreign policy.[2] In a Brookings Institution Report, scholars argued that "public diplomacy" is the "primary tool" through which the United States could harness "soft power." The term "soft power" was first coined in the late 1980s by Joseph Nye, outgoing Dean of the Kennedy School of Government at Harvard University. It has been defined as "the ability to get desired outcomes because others want what you want. It is the ability to achieve goals through attraction rather than coercion." It is also described as "the most efficient" means of power "as it does not require the use of force or huge financial payoffs to achieve or sustain one's policy objectives."[3]

In the context of America's relations with the Islamic world, "public diplomacy" has become vital to the country's "battle for the hearts and minds" of the citizens of the Islamic world. It has been suggested even by realists that something should be done for the sake of the "non-kinetic aspects of the war." For example, Donald Rumsfeld, US Secretary of Defense, has talked positively about the necessity to do a better job "with respect to the nonmilitary aspects of the challenge."[4] Consequently, the Pentagon established special offices to help reach public diplomacy goals.

Since September 11, the public diplomacy divide between how Arabs and Americans perceive their relationships has steadily increased, leading to an unprecedented level of tension between the two sides.[5] As communication conflicts intensify, public diplomacy is likely to play an important role. "Once the stepchild of diplomats, it has recently assumed its rightful place in international relations," as one commentator rightly put it.[6] The importance of the media factor in international relations and diplomacy has become evident. Media coverage of an event has profound implications for international relations. As Madeleine Albright, former Secretary of State, contended, "CNN is the sixteenth member of the U.N. Security Council."[7] World politics is played by word politics. However, in a globalized and digitalized world, characterized by 24/7 news channels, public diplomacy is as relevant as ever. Communication is being treated as integral to the structure of the international system, and this explains the rapidly growing role of international broadcasting for public diplomacy in the context of US foreign policy.

According to Kenneth Y. Tomlinson, chairman of the Broadcasting Board of Governors, it was September 11, 2001 that changed the US approach to international broadcasting.[8] The function of public diplomacy and broadcasting is the confrontation of "an iron curtain of misunderstanding" that separates America from the Arab and Islamic world. Aware of its declining image among the public in the Arab and Islamic world, the United States was forced to fight back with its own communication efforts. Americans have paid attention to the role the media plays in feeding international conflicts. The American "information edge" proclaimed by Nye has not solved America's image problems. However, in an age characterized by an information overload, attention rather than information is the scarce resource. The new public diplomacy will not be determined by the "information edge" but by what we call the "communication edge." Therefore, communication has assumed a central place in the public diplomacy paradigm.

US Public Diplomacy

Realist, unilateralist, short-term state-centered paradigm

After the dramatic events of September 11, 2001, public diplomacy has regained its importance in communicating US foreign policy. The Bush Administration announced a program of public diplomacy to reach out to the Islamic world. The White House believed that such an initiative, based on public diplomacy practices coupled with marketing expertise, would bring an accurate understanding of America to the Islamic world and thus reduce the potential for future conflict. Henry Hyde, the Chair of the House International Relations Committee, called for the State Department to consult "those in the private sector whose careers have focused on images both here and around the world."[9] The immediate task was to try to figure out how to mediate its message and communicate with the Islamic world. The United States launched an intensified public relations offensive at the State Department. In less than a month, on October 2, 2001 the State Department hired Charlotte Beers, a veteran Madison Avenue advertising executive, as Under-Secretary for Public Diplomacy and Public Affairs, with the main mission of "selling" American policies and viewpoints to Arabs and Muslims. According to her, public diplomacy is "not really about advertising...it is about informing, engaging and influencing key international audiences...to advance US interests and security and to provide the moral basis for US leadership in the world."[10]

To "brand" the United States in a positive way, the State Department launched in late 2002, a marketing campaign film titled "shared values," which involved a series of television advertisements, depicting the daily lives of Muslims being treated well in the United States. To the surprise of many Americans, the intended audiences derided the film for being amateurish and for not addressing Muslim concerns about US policies toward Iraqis and Palestinians. A number of Arab countries even refused to air it, with Egypt and Lebanon turning it down outright and Jordan withdrawing its clearance. [11]

As Americans learned that the Arab and Islamic world rejected its vaunted "shared values" campaign about the Muslim community in the United States, Beers described the gap between the US view of itself and how others perceive the country as being "frighteningly wide."[12] Public diplomacy could not successfully manage the declining US image. Beers' conclusions were supported by recent polls that showed rising anti-US sentiment in the Arab and Islamic world and a dramatic decline in support for the United States. Polls released by the Pew Research Center for People and the Press in highlighted the depth and breadth of the anti-US sentiment in the Islamic world in the aftermath of the Iraq War of 2003. In several Arab countries, more than 90 percent hold an unfavorable view of the United States and negative perceptions have spread across the Islamic world. [13]

Consequently, there was greater pressure on the professionals behind the management of US public diplomacy. On March 7, 2003, Charlotte Beers resigned amid mounting criticism of her performance.[14] The State Department's marketing television advertising campaign film was seen as insincere and artificial and was ultimately counterproductive. Mamoun Fandy, President of a Washington-based think-tank and an expert on Arab politics and media, described it as "expedient, insincere, and likely to inflame anti-American sentiment."[15] The Arab press called it a propaganda machine designed to distract attention from American anti-Arab policies.[16]

Much of the current debate about US public diplomacy has focused on which methods are appropriate for dealing with the Arab and Islamic world. After the Cold War ended, many Americans believed that victory was a direct result of public diplomacy via radio broadcasts including *Voice of America (VOA)* and *Radio Free Europe/Radio Liberty (RFE/RL)*.

The conventional wisdom was that public diplomacy programs changed the minds and attitudes of target audiences. Consequently, Americans concluded that public diplomacy can also help to overcome anti-US sentiment, particularly in the Islamic world.

Advocates of public diplomacy have debated over which mechanisms such programs should rely upon and which instruments, including radio and television broadcasts, and cultural exchanges, are more effective. Nye distinguishes between three types of public diplomacy, all of which have equal importance. The first type is daily communications, which involves explaining the context of domestic and foreign policy decisions. The second type is strategic communication, which involves special focus on particular policy themes or initiatives. The third type is public diplomacy through scholarships, exchanges, training and conferences.[17]

Nye's categorization is useful in understanding the Bush Administration's preferred type of public diplomacy. In fact, the Administration's first approach was to rely on broadcasting to send messages to the Muslim world. Indeed, the US Fulbright program is designed to develop mutual understanding between the people of the United States and those of other countries. However, many US voices criticized the government for devaluing such international exchanges of students and scholars as a tool of public diplomacy.[18] The Bush Administration focused on broadcasting while underestimating the worth of educational, cultural and intellectual exchange. According to K. Tomlinson, the former Director of the Voice of America (VOA), Washington focused on electronic media for three fundamental reasons: First, "television has already become the most important medium in the region for news and information, since more than four out of five people get all or almost all of their news from television and they trust television more than any of the other media channels." The second reason is that "satellite television offers the chance to break the grip of the regime over audiovisual media outlets to promote pluralism of opinions." The third and most important reason is to win "more long-term and reliable friends through the provision of accurate, balanced and reliable information." In addition, there are other reasons behind the US determination to focus on broadcasting: first, because there has been a broadcasting tradition in American public diplomacy, and second, in the media age, the United States was determined to fight media with media.

Radio programs such as the Voice of America are funded and managed by the US government. These programs are supposed to disseminate international news and reports as well as to explain US policies. The aim of these communication channels is that Americans can "tell America's *own* story" to foreign publics. This has been done by a combination of powerful medium-wave and FM transmitters, as well as popular regional satellites. The broader international broadcasting strategy of the United States has relied on a "combination of *Radio Sawa*, RFE/RL's Radio Free Iraq, Arabic language Internet, and a US Arabic language satellite television" as the best strategy.[19]

As Joseph Nye observed, "the world's leading communications country has proven surprisingly maladroit" in conveying its message. Nye argued that US soft power has been declining, "because many of its crucial resources are outside the control of governments, and their effects depend heavily on acceptance by the receiving audiences."[20] For Americans, the success of public diplomacy requires that Arabs be kept in the passive mode of being receivers of US views and programs. According to Washington, Arabs are short of objective information and the United States can provide them with balanced news. Americans think that the problem is simply lack of information, and that if the Arabs knew what Americans know, they will see things in the same way. However, no longer do audiences in the Arab and Islamic world depend solely on the broadcasts of the British Broadcasting Corporation (BBC), Voice of America (VOA) and Deutsche Welle for reliable sources of information. Gone are the days of the First Gulf War when Arabs could only receive reliable information from the Cable News Network (CNN).

The exercise of soft power in the "Age of Al Jazeera," when the US government is no longer the sole player in the arena of public diplomacy, has become increasingly difficult. *Al Jazeera*, an Arabic satellite television channel, was established in Doha, Qatar, in the Arabian Peninsula in November 1996 with $137 million-plus from the Qatari government.[21] Since 2001, *Al Jazeera* has aired tapes from Osama bin Laden and was the only foreign network to broadcast from Afghanistan, which made its reports "a staple of America's nightly news."[22] The channel claimed an estimated 45 million viewers.[23]

During the US involvement in Afghanistan and Iraq the real focus of public diplomacy was to shape public opinion in the Arab and Islamic world, rather than to focus on the military interventions themselves. Americans were aware that *Al Jazeera* has a wide audience in the Arab and Islamic world and its impact is "far greater than any other media outlets." Consequently, *Al Jazeera* turned out to be a major focus of US public diplomacy efforts, because it carried reports and commentaries that helped to communicate American arguments and views.

American acknowledgment of *Al Jazeera's* credibility was indicated by the appearance of senior US policy-makers and heavyweight politicians on the channel. Within days of the 9/11 attack, US Secretary of State Colin Powell appeared on *Al Jazeera*. Following Secretary Powell's lead, US Secretary of Defense Donald Rumsfeld and National Security Adviser Condoleezza Rice also appeared on the channel. However, US officials accused it of an anti-American bias and later highlighted the station's alleged connections to Al-Qaeda.

The Iraq War presented *Al Jazeera* with an opportunity to prove its worth to an enlarged audience. *Al Jazeera* was perceived by many people around the world as the most accurate source of information on the Iraq War.[24] It aired gruesome images of dead US soldiers and prisoners being interrogated by the Iraqis. Moreover, it featured statements by Saddam Hussein before his capture and aired insurgents' messages.[25] According to many critics, *Al Jazeera's* coverage of Iraq, especially its airing of hostage videos and beheadings was controversial.

Decisions about what aspects to cover have enormous consequences for international diplomacy. Americans wanted *Al Jazeera* to perform their public relations role for them as other Arab regimes always did.[26]

[306]

Finally, the United States boycotted *Al Jazeera* because it was assumed that the latter was airing hostile interviews and verbal attacks on the United States and that its coverage was biased. While campaigning to promote press freedom in the Arab world, Washington has constantly pressured the Qatari government to exercise control over *Al Jazeera*. This move has greatly undermined the US communication-based public diplomacy.[27]

In October 2001, Colin L. Powell, former US Secretary of State complained to Qatar's Ruler, H.H. Sheikh Hamad bin Khalifa Al Thani, that the station was helping Al-Qaeda by broadcasting Osama Bin Laden's messages without comment. As tensions increased after the US intervention in Iraq, the White House complained again. Powell told the Qatari Foreign Minister, H.E. Sheikh Hamad bin Jassim bin Jabr Al Thani in April 2004 that *Al Jazeera* was inciting the Arab people to commit violent acts against US troops, and that its news coverage was undermining relations between the United States and Qatar. In the same vein, Donald Rumsfeld, the US Secretary of Defense, accused *Al Jazeera* of "vicious, inaccurate and inexcusable reporting."[28] A number of US officials have made *Al Jazeera* a natural target, holding it responsible for the pervasive spread of anti-American attitudes in the Arab and Islamic worlds.[29] However, recent research by US scholars was unable to substantiate such charges.[30]

During the Iraq War, *Al Jazeera* faced reporting restrictions and its reporters were banned from some places in Iraq. Moreover, its offices in Iraq were attacked, just as they had been in Afghanistan in 2001. On April 2, 2003, *Al Jazeera's* offices in Basra were shelled and a car clearly marked as belonging to *Al Jazeera* was shot by US soldiers a day before the Palestine Hotel incident. On April 8, 2003 *Al Jazeera* once again came under attack when a US army missile hit its Baghdad office, killing one of its correspondents, Tareq Ayoub.[31]

Indeed, the United States' powerful military intervention could have destroyed *Al Jazeera's* offices and killed its journalists, but could not undermine its credibility and its effect—key resources of power in the "battle to win minds and hearts" in the Arab world. Ultimately, it is *Al Jazeera's* coverage that has emerged triumphant. What made *Al Jazeera* unbeatable in the competitive international arena is its capability to present stories in the Arab context. US public diplomacy efforts will be rendered even more difficult, when *Al Jazeera* develops and launches comprehensive English language programming by early 2006. Consequently, one of the serious challenges that US public diplomacy has encountered is "how Washington confronts Arab media" successfully.[32]

Radio: Radio Sawa

On March 23, 2002, the US Broadcasting Board of Governors, the advisory group that oversees media programs, launched Radio Sawa, which means "together" in Arabic. It is a new US government-funded Arabic language program of international broadcasting to reach out to young listeners in the Arab world.[33] Radio Sawa is a 24-hours-a-day, 7-days-a-week service with 48 daily newscasts in Arabic being transmitted by various means: AM, FM, shortwave, transmitters, digital audio satellite and the Internet.

Radio Sawa airs news, analysis, editorial comment, talk and music. It not only delivers a mix of news bulletins and popular music, but provides an ideal access to American opinion. It plays mostly music for young people, which makes its content heavy on pop music and light on news (10 to 20 minutes out of 60). Radio Sawa's motto is "you listen to us; we listen to you." Its programming format throughout the day is aimed at appealing consistently to a particular target audience and does not vary from hour to hour.

Radio Sawa targets young Arabs under 30, who constitute more than 50 percent of the population in the Arab world. According to informal US survey data, Radio Sawa is already the most popular station in many Arab capitals and has gained a significant audience. Other sources reported that Radio Sawa has little penetration in the Arab world.[34] However, it is too early and thus too difficult to assess the effectiveness of Radio Sawa in quantitative terms. According to Gary Thatcher, the Director of the

Middle East Radio Network, based on the Voice of America, which has never had good penetration in the Arabic world, surveys showed Radio Sawa having a regular audience of 2 percent. For him, this percentage is likely to double, given the "huge potential."[35]

Satellite Television: Al Hurra

After launching Radio Sawa, plans were developed for an Arabic-language television network to compete with other Arab satellite televisions and to promote favorable images of the United States to the Arab public. More importantly, senior US officers think that a television station can resolve America's reputation problems. The Broadcasting Board of Governors has proposed the creation of a television station to challenge the views expressed on *Al Jazeera* and other Arab satellite television stations. According to some US officials, President Bush's 2004 budget request, which helped to create a US Arabic-language television network, is "the most important public diplomacy initiative of our time."[36]

On February 14, 2004, the United States launched a new $62 million Arabic language satellite television channel, *Al Hurra,* which means in Arabic "the free one," to deliver US messages in Arabic across the Arab world. The decision to launch *Al Hurra* was seen by many in America and in the Arab world as one of the clearest examples of the strategy to combat and counter competing messages from Arab news organizations such as *Al Jazeera. Al Hurra* broadcasts its programs from a state-of-the-art studio in Springfield, Virginia. Many who have watched *Al Hurra* programs reported that it resembles state-run Arab television channels that carry only pro-regime propaganda.[37] On launch day, it interviewed the US President, following a well-established tradition in the Arab media landscape. It not only broadcasted to the whole region, but also produced, adapted and aired programs for certain countries such as Jordan, Sudan and Egypt.

Initial indications were that young people watched *Al Hurra* for its music and turned to *Al Jazeera* when they wanted to obtain information and news. However, some reports said that *Al Hurra's* audience includes not only the young but also older people who turn to it for news and information. According to Jon Alterman, Director of the Middle East Program at the Center for Strategic and International Studies (CSIS), a Washington think tank, *Al Hurra* cannot serve the needs of American public diplomacy, partly because governments generally do not produce good television, and partly because of questions about journalistic independence and the potential for propaganda.[38] While W. Rugh considered the launching of these media outlets as a step in the right direction, he asserted that the content has severely reduced the effectiveness of American broadcasting in terms of public diplomacy.[39] Whether *Al Hurra* will establish the necessary credibility remains unclear.

The Internet

Internet technologies, including the World Wide Web, electronic mail, desktop and laptop computers, as well as streaming and compression technologies that enable audio and video images to traverse the world, have fundamentally changed the way governments interact with people. The Internet is affecting cross-cultural and political relationships in international affairs and has become a fundamental medium for communicating the foreign policies of governments to the international public and to audiences previously beyond reach. The State Department has used the Internet intensively in its public diplomacy efforts to win minds and hearts in the Arab and Islamic world.

After the events of New York and Washington, the State Department's Bureau of International Information Programs (IIP) compiled evidence linking Al-Qaeda and the 9/11 attack into a brochure entitled, "Network of Terrorism." This pamphlet was designed to convey the State Department's version of September 11, 2001, to overseas audiences and to persuade governments that Al-Qaeda is operating worldwide by relying on its global networks, and that defeating it requires a global solution.

The general text of the Network of Terrorism pamphlet was posted on the IIP's website and made available in more than 30 languages, making it accessible to the international public, including embassies, media and scholars. The website of the IIP attracted a worldwide audience of a million visitors. It was reported that some media could widely distribute it because it was easy to download and they could reproduce it at minimal costs. A well-known example was *Panorama*, Italy's most influential weekly news magazine, which published the document in the Italian language.

Internet use by American public diplomats has made information more accessible to an unprecedented number of people of all backgrounds. However, as argued earlier, information is available in plenty, but credibility is crucial. Reputation has always counted in international communication, but it is credibility that occupies the center stage. Thus, US public diplomacy has encountered what Nye calls the "paradox of plenty."

In his illuminating article in the *Foreign Affairs,* Marc Lynch criticized the American government for not taking Arabs seriously. According to him, US public diplomacy involving "advertising and the promotion of radio stations featuring popular music" has proven "ineffective, if not alienating. A number of people in the Arab and Islamic world considered the American intensive and market-based public diplomacy as mere propaganda campaign designed to promote American "national interests."[40] Nye argued that the public diplomacy that "appears as narrowly self-serving or arrogantly presented are likely to consume rather than produce soft power...public diplomacy that appears to be mere window dressing for hard power projection is unlikely to succeed."[41]

The credibility crisis stems from the fact that many in the Arab and Islamic world perceive a sharp discrepancy between the words of US public diplomacy and the actions of US foreign policy.[42] International broadcasting is most effective when it operates first and foremost according to the highest standards of independent journalism. It is based on establishing a direct line of trust between those delivering news and information and those consuming it. Consequently, reliable and accurate news is imperative for success. The question that remains unanswered is: To what extent can the US "broadcasting, broadcasting and broadcasting" strategy convert Arabs and Muslims to a world view that the White House seeks to promote? Or will the intensive and varied use of media outlets have the unintended effect of promoting the worldview of those whom it seeks to convert?

German Diplomacy of Dialogue

Idealist, multilateralist, long-term civil-society centered paradigm

Much contemporary research on international communication is taking place in the field of public diplomacy, including its nature and strategies. A number of publications have been written about public diplomacy in the United States[43] in England[44] and in Canada.[45] This chapter offers a systematic comparison between two approaches to public diplomacy, namely the American and the German. Germany has developed and used a new concept of public diplomacy, based on what we call "diplomacy of dialogue." Therefore, Germany is a good example of those countries with limited public diplomacy resources that used soft power very adeptly.

The German diplomacy of dialogue is consistent with Nye's third type of public diplomacy. Germany accomplishes a great deal of its public diplomacy through a range of instruments such as international broadcasting, cultural activities, educational exchanges and scholarships, programmed visits and conferences. In 1998, the Red–Green (Social Democratic Party–Green Party) coalition government redefined German foreign policy in a manner consistent with ideological orientations.[46]

Table. 17.1: Comparative Investments in Soft and Hard Power: United States and Germany

	Public Diplomacy	Defense	Year
United States	US$1.12B	US$347.9B	2002
Germany	US$218M	US$27.5B	2001

Source: Joseph Nye, "Soft Power: The Means to Success in World Politics," 2004, 23.

Since the reunification, Germany has witnessed a growing debate on the presumed role of the "dialogue of cultures" in reducing and easing political tensions between Europe and the Islamic world. Germany is keen on what senior officials call "fair and balanced communication and interaction between the two sides, which can energize and enhance the type of understanding that allows for peace and cooperation."[47] After the end of the Cold War and the peaceful reunification of Germany in 1989-90, German interest in the role of public diplomacy increased and the diplomacy of dialogue has become a constant pillar of German foreign policy with the Arab and Islamic world. With the arrival of the Red–Green coalition government in 1998, the trend has been intensified. From the outset, the pacific message of Joschka Fischer, the German Foreign Minister, was obvious. The style and substance of the German diplomacy of dialogue grows out of Germany's political culture, including its modern history.

For many years now, dialogue with the Muslim world has formed a fixed component of German foreign cultural and educational policy. In the aftermath of September 11, 2001, Germans rediscovered the importance of dialogue with the Arab and Islamic world. A content analysis of Fischer's speech at the United Nations on September 12, 2001, indicated the continuity of interest in public diplomacy and dialogue with the Arab and Islamic world. The tenor of Fischer's speech was in keeping with the idealist and "integrationalist" traditions of German foreign policy since the Second World War.

The dialogue was intended to serve as a long-term strategy to campaign against international terrorism and as a means of pursuing foreign policy, particularly with the Arab and the Islamic world. A number of useful steps have been taken to coordinate and intensify this dialogue. In 2002, for instance, the post of Commissioner for the Dialogue with Islam/Dialogue among Civilizations was created at the Federal Foreign Office and was directed by former ambassador Dr. Gunther Mulack.[48] This appointment was made despite severe budget cuts that year, which led to a reduction in the German diplomatic corps assigned abroad.[49] Germany has taken more proactive measures to build a long-term understanding of Arab and Islamic societies, cultures and ideas and to intensify the "cultural and educational exchange programs."[50]

In contrast to conventional forms of diplomacy that focus only on dialogue between governments, the German diplomacy of dialogue aims to communicate with non-state civil society actors, such as NGOs, the media and the general public to promote greater understanding between Germany and the Arab and Islamic world. According to Rainer Schlageter, the General Director of Communication at the Federal Foreign Office, public diplomacy is "the sum of all communications activities directed towards selected elite, contact organizations, and the broader public worldwide."[51] With its international reputation and experience with civil society groups, Germany has positioned itself to strengthen multilateral international institutions as well as to cooperate with international organizations. The target of the German diplomacy of dialogue is to build long-term relationships that create an enabling environment for dialogue between cultures. This is designed to build goodwill between Germany and the countries of the Islamic world over time.

Germany lacks the communication capabilities and the resources to engage in international promotion on the scale of the United States. However its approach, based on mutual understanding, has enjoyed good acceptance. The German diplomacy of dialogue is formulated in consultative ways that involve the views and interests of Arabs and Muslims. A case in point was the Frankfurt Book Fair in 2004, at which the Arab world was given the status of Guest of Honor, and thus provided with a platform to project its image not only in Germany but also across Europe.

The development of a cultural public diplomacy intended to build a long-term relationship based on educational exchanges has become an objective of German foreign policy. According to Fischer, foreign cultural and educational policies should be integrated into the formulation of German foreign politics.[52] All programs involved in cultural public diplomacy such as student exchanges and language training have played a role in enhancing better understanding between people in different cultural contexts. Increasing scholarly exchange programs have given German culture more visibility at Arab universities and libraries.[53] The aim of cultural public diplomacy is not to influence those same people to accept its values but to gain a long-term, cumulative effect.

**Table 17.2: Comparative Campaign Characteristics:
United States and Germany**

Characteristics	United States	Germany
Type	Public Diplomacy	Diplomacy of dialogue
Philosophy	Realist	Idealist
Approach	Unilateralist	Multilateralist
Objective	Win/lose	Win/win
Nature	competitive	cooperative
Orientation	State-centered	Civil-society centered
Means	Media relations	Cultural programs
Emphasis	Image	Message
Intensity grade	Intensive	Extensive
Term	Short-term	Long-term
Institution	Under-Secretary for Public Diplomacy and Public Affairs	Commission for the Dialogue with Islam/Dialogue among Civilizations
Style of Leadership	1. Advertising Executive 2. Former diplomat & Acting Executive 3. Former Entrepreneur	1. Former Diplomat 2. Former Diplomat

Source: Author

By focusing on a culturally and educationally-based comprehensive dialogue, the German diplomacy of dialogue has played an important role in projecting an acceptable image of Germany and a great amount of goodwill in the hearts and minds of a number of citizens in the Arab and Islamic world. The diplomacy of dialogue by the Red–Green coalition government has enhanced the credibility of German foreign policy and thus increased Germany's soft power based on non-coercive influence.

German Broadcasting: Deutsche Welle

Since 1953, Germany has developed its broadcasting presence through *Deutsche Welle*. This broadcasting service has been dedicated to providing interested radio and television audiences and Internet users abroad with a comprehensive picture of political, cultural and economic life in Germany, and explaining German positions on national and international issues. Since 2002, the Arabic programs of *Deutsche Welle* have been increased to about six hours a day. *Deutsche Welle* focused on issues pertinent to the dialogue of cultures.[54] It also produced and broadcasted special programs on inter-cultural dialogue. This trend has intensified with the proliferation of audiovisual media and technological advances. *Deutsche Welle* even exploited new broadcast niches. For instance, in 2002, it launched a three-hour long Arab television program.

While using broadcasting as a means to promote the diplomacy of dialogue, the German government has not sought to determine the content of *Deutsche Welle* broadcasting. Hearts and minds in the Arab and Islamic world will not be won by excessive or manipulated information but by media values such as reliability, constancy and authority. Accuracy and truthfulness are the keys to maintaining credibility and trust among targeted audiences. A content analysis of the *Deutsche Welle's* coverage of the Iraq War showed that the government had not interfered with the editorial functions of *Deutsche Welle*.[55] The channel's standards of objectivity in handling the news were respected. Between Germany and the Arab and Islamic world the gap in trust is minimal. International observers said that the *Deutsche Welle* has acquired some advantages over other international broadcasting outlets. At a time, when Arab people have grown distrustful of government-sponsored media, the *Deutsche Welle* has gradually gained a good penetration in the Arabic world and has not faced a high level of skepticism.

Deutsche Welle is a part of Germany's communication efforts and as a media platform, has proven far more fruitful in building trust between cultures than any overt propaganda. It has been regarded as a credible dialogue partner. The diplomacy of dialogue has raised Germany's credibility, a scarce resource in a world inundated with information.

Public Affairs Agencies: Institute for Foreign Affairs

The *Institut für Auslandsbeziehungen* (Institute for Foreign Affairs, IFA) was founded in June 1951 as a successor to the German Overseas Institute. Germany has gradually developed professional public affairs agencies, specialized in managing German public diplomacy and the diplomacy of dialogue. In 2001, the IFA marked 50 years of its existence.[56] One major focus of the IFA is the coordination of German international cultural relations. The IFA views itself as a service provider for foreign cultural policy and as a future-oriented workshop for intercultural and civil society dialogue.[57]

With regard to the Arab and Islamic world, the IFA's aim is to manage the dialogue with Islamic world through several cultural activities. Cultural exchange is perceived as "give and take" and not just as a one-way street exporting German culture or a German "Leit-Kultur" (leading culture).[58] It is about an exchange of experiences, perceptions, ideas and visions. One of the highlights of this dialogue is the two-way street media dialogue forum, involving multipliers such as journalists, academics and elites from both sides, who can successfully convey the message to their respective audiences and societies. The media dialogue forum has served as a platform where participants such as journalists, opinion-builders and intellectuals exchange perceptions on the workings of the media, media systems and its role in facilitating communication between the two cultures. This exchange helps participants to understand the root cause of cultural misunderstandings and address these communication problems through concrete projects. Measures were adopted that gave more

[317]

concrete form to the dialogue and served to make participants view the cultural exchange as an enriching experience.

The diplomacy of dialogue is "accomplished not through nice words on high levels but through concrete projects and programs."[59] The German diplomacy of dialogue has taken into consideration the interests of local civil societies and focused on cooperation with them as local partners in order to work out concrete programs. Islamic organizations with which there was no previous contact are identified as target groups and included within the ambit of the diplomacy of dialogue. The IFA works with NGOs and institutions to support the development of reliable, independent media outlets across the Arab and Islamic world.[60] The underlying purpose is to influence powerful non-state actors who have a more relevant role in highlighting the achievements of dialogue.

Germany does not have the advantage of widespread use of the English language as a medium. However, the use of English as a *lingua franca* has impeded a successful diplomacy of dialogue with the Arab and Islamic world. The use of European languages such as English and French in previous forms of dialogue has excluded significant segments in the Arab and Islamic world. Until recently, the dialogue did not even consider Arabic as a language of communication. The masses and Islam-oriented elites who communicate predominantly in Arabic were practically excluded. The use of Arabic has considerably expanded the reach and scope of dialogue to these segments, which represent dynamic forces in the Arab and Islamic world and thus triggered a significant change in terms of communication.[61] By using Arabic as a language of communication and thus including new Islam-oriented elites the dialogue has attained a degree of credibility, which in turn, has guaranteed that the results of conferences, workshops and seminars have reached important segments of the Arab and Islamic worlds.[62]

Educational and Cultural Institutions: The Goethe Institute

The diplomacy of cultural dialogue is accomplished through educational exchange programs for students. One of the main focuses of the German diplomacy of dialogue is education. The Goethe Institute has played a central role in the cultural and educational policies of Germany for over 50 years. This institute is the Federal Republic of Germany's main cultural organization, which operates all over the world. The Goethe Institute operates language centers, reading rooms, libraries and cultural societies all over the Arab and Islamic world. This cultural presence has created a large network of people familiar with Germany and its people.

The Goethe Institute is a politically independent, autonomous body. Yet the institute's interaction with the Foreign Office is governed by general agreement.[63] The Goethe Institute cooperates with partners from public as well as private cultural institutions, including the federal states, local authorities and the private sector. Despite a small budget of approximately €278 million at its disposal compared to other cultural institutions, it actively supports all those involved with Germany, its language and culture.

The institute promotes the study of the German language abroad and encourages international cultural exchange. The Goethe Institute's key principle is "dialogue and partnership." According to its President, Jutta Limbach, dialogue is achieved through communication and exchange. Further, she considers "cultural diversity" as an enriching element of German society.

Conclusion

Today, the United States has a serious image problem across the world. Moreover, the gap between America's own perceptions and how the world perceives the country is dramatically widening, particularly in the Arab and Islamic world. What makes this problem more serious is that American public diplomacy, designed to solve the country's image problems has actually proved to be counter productive. In this chapter it has been argued that the success of a country's foreign policy, which relies partly on soft power, is an indication of a new mode of competition in world politics that is much broader in scope. In the conduct of world politics, including public diplomacy, the media has become a central player. In an age that is awash in information, the issue is not only which actors own communication outlets, including satellite television, radio stations and websites, but the issue is who pays attention to these sources of information.[64]

Focusing exclusively on mass media public diplomacy, which may have been an efficient Cold War strategy, cannot guarantee immediate success in the post-Cold War era. Fruitful public diplomacy is about effective communication with foreign public opinion and will not succeed if the target audience perceives it solely as propaganda. As Nisbet et al. assert:

> A US-sponsored news channel is only likely to have the same slight buffering effect that our study demonstrates for Western news networks such as CNN or BBC, with the Muslim public selecting and sampling that portion of the "balanced" news that only conforms to their anti-American predispositions.[65]

The most pressing challenge that has faced American public diplomacy in the Arab and Islamic world is its lack of credibility.[66] The effectiveness of public diplomacy relies heavily on credibility, which is understood as a form of "symbolic capital" to use French sociologist Pierre Bourdieu's term. The value of credibility thus is its power of persuasiveness. A public diplomacy without credibility and reputation is often counterproductive. Not only are soft power and the politics of credibility coming to the fore, but they are transforming some fundamental terms of power in international affairs.

The new global communications infrastructure of the Internet, films, television and music represents a serious new challenge for public diplomacy. For instance, the control of information, necessary during crisis and war, has been rendered difficult. Al Jazeera's coverage of US-led intervention in Afghanistan and Iraq was considered as having contributed to the pervasive spread of anti-American attitudes in the Arab and Islamic world.

While the US approach to public diplomacy appears rather competitive, unilateralist and realist, the German diplomacy of dialogue

[320]

appears more cooperative, multilateralist and idealist. US public diplomacy is heavy on film-type image and light on message.[67] The Germans focus more on relationship-building strategies by developing reciprocal connections between people and civil society. While US public diplomacy appears to have its share of problems in the Arab and Islamic world, German diplomacy of dialogue enjoys a reasonable degree of soft power. By adopting this strategic and long term approach to public diplomacy based on relationship-building, Germany is developing a reputation for its diplomacy of dialogue. Should other European and Asian countries follow and promote the diplomacy of dialogue in the name of international cooperation and understanding, they would reduce the risk of creating an environment in which public diplomacy might become hegemonic.

The increasing reliance of the United States on public diplomacy as a foreign policy instrument does not reflect a commitment in military disengagement as McEvoy-Levy concludes.[68] Rather it can be understood as a new "non-violent" mode of intervention. It is worth bearing in mind that the notion of "soft power" was elaborated in a context of international competition. The same holds true for US public diplomacy. It would not be an exaggeration, if US public diplomacy was described as a hard "soft power." The question that arises is whether the critical assessment of current US public diplomacy by American scholars will result in a shift towards the diplomacy of dialogue.

18

The New Anti-Semitism: Hollywood's Reel Bad Arabs: Impacting Public Opinion and Policy

Jack G. Shaheen

History teaches us that repetitive and severe stereotypes can damage an entire people. Such counterfeit words and images do not exist in a vacuum but have an impact on public opinion and political policies. As the Greek Philosopher Plato wrote in *The Republic*, "Those who tell the stories [also] rule society." The French monarch Louis IV noted in 1663, "The arts symbolize the power of the state as much as feats of arms." French Nobel Laureate Albert Camus affirmed "Words [and images] are more powerful than munitions."

American scholar Peter C. Rollins notes that since the creation of motion pictures, government leaders from Russia to France, and from the Third Reich to Italy, "were fascinated with what could be done with movies to advance propaganda. Early on, they recognized that film shaped the minds of citizens, shaped the perceptions and social attitudes of mass audiences." In 1924, soon after World War I, when cinema was only in its infancy, Russian revolutionary leader Vladimir Lenin recognized how film could be used for propaganda. "The cinema must and shall become the foremost cultural weapon of the proletariat," said Lenin. "For us, it is the most important of all the arts." Concurrently, in the United States, Arthur Zukor, the President of Paramount Pictures, echoed Lenin's beliefs, saying, "As an avenue for propaganda, as a channel for conveying thought and opinion, the movies are unequaled by any form of communication." In 1932, Pope Pius XI concurred with Zukor's view stating: "There exists today no means of influencing the masses more potent than the media." At about the same time, Joseph Goebbels, Nazi Germany's Minister of Propaganda, declared, "The most brilliant propaganda technique confines itself to just a few points…and repeats them over and over."

Flash forward to 1998. Jack Valenti, Chair, Motion Picture Association of America, solidifies the relationship between escapist cinema and political propaganda, saying: "Washington and Hollywood spring from the same DNA."

Negative Stereotyping

The negative stereotypes of Arabs are deeply entrenched in Western popular culture—they are as solid as prehistoric rocks. This is nowhere more apparent than in Hollywood films where Arab Muslims, unlike other racial and ethnic groups, continue to be demonized on movie screens. With very few exceptions, Arabs are portrayed as hate-figures to a degree that the studios would no longer dare with any other ethnic group. Although many negative images of racial and ethnic groups have dissipated since Hollywood's early days, the Arab stereotype endures. The Arabs still remain the most vilified group of people in the history of Hollywood. This negative stereotyping has been a feature from the beginning, explains critic Brian Whitaker:

> Arabs and their descendants were portrayed as…dark creatures living in desert tents, riding camels, fighting against legionnaires and among themselves, hawking goods at outrageous prices, as well as enslaving and buying women at slave markets.

By the 1970s, two decades after Israel was created, Hollywood's characterizations of Arabs (the *reel* Arabs) were often as amorous sheikhs, who were portrayed as rich, vengeful, corrupt, sneaky and invariably fat. In part, the ugly, refurbished images most probably intensified as a result of the 1967 and 1973 Arab-Israeli wars, the oil embargo precipitated by

[324]

the Arab Gulf states, as well as the 1979 Iranian Revolution. From the 1980s onwards, as the Arab-Israeli conflict dominated headlines, Hollywood simply enhanced its portrayals of Arabs as desperate Islamic "fundamentalists."

Reel Arabs are almost always portrayed as Muslim terrorists—even though in the last decade more Muslims have been victims globally, than non-Muslims. Consider the deaths in Bosnia, Israel/Palestine, Kosovo and Chechnya. Partly as a result of the stereotype, movie-goers have no opportunities to witness real Arabs or Muslims or empathize with them as victims of oppression. Decades of Hollywood's reel prejudices have denied them such opportunities. Instead, Islam and its followers have been viewed with suspicion and anxiety. Selectively framed images of violence lead many Americans and Europeans to believe that Muslims cannot live with the post-enlightenment values of the West, modernity or human rights.

Many Americans have difficulty distinguishing between "Arabs" and "Muslims." The term "Arab" is essentially a linguistic category referring to about 275 million people from Arabic-speaking countries. However, the term "Muslim" is a purely religious distinction, referring to 1.1 billion Muslims, the majority of whom are Indonesian, Indian and Malaysian. Only 12 percent of the world's Muslims are Arabs. Yet, media images intentionally frame and are almost always hostile towards one group of Muslims—*Arab* Muslims. As a result, the Arab Muslim lacks a human face. The absence of positive, realistic images continues to nurture suspicion and stereotype. In fact, Hollywood has collectively indicted all Arabs as Public Enemy No.1. When was the last time one can recall any movie or TV show that depicted an Arab as an ordinary person?

Hollywood's motion pictures are some of the most powerful teaching tools ever created. Their deeply ingrained stereotypes dominate the universe, playing a major role in influencing world opinion and public policy. In over 100 nations worldwide, on a daily basis, viewers see American movie stars – Arnold Schwarzenegger, Samuel L. Jackson,

[325]

Harrison Ford, Chuck Norris and others – invading countries in the Middle East and blowing up Arabs. Scores of feature films misleadingly show Arabs as the enemy of humankind. As a result, Hollywood's "Arab-as-enemy" films, although not specifically released or labeled as overt propaganda, indeed function as propaganda in the guise of entertainment.

Hollywood first went to war against the Iraqis in the 1943 movie, *Adventure in Iraq*. This World War II thriller projects oil-rich Iraqis as pro-Nazi "devil worshipers." In the end, however, the Arabs are defeated in the movie, brought down by the US Air Force's "shock and awe" bombing. One effect of *Adventure in Iraq* and other "us" versus "them" movies is to help condition audiences to perceive Arabs – and by extension all Muslims – as unrelenting enemies of Western values. Projected along racial and religious lines, Hollywood's continuous denigration of Arabs conveys a negative message: "We Americans despise you and your religion!" A 1993 *New York Times* editorial confirms this negative stereotyping of Arabs:

> Disparaging stereotypes [that demean Asians, Blacks, Jews, Latinos and others] are now so unacceptable that it's a shock to hear them mentioned. However, one form of ethnic bigotry remains an aura of respectability in the United States: prejudice against Arabs.

For more than a century, from 1896 until the present, Hollywood has vilified all things Arab. Long before the tragic September 11 attacks, Islam was perceived as a threat to the West. More than one thousand *pre-9/11* films conclusively demonstrate that Arabs were the most maligned group in the history of Hollywood—the most enduring stereotype in movie history! Most people from Iceland to Isfahan – children as well as great-great-grandparents – have been exposed at some time or the other to Hollywood's false, damaging images of Arabs as bloodthirsty, barbaric and conservative.

Hollywood's manufactured prejudices form the main focus of this chapter. After defining the industry's Arab and Arab American screen stereotypes and revealing basic character types, it will explain why these images persist, and discuss their impact on individuals, public opinion and public policies. President George W. Bush's media campaigns designed to influence the hearts of minds of Arabs are noted. Finally, specific solutions are offered to resolve the stereotyping issue.

Hollywood's Arabs: An Overview

How did it all begin? Obviously, it did not begin with Hollywood. Movie-makers simply acquired and elevated Europe's pre-existing stereotypes, those wild, exotic caricatures that were created by French and British writers and artists during the 18th and 19th centuries. Then, in the 1900s, French film maker George Melies borrowed a page from the *Arabian Nights* stories. He projected subservient maidens attending a greedy black-bearded potentate in his *The Palace of Arabian Nights* (1905). Hollywood went on to duplicate and expand on Melies' mythical Arabia, one which depicted Arabs in ornate palaces and desert tents, wielding huge scimitars and abducting the blonde Western heroine, and killing one another. Many films show Arab caricatures surfacing invariably in a uniform desert setting, which I call "Arab-land"—a make-believe theme park, complete with oases, oil wells, palm trees, ornate palaces, souks and the inevitable camels. To complement this setting, producers insert fictitious locales, like the "Shish-Ka-Bob Cafe" and "The Pink Camel Club." Then they provide actors and actresses with props and costumes from an "Instant Ali Baba Kit." The kit contains magic lamps, giant feather fans, curved daggers, nargilehs, chadors, sheer pantaloons, veils, dark glasses, fake black beards and burnooses.

For thirty years, I have studied how Arab peoples are depicted in American popular culture, giving special emphasis to "entertainment" images of television programs and motion pictures. My research offers convincing evidence that lurid and insidious portraits are the media's staple fare. Almost all of Hollywood's portraits of Arabs are dangerously threatening. Stereotypical profiling has gone on for more than 100 years.

[327]

Hollywood's *reel* Arabs have been repeatedly projected as being anti-Christian and anti-Jewish.

On a canvas far broader in terms of ethnic coverage than its title indicates, my pre-9/11 book, *Reel Bad Arabs: How Hollywood Vilifies a People* paints the dangers of rigid and repetitive stereotypes when we lump "those people" together indiscriminately. In the book, I analyze virtually every feature film that Hollywood has ever made about Arabs, more than 1,000 feature films, the vast majority of which bombard audiences with rigid, repetitive and repulsive depictions. The term "Hollywood" is used here in the generic sense, as some movies were produced by independent American film makers, and a few others by producers from other nations, such as Australia, Canada and Israel.

These movies have tarred an entire group of people with the same sinister brush. Screen images falsely imply that Islam, a faith followed by more than one billion people, advocates violence. Producers projecting racist images of Arabs get away with it because standards of decency that are made applicable to others do not apply yet to Arabs. Movie makers have repeated and embellished those stereotypical characters from silent films, portraying Arabs in trashy roles as junk dealers who smash automobiles. In the process, both automobiles and Arabs are recast and associated with refuse.

For a whole century before the September 11 tragedy, the Arab has been portrayed as America's bogeyman. From *Fatima* (1896) to *The Mummy Returns* (2001), status quo prejudices dominated silver screens. The United States was never at war with an Arab nation until the 1991 Gulf War. Yet, prior to 1991, Hollywood churned out 800-plus movies ridiculing and debasing Arabs. Some movies, notably those released in the 1980s, presented American civilians as well as members of the US military and Israeli forces at war with the Arabs, easily killing scores of reel burnoosed villains.

Pre-9/11 stereotypes are identical to post-9/11 caricatures. In the cinema, the misleading "Arab-as-evil" image remains fixed. Hollywood continues to project them as subhuman beings, *untermenchen,* a term applied by the Nazis to gypsies and Jews. Yesteryear's Shylocks have been replaced on celluloid today by sheikhs, triggering fear of the "other." Writer William Greider observes:

> Jews were despised as exemplars of modernism; Arabs are depicted as carriers of primitivism—threatening to upset our cozy modern world with their strange habits and desires.

Producers ignore or exploit the fact that the Arab 'other' of today is cast in a stereotype much like the Jewish 'other' of yesterday. Consider the familiar reel formula of the Arab/Jew as the seducer. Back in the 1930s, Nazi cinema projected the defiled Jew lurking in the shadows waiting to assault Aryan virgins. Hollywood similarly casts the Arab in the guise of a villain waiting in the alley to attack Western heroines. In the mythology of Hollywood, people of color – the Red Indian, the black buck, the sneaky Asian, the unkempt Mexican, and the bearded Arab – all moved to abduct the white, fair-haired heroine. Fortunately, these injurious rapist myths are gone, with one exception, the villainous Arab—the only 'reel rapist' who is still prowling around on the movie screens.

We strongly deplore, as we should, the false portrait of Jews as hook-nosed swindlers, or as a lascivious, swarthy menace. Yet, we remain silent when equally negative portraits are transferred to another group of Semites—the Arabs. Though Arabs, like Jews, are Semites who share a common genetic make-up, films continually advance this other anti-Semitism, projecting Arabs as carriers of primitivism, with strange habits. I use the word "other" not because anti-Semitism against Jews is passé (it is not) but because the most damaging films directed against Arabs were released in the last third of the twentieth century, at a time when Hollywood was eliminating stereotypical portraits of other groups. It is still considered acceptable in films to keep projecting anti-Semitic portraits—provided the Semites are Arabs. Israeli-born actress Natalie Portman expresses her view:

> Jews and Arabs "are historically cousins…Until we accept the fact that we are the constituents of the same family, we will blunder in believing that a loss for one 'side' is not a loss for all humankind."

[329]

Since cameras began cranking, Hollywood's movies were universal. Overseas viewers also witnessed hate-filled images on movie screens, depicting Arabs as evil and less-than-human. In the process of disparaging a people and their faith, defamation itself gained strength by impacting viewers, especially youngsters in the Middle East, as well as extending its ruinous power far beyond the people it was defaming. Why is it important for the average individual to know and care about the Arab stereotype? One main reason is the July 2004 poll by the Council on American-Islamic Relations (CAIR), which reveals that one out of every four Americans believe that Islamic teachings condone violence and hate. This poll reflects the dislike of "the stranger" image, often expressed in the term "xenophobia." It forewarns us that when one ethnic or racial or religious group is vilified, innocent people suffer. The onslaught of the reel Arab contributes to myths about Islam and helps to condition how young people, Arab Americans as well as Arabs, perceive themselves, and how others perceive them as well. One Arab American college student explains:

> The most common questions I was asked [by classmates] were if I had ever ridden a camel or if my family lived in tents. Even worse, I learned at a very young age [that] every other movie seemed to feature Arab terrorists.

Screen Villains

In the course of my research, I discovered that from the beginning most Arab men are relegated to stereotypical **"B"** images, appearing as **b**ombastic **b**illionaires, **b**eastly **b**ombers, **b**lundering **b**uffoons, and **b**oisterous **b**argainers. Beginning with *Arabian Dagger* (1908), up to and including Disney's *Hidalgo* (2004), a synergy of images equates Arabs from Syria to the Sudan with quintessential evil. For more than one hundred years Hollywood has depicted Arabs as villains. The vast majority of villains fall into four major categories, many of which overlap. Viewers witness scores of despicable and devious Sheikhs, Palestinians, Egyptians, and maidens. On occasion, Hollywood has tossed into this unsavory group of caricatures some other dark-complexioned villains:

[330]

Algerians, Iraqis, Jordanians, Lebanese, Libyans, Moroccans, Syrians, Tunisians and Yemenis. Locked into a cycle of predictable film scenarios, all these evil-doers pop up in a hodgepodge of melodrama and mayhem. Shockingly, some of the industry's most reputable film makers—Steven Spielberg, Francis Ford Coppola, Sir Ridley Scott and others have helped perpetuate the stereotype.

Given the fact that Arab villains appear in one thousand or so movies it comes as no surprise that they surface in every sort of film imaginable:

- Sword-and-sandal soaps: *Samson against the Sheik* (1962), *Devil of the Desert against the Son of Hercules* (1964).
- The Foreign Legion: *Beau Geste* (1939, 1966), *March or Die* (1977)
- Terrorist shoot-'em-ups: *True Lies* (1994), *Executive Decision* (1996)
- Camel-operas: *Road to Morocco* (1942), *Ishtar* (1987)
- Licentious Sheikhs: *Jewel of the Nile* (1985), Jackie Chan's *Gen-Y Cops* (2003).
- Scandalous Slavers: *Tarzan the Fearless* (1933), *Ashanti* (1979)
- Musical comedies: *Kismet* (1920, 1930, 1944, 1955)
- Magic carpet fantasies: *The Thief of Baghdad* (1921), Disney's *Aladdin* (1992)
- Comedies: *Abbott and Costello Meet the Mummy* (1955), *Ernest in the Army* (1997)
- Historical dramas: *King Richard and the Crusaders* (1954), the Crusades film, *Kingdom of Heaven* (2005).
- Egyptian desert shoot-'em ups: *Raiders of the Lost Ark* (1981), *Indiana Jones and the Last Crusade* (1989)
- Movie serials: *Radio Patrol* (1937); *Adventures of Captain Africa* (1955)
- Cowboys-and-Indians: *Desert Pursuit* (1952), *Hidalgo* (2004)
- Secret agent (007) movies: *Diamonds Are Forever* (1971), *Wrong Is Right* (1982), *Never Say Never Again* (1986).
- Science Fiction: *Metalstorm: The Destruction of Jared-Syn* (1983), *Raptor Island* (2004)

In addition to these mortifying movies, many decades before the 1991 Gulf War, dozens of films ranging from *The Lost Patrol* (1934) to the more recent *Rules of Engagement* (2000) depicted French, British, Israeli and American forces eradicating Arab villains.

Egyptians

More than 100 films display frightening Egyptian caricatures. From the start, movie makers linked Egypt with the walking dead—over two dozen mummy movies prowl around the screens. It began early on with George Melies' short film, *The Monster* (1903), followed by *The Mummy* (1911), *The Mummy* (1932), *The Mummy's Revenge* (1973), and other "here-comes-the-mummy" movies. Historically, viewers witnessed reel Egyptians – pharaohs, swindlers, fascists and menacing mummies – routinely descending upon Westerners, Israelis, and fellow Egyptians in contemporary dramas such as *Sphinx* (1981) and *Deception* (1992), animated films, *The Prince of Egypt* (1998) and sundry mummy scenarios.

Mummy plots are relatively simple. Revived mummies and their caretaker "priests" contest Western archaeologists. In most beneath-the-pyramids films, the ambitious Western grave-diggers ignore tomb warnings. So, they suffer the consequences for daring to reawaken Egypt's sleeping royals. Once fully revived, the bandages-with-eyes mummy lusts after the archaeologist's fair-skinned daughter. As long as mummy-on-the-move features remain popular they will continue surfacing on silver screens. These features make money, a lot of it, as demonstrated by the box-office success of Universal's recent releases *The Mummy* (1999) and *The Mummy Returns* (2001). In 2004, Universal even launched a mummy amusement park ride entitled *Revenge of the Mummy*.

Sheikhs

More than 160 films such as *The Power of the Sultan* (1907), *The Sheik* (1921), *Ali Baba Goes to Town* (1937), and *Secondhand Lions* (2004), project Arabs sheikhs the same way that German cinema once portrayed

Jewish money-lenders. Cinematic Arabs have never been likeable characters. In the early 1920s, the swarthy movie sheikh kidnapped and chased the Western heroine around sand dunes. Almost always, the reel sheikhs move to *take* the heroine, not to court her or to fall in love with her. For example, the villainous sheikh in *The Adventures of Hajji Baba* (1954) threatens: "Give her to me or I'll take her."

Hollywood's reel sheikhs are portrayed as potentates who plan bomb attacks on the West and seek to enslave blacks and pale-faced blondes. More than 60 movies ranging from *The Fire and the Sword* (1914) to *Spartan* (2004) show rich sheikhs abducting, enslaving and/or moving to seduce the fair Western maiden. The sheikh genre never includes scenes with Western heroines playing the role of willing lovers. Producers experiencing desert mirages dared not imagine such unions. Nor do Hollywood movies project devout sheikhs with their families, caring for their children, respecting and loving one Arab wife. Instead, a number of films such as *John Goldfarb Please Come Home* (1964), *Protocol* (1984), and *Harem* (1985), show sheikhs disregarding Arab women and preferring Western maidens. For example, consider Valentino's classic 1921 film *The Sheik*. Only when Diana, the western heroine, finds out that Ahmed (Valentino) is not an Arab does she truly fall in love. Ahmed's father, it turns out, "was an Englishman, his mother a Spaniard." During World War II, scores of Arabs sided with the United States but movies exclude this reality. Instead, many 1940s war dramas, *A Yank in Libya* (1942), *Action in Arabia* (1944) and others, show shady sheikhs and their cohorts supporting the Nazis against the Allies.

Contemporary films, notably movies of the 1980s—*Wrong Is Right* (1982), *Protocol* (1984), *Bolero* (1984), *Jewel of the Nile* (1985), *Never say Never, Again* (1986)—display mega-rich, self-indulgent extremists positioned atop missile bases. These anti-Christian, anti-Jewish zealots are supposedly armed with nuclear weapons. These movie characters are shown as misinterpreting Islam to justify violence against the West, and trying to seduce movie starlets—Brooke Shields, Kim Basinger, Bo Derek and Goldie Hawn.

Palestinians

Forty-three Palestinian fiction films that are discussed in my book *Reel Bad Arabs* represent dangerous hate propaganda. What is absent from such Hollywood movies is Palestinian humanity. Only two scenarios reveal Palestinians with families. Not one film movie shows Palestinians as victims and Israelis as oppressors. No film shows Israeli settlers uprooting olive orchards. The Associated Press reported on December 9, 2004 that the Israeli army killed 148 unarmed Palestinian civilians in the West Bank. Yet, no movie has ever shown Israeli soldiers gunning down innocent Palestinian men, women and teenagers in Palestinian cities. No movie depicts Palestinian families struggling to survive under occupation, living in refugee camps, striving to have their own country with postage stamps and passports issued by the "State of Palestine." Regrettably, Hollywood's unwritten cinematic code still prohibits movies from projecting Palestinians as normal peace-loving folk—computer specialists, engineers, farmers, teachers and artists.

Dictating numerous "Palestinian-as-terrorist" scenarios is the Israeli connection. More than 50 percent of the Palestinian films were filmed in Israel, with the cooperation of the Israeli government. Golan and Globus' now defunct Cannon company produced seven films, displaying Palestinians as violent extremists fighting Westerners, Israelis and fellow Arabs. Twenty eight of the forty three movies were released between the years 1983 to 1998. Movies such as *Sword of the Desert* (1948), *Cast a Giant Shadow* (1966) and *Judith* (1966) advance the myth of Palestine as a land without people. Many films such as *The Delta Force* (1986), *Navy SEALS* (1990), *True Lies* (1994), *Executive Decision* (1996), and others—show the US military and special agents gunning down "evil" Palestinians. More than twelve films, *Half-Moon Street* (1986), *Terror in Beverly Hills* (1988), *Appointment With Death* (1988) and *Black Sunday* (1977), project Palestinian evildoers injuring and threatening Western women and children.

[334]

Collectively, these films convey harmful and false information about an oppressed people under occupation. Those viewers arguing that these reel images reflect real Palestinians are either ignorant, biased or both. Obviously, viewers watching Tarzan movies do not believe they are acquiring accurate knowledge of Africans. Similarly, viewers seeing Fu Manchu films certainly do not all believe that all Asians are clones of this mythical arch villain.

Maidens

Scholars have ignored Hollywood's stereotypical depictions of the Arab woman. Ever since the beginning of cinema, Hollywood's movies have humiliated, villainized and eroticized them. Obviously, film makers did not create these images but inherited and embellished Europe's pre-existing Arab stereotypes. In the eighteenth and nineteenth centuries, European artists and writers offered fictional renditions of women as easily influenced and submissive exotic "objects." This stereotype came to be accepted as valid, becoming an indelible part of European popular culture, and eventually, such skewed images made their way to Hollywood.

Stereotypical idiosyncrasies abound, linking Arab women to several warped and repetitive 'B' images. It began with two silent shorts – one censored and the other uncensored – *Fatima* (1897) and *Fatima's Dance* (1907). Both feature Fatima, the star of Chicago's 1896 World Fair, as a veiled buxom belly dancer. To see seductive Arab belly dancers appearing in early films is not surprising. At the turn of the century, they were familiar fare in vaudeville and burlesque circles, dancing to entertain audiences. Hollywood simply emulated and enhanced this image.

The image of Arab women as black magic vamps, "serpents" and "vampires" began in 1917, with Fox's silent *Cleopatra*, starring Theda Bara. Subsequently, the word, "vamp," was added to English dictionaries. Movies such as *Saadia* (1953) and *Beast of Morocco* (1966) display the Arab women as black magic vamps, and as enchantresses often in league with or even "possessed" by evil forces.

In Arabian Nights fantasies such as *The Sheik* (1921), *Slave Girl* (1947), and *John Goldfarb, Please Come Home* (1964), Arab women often appear peeping out from diaphanous veils, or as disposable "knick-knacks" lounging on ornate cushions, seductive harem maidens with bare midriffs, closeted in the palace's women's quarters and/or on display in slave markets. The fantasy of the harem persists. Not much has changed since 1961, when William Zinsser defined Hollywood's Arabia as "a place where young slave girls lie about on soft couches...ready to do a good turn for any handsome stranger who stumbles into the room...This is history at its best." Typically, Disney's remake of *Around the World in Eighty Days* (2004) advances and solidifies the myth. Here, Governor Arnold Schwarzenegger acts as a sheikh surrounded by scores of dancers and wives.

The bomber image began with Republic's movie serial, *Federal Agents vs the Underworld Inc.* (1948). Since then, Hollywood has released several feature films portraying Palestinians, Moroccans and other Arab women in the role of terrorists invading the US and killing American civilians. In *Underworld*, Nila, the Egyptian "female fanatic" and her Arab associates move to bring down US federal agents. Though Nila, Hollywood's first-ever Arab terrorist, tosses a bomb at the American "infidels," she's no match for the Western agents. At the end of the film, a huge statue crushes her and Nila succeeds only in destroying herself.

The film *Black Sunday's* images are firmly implanted onto the TV landscape. Every year, usually days before the annual Super Bowl game, *Black Sunday* (1977) is viewed by at least 20–25 million viewers. For nearly 30 years, viewers have witnessed Dahlia, a Palestinian, helping to gun down American citizens in Los Angeles and Washington DC, and then trying to detonate a cluster bomb, massacring 80 thousand Super Bowl spectators in Miami, including the American President. In time, an Israeli officer, not an American agent, terminates her. Interestingly, *New York Times* critic Vincent Canby criticized Marthe Keller, the actress who portrayed Dahlia, in his report dated April 1, 1977. She did not fit Canby's

[336]

preconceived image of a Palestinian woman. He writes: "Miss Keller has some difficulty playing a Palestinian terrorist, looking as she does, as beautiful and healthy…as a California surfer."

Four years later Shakka, a dangerous Moroccan terrorist surfaced in the 1981 New York-based drama, *Nighthawks*. Born in Tangiers of wealthy parents, Shakka is depicted as a woman who has been indulged and who kills without provocation. Shakka and her associate, a German assassin, hold the families of UN officials as hostages in a dangling cable car 250 feet above the East River. However, the police save the day and she is eventually shot dead in the film.

Wrong is Right (1982) depicts enraged Arab students in the role of terrorists. Clad in robes and checkered *kuffiyehs* the students march on Times Square and tussle with New York policemen, shouting, "Death to the Jews;" "Death to America." One young woman implants a plastic bomb into her body, blowing up herself and injuring onlookers. Moreover, in the James Bond thriller, *Never Say Never Again* (1983), Fatima, playing the role of a nuclear terrorist working with SPECTRE, attempts to detonate two nuclear bombs in the West. She fails and eventually Bond terminates her.

Set in Los Angeles, *Wanted: Dead or Alive* (1987) shows Palestinian and home-grown Arab Americans causing an explosion and killing more than 200 men, women and even children. An Arab-American terrorist factory contains 50-plus chemical weapons and the weapons are about to be released into the atmosphere, killing millions. When Malak, the primary villain and Jamilla, his loyal assistant, find out that the powerful explosions could also kill them as well as their fellow conspirators, Malak cancels the mission and the angry Jamilla protests. Determined to launch the weapons, she is willing to die for "the cause." Malak ultimately shoots her dead.

True Lies (1994), presents Juno, a Palestinian terrorist. She and her fellow Palestinians, members of the "Crimson Jihad," move to launch nuclear missiles over American cities. Final frames show the movie's hero and the Marines defeating the Arabs and thwarting their plan.

In all seven films, six showing the "alien" Arab woman being shot dead, and four portraying her as a *nuclear* terrorist, the general message conveyed is: "Rid the United States of Arabs and we will all be safe."

Only a handful of out-of-date movies – *The Return of Chandu* (1934), *Baghdad* (1949), *Flame of Araby* (1951) and *Princess of the Nile* (1954) – present the Arab woman as one who is characterized by intelligence, courage and beauty. Admirable Egyptian queens appear in the 1934 and 1963 versions of *Cleopatra* and in *Caesar and Cleopatra* (1946). On rare occasions, when the dark-complexioned, heroic Arab woman tries to court a Western protagonist, she is disappointed. Films such as *Outpost in Morocco* (1949) and *Secondhand Lions* (2003) project the view that an Arab woman in love with the American protagonist must die.

For decades, these rigid stereotypical 'B' portraits have projected false realities. Producers never show Arab women at home with a devoted husband and children, or in the work place, functioning competently as doctors, computer specialists, school teachers, print and broadcast journalists or as successful engineers. Instead of revealing a common humanity, the movies contend that Muslim women are in a pathetic state, thus helping to alienate the Arab woman from her international sisters and vice versa.

Arab Americans

Not surprisingly, the century-old Arab Muslim stereotype has impacted Americans of Arab heritage. Despite the rich history and numerous contributions of Arab Americans, movies have also singled them out for discrimination, portraying them as terrorists, who are intent on destroying America. Hollywood has failed to reveal their individual accomplishments and movies have failed to humanize them. Not a single film has ever projected an Arab American family, with grandparents and children, as an integral part of America's cultural mosaic. Although a fair proportion of Arab Americans are Christians, no movie has ever shown them worshiping in a church. In fact, films display most Americans of Arab

[338]

heritage as Muslims and wrongly link the Islamic faith, which is a religion of peace, with violence. Nor do films project Arab Americans as distinguishing themselves in the military. Consider, for example, two typical families—the Jacobs and the Rafeedies. My grandfather, Jacob Mike Jacob, was a chanter at our church and worked in the mills outside Pittsburgh for nearly two decades. Albert Rafeedie, my father-in-law, served in the United States Army during World War I. Following the war he ran dry goods stores in Minneapolis and Los Angeles. Both Albert and Jacob emigrated to America in the early 1900s. Their families served their country during World War II and the Korean War, enlisting in the US Army, Navy and Air Force. Inexplicably, the presence of Arab Americans, Christians and Muslims, and their manifold contributions to America remain invisible on movie screens.

For example, for more than a century, Hollywood has released literally thousands of movies, many of which focus on America's many racial and ethnic groups. Amazingly, during its 100-plus years of movie making, Hollywood has only released 23 movies with Arab American characters. Seventeen of these 24 films display them not as they are – typical hard-working Americans like the Irish, Italian, French, and others – but as carbon copies of Hollywood's stereotypical Arab Muslims. Especially offensive are Hollywood's vilification of Arab Americans in movies such as *Wanted Dead or Alive* (1987), *Terror in Beverly Hills* (1988) and *The Siege* (1998). In these movies they appear as terrorists, intent on blowing up sections of the cities of California and New York.

Animated cartoon stereotypes also play a role in negative stereotyping. From an early age, Arab American youngsters view dozens of their favorite cartoons that once appeared in movie theaters, witnessing their cartoon heroes bringing down dastardly Arabs. Superman crushes a rampaging mummy; Batman punches out scores of Egyptian baddies; Heckle and Jeckle pull the rug from under Ali Boo-Boo the Desert Rat; Popeye trashes Sinbad and Ali Baba; and Porky Pig and Bugs Bunny beat up Hassan and Ali Baba, portrayed as desert villains. Whatever happened, our children must wonder, to Aladdin's good genie?

Hollywood's Arab American actors are affected as well. Some have disguised their roots. Soon after his film debut in *Blackboard Jungle* (1955), Jameel Farah, star of the hit TV series, M*A*S*H, changed his name to Jamie Farr. Actor Siddig El Fadil, a regular on *Star Trek: Deep Space Nine*, changed his name to Alexander Siddig. Then there's F. Murray Abraham. When asked what the "F" stood for, Academy Award winner for *Amadeus* (1984) Abraham said: "F stands for Farid." However, he dumped Farid because he feared that he would be relegated to portraying only "sour Arabs." Actor Nameer El-Kadi has Iraqi roots; he changed his name to Nicholas Kadi but this did not help. Kadi is still obliged to make his living playing the role of terrorists in films like *Navy SEALS* (1990) and *Freedom Strike* (1998). Kadi laments, "in these movies, I do little talking and a lot of threatening—threatening looks, threatening gestures." On screen, he and others who play Arab villains supposedly despise America. "There are other kinds of Arabs in the world," says Kadi, "I'd like to think that some day there will be an Arab role out there for me that would be an honest portrayal."

Nine million Arab Americans and American Muslims – from physicians to female police officers – are as courageous, as patriotic as their neighbors, and every bit as intent on wiping out terrorism. Yet, these TV shows and others falsely imply that they are a threat to their neighbors and their country. For the first time, these shows portray all Arab Americans as unsavory terrorists—Al-Qaeda clones or disloyal thugs, who are waging a war against their next door neighbors. The TV shows give viewers the wrongful impression that they conspire with Al-Qaeda, use mosques as hideouts, shoot dead their fellow Americans, and use dirty bombs to nuke Washington, D.C., Los Angeles and Texas.

During the 1950s, Wisconsin Senator Joseph McCarthy's "black list" unfairly painted Hollywood's producers and writers with the same sinister brush, labeling them as "dirty commies." McCarthy and the FBI claimed Hollywood's communists were "injecting small portions of propaganda into their movies that glorified the Soviet Union." However, no evidence was uncovered of communists engaging in film propaganda nor did the FBI locate any evidence that movie makers violated any federal laws. So why did the agency and McCarthy slander and go after the "Hollywood Ten?" Not because of facts, but because of fear. They feared that their "subversive ideas might influence popular culture." Subsequently, the Senator's witch hunt resulted in innocents losing their jobs.

Currently, Arab and Muslim Americans are experiencing an updated version of McCarthy's 1950s black list. This time, it is not a US Senator but Hollywood being responsible for impugning innocents. The victims of the refurbished witch hunt are Arab Americans who are secretly being blacklisted by Hollywood's unwritten policy: "No Arab Americans Wanted." There are, however, exceptions to this policy. Producers welcome those few "Uncle Abdul" actors who are willing – for the sake of financial or professional survival – to portray passionate sheiks and Muslim terrorists. Offering only stereotypical roles to Arab American performers creates a chilling scenario for the ultimate dehumanization. The fact remains that positive and humane portraits of Americans of Arab heritage continue to be excluded from movie and TV screens. The exclusion process, combined with the ever-present stereotype, is especially injurious to Arab American children. It is like looking into the mirror and seeing a void! These positive images do not exist at all.

Why the stereotype?

The extraordinary longevity of the Arab stereotype has resulted from a combination of factors: the lack of public critique and the failure of government officials and Christian and Jewish leaders to brand these 1000-plus movies as anti-Semitic. Our leaders know full well that Arabs are also Semites to whom a reasonable sense of fairness might give the nod by recognizing "the other anti-Semitism" that manifests itself in, for example, the anti-Palestinian tilt of American foreign policy.

Though some movies reflect the image maker's prejudices, not all script writers start with a plan to harm Arabs. Novelists, cartoonists, educators, religious leaders and others form their opinions of people based on what they learn in school, read in print, hear on the radio and see on TV and at the movies. They are influenced by a continuous flow of popular cultural images which suggest that if you have seen one, you have seen them all. Serving to eternalize Hollywood's stereotypes are artistic laziness, "if it bleeds, it leads" newscasts, lack of presence, insensitivity, greed, lack of vibrant film criticism and especially politics. The Arab remains the politician's favorite whipping boy. In his memoirs, Terrel H. Bell, Ronald Reagan's first Secretary of Education, writes about an "apparent bias among mid-level, right-wing staffers at the White House."

Fast forward to Israel and Menachem Golan and Yoram Globus, two Israeli film makers with a political agenda. They formed an American film company, Cannon. Under the Cannon label, the two producers churned out upwards of 26 hate Arab movies, ranging from *Hell Squad* (1985) to *Killing Streets* (1991). The post 9/11 movie, *Air Marshal* (2003), is also a product of Israeli-born producers, Avi [Danny] Lerner, Boaz Davidson and Alain Jakibowicz. *Air Marshal* not only shows vicious Arab terrorists taking over a passenger plane and killing innocents, the film shamelessly exploits 9/11 victims and their loved ones. The three producers are responsible for other vicious anti-Arab scenarios. They have churned out many Arab-bashing films: *The Delta Force* (1986) and other *Delta Force* movies, *Chain of Command* (1994), *American Ninja 4* (1992), *Hostage* (1986) and *Executive Decision* (1996).

A few critics are critical of the stereotype while some are silent. Others accept reel Arabs as real ones. As Jawad Ali explains, "I always tuned in to watch the late Gene Siskel and Roger Ebert discuss movies. Back in 1996, they did a show on hateful movie stereotypes. They went down the list, one by one, of Hollywood's racist and sexist offences: Blacks, Italians, women, gays and so forth. And then," says Ali, "they got to the part I had been waiting for: Arabs and Muslims. But, Siskel brushed off the entire history of Hollywood's hateful Arab portrayals with a single sentence that went something like this: 'Oh well, as long as Arabs are our enemy and are blowing up innocent people, our movies will show them as terrorists.' Sadly, Ebert let the slur slide and they moved on to other topics."

When considering stereotypes, the role played by the US Department of Defense (DOD) must be considered. To date, over 14 movies, ranging from *Death before Dishonor* (1987) to *Rules of Engagement* (2000), depict members of the US military gunning down scores of Arab men, women and children. Regrettably, the DoD willingly provided needed equipment, personnel and technical assistance to the films' producers. Then there's Morocco. Hollywood's image makers searching for a safe place to film bash-the-Arab scenarios without any complaints, travel not only to Israel, but to Morocco. Dozens of movies, from *Ishtar* (1987) to *Hidalgo* (2004) are filmed in Morocco and Arab officials remain silent on the issue.

Apathy, greed and presence play important roles. "Kill-the-Arab" movies make money; and some studios eagerly exploit the power of the stereotype for profit. Moreover, Arab Americans share the blame. As a group they have been reluctant to mobilize, to actively strive for accurate and balanced portrayals. The lack of presence is another major factor. No Arab American or Muslim American lobby exists in Hollywood. Not many Arab Americans are involved in the film industry and none of them is a famous Hollywood mogul like Ted Turner or Michael Eisner. As a result, their all-too-rare and not-so-well-organized protests are rarely heard in Hollywood. Even when heard, the protests are too faint to get the offenders to back off. As for the future, history shows that stereotypes can be alleviated by information.

Yet another reason is that familiar and "comforting stereotypes make everyone's job easier." Columnist Maureen Dowd observes that stereotypes are offensive, but they are also comforting because they "exempt people from any further mental or emotional effort. They wrap life in the arch toastiness of fairy tale and myth. They make complicated understandings unnecessary." Consider also the marketable news headlines. They are picked up and repeated by global news services. Nightly "if it bleeds it leads" newscasts tend to focus selectively on a minority of radical combatants intent on killing Americans. Extremists chanting "Death to America!" abduct and murder innocent civilians. These "all-Arabs-are-villains" images gratuitously equate 1.2 billion people as clones of either Osama Bin Laden or Saddam Hussein. Additionally, violent news-media projections of extremists beheading captives and fiercely fighting the US military in Iraq keep driving home the myth that many Arabs are evil.

The violent news images reinforce already existing stereotypes, and serve as an excuse for film makers to exploit the issue. "We're not stereotyping," say some. "Just look at your TV set. Those are real Arabs." Such responses are dishonest, and trigger further misunderstandings. Since 1991 nightly newscasts have for the most part, excluded Iraqi suffering. Seldom do viewers see starving and/or injured Iraqi children, or devout Iraqi families praying in mosques, trying to live peaceful, normal lives. Movie makers have a moral obligation to see the stark realities taking place on the ground in Iraq that go beyond the news media's sins of omission and commission.

Islamophobia was in vogue decades before 9/11. However, the continued denigration of all things Arab and Muslim in popular culture, especially racist comments made by radio talk show hosts such as Don Imus, and religious zealots such as Jerry Falwell and Pat Robertson, have recently intensified. Regrettably, embedded stereotypes advanced by journalists such as Steven Emerson (*Jihad in America*), scholars like Bernard Lewis (*What Went Wrong*), and political leaders like former Attorney General John Ashcroft continue to vilify the Islamic faith as a religion that condones violence. Such prejudiced rhetoric helps to nurture the image maker's mythology.

Silence is also a factor. When it comes to publicly condemning the Arab stereotype, civil rights leaders, scholars, entertainment personalities, and others fail to speak out, reminding Hollywood and the public at large of their responsibilities to eliminate insidious stereotypes, explaining that xenophobia and prejudice are the flip sides of harmony and togetherness. When they eventually speak out, what will be the result of their actions? Films would begin to illuminate, not denigrate, an entire people and their faith. We see many more humane and down-to-earth African-American images on TV and in film today because for decades the National Association for the Advancement of Colored People (NAACP) and others worked together as a lobby to break the silence surrounding the black stereotype. The NAACP drove home with the public and the press the message that the entertainment industry was discriminating against American blacks.

To date, no significant element of public opinion – either in America or in the Arab world – has vigorously contested and condemned the stereotype. No group has yet driven it home with the press and the public that the entertainment industry discriminates against all things Arab and Muslim. Even Arab diplomats ignore the problem. Why have they not vigorously protested Hollywood's pervasive stereotypes with their counterparts in Washington, DC? Even liberal American politicians remain silent. When New York's Andrew Cuomo ran for Governor of New York, a state where many Arab Americans reside, he spoke out against "discrimination and...vulgar stereotypes in popular culture." Image-makers, he says, are "still stereotyping Italian-Americans, Irish-Americans, African-Americans, Indian-Americans and American Jews." However, Cuomo did not mention coarse stereotypes of Arab Americans. Silence means acceptance of the *status quo* images. If ever we are to illuminate our common humanity, should not Cuomo and political leaders of all nations reveal and challenge hateful stereotypes?

Impact on Innocents, Opinion and Policy

Cinema plays a major role in helping to shape the public's perception of historical events and nations. In 1957, the Soviets made an effort to win the hearts and minds of Egyptians. Aware that Cairo film-goers loved American films, Russian propagandists took steps to eradicate

Hollywood's influence. They gave Cairo's motion picture theater owners wads of cash. In return, the owners agreed to stop screening American movies, and to show Egyptians more than 300-plus newly imported Russian films. As for the cinema's impact on historical events, scholar Robert Brent Toplin explains that film makers selectively "illuminate these historical events in ways capable of reaching mass audiences that few historians can ever hope to reach." According to Toplin, producers often design their stories by presenting only one viewpoint—good versus evil, Western hero versus Arab villain. Film makers continually respond to current events and to earlier films, as well. To stimulate audience interest they mix old and familiar character types and plots with new and intriguing variations. Hollywood's scenarios and characters regularly change and evolve. As a result, reel Arabs are never static. Movie-goers recognize familiar characters from the past movies and also experience fresh stereotypical surprises in contemporary films.

To their credit, the American government and media were careful not to blame Islam and all Arabs and Muslims for the tragedy of September 11. Initially, thanks to their wisdom, there was no surge in animosity against the American Muslim community. However, soon after the events of September 11, and the ensuing "war on terror" in Afghanistan and Iraq, Arabs and Muslims, worldwide felt a deep sense of alienation. The image of all "those people" as a threat has led to an alarming increase in hate crimes and hostile attitudes towards Arabs and Muslims, giving prejudice a free pass. Arab and Muslim Americans have experienced attacks on churches and mosques, harassment in schools, physical violence, loss of jobs, rude profiling at airports and even arrest and imprisonment in violation of civil rights. Some politicians have used this atmosphere of hate for political gain, by further alienating opinions against scholars, performers, and immigrants.

Taken together, the crimes committed and the deeply entrenched stereotypes of Arabs and Arab Americans being transmitted reflect the earlier abuses of Asians, American Indians, blacks and Jews. Negative stereotypes are not harmless, because innocent people suffer when media systems regularly portray any ethnic group as sub-human. Stereotypes perpetuated by Hollywood's films and the newspapers of William Randolph Hearst enabled the American government to incarcerate more than 100,000 Japanese-American citizens in 1942. In addition, abhorrent media stereotypes served to deny blacks their basic civil rights—some were even lynched. The dime novels helped demonize American Indians and scores were uprooted and murdered. Moreover, Nazi Germany's propaganda and prejudiced portrayals of Jews and other minorities helped to expedite the deaths of millions. "Prejudice," the novelist Pearl S. Buck writes, "is a shadow over all of us, and the shadow is darkest over those who feel it least and allow its evil effects to go on."

Which came first – the politics or the stereotypes – is a moot point. However, both are interlinked. The stereotypes help to justify the foreign policies of the United States and other western governments. At the same time, government policies help to legitimize the stereotypes. Unlike the movie images of Judaism and Christianity, Islam continues to be presented as a faith that condones violence. Mickey Mouse cartoons and Spielberg movies may thus outweigh scholarly studies from Harvard and Stanford. While many policy makers mistakenly dismiss Hollywood's influence on opinion and policy, actor Richard Dreyfuss does not. "There are film artists that affected me more than any textbook, civics teacher, or even a lot of what my parents taught me, and that's big," he comments.

Films last forever, just as books do. Their pervasiveness is even more far-reaching and influential. For example, about six months after movies first appear on American movie screens, the films are released throughout the world, to approximately 150 nations. Months later, in the United States and abroad, they can be purchased or rented from e-Bay, video stores and Wal-Mart outlets. Next, the films appear on cable TV outlets, followed by showings on commercial TV networks. Movies are then screened in airplanes, hospitals, schools, universities, prisons and even in dental clinics. The more successful movies lead to TV shows, video

[347]

games, musical toys, records/CDs, toys, games, trading cards, cereals, coloring books, theme park rides, magazines and "the-making-of-the-movie" books.

More than any other medium of communication, television systems immortalize the stereotype. On a weekly basis, 20–24 recycled movies in small towns project Arabs as villains. Take a single evening—August 8, 2004. On this day, TV viewers and their families could watch the following films.

- *Patton*, in which ugly Tunisian scavengers are equated with vultures.
- *The American President* in which the US Air Force opts to bomb Libya.
- *Broadcast News* in which the US Air Force bombs Arabs.
- *Navy SEALS* in which US forces in Lebanon demolish scores of Palestinian "terrorists."
- *Executive Decision* in which US Special Forces wipe out Palestinian "terrorists."

When movies that vilify Arabs leave movie theaters, they do not fade into oblivion. Rather, the films endure forever, appearing in over 150 nations. American troops, for example, arrive in Iraq with a rifle in one hand and a lot of pop culture – satellite dishes and portable DVD players – in their rucksacks. Too much technology may do more damage than good, preventing them from learning or understanding anything about the Iraqi people, Islam or Arab culture. Why? Because technology allows them to view US television and the latest movies and most of these screen images vilify all Arabs and Muslims, portraying them as arch enemies of the United States. Does the soldier's stockpile of Hollywood images help to encourage tolerance and peace? Or do all those movies on DVDs serve to escalate intolerance by teaching young men and women in uniform to hate Arabs?

What about the impact reel Arabs have on Arab audiences? In Egypt and in other Arab countries, youngsters can rent Disney's *Aladdin* (1992) and scores of other Arab-bashing films for the equivalent of twenty-five US cents. The Yemeni Ambassador to the United States cited one such example. When Paramount's *Rules of Engagement* (2002), a film depicting US Marines shooting dead 83 Yemeni men, women and children, became available in Yemen, residents who were shocked at seeing so many anti-Arab images copied the film onto video tapes and distributed them to every city and village in Yemen. Their objective was to illustrate the extent to which Hollywood hates Arabs.

At Washington DC's Islamic Center, soon after the 9/11 attacks, President Bush stated:

> America counts millions of Muslims amongst our citizens, and Muslims make an incredibly valuable contribution to our country...And they need to be treated with respect.

A year later, on September 10, 2002, at the Afghan Embassy, he repeated his post 9/11 position, saying:

> It is important for our fellow Americans to understand that Americans of Muslim faith share the same grief that we all share from what happened to our country on 9/11. [American Muslims] love our country as much as I love our country...no American should be judged by appearance, by ethnic background, or by religious faith.

Recognizing the need to address anti-US sentiment in Arab and Muslim nations, Senior Advisor Karl Rove and other White House officials met with 40 Hollywood executives to enlist their help to "win the war on evil." While concurring that the war against terrorism was not a war against Islam, they agreed on the desperate need to convince peace-loving Muslims that they were not being targeted. Intent on reinventing America for 1.2 billion Muslims, President Bush appointed a former advertising executive, Charlotte Beers, as Undersecretary of State to lead a $15 million public diplomacy campaign to win hearts and minds in the Muslim world. What was the purpose of the government's PR campaign? To crush decisively the myths that the war in Iraq has anything to do with pitting Islam against Christianity or the Arab World against the West. Instead, the President and his supporters believe that this war has everything to do with defeating the marginalized fanatics responsible for 9/11 and other terrorist actions.

Yet some experts feel the government-sponsored diplomacy campaigns not just failed but helped to advance anti-Americanism in the Arab Street and that Arabs were not buying the US government's "We love you" propaganda. Perhaps one reason for the failure was the fact that pro-Bush supporters and the media were comfortable with posing only one misleading question: "Why do they hate us?" More accurate and less generalized questions should have been asked: "Why are they angry with us?" [after all, anger implies dialogue], and why do our media systems hate them and their religion?" Within a year, the President and his administration's actions began to contradict his earlier message of tolerance. The US administration's actions resulted in increased harassment of Muslim and Arab Americans, such as airport profiling. Also, the behavior of the Justice Department toward scores of innocent Muslim immigrants, and vicious anti-Arab Muslim media images combined with racist comments made by media talk-show hosts, religious conservatives close to the White House, and by some administrative appointees, stand in stark contrast to the President's statements.

Not surprisingly, US actions or inactions at home and in Iraq have driven the United States' favorable ratings "in most Arab countries down to single digits," notes Dr. James Zogby, President of the Arab American Institute (AAI). One reason for the dramatic drop, according to Professor John Esposito is because, "in most parts of the Muslim world, America's war against global terrorism has come to be viewed as a war against Islam and Muslims." According to Esposito, the administration has not only "failed to support Palestinian human rights, but also failed to prove a substantive Iraq–Al Qaeda connection." America's moral leadership and credibility, writes Esposito, "were further eroded when people saw the disturbing photographs of tortured Iraqis, taken at the Abu Ghraib prison and when the International Red Cross reported that prisoners were being abused at the US Navy Base at Guantanamo Bay." Some of the horrible treatment of Arabs, whether in Palestine, Iraq or the United States can be traced to Hollywood's indelible "Arab-as-villain" image.

The Bush administration has repeatedly failed to acknowledge and offer corrective measures to counter the entrenched stereotypes. Instead, in December 2003, it launched *Al Hurra*, a slickly produced Arab-language news and entertainment network, which is beamed by satellite from a Washington suburb to the Middle East. Although *Al Hurra* is meant to be America's answer to outlets like *Al Jazeera*, Middle East viewers are not convinced. An Arabic video produced in 2003 by the State Department highlighting Muslims living prosperously in the United States was greeted with skepticism by Arab viewers. In addition, after 9/11, the government launched Radio Sawa, an Arabic-language radio network, which according to media specialists, has achieved only some moderate success. These projects and others continue to cause considerable frustration and much disappointment in American diplomatic circles.

Possible Solutions

Pulitzer Prize-winning columnist Mike Royko once wrote, "I never went to a John Wayne movie to find a philosophy to live by or to absorb a profound message. I went for the simple pleasure of spending a couple of hours seeing the bad guys." What America needs now, is to reverse the portrayal of Arabs as "bad guys." What should be done to compensate for the way Arabs and Americans of Arab heritage have been ruthlessly vilified in American popular culture? Who will step forward and convince Hollywood to roll back those heinous portraits which savage the human spirit across the region stretching from Morocco to Sri Lanka? How can Arab Americans acquire the necessary power to present humane images of themselves and their culture?

Visibility in Hollywood would certainly help. It is difficult to demean Arab Americans when they are standing in front of you, especially if they are your friends and/or bosses. Since 1988 I have encouraged Arab American students to major in media studies with a view to establishing more of an Arab American presence in Hollywood. To date, I have awarded fourteen Jack G. Shaheen Mass Communication Scholarships to outstanding students. This is necessary because Americans of Arab heritage are currently being stereotyped as terrorists, and because their humanity is invisible in the media. By their very presence, Arab and Muslim American image makers will portray themselves on movie and TV screens as decent human beings, like every other ethnic group. Several scholarship recipients have already produced award-winning independent films. Film maker Spike Lee cited one scholarship recipient's outstanding skills as a cinematographer while others are excelling in journalism, writing for magazines and newspapers.

Arab Americans who want to become an integral part of the industry should be supported. If members of the community fail to help themselves, media systems will have a free pass to continue vilifying Islam and poisoning the hearts and minds of our children and grandchildren. However, by working together to support future image makers, Arab Americans can help to trash this sinister anti-Arab agenda. Such an endeavor can be supported through grants made to the American Arab Anti-Discrimination Committee's Research Fund. When there are a number of high-level Arab Americans working in the industry, such negative myths will be relegated to a video necropolis.

To demolish prejudices, commonalities should be made visible. Islam, the fastest growing religion in the world, is a faith that brings comfort to more than a billion people around the globe. The name is derived from the Arabic word *salaam* meaning "peace." The three religious traditions – Christianity, Islam, and Judaism – have their own integrity and share commonalities. In medieval times, it was commonplace for Christian, Jewish and Muslim philosophers to read each other's works, study in the same academies, and share one another's insights when discussing the nature of God and religious revelation. Historically, all three traditions share the same philosophical/theological discourse. All three emphasize humane behavior; recognize the Prophet Abraham as a father in faith; worship one God who has revealed His will through the sacred scriptures; and also believe in the ultimate triumph of divine justice.

[352]

Not so long ago, women and minorities were excluded from studio executive offices. Not anymore. Director Spike Lee explains:

> Look at the number of women in the film industry now – Amy Pascal is running Sony, you have Sherry Lansing at Paramount, and Stacey Snider at Universal – and twenty years ago there were no women heads of studios…This is a gradual process.

Moreover, the Civil Rights Movement of the 1960s helped bring about more realistic depictions of various groups. It curbed negative images of the lazy black, the wealthy Jew, the greasy Hispanic and the corrupt Italian. Conscientious image makers committed themselves to eliminate the racial mockery that had been a shameful part of the American cultural scene. These images are mercifully rare on today's screens.

The late CBS journalist Edward R. Murrow reminds us, "What we do *not* see is as important, if not more important, than what we do see." Missing from Hollywood scenarios are images of ordinary Arab men, women and children, families who live normal lives, practicing law, driving taxis, healing the sick, attending school, worshiping at mosques and churches, partying at picnics, going on holiday, getting married and raising children. Another practical and feasible solution for this century-old stereotype is to see movie characters patterned after Arab scholars, those innovative individuals who provided us with the fundamentals of science, mathematics, medicine, astronomy and botany. America's "movers and shakers" need to encourage and foster a powerful movement in the motion picture industry to create films that reflect the positive, beautiful and remarkable aspects of Arab culture, as well as the humanity of its people and their faith. The Arabs have made numerous contributions to civilization. Arab seamen, for example, pioneered navigational techniques enabling them to traverse oceans. The Arabs brought a fresh and vigorous religion, new technology and new knowledge to Indonesia and Spain and in the process, helped to transform these civilizations. These and other contributions should figure strongly in the film producer's image of corrective films about Arabs.

[353]

Waiting for ethnic stereotypes to fade out is no solution, because stereotypes do not die a natural death. Instead, victims of the stereotype, in this case Arabs and Arab Americans, must hunt them down and eradicate them. However, many Arab Americans fail to act. Well-qualified and affluent people must be urged to fund and empower their own maligned community to organize and protest against this dedicated misrepresentation. American Arabs and Muslims must be encouraged to begin working together and invest time, money and expertise in creating a west coast lobby and/or a media institute that would not only contest the stereotypes, but project more honest images. To date, not a single group has taken such an initiative. Other groups know Hollywood is the world's foremost industry for molding the public opinion that helps to shape public policy. This explains why practically every racial and ethnic group has a lobby in Los Angeles, unlike the Arab Americans and Muslim Americans.

How can we improve US perceptions of the Arabs? At the very least, Arabs should enjoy relative immunity from prejudicial portrayal. To dispel stale portraits, they should produce some of the great classic stories about Arabs. CBS-TV's *Misunderstanding China* and the feature film *Gentleman's Agreement* (1947) helped to break down myths about the Chinese and Jewish people. Fresh images patterned after these films and others would certainly help to shatter stale Arab myths, as well as to advance tolerance and unify people.

The evidence documented here about Hollywood's mythology serves as a wake-up call. As the world continues its war against terrorism, Arab and Muslim lobby groups should more actively address the virus of "Islamophobia" by capitalizing on the growing interest in Islam among wider populations. Millions of Muslims and American Arabs could begin forming sustainable bridges between Islam and the West. After all, they are people who represent both Islam and the West. Continued support should be given to informed academics, journalists, writers and broadcasters who are committed to challenging prejudices and presumptions.

Political leaders and image-makers must not allow themselves to fall into the "seen one, seen them all" quagmire. They should cease attributing the 9/11 attacks by the lunatic fringe to the vast majority of peaceful Arabs and Muslims. No individual and no nation should cast judgment on an entire race, culture, nation or religion based solely on the actions of a few fanatics. The nineteen Arabs responsible for the 9/11 tragedy do not represent Muslims any more than the Ku Klux Klan represents Christians.

A step in the right direction would be for image makers to ponder movie hits such as *My Big Fat Greek Wedding*, and *Driving Miss Daisy*, and blockbuster TV series such as "Seinfeld" and "Everybody Loves Raymond," in which the families are Jewish and Christian. Religion forms a normal part of the protagonists' lives. However, no Hollywood movie, and no TV series has yet to feature an Arab Muslim family. It would be truly refreshing if audiences could finally see and begin to understand the Islamic faith better, via a TV series or a smash hit movie, in a warm, realistic setting, as a normal part of a Muslim family's life.

It would help if studio heads would actively seek out and employ highly talented Arab American image makers. In a democratic society every racial and ethnic group should rightfully have a place at Hollywood's table. No industry should have the power to exclude or vilify an entire people and their religion whether unintentionally or by deliberate acts of exclusion. Inclusion would help offset the negative film images of Arabs. In addition, Hollywood's elite and its policy makers should break their silence by condemning and/or eliminating the stereotypes. For example, when actor Danny Glover first read the screenplay for *Lethal Weapon 2* (1989), the villains were Arab terrorists. Glover objected and the studio offered to use Latino "druggies" instead. "No way," said Glover. In the end, thanks to Glover, it was South Africans rather than Arabs or Latinos who became the villains in the movie.

Some film makers refuse to advance the stereotype. The book, *The Sum of All Fears* and early drafts of the screenplay for *Collateral Damage*, featured Arab terrorists as villains, exploding a nuclear bomb in Baltimore and blowing up a US consulate. However, *Collateral Damage* shows Governor Arnold Schwarzenegger in South America eradicating Columbian villains and *Sum of All Fears* displays crazed neo-Nazis as the

[355]

evil characters. Other image makers are projecting humane Arab characters. For example, in Al Pacino's *The Recruit* (2003), the CIA heroine is an Arab American; she saves the American protagonist's life, and nabs a corrupt agent. In the independent feature film *Yes* the actress Joan Allen falls in love and has an affair with a compassionate Lebanese surgeon. In January 2005, the Sundance Film Festival screened two fresh documentaries at their annual Park City festival in Utah. Jackie Salloum's *Planet of the Arabs*, a montage of movie clips based on my book, *Reel Bad Arabs: How Hollywood Vilifies a People,* and Sean McAllister's *The Liberace of Baghdad*, about a famed Iraqi pianist stranded in a hotel while awaiting an American visa.

A small number of film makers from other nations are also offering refreshing portraits. Consider the Israeli film, *Syrian Bride*, the 2004 Montreal Film Festival winner. *Syrian Bride*, co-written by a Palestinian, Suha Arraf, focuses on a Druze woman from the Golan Heights engaged to marry a Syrian TV star whom she has never met. There is also the Dutch-made film *Shouf Shouf Habibi* (2004). Directed and written by Albert Ter Heerdt, this comedy concerns a Moroccan family trying to find their way in Dutch society. In the end, the treatment of the collision between two cultures earns the viewer's respect. Finally, the Youth Film Prize at Amsterdam's 2004 International Documentary Film Festival was awarded to *Nabila*, about a female Muslim rap artist in Sweden.

Arabs are also portrayed in three major movies released in 2005. First, there was *Kingdom of Heaven*, the controversial Ridley Scott film about the Crusades. The film *Jarhead* concerns American Marines in Iraq and *Syriana* stars George Clooney as a CIA agent who must cope with power and corruption in the United States and the Middle East. Whatever the nature of these portrayals and the verdict on them, the continuing awareness and sensitivity displayed by image makers could help to restore a degree of equity. If and when such a transformation takes place, Arab opinion might reach a greater level of understanding and appreciation of the United States. That would be a demonstration of public diplomacy at its best.

[356]

Conclusion

History teaches us that a major obstacle to world peace is the tendency of governments and image makers to dehumanize "those people" by creating and embellishing enduring myths. For more than a century, it has apparently been impossible for a reel Arab to be portrayed as a genuine human being. Hollywood continues to bombard audiences with negative images. From 2001 to 2004 over two dozen films have demeaned Arabs and Islam. To name a few, Steven Seagal's *Out of Reach* (2004), *Raptor Island* (2004), *Flight of the Phoenix* (2004), *Secondhand Lions* (2003), *Fire Over Afghanistan* (2003) *Black Hawk Down* (2002), and *Four Feathers* (2002).

To turn the tables on a century of Hollywood bias against Arabs, we should seriously reflect on the power of myths and how they affect policies. Former US President John F. Kennedy cautioned:

> The great enemy of [peace and] truth is very often not the lie, deliberate, contrived and dishonest but the myth: persistent, persuasive and realistic.

Four decades later *Los Angeles Times* critic, Kenneth Turan affirmed Kennedy's thesis by writing:

> [Hollywood's manufactured myths] are so hard-wired into our psyches [that they] change minds politically, shaping how we view the world...It's when politics infiltrates entertainment that it is most subversive—and most effective...Movies change minds politically [because] artful entertainment easily beats full-on propaganda [films].

Advancing his entertainment-as-propaganda thesis, Turan points out that back in the 1930s, in the pre-war years "all the Germans were watching Leni Riefenstahl's entertainment movies. [They] had so permeated German popular culture that her films formed a background [against] which the nation came to judge the emerging Nazi Party and its Aryan superiority."

Flash forward to 2004. Hollywood's 1,000-plus Arab movies have also played an important propaganda role. According to Turan, "they feed the unusual haste with which we [the United States] became involved in

Iraq." Why? Because the cinema of Hollywood has always assured us that "we were the good John Wayne guys, sure to win easily [over the bad Arab guys] because we had right on our side."

Some US officials contend that "the United States' problem in the Middle East is its failure to effectively communicate with the Arab people." Assuming they are correct, what actions, if any, should Hollywood take, and what steps, if any, should the government take regarding Arab stereotypes in films? Journalist Ann Marlowe, who is Jewish, offers these telling insights, "We [Americans] need to rid ourselves of our perverse myths about Middle Eastern men and women." Slurs against Arabs are, after all, just another form of anti-Semitism. "These bigotries," writes Marlowe, "show an American inability to see Arabs as fully human." Image makers should heed her wisdom, keeping in mind that what is helpful to any Middle East peace are motion pictures that certify commonalities—movies that reveal we are more alike than different. After all, Christianity, Islam and Judaism are religions of peace, advocating that all mankind is one family in the care of God.

Deteriorating relations between the United States and Arab nations are serious and attention must be must paid to this situation, argues Graham Fuller, a former CIA analyst on the Near East:

> I have never felt such an extraordinary gap between two worlds. Clearly, in a region where we desperately need friends and supporters their number is dwindling, and we are increasingly on the defensive.

In her February 2003 testimony before the influential US Senate Foreign Relations Committee, Charlotte Beers, Undersecretary for Public Diplomacy and Public Affairs, summarized the degraded state of American diplomacy. Beers noted, especially, how negative images are influencing behavior on the Arab street, telling members of the Committee:

> We are talking about millions of ordinary people, a huge number of whom have gravely distorted, but carefully cultivated images of us—images so negative, so weird, so hostile that I can assure you a young generation of terrorists is being created.

[358]

Dr Tariq Ramadan, the Geneva-based Islamic thinker whose US visa was revoked in the fall of 2004, explains why those "negative" and "cultivated images" of Americans exist. Professor Ramadan wrote in the *New York Times*:

> In the Arab and Islamic world, one hears a great deal of legitimate criticism of American foreign policy. This is not to be confused with a rejection of American values.

Arab American Institute President, Dr. James Zogby confirms this point:

> Most Arabs like almost everything about America (its values, its democracy and freedom, its education, science and technology, and its people)...The main problem between the United States and the Arab world, is our unwillingness to act as an honest broker between Palestinians and Israelis. Our pro-Israeli policies help alienate and anger Muslims.

Most probably, the average Arab on the street will form his opinion of the United States, says Zogby, based on American actions in the region.

Obviously, fresh Hollywood movies alone will not necessarily change foreign policy minds, on either side. However, a much-needed more favorable impression of the United States could be created, provided new-and-improved films debunk two major myths:

- Islam is equated with violence
- All Arabs are categorized as terrorist-thugs.

Here, Hollywood's role is pivotal. The industry must eradicate and not advance discriminatory images of demagoguery, hate and prejudice. There is no doubt that America's standing within the Arab world will be enhanced when Hollywood begins to erase harmful myths.

Why should Hollywood not embrace and apply the same ethical standards that prevent insidious movie images of Asians, Blacks, Latinos and others from being shown on TV screens? Shouldn't TV repeats of Arab-bashing movies also cease and desist? Why should the industry not shift gears and start churning out movies that help to enhance understanding and unify people? Finally, why should Hollywood not

[359]

begin to portray Arabs as neither saints nor sinners, but as fellow human beings, with all the potentials and frailties that this condition implies?

The foregoing discussion should help to bridge the barren desert between Hollywood's film makers and the Arabs that until now apparently could not be traversed. The evidence documented here will alert readers, notably politicians and movie makers, that discriminatory portraits boost bigotry and prevent peace. Still, openness to change has always been an American tradition. Not so many years ago film makers projected other groups – Asians, blacks, Italians and Latinos – as the cultural "other." They do not do so any longer. Aware that heinous stereotypes injure people, these communities formed pressure groups and acted aggressively against discriminatory portraits. Eventually, these minorities not only eradicated injurious portraits, but they became an integral part of the industry's creative work force. They now function as executives, producers, writers and directors.

What is needed today, in this hour of global crisis, is for President George W. Bush to host a major international summit, one which focuses on shattering myths and enhancing tolerance. The purpose of this summit, attended by image makers and policy makers, would be to help advance peace and diplomacy. High on the agenda would be the role that Hollywood and the Arab world can and should play to eradicate heinous images. The summit could be patterned after the successful 1986-1987 Entertainment Summit, which took place in Los Angeles and New York, and in Moscow and Tibilisi. The summit was a project of Mediators Foundation, a non-profit educational foundation that specializes in global bridge-building to prevent conflict and promote understanding across cultures.

At the time of the Cold War, during the mid-1980s, Foundation president, Mark Gerzon, was working as a Hollywood screenwriter-producer. Gerzon was deeply troubled by Hollywood's movies that projected most Russians as evil Soviet communists, and equally concerned by the movies from Moscow that stereotyped Americans as ruthless, heartless capitalists. Gerzon and his colleagues took steps to break these stereotypes; they brought together delegations from both the Soviet and American film industry to "end the Cold War on the big screen." The results of this citizen diplomacy project were that the major studios and entertainment guilds on both sides of the Iron Curtain formed a partnership to foster more accurate films. They also agreed to promote co-productions that would serve to create deeper understanding and respect between the peoples of both nations. The summit helped to bring about an abrupt halt to depictions of Soviet Communists as bogeymen.

"When film producers, directors and movie stars of a culture move beyond stereotypes of 'the other,'" says Gerzon, "the mainstream population soon follows." His Russian-American summit helped defuse the "real generator of the Cold War, which was human hatred." An American Arab summit could defuse Islamic-American tensions and also "help reduce dehumanizing stereotypes, which fuel the fires of war, terrorism and revenge." Moreover, it could underscore the possibility of peace resolutions and decrees that would help erase dehumanized caricatures of the Arab "other." Gerzon contends, and rightly so, that such a summit would help improve the understanding of each other's interests and concerns.

It is imperative that an entertainment summit take place, one which allows Americans and Arab image makers an opportunity to meet and exchange views. Its impact would be significant. Not only would the proceedings be telecast and seen by viewers throughout the world but *for the first time ever*, Americans and Arabs could begin working together to dispel stereotypes. As a result of the summit, the word, "Arab," an invective used to profane and defame a friendly and hospitable people and their Islamic faith, might no longer be seen as a synonym for "terrorist." In 1999, Senator Hillary Clinton addressed the urgency of breaking down malicious mythical barriers, remarking, "For too long, our close ties with the Arab world have been compromised by negative stereotyping."

Consider the alternatives. Is the time not long overdue to dispel prejudices? Should not Hollywood's future reel Arabs emerge on silver screens not as stereotypical terrorists but as hospitable and peaceful men, women and children who cherish life as much as Americans and others do? Who benefits from status-quo prejudices? Should not movies elevate rather than denigrate the human spirit? This proposed summit will give both Americans and Arabs much-needed opportunities for an innovative beginning. As Muhammad Ali reminds us, "Rivers, ponds, lakes and streams; all are unique. Yet, all contain water, just as religions all contain truth."

Ali's heartfelt words serve as an important reminder as to the importance of the stereotyping problem, and the urgency of a summit. Hosted by American and Arab political and entertainment leaders, the summit would enable men and women of goodwill to unlearn prejudices, and to illuminate justice. As the classic Arab proverb reminds us: *Eed wahdeh ma fiha tza 'if* (one hand alone does not clap).

[362]

CREDIBILITY AND IMPACT OF NEWS CHANNELS

19

Credibility of News Channels: Competing for Viewers

Waddah Khanfar

Media is more an art than a pure science. While the sciences involve rules, equations and facts, the arts fit into the worlds of aesthetics, beauty and opinion that are closely associated with social, psychological, and cultural factors, as well as human experiences.

Media is an art, and formulating clear definitions for relevant terms such as professionalism, credibility, objectivity and independence is like sailing in a rough sea where it is extremely difficult to follow the compass and navigate boats in the right direction.

Generally speaking, there are parameters that the media can set for itself so as to consolidate its credibility and produce reliable coverage. It is beyond the scope of this discussion to delve deep into such terms as each of these words has many connotations.

Before presenting a thorough, comprehensive definition of the term "credibility," which is the focus of this chapter, it may be observed that credibility is the conviction developed by the recipients that what they see or listen to is honest, impartial and closely reflects reality.

From the perspective of heritage, credibility can be traced back to traditional narrators and ancient storytellers. Pioneering Arab scholars have played a significant role in designing rules and guidelines for assessing the news in order to distinguish between sound and weak stories. Hence, they have laid the foundation for the modern media to build upon in its endeavor to ensure the accuracy, impartiality and honesty of the news.

On the other hand, the biggest challenge faced by the Arab media is the domination of some ruling regimes that continue to control the level of freedom in the Arab world. In spite of the independent news media experiences that have emerged during the past decade, the greatest threat to the future of Arab media still lies in such dictatorial regimes and not in media tyranny. In my view, if journalists and media personnel were allowed the opportunity to regulate their profession themselves, they would be capable of developing, and abiding by, certain guidelines and codes of conduct, with a view to producing positive and beneficial journalism to serve their audiences.

Ruling regimes have always been the dominant power and the absolute masters in the Arab countries. Yet, no culture has developed where opinion is respected and journalists are free from many political pressures, even though such pressures exist in every society, including Britain. There, the government sometimes has the right to criticize the media organizations, but it cannot under any circumstances close media outlets, confiscate media materials and equipment, or put journalists behind bars. This issue must be strongly taken up by Arab journalists who must also devote strenuous and practical efforts to assert the independence of journalism and journalists. In this respect, an important question emerges, namely, competition between Arab satellite channels.

Arab journalists must compete in terms of media credibility and professional commitment, not in terms of institutional loyalty. If Arab journalists successfully transcend such loyalties to discuss the profession and its traditions, and support each other when faced with political or oppressive pressures, they will then be in a position to talk about a true Arab media doctrine and real Arab media credibility.

The other important question that emerges from practical and realistic experience is that the Arab media is still in its infancy, since it is only a few years, not decades, during which traditions ought to have been consolidated, theories propounded, and research studies conducted. The discussion revolves around a media that has proved immature in most cases and one in which journalists are moving from print outlets to satellite television channels, which often entail differences in dealing with certain events and attitudes.

In this connection, it is my conviction that the television media in the Arab world is much poorer than print journalism in terms of reporting and analytical content. The former is more involved with analyzing and pursuing the mechanism of the story from the moment it occurs, in a situation in which time is of the essence. Therefore, if the television medium is not employed in a proper way, it would become a superficial and simple news gathering and monitoring tool, thus depriving the viewer of the ability to analyze and contemplate the issues debated. Hence, this problem needs to be discussed among Arab media personnel with a view to arriving at specific solutions.

However, self-criticism on the part of the media should not become a tool used by governments to set their own media restrictions and controls. Rather, self-criticism should help to determine the parameters that journalists create for themselves. Any ideas for forming codes of ethics or professional conduct must stem from the core of media experiences and not be dictated by the censorship authorities or ruling regimes. In this way, mass media and media personnel can rise to the level of the commitments they have authored in their codes of ethics or professional conduct.

At the *Al Jazeera* channel, journalists have entered into a candid, serious dialogue about all questions related to media credibility—including news handling approaches, different editorial policies, use of pictures and photos and the selection of guests. An important decision was made to set up an editorial board so that the choice of programs and shows presented through the channel will not depend on the mood of any particular individual, or be influenced by a certain party, and editorial decisions will be taken collectively to avoid any unprofessional "slips."

The channel has also adopted the *Al Jazeera* Code of Ethics, the outcome of four months of internal discussions. At that time it was stated that the Code's provisions are purely statements of intent without implementation mechanisms. Therefore, *Al Jazeera* has now drawn up a Code of Professional Conduct as detailed field guidelines for its correspondents, reporters and journalists. Using this as a guide, they can translate the Code of Ethics into concrete realistic steps derived from their daily experience. Moreover, in order to achieve genuine adherence to the Code of Professional Conduct, the channel has established the *Al Jazeera* Training and Development Centre, where scores of courses have been organized for hundreds of journalists from *Al Jazeera* and other channels, so that they can benefit from the experience and expertise of important global media schools, like that of the British Broadcasting Corporation (BBC).

Moreover, a Quality Control Commission was set up to ensure that what is presented on the screen is in harmony with the letter and spirit of the Codes so that these will not remain purely statements of intent. Thus, to be able to fulfill social obligations it is necessary to create and honor such institutional controls and parameters.

The tough questions that the *Al Jazeera* journalists asked themselves were: Who are we? What is *Al Jazeera* channel? How do we see ourselves? The channel conducted an in-depth dialogue with its journalists and reporters. All agreed that *Al Jazeera* is a media service and a multiple forum representing Arab identity with a global orientation, respecting various and diverse opinions, striving for the truth, and abiding by institutional professionalism. This is the vision *Al Jazeera* has set for itself.

A heated debate broke out about the mission of *Al Jazeera*. The channel does not regard itself as a political party or driving force for social change within the framework of civil society organizations that pursue specific ideological and direct projects for immediate reforms. The channel views itself as a media organization devoted to supporting important social causes, and in discussing *Al Jazeera's* mission, three fundamental elements were cited:

- The right of humankind to knowledge.
- Democracy, freedom, human rights and reforms.
- *Al Jazeera* as a bridge for communication between different cultures.

It cannot be assumed that the media in the Arab world has reached the adult phase of maturity. I would acknowledge that the media has made several mistakes, and certain mechanisms must be established to remedy these mistakes. That is why the *Al Jazeera* Code of Ethics provides for the channel to "acknowledge a mistake when it occurs, promptly correct it and ensure that it does not recur."

If journalists are to expand the circle of freedoms and human rights through their media activities, they must begin by criticizing themselves, acknowledging and apologizing for their faults in order to become models worthy of being emulated. They should not remain mere advocates of values and ideas without effectively putting them into practice.

The Arab satellite media scene is not too crowded, compared to other places in the world, so competition, in principle, is welcomed because it offers more choices to the recipients and lifts up the standard of the media industry in general, but they have to be governed by codes of ethics. In this respect, I would appeal to all journalists and satellite channels to hold dialogue meetings to formulate a professional code of ethics under which each channel is recognized and respected for its distinct characteristics.

However, journalists will have to agree upon the quintessential principles associated with the ethics of this profession, including those prohibiting the use of the media to humiliate or dishonor other colleagues and organizations. By exchanging accusations in the arena of competition journalists will only lose the respect of their audiences.

In the context of *Al Jazeera's* discussions on high media values (such as objectivity and impartiality), it was suggested that the journalist must have the ability to make crucial decisions at certain times. For example, in covering wars and armed conflicts, the media tends to concentrate on issues such as warfare technologies and weapons, the advances and withdrawals of troops and the losses and gains of warring parties. Nevertheless, such coverage often misses a very important issue, which is the coverage of the human angle, whether from the perspective of a warrior or a victim.

At this point I would like to recall a personal experience. While covering the War in Iraq from the city of Mosul, the media team found itself in the midst of a truly chaotic situation of looting and plundering. The most painful aspects of that situation were the setting of fire to the city's ancient university and the looting of the assets in its historic museum. There, the media team faced the following options: Should they handle the acts of looting and robbery with absolute objectivity and impartiality as a mere news story? Alternatively, should they speak to one of the looters to ascertain his attitude? Or, does the rule of media impartiality not apply to this case?

The decision that the media team took was to support what was right and ethical, and appeal to people to save that valuable heritage. Hence, by addressing the issue of media and credibility, journalists are indeed talking about total commitment to the lofty virtues recognized by all of humanity, which are commonly accepted by moral and ideological institutions anywhere in the world.

If journalists can attain such a level, I am confident that one day they will lay the foundations of what will hopefully become an Arab media doctrine that embraces the cultural particularity of Arab societies, although it may derive benefits from the experiences of well-known media schools.

20

Impact of Global News Channels on International Relations

Greg Dyke

The invasion of Iraq and its aftermath as well as the tragic loss of life in Asia resulting from the tsunami were just two of the major stories covered night and day by the world's global news channels. However, the risks that media personnel often take to provide such news coverage are not readily recognized. The public should pay tribute to the media teams on the ground, which work long hours under the most difficult circumstances to bring these stories to the world, not just risking but sometimes even losing their lives in the process.

These journalists are now part of a 24-hour news culture, a culture more apparent than ever with the steady development of new channels. Twenty four hour news channels are being set up all over the world. Some of these new channels are global, while many others are local. However, such channels are no longer the preserve of the big western corporations.

The market hold of traditional global players such as the British Broadcasting Corporation (BBC) and Cable News Network (CNN) is being challenged and channels such as *Al Jazeera* and *Al Arabiya* have emerged as big players in the field. In the US, Fox News has found success with its own brand of "news with a view" and former Vice President Al Gore is currently developing yet another 24-hour US news channel—presumably to reflect a different approach to news than that of Fox News. However, this is only the beginning. Ironically, while *Al Jazeera* is setting up an English-speaking network, the BBC is being encouraged by the British government to request funding to establish an Arabic-speaking channel. Moreover, the French government, unhappy with what it perceives as the Anglo-American view being reflected around the world, is also seeking to establish its own 24-hour international news channel. Undoubtedly, something truly remarkable is happening—it is possible to watch Fox News in New Delhi, *Al Jazeera* in New Orleans and CNN in New Zealand. Never has there been so much news, nor have there been so many views.

Proliferation of Channels

What are the factors that have led to this proliferation of news channels? The economics of such channels is changing rapidly, making it cheaper to set up an international news channel. First, more and more people can receive them. In Asia alone, where economies are growing at between 7% and 15% per annum, the number of multi-channel television homes has reached 200 million—representing over 30% of all TV households. However, the real change in the economics is that the costs involved in newsgathering are falling rapidly and with them, the entry barriers to the 24-hour news business are also falling. It is new technologies that are dramatically forcing down the cost of newsgathering.

While covering the conflict in Kosovo in the 1990s, broadcasters needed flight cases full of satellite equipment weighing around two tons to be able to transmit their reports. Broadcast news required big teams, heavy equipment and often huge expense. However, that scenario has changed rapidly. In November 2003, the BBC was covering the arrival in the United Kingdom of four decrepit US ships carrying toxic waste. In a move opposed by the public and by environmental groups the vessels were scheduled to be scrapped by the British firm Able UK at the northeastern port of Hartlepool. Traditionally, the BBC would have needed a satellite dish on the shore to transmit scenes of the ships as they arrived. However, the pictures of these ships actually sailing into port were transmitted live from a small boat—by the reporter via his mobile phone.

The Internet has also changed the face of newsgathering, not just through provision of content, but as a means of transmission. The BBC now regularly goes into live visual transmission to its correspondent in Beijing, on a phone line. In 2003, the BBC had to pay £800 for every story it filed from Mexico by satellite. At present, it files stories by broadband Internet at a cost of £500 for a whole year. Imagine that—a permanent 24-hour open line *costs less for a whole year* than one 10-minute satellite feed! Newsgathering is getting cheaper, faster and infinitely more mobile besides offering unprecedented access to places. A story which needed a team of five until recently can now be covered by just two people – sometimes just one – equipped with a camera, laptop and phone. Moreover, as teams get smaller, various professional roles such as those of reporter, cameraman and editor are no longer distinct but blurred together.

Despite all these developments and the fact that the market is getting bigger while news-gathering costs are falling, few of these international channels seem profitable. Today, it is not a business agenda that is mainly driving this trend towards 24-hour news, particularly towards international 24-hour news channels. I suspect that there are several motivating factors involved, but the desire by governments and corporations to have worldwide influence for their brands, and arguably, their views, is probably the single most important factor.

It may be recalled that the British Broadcasting Corporation launched BBC World with two broad aims—having influence and making money. What the BBC discovered was that the latter aim was very difficult to achieve. Today BBC World remains heavily subsidized by the BBC's other more successful commercial activities. Furthermore, I suspect that if the BBC decided to stop BBC World for commercial reasons, as it might have to in the years ahead, the British Government would probably step in and fund it in the same way as it funds the BBC's international radio services. This is because the world has changed since 9/11 and today, the continued existence of BBC World clearly matters to the British Government.

[373]

Diversity of Views

This proliferation of 24-hour news channels – and the diversity of views that this multiplicity implies – ought to be a welcome development. Ted Turner, the father of global television, once said: "My main concern is to be a benefit to the world, to build up a global communications system that helps humanity come together." Turner's notion was that the greater the level of information we received about one another, the greater the level of international understanding that would prevail. His vision was that the globalization of the media would knit the world together. There has been progress in terms of making that information accessible. A young man in Uganda can watch the US elections live, while Americans can hear about Fallujah or Ramallah on a minute-by-minute basis. As yet, I am not convinced that this technological togetherness has quite created the human bonds that were promised. Today, I want to sound a few warning bells. I have a number of concerns about the pattern emerging from these channels and the way they inform our lives. I can even foresee a situation in which the growth of 24-hour global news networks and easy Internet access could actually make the world a less understanding and less tolerant place, which in itself has repercussions for international relations.

Let us first consider the issue of rapid growth in the number of channels. Diversity of voices must be a good thing, but only if we all hear these diverse voices. Understanding the world and the way it works is achieved by understanding a wide range of viewpoints but that does require us to hear the full range of opinion. Assuming that we are all likely to have a favourite 24-hour news channel, the question we need to ask is: Can we be certain that we will hear the full range of voices on that channel or will we only hear news from a particular perspective?

We all have different ideas, come from different cultural backgrounds and our starting points on any given story will be very different. As a former BBC colleague expressed it, there is more than one truth in any given story. [She worked in the Middle East, naturally.] This would explain why it is vital for news channels to reflect a range of voices and not a single voice.

[374]

We need journalists to challenge those in authority and to hold them to account. However, we sometimes need them to challenge us as well by challenging our pre-conceived notions of the world and by challenging the pre-conceived views of their audiences. The short-hand language and dependence on pictures that 24-hour news channels demand can often create stereotypes of the world. Too often, the Western stereotype of a Palestinian is that of a teenage boy throwing stones—because people in the West rarely see other aspects of life in the occupied territories. I have long thought that bad journalism reinforces stereotypes, while good journalism challenges them by making us think again, look twice or reappraise our perceptions.

This leads me to my principal worry—that too much of what we are seeing today is reinforcing stereotypes and views already held. The danger here is not that there are too many channels but that they pander to what they think their politicians, proprietors or audiences want. Consequently, they present a world view which tends to mirror a particular perspective and this in turn means that audiences will tune in to specific channels, not because they are fair or objective, but because they will reinforce their own world view. They will turn to channels precisely because they do not offer a range of voices.

Let us take the United States as an example. I have said on many occasions how shocked I was during my US trip by how unquestioning the broadcast news media was during the Iraq War. The US networks did not seem to be posing tough questions to the US administration. Instead, led by Fox News, they became cheerleaders for the war. In Britain, we believe the job of a broadcaster is to be impartial and that makes it necessary to broadcast a range of views, including those critical of our own Government's position. This does not always create a happy relationship between the broadcasters, particularly the BBC and Government. However, that is not the role of good journalism.

When Prime Minister Tony Blair wrote to me as Director General at the start of the Iraq War complaining that the BBC was taking an anti-war stance my reply was very simple—we were trying to be impartial by reflecting a range of opinion. I then challenged him: How could he possibly be the judge of impartiality, being a committed politician who had staked his political future on supporting the war? Our job was to reflect all opinions and this was particularly so given the strength of public opposition to the war in the United Kingdom. John Simpson, the BBC's World Affairs Editor summed up the position brilliantly in an article published just weeks before the Iraq war in which he said:

> At the times of Suez, Biafra, Vietnam, the Falklands, the American bombing of Libya and the NATO attacks on Kosovo and Serbia, the BBC reported the opposition to these wars fully. On every occasion the Government – Labour or Conservative – tried to bully the BBC into supporting the official line. On every occasion the BBC resisted; sometimes energetically, sometimes not as energetically as it ought to have done...Governments have as much right as anyone to put pressure on the BBC; it's only a problem if the BBC caves in.

I think in the United States, particularly since September 11, such an approach would be viewed as unpatriotic. Of course, impartiality in Britain is a *legal* requirement and remains the hallmark of good journalism. A professional journalist tries to reflect all sides of the story, whether or not it is a legal obligation. Of course, this line is tougher to maintain during war time – as I know to my cost – but to adopt any other line is to replace journalism with patriotism and to substitute analysis with propaganda.

One of the US networks that surprised me the most was Fox News. This channel has taken a committed political position, which has paid off in a commercial sense. It now has the highest audience of any 24-hour news network in the US but it is the nature of that audience which is most revealing, and which reflects a troubling trend. Research published by the Pew Centre last year showed that the overwhelming majority of viewers to the Fox News Channel were supporters of George Bush's Republican Party. In other words, people were choosing to watch the channel in order to have their own world view reinforced. They certainly were not watching it for something different or surprising or to have their own views challenged.

[376]

If this trend was to be repeated globally – and there are some signs it might be – it could prove to be very divisive indeed. If 24-hour channels seek, for commercial or political reasons, to pursue a certain world view, without a proper context, then we run the risk of the Information Age making the world a less tolerant, less understanding and more dangerous place. In fact we could end up with the very antithesis of Ted Turner's vision of humanity coming together. Indeed, should this happen, lack of tolerance and lack of understanding is likely to increase rather than decrease as more and more new channels are launched. Our global villagers will be seeing and hearing each other faster and better but with no corresponding improvement in their ability to learn from or understand one another because they will only be getting news from a particular perspective.

I am not making a case for some kind of neutered journalism and I am certainly not arguing that all networks should look and sound the same. Otherwise all the benefits of diversity are lost. There are cultural differences that should be reflected in different approaches to news. The BBC held a different view from *Al Jazeera* on the issue of broadcasting scenes depicting the bodies of dead civilians or dead soldiers. This is based on a cultural rather than a political difference. However, reports and stories need to be put in a proper context with a range of voices that explain the rationale behind the actions of all players, whether or not they support the national government of the broadcaster. That is the aim of good journalism. Without this breadth of views there will be a built-in bias against understanding and we will be doing our audiences a disservice.

The role of the international news broadcaster must be to reflect a broad range of opinions and not merely the particular views of its government, its proprietor or even that of its likely audience. Of course, there is a group of people who will always complain about news organizations whatever they do—politicians and diplomats who have no shortage of advice for broadcasters. They generally regard media

[377]

reporting and analysis of crises as random and because of that sometimes dangerous. In Britain, particularly during times of major conflict, government attacks on the BBC are a matter of course but they are often savage nonetheless. When British policymakers face a real crisis – such as Afghanistan in 2001-2002, or Kosovo in 1999 and Iraq in 2003-2004 – you can guarantee that the government will fire off a letter reminding the BBC of its obligations to be impartial, just as Tony Blair did to me. What they are really hoping to achieve is to influence the BBC's output in favor of their position.

The crisis in Iraq is just the latest case in which British Government ministers have lined up to criticize news organizations and their 24-hour demands. Home Secretary David Blunkett complained that British journalists were reporting the conflict in a manner that lent "moral equivalence" to the Iraqi regime. According to Blunkett, we were encouraging a "progressive and liberal public" to believe this distorted version. Foreign Secretary Jack Straw developed this theme further, arguing that there were no TV cameras in Saddam's torture chambers. His reign of terror had been conducted off-camera, and therefore – unlike Milosevic in Kosovo – Iraq had not pricked the world's conscience through our TV screens. Saddam had waged a war, but a hidden one, against the Iraqi people. I cannot speak for other news organizations, but what both Blunkett and Straw had conveniently forgotten, was that the BBC, over at least 15 years, had consistently documented human rights violations in Iraq, along with the effects of sanctions on Iraqi civilians.

Sustaining Media Coverage

This raises another important point. News organizations cannot fulfil their remit simply by parachuting in correspondents, satellite dishes and videophones when a crisis happens. The best defence against claims that the media are too often reaching snap judgements are for newsrooms to make long-term commitments to covering the most important stories. The best and most responsible coverage of any news story comes from journalists who have reported it over a long period and those who find the time and space to return to those stories afterwards to find out what happened.

The media circus sometimes appears to move *en masse* from one major crisis to another. This must be irritating to policymakers, who cannot simply drop a problem and move on to something more entertaining or engaging. However, in truth, I suspect that policy makers may well have mixed feelings about the short attention span of the broadcast media.

On the one hand, you can sympathize with politicians and diplomats who feel they came up with worthwhile solutions to international, regional or national problems only to have their efforts ignored by the broadcasters. Little credit was given to those who managed to create a more stable Sierra Leone in 1999 or a more peaceful Cambodia after the UN intervention there in 1992. Yet some politicians and policy makers must surely be relieved when the media caravan moves on *without* tough questions being posed. What ever happened to all that media concern about the Chechens in the mid-1990s? Or the Tibetans after the Chinese moved in on the Dalai Lama's supporters? Instead of making life too complicated for the politicians and diplomats, on these occasions I am more inclined to think that we let them off the hook too frequently.

Whatever happened to reporting in Afghanistan after the Russian Army departed in 1989? More regular reports would have revealed the brutality of the rule of the tribal warlords in Afghanistan followed by the rise of the Taliban supported by the US Government. It would also have made western politicians – US politicians above all – confront the notion that the desire to get the Russians out was unmatched, even to the remotest degree, by any concern for the prospects of the Afghan people.

It is not a question of praising or condemning the policy makers. It is just worthwhile for news organizations to find out what happened to those not-so-recent crises. As an industry we need to be better in returning to stories to find out the answer to that most compelling of narrative questions: What happened next? There is definitely scope for international broadcasters to raise the standard of their game in this regard.

Some politicians have argued that the media are inevitably actors as well as spectators in foreign affairs, because of the way they choose to cover some stories rather than others. I am not convinced that diplomats or politicians have a list of concerns that is actually much more rational than many media organizations—but I do have some sympathy for this view. Despite significant technological advances in newsgathering, broadcasters have neither the money, nor resources, nor even the logistical range to be everywhere all the time. In some places, they cannot get in at all—even if they wanted to. This means, of course, that they are selective in what they do.

Let us consider the numbers killed in the civil war in the Congo—estimated at well over a million and possibly as high as three million. Where was the in-depth reporting and analysis? Where were the challenging interviews with policymakers about that conflict? The truth is that journalists could not get in and as a result the story was not comprehensively reported. However, we have to ask ourselves: Did we try hard enough or did we just dismiss the Congo as a second or third level story? At times, it is also hard to defend ourselves against accusations that we have tunnel vision, or at least a one-sided view of what is important in the world.

This point was made eloquently by a former British Foreign Secretary, Douglas Hurd. He argued that Bosnia, and within Bosnia, Sarajevo had been selected for media coverage. These selections thereafter determined the nature of the coverage. He thought that too many journalists had become members of the "something must be done club." The question he raised was: What would our reaction have been if doing "something" *had* led to a lot of casualties? Had this been the case, the journalists would have rounded on the politicians for embarking on a disastrous misadventure. Hurd argued that journalists were trying to force intervention by plucking on the heartstrings of their audience and bombarding them with human suffering to the exclusion of thought.

Watching the coverage of the Asian tsunami, there were occasions when journalists became part of the "something must be done club" although the scale of the disaster is so large that doing anything was bound to take time. That is when journalism is at its worst. Much has been said and written about this – it has often been called "the CNN effect" – and I will not go into this matter at length. Yet there is some evidence to suggest that if policymakers do have a decently formulated policy they can survive the impact of media attention, which seeks some form of intervention without specifying what may be the likely solution to a crisis.

However, if the politicians and diplomats do not have a properly considered, robust policy –and in Yugoslavia they certainly did not – then they are more likely to get pushed around in their view by the intensity of 24-hour television and radio. Obfuscation is harder in an age of 24-hour scrutiny. Politicians dislike ceaseless coverage not because it masks the truth but because it sometimes exposes their own inertia. In other words, I would argue that 24-hour news most affects public policy where there is inertia in policymaking in the first place.

Obviously, it is not just for the broadcasters that policy makers need robust policies. They need such policies to gain the support of the general public. Military strategists seem to take it for granted that the public will not accept flag-draped coffins being sent back from a conflict. I simply do not know whether that is right or not. However, I think it *is* true that a broad public understanding and approval for war or for intervention is a necessary precondition for the tolerance of high casualties. I may be wrong and that may not be enough. Britain's Foreign Secretary Jack Straw has argued recently that the First and Second World Wars might never have been won if they had been covered by 24-hour news channels. To an extent I agree with him. I find it hard to imagine that the First World War would have continued if television cameras had been covering the battlefields of Somme, Ypres or Verdun and beaming back nightly news. However, would that have been a bad thing? Would it not have prevented the wholesale and unnecessary slaughter of millions of young men for a cause that ultimately proved to be pointless? On the other hand, I hope that if the news channels had been there on D-Day in June 1944 – the

[381]

public in the US, the UK and France would have stood firm and accepted it – even though it was war on foreign soil for both sets of troops. Here there was a real cause.

Looking back through time can be instructive and I want to put in a word for documentaries here. Many painstaking documentaries about recent crises have not only produced compelling drama, but genuine insights. In the constant hustle of our 24-hour culture, pausing and looking back in detail can be hugely enlightening and our 24-hour news channels should do this. At the very least, documentaries can destroy some of the certainties that marked elements of our reporting at the time. It also teaches us to beware of the seductive possibilities of technological and military claims, backed up by neatly packaged video provided for journalists by a willing briefing machine.

Documentaries made in the aftermath of the Bosnian conflict and Middle East peace process also served to remind us just how limited our coverage was at the time. We probably did have access to enough information to have provided audiences with a richer picture than we actually did. It may just be another example of broadcasting's short attention span. Perhaps we should have thought more for ourselves. Whatever the reason, these documentaries showed that, with hindsight, we were too lenient on politicians and diplomats—not too troublesome.

Media Credibility Issues

In this chapter I have underlined the need for news organizations to reflect a true diversity of voices and present their coverage in the proper context. I have also tried to reflect my belief that a long-term commitment to stories, both before and after the point of crisis will better serve our audiences and better hold politicians to account. To conclude I want to look at an emerging issue which concerns me greatly and which affects our most important asset as news organizations—our credibility.

Consider for a moment the infamous photographs taken inside the Abu Ghraib prison in Iraq. The US government's efforts to paint a picture that things were going well in Iraq, despite some setbacks, were quickly and completely undermined by the images of American soldiers posing for the camera while humiliating naked and hooded Iraqi detainees. The photos were snapped by soldiers equipped with digital cameras and burned onto CDs. There is no better testament to the ability of the digital revolution to bring a new transparency to the brutality of war.

In this age of interconnectivity and 24-hour news channels the images had an immediate and profound impact around the world in ways that simple words could not. Views around the world hardened. Pictures on a tiny digital smart card, no bigger than a postage stamp, led to Congressional hearings in Washington. Things may have looked bleak for the American and British forces but they were to get worse. Shortly afterwards, another set of photographs appeared, this time in a London newspaper, the *Daily Mirror*. They showed British soldiers in similar poses. The photographs appeared in the morning and by tea time a BBC correspondent was interviewing an Iraqi sheikh, holding up the *Daily Mirror* front page for the cameras.

Such is the speed and interconnectedness of this Information Age that the pictures reached all around the world in a beat. The photographs renewed and compounded the disgust and tensions generated by the American pictures. Yet there was a difference—a crucial difference. These pictures were not genuine and indeed, formed part of a hoax. However, by the time the hoax was discovered, some weeks after, substantial damage had already been done, given the strong views in the Arab world about these images. Of course it was the newspaper that was hoaxed. Yet news organizations all over the world carried not only the story but also the pictures.

In December 2004, the BBC broadcast an interview with an executive from Dow Chemicals, who admitted Dow's liability for the deadly chemical leak at the Union Carbide plant in Bhopal, India on December 3, 1984 (based ostensibly on its subsequent takeover of Union Carbide). He promised a twelve billion dollar compensation package for the thousands of people affected by this disaster. Reuters and Associated Press flashed the news around the world. Indian victims were interviewed, weeping with joy. It was a great scoop, achieved through simple means. The BBC had gone to a Dow Chemicals website, then on to the press office and negotiated an interview. It was only when Dow Chemicals contacted the BBC – after the interview had been broadcast twice – that the BBC realized that something was amiss. The BBC had visited a fake website and press office, conducted a fake negotiation and interviewed a fake executive. I happen to know that the BBC's systems are better than most news organizations—but despite these systems, it had been well and truly hoaxed.

The problem here clearly stems from a conflation of two key aspects of this Information Age— the voracious appetite of the 24-hour news cycle, and the rise of the Internet and the ability to use and manipulate it to whatever ends. It means that the chances of news organizations being hoaxed are greater than ever. As I have already observed, the digital revolution has brought with it not only fantastic advances in newsgathering but also the ability to manipulate images—and responsible broadcasters will increasingly have to confront this phenomenon.

Nowadays, in one sense, everyone is a journalist. Much of the major networks' coverage of the tsunami of December 2004 which so tragically devastated large coastal areas of Asia came from the digital cameras, amateur videos and 3G phones of ordinary people involved in the disaster. The media is being democratized, which is a positive thing in some ways. We are witnessing the empowerment of large numbers of people through cheap newsgathering technology and a medium of their own—the Internet. However, the need for careful authentication of sources and information is paramount. Being right *has* to take precedence over being first. The BBC has now trained producers in identifying hoax websites, which is actually very easy.

Conclusion

I am aware that the foregoing discussion may have painted a somewhat gloomy picture. Yet I am not pessimistic. Despite the extraordinary technological advances of the past few years, it seems to me that global news providers are still in the initial stages of what promises to be an incredibly exciting new world.

We all need to evolve and modernize rapidly but this progress must be founded on traditional journalistic values. If we lose those values, we lose our credibility and with that we lose everything. Global news organizations have a massive responsibility on their shoulders if they are not to inflame already existing divisions around the world. They must broadcast a diversity of voices, set in their proper context. They need to spend more time focusing on their stories instead of descending on them only when there is a crisis. In addition, as broadcasting and the Internet converge, journalists will need to work harder to authenticate all the available information and sources. None of these tasks are likely to be easy but they will go a very long way to helping the world's broadcasters to discharge their heavy burden of responsibility.

[385]

MEDIA IN THE SHADOW
OF WAR AND OCCUPATION

Media Credibility in War:
The Phenomenon
of Embedded Reporters

Richard Caplan

The US-led war against Iraq witnessed a new approach to governmental management of the media's war coverage—the practice known as 'embedded journalism.' In the Gulf War of 1991, the Pentagon sought to control media coverage by the establishment of restrictive "press pools." However, in 2003 the US military loosened the reins significantly and allowed some 700 US and foreign journalists to live, eat and travel with the American troops. It is often said that truth is the first casualty of war, and the practice of embedding journalists raises important questions that are relevant to media credibility during times of war. Although better access to soldiers and combat operations affords journalists some obvious advantages, what effect does embedded journalism have on the quality of media coverage? Does it create undue bias and sympathy for the troops with whom the journalists keep company? Does it foster a narrow, one-dimensional perspective? Or are journalists able to maintain independent judgement and transcend the limitations of their circumstances?

A Novel Policy

Although the term "embedded journalism" originates with the most recent US war, there is nothing particularly new about the practice of journalists reporting from within the ranks of soldiers at the war front. Journalists have worked alongside soldiers before—in World War I, World War II, Vietnam, and in many other combat situations. The novelty lies in the Pentagon's efforts to facilitate reporting by actually inviting journalists into their fold.

Why would the US military be interested in facilitating media coverage of the war in this way? In the past – especially since the Vietnam War – the US military has been rather wary of the media. Media coverage of the Vietnam War is thought to have been one of the factors responsible for turning the US public against the Pentagon's war effort. For many in the military, the lesson learnt from the Vietnam experience was that journalists should be mistrusted, information carefully guarded and battlefield access denied. Accordingly, in subsequent US wars – notably in Grenada (1983), Panama (1989), the Gulf War (1991) and Afghanistan (2001) – the US government sought to restrict media coverage. Characteristic of this wariness was the comment by Dick Cheney, then US Secretary of Defense, at the time of the 1991 Gulf War: "I do not look on the press as an asset. Frankly, I look on it as a problem to be managed."[1]

The Iraq War of 2003, and the policy of embedded journalism that it initiated, thus marks a significant shift in US governmental policy.[2] Two factors accounted for this shift. First, the military was concerned that the Saddam Hussein regime would seek to manipulate domestic and international opinion with its distorted accounts of the war—as the regime had done in 1991, and the Taliban regime and Al-Qaeda did more recently in Afghanistan. The most effective way to counter disinformation, it was thought, would be to have professional journalists on the ground to tell the story as they saw it. So when, for instance, the Iraqi Information Minister Mohammed Saeed al-Sahhaf claimed on national television that the Iraqi forces were "burning the Americans in their tanks," the claim had absolutely no credibility – internationally at least – because the embedded reporters saw no evidence to support it.[3]

The other reason for this policy shift was that the US military expected to perform well in combat and wanted the media to be on hand to report it.

The military could, of course, publicize their own achievements, as in the past. However, to a journalist and to the viewing, listening or reading public, there is a big difference between reporting what a military spokesperson standing behind a podium says and reporting directly on the event itself.[4] The US military also expected that their troops would be welcomed as liberators and that this would make good television coverage and help to sell the war to a sceptical public that might otherwise be inclined to raise questions about the war effort. As one commentator put it, the Bush administration anticipated that Operation Iraqi Freedom would be the "War of the Happy Iraqis" and that the best way to capitalize on this success would be for the happy Iraqi faces to be broadcast live at home and around the world.[5]

The "rules of embeddedness" were not particularly restrictive. The Public Affairs Guidance (PAG), which was sent to all commanders in the field, indicated:

> Department of Defense (DoD) policy on media coverage of future military operations is that media will have long term, *minimally restrictive* access to US air, ground and naval forces through embedding.[6]

Media representatives – which, incidentally, included *Al Jazeera* and other openly critical correspondents – were to be allowed to "live, work, and travel as part of the units with which they are embedded to facilitate maximum, in-depth coverage of US forces in combat and related operations."[7] For the most part the rules reflected the need to balance media freedom with reasonable security requirements, and imposed certain restrictions, such as reporting on the following matters:

- specific geographic locations of military units
- specific numbers of troops, aircraft or ships below very large levels
- postponed, cancelled or future operations
- force protection measures
- intelligence collection activities
- effectiveness of enemy security measures

While unit commanders could and did exercise their discretion in applying the rules –thereby creating some variation from unit to unit – there is little evidence to suggest that unit commanders were unduly restrictive. Indeed, it appears that the military did not receive as many complaints about restrictions from journalists in the field as they had expected.[8]

Strengths and Weaknesses

Even if the rules of engagement were not particularly onerous, were the media compromised by the military's agenda? After all, the military was not indifferent to media coverage and its policy of embeddedness might allow it to exercise control or influence over the media—indirectly if not directly. Here we get to heart of the matter: the strengths and weaknesses of embedded journalism.

One obvious benefit that embedded journalism affords is first-hand exposure to the battlefield, and it is difficult to see how more rather than less access to the combat environment can be negative. The 1991 Gulf War provides a useful contrast. Then, for instance, the US military made exaggerated claims about the success rate of its Patriot missiles in shooting down Scud missiles. Partly because of restricted access, journalists were not able to verify these claims easily. Consequently, there was a lot of false or misleading reporting about the Patriots. The media did sometimes fall for Pentagon spin even under the embedded scheme, but they were less susceptible as they were often first-hand witnesses to the events in question.

Of course an embedded journalist's view of the world can only be a limited one—a slice of a much broader and complex reality. By the very nature of their positions, embedded journalists cannot know much more than what they can glean from their immediate experience. As one journalist has described it:

> You are someone like the second dog on the dog sled team, and you see an
> awful lot of dog in front of you and a little bit to the left or to the right. But
> if you see an interesting story to the left or to the right, you can't [just]
> break out of the dogsled team.[9]

In short, an embedded journalist's view is necessarily a narrow one. However, this is only a problem if media outlets rely on embedded journalism as their sole or principal source of information, which they generally have not done. Rather, embedded journalists have been used as part of a broader media strategy that integrates reports from other sources, including "unilateral" (non-embedded) journalists; correspondents from military command headquarters, Washington, and other locations; and the commentary of retired generals and other independent analysts. Some media outlets have been better than others in providing background and context but the failure by some to paint a bigger picture cannot be viewed as a weakness of embedded journalism.

The practice of embedding journalists with soldiers creates another potential problem—the sympathy that may develop between them. As one veteran war correspondent has described the situation:

> [The journalists] depend on the military for everything, from food to a
> place to sleep. They look to the soldiers around them for protection. When
> they feel the fear of hostile fire, they identify and seek to protect those who
> protect them. They become part of the team. It is a natural reaction.[10]

And, indeed, the empathetic tone of some coverage suggested that journalists were sometimes a little too close to their subjects. As an embedded reporter from the *Los Angeles Times* explained:

> When you're living in tents with these guys and eating what they eat and
> cleaning the dirt off the glasses, it's a whole different experience. You
> definitely have a concern about knowing people so well that you
> sympathize with them.[11]

Under such circumstances, how can journalists be anything but partial? How can they maintain the distance necessary to report critically? Yet the fact remains that in many cases they have been critical. Consider the two following examples. On March 31, 2003, *Washington Post* correspondent William Branigin, embedded with the US Army's Third Infantry Division, reported on US troops firing on a Land Rover packed with 13 Iraqi civilians after the driver ignored shouts and warning shots. These warning shots, however, were fired too late to allow the driver time to react before the platoon leader ordered the vehicle to be destroyed. Had it not been for Branigin's embedded reporting, we are unlikely to have known the truth of the matter. Indeed, the Pentagon gave a very different version of events, describing an orderly, by-the-book process, which if Branigin's account is to be believed – and there is no reason why it should not be – was not the way the events occurred.[12]

A similar incident arose during the US assault on Fallujah in November 2004. In this case, Kevin Sites, an *NBC Television* correspondent embedded with US Marines, captured on video the shooting of a wounded and unarmed Iraqi fighter who had been discovered the previous day and left to await the necessary medical attention. The dramatic footage shows a US marine standing above the injured, helpless man, pointing his rifle at his head, and firing a lethal shot. Again, if it were not for Sites' position as an embedded journalist, it is unlikely that this particular story would have been reported, resulting in a criminal investigation of the incident.

Branigin's and Sites' stories show that embedded journalists are not necessarily in league with the military but rather, that they are capable of filing honest and accurate reports, despite the empathy they may feel for the soldiers in their company. (In Sites' case, the empathy resulted in an "open letter" that he wrote to his Marine companions, explaining the reasons why he chose to file the story, but the sentiment does not appear to have compromised his reporting.)[13] Even though the military must have been unhappy about these incidents, they did not prevent the reports being filed. As Bryan Whitman, the Pentagon's Deputy Assistant Secretary of Defense for Public Affairs, and the chief policy architect of embedding, explained subsequently: "We knew…that we were going to get reporting of the good, the bad, and the ugly."[14] And so they did.

It is important to stress that much of what is known about embedded journalism is rather impressionistic and anecdotal. There have been very few *systematic* analyses of embedded journalism. The few studies that have been conducted to date—notably a study by Columbia University's Project for Excellence in Journalism and another by the Cardiff School of Journalism in Britain—suggest that on balance, viewers are better served by embedded journalism than by the more limited press pools during the Gulf War of 1991 or the halting access to events in Afghanistan since 2001.[15] For what popular opinion may be worth, a survey conducted by the Pew Research Center for the People and the Press in March 2003 found that 58 percent of Americans thought that embedded reporters "were a good thing." Of the 34 percent who thought they were "a bad thing," most were worried that embedded reporters were or would be providing information that could help the enemy.[16]

More Fundamental Problems

The more serious problems for media credibility have less to do with embedded journalism *per se* than with tendencies that characterize Western reporting generally. Just three of these problems are discussed below:

1-Insufficiently Critical Reporting

This may seem a curious charge against the Western media—an institution that is famous (if not infamous) for challenging authority. However, when it came to reporting on the war against Saddam Hussein, major US media organizations were insufficiently critical of US government claims, as they themselves admitted subsequently. For instance, in an extraordinary admission on August 12, 2004, the *Washington Post* acknowledged that it had underplayed scepticism of White House claims that Iraq had weapons of mass destruction, thus making it easier for the Bush administration to pursue a pro-war policy. In a 3,000 word front page article, the newspaper said that it "did not pay enough attention to voices raising questions about the war." Three months earlier, in May 2004, the *New York Times* had published its own *mea culpa* in which it confessed:

> Editors at several levels who should have been challenging reporters and pressing for more skepticism were perhaps too intent on rushing scoops into the paper.[17]

2-Lack of Local Knowledge

Western journalists, whether embedded or not, too often lack local knowledge and are thus prone to misinterpreting the situation on the ground or even missing important stories altogether. One embedded correspondent, writing for the *Washington Post* during a US marine attack on Fallujah in April 2003, described, almost poetically, "the indecipherable chanting of muzzeins," coming from the city, "filling the air with...Koranic verse." By contrast, *Al Jazeera*, with its intimate knowledge of the local culture and language and having a correspondent and crew posted in the city, described more accurately what the *Washington Post* correspondent was hearing—urgent appeals for medical assistance and calls on the local population to rise up and fight the Americans.[18] This is weakness of a more general nature that characterizes a lot of Western, especially US journalism. It is not a weakness that is restricted to embedded journalism. The *Washington Post* was, in fact, in a better position than many other Western newspapers because it at least had correspondents in Baghdad who could speak Arabic.

3-Self-censorship Tendency

The rules of engagement for embedded journalists, as already noted, were fairly relaxed. For the most part, formal restrictions were minimal and reasonable. It is not hard to see that violations of these restrictions could jeopardize operations and endanger lives. While there might be disagreement as to what constitutes "operational security," generally speaking, the military does not appear to have unduly suppressed news reporting. Indeed, as noted above, the military oversaw, and indirectly facilitated, reporting on some serious misconduct by soldiers. However, if military censorship did not prove to be a serious problem, self-censorship did. For instance, there have been few images of wounded or dead US or British soldiers. The Cardiff University study found that although reporters who accompanied the British and US military could be objective, they avoided images that they considered to be too graphic or violent for British television, leading some to charge that journalists were "sanitizing" the war. By contrast, regional media, such as *Abu Dhabi TV* and *Al Jazeera*, did not shy away from showing civilian casualties and other "uncomfortable" scenes.

Along with self-censorship there is the highly questionable but now established practice of using euphemisms to conceal the harsh realities of war. These include, for instance, references to Iraqi forces being "degraded" or even "attrited" (a neologism) to describe the killing of Iraqi soldiers, and "collateral damage" to describe civilian casualties.[19] There has also been scant coverage of the effects of military attacks on Iraqi civilians. Such limited coverage can only partially be attributed to problems of access. Much of the Western media were simply less interested in covering such matters as anti-American rallies or civilian casualties.

Conclusion

The policy of embedding journalists with military units was devised by the Pentagon as a means to improve its media image after attempts at restricting access during earlier wars yielded unsatisfactory results and drew considerable criticism. A key assumption behind the embedding process was that there would be more positive coverage rather than negative coverage, and that the risk of a few unfavorable stories by embedded reporters was outweighed by the expectation of overwhelmingly favorable coverage. On the whole, the Pentagon's assumptions appear to have been validated. Moreover, many analysts seem to agree that embedded journalism has added useful perspective to media coverage of the war. There have certainly been weaknesses stemming from that coverage, but most journalists involved have been able to maintain their objectivity and, in some cases, have even provided critical reporting that would otherwise not have been available. Indeed, the Cardiff School of Journalism study concluded:

> The embeds provided a much *more* balanced account of events than some non-embedded reporters—especially studio-based anchors, whose scripts could be seen, on some issues, to be inadvertently tilted toward certain pro-war assumptions.[20]

The problems for media fairness, accuracy and thus credibility, do not derive principally from the nature of embedded journalism but from more general tendencies – notably the uncritical use of government information and analysis, a lack of local knowledge and self-censorship – occupational hazards that all journalists, whether embedded or not must tackle effectively.

22

The US Military and the Media: War Coverage and Credibility

Robert Hodierne

Since the rise of the popular press in mid-19th century America, journalists have traveled into war with US forces. From the start there has been friction—the inevitable collision between military people who are accustomed to secrecy and control and reporters who chafe at both. For a century and a half, that friction has defined both the nature of the relationship between the US military and the media and the credibility of those two institutions with the public at large.

The uncomfortable truth for most journalists is that the American public is more likely to believe the military than the press, especially when there is wide support for war. During what Americans call the First Gulf War (1991), nearly all journalists were excluded from front-line coverage. They were reduced to covering press briefings at military headquarters. A RAND study concluded:

> ...the military was successful in implementing some of the most extensive controls ever on information and press coverage, and the public appears to have been largely indifferent to, if not entirely satisfied, with the performance of the press and the military in keeping the public informed.[1]

In the years after the First Gulf War, the military came to realize that the pending war with Iraq was going to be a war not just with bombs and bullets, but with information. The military needed the work of a free and unfettered press to counter what was expected to be a vigorous information campaign from the Iraqis. That need, as much as anything else, motivated a return to the kind of unregulated and uncensored coverage not witnessed since the Vietnam War.

The results of embedding large numbers of journalists with frontline troops were obvious to all. For the first time, stunning live images of combat were broadcast into homes around the world. Thousands of stories portrayed American troops in just the way the government wanted—as skillful, well-trained men and women who, in general, performed honorably. It is only now, in the occupation stage of the war, that embedding has started to reveal the other, darker and inevitable consequence of war—the abominable behavior of some troops and the grinding, seemingly never ending lists of casualties.

In the short term, the coverage by embedded journalists boosted the sagging credibility of the US press. Yet, as the war drags on, the simple story line of a lightning-quick invasion has given way to more complex and often unflattering coverage. Likewise, there is a swelling disenchantment with the war among the US public. And with that, media credibility has started to droop. However, without the frontline accounts, the press would be reduced to parroting the government version of events and that would do even deeper, more far-reaching damage to press credibility. As US Senator Hiram Johnson said in 1917: "The first casualty when war comes, is truth."[2]

To understand how the media performed – and was used – in the Iraq War, it is necessary to understand the historical background. The stage for such media reporting was set in Mexico a century and a half ago.

The Historical Background

In 1846, an expansionist United States went to war with Mexico. The Mexican War (1846–48) was the first US war covered by professional journalists at the front lines. Much of the press handling of the Mexican War presaged the way the US press has covered wars ever since. While much has changed since then, much remains the same. For example, the vivid descriptions of combat and atrocities in the Mexican War fueled an anti-war movement back home, something that would be echoed 120 years later in Vietnam.

The Mexican War came just as the US newspaper business was going through dramatic changes. The invention of the fast rotary press in 1843 allowed newspapers to increase their press run and lower their costs. The so-called penny press became America's first truly mass media, catering to the tastes of an ever-widening range of literate Americans who bought papers on the streets from boys hawking that day's headline.

Much of the press fueled the drive to war with uncritical and unquestioning acceptance of government pronouncements, not unlike the US press treatment of the run up to the current war in Iraq. *The Boston Times* said of the pending Mexican War that an American victory "must necessarily be a great blessing," because it would bring "peace into a land where the sword has always been the sole arbiter between factions" and would introduce "the reign of law where license has existed for a generation."[3]

Once the war began, it became America's first media war. Robert W. Johannsen, writing in *To the Halls of the Montezumas: The Mexican War in the American Imagination*, commented:

> [The war]...touched the people's lives (especially if they were readers), a war that was experienced more intimately, with greater immediacy and closer involvement than any major event in the nation's history. It was the first American war to rest on a truly popular base, the first that grasped the interest of the population, and the first people were exposed to on an almost daily basis. The essential link between the war and the people was provided by the nation's press, for it was through the ubiquitous American newspaper that the war achieved its vitality in the popular mind.[4]

Prior to the Mexican War, newspaper accounts were based on letters from soldiers or official dispatches. (In a sense, one might say that the proliferation of Internet blogs by troops at the front lines is a throwback to that earlier time.) In the Mexican War, professional reporters traveled to the front with the troops—being "embedded," to use the popular

[401]

contemporary term. However, unlike modern wars, those reporters frequently blurred the line between observer and participant. Some took up arms and some even advised military and diplomatic leaders. One of them, James L. Freaner of the *New Orleans Delta,* actually carried the signed peace treaty from Mexico to Washington.

If it is true that wars are good for the careers of military officers, it is equally true that journalistic careers have been made by wars. The man often described as the first modern war correspondent was George Wilkins Kendall, who founded the *New Orleans Picayune.* His coverage of the war made him nationally famous, probably America's first celebrity journalist. Whatever the shortcomings in accuracy and objectivity, Johannsen said, "Americans were better informed about their war than any people in wartime had ever been."[5]

That access to information turned out to be a double-edged sword. Reporters traveled where they wanted and reported what they saw. They reported on the hardships experienced by the troops, the horror of combat and the atrocities that some US troops committed against Mexican civilians. Such reporting helped to build a vibrant anti-war movement in America that included such people as Henry David Thoreau and Abraham Lincoln.

The war ended with the United States annexing California and much of what is now the American southwest—excluding Texas. The expansionists, who had led the charge to war, felt that the United States got less than it deserved. In fact, before the war, the United States had offered to buy those same territories from the Mexicans. Many American historians believe that US government settled the war because the American public, once enthusiastic about the war, had grown tired of its costs—both in terms of dollars and lives. At both ends of that equation was the press. The American public believed the press when it said the war was a good idea and many also believed the press accounts of the war's true gruesome nature.

By the time the American Civil War (1861–65) began, the newspaper business had flourished. Northern newspapers put 500 journalists in the field. One paper, the *New York Herald* spent $1 million covering the war and had 63 journalists covering it.[6]

The technology of gathering news had improved dramatically. The country had gone from having no telegraph at the start of the Mexican War in 1842 to having 50,000 miles of telegraph wires at the start of the Civil War. The technology of printing newspapers had also improved. Presses powered by steam engines were faster, which meant that the time between the arrival of a wire report from a distant city and the appearance of a paper on the street was cut from days to hours. Newspapers often had stories about battles before government officials in Washington had accounts from their military officers.

What had not improved was the professionalism of journalists. A journalist of that era would not have understood the term "objective reporting." Papers were partisan, and so were the journalists reporting for them. Sourcing standards were practically non-existent. Phillip Knightley, in his book *The First Casualty*, said that the battalion of Civil War journalists "measured up poorly to the task." According to him, they were "ignorant, dishonest, and unethical...the dispatches they wrote were frequently inaccurate, often invented, partisan, and inflammatory."[7] Editors and publishers did not care much about such matters. They cared more about selling newspapers. Knightley said a New York newspaper "could sell five times its normal circulation when it ran details of a big battle …"[8]

However, if the newspapers were dishonest, so, too, was the government.

> The Secretary of War, Edwin M. Stanton, began to dicker with casualty figures. He altered an account of (Gen. Ulysses S.) Grant's failure at Petersburg, reducing the losses to about a third of their actual number. His department withheld news of the surrender of Harper's Ferry for twenty-four hours and changed '10,000 Union troops surrendered' first to '6,000' and in later dispatches to '4,000.' The actual figure was 11,200. Stanton

[403]

took to suspending newspapers that had broken his censorship rules, arresting editors, threatening proprietors with court-martial, and banning correspondents from the front, and he actually issued orders for Henry Wing of the *New York Tribune* to be shot for refusing to hand over a dispatch he written for his newspaper.[9]

By 1898, at the start of the four-month Spanish–American War, the US press had nearly reached the zenith of its sensationalist partisanship. The role that the press played in creating the war continues to be debated. However, 200 journalists went to Cuba to cover the fighting there.

By 1917, the start of US involvement in World War I, the number of newspapers in America had reached 17,000, the greatest number that would ever exist in the United States.[10] The press had matured and standards of accuracy and objectivity had become more widespread. Governments, too, had matured in their understanding of how to manipulate the press. Before America's entry into the war, the US press struggled to remain neutral and objective, siding with neither the British and French nor the Germans. The British government launched a campaign to win over the US press and bring the country to its side in the war, which Knightley said was notably successful.[11]

Once the United States had joined the war, reporters needed military credentials to travel with the American forces. On the subject of war correspondents and their accreditation procedures, Knightley writes:

> The rules for accreditation of a war correspondent to the American Expeditionary Force have to be read to be believed. First, the correspondent had to appear personally before the Secretary of War or his authorized representatives and swear that he would 'convey the truth to the people of the United States' but refrain from disclosing facts that might aid the enemy. Then he had to write – and the authorities defined 'write' to mean with a pen, not a typewriter – an autobiographical sketch, which had to include an account of his work, his experience, his character, and his health. He had to say what he planned to do when he reached Europe and where he planned to go. Then he or his paper had to pay $1,000 to the army to cover his equipment and maintenance and post a $10,000 bond to ensure that he would comport himself 'as a gentleman of the Press.' If he were sent back for any infraction of the rules, the $10,000 would be forfeited and given to charity. He was allowed to take an assistant – for a

[404]

further $500 maintenance fee – and if he did not wish to use army transport he could buy a car or ship one overseas for his personal use. Correspondents wore no uniforms, but were obliged to wear a green armband with a large red 'C'.[12]

While certain rules seem stark by today's standards – no journalist would ever post a bond to ensure his good behavior – many other regulations are not so different from those imposed on journalists by the US forces in Iraq. Reporters working in Iraq were prohibited from describing the success of enemy weapons against US forces, nor were they allowed to report which Iraqi defensive measures were successful (For details, see Public Affairs Guidance rules on embedded media reporting available at: www.hodierne.com/groundrules.htm).

During World War I (1914–18), all the stories about US forces were censored. The same practice continued during World War II (1939–45). Among the bizarre results of that censorship was that although the Japanese public saw newsreels showing how many ships its navy had sunk at Pearl Harbor, and every person in Hawaii knew it too, the US public was purposefully misled until well after the war.

When commanders in the field made errors, when supplies were short, when the enemy managed victories, the American public never knew. While reporters chafed and groused, there was never an organized effort to either circumvent or change the censorship rules. The journalists, like the military, believed in the greater good. After the war, the American author John Steinbeck wrote:

> We were all part of the war effort. We went along with it, and not only that, we abetted it. Gradually it became a part of us and the truth about anything was automatically secret and that to trifle with it was to interfere with the war effort. By this I don't mean that the correspondents were liars. They were not...It is the things not mentioned that the untruth lies...Yes, we wrote only a part of the war but at that time we believed, fervently believed, that it was the best thing to do. And perhaps that is why, when the war was over, novels and stories by ex-soldiers, like the 'The Naked and the Dead,' proved so shocking to a public which had been carefully protected from contact with the crazy, hysterical mess.[13]

In the early months of the Korean War (1950–54) there was no formal censorship and reporters filed vivid and often chilling accounts of the war, which at the start went especially badly for the Americans. The military accused the reporters of being traitors (a similar accusation was made against me twenty years later in Vietnam). However, the press had a different view of its mission in Korea than in any previous war. Their mission was to tell the truth. Marguerite Higgins, a reporter for the New York *Herald Tribune,* wrote as follows:

> So long as our government requires the backing of an aroused and informed public opinion…it is necessary to tell the hard bruising truth…It is best to tell graphically the moments of desperation and horror endured by an unprepared army, so that the American public will demand that it does not happen again.[14]

After the Korean War, Higgins was one of the earliest Americans reporters to cover the war in Indochina. She was with photographer Robert Capa when he stepped on a mine in 1954 and was killed. In 1965 while in Vietnam, she contracted the tropical disease leishmaniasis and died early the following year.

Depending on your point of view, coverage of the Vietnam War (1961–75) was either the high point or low point of American war coverage. During that war, journalists traveled anywhere in the country, limited only by their nerve and their ability to hitch rides on helicopters. There were few restrictions on what they could publish, resulting in the most unvarnished coverage ever of a major war. It was the first war played out on television— bloody color war images on every TV set in the United States. Along with stories of heroism came stories of atrocities. An entire generation of US military leaders believed firmly that what they viewed as negative press coverage lost the war in Vietnam. And for a generation, US journalists believed that you could tell if a military officer at a press briefing was lying simply by looking to see if his lips were moving.

The same year that Higgins died, I dropped out of college and paid my way to Vietnam to work as a freelance war photographer, a stringer. I mention this as an illustration of how accessible that war was to journalists: Even a 21-year-old freelancer with no other professional experience could get a press card and set forth wherever he wanted.

Correspondents who covered the Vietnam War sometimes speak wistfully about it as the last good war for journalists. The military provided transportation and placed few restrictions on where we could travel. We did not need to clear our travel plans with anyone. Our stories and photographs were uncensored. Of course, there were some ground rules. We could not report on a military operation until contact had been made with the enemy. We could not report exact casualty figures. Instead we used terms like "light," "moderate" or "heavy."

Technology was also moving ahead rapidly. Just as the telegraph enabled reporters covering the Civil War to bring the war news home with unprecedented speed, television was not only bringing the news home faster but bringing it right into American living rooms.

Until the late 1960s, many journalists covering the war sympathized with US government goals. Many of the older correspondents who had begun their reporting during World War II and the Korean War tended to view the government with little or no skepticism. However, as the war dragged on, the conflict between the reality that was plainly visible to reporters in the field and the picture painted in official briefings became starker.

The daily military briefing, conducted at five in the afternoon, became known as the "Five 'O'clock Follies." By 1969, the push was on to turn the war over to the South Vietnamese army so the US forces could declare victory and depart—a policy that sounds eerily like US policy today in Iraq. An early test of that policy came at an isolated Special Forces camp near the Laotian border called Ben Het. I had spent several days at the camp in June 1969. It was surrounded by North Vietnamese soldiers who lobbed in scores of rocket and artillery rounds each day. The only way in and out was by helicopters that were inevitably shot at. I left the camp and flew back to Saigon, arriving just in time to hear the briefer at the Five O'clock Follies upbraiding the gathered press for insisting on referring to

[407]

the "siege" of Ben Het. He said, with utter sincerity, that the camp was not under siege, and that the South Vietnamese army had the road to Ben Het open and was regularly supplying it. I never believed another word the man spoke.

Several months later I wrote an article about soldiers who, after several days of bloody fighting, had refused to fight. The chief spokesman for the US Army in Vietnam gave a speech in which he said "whether the story was true or not was beside the point." My story, he said, "did not border on treason, it was treason."

For the press at least, the statement "Whether it was true or not is beside the point" pretty much defined the US military's attitude toward truth. For its part, the military came to believe the reporting from Vietnam was unrelentingly and unfairly negative. When the North Vietnamese and Viet Cong staged their coordinated, countrywide attacks during the Tet holiday in 1968, the military, quite correctly, noted that thousands of the enemy had been killed and that they had been unable to hold a single city (though it did take the US Marines weeks to drive them out of Hue). It took the military years to understand that the lies they had told in the years leading up to the Tet attacks had led the American public to believe the enemy was crippled and incapable of the stunning military action that they watched in horror on the evening television news shows. Thus the US military, while handing the North Vietnamese a staggering military defeat, itself suffered a staggering public relations defeat from which it never recovered during that war.

The military vowed to never let it happen again. Through the next three decades, as they fought in Grenada, Panama, Haiti, Somalia, Bosnia and Kosovo, the military kept the press away from the action or let so few have such limited access that it never faced the unrelenting scrutiny it believed had undone its efforts in Vietnam. In the First Gulf War that policy reached its zenith. The military, whose telegenic officers and whiz-bang smart bomb videos entranced an American public, totally controlled the message.

Lurking in the background, however, was the unlearned lesson from the Vietnam War—that you must be credible to succeed in the Information Age. For the US military to be credible with its public, it must allow the press the access and ability needed to perform its watchdog role. Unrestricted coverage may prove painful from time to time—the video of a Marine shooting an apparently helpless wounded Iraqi insurgent was not the best public relations exercise for the military. Nonetheless, in the larger scheme of things, it is the only successful route for the military as it functions in a democratic society, which depends as Higgins put it, on an aroused and informed public.

The Birth of Modern Embedding

When Washington decided to invade Afghanistan and search out the Al Qaeda forces behind the September 11, 2001 attacks as well as the Taliban regime that supported them, it enjoyed public and worldwide support not seen since World War II.

The early military operations in Afghanistan, relying as they did on special operations teams, did not lend themselves to media coverage. The techniques and weapons were secret and even the very fact that they were present on the battlefield was secret. Moreover, there are not many journalists who could hope to physically endure what the special operations teams endured.

Once conventional forces entered the fight, the American military's response to the press was reflexively controlling and secretive. Here is a description by *Washington Post* reporter Carol Morello of the first group of reporters allowed with US Marines in Afghanistan in late November 2003:

> The first news media pool, a small grouping of reporters who are the eyes and ears of their colleagues and share their reports with others who are not present, was airlifted to the Marine base in Afghanistan for five days that ended early this morning. While at the base, the reporters were not permitted to accompany troops on expeditions from the base, were prohibited from reporting much of what they saw, were diverted toward

feature stories such as church services and promotion ceremonies, were not allowed to speak to senior commanders (except one produced in their final hour with the Marines) and were barred from reporting details even after they were leaked – and announced – by the Pentagon. Working under Pentagon guidelines that require public affairs escorts at all times, reporters could cover everything but the news. [15]

Morello went on to describe what happened when some wounded Americans were brought to the Camp Rhino base. The journalists were confined to a windowless warehouse when the wounded US and Afghan troops arrived. The men had been wounded when a US B-52 dropped bombs near them and the military did not want the negative coverage they believed would follow if reporters had access to the men. So, the reporters were not allowed to interview the wounded nor the doctors who treated them. They were not even allowed to see them. For many in the press, it seemed like the bad old days of the First Gulf War had returned. "We had greater freedom of coverage of Soviet military operations in Afghanistan than we had at Camp Rhino," CNN reporter Walt Rogers was quoted as saying in Morello's story. [16]

Then a remarkable thing happened. In Washington, the Defense Department spokeswoman, Victoria Clarke, issued a memo to the press saying "we owe you an apology" for the "severe shortcomings" in the treatment of reporters at Camp Rhino. Even more remarkably, for those accustomed to a far different message, Defense Secretary Donald Rumsfeld said he was "committed to the principle that the media should have access to both the good and the bad in this effort." [17]

The military made good on those words. When the US Army staged its largest operation of the Afghanistan war, the assault into the Shahikhot Valley, it took reporters into combat. A reporter and photographer from *Army Times,* reporters from Agence France-Presse, the Associated Press and a two-man team from CNN went in with the first waves of Operation Anaconda. The reporters were given the sort of pre-operation access they had dreamed about for a generation. They sat in on sand table briefings in which the entire operational plan was laid out. These were not special, sanitized press briefings. These were briefings for the officers who would lead the fight.

Such access posed enormous risks for the military leadership. If the plan fell apart – and the axiom in military life is no battle plan survives the first contact with the enemy – the reporters on the scene would witness the unraveling. The best hope of the military in that situation was that the reporters would put any change in the plan into its proper context. Operation Anaconda was a tactical military success in that the several hundred Al Qaeda and Taliban fighters in the valley were either killed or driven off. It was also a public relations success. The stories and photographs that came from that small team of embedded journalists in general portrayed the American soldiers as brave and competent, their leaders as savvy and the enemy as defeated.

It may be noted here that one of the embedded reporters, Sean D. Naylor of *Army Times,* completed a book on the operation that delves far more deeply into both the heroics performed by American troops and their mistakes. It is unlikely that he would have been able to produce such a definite analysis had he not been present for the fight. The fact that he was there, suffering the same physical hardships as the troops, including being shot at, increased his credibility among the men whom he had later interviewed for his book.

At the urging of military public affairs officers who had been in Afghanistan and who had helped push through the small-scale experiment in embedding, Victoria Clarke, the Defense Department spokeswoman, and her deputy, Bryan Whitman, began enlisting the support of major US media organizations. Both knew they would have a tough time selling the idea to their boss, Defense Secretary Donald Rumsfeld, and his boss, President George W. Bush[18] Their goal was simple, as Whitman explained:

> We wanted to neutralize the disinformation efforts of our adversaries. We wanted to build and maintain support for US policy as well as the global war on terrorism. We wanted to take offensive action to achieve information dominance. We wanted to be able to demonstrate the professionalism of the

[411]

US military. And we wanted to build and maintain support, of course, for the war fighter out there on the ground.

In short, as Whitman put it, they believed that "robust media access" would "counter Iraqi lies" and highlight the professionalism of US forces.[19]

Getting Rumsfeld on board proved easier than getting the President to approve:

> 'Rumsfeld and Torie Clarke ran against the current,' said (Walt) Rogers (of CNN). 'I know personally, and won't go into any detail, that the President of the United States thought embedding was 'a crazy idea' and was initially opposed to it but reluctantly went along. I know personally that the Vice President of the United States did not think it was a good idea. It was Torie Clarke and Don Rumsfeld who pushed this through over the objections of their superiors.'[20]

The decision to embed large numbers of journalists with the armed forces preparing to invade Iraq, while different in scale, was consistent with what the published public affairs policy of the military had been since 1993. "Open and independent reporting shall be the principal means of coverage of the US military operations," those guidelines say. "Journalists shall be provided access to all major military units."[21] The major difference was that this time the military meant it.

Once the decision had been made to embed journalists with military units, both the military and the media had many decisions to make. On the military side, it was mostly logistical. How many journalists could any given military unit accommodate? How would the military move the journalists around the battlefield? Should the military provide protective gear? However, those are the sorts of logistical matters the US military is expert at handling.

For journalists, there were more troubling issues, mostly dealing with the risks to their credibility if they were perceived as being in partnership with the military, rather than merely embedded with them.

> The psychological phenomenon in which hostages begin to identify with, excuse, and in some cases even actively protect their captors is called 'the

> Stockholm syndrome.' While this term is not wholly applicable to the embedded press, there is little doubt that similar pressures are placed on embedded reporters. From the military's perspective, journalists' identification with soldiers can be beneficial since it increases the likelihood of good public relations. But from the perspective of journalists and the public, this closeness can be somewhat alarming.[22]

In the end, all the major US news organizations took up the military's offer to embed journalists. In all, 775 journalists were embedded with US ground forces, on Navy ships and at airbases in Kuwait (though much to the frustration of reporters there, they could not identify even the country of their location due to Kuwaiti sensitivities). Yet, for all the sound and fury surrounding the number of embedded journalists, only 40 or 50 would witness actual combat. Moreover, despite the large number of embedded journalists, they were outnumbered by those acting outside the military embrace. Such "unilaterals," as they became known, were based in Kuwait, Qatar and Baghdad. Some roamed the battlefield, while others reported from the roofs of their hotels in Baghdad.[23]

The Outcome

For the US military, the embedding of journalists during the first stage of the war was a major success. As a RAND study concluded:

> Embedded press during major combat operations in Iraq, coupled with the decisive military victory and the by-and-large exemplary performance of US forces, resulted in excellent public relations for the military. Public support for the military remained high, even during the second week of the war…when several negative stories appeared.[24]

The RAND study added that the military's commitment "to the embedded press system, even in the face of events that did not show the military in a favorable light (such as the reporting of accidental civilian casualties at a checkpoint), served to increase and maintain military credibility."[25]

As Alicia C. Shepard concluded in her study:

Americans gained a better comprehension of what the military does and of the sacrifices and hardships thousands of Americans make on a daily basis. And it renewed pride in the US military.[26]

Having the independent press along to bear honest witness paid off, just as the military planners had hoped. After the war, Victoria Clarke, while speaking at a Brookings Institution panel, made the following observations:

> I've used this story several times, but I knew with great certainty if we went to war, the Iraqi regime would be doing some terrible things and would be incredibly masterful with the lies and the deception. And I could stand up there at that podium and Secretary Rumsfeld could stand up there and say very truthfully the Iraqi regime is putting its soldiers in civilian clothing so they can ambush our soldiers. Some people would believe us and some people wouldn't. But we had hundreds and hundreds of credible, independent journalists saying the Iraqi regime is putting their soldiers in civilian clothing. So we knew that would be a very effective tool.[27]

Contrast this with Gen. William Tecumseh Sherman in 1861, who declared, "We don't want the truth told about things here…We don't want the enemy any better informed than he is."[28]

At no point was the strategy of using the media to bolster the credibility of the military more apparent than in the closing days of the drive to Baghdad. Had there been no embedded journalists, the story would have played out this way: Gen. Vincent Brooks, the US military's chief spokesman operating out of Camp Doha in Qatar, would have told the 200 or so assembled press that American troops had moved into Baghdad airport and were in the outskirts of Baghdad. The world's media then would have broadcast Iraq's Minister of Information, Mohammed Said Sahaf, saying that Baghad is "safe and secure," that the invading "louts" and "mercenaries" were being "slaughtered." According to Sahaf, "We have killed most of the infidels, and I think we will finish off the rest soon."[29]

Who would have known what to believe? The conventions of "objective" news coverage would have required journalists to offer up both views and let the audience decide. However, with live television images showing US tanks at the airport, Sahaf was reduced, at least to American eyes, to a comic figure. He may have been viewed differently in the coffee shops of Cairo and Amman, but there was nothing the US military could have done about that. In America, the Iraqi regime was reduced to farce.[30]

Polling by the Pew Research Center for the People and the Press showed that the military's credibility with the American public was high. At the end of March 2003, 84 percent of Americans were saying they had confidence in the accuracy of the military's reports about the war.[31]

Although embedding was a boon to the military's credibility, the results are more ambiguous for the press. As the RAND study noted:

> Credibility is particularly hard to nail down for the press because of its atomized nature: different press agencies deserve different levels of credibility; however, different people will mentally aggregate 'press' at different levels; some might distinguish between print and television, while other might single out specific agencies for greater skepticism, and still others might consider the press as a single monolithic enterprise.[32]

At the height of major combat operations, the Gallup pollsters asked the American public to rate the job done by the news organizations in covering the war. During the first week of the war, a resounding 84 percent said the press did an "excellent" or "good" job, numbers that slipped a little during the second week to 79 percent. Those laudable numbers came in an era when large segments of the American people (ranging from 58 to 62 percent) said that in general, news organizations were often inaccurate. Only slim majorities described themselves as having any level of trust and confidence in the media. In short, the public believed the war coverage more than they typically believe the media.[33]

Before drawing any link between that level of public trust and the embedding process, it is instructive to look back at similar polling during the First Gulf War when most journalists were kept far from the fighting. The public ratings then were, if anything slightly higher.[34] These conclusions were essentially duplicated by polling done by the Pew Charitable Trust in May 2004.[35]

The increased press credibility may have rubbed off from the generally high credibility that military pronouncements had in the minds of the general public. Nonetheless, there is evidence that embedding had bolstered news media credibility. A *Los Angeles Times* poll found as follows:

> 55 percent said the greater media access is good for the country because it gives the American people an uncensored view of events. By contrast, 37 percent said embedded coverage is bad because it provides too much information about military actions as they unfold...[36]

Fred Cowardin, a Florida respondent in the *Los Angeles Times* survey, commented:

> I think all the reporters we have over there are showing us the battlefield, the way it really feels, and I suppose that's as good a kind of coverage as you can get. I can't personally verify the accuracy of everything I'm seeing, but it's much easier to believe with this access.[37]

However, Pew asked several other questions that raise concerns about the credibility of war coverage among the American public. Thirty eight percent of respondents told Pew pollsters in May 2004 that news reports are portraying the situation in Iraq as worse than it really is, 14 percent said the news reports portray it better than it is and 36 percent say the media tells it the way it really is. Or to put it another way, a clear majority thought the media had it wrong.[38]

There is also an appetite among American news consumers for fair coverage of the war on terror. In excess of two-thirds told the Pew pollsters that they preferred coverage of the war on terror that was "neutral" instead of "pro-America." About half of the same respondents told Pew that media criticism of the military helps keep America's military better prepared.[39]

All of which raises the question: Did the embedding of journalists help the US media to produce accurate and objective war coverage? Journalists hold as an article of faith that if they are accurate and objective they will be credible. There is, of course, no obvious metric for objectivity. One man's objectivity is another man's propaganda.

The Project on Excellence in Journalism, part of Columbia University's Graduate School of Journalism and underwritten by the Pew Charitable Trusts, reported: "The review of embedded reports shows that the inevitable bias that comes with [a] point of view is a risk journalists and viewers must beware of."[40] The Project on Excellence report offers as an example a story on March 22, 2003, by Oliver North, who was embedded with Marines and reporting for Fox News. North is a former Marine lieutenant colonel who was the central figure in the arms sales to Iran and the diversion of some profits to the Nicaraguan rebels in the 1980s. He was convicted of felony charges in that scandal but the convictions were later overturned. Regarding North's report of March 22, 2003, the Project on Excellence says:

> [North]…talked about a 'remarkable display of military prowess and might' on the part of 'my marines.' North also covered the Marines aiding a wounded Iraqi teenage girl and transporting her to medical attention. 'A remarkable display of humanitarianism by our armed forces as well,' the Fox anchor added. Some may question how representative North's reporting may be. North, however, is employed as a journalist by Fox News.[41]

It is easier to measure accuracy than objectivity, although as we will see those two concepts are interwoven. *Editor and Publisher* magazine is the major trade journal of American newspapers and magazines. Its editor, Greg Mitchell, kept a tally of what he viewed as errors in the first week alone. He listed 15 of these, including: Saddam may well have been killed in the first night's surprise attack (March 20); Umm Qasr has been taken (March 22); Iraqi citizens are greeting Americans as liberators (March 22); Umm Qasr has been taken (March 23); a captured chemical plant likely produced chemical weapons (March 23); and, Umm Qasr has been taken (March 24).[42]

Yet, factual errors of that sort are inevitable in a fast-moving war. It is not for nothing that the military refers to the "fog of war." More important were stories that the embedded journalists missed entirely, some understandably, some inexplicably, all contributing to a distorted view of the war that damaged the overall credibility.

[417]

Embeds saw only what their own military units saw. If the embedded journalist was with a combat unit, he typically had a view out of the window of his Humvee as it sped north. There was little time to stop to see what impact all those bombs and artillery shells had on ordinary Iraqis. Or to ask the Iraqis what they thought of the US military juggernaut. Such stories were largely left to the Arab media. However, the US military was outraged when *Al Jazeera* showed video footage of wounded Iraqi civilians. In the documentary film *Control Room*, Rumsfeld is seen accusing the network of faking the scenes of Iraqi suffering:

> We know that Al Jazeera has a pattern of playing propaganda over and over and over again. What they do is when there is [a] bomb [that] goes down they grab some children and some women and pretend the bomb hit the women and children. It seems to me it's up to all of us to try to tell the truth, to say what we know, to say what we don't know and to recognize that we're dealing with people that are willing to lie to the world to attempt to further their case.[43]

On US television and in its newspaper photographs there was a real absence of suffering. The American public may have read about wounded and dead troops, but they seldom saw them during the early stages of the war. One exception was a stark photograph published in the *Army Times*, April 21, 2003, of a wounded soldier being carried off for medical treatment.[44] The soldier later died. When the *Army Times,* an independent newspaper published by the Gannett Co., printed that photograph, the Army tried to throw out all of the paper's embedded journalists. At that point, there were only three *Army Times* journalists remaining with Army units as three others had already left the combat zone. The Army was overruled by the Department of Defense Public Affairs Office, which had to admit grudgingly that the paper had not violated the ground rules governing the publication of photographs of wounded soldiers, which read as follows:

> Battlefield casualties may be covered by embedded media as long as the service member's identity is protected from disclosure for 72 hours or upon verification of (next of kin) notification, whichever is first.

[418]

As the war has dragged on, photographs of wounded Americans have become more common in American newspapers and magazines and on television. The *New York Times*, in particular, has published images of wounded troops that are remarkable both for their graphic nature and the lack of a negative response from the Pentagon.[45]

One other aspect of the embedding process that affected credibility was the varied treatment that different media got. Some were favored, some were not. As indicated earlier, the Army tried to kick out all of the *Army Times* journalists after the newspaper published the photograph of the dying soldier. Yet, when Fox News reporter Geraldo Rivera gave away his unit's location by sketching a map in the sand on live television on Sunday, March 30, 2003, he was *asked* to leave briefly and reinstated but no action was taken against any of the other Fox reporters covering the war. The Fox network is generally viewed as the most conservative of the American television networks.

Capt. David Connelly, an Army media relations officer at the US military headquarters in Kuwait during the war, said of Rivera:

> He went live on air and basically violated everything you would normally protect: timing, intentions, and things an adversary can use against you...He scratched out a sketch in the sand that showed their formation, where they were, how far and fast they had traveled, and when they would be at their next location.

When higher headquarters ordered that Rivera be removed, Connolly wrote about Rivera's unit, the 101st Airborne Division:

> [The Division]... who did not have the benefit of live television, was upset because, 'he was their man.' Say what you will about Geraldo, but he is great for morale...He was eventually pulled, knowing he would go back because the division wanted him back. This was after a heartfelt apology, of course. Luckily, it did not appear that his actions ever got anyone killed.[46]

Yet when Philip Smucker, a freelance reporter working for the *Christian Science Monitor* and the *London Daily Telegraph,* did much the same thing – he gave away a unit's location during a live television interview – his treatment was far harsher, even though he was a unilateral and not embedded with any American military unit.

> US troops escorted the veteran correspondent out of Iraq for reporting information that "could harm him and the unit." Monitor Editor Paul Van Slambrouck maintains that Smucker did not disclose anything that wasn't already known. Smucker told colleagues he had been handcuffed and had equipment confiscated.[47]

The process of embedding journalists with the military did clearly build media credibility among members of one group—the military. Bob Franken of Cable News Network (CNN), speaking at a Brookings Institution panel, commented:

> You were there. You experienced everything. That was part of it. The other part of it is that the military people got to see firsthand that we weren't just a bunch of lazy pencil necks, to use the expression, who would sit at our desks in Washington drinking coffee and reporting ignorantly. One of my proudest moments came when this Marine colonel, a John Wayne type if there ever was one, came up to this riffraff group of reporters, all of us were dirty, none of us had bathed, we were all eating the MREs (military rations) all that type of thing. And he said, 'You guys are like the Marines.' I was embedded with the Marines. 'That is to say, you'll do whatever it takes to get the job done. Whatever it takes, no excuses.'[48]

Liz Marlantes, in the *Christian Science Monitor*, got it right when she wrote:

> While there should always be some distance between reporters and the subjects they cover, the gap between the media and the military has in recent years become a chasm…With the rise of an all-volunteer military, and with fewer and fewer journalists volunteering, one upside to embedding is that it essentially offered journalists a crash course in military service. The program gave many reporters a first-hand understanding of how the military conducts warfare, and, many say, a greater respect for service members. Similarly, the troops and commanding officers in the field had a chance to observe the dedication and professionalism of journalists —and see them in a more sympathetic light.

> 'This was a very valuable experiment, in having the military…perhaps discover that reporters are people, too, and vice versa,' says Chris Hanson, a journalism professor at the University of Maryland and a former Pentagon reporter. 'I think this might help media-military relations in the

future, and cut back on the mutual stereotyping that has been a problem for so long.'[49]

The military has shown a remarkably durable commitment to embedding, perhaps because it realizes how effective overall it has been. Even when embedded journalists have produced the worst imaginable news stories, the military has stood up and protected the rights of journalists to stay in the field.

On Nov. 15, 2004, NBC broadcast video footage shot by Kevin Sites, who was embedded with Marines in Fallujah. The video showed a Marine shooting a wounded and apparently helpless Iraqi. The video created a firestorm of bad publicity for the US military, especially in the Arab world. Two days after the video was first aired, the Armed Services Committee of the US House of Representatives, had the Marine Corps commandant before it. The committee chairman, Republican Representative Duncan Hunter of California, asked:

> Can we abandon that plan about embedded reporters? War is hell....I don't think it's a good idea to have embedded reporters in combat to the extent that we have them. And I hope we abandon that.

Another committee member, Democrat Representative Silvestre Reyes of Texas, supported this view:

> Not that we want to keep anything secret. But having had the experience of combat, it's an ugly situation. And people get into different kinds of situations. And we should not be providing Al Jazeera with the kind of propaganda that they have had the last couple [or] three days.

However, the Marine commandant, Gen. Michael W. Hagee, remained firm:

> I understand the comment about embedded reporters. Obviously, I know the incident you're talking about. But sir, in my personal opinion, embedded reporters have actually worked very well. They inform the American public about what these great, young Americans are doing over there. And the large, large majority are doing, as you have – as the members here have already articulated – are doing a tremendous job. And the American press is an important part of getting that information out. So I would not want – I personally, Mike Hagee – would not want to do away with something that's working very well.[50]

[421]

Conclusion

For the military, telling the truth is not a moral imperative, it's a tactic. For the media truth is not a means to an end, it is the end. To be sure, it is a goal that the media often misses for any number of reasons: deadline pressures, financial restraints, competitive pressures and – never underestimate this one – incompetence. Yet, among America's major media organizations it is seldom the result of a conscious decision to lie.

When the military decided to allow journalists unusually broad access to its operations during the Iraq War it was not lifting the curtain and revealing what the wizard was doing behind the scenes. Neither the media nor the media's public should ever believe that. It is instructive to read what the military people behind the scenes of the embedding process were doing and thinking.

Capt. David Connolly was a media affairs officer at the US military headquarters in Kuwait during the war. Writing later in *Infantry Magazine*, he said:

> The media should be considered as a component of non-lethal fires/non-kinetic targeting, another tool at our disposal to help accomplish the mission. The media will write their stories, with or without our input. It only makes sense to engage the media to ensure the whole story is told. The media is a venue in which we can pass along our command messages, which contain truthful and factual information. The bottom line is that we should always keep in mind what we are there to do. Always remember the soldiers, sailors, airmen, and Marines that are on the ground sacrificing every day. If we can help their morale and ultimately make their job easier by using the media, we should. It is safe to say that 99 times out of 100, we – the members of the US military – are acting with the right intentions. Meaning, we have nothing to hide. We have been given our orders and are attempting to carry them out within laws of land warfare. But bad things happen in war. Not everything goes our way. During these times it is best to confront the media and articulate to the world our side of the story.[51]

And while portions of that may sound benign, he goes on later in the same article to talk about the role of Information Operations, which is the military branch charged with carrying out propaganda and disinformation operations intended to confuse the enemy, and Public Affairs, which is meant to be the honest voice of the military speaking to the media.

> During the initial phases of (Operation Iraqi Freedom), (headquarters) always ensured that Public Affairs planners were involved in the Information Operations Working Groups (IOWG)...In that case, they could bring that information to the media director. The media director would then have a clear picture of what the commander's intent was and what the staff was attempting to accomplish. Armed with this knowledge the media director could prioritize which of the thousands of media queries to work on while maintaining a level of fairness and equity to all reporters. As an example, prior to crossing the line of departure (LD), IO was pushing themes to the enemy concerning capitulation. Knowing this, the media director could push reporters out to units responsible for dealing with large numbers of enemy prisoners of war (EPWs). These types of stories would send a message to the enemy and the world. The enemy would see how they would be fed, clothed, and provided shelter. Capitulation might appear to be a good option given their current status. The world would see that we were trained and ready.[52]

Despite the grave risks of being manipulated by the military, the media should continue to take every opportunity to embed with the military. The more experience reporters have covering the military, the more difficult it will be for the military to misuse the media and deceive it. Stephen Hess, a Senior Fellow at the Brookings Institution, summed it up nicely:

> We sometimes talk about win-win propositions, but I think (the Department of Defense) produced one of the most remarkable win-win-win propositions. It's clear that journalists, who want access more than anything else, were given remarkable access. It seems to me clear that the military got much more favorable coverage than they would have had had there not been embedding. And it's clear that the public saw a type of picture that they had never, never had an opportunity to see before.[53]

And all other considerations aside, the public loved the coverage. According to the *Chicago Tribune*:

> For the week of March 17 (2003) each of the 24-hour news cable channels saw huge gains in viewers following word [on] the night of March 19 that US-led forces had launched the attack on Iraq...Fox's viewership was up 379 percent over the same time last year, CNN increased by 393 percent, and MSNBC soared by 651 percent, according to figures from Nielsen Media Research.[54]

The mass media will never ignore an audience that massive.

[423]

23

The Impact of Occupation on Media Freedom: The Cases of Afghanistan and Iraq

Abdul Wahab Badrakhan

The freedom of the media under occupation is a complex and confusing issue which is difficult to assess within a specific and limited time range, especially because it involves two opposites: freedom and occupation.

Certainly, in Iraq and Afghanistan, we have witnessed two unprecedented cases of US occupation—albeit an occupation that wants to be viewed as a 'friendly' and 'amicable.' This remains the case although the formal American discourse has turned this occupation into the vanguard of surgical interventions in modern international relations. At least from the American perspective, the terrorist attacks on the United States on September 11, 2001 were cited as a direct cause to justify these interventions.

There are few serious studies of the two cases of Iraq and Afghanistan with regard to the issue of media freedom under occupation. At the academic level, researchers are still in the stage of gathering information and analyzing several facts made available by organizations and authorities which employ correspondents or envoys in the field. It would be a truism to say that the first inclination is to compare these two cases with the occupation of Germany and Japan in the wake of the Second World War. It is also plausible to make a comparison with the experiences of NATO troops both in Bosnia and Kosovo. However, for those who had planned for the war and its aftermath the difference was that the invading force was not forced to control the media, whether in Afghanistan or Iraq. On the contrary, there was a realization that both necessity and interest dictated the need to build up the media and rely on it to understand the population and facilitate the process of building a new regime.

Despite the iron-fisted control that characterized the former Iraqi regime, the media structure associated with the existence of the state and its rule was destined to collapse with it. Moreover, it was not founded on the basis of professionalism or scientific propaganda as was the case with Nazi Germany or Imperial Japan. On the contrary, the Iraqi media were dedicated to the glorification of the leader and centered round his personality. At the same time, the media was not part of a cultural system with correlated tasks unlike the Baath Party circles. While the party and the state were undistinguishable in Iraq, the organizational skills of the Baath Party could not compare with the masterful organization of the Nazi Party, which necessitated "uprooting" both the media-culture and the political, military and social structure of Nazism. Nevertheless, the doctrine of "uprooting the Baath" was proposed and embarked upon since those Iraqi and Americans who advocated such rooting out believed that they were confronting a phenomenon similar to Nazism. This rooting out occurred before they were forced to review this mission.

The Americans and the British entrusted their officers and civil envoys with media-related work. However, the task that was set for them was a far cry from that of their counterparts following the occupation of Germany and Japan in the mid-1950s. Major-General Alexis McClure, who was assigned the task of organizing the German media after World War Two, was a pioneer in psychological warfare. During the military operations he supervised a psychological war aimed at "winning the cooperation of Germans, especially via securing all services, and creating a public opinion sympathetic to the Allied forces." As soon as the Nazis were defeated, McClure reorganized his unit from "Psywar Unit" to "Media Control Unit." In July 1946 he wrote to his friend, C.D. Jackson, Vice President of Time-Life Inc. as follows:

[426]

> We control 37 newspapers, 6 radio stations, 314 theatres, 642 movies, 101 magazines, 237 book publishers, 7384 book dealers and printers, and conduct about 15 public opinion surveys a month, as well as publish one newspaper with 1,500,000 circulation, 3 magazines, run the Associated Press (DANA), and operate 15 library centers …

Eradicating the effects of Nazism, which had pervaded the entire German body politic, was clearly an educative concern. It was the same concern which guided the experience in Japan, albeit the occupation forces in both cases faced two different countries, two distinct nations and two organized societies with deep-rooted traditions. Inevitably, in such case, it was a huge task to transform ideas, implant the principles of democracy and to push the Germans and Japanese to adopt two new constitutions involving such values and principles. In the case of Japan, it was sometimes necessary to impose some constitutional provisions, especially those relating to outlawing discrimination between social classes, transforming public service from a system of enslavement to one of rights and duties, recognizing religious and gender equality and modernizing and democratizing education.

In the cases of Afghanistan and Iraq, there has not been much of this kind of principle-based work. This is so despite the fact that the discourse which theorized about the virtues of war practically used all the familiar arguments, especially in its emphasis on establishing democracy in Iraq as a model for its neighbors. It is true that there was no urgent need for media control in Afghanistan because the media was practically non-existent under the rule of the Taliban. In Iraq too, the media was not actually controlling the views of the people. However, there was an urgent need to win public cooperation at a time when all the segments of the public viewed the foreign troops in a hostile manner. It must be noted that this urgent need still remains.

The intervention in Afghanistan is still viewed as having international legitimacy. However, in the case of Iraq, the intervention is seen as a violation of international law. The former case gained international consensus because of the general conviction that intervention took place in the context of the war against terrorism—a war to which the international community is still committed both at the external and internal levels. However, the second case, that of intervention in Iraq was obviously contrived and arbitrary. This is evidenced by the state of pervasive chaos it has produced in Iraq and the region. Moreover, it has created a deep rift within the international community, undermined the authority of the United Nations and exposed it to the danger of complete marginalization.

In both cases there were worthy goals, the achievement of which necessitated international intervention—the overthrow of two iron-fisted, despotic regimes that ruled police states, curtailed liberties, violated human rights and practiced repression. The world was confronting two different regimes whose existence and continuity were no longer untenable. As for intervention in both these cases, it was considered by many scholars at the heart of the new world order, the objective being to liberate people and give them an opportunity to build a future based on development and the rule of law.

However, the problem still relates to the nature of intervention and how it could be steered in a way that achieves its declared objectives, assuming that these are genuine and credible. The problem also relates to the fact that the world, as represented by the leading, developed countries with military capabilities failed to achieve a consensus either on the ethicality of this intervention, its mechanism, the prerequisite steps, or on the obligatory international legal framework, which exercises checks on the intervening power, conferring legality on it. Perhaps the expected reform of the United Nations will signal the start of a process to remedy these gaps and overcome these obstacles.

Such questions were never raised in the case of Afghanistan because after the Soviet occupation ended, it plunged into a civil war that resulted in a state of chaos, with the country divided into sub-states and areas of influence. Moreover, the dominance of the Taliban regime led the country into a dark phase during which terrifying human rights violations occurred. This happened while the state failed utterly in reviving the economy or ending the internal war.

Moreover, in the Taliban era, Afghanistan was transformed into a focal point for and a safe haven for establishing the Al Qaeda organization. This in turn became the core nucleus of terrorism that produced the terrorists who carried out the 9/11 attacks. Thus the international community did not find any reason to reject the invasion of Afghanistan, which was carried out with the avowed objective of formally 'striking terrorism' and the regime that provided it with sanctuary. This intervention was undertaken after the UN resolutions declared that any state which supports terrorism or offers it logistical and financial support will render itself internationally accountable.

On the other hand, the case of Iraq was completely different. Though the Iraqi regime did not enjoy international sympathy due to its record of ruthlessness and violations, it was not an isolated regime. Rather, it had a network of regional relations and international affiliations that it had knitted together during the time when it enjoyed huge oil wealth. Iraq was able to renew these ties when it was under siege via the Oil-for-Food Program. The regime of international sanctions imposed on Iraq after its invasion of Kuwait was well-considered and designed to lead to an inevitable outcome—weakening the regime and precipitating its downfall. This was the farthest that international action could reach in its attempt to topple the regime. Although the sanctions inflicted much suffering on the Iraqi people in different spheres (such as health, education, food and standard of living), the regime was able to survive. Later, it turned out that all the justifications that the United States put forward for waging war in Iraq were false: the American inspectors did not find WMD and the relationship between the former Iraqi regime and Al Qaeda, or any other known terrorist organization, was not proven. The excuse always cited was that it was a suspect regime, capable of resorting to terrorism—that it operated on a "terrorist logic." Hence it was impossible to wage war against terrorism without considering a removal of the Iraqi regime on the basis of a pre-emptive war, or as a second step in striking against the "axis of evil." This American logic might have seemed theoretically acceptable but it was not practically preferable for most allies and friends who warned the United States of the repercussions of this war and the difficulties that would follow. Also, they were not yet prepared to accept such an intervention, believing that the desired objective could be achieved by other means that might be slower, but equally effective.

However, later events have shown that hasty US action led to consequences that were not anticipated by the Americans themselves. Military power might have accomplished the mission and toppled the Iraqi regime but this was the easy part and the most difficult part is still ahead. As for the political authority of the occupation, it committed a series of errors, beginning with the dismantling of state institutions and disbanding the military and security forces, and capping all this by formulating a provisional constitution (Law of Administration for the State of Iraq for the Transitional Period) in accordance with political deals reached with different Iraqi factions. Certainly, this will lead to conflicts at a later stage when the Iraqis focus on formulating their permanent constitution. The United Nations set itself the task of overseeing the formulation of a provisional constitution in Afghanistan but in Iraq this kind of UN role was impossible.

It was natural that a new state of affairs would emerge on the basis of many factors: regime change in Afghanistan and Iraq, military administration of the two countries by an occupation force, and continuing statements, especially by the United States that the war was waged for the liberation of both countries. It would be a truism to say that the emergence and expansion of the media and its active and prominent role reflect ongoing change. The occupying troops and their administration, coming from countries accustomed to the media presence in the public arena and familiar with its role in preserving law and social norms within the community, adopted a policy of encouragement to promote all forms of the media in these two states—print media, radio stations, television stations, websites and Internet cafes.

[430]

The appearance of Mariam Shekeba on the state-owned Afghanistan Television had a significant effect in view of the segregation and persecution she was subjected to under the Taliban. In Iraq, the shift was effective. From a media monopolized by one man's image for about a quarter of a century, to a media where many faces appear in the media scene, reflecting an unprecedented multiplicity. The occupation authority had a vested interest in showing the difference, and in making the freedom of expression and news a reality. No doubt this in itself was an achievement. However, it is obvious that there is a distance between this emerging new reality and freedom which is bound to grow gradually. Freedom and occupation are opposites. The emergence of the media is a definite expression of some sort of freedom, yet considered in isolation, it is not sufficient to confirm that freedom has been restored and consolidated.

On the contrary, the freedom of media activity could lead to a conflict of interests, especially when security itself is in a state of turmoil and not assured. The three years that have elapsed after the fall of the Taliban regime have not been enough to create an atmosphere free of the kind of intransigence and tribalism that have solidified during the years of *Jihad* against the Soviets and internal conflict. Still the warlords cling to their spheres of authority and influence, controlling politico-social affairs, and sometimes engage in practices and adhere to concepts that are not very different from what prevailed during the Taliban era. In Iraq, all American dreams about quick stability after the fall of the Baath regime was shattered and the former Iraqi military, after its disbandment, became an army of unemployed persons seeking jobs. Hence many of its members joined the ranks of militias for various reasons: resisting the occupation in order to obtain gains and assert their political presence (as in the case of the "Mahdi Army" militia led by Al Sadr), or to compensate a real loss suffered due to the fall of the regime (as in the case of the militias that appeared in the "Sunni Triangle"). Although the Iraqi media grew rapidly under these circumstances, it suffered as a result of this instability, and

[431]

from the pressures applied by the Coalition Provisional Authority (CPA), the Interim Iraqi Government (IIG), and all the militias.

What is specially striking in Iraq is the way both the occupation authority and the Iraqi government complain about the media. This specifically indicates failure to control the situation. This was not confined to the explicit and powerful criticism of particular channels (*Al Jazeera*, *Al Arabiya* and Abu Dhabi TV in the first stage of the war and after), nor to issuing decisions forbidding *Al Jazeera* (and *Al Arabiya* to a lesser degree) to operate from Iraq. In addition, many journalists were shot by the occupation troops or by the shelling of places where they were based (as in the case of the Palestine Hotel). The last issue remains a subject of controversy between the US Department of Defense and Reuters agency, though the file of the US investigation into this event was closed without determining the responsibility for killing and wounding three of the agency's reporters.

These positions clouded the atmosphere of media freedom in Iraq, making it the most dangerous country for journalists. The worsening of the dangerous security situation was reflected in the media coverage and it weakened the ability to gather information. Here we should recall the Abu Ghraib prison scandal, which was first revealed and discussed in the American media. However, its revelation was the result of regular leaks from government sources and was explained by the American press as being politically motivated and linked to the struggle within the American Administration. The second scandal involved photographs of a soldier killing a wounded man in a mosque in Fallujah. It was taken by an American photo-journalist embedded with the American troops. That was the first time that one of these journalists was able to release materials that the military did not wish to make public. It was obvious that the attacking forces in the second battle of Fallujah, which broke out in November 2004, were anxious to keep away the Arab media. However, American and Iraqi officials did not stop criticizing the Arab satellite channels that gave some Fallujah residents the opportunity to comment on what was happening in their city.

[432]

The following observations can be made in both cases (Iraq and Afghanistan):

- The occupation authority allowed the media to emerge, expand and crystallize. Moreover, the occupation authority encouraged this phenomenon in the case of private media and it used the existing structure to make the media its voice.
- The occupation authority did not seek to control the emerging media. However, either directly (via the power of the Coalition Provisional Authority in Iraq), or indirectly (via the Afghan Transitional Authority) it was able to draw red lines which no media organization was allowed to cross, especially in the absence of a national rule and legislations that regulated media work.
- The question of media freedom remains a protracted one. It was non-existent and therefore cannot be achieved automatically. It has to build itself gradually in synchrony with other freedoms that are presumably respected by the emerging democratic system.
- Undoubtedly, the atmosphere of freedom which emerged immediately after the occupation led to clashes in the absence of the professionalism necessary to support, accommodate and deepen it. Hence reliance must be placed on current active training programs, which must be pursued diligently to acquaint journalists not only with means and methods of work, but also how to deal with the available freedom and uphold the ethics of the profession.
- The unstable security situation might curtail the atmosphere of freedom. Hence the emerging media experience is in a state of transition. The continuing risks and reliance of the occupation authority on strong security measures negatively affect the progress of media operations. This leads to frustration for journalists and strengthens the desire on the part of the governing authority to dominate, whether it is totally affiliated to the occupation forces or more independent.
- It is expected that the provisional legislations for regulating the media scene and the respect for the principle of freedom will be affected by

security requirements. Therefore, it presumed that reliance will be on maximum flexibility to keep any legislation receptive to accelerating changes whether in technology or the state of the country itself.

In the two countries under consideration, despite regime change via a foreign military campaign, and all attempts to move the media in the direction of freedom, both are ranked low in terms of standards of media freedom. In a survey conducted by the Reporters Sans Frontières (Reporters Without Borders) organization, fifty questions were put to journalists from all over the world. The questions centered round incidents involving the killing of journalists, imprisonment verdicts, censorship, pressures, media monopoly and legal penalties. Afghanistan was ranked 104th and Iraq was in 130th position. As for the scale of liberties assessed by the American organization Freedom House, Iraq was ranked 142nd and Afghanistan was placed in the 159th position.

Afghan Media under Occupation

During a decade of Soviet occupation, the civil war era and the rule of Taliban, there was no media activity of note. The media was weak and was monopolized by the state. It was an apparatus affiliated to the state. In view of the vast expanse of the country and the diversity of its politics and demographics, the radio was the most frequently used means of disseminating information. It is not only cheap but can also communicate with the uneducated and the illiterate. The print media focused on governmental newscasts which were unavailable in all the local languages. The status of television was no better than that of other media, especially at a time when there was an increase in the number of satellite channels and private stations at a time of domestic turmoil. Also, the Taliban regime dominated most parts of Afghanistan since 1996. It pursued a policy that ignored domestic media though it showed some concern with external media. This was in accordance with its campaign to project its image and impose its dominance from the outset as the ideal solution to end the chaos and civil wars that devastated the country.

[434]

When the features of the Taliban administration began to take concrete shape, especially the way it regarded "Islamic governance" and despised women, denying them education, as well as its disrespect for any modern concepts of organization – from human rights to public liberties, and its isolation from the international community – the regime was treated as the "sick man of Central Asia," with which no one wanted to deal or cooperate.

In fact this state of affairs was an extension of earlier periods of rule when the international community stopped concerning itself with this country. British colonization neither achieved stability in this country nor did its leaders embark on a process of universal and purposeful development. Centralized royal rule did not succeed in knitting powerful ties between regions inhabited by different clans and ethnic groups. Instead, it relied on an elite group comprising military personnel in particular, to impose dominance and order. Therefore, the Soviets resorted to infiltrating the army, supporting the coup against the monarchy in the early 1970s. They staged a communist coup against the ruling military junta to pave the way for invading the country in late 1979. Since the first coup, an Afghani emigration movement to Pakistan started and then escalated and intensified towards the south after the Soviet invasion. These emigrants were distributed in accordance with ethnic and tribal affiliation. They were first organized into seven organizations, which were known to the world by one name—Mujahideen. At the same time, some resistance groups were formed in the north and one of them, under the leadership of Ahmed Shah Masoud, gained prominence.

During the whole phase of Soviet occupation, the interior regions of Afghanistan and the areas dominated by the Mujahideen were locked into Cold War conflicts. The West, particularly the United States considered the occupation as a trap in which the Soviets had become entangled. The occupation turned into daily bloodshed and the Americans made Afghanistan a focal point for confrontation with the Soviets. They did not need to involve their army but only provide munitions, money and training. Yet the outcome was of paramount importance. The religious

[435]

motive that attracted and impelled the Mujahideen was an anti-Soviet and anti-communist ideology. It was readymade, as it were, and did not have to be produced or nurtured. Thus the Americans achieved in the field what was hitherto only a theoretical goal that regarded Islam as a possible means to confront the tide of communism. Having achieved this, the doors were opened to a wider mobilization with fighters from all over the Islamic world joining the Afghan Mujahideen. Within a few months, this mobilization became more formal and governmental. Several governments in the Arab and Islamic worlds were invited to encourage youth to partake in the fight against "apostate infidels" who had taken over an Islamic state. Many governments were induced to give financial incentives to their young men and those of other countries to encourage them go to Afghanistan.

As the Soviets withdrew in 1989, the Mujahideen found themselves with no plan for controlling and managing the country. They did not have a clear vision of the kind of rule and organization which were supposed to prevail. In reality, there was no single and decisive leadership among the Mujahideen. The international powers that managed their affairs and funded their movement throughout the jihad against the Soviets seemed unconcerned and abandoned them to their internal struggles. The United Nations was prepared to help, but its efforts floundered because of the severity of these domestic struggles and the inability to reconcile the Rulers of Kabul, (who were initially supported by the Soviets but later abandoned and left to face their own destiny) with Mujahideen factions. Thus the situation that transpired after the end of the Soviet occupation was ideal for sustaining the authority of the warlords who relied on their clans and supported the kind of ethnic fanaticism which thrived on regional affiliations. To start a more serious attempt to build a state, an army and other institutions took ten years—from 1992 when the Mujahideen reached Kabul and began embittered attempts to engineer a social contract and build a new state, till late 2001 and early 2002 when the American troops and the Northern Alliance troops eventually reached the capital.

However, during that difficult decade, the Taliban appeared on the scene to carry out tasks assigned by Pakistan and found that the circumstances were ripe for spreading their dominance over the country. This dominance was partially achieved when they entered Kabul in 1996 and started extending their power to the west and the north. However, till the end of their rule they could not gain control over all the territories of Afghanistan, particularly the Tajik regions in the north.

Meanwhile many Arab Mujahideen, or "Arab Afghans," as they became known, returned home after the Soviet occupation had ended and they had completed their mission. However, many of these Arabs resided in Afghanistan and severed ties with their families and countries. The severity of their experience shaped their political outlook and life convictions and they also acquired the title of "warlords." They organized themselves and the Taliban relied on them during their struggles. They found a suitable leader in Osama bin Laden, a former comrade-in-arms, who returned to Afghanistan in 1996. Thus the rule of the Taliban began and a center of terrorism emerged. The bitter neglect that Afghanistan suffered after the Soviet withdrawal led to the association between the Taliban and the organization that became known as "Al Qaeda." The complexities stemming from neglect and abandonment still arouses anxiety among the Afghans today for two reasons. First, internally their country could not rid itself of the domestic factors and circumstances that might restore Taliban dominance, especially since the Taliban had always enjoyed the support of the Pushtun ethnic group to which most of their warriors belonged. Pushtuns comprise the largest ethnic group and are therefore capable of dominating the country. Second, they are aware of the lack of skilled personnel necessary for rebuilding the country, sustaining security and launching development.

The invasion and occupation of Afghanistan in 2001 was led by a broad international coalition, which was capable, after the downfall of the Taliban regime, of guaranteeing a reasonable degree of security. However, what was more important after the war was the commitment of this

[437]

coalition to provide aid and assistance to manage and run the country. This was especially so because the country needed almost everything. After notable efforts, Kabul received promises from donor states to provide aid amounting to $8.2 billion over a three-year period. Of these, one billion was to be in the form of immediate aid. However, the aid was not received in a timely manner and the invasion of Iraq slowed down aid efforts because the American administration was preoccupied with the crisis there. Despite this, the presidential elections which took place on October 9, 2004 were successful. Most observers considered it acceptable though it was tarnished by some wrong practices and violations. American President Bush paid tribute to the elections for being a model exercise of freedom. The next important achievement was the parliamentary elections of September 2005 since this step would give the United States an opportunity to withdraw its troops from Afghanistan. However, the country needs round 25,000 foreign soldiers to maintain security and keep the elections on track. The greatest achievement that Afghanistan witnessed under the occupation was the approval by the *loya jirga* (the tribal parliament) on January 4, 2004 of a new constitution emphasizing equality between women and men and guaranteeing respect for fundamental freedoms including media freedom.

The Political and Media Scene during the Taliban Era

Immediately after the Taliban seized power in Kabul, the regime adopted a literal concept of applying the *Shari'ah* law. It held executions in public squares and stoning to death punishments were carried out in football stadiums. In order to eradicate all non-Islamic influences, the Taliban banned television, music and the Internet. It made the growing of beards mandatory for men, on pain of punishment. Their treatment of women was more ruthless. Girls were banned from attending schools and women were forbidden to leave homes unless accompanied by a relative of the first degree. Those who did not observe this rule risked being whipped or shot by officials from the Ministry for the Promotion of Virtue and

[438]

Suppression of Vice. Members of the Taliban could not halt smuggling activities. Initially, they benefited from opium revenue but in 2000, they banned opium-related cultivation and growth, reducing the world production of opium by two thirds. However, they did not provide alternative avenues for the thousands of people who lost their only source of income. In any event, the Taliban regime used this move as part of a diplomatic campaign aimed at gaining recognition from the United Nations. The Taliban also held out the possibility of a trial for Osama bin Laden whom the United States accused of plotting the bombings of its embassies in Kenya and Tanzania in the summer of 1998. They proposed an Islamic court based in Europe to carry out this task. In addition, they improved their cooperation with the UN agencies and non-governmental organizations that had representatives and were carrying out work programs in Afghanistan.

In return, the United Nations revived its attempts to look for a political solution to end the civil war. However, the bombing of the USS Cole on October 12, 2000 in Aden port led to renewed confrontation. In December 2000, the Security Council passed a resolution imposing sanctions on the Taliban regime if it did not halt completely its support for "international terrorism," particularly since the United States accused Al Qaeda of bombing the destroyer Cole. This signaled a point of departure in the Taliban's relations with the world. A month later, sanctions were implemented by closing the offices of the Taliban regime's consular representations abroad and banning the flights of the Afghan airline Ariana. The reaction of the Taliban was very violent internally. It recaptured the central highland regions from the Hazāra (an ethnic Shia community) after great massacres that afflicted civilians and enabled the Taliban to control Bamiyan where there were two huge statues of Buddha. In March 2001, Taliban leader Mullah Mohammad Omar ordered the destruction of the two statues in a move reflecting political vengeance, despite international appeals to preserve them. He responded to these appeals by citing the imposition of international sanctions on Afghanistan.

[439]

The year 2001 heralded the end, but prior to the downfall of the regime, the country witnessed a more ruthless approach on the part of Taliban in dealing with both Afghan citizens and foreigners. For instance, non-Muslim religious minorities were asked in May to wear special cloth badges that would distinguish them as non-Muslims. Hindu women were ordered to follow the example of Afghan women in wearing the *burqa*. In July, the regime's fanaticism extended to banning the Internet, playing cards, floppy discs, films, satellite dishes, musical instruments and chess, all of which were considered as contravening Islamic laws.

In this atmosphere, there was no scope for media activity. In fact, media activity during Taliban reign was restricted to foreign reporters who faced many difficulties with the regime, which even accused them of espionage. It was quick to charge them in the courts and pronounce them guilty. In January, the Afghan authorities forbade reporters from going to Yakaolang in Bamiyan province (in the central highlands) where the United Nations had documented massacres. Mullah Omar justified this prohibition by saying that foreign media transmitted "fabricated and hostile news" about Afghanistan. After that, a BBC reporter was expelled and its office, which had been operating since 1990, was closed. The decision to expel the reporter was made after the Pashtun language service in the BBC broadcast an interview with Ashraf Ghani, an Afghani intellectual living in exile, in which he described Taliban members as being "illiterate" and "ignorant." He considered the destruction of the Buddha statues in Bamiyan as un-Islamic. The Afghan Minister of Information accused the BBC of broadcasting news "hostile to Afghanistan" and ignoring the viewpoint of the Taliban's government and "the realities on the ground" in the country. Later, negotiations were held between the government and the BBC and the Taliban regime agreed to reopen the office on condition that the BBC reporter was an Afghan and not a foreigner. However, prior to this, in December 2000, the Afghan authorities had arrested an Afghan national who worked as an assistant and translator with the BBC for contravening the law and working with a foreign institution.

Six months before the fall of the Taliban regime, the authorities imposed new rules on foreigners. According to these rules they were obliged to sign a permit in which they undertook "not to promote immoral goods, drink alcohol, eat pork, listen to loud music or distribute anti-Taliban literature." Failure to comply with these rules would lead to one month's imprisonment or expulsion from the country. These new restrictions put increased pressure on journalists whose presence since August 2000 was subject to an order issued by the Ministry of Information containing 21 points specifying the working regulations for foreign journalists in the country. These regulations included prohibiting journalists from entering any Afghan house, interviewing an Afghan woman without permission from the designated authority and taking a photograph of any person. Journalists were asked to inform the designated authority of their travels outside Kabul and to respect the "prohibited areas." They were also not permitted to hire translators or local assistants unless they were licensed by the authority. Finally, reporters were ordered to attend press conferences held by Afghan officials, and refer to the country as "the Islamic Emirate of Afghanistan."

On 13 July 2001, the Islamic Afghan Press Agency, whose headquarters were in Pakistan, announced that the Taliban had banned the use of the Internet. The Ministry of Foreign Affairs justified this decision by saying its goal was to block access to "anti-Islamic immoral websites." At that time there were a small number of Afghan officials and foreign residents working for international organizations who were using the Internet via telephone links connected to Pakistan.

That summer, during the same period, the relationship between Afghan authorities and the press reached maximum tension levels. Journalists were forbidden to cover the trial of eight foreigners, which took place behind closed doors. An Afghan journalist working for Agence France-Presse (the French news agency) was forced to flee to France after receiving arrest threats. A Pakistani journalist was expelled because he quoted announcements made by the Minister of Foreign Affairs in a way that did not please the minister. In mid-September 2001, four days after

[441]

the terrorists attacks in the United States, all foreign journalists were ordered to leave the country with exception of the *Al Jazeera* channel reporter. This channel and the official Afghan news agency became the only sources of news. Afghan reporters working for foreign agencies were allowed to work under strict monitoring.

The Media Scene under Occupation

After the fall of Taliban regime, Afghanistan moved from being an arid media desert to a land that witnessed an uncontrollable media flurry. The media scene became crowded with many publications under different titles and names in different languages and orientations that ranged from fanatical conservatism to uncontrolled liberalism. All social groups, from clergymen and Mujahideen to intellectuals found their niche in this scene— with publications ranging from the archaic to the modern, and from state television and radio to private institutions, all the way to electronic media via the Internet.

The print media first appeared in Afghanistan over a century ago in 1873 specifically with the appearance of *Shams al Nahar* (Daylight Sun) newspaper, it remained under governmental control throughout this period, with the exception of a very short period called "the decade of democracy" (1963-1973). Prior to this, the print media experienced intermittent periods of freedom. In the era of Soviet occupation some newspapers became known, such *Anis, Hewad,* and the *Kabul Times.* These were supportive of the regime, which remained loyal to Moscow. Some newspapers were published abroad, specifically in Pakistan and Iran. These expressed the views of the Mujahideen who were resisting the occupation. The Taliban regime used all available means as megaphones, but purely from an ideological standpoint, closed down the country's television outlet and gave the radio a name expressive of its function: *Shari'ah Radio.*

In April 2002, about five months after the fall of Taliban, the Media Act was issued. This act gives every citizen the right to issue a publication independently and allowed criticism of the government in principle. After the Media Act was issued, about a hundred publications appeared (daily, weekly, bi-monthly, monthly and quarterly); and the numbers increased rapidly. There were still 45 government-affiliated publications in different parts of the country. The government was the biggest publisher, owning three daily newspapers and other publications with different frequencies. Although tens of independent publications appeared, the report of the Bureau of Public Services in the US embassy in Kabul noted the existence of sustained self-censorship. It attributed this to the "insufficient legal protection of journalists." The report demonstrated that this insufficient protection hampered coverage of some causes that "put journalists in a confrontation with warlords who still enjoy great authority in the country."

Among the most important publications are *Anis* the oldest daily newspaper in the Pashtun language (with a circulation of about 6,000), *Islah*, the voice of the government, published in 1930 (with a circulation of 3,000) *Hewad*, founded by King Zahir Shah in 1949 (with a circulation of 6,000), *Kabul Times* the only English newspaper (with a circulation of 3,000 to 5,000). Among the most significant non-governmental publications are *Afghanistan*, a weekly (with a circulation of 3,000), *Afghanistani Juan* a bi-monthly published in Dari (with a circulation of 2,000) and *Afghan*, a weekly (with a circulation of 5,000). This publication was issued under the same name in Kabul in 1971 and under the name *Afghan Mujahid* in Peshawar in Pakistan in 1982 before the Pakistani authorities closed it down and imprisoned its publisher Mohammad Hassan Walosmal. Walosmal took refuge in Norway and resumed publishing *Mujahid Walos* in which he criticized the leaders of the Mujahideen. Other publications include *Ain Zan*, a woman's weekly (with a circulation of 3,000), *Bazaar* a weekly issued by the Unity Party in Dari (with a circulation of 3,000), *Shiragh* a weekly issued in Pushto, Dari and English (with a circulation of 3,000), *Mallali*, a woman's monthly, *Mujahid*, a weekly issued by former Afghani President Burhanuddin

Rabbani, *Mardom*, issued by the Shiite Afghanistan Islamic Movement in Dari, *Bakliana*, founded in April 2003 by Mohammad Shinowari, a emigrant Pushtun businessman (with a circulation of 7,000), in addition to *Demoghratiya, Insaf, Arada, Ightidar Meli, Islahat, Fajri Omeed, Farda, Jamhouri Ghanj, Kabul, Mithagh Al Wihda,* and *Misha'l al Demoghratiya.*

Television broadcasting in Afghanistan began during the first communist government. It was established in 1977 with financial and technological help from Japan and used to cover the whole country. However all transmission installations were bombed by the Mujahideen. Television broadcasting was stopped altogether in the Taliban era. After the fall of Taliban, television resumed broadcasting with technological aid from Iran. Japan undertook to modernizing television installations by 2004 and the US embassy in Kabul a provided a new transmitter in early 2003. At present, broadcasting continues for 4 hours daily. Afghan Television has 14 branches working in a semi-autonomous manner.

In early 2004, the Afghan Ministry of Information launched the first private television station Ina Television, in the Jowzjan province with a funding of US$3 million from the engineer businessman Said Faheem Faryabi. The station covers five Afghan regions and operates under loose censorship. The popularity achieved by the station encouraged many companies to compete in obtaining licenses for private television networks. This trend enraged conservative circles, which launched a campaign to prohibit private television stations, whereas the government sought a regime to control this activity.

After the *Shari'ah Radio*, which monopolized the ether during the Taliban rule, about twenty stations compete to attract listeners. Germany funded the first Afghan state-owned station in 1929. Since then the radio has become – and still remains – the foremost and almost the only means of information and entertainment in Afghanistan. The formal radio broadcasts 19 hours daily and transmits records to its branches, mostly in Pashto and Dari languages. Some are in Uzbek, Balochi and Pashto

[444]

languages. Among the new radio stations we find *Balkh, Nangahar, Kandahar* and *Herat* (which broadcasts 7 hours daily). However, the period of turmoil, war and disruption of broadcasting encouraged international organizations, especially the *BBC, Radio France Internationale, Liberty Radio* and the *Voice of America*, to transmit special broadcast in local languages. After the fall of Taliban, many radio stations appeared broadcasting on the "FM" wave, while the Internet sector is witnessing an anticipated rapid growth as the electricity and telephone networks are modernized.

The Media Returns to Confront Traditional Enemies

When war broke out on October 7, 2001, the radio and television stations and the buildings housing printed material were subject to bombing in Kabul, Jalālābād, Kandahar and Pol-e-Khomri. In any case, the television was suspended by a decision from Taliban since 1996. Taliban relied specially on the radio whose broadcasting was stopped by the bombing. Partial broadcasting was resumed before it was finally silenced on October 25. The Americans soon started using the same wave which was employed by the Shari'ah Radio to broadcast news of interest to the listeners and music which was banned by Taliban. Immediately after the fall of Kabul, responsibility for Afghan Television was given to the Ministry of Information, which soon resumed partial broadcasting.

During the war, journalists were ill-treated. In the Northern Alliance region, the Belgian Television team was stopped and its members were ordered to leave the country. The reason was that the bogus journalists who murdered Ahmed Shah Masoud were carrying Belgian travel documents, and because the Belgian government did not investigate this affair seriously. As the American troops entered Kabul on November 12, 2001, the *Al Jazeera* office was shelled on the pretext that it was giving homage to Al Qaeda fighters, as claimed by an American spokesman.

As the war drew to a close, Arab journalists in Afghanistan felt that they were being targeted by both sides—the Americans and their Afghan allies. They were forced to withdraw. The new authorities started harassing Pakistani journalists too.

Six weeks after the fall of the capital, a group of ladies issued the *Sira* magazine. On the cover was a picture depicting a shackled woman being set free by a pen. This heralded the birth of a new Afghan press. Female journalists had requested permission from the Ministry of Culture to publish a magazine. A committee from the Ministry checked the magazine's articles prior to printing.

Various media outlets began to emerge and expand gradually in Afghanistan. Within months, the number of publications reached two hundred. These publications relied on aid from international organizations or on funding from local parties. At the same time, the media confronted its traditional enemies: warlords, fanatical judges, and even the dispersed Taliban fighters. Although the provisional constitution guaranteed the freedom of the press, it also approved imprisonment for "opinion crimes." The Blasphemy Act remained the greatest threat to journalists. In fact, two journalists were sentenced to death for their writings and had to flee the country.

As the Americans distributed two hundred thousand radios, radio stations made a significant breakthrough in the new media scene. For the first time a commercial radio station by the name of *Arman* (Hope) appeared, broadcasting music and discussions in which males and females participated. These discussions touched on social and life issues avoiding political ones. Of course, conservatives objected to this radio station where "the laughs of young women could be heard." This is regarded as *'awra* (taboo). However, the radio station attracted audiences from other radio stations including international stations. The American troops and international organizations supported broadcasting activities because of their efficacy in communicating with Afghans through different regional languages.

In January 2002 the *Sadaee Moqawemat* (Voice of the Resistance) radio appeared. It was branded illegal because it called for the killing of

American soldiers and for overthrowing the government of Hamid Karzai. The former Afghan leader, Gulbuddin Hekmatyar, was behind the launch of this radio station in Khost.

The story of television in Afghanistan is different and more complicated. Its entry was rather timid and limited. Emphasis was on improving the standard of official television. However, the programming content was trivial and subject to censorship. Nevertheless, a special network appeared in Samangan province and started broadcasting for six hours daily in four languages. In Kabul, four companies competed to obtain licenses for the establishment of private television stations.

The entry of Afghan women into the media field was a difficult challenge but they were given the opportunity to work in radio stations and television in the Herat province. On March 8, 2002 which coincided with International Women's Day a women's magazine appeared under the title of *Morsal* (The Rose). On the same day the *Voice of Afghan Women* started broadcasting from Kabul. This was the first radio station specifically intended for women and its broadcasts included music, educational programs as well as local and world news. Yet another radio station *Rabia Balkhi* was set up in Mazār-e Sharīf. A third station was launched in Herat under the name of *Radio Sahar* (Dawn). In Kandahar the *Afghan Independent Radio* was launched with support from international organizations.

As the elections of 2004 drew near, dialectical confrontations occurred through the media. This "war of words" showed the intensity of the paroxysms taking place within the Afghan government itself—between extreme conservatives and open-minded liberals. For instance, one newspaper, supported by former Mujahideen, attacked "those who owe their allegiance to the West and follow in the footsteps of the communist regime." The newspaper said, "These have fled the country when the situation was bad, and have now returned to occupy the highest ranks." One these "emigrant Afghans," Abdul Hamid Mubariz, the Assistant to the Minister of Information and Culture, responded through an article in

Anis, the state newspaper, entitled "Those who have returned from the West are the true sons of this country." He drew attention to the fact that they had contributed to rebuilding the country. The discussion extended to another state newspaper *Arman-e-Mili,* which tried to soften the situation by saying, "We have gained the freedom of the press. We should not lose this opportunity by using vicious words that will lead our country into tribal and territorial conflicts."

In practice, the new "free media" became a point of conflict between the extremists and the "emigrants." This conflict surfaced specially in the decision made by extremist judges to prohibit the establishment of cable television stations. When a journalist criticized this decision, one of the members of the Supreme Court replied by leveling the charge of "infidel" against the journalist. The attitudes of the extremists escalated with respect to independent media. The case of the *Aftaab* weekly emerged as an example of how the authorities would deal with such media, especially since the publication was accused of "blasphemy." This occasioned a return to self-censorship on the part of journalists in all matters pertaining to the former "warlords."

At this time, when the media conflict was taking shape, journalists were subject to repeated attacks and harassments. This forced the Ministry of Information to put in place a system for protecting them in coordination with the Ministry of Interior. The spokesman of the UN Mission condemned those attacks because they "spread an atmosphere of restricted freedom of expression." Abdul Ahror Romizpour, head of the Afghan Independent Human Rights Commission, confirmed the existence of threats and pressure on the press coming from senior officials, politicians, warlords and Mujahideen. This committee had a successful experience in Mazār-e Sharīf when it managed to get a female Afghani writer who was accused of "blasphemy" acquitted. This writer was sentenced by a local religious society to death for an article on the presumed role of women in the new constitution.

The *Aftaab* Case: A Warning to all Journalists

As mentioned earlier, the charge of blasphemy was leveled against the weekly magazine *Aftaab* (The Sun), published in the Dari language. This became the most serious and well-known case in the post-liberation media and under the occupation. The Editor-in-Chief of the magazine, Sayeed Mir Hussein Mahdavi and the journalist Ali Reza Payam Sistany were arrested because they published an article on June 11, 2003, which was considered blasphemous. Copies of the magazine were confiscated and its offices were closed. The article had raised questions about Islam's place in politics and methods of interpreting religious texts. It also criticized the practices of some Mujahideen and religious leaders, extending its criticism to the President (Chief Justice) of the Supreme Court, a conservative cleric associated with warlord Abdul Rasoul Sayaf. This article was published amidst discussion on the new constitution, and thus embarrassed the government, which was forced to support the Supreme Court. It is worth mentioning that the magazine was as severe in its criticism of government as it was in its criticism of the Mujahideen.

The arrest of the journalists angered various international bodies. The United Nations Special Envoy for Afghanistan, Dr. Lakhdar Brahimi urged their immediate release and asked for reform of the judicial system to provide for a better protection of the freedom of expression. President Hamid Karzai, who had issued the order to arrest the journalists, directed their release till they appeared before court. The conservatives responded by demanding a death sentence. *Al Islami* newspaper published a *fatwas* (a formal legal opinion) legalizing their execution. The journalists disappeared and this prompted the Supreme Court President to accuse the Minister of Information and Culture, Sayed Makhdoum Raheen of helping them to leave the country to escape accusations. The organization Reporters Sans Frontières disclosed a confidential document revealing that the Supreme Court had urged the death penalty for the two journalists. President Karzai intervened to transfer the case to a Kabul civil court lest the Supreme Court took decisions such as ordering the execution of the journalists, which would have been binding on the government. Acts of persecution and serious threats drove these two journalists to leave Afghanistan with their families. They fled to Pakistan and gained asylum in a western country with the help of the office of the UN High Commissioner for Refugees.

At the same time, acts of violence against journalists increased, especially on the part of the warlords. On March 19, 2003 Ahmed Shah Behzad, the correspondent of Radio Free Afghanistan was covering the inauguration of the office of the Afghan Independent Human Rights Commission in the city of Herat. However, Ismail Khan, the Governor of the province, was irked by questions that the journalist addressed to officials present, so he ordered him to be ejected. Outside, Behzad was beaten by security officers and by members of Ismail Khan's entourage. He was then taken to the police station for interrogation. He was only released some hours later following intervention by Ahmed Jalali, the Minister of Interior, a former Director of the Pashto language service in the *Voice of America*. However the press continued to face troubles with Ismail Khan. He was quoted as saying that the money that journalists received from their foreign organizations "should be spent on their graves after their burial." He targeted the same journalist again and ordered him to leave Herat although he was a native of the province. Other journalists expressed solidarity with their colleague and complained to the President Hamid Karzai, and Ismail Khan was ultimately forced to compromise.

In the Zābol province, soldiers of Hamidullah Khan Tokhi, the Governor of the province detained a journalist working for the Pashto language service of the *Voice of America* claiming that his coverage of the security situation in the region was biased. In Khost, the correspondent of *Radio Azadi* (Radio Free Europe) was arrested for several days by the militia of Pasha Zadran, the Governor of the province, because the journalist had interviewed the Governor's opponents in one of his articles. In Kabul, the police arrested Zahoor Afghan, the editor of the independent daily called *Arada* (The Decision) after he had published an article that angered Younis Qanooni, the Minister of Education, and those in his inner circle. In Mazār-e Sharīf, supporters of Mohammad Atta, the strong man in the region, attacked Syed Khalid Meerzada, a journalist affiliated to Reuters and beat him up, making violent threats against him because he was "a spy for foreigners." This journalist eventually escaped to Pakistan and applied for refugee status to the UN High Commission for Refugees in Peshawar.

In Nangarhar, elements from the local police force beat up two officials of the local television station. The US Human Rights Watch organization reported that the police commander of the region was angry because the television station did not broadcast news about a public meeting he had convened that day. In Kabul too, two persons assaulted Abdul Samay Hamed, writer and editor of *Telaya* magazine, published in Mazār-e-Sharīf. Two days prior, he had spoken to the BBC's Dari-language service, voicing criticism of the warlords. In 2002, the authorities in Mazār-e Sharīf had banned his magazine because of articles reporting abuses of the law by the local warlord's militias. This writer had to ask the Minister of Information to intervene and allow the magazine to resume publication. He told the Committee to Protect Journalists (CPJ) that the "danger for us comes from all sides, but the main problem is that of self-censorship which forces journalists to refrain always from criticizing the authorities." On the highway between Lowgar province and Kabul an armed group attacked Faiz-ul-Rahman Uryo, the editor of the weekly magazine *Mish'al al dimoqratiya* (The Torch of Democracy), hitting him with the butts of their rifles. They said that he should have known better than to publish criticisms of the Mujahideen.

Threats, Intimidation, Constraints and Flaws in Legal Protection

In the following section more specific examples are presented of the threats, intimidation and constraints faced by Afghan journalists. These indicate the kind of dangerous interaction that has brought the press into conflict with many actors in Afghan society.

[451]

- Before Sayeed Mahdavi, the Editor-in-Chief of *Aftaab* magazine, was arrested in June 2003 and accused of blasphemy, he was subjected to threats for weeks. In March he was increasingly harassed because of articles criticizing the Mujahideen and a caricature of the former President Burhaneddin Rabbani. Electricity was cut off from the *Aftaab* offices by an order from the Minister of Agriculture, Sa'eed Anvari, who was criticized by the magazine. After an article criticizing the warlord Abdul Rasoul Sayaf, he received abduction threats and threats to massacre members of the Hazāra, the ethnic group to which he belonged. He also received threats from security circles. In April, threats to kill him intensified. In a telephone call, the speaker declared, "We will stalk you like your shadow. We can easily kill you." This followed the publication of an article calling for the establishment of a secular government in Afghanistan. Mahdavi reported these threats to the Ministry of Information, which gave him a letter to the Ministry of Interior. A police officer visited him to discuss protection measures. However, during their next meeting the officer told him that his superior officers refused to protect him because of orders by Ministry officials. In their view the journalist had insulted people and Islam and should be prepared to bear the consequences. Mahdavi sought the help of international organizations but he was soon arrested.
- In March 2003, a journalist in working for Human Rights Watch reported that he was threatened after publishing a caricature of the Afghan President Hamid Karzai and the Minister of Defense, Muhammad Fahim. He added that the security men "visited" his house and office. He had also received a threat after publishing an article about the former President Burhaneddin Rabbani. Also, Governor Ismail Khan personally contacted him and told him that he would take measures to respond to an article in which he criticized him. In the same month a journalist working for Radio Gardēz (in the eastern part of the country) revealed that he was harassed by police officials in the province. He commented to the Human Rights Watch

organization: "We must say that everything is well even if people are dying of hunger...this is the freedom of expression which we enjoy." In mid-April, Mirwais Afghan, a BBC World Service stringer, was in Kandahar covering the combat between the Afghan army and Taliban fighters in the Zabol province. A soldier approached him and asked him to surrender his equipment. He refused and the soldier fired in the air. The journalist learned that the Governor of the region had given an order to intimidate him. Some days prior, he had received death threats from the Governor himself because he reported that a group of Taliban fighters had captured part of Zabol. In mid-April the office of the Attorney-General threatened to liquidate Latifa Barakzay the Editor of *Saboon* magazine, after the magazine published pictures of Indian cinema stars. In late June, two journalists working for *Mish'al al dimoqratiya* magazine received threats from officials in the ministries of Transport and Women's Affairs after the magazine published articles criticizing the bad management of senior officials in these two ministries.

• In January 2003 the Supreme Court Chief Justice Fazil Hadi Shinwari prohibited cable television broadcasting, explaining that "some people complained about cable channels broadcasting pornographic films that contradict Islamic teachings. We are Afghan[s] and Muslims and we have Islamic laws and values in our country. It is our responsibility to take this decision and the government must implement it now." Broadcasting by the cable TV operators was halted on the same day although the Minister of Information publicly opposed this ban, declaring that permitting or prohibiting broadcasts was his authority: "Our policy toward cable television is one of freedom but also a policy of respecting the new legislation that we have formulated. Of course channels that contradict Islamic and Afghan traditions are prohibited." In the same month the Supreme Court Chief Justice requested banning all foreign channels that "contradict Islam." President Karzai formed a commission of enquiry comprising four ministers to screen the programs of foreign channels transmitting

[453]

cable broadcasts. After three months, the BBC, CNN and *Al Jazeera* channels resumed broadcasting. However, the regulations listing certain permitted television channels excluded all foreign music channels and those that broadcast American and Indian films.

- On July 17, 2003 the authorities confiscated *Risalat al Mujahideen* magazine because of an article suggesting that President Hamid Karzai should resign. This conservative magazine, which was close to the Minister of Defense, published an editorial accusing the President of cowardice because he had apologized to the Pakistani authorities after the looting of the Pakistani embassy in Kabul. However, the Assistant to the Minister of Information confirmed that he did not order the confiscation of the magazine and that those responsible for it undertook to collect copies from the market.

- In late August 2003 the US troops asked the authorities in the Zabol province to expel Afghani and foreign journalists because they were about to launch a wide campaign against Taliban elements.

- On October 11, 2003, the Dari-language state newspaper *Arman,* stopped publication after a government order. The Minister of Information Sayeed Makdoum Raheen gave budgetary reasons for this move. He said that since there were five government-funded publications and in most cases they carried similar articles and pictures, "we had to stop one of them." However, the Editor-in-Chief of the newspaper, Mir Haider Motahar, ascribed the reason behind the stoppage to the newspaper's increasingly independent political orientation, and its reporting of public discontent with government measures. Later on he said that it was closed after it had refused to publish materials sent by the Ministry of Information. He revealed that the government had proposed selling the newspaper to the private sector but the decision to halt its publication was hasty. In his view, this decision was dictated by internal conflicts between the different wings of the government.

Iraqi Media under Occupation

Different Atmosphere from Afghanistan

In contrast to the simple and limited capabilities observed in the case of the Afghan media, which began to witness a flood of investments from businessmen and capitalists, the Iraqi media scene after the fall of the former regime seemed to pulsate with activity. The occupation authority injected millions of dollars into the field as an integral part of the invasion and occupation plan, so that offers and incentives started weeks before the war began. This was also a part of the democratic transformation in the country, and a response to the occupation authority's need for rapid and reliable communication with all social groups. All the parties which supported the war, with a few exceptions, got special aid for media purposes. Some of this aid was used for its specified purposes whereas most of it was used for other purposes and simply evaporated. There were factors that collectively rendered media activity a futile effort. These included the changing circumstances for the occupation force, disharmony between the occupation force and the people of Iraq, the state of chaos which emerged after the occupation, the collapse of basic public services and the disbanding of the army, security forces and most state institutions. True, there was a good response to the desire for reviving the media as a proof of the vitality of freedom. However, the sad state of public affairs hindered the pace and achievement of this objective. A number of factors account for this situation. First, the "free media" had to create space for itself in an environment unaccustomed to media freedom for almost half a century. Second, it had to gain its freedom with respect to delivering information and expressing opinions. Third, it had to embark on this mission amidst serious Iraqi divisions. Fourth, it had to look for national consensus in order to follow a particular plan, or align itself with the sectarian political currents that had crystallized rapidly with support from the occupation authority.

The occupation authority and the people of Iraq were diametrically opposed, more so than in Afghanistan. This situation was exacerbated

[455]

because the Iraqi people could not adjust to the dismantling of the state and its institutions even before they had time to absorb the initial shock of the occupation. As for media freedom, there was no comparison with the earlier situation. The print media quickly grew active while radio stations, television stations and electronic media were active to a lesser extent but in unprecedented numbers, having suddenly gained permissibility. Internet cafes sprang up and trading in previously banned satellite dishes flourished. However, the presence of the occupation troops did not negate the fact that Iraq was, and still is, the most dangerous country for journalistic work. Also the difficulties encountered by the occupation authority and its hand-picked government created a confrontation between them and the media, especially the Arab satellite channels. Therefore, they repeatedly took decisions to stop particular satellite channels from working in Iraq.

Obviously, the atmosphere of open freedom which prevailed in the first months after the occupation soon receded in the interest of self-censorship in the case of local newspapers. Criticism abounded from military leaders and political officials in Baghdad, Washington and London. Among these were, particularly, the US President George Bush, the British Prime Minister Tony Blair, and their ministers—Donald Rumsfeld, Colin Powell, Jack Straw and Geoffrey Hoon, in addition to other senior officials. Colin Powell and Paul Bremer, the American civil administrator in Iraq, went so far as to stop the publication of *Al Hawza*, the newspaper published by Muqtada Al-Sadr's faction. Al-Sadr waged a bloody fight on US troops in Karbala, An Najaf and some Baghdad quarters. While the Interim Iraqi Government (under the premiership of Iyad Alawi) decided to ban *Al Jazeera* from working in Iraq from August 2004, it was noteworthy that during the second battle of Al Fallujah in November 2004, the US troops were keen to distance the media completely from the battle. However, at the end of the battle they permitted certain media teams to be present, while excluding some Arab and Iraqi media organizations. The expulsion of the media during the battle was based on decisions taken by the Coalition Provisional Authority to ban any media outlet that "instigates violence or spreads instability."

In any case, the Iraqis finally had access to new sources of information. The state media was no longer their only source of information and they ended up totally ignoring it. Within a year after the beginning of the occupation, a report by experts of the Freedom House organization counted more than two hundred newspapers and about 90 television and radio stations. However, the content quality of these publications was varied. The report stated that media freedom in Iraq was still in danger and far from being consolidated. Also, media circles were still preoccupied with suspicions arising from the complications of the provisional phase and the uncertainty surrounding the future of the political system.

The Iraqi Media Scene before the Occupation

Before the Baathists seized power in 1968, the Iraqi media was relatively free and diversified. In that year, Decree No. 840 was passed, according to which any one who criticized or insulted the President could be sentenced to death. During the 35-year rule of Saddam Hussein, both the opposition and independent newspapers were silenced and the media became merely a means of glorifying the regime and the President. In the regime's last years, Saddam's son Uday dominated the media via his newspapers, radio and television stations. In 1992 he became the chairman of the Iraqi Journalists Union. The Iraq–Iran War helped in the growth of various media outlets. However, these did not reflect the rapid progress in the field of communications despite the availability of material resources. Satellite dishes were not only banned, but the penalty for using them included fines and imprisonment. Also, satellite channels and foreign radio stations were jammed.

When the country was connected to the Internet in late 1998, its use was controlled and e-mails were sent via special offices. Non-Iraqi newspapers were banned. Foreign journalists were only allowed to work in the company of government officials. On the other hand, in the Kurdish northern region, tens of newspapers and nearly 20 radio and television stations were founded as of 1991. The radio channels of the *BBC, Monte*

Carlo and *Sawa* could be heard there. The inhabitants were allowed to receive transmission from various television networks without any restrictions. Although the Kurdish press enjoyed greater relative freedom than was prevalent in the rest of Iraq, it was also committed to self-censorship.

In the rest of the country, the iron fist continued to strangle all media. The media continued its propaganda activity under Uday's supervision. This activity was carried out through his newspapers, television stations, especially the *Youth Television* and radios such as *The Voice of Iraq* which used to transmit via FM in English. In March 2001, thirty journalists were expelled from the journalists' trade union by an order from its Secretary-General Uday claiming that they were incompetent. In fact they had refused to work under new Editors-in-Chief appointed by the President's son.

The journalists' trade union counted as many as fifty journalists who fled the country during the year 2001. As for the Ministry of Information, it asked press attachés in the Iraqi embassies to provide it with the names of journalists who worked with the opposition. A list of 300 journalists and writers was compiled. Internally, it was difficult to count the number of journalists who were under arrest. The authorities did not allow any queries or investigations by a foreign body. In spite of this, the cases of three journalists were documented. Ahmed Aziz Al Saiyd Jasim, who worked for *Al Qadisiya*, *Al Ghad* and *Al Thawra*, was arrested in 1999 and detained in a secret place, after refusing to author a book about Saddam Hussein. The journalist Hashim Dram from *Al Qadisiya* disappeared in April 1991 and was never seen again. Hashim Hassan, the Editor-in-Chief of *Al Thawra*, was arrested by the Iraqi intelligence at the Jordanian border in late September 1991. Hassan sought to escape after receiving threats from Uday because he refused to take up the position of the Editor-in-Chief of *Al Rafidein* magazine.

Media freedom existed in Iraq within the limits determined by the regime. Journalists were only able to express what orders dictated. For this reason they demonstrated in late March 2002, for instance, and burned Israeli and American flags, appealing to the Arab leaders, who were attending the Arab Summit Meeting in Beirut, to reject any military action against Iraq. Likewise, many journalists called on April 27, 2002 for commemorating the 65th anniversary of the birth of the President Saddam Hussein in a demonstration in front of the US embassy in Baghdad, which had been closed for ten years at the time. Six months later, on October 15, orders were issued to cover the new and repetitive *Mubay'a* (pledge of allegiance) to Saddam Hussein through a referendum. *Al Thawra* newspaper urged turning the referendum into an expression of love for the President. All newspapers were published carrying the same headline: "Yes to Saddam." Saddam officially got 100% of the votes and his Deputy Izzat Ibrahim called this "an exceptional expression of a democracy which is superior to all other democracies, including those in the countries besieging Iraq in an attempt to strangle it."

After the referendum, Saddam took a number of steps, including the release of prisoners and urging those in the opposition to return to the country. Nevertheless, a month later, in November 2002, increased movement was detected among citizens seeking to emigrate through Jordan and Turkey. There was no sign of any atmosphere of confidence. The Iraqis grew fearful as the US threats mounted. They were also suffering from domestic pressures because of measures taken to confront any possible popular uprising in case of an external attack. This possibility was evidenced by some unknown elements who wrote "Down Saddam" on a wall in the *Al Jadida* quarter in Baghdad. This resulted in a brutal house-to-house inspection and led to the arrest of tens of people whose fate remains unknown. This was followed by forcing employees to take an oath confirming that they would not leave their offices even when the US air raids began. During the same period, Baghdad agreed to the new mission of the international inspectors and allowed journalists to cover the work of the inspectors provided they were accompanied by government officials.

Since 1992 when Uday was elected leader of the journalists union, the Iraqi media lived through its darkest era. There was constant pressure on a

[459]

daily basis, and all journalists were forced to join the Baath party. Journalists who did manage to escape abroad gave shocking testimony. Some spoke of tongues being cut as punishment and of torture rooms in Uday's headquarters at the premises of the Olympic Committee, which he chaired. Others spoke of pressures that ranged from legal intimidation, insults, extortions, arrest and physical liquidation.

In the last years before the fall of Saddam Hussein's regime, the Liberty TV station was able to broadcast to Iraq from neighboring countries. The Iraqi National Congress had launched this station but stopped broadcasting in late 2002 because of budget cuts by the US Congress. At the same time, *Radio Free Iraq*, which was affiliated to the CIA, was broadcasting for a few hours daily from Prague. Its broadcasting was so well received in Iraq that the Iraqi Foreign Minister protested formally to the Czech government for allowing the CIA to broadcast news hostile to Iraq. As for Iraqi journalists abroad, they were also subject to intimidation and some of their family members inside Iraq were threatened and arrested. Although *Al Jazeera* channel managed to establish a successful working relationship with Baghdad, it continued to receive warnings whenever it hosted opponents in its programs. Its office in Baghdad was closed more than once and its correspondents were prohibited from working frequently for various reasons relating to the editorial stand taken by the channel. Yet the relationship between the channel and Baghdad remained strong. For this reason, Iraqi officials adopted a hostile attitude towards the channel after the fall of Saddam's regime.

Rapid Development of the Emerging Media during the Occupation

The US-led War in Iraq was considered the primary event that polarized media coverage but it was also the bloodiest in the history of the media as evidenced by most organizations concerned with media freedom. Journalists were, literally speaking, caught in the crossfire. They had to deal carefully with the invading troops and the Iraqi authorities before the collapse of the regime. On the American–British side, 800 journalists were invited to accompany the military forces as embedded journalists, in accordance with strict conduct rules. The success of these embedded journalists was mixed. While they could give an idea about the casualties and talk of the wounded, they had to refrain from revealing progress made in the tasks assigned to the forces they had joined. On the Iraqi side, the authorities tried to the very last minute to control the work of hundreds of journalists. During the military operations the *Al Jazeera* channel was harshly criticized in Washington and London because it had broadcast pictures of US prisoners of war. Even before the fall of Baghdad on April 9, 2003, twelve journalists were killed and two were missing. In addition, four media support staffers were killed. The Americans, who were held responsible for the death of five journalists, failed to carry out serious investigations into these incidents.

In the period following the end of the major operations in the war, the Americans seemed tense and more prone to violence, especially towards the Arab satellite channels. This led US journalists to protest strongly to the Pentagon, which officially announced that although clear instructions forbidding intervention in the work of journalists were given some individuals do not follow these instructions.

Soon after the fall of Baghdad, the Iraqi Ministry of Information was bombed and looted. Then it was announced as having been dismantled, heralding the unemployment of five thousand journalists. The Coalition Provisional Authority immediately established the Iraqi Media Network, which issued *Al Sabah* (The Morning) newspaper and made the radio and television channels operative. Within weeks, tens of newspapers appeared to replace the four formal newspapers. A new era had begun but media freedom depended on stability being achieved in the whole country. This new media era is still undergoing an experimental phase.

Three days after the beginning of the military operations, on March 22, 2003, Paul Moran, an Australian photographer working for the ABC network, became the first media victim of the war. He was killed in a car bombing at a military checkpoint on the Iranian border with Iraqi Kurdistan. On the same day, the British journalist Terry Lloyd, who worked for ITN, was killed in a fight between US and Iraqi troops near Al Basrah. On April

[461]

8, 2003, one day before the fall of Baghdad, the offices of *Al Jazeera* and Abu Dhabi Television were damaged in US bombing. Tariq Ayoub, *Al Jazeera's* correspondent, was killed in this blast, the first Arab journalist to die in the war. Although the war had practically ended, it did not remove the danger accompanying the work of the journalists, about 17 of whom were wounded and at least one was abducted. Before the fall of the regime, the Iraqi authorities arrested five western journalists and sent them to the infamous Abu Ghraib prison. They also put ten journalists under house arrest in the hotel where they were staying.

After the fall of Baghdad, the Americans took over the task. With the Iraqi police they arrested about thirty journalists for varying periods. During and after the war, about 15 journalists were assaulted in Chamchamal in Kurdistan, Al Najaf, Baghdad, Al Fallujah and Kirkuk. As for the residences, offices and cars of journalists (those working for *Al Jazeera*, Abu Dhabi Television and CNN in Tikrit, the Associated Press in Al Khalidia, NBC in Baghdad and the Turkish Anadolu News Agency in Arbil) as well as the hotels where journalists were staying (such as the Meridien, Palestine and Sheraton in Baghdad) were all targeted by fires. From January to March 2003, Iraqi authorities successively expelled journalists from Indonesia, USA, Canada, Spain, Iran, Britain, Australia and South Africa. They also expelled Turkish journalists.

The new media era in Iraq was soon tarnished, even before the operations against the US troops intensified. On April 15, 2003, just six days after the invasion troops entered Baghdad, they prohibited journalists from covering a demonstration in front of the Palestine Hotel where media personnel were staying. The demonstration demanded better electricity supplies and protested against the lack of security. On July 22, the occupation authority for the first time ordered the closure of *Al Mustaqila* (The Independent) newspaper, after accusing it of instigating the killing of Americans. Ten days earlier, the newspaper had published an article titled "Death to the spies and collaborators (of the Americans)—their killing is a religious duty." The newspaper resumed publication after a month. On September 23, the Iraqi Governing Council made a decision to impose severe punishments on *Al Arabiya* and *Al Jazeera* channels, accusing them of encouraging political violence, the killing of Council Members and broadcasting terrorists' tapes. The two channels had broadcast verbal messages from former Iraqi President Saddam Hussein. The two channels were banned from covering official activities for two weeks. This decision came two weeks after the assassination of Council's Member Aqilah Al-Hashimi. At that time, the occupation authority declared that it could not avoid punishing those Arab satellite channels that focused a large segment of their programming on the coverage of attacks against US troops.

In late October 2003, the US troops closed *Sada Tall 'Afar* (The Echo of Tall 'Afar) a newspaper published by the Turcoman Front in Tall 'Afar (north of Mosul) on the charge of inciting violence against Americans. This newspaper had published an article titled "Al-Mawsil [Mosul] for Turks." On November 24 the Iraqi Governing Council decided to close the offices of *Al Arabiya* channel and banned it from working in Iraq until it ceased to broadcast verbal messages from Saddam Hussein. Washington backed this decision on the basis that *Al Jazeera* and *Al Arabiya* channels incite "violence against the coalition." *Al Arabiya* resumed working from Baghdad the day the former Iraqi President was captured.

Increasing Reliance on Iraqi Journalists

In 2004 the International Union of Journalists announced that 62 journalists were killed in Iraq since the start of the US intervention in this country. Although the "formal" war itself had a high toll of deaths and casualties, the toll of "the war after the war" is increasing by the day. In May 2004, a report by the Committee to Protect Journalists documented the death of 14 journalists since the beginning of the year. Among them were 12 Iraqis, with 6 of them working for foreign media organizations. Obviously, the same year witnessed the emergence of more Iraqi journalists as the foreign media increasingly relied on them, mainly for security reasons. The risks of abduction and assaults for journalists became a concrete reality. Also, antagonistic sentiments towards foreign journalists in particular were exacerbated. Moreover, Iraqis proved that they were increasingly adapting to the media, and their ease of mobility was much greater than foreign journalists. The events in Al Fallujah and An Najaf made greater reliance on local journalists inevitable because they could communicate more easily with the locals, avoid the suspicions that regarded foreigners as "spies" and need not fear acts of retaliation.

It must be noted that work in different sectors became dangerous. Iraqi journalists, who were unemployed, had no alternative but to risk danger to keep their jobs and livelihoods. In April 2004, foreign journalists were forced to stay in their hotels and not to approach hot spots because of the heightened risk of abductions, especially after six journalists were abducted during that period. This led to Arab satellite channels enhancing their ability to broadcast news reports from within besieged cities, because they relied more on Iraqi correspondents and informers. A *Los Angeles Times* correspondent explained that foreign journalists used to move around with the support of other journalists even inside Baghdad. Sometimes they would remain inside their cars and send translators with a list of questions to put to their sources, many of whom they could not reach personally without exposing themselves to danger. Although the ability of Iraqi and Arab journalists to reach any place quickly, especially bombing sites, was understandable, the US troops were not pleased with this rapid, uncontrolled coverage. For this reason, the dangers facing Iraqi and Arab journalists escalated, and they were subject frequently to assaults or firing. Sometimes, public anger following an event used to be vented against media personnel, holding them responsible for what happened.

The dangers did not stem solely from the areas of coverage. Journalists and translators working for the US media also became targets. In March 2004 armed men attacked a translator working for the *Voice of America* and another working for *Time* magazine. Many Iraqis working for American media institutions received death threats. Two journalists were arrested in Al Fallujah because they were suspected of working for *Al Hurra* channel. This forced other journalists to conceal the identities of the institutions they worked for and take strong precautions. In press conferences they avoided giving the names of their institutions and some were even forced to give up their jobs.

Iraqi journalists said that during the war coverage they feared US firing in particular and felt that they were being targeted, especially after seven Iraqi and Arab journalists were killed by US fire. In March 2004, Arab journalists walked out of a press conference held by the US Secretary of State, Colin Powell, in protest against the death of two Iraqi journalists— Ali Al Khateeb and Ali Abdul Aziz from *Al Arabiya* channel. These journalists were shot and killed by US fire at a US-manned checkpoint in Baghdad as they were leaving the site of a missile attack that they were covering. This heightened worries among journalists as they passed any US checkpoint because they feared sudden reactions.

It must also be noted that journalists who dealt with US troops or worked near them were subject to different forms of intimidation, including arrest, physical harm and confiscation of films or equipment. For instance, in August 2004, US soldiers arrested a journalist and photographer who worked for the Associated Press agency near Abu Ghraib prison. Both were bound up, forced to sit in the sun for three hours and not given anything to drink nor allowed to use the phone. Later on, the officer in charge apologized to them and to the agency saying that the whole matter was just a "misunderstanding." Prior to this, in November 2003, Salih Hassan, an *Al Jazeera* photographer, was arrested as he arrived at a site in Ba'qubah where an implanted bomb had exploded. The site was on the side of a road along which a US convoy passes. The American magazine *The Nation* said that the soldiers accused him of knowing about the attack even before it occurred. They put his head in a sack and sent him to Abu Ghraib prison where he was stripped by the soldiers, who called him "*Al Jazeera's* boy," hurled foul insults at him, and forced him to stand for hours with his head inside the sack. He was released after a month and a half when a court affiliated to the Iraqi Governing Council failed to find any evidence against him. Journalists working for Reuters

[465]

were arrested by US soldiers near Al Fallujah. The British newspaper *The Guardian* said on January 23, 2004 that the soldiers blindfolded them and forced them to stand up for several hours with their arms raised. The newspaper reported that the family of one journalist said that he was forced by US interrogators to strip naked and put his shoes in his mouth.

The US military refused to comment on many such events and treated Arab and Iraqi journalists on the basis of their having pre-knowledge of the attacks on US soldiers. They continued to accuse *Al Jazeera* and *Al Arabiya* channels of instigating anti-American sentiment. Even the US Secretary of Defense Donald Rumsfeld announced that the two channels "obtain from time to time information about attacks before they occur. Because of this they broadcast false reports and work in coordination with the terrorists." Iraqi journalists responded by saying that they knew the places very well and that enabled them to locate the sites of attacks quickly and arrive minutes later in order to convey the news and this caused both anger and astonishment among the Americans.

These risks made it necessary to identify the best means of protecting journalists. One ABC correspondent, Dave Marash, a member of the board of the Committee to Protect Journalists, proposed providing local news teams with better safety devices like protective jackets and even armored vehicles. Marash was able to witness closely the dangers in Iraq, especially when an Iraqi photographer working for his own network was killed after being hit by bullets coming from the American side in Al Fallujah.

As the accidents targeting journalists increased, the US military did not care about calls for immediate, comprehensive and public investigations in which American soldiers were accused of inconveniencing and arresting others, or of shooting at journalists to inflict mortal wounds. The Pentagon's investigation in March 2003 into the accident in which three Reuters journalists were killed was concluded by accepting the story of the US soldiers—that the journalists were in a location from which hostile fire was coming. However, the reality is that they were gathered in one of their own hotel rooms when that hotel was shelled by the Americans. The

Reuters management did not accept the conclusion reached by this investigation and held Washington responsible for the death of its journalists.

A Varied and Expanding Media: A Preliminary Evaluation

Amidst all these dangers, there was an unprecedented flurry of media activity in the first few months that followed the fall of Saddam's regime. Observers found it difficult to count the exact number of emerging newspapers and magazines. It was estimated at two hundred but only half of these managed to survive and continue after a year. In late 2004, official sources confirmed that they had registered 105 daily and weekly publications. At the same time there were about 90 radio and television stations all over Iraq. After being silent for decades, Sunnis, Shi'ites, Kurds, communists and liberals competed in the media field.

Within this short period it is possible to evaluate this media phenomenon, which appears to have been programmed by the Americans to a great extent. The following observations may be noted:

First, external political forces, as well as potential forces within the country, realized the importance of the media and the symbolic significance of having media operations that could exercise new freedoms. Newspapers, radio stations and television channels seemed very concerned with the bodies funding them and their activity, and thus focused on party leaders rather than on general coverage and objectivity.

Second, observers soon noted that this diverse media suffered from a deficit of professionalism since media standards were varied and obscure, and they were "inclined towards sensationalism, amplifying rumors and conspiracy theories. This gave rise to concerns about the possibility of media contributing to incitement and eruption of violence," according to the report of the Freedom House organization in August 2004. However, the report itself noted the existence of new newspapers trying to raise the general standards such as *Al Mada* (The Range), which appeared in mid-January 2004. It was reputed for publishing the names of politicians,

[467]

companies and institutions that allegedly received "oil coupons" from the former regime.

Third, Iraqi journalists gave testimonies showing that their work environment lacked freedom, and they could not deal freely with news. The fears of the journalists stemmed two sources: the political parties and the unstable security situation. Therefore, self-censorship flourished and journalists could not speak of a "free press" in a country "under foreign occupation." Decree No. 7 issued by Paul Bremer was a sort of red line for the freedom of the media. It banned the instigation of violence against the coalition forces and the incitement of ethnic and religious hatred. The widespread use of arms coupled with the lack of police presence did nothing to encourage journalists to go out and cover certain areas or write about sensitive issues (like those discussing clans, women and sects). Some journalists, as those in *Al Aswaq* (The Markets) said that any militia could come and attack the newspaper's office, which consisted of a single room.

Fourth, the new Iraqi media did not pose a problem to the Coalition Provisional Authority (the occupation). The difficulties arose from the Arab television media (as represented by *Al Jazeera* and *Al Arabiya* channels). This confronted the authority with the challenge of finding "a balance between media freedom and responsible coverage."

Fifth, there is the problem of interference by regional players through connections with the Iraqi political forces, regardless of whether the particular state had supported the war (such as Kuwait and Qatar), or apparently opposed it (such as Iran and Syria), or was neutral (such as the Kingdom of Saudi Arabia, Turkey and the UAE). What was especially notable was that Iran involved itself in media affairs either by supporting political parties close to it, or by strengthening official Arabic television broadcasting directed towards Iraq, and by launching the *Sawat al Mujahideen* radio station, which was affiliated to the Supreme Council for the Islamic Revolution in Iraq (SCIRI). Also, Iran funded the emergence of channels such as *Al 'Alam* (The World) and *Al Sumariya* (The Sumerian).

[468]

The CPA: Seeking a Balance between Freedom and Media Control

The Coalition Provisional Authority (CPA) was the first to encourage interested persons to engage in media activity. It distributed generous funds that contributed to the publication of several newspapers and launched radio and television stations in accordance with criteria specified by Decree No. 65 and 66 issued by the CPA Administrator Paul Bremer. Also, the United States realized that it was time to challenge *Al Jazeera* and *Al Arabiya* channels and thus launched *Al Hurra* in February 2004 to project the desired American viewpoint. However, this move did not lead to the expected audience penetration. American financial contribution did not stop, but was diverted in later months away from the media and towards research centers and promising individuals.

Improving professional performance became the main focus of several government and private initiatives. This was necessary because the so-called "official" media was there, as the state radio and television resumed its activities, in addition to the state newspaper *Al Sabah* (The Morning), which was approved by the occupation authority prior to the process of power transfer in late June 2004. Also, there were the private media organizations which surpassed state media in terms of number and vitality. Iraqi journalists were invited to training sessions abroad and developed a new awareness about the role of the media in Iraq. The freedom available in Iraq after the fall of the former regime was real but because of inadequate experience and competence it plunged into chaos. Also, the media could play a basic role in shaping the future of the country provided it could defend inalienable rights. However, this kind of awareness is still in its infancy and it is uncertain whether it will evolve rapidly, especially because prevailing political forces have imposed the kind of models they want to perpetuate.

The Interim Iraqi Government hesitated to formulate a comprehensive national media vision. Decree No. 66 issued by Bremer was considered his best decree, particularly as it provided for the establishment of the Iraqi Public Authority for Broadcasting Services, which Bremer preferred to call "public service." However, the Interim Iraqi Government

[469]

abandoned this concept when it established the Higher Media Council, which several experts viewed as a revival of the former regime's system and an attempt to restore the control exercised by the defunct Ministry of Information. This was especially true in terms of controlling licenses for publishing newspapers, imposing restrictions on publishing content and taking measures against newspapers that criticized the government.

In any case the media is expected to witness the revival of some restrictions so that the state can determine its working criteria. Decree No. 14 issued by Bremer on June 10, 2003 set out some provisions. The most important provision was the ban on incitement of violence and attacks on coalition forces as well as demanding any change in Iraqi borders for any reason. It also prohibited calls for the Baath party to return to power. It was clear that the aim of the decree was to sustain civil stability. However, the critics of this decree say that it opened the door for unnecessary censorship. It was Decree No.14 that Bremer relied upon when he closed *Al Mustaqila* newspaper less than month after issuing the decree, on the pretext that it called for the killing of spies who collaborated with the Americans and considered this a religious duty. This decree was also a "legal" cover for banning *Al Arabiya* and *Al Jazeera* channels from working in Iraq. They were accused by the Coalition Provisional Authority and the Iraqi Governing Council, as well as the Interim Iraqi Government, of "collusion with terrorists." *Al Arabiya* followed a more conciliatory policy, which led to a stable relationship with the interim government. However, *Al Jazeera* exerted efforts to find a new equation for its relationship with that government.

Decree No.14 was also the basis of Paul Bremer's decision to close *Al Hawza* newspaper (which projects the viewpoint of Muqtada Al Sadr's faction). This decision was made after the newspaper accused US helicopters of launching missiles that killed 50 volunteers for the Iraqi police, and likened Paul Bremer to Saddam Hussein. However, the decision to close the newspaper was regarded as a political decision in the first place because it coincided with the US desire to arrest Al Sadr and

[470]

the waging of a campaign against him in An Najaf on April 10, 2005 and in the summer of the same year.

Even if the ban and closure decisions could be justified by security and other considerations, those moves, as well as the harsh criticisms of Arab satellite channels by US civilian and military officials did not reflect favorably on the occupation authority. The US military had presumed – as in its war plans – that it would encounter a submissive country and a population that would welcome the arrival of the invading forces. However, even a quick and superficial analysis of the Iraqi society would have given the planners a fair idea of what awaited the invading troops in Iraq, where sectarian, social and political divisions are well known. These divisions became more dangerous and complicated during the ruthless era of Saddam when Iraqi groups were forced to operate underground to maintain their religious and political identities.

One aspect of the kind of press that flourished in Iraq after the occupation was that it was not only political but included several religious newspapers. There are also sport newspapers and those specialized in economics and culture, as well as tabloids.

Political newspapers expressed the viewpoints of parties and groups, such as *Al 'Adala* the newspaper of the Supreme Council for the Islamic Revolution in Iraq. The *Al Manar* newspaper, which was first published in 1945 and has been reissued after a long gap in a tone critical of the US presence. *Al Ittihad* is the newspaper of the Kurdistan National Union under the leadership of Jalal Talbani. *Al Taakhi* is the newspaper of the Kurdistan Democratic Party under the leadership of Massoud Barazani and the most prominent Kurd newspaper in Arabic. Since 1991 the last two papers have been enjoying a freedom that was non-existent in Iraq prior to the occupation. The most widespread newspaper is *Al Zaman*, published by Sa'ad Al Bazaz. It quickly established a network of correspondents and opened an office in Baghdad and in the major cities. It kept its official address as a newspaper published in Britain. There is also *Al Mu'tamar* newspaper, which used to express the viewpoint of the former opposition. Also, *Habzboz* newspaper was relaunched and is

[471]

described as a newspaper reputed for "news, cynicism and independence since it has allegiance neither to the west, nor to the east." Ashtar Al Yassiri, the Editor-in-Chief, maintains that it circulates between 3000–6000 copies daily. As for *Al Sabah* newspaper, it is published in the offices of *Al Thawra*, the former being the first newspaper published after the fall of the former regime, and it was practically the newspaper of the Coalition Provisional Authority.

The CPA and the Establishment of a New National Media

In the spring of 2003, the Coalition Provisional Authority attempted to establish a new national media, according to the models of the British Broadcasting Corporation (BBC) and the American National Broadcasting Company (NBC). To achieve this, it summoned Simon Hazelock, who worked with the United Nations in the interim administrations after the war in Bosnia and Kosovo. He was appointed Chairman of the Authority and was assigned the task of developing the Iraqi media. The Coalition Provisional Authority also established the Iraqi Media Network (IMN) which supervises *Al Sabah* newspaper and the *Al Iraqiya* television channel and radio. The Coalition Authority then contracted Scientific Applications International Corporation (SAIC) to build this new media. This company has an experience in modern media technologies but lacks one in training. In the months following its inception, the Iraqi Media Network suffered a shortage in personnel and faced administrative problems. It also specially suffered from directives, which rendered it vulnerable to charges of being a propaganda machine for the Coalition Provisional Authority. All this drove its Chairman, Ahmed Al Rikabi to resign in protest against the low budget and lack of independence from the Coalition Provisional Authority. The situation was such that Don North, the former Advisor and Trainer at *Al Iraqiya* channel wrote a message to the Associated Press in which he said that the channel had become "a propaganda megaphone for the Coalition Authority by virtue of its directed news and trivial external programming." The Iraqis used to call it "America Television."

[472]

The lack of management and training experience on the part of SAIC resulted in some disorder. This was evidenced by contradictory and sometimes unwise and imbalanced decisions. Journalists were asked to stop interviewing citizens in the streets because their anti-occupation sentiments were unmistakably clear. Journalists alleged that they received instructions from their superiors to exclude the recitation of the Holy Quran from cultural programs. Radio and television programming were prepared in the Convention Center near the headquarters of the Coalition Provisional Authority in the Green Zone. Also, the location of the Iraqi Media Network was subject to criticism because it isolated journalists and robbed them of the mobility and independence needed to keep pace with rapid events.

In the autumn of 2003 protests mounted against the Iraqi Media Network. In November the Supreme Council for the Islamic Revolution in Iraq threatened to wage a protest campaign and issue *fatwās* (formal legal opinions) against the network for broadcasting "immoral" programs. An investigation committee sent by the Pentagon acknowledged that the SAIC did not do its duty. Two months later, in January 2004, the new contractor, Harris Establishment was given the responsibility of developing the Iraqi Media Network in collaboration with the LBC and the Kuwaiti Al Fawaris Establishment with help from Microsoft. Harris Establishment succeeded in solving several problems. In March, the Coalition Provisional Authority designed a new framework that specified the build-up and work of the Iraqi Media Network. Bremer issued Decree No. 66, which placed the network under the supervision of a Council of Governors, a Financial Committee and a Director-General.

This coincided with an opinion poll conducted by the CCN, *US Today* and Gallup. The poll showed that 95% of the Iraqis owned television sets, and 74% watched *Al Iraqiya* channel over the seven days preceding the poll. This made the channel the most popular in the country. A quarter of the audience watched *Al Jazeera* and *Al Arabiya*. Another poll by Oxford Research International in February 2004 showed that 50% trusted *Al Iraqiya* channel while the corresponding number was only 11% in

[473]

November 2003. The explanation behind these figures is that *Al Iraqiya* is the only terrestrial station and therefore does not require a dish. Despite the popularity of *Al Iraqiya,* the participants in the CNN/Gallup poll gave it less credibility than *Al Jazeera* and *Al Arabiya* in terms of objectivity and quick broadcasting of news.

The Iraqi public did not accept the reform achieved by Harris and the LBC, especially since the latter "Lebanized" *Al Iraqiya* to the surprise of viewers. The concerned Iraqi officials were not pleased with the way the US company and its Lebanese associate dealt with them, since they found that their establishment had no budget and there was no visible progress in the training process. It is worth mentioning that they read the contract made between the Coalition Provisional Authority and the company and realized that 120 million dollars were spent to activate the Iraqi Media Network. However, they also found that accounting procedures were faked by huge internal bills, something which made the budget evaporate quickly. According to an Iraqi official in the network, the LBC featured old serials and records from its archive and issued bills that were several times higher than the original production cost. Thus an internal controversy raged and continued for months till the Executive Director of the radio and television stations resigned. The Council of Governors was reformed and a new Director was appointed without remedying the causes that had led to the resignation of the former. The main complaint of media personnel who came to work for the Network was that the real supervisor was a former intelligence officer—a security man with no media experience. It would be a truism to say that his heading of the Network undermined confidence in the Network, and the manner in which it was developing a new media in a new Iraq.

In the process of preparing for the transfer of authority to the Iraqis in late June 2004, the Coalition Provisional Authority established a new authority called the Iraq Communications and Media Commission (ICMC). Decree No. 65 (issued in March 2004) described the authority as "an independent establishment for public services responsible for licensing communications and broadcasting means and media services."

[474]

Bremer appointed Siyamend Ziyad Othman as Executive Chairman and specified certain tasks for this commission—organizing the Iraqi media scene and proposing a new act for advertising and communications to the incoming government. Directly after this public announcement, the *Al Sabah* newspaper, although affiliated to the Coalition Provisional Authority, did not hesitate to criticize the fact that the commission had power and influence far exceeding that enjoyed by the Ministry of Information during the rule of Saddam Hussein. The Interim Minister of Communications, Hayder Al 'Abadi said that the commission had replaced him and that the officials of the Authority did not intimate him of their plans. Some analysts warned that Decree No. 65 and the commission it had formed would give the new government the chance to dominate the private media that had emerged and grown after the fall of the former regime.

In any case, the vast gains made in terms of media freedom since the fall of the former regime cannot be ignored. These advances sustain hope in the future of Iraq. However, the continuing violence not only poses major problems in practicing professional journalism and safeguarding the right to information, but constitutes a danger to the country, the unity of its people and integrity of its territories.

[475]

24

The Iraqi Press after Liberation: Problems and Prospects for Developing a Free Press

Hussein Sinjari

Since the formation of the state of Iraq, the press in this country has never been free in the western sense. In one way or the other, the media was directed to serve the government or the authorities and their orientations. It also served the interests of a particular class at the expense of the others. In this sense, there was no national media or press in Iraq. The media was an apparatus for distorting facts and sometimes engaged in a repressive role. The press always served some sections at the expense of others, praising them and portraying them in a positive light, as well justifying or covering up their mistakes, while concealing the aspirations or achievements of others. Kurds and Shi'ites were marginalized and political opponents and anyone who disagreed with the government were smeared although they constituted the majority. This marginalization marred the image of the media in the eyes of the citizens. Media reports were disparagingly referred to as "newspaper talk" which should not be taken seriously [and became synonymous with "immaterial" in local parlance]. It was ridiculed and despised by the citizens because the state itself was not founded on the values of justice, freedom and equality. This public attitude, which formed in the early 1920s, ever since the arbitrary formation of the Iraqi state without respecting or heeding the majority, snowballed under authoritarian rule until it gained awesome proportions during the tenure of the despotic President Saddam Hussein.

Iraqi newspapers (*Al Thawra, Al Qadisiyyah, Al Jamhoriya, Al Iraq, Babel*) used to convey the same lengthy, boring news as well as reports and speeches of the sole leader. The instructions issued by the high command and from the apparatus of repression used to stifle any possibility of developing the form and content of the press. This changed the Iraqi press into a party circular and a laudatory instrument for the dictator, enhancing his image and justifying his mistakes, as well as camouflaging the destruction suffered by the country as a result of his policies.

On the other hand, no one could work in the press unless he was a prominent, high-ranking Baathist in the party, and knew at least one influential official who would come to the rescue when nepotism was involved. For Baathists, work in the field of journalism was sensitive and dangerous and required people with special attributes. Thus journalists had to sit for tests and examinations to assess their loyalty to the regime and the party. They were required to participate in contests and party activities in which efficiency and professionalism were categorically excluded. Hence it was not surprising to find illiterate persons working in some newspapers. When Uday Saddam Hussein became Chairman of the Iraqi Journalists' Union, the field of journalism deteriorated and declined to its lowest level. The union headquarters was turned into his club, where personal activities including sexual adventures took place, and this became yet another security apparatus along with the other instruments of repression. Often journalists, even those who were loyal to the regime, had to endure the meanest insults including personal beatings, shaving of hair and being urinated upon them during public meetings.

The Baathists' repressive management of the media, and the restriction of freedoms in the mid-1970s, led to Iraqi journalists and media personnel fleeing the country. In addition, hundreds of journalists were arrested and liquidated. This was a grave loss to the Iraqi media. From its pioneering position in the Arab world in the 1970s the Iraqi media regressed to a very backward state by the end of the 1990s. Despite several reform attempts in

[478]

the Ministry of Information, the urging of intellectuals from abroad, and the attempt to encourage weekly newspapers and distribute money, there was no real change in the Iraqi media under Saddam's regime because of the lack of freedom—the essential foundation for the building of a good press.

However, with the fall of the former Iraqi regime, the situation has changed. A great transformation has occurred in the situation of the Iraqi press in particular, and the Iraqi media in general, under the wide margin of freedom which the Iraqis gained.

A comparison between the situation of the press and media in pre-liberation and post-liberation Iraq, as shown in Table 24.1, will serve to clarify the magnitude of the change taking place.

Table 24.1

The Press Situation in Iraq Before and After Liberation

	Pre-Liberation	Post-Liberation
1	All newspapers and magazines were owned by the state or by persons in the authority.	The state owns only one daily newspaper.
2	The number of newspapers was not more than fifteen and all expressed the same ideas and trends. Of these five were daily newspapers.	The number of newspapers is more than one hundred and fifty, expressing different trends and ideas. There are nearly twenty daily newspapers.
3	The state owned all television broadcasting stations.	The state owns only one television station.
4	The state owned all radio broadcasting stations.	The state does not own a single radio broadcasting station.
5	The media channels were controlled by one party which was the ruling party.	Media channels are not dominated by one party and there is no ruling party.
6	There were three state radio stations broadcasting in Arabic.	There are tens of radio stations broadcasting in Arabic, and they are not owned by the state.
7	There was one state radio station broadcasting in Kurdish.	There are tens of radio stations broadcasting in Kurdish, and they are not owned by the state.

[479]

	Pre-Liberation	Post-Liberation
8	There were no radio or television stations broadcasting in the Turkmen or Assyrian languages.	There are several radio and television stations broadcasting in the Turkmen and Assyrian languages.
9	There was one state satellite TV station.	There are nearly ten independent satellite TV stations.
10	There were no radio stations, or newspapers issued outside the capital Baghdad.	There are newspapers and media channels outside Baghdad and in different Iraqi cities.
11	Reception of satellite broadcasting was prohibited.	There is no prohibition on any kind of broadcasting.
12	Anyone who criticized Saddam or the Baath Party could incur the death penalty.	No penalties are incurred for criticizing the government.
13	Printing presses were under censorship.	No censorship of any kind is imposed on printing presses.
14	Distribution was state controlled.	Distribution is private and free.
15	Advertising was state controlled.	Advertising is private and free.
16	Publishing a newspaper or magazine in any form or under any title was prohibited.	Publishing newspapers and magazines is completely free and without monitoring by any authority.
17	It was strictly forbidden for Kurds and Shi'ites to express their aspirations.	Kurds and Shi'ites are free to express their aspirations.
18	A writer was subject to self-censorship in addition to state censorship.	A writer is free to write on any subject.
19	There was no freedom of expression for religious and ethnic groups like Christians (Assyrians and Chaldeans) Turkmen and Yazidis.	All religious and ethnic groups enjoy freedom of expression.
20	State secrets and lists of forbidden things were infinite.	There are no limits on freedom and no confidentiality and there is absolute transparency.
21	No press or media existed for organizations of civil society and non-governmental organizations.	Non-governmental organizations have their own press and media.
22	The photograph and news of the leader had to appear on the front pages everyday.	The press is not obliged to publish any photographs or news of officials.

	Pre-Liberation	Post-Liberation
23	The achievements of the party and officials had to be published.	The press is not obliged to publish the news and achievements of the government.
24	There was a Ministry of Information directing the media.	There is no Ministry of Information and the media is not subject to direction.
25	No foreign correspondents (or the number was very limited and subject to complicated formal approvals which included many restrictions).	No limits or restrictions on foreign correspondents.
26	There were no offices of global organizations for training journalists.	There are offices and organizations and training sessions to train journalists and confer qualifications.
27	The Internet and Internet cafes were non-existent.	Internet services are freely available.
28	There were no mobile phones or necessary mobile phone services for journalists.	Mobile phones are available and are not subject to any restrictions.
29	There were restrictions on computers and photocopiers and they had to be registered with security apparatuses.	There are no restrictions on selling and buying computers and photocopiers.
30	The media personnel including press employees were members of only one party—the Baath Party.	Media personnel and the press are free to join any party of their choice.
31	There was a lack or scarcity of foreign newspapers, magazines and publications and they were all subject to censorship.	Foreign newspapers and publications are available without restrictions.
32	There was strict monitoring on the printing and publishing books.	There is no monitoring on printing and publishing.
33	Importing foreign books was prohibited or subject to restrictions.	There are no restrictions on importing foreign books.
34	There were no cartoons or caricatures criticizing the authorities and officials.	There are no restrictions on cartoons or caricatures criticizing the government or any other authority.
35	Journalists used to gather most of their information from the Ministry of Information.	Journalists gather their information from the street and any other quarters they choose, without any state restrictions.

	Pre-Liberation	Post-Liberation
36	There were many authorities or state agencies authorized to monitor the media, or distort foreign television and radio stations.	There is no censorship or distortion of foreign television and radio stations.
37	Nearly all newspapers used to publish the same news and political issues.	Newspapers publish what they choose, and the press is free to decide what it deems appropriate, regardless of the source.
38	The government used to sponsor the press and prohibit any foreign or private sponsorship.	There is foreign sponsorship of the press in addition to private sponsorship.
39	There was a lack of press coverage on pluralism, democracy, religious and ethnic tolerance, the rights of religious and ethnic minorities, parliamentary practices, coverage of parliamentary sessions, coverage of elections, party activities, party slogans, activities of non-governmental organizations, trade unions, anti-government demonstrations, calls for protests and demonstrations, and complaints against parties and the government.	There are no restrictions on publishing, coverage and writing on any issue or activity, and no ban on any kind of concepts and activities.
40	Journalists used to have low salaries that ranged between $10 and $20 per month.	The salaries are more reasonable and range between $170 and $300 per month.
41	The press was a convenient profession and journalists used to be treated as state employees.	The press is a dangerous and hard but free profession.
42	There was no national press.	There are very few newspapers that can be considered national.
43	Journalists were incompetent in English and did not need a foreign language.	Journalists learn foreign languages and need them in their work.

	Pre-Liberation	Post-Liberation
44	Journalists did not read or follow what was written in the newspapers.	Journalists read and follow what is written in the newspapers.
45	There were only a few printing presses but most were obsolete and dated from 1980s.	Tens of printing presses with different specifications have been imported, and there is an expansion in printing and technology development.
46	The technical cadres of journalism were very few in number.	Hundreds of technicians working in publishing and design have emerged in the field of journalism.

The Iraqi Press Today: Problems and Expectations

The current Iraqi press can be divided into two categories. First, there is a free press that is connected with individuals, authorities or private companies and which enjoys a large margin of freedom as regards presentation and criticism. It is also not obliged to comply with any rules or restrictions in the process of conveying information but is generally characterized by technological weakness. Second, there is the party-oriented press which may be regarded as an extension of the Iraqi opposition press abroad. This section of the press is heavily bound by ideology, party traditions and sloganeering. It has not liberated itself from this heritage and this has led to monotony and weakness in form and content. It puts the pictures of its leaders on the front page and reports news of these leaders, their meetings with visitors, farewell ceremonies, receiving felicitations on different occasions, in addition to presenting news in the style of monotonous propaganda, maintaining political correctness, and reporting events in an unprofessional style as well as selecting materials and news in a way which is governed by party doctrine.

The party newspapers that came with the parties from abroad attracted many readers in the beginning because it monopolized the field. It also enjoyed wide readership for lack of alternatives and because people were thirsty for news, articles and ideas opposing the former regime after the complete absence of contrary opinions for decades, and also because of the curiosity and interest associated with the new situation. However, the readers diminished in number gradually and the party press ceased to enjoy popularity with the passage of time. This was particularly so because tens of private newspapers had appeared and there was also a spread of radio and television stations. The Internet and the availability of Arab and international newspapers in the Iraqi market, coupled the continuing boredom of Iraqis and their despair over the lack of rapid improvement in the security and economic situation meant that Iraqi newspapers had fewer readers in general, especially in the context of its dominant verbal culture.

However, this does not mean that the number of readers dropped from its previous level after the collapse of the former regime. On the contrary, daily Iraqi newspapers, such as *Al Thawra, Al Jamhoriya, Al Iraq* and *Al Qadisya*, did not publish more than three thousand copies. *Babel*, which was the most popular, used to publish more than this number. Now there are Iraqi newspapers which publish more than twenty thousand copies (such as *Al Sabah* newspaper), and there are more than ten newspapers that publish more than three thousand copies. There are also several newspapers which publish between five thousand and ten thousand copies daily (*Al Zaman*, *Al Shahid* and *Al Mushriq* and others). It is worth mentioning that the number of newspapers (daily and weekly) during the tenure of the former regime did not exceed fifteen newspapers while the number now exceeds a hundred and fifty newspapers located in the different regions of the country.

The relative lack of literacy has encouraged many people to watch television, especially since the fall of the dictator availed them the chance to watch forbidden satellite channels. Journalists also watch satellite channels. Newcomers to the profession view these satellite broadcasts during the day as a source of news and write their reports in the afternoons to be published in the newspapers of the following day, especially since most are not yet skilled in Internet usage.

Journalists were accustomed to idleness and inactivity under the former dictatorial regime. They used to collect their information from the Ministry of Information directly. Now that there is no such ministry, journalists turn to satellite channels like *Al Jazeera* and *Al Arabiya*, or international agencies for their information, without scrutinizing or verifying it and often without exerting any effort to look for news. Of course, there are some exceptions. Journalists who do not personally go to the site of events, and who rely on ready-made news are still the dominant model.

Another important issue relates to the danger of regression in press performance. Many journalists who worked with Uday Saddam and helped to sabotage the Iraqi press for two decades have succeeded in infiltrating several new Iraqi newspapers, and established themselves in the press. This situation has worsened so much that these journalists not only determine the policies of those newspapers but at the same time they get sponsored by foreign parties. This has encouraged the emergence of a Baathist work style in many Iraqi newspapers. Moreover, many parties have relied on such persons in founding their newspapers because they are more capable of understanding Iraqi realities, and in dealing with printing presses and distributors. Also, such journalists are more adept at hypocrisy and paying lip service to climb up the ladder and many have had special links, even scandalous connections in the past with many officials of current political parties before they became national opposition figures. Every party understands that preserving its own special interest requires covering up the scandals and mistakes of other parties. Hence the language of interests gains the upper hand and negative styles of functioning rather than professionalism pervade journalistic work. This jeopardizes the building of a new Iraqi press.

However, these developments are only the beginning. Another aspect is that a new generation of journalists has started to emerge and their skills will develop quickly after a reasonable period of training which enables them to acquire the required values and professional expertise to succeed in the field of journalism.

Sensationalism in Party and Private Newspapers

Several newspapers have closed their offices because of the limited support they get and the scarcity of commercial advertisements—they are unable to continue publishing. On the other hand, party newspapers have endured because of available financial support. Yet these newspapers face a gradual drop in readership because of their monotonous content and lack of credibility, or because they do not disclose exciting events which may negatively affect either the parties that publish these papers or other parties with which they have particular relations. They also continue to suffer from the viewpoints of the parties publishing them, as well as their associates and interests, which put shackles on these newspapers and draw red lines that the journalists cannot cross. Thus they lack freedom and professionalism to a very great extent. In addition, they avoid presenting issues with courage and credibility and are disinterested in the vital issues affecting the country and the problems plaguing its people. As they are not concerned with press competition and are focused on private party propaganda, these newspapers are constantly declining in circulation despite their huge financial capabilities and modern technologies. All this makes party newspapers monotonous and drives them every now and then to renew themselves by crossing the red lines to win back their readers, especially since they are competing with other parties and are concerned about maintaining their influence on public opinion. As the reality of most party newspapers is obvious and as parties pursue increasing readership, they have started employing more effective methods of winning audiences—namely, radio and television stations, both terrestrial and satellite ones. These are tools which are effective in influencing and polarizing people. This has created an arena of competition between certain parties.

The decline of party newspapers, in the light of readers' indifference, has led to the emergence of private newspapers. These papers distance themselves from ideologies and party constraints and are sponsored by merchants, former politicians or media companies. This creates more positive competition and expands the freedom of the press. To face the huge technological capabilities of party newspapers, private newspapers depend generally on sensationalism, criticizing party policies and conveying political news which uncovers the scandals of senior officials. They also rely on western-style headlines and exciting pictures which attract readers. With nearly complete absence of censorship and the lack of any kind of accountability, private newspapers publish thrilling reports or news about some politicians, and these are often not objective and even border on defamation. They publish subjects and articles attacking certain authorities without evidence and turn themselves into paid instruments of accusations and untruths. They may also do so just to boost their sales. Private newspapers draw many of their topics from websites without acknowledging their sources and this robs them of their weight in the cultural and political street by the passage of time. This can apply to newspapers such as *Al Shahid, Al Yom Al Akhar, Al Madar* and others.

However, not all private newspapers are sensationalist newspapers. There are serious and objective ones which rely on conveying the truth and are committed to professionalism in their work. They also depend on gradually developing themselves as the situation in Iraq improves.

To counter the huge financial capabilities of party newspapers, which attract the most competent journalists by paying good salaries, private newspapers rely on young writers who are not obliged to any authority or committed intellectually or to any party. They are also not fettered and do not suffer the malaise of sloganeering or rhetoric which drowned their journalistic predecessors within the country. This creates an opportunity for the emergence of new journalists with different ideas, concepts and aspirations.

There is a struggle between party and independent newspapers to attract more advertising. Party newspapers almost completely dominate advertisements, which are essentially limited because of the situation in the country. This stems from two reasons: first, relations between the

[487]

parties and the government, which provides most of the advertisements are good, and second, party papers are published daily whereas most private newspapers are not because of their weaker situation. Thus private newspapers are deprived of advertisements from the government and construction companies. This threatens private newspapers with loss as they are deprived of the most important source of revenue to ensure their continuity and profit. Hence they are forced to accept whatever is offered to them by certain commercial companies in return for certain press services, or to rely on the assistance of international organizations or authorities. It should be pointed out here that newspapers are sold at a low rate, especially party newspapers.

In addition, there are many problems in newspaper distribution because there are no modern marketing companies in the country. Reliance is placed on distribution offices in Baghdad which randomly circulate the newspapers. According to the inclinations of the owner of the office, there is preference for some newspapers at the expense of others. This happens because of party intervention and a tendency to obstruct this or that newspaper, in addition to the spread of unfair competition. In certain quarters people buy thousands of copies of a newspaper and burn them in order to prevent their distribution. Moreover, there are other terrible pressures, which include the burning of distribution offices, the deteriorating security situation and the difficulty of movement between the provinces and Baghdad.

Shaping Public Opinion: A Task in the Far Future

One of the major tasks of the press in civilized, advanced societies is to shape or form public opinion, in addition to drawing the attention of the authorities to the mistakes committed by their officials or agencies, and to urge the correction of these mistakes and punish those who have committed them. The press also uses its authority to guarantee the rights of citizens if these rights are overlooked, provides information for those who want it and identifies trends and opinions that are being formed in societies. This is what is done by the independent press in advanced societies. However, the new Iraqi press is still a long way off from this ambitious situation for many reasons. This raises the question whether progressive forces and efficient personalities can win leadership positions through elections when they do not possess the necessary financial capabilities to canvass support, and the press – even the independent press – does not possess the ability to direct or shape public opinion to make the best possible choice.

Political and external reasons have hindered the Iraqi press, even after a year and a half of freedom, from reaching the stage of affecting public opinion. However, an obvious professional reason is the absence of the Iraqi correspondent or journalist in general from the field of events—and the consequent reliance on conveying news from other sources. This weakens the standing and objectivity of the Iraqi press. The correspondent should report the incident from its actual location as this will raise the credibility of the news and make it distinct from the news conveyed by the correspondent of another newspaper or a satellite channel as is the case now.

Generally, Iraqi newspapers depend on international agencies as sources of news, especially the French and German news agencies which are active in Iraq and provide advanced services at reasonable prices. The outcome is that the same news items are published in most newspapers in the same words. In most Iraqi newspapers, the special correspondent is only relied upon in conducting interviews and investigative reports which are essentially few. Thus there is a great difference between the capabilities of the correspondent working for an international agency, which provides him with his needs and the local correspondent who has been out of touch with journalism for decades, is technologically semi-illiterate and does not speak a foreign language. What happens in the realm of news repeats itself in the realm of pictures. The same pictures are repeated in the many newspapers because they are all sourced from the

[489]

same foreign agency, while the exclusive pictures taken by the staff photographer or special correspondent of the newspaper are almost completely absent.

The Search for a National Press

Today, the Iraqi press faces the problem of being split into local, regional, sectarian, ethnic and partisan segments which are not concerned with the whole of Iraq. There are no strong national parties with broad capabilities. Also, the state is currently absent from the field of information. In the light of this it may be said that there is no national Iraqi press at present. The press is either Sunni Arab, Shi'ite or Kurdish, the last being divided between the two major parties—the Patriotic Union of Kurdistan and the Democratic Party of Kurdistan. The Christian press is sub-divided into Chaldean or Assyrian segments while the Turkmen press is sub-divided into Sunni and Shi'ite groups.

All these religious, national and sectarian groupings have their own press and they publish things that relate to conflicts, emotions and concepts that are tinged by sectarianism, ethnicity, territorialism and doctrinal stances even if they claim otherwise. This kind of sectarian press fails to create a national consciousness in the absence of a national leadership that accommodates Iraqis of all groupings, political allegiance, ethnicities and creeds.

If it is customary that each newspaper has an intellectual, cultural, political, or social orientation, or a certain color, the problem of Iraqi newspapers is that most of them, if not all of them, represent doctrinal, national or sectarian trends and there is a lack of intellectual and cultural diversity. The absence of an integrated press which can bring Sunnis, Shi'ite Arabs, Kurds and Assyrians together means that no national press exists that represents Iraq as a whole.

Lack of Collective National Interest: Who Believes Whom?

When one family and one party controlled the country, the Iraqi media used to speak of the national interest. The Baath Party used to speak incessantly about the national interest, Arab nationalism, Palestine, Pan-Arabism and the glorious and heroic deeds of Islam, as well as illusory victories. It used to repeat this millions of times, turning these things into a facade that protected the interests of a narrow, limited class.

Such a press heritage could not serve the emergence and ascendance of a democratic regime in the new Iraq. Moreover, this process could not have helped in the emergence of existing Arab satellite channels. Many Iraqis are currently afraid of the effects of these channels on their country since they have become their primary enemy by encouraging terrorism; describing sabotage acts as resistance and the killings of the national police as *jihad*. The absence of a successful, central television channel that positively affects the formation of public opinion and convinces the viewer that it expresses his views and represents his interests, increases this danger and places hurdles on the road to democracy. The existence of local party television stations, as well as local, ethnic party newspapers, does not help in creating good professional cadres because the journalists express their ideologies and those of their parties without commitment to professionalism. How can one create public opinion when the factors of objectivity and professionalism are absent? Also, party news reports suffer from limited horizons, weak structure and inability to describe and provide the greater part of the truth. It also lacks the excitement generated by a scoop.

Under the rule of dictatorship the press was not national because it excluded the interests of Kurds, Shi'ite, Christian groups and Turkmen who form the majority of the population. Thus the press failed to create either a national public opinion or a national feeling. The national press helps in the emergence and ascendance of democracy because it affects public opinion by reflecting the democracy of consensus—the act of

[491]

preserving the self and harmonizing with the other. Without a consensus based on the recognition of the rights of all, it will not be possible to create a national spirit in a country with multiple ethnicities, regions and religions.

Ways to Build an Independent and Liberal Press

The most important measures needed in order to support the establishment of a liberal, independent press may be summarized below:

- Supporting the establishment of a national independent authority, which is supervised by efficient media cadres known for independent and liberal tendencies

- Establishing professional, independent civil unions to improve the situation of the journalists and protect them

- Supporting liberal, independent newspapers financially and technologically through international non-governmental organizations

- Opening special centers to improve the capabilities of journalists and encourage and reward professional excellence.

Many journalists believe that there was a good opportunity to build a liberal press in Iraq when the former CPA Administrator in Iraq, Ambassador Paul Bremer, issued Decree No.66. It was hoped that the implementation of that decree would lead to the establishment of an independent national authority for radio and television in accordance with the principle of public service. That decree could have made Iraq the first state in the region to adopt the principle of public service in media broadcasts. However, some obstacles came in the way of implementing that enterprise. At present, the relevant authority tends to inconvenience the Iraqi media by drawing many red lines, and justifying this by pointing to the abnormal situation and the need to confront terrorism and instigation of violence in the media channels, in addition to imposing censorship and restrictions.

Decree No.66 provided for establishing the general authority for broadcasting in accordance with the principle of public service and this meant obtaining funding from taxpayers—and hence independence from the state. Its administration consists of a board of governors whose members are not allowed to hold any administrative, legislative or judicial position in the government, or a political position in any party. The authority was supposed to be responsible for radio and television broadcasting in the country.

However, the authority faced obstacles and challenges in its operations when Prime Minister Ayad Allawi announced the formation of the Higher Media Commission without specifying its functions. Its authority appeared to border on those of the dissolved Ministry of Information and it seemed to seek media control by licensing of newspapers, imposing restrictions on publishing content, and taking action against newspapers when they went beyond the limits imposed by government employees in the authority. This betrayed a move backwards by building an apparatus subject to the authority of the government, bent on preserving the interest of the government and not the citizens and paving the way for censorship on printed material and media content. This move threatened to lead to harassment of journalists, and even denial of the freedom of expression.

Towards an Independent and Developed Press

The new press that Iraq needs involves rebuilding the existing Iraqi press in terms of form and content. It must go beyond the press of individuals, parties and tribes and become the press of the homeland. It must also be a professional, objective press capable of scrutinizing events and presenting them to the reader without misrepresentation and distortion of truths. It must also be capable of distinguishing between what is genuine national interest on the one hand and what is official, party and class-oriented interests on the other. This presupposes changing the fundamentals of journalistic work, as well as its rules and general concepts through developmental and transparent programs.

[493]

It is worth mentioning here that the establishment of a free press does not mean adopting the positions of those who oppose the government and the authority in general. It also does not mean siding with the government and the authority on everything under the slogans of nationalism, unity and preserving the interests of the country. The interests of the country cannot entail hiding truths and mistakes and overlooking negative aspects and corrupt dealings. The new Iraqi press must report truths and must be professional and objective in revealing mistakes and negative aspects. It must mention the positive aspects, protect the citizen and play the role of watchdog over the first three estates to build a developing society, functioning truly as the fourth estate and not merely a vehicle for rhetoric and slogans.

This requires reviewing the roles of the trade unions and press unions so that they are no longer merely formal instruments without any real work and role—ones that serve the authority and subordinate themselves to the government. They must become a base and a haven for all true journalists by defending and protecting them and remaining devoted to developing their capabilities. Press unions must go beyond a state of subordination to the authority, formalism and demands, to a state of doing real work and exerting influence by performing effective trade union functions. This begins with the selection of genuine press representatives and ends with these unions activating the press to influence and direct public opinion. Moreover, they must be pioneers in the process of development and democratization of the country by criticizing, assessing and directing different events.

An Effective Iraqi Press: Not a Voice in the Wilderness

The development of the Iraqi press after the fall of the Baathist regime can be viewed as slight considering that the transformation occurring now is a shift from a state of silence and acts of embellishing the mistakes of dictatorship to a state of yelling and clamoring without impacting on political reality.

The role of the press and the media in civilized societies is not restricted to monitoring the three estates, drawing attention to their mistakes and posing ideas to correct these mistakes. It goes beyond this to a stage of directing and creating public opinion. Hence the press in civilized societies possesses a power and authority feared by all—from the employees of the smallest institution to the head of the state. This fact makes all institutions accord a special status to the press because its judgment directs the man on the street. The press affects the rest of the media and may lead it in a direction that influences the public and forms public opinion. However, this significant position cannot be attained easily even if freedom of speech is available. In societies that have recently experienced liberation, freedom can easily turn into disorder. In this state of freedom-disorder saying something or remaining silent may result in the same outcome. Saying something which no one hears or takes seriously amounts to a mere voice in the wilderness—a voice without a value, a futile directive or guideline. The last description seems to apply to the Iraqi press, which has shifted from a state of suppression and deprivation to that of freedom—but a freedom that has had no results or impact.

Although this process of transformation is important, it has its negative aspects. The press might become a safety valve for giving vent to rejection and grudges of the public, which seeks effective change and real development in general services or policies—a change which bombards corruption and errors and provides people with a better life. This has not been achieved by the Iraqi press. The Iraqi press remains largely without readership, because what it publishes about corruption and misuse of state funds does not attract attention. There is no follow-up of issues that are raised in the press and thus what is published is never taken seriously although some of it is of a very serious nature.

It may be said that the press does not currently have an impact on the policies and tendencies of the authority or the political parties—it does not even represent a threat to individual illegal acts. Thus, what is published does not provide an opportunity to correct the course of action, to hold

[495]

those who fail to deliver accountable and to create positive change. The battle of the journalists and press unions must be focused on having a highly valued voice in the process of change. Their writings must be endowed with the ability to influence others and be echoed within the ranks of the highest authority in the country. This can only be the case if these writings influence the public in the first instance, and are echoed within its ranks.

Journalists must go beyond general criticism and cynicism to a stage of analysis—directing and driving the country to move towards a stage in which the citizen enjoys all his rights. Such rights will not be achieved if corruption endures, goes unreported in the newspapers, and does not elicit a response through strikes, sit-ins and total civil rebellion. And all this should be done in pursuit of change and development, and a state in which the press plays its real role in influencing, directing and forming public opinion.

The press in Iraq now faces widespread indifference on the part of the government authorities. These authorities do not respond to complaints and reports that incriminate ministries, state agencies and governmental officials. This state of matters must be changed.

No country can be built without a free and developed press. This necessitates establishing an independent information authority, led by qualified, liberal media professionals, to lay the basic foundations for an independent, advanced press. This is very important for building a democratic country where government institutions work with transparency under the watchful eyes of the fourth estate and its lenses which are everywhere.

In the region of Iraqi Kurdistan the press has witnessed a notable development in terms of quantity and quality during the last five years. Party and government newspapers and magazines appeared in the Kurdish, Arabic, Assyrian and Turkmen languages. In addition, liberal, free and independent newspapers appeared, supported by intellectuals, merchants and international organizations. The party-oriented press started in the region in the early 1990s and expanded and developed gradually. The number of publications exceeded 100 newspapers and magazines. However, this number has dropped relatively in the last years. There are now tens of newspapers, magazines, radio stations and television channels that present their content and contributions without censorship. There is a section in the act passed by the Parliament of Kurdistan relating to the press which stipulates that there will be "no censorship on publications." This development goes back to the period when the region was liberated from Saddam's regime more than 14 years ago. Since that time Iraqi Kurdistan has been enjoying democracy.

The Iraqi newspaper *Al Ahali*, which publishes in Arabic, was founded on April 23, 2002 with funding from the Iraqi Institute for Democracy, which is chaired by this author. The newspaper is meant as a parallel to the development of the newspapers published in the Kurdish language and the emergence of independent Kurdish newspapers. The emergence of *Al Ahali* was an important step in the development of the Iraqi press because it was the first liberal Iraqi newspaper to attract tens of Iraqi writers from inside and outside Iraq. It has successfully presented different ideas and trends very freely and continues to embrace liberal thought and supports the building of the foundations of civil society.

INFLUENCE OF ARAB GOVERNMENTS ON THE MEDIA

25

The Independence of the Arab Media

Edmond Saab

The independence and freedom of the Arab media have not received the consideration they deserve from media circles in general. That is due on the one hand to the close link between the issue of liberties, the nature of the ruling regimes and ways of generating power in Arab world and on the other hand, to the financial hegemony over the ownership of newspapers and political publications in most Arab countries, whether such control is exercised via the ruling regime or otherwise. Moreover, the high illiteracy rate in Arab societies has resulted in limiting the readership numbers, which is considered the natural guarantee of a newspaper's life and sustainability.

A free media is a basic element in democratic countries, but in other countries, there is no opportunity to discuss the concept of a free media or its role in enhancing awareness, supervision or development. Through a free media, the public can scrutinize government performance, criticize the ruling regime and disclose its faults, to pave the way for reforms through elections held within a fixed period.

A free media enjoys power and efficiency at the level of public opinion in some countries. It was the media that compelled Richard Nixon, the President of the United States, the global superpower, to resign in August 1974. This resignation was forced upon him in the aftermath of the Watergate scandal, which was reported in the *Washington Post* by its

[501]

journalist, Bob Woodward. Woodward uncovered the involvement of President Nixon in implanting wiretaps in the headquarters of the Democratic National Committee (at the Watergate Hotel in Washington, DC). President Nixon initially denied any involvement in the scandal but later confessed the truth and handed over the tapes of phone calls to the relevant court.

In this context, the following question arises: Can anyone in the entire Arab world, imagine that the proprietor of any newspaper would allow the publication of an article that might topple a ruler, a king or a president? Are there any Arab writers who can write an article powerful enough to overthrow a president, relying on the constitution and the judiciary system? Is there any ruler in the Arab world willing to subject himself to the rule of law and the constitution, who would resign if he had violated any law, as US President Richard Nixon did?

Democracy and its mechanisms for managing the affairs of the nation have not been adopted by many regimes in Arab world – which are either republics, monarchies, emirates or sultanates with unelected and unaccountable rulers. However, all these barriers did not prevent the spread of the press in the Arab countries. In form, these Arabic newspapers are similar to the press of democratic nations, although the laws and regulations of these countries do not provide sufficient rights and guarantees to practice the media profession freely. Furthermore, the media should be an instrument at the service of citizens and not rulers, making the government subject to accountability and criticism, and laws should give citizens the freedom to reject, not merely the freedom to accept the official truth and nothing else.

There are thus two types of press. The first is the press of objective truth as perceived by public opinion, which plays an enlightening role and facilitates the functioning of a prudent and judicious leadership, and the second is the press of the official truth or "the Truth of the Sovereign" as it is understood by the totalitarian ruler who deals with members of society as subjects and not as citizens with fundamental rights, especially

[502]

the right to use the media. Perhaps the most common factor between these two presses is the right to express opinion and knowledge, followed by the right to monitor public affairs and hold the government accountable. Given that the legitimate source of power is free will and not any tribe, religious sect, political party or external interference, another common factor between the two presses is that these nations regardless of their ruling regimes, on becoming members of the UN and its associated agencies, have adopted in their national constitutions – if and where there is one – the international and regional conventions on human rights, particularly the right to freedom of opinion and expression.

In addition to these conventions, there is an accumulated national heritage replete with struggles to secure various types of freedom. This includes the freedom of expression, on the altar of which much heroic blood was shed and many martyrs were hanged in Beirut and Damascus by "the Butcher" Ottoman Sultan Jamal Pasha, in May 1916, half a century before the issuance of the Universal Declaration of Human Rights.

With the light of these two "lanterns" – the International Conventions on Human Rights, and the heritage of the struggle for freedoms – an attempt will be made to track down in an objective way the margin of freedom enjoyed by the media in Arab world. There is already a realization that rulers in many Arab countries control the press and other media organs and exploit them to obscure the truth, misinform the people and prevent the free expression of public opinion. Therefore, the media mission has been diverted from its main objectives which should be to guide and lead society to its vital interests, not the interests of the rulers, nor even the interests of journalists and newspaper owners. A society's vital interests are perceived as progress, knowledge, openness and development.

Press and Power

Salah Al-Deen Al-Hafiz, Managing Editor of *Al-Ahram* newspaper and Secretary General of the Arab Journalists Association observes:

[503]

There is a clear tendency by the government to be openly strict with newspapers, magazines and books. This strictness not only seeks to suppress freedom of opinion and freedom of expression, but also to enhance the control of the government over the media and the tools for formulating trends in public opinion.

Al-Hafiz goes on to observe:

Government policies constantly impose their hegemony on the ownership of newspapers, define their guidelines, impose direct censorship and control over the freedom of publication and distribution, and use various evil methods for propaganda; Apart from that, government authorities choose to impose a "siege" on journalists, media-personnel and intellectuals and track their movement through unfettered legal and extraordinary procedures to deliberately restrain freedom of opinion and expression in society.[1]

This description of restraining freedom of opinion and expression through laws, not merely through administrative procedures, is borne out by the conclusions of the *MacBride Commission* (an international commission for the study of communication problems), which is a subordinate agency affiliated with UNESCO. The Commission stated:

Given that practices violating the right to freedom of opinion and expression are based on written laws, does not deny that they are irrelevant when they are not in compliance with international conventions, especially in signatory countries. Freedom to launch societies, labor-unions and political parties, freedom of gathering and demonstration, freedom of opinion, expression and publication, all of these are basic components of the human right to use media and communication.[2]

In this context, a similar view has been expressed by Ghassan Tuwainy, when he was Editor-in-Chief of the Lebanese *Al-Nahar* newspaper:

Free media or media which is independent of political power is the one kind which enjoys financial self-sufficiency through legal resources accrued via selling its products and advertisements. Such media (particularly newspapers) enjoys also a spiritual partnership with its readers and a constant daily dialogue...On the other side, there is a directive media which exemplifies the opinion of power and regime. Since media organs speak for the ruling regime and power, the proprietorship of these organs may go to the governments, or at least be subject to the censorship of governments. Meanwhile, a journalist in the free media feels that he is doing significant work, more than just being the owner of a newspaper or a magazine. He is an advocate of a human principle that no state or society can be established without freedom, and no journalism can flourish without freedom, and no freedom can thrive without the press. That means almost all types of freedom can be embodied in the freedom of expression, which summarizes in its role all types of freedom, because it is the expression of the knowledge of free people, their trends, culture and views.[3]

The Historical Background

Freedom is the Genuine Norm, Restriction is the Exception

It is not irrelevant here to mention some examples from history. In 1855 Rizq Allah Hassoun, a Syrian from Aleppo, published the first Arabic language newspaper in Istanbul, the Capital of the Ottoman Sultanate. He called the paper *Mirror of Circumstances* and its mission was independence. Its founder made it "a forum for freedom and a minaret for knowledge." As the Sultan did not appreciate such a mission, he ordered its closure, and sentenced its founder to death, so Hassoun sought asylum in Russia. Nevertheless, the repression against Hassoun and the closure of his *Mirror* did not deter Khaleel al-Khoury from publishing a newspaper dubbed *News Garden* in Beirut in 1858. According to the historian of the Arabic press Viscount Philip Tarzy, this newspaper's mission was as follows:

> Spreading knowledge and arts in the Ottoman Sultanate; and providing progress and education for the subjects of the Sultanate, who enjoyed luxury and security under the abundant shadow of the Sultanate…to include matters necessary for human benefit. The newspaper was launched with full freedom, publishing news as it is, whether bad or good.[4]

This freedom did not last long, because Sultan Abdul-Hamid closed the *News Garden*. After being deposed and sent to exile, the Sultan was asked what would be the government's first action if he were restored to power. He answered that he would "throw journalists into hell."

Ghassan Tuwainy commented on that particular statement by saying:

Needless to say, Abdul-Hamid did not regain power, and therefore he could not throw journalists into hell, but this does not mean that there are no Sultans subjugating us. These modern rulers have emotions towards the press which are no less "blazing" than the hell of Abdul-Hamid. Although the suppression of journalists has continued in various forms and types, the press flourishes and becomes more influential among people day after day…The struggle of the press takes on new dimensions because it has become a tool to defend freedom, freedom as a demand, then freedom as a right (for individuals and/or societies) which can express itself through the press, which finds itself isolated in its confrontation with the tyranny of the ruling power, as if it is a call from the wilderness.

The interesting outcome is that reading newspapers is no longer a privilege reserved for the elite, especially after the liberation of the public and the emergence of the masses who have realized that their real interests are served by their cooperation and solidarity against tyrannical rulers and Sultans, and that they should not be content with the rights already achieved through their struggle, but should demand more. So, the press was effective whenever there was a risk threatening freedom; and it was ready to provide care and protection for the right people. In many countries, the press replaced political parties in its role as a supervisor of the government performance. Soon, newspapers became very strict in their supervision over the ruling power, winning support from the increasing number of readers, who gained more influence in society.

Tuwainy goes on to add:

Thus freedom is no longer mere ideology or abstract theories but a concrete fact. Freedom issues were reflected by the press and used as a supporting force that helped freedom to endure. The press turned freedom into a tradition and a historic fact. It became an independent institution represented by the press which continued to struggle after the collapse of the Ottoman empire for national independence, to foster the right of any citizen to live a free life in a system where the rule of law prevails, and for a situation where justice, equal opportunities, social development and cultural and religious diversity are available for citizens.[5]

With Tuwainy's vision about press freedom, it appears that freedom is the origin, foundation and norm, while restriction is the exception. The gap between the two will widen to the extent that the ruling regimes forsake democracy and the heritage of freedom and human rights.

Media Freedom and Human Rights

In a study about the "Regulation of the Arab Media from the Perspective of Human Rights" edited by the Egyptian lawyer Abdullah Khaleel,[6] the former Chairman of the Legal Committee at the Arab Organization for Human Rights, the writer makes a comparison between two press systems prevailing in the Arab world, in terms of respect for human rights, particularly the right of expression and the right of voicing opinion. These systems are, first, the totalitarian or dictatorial and restrictive regime, where the margin of freedom decreases to the minimum, and second, the liberal regime, which is originally founded on freedom. Most of the Arab ruling regimes belong to the first category.

This writer observes that the beginnings of these totalitarian regimes was in tandem with the launch of newspapers in Western Europe at the end of the 16th century and early years of the 17th century. This type is considered the oldest press system in history. The key principles of this system can be summarized as follows:

- The press should constantly support the ruling regime.
- The press is prohibited from publishing any criticism of the government or any other material which might weaken the regime.
- The press is prohibited from publishing anything that might hurt the elite and ruling class, or which might violate basic and ethical norms.
- Any (media) attack against the ruling power or the official policies is considered a criminal act. Journalists under such system would be subject to various punishments.
- Journalists do not enjoy any kind of independence or freedom within their press institutions, or the media organizations that they work for.

These principles are being imposed through various methods: regulatory restrictions; a compulsory condition to get a license (from the government) to publish newspapers; warnings to newspapers and temporary closure through legal decisions in compliance with the laws promulgated by the ruling regime, closure through administrative procedures without reference to legal validation; censorship of all kinds whether military, civil, direct or indirect.

[507]

In contrast, the liberal press system is based on the following foundations and principles:

- Publishing should be free of any kind of censorship.
- Any individual or group should have the right to own newspapers and other media organs and administer them without a prior license from the government.
- Criticism of the government or any political party or official dignitaries should not lead to punishment, even if it is published.
- There should be no restrictions on gathering information for publication through legal methods.
- There should be no restrictions on information being circulated and transferred across national borders.
- Journalists should enjoy professional independence within their press institutions.

Khaleel indicates that lawmakers – when they classify freedoms within one of these two types and select one category – are usually affected by the ideology adopted by the regime, their real view of freedom and the dominant political trend. He also explains that an open choice is made from these two systems. The first is the deterrence system, which usually reflects the trend towards a democratic vision in regulating liberties. This system gives the individual a chance to carry out activities and exercise freedom without pre-arranged restraints or procedures which might limit freedom. However, if the individual misuses freedom or conducts unethical activities he will be held accountable. Prior notice is an important aspect of this system. The intended person gives prior notice to the relevant authorities about his plan to exercise a specific freedom or activity. In turn, the relevant authorities do not have the right to prevent the individual from practicing that activity or exercising freedom.

The second system is the preventive system, which reflects a restrictive view that imposes constraints on individual liberties. This system is considered a demonstration of the totalitarian regime. The individual in such system cannot experience freedom without prior permission or a license from the administrative authority. Enjoying freedom is completely dependant on the will of that authority, which might grant or deny the right to practice freedom.

Legal Restraints vs. Universal Declaration of Human Rights

There is a striking contradiction, ironically described as an "Arab talent," which is the ability to combine freedom of expression with the suffocation of such freedom. The 2003 Report of the Egyptian Human Rights Watch stated that since 1923, consecutive Egyptian constitutions promulgated the right to freedom of opinion and expression, particularly freedom of press. However, this constitutional right was always restrained by legal and procedural "chains," such as the Laws of Publication and the Penal Law.[7]

One of the resolutions of the Egyptian Constitutional Court states that the constitution guarantees the following freedom in Article 47:

> Freedom of expression of opinion and the capability to publish such opinions and broadcast them, whether in words, photos, printing or writing…or via other means of expression.

The court describes freedom as follows:

> It is the original norm, and no open dialogue can be established without freedom. Since the freedom of opinion and expression which is guaranteed by the 1951 constitution is considered the essential foundation for every democratic structure, violating such a basis is merely denying the truth that freedom of expression should not be separated from its instruments. The means for practicing this freedom should be linked to its ends, in a way that no one can impede its essence, nor blight the means of enhancing freedom.

Although the Egyptian constitution mentions clearly that it guarantees freedom of opinion and expression, publishing, scientific research, literary and artistic creativity, it also forbids the imposition of any censorship on the press. However, the guarantees mentioned in the constitutional articles which are linked to such freedoms – as with many other articles of the same constitution – refer the issue to the courts and legal procedures. Legislators managed to restrain freedom of opinion and expression in a "creative way," according to the reports of the Egyptian Human Rights

Watch, through legalizing procedures "which make censorship of the press a central issue without the need to maintain censorship or to apply an emergency law (martial law)."

The scholar Jamal Al-Deen Al-Afghani predicted the effects which seizure of power might have on freedoms, when he talked about "the power of the tyrannical ruler" in late 1890s. Al-Afghani commented:

> The Nation which does not have a say in its affairs and policies, and is not consulted about its national interests, and which has its will neglected in its public welfare, while it is subjugated to one ruler whose will formulates the law, and whose desires embody the public order, who rules at his convenience and does whatever he wants: such a nation cannot maintain stability, nor control the pace of development, and therefore it will face prosperity and misery, it will experience knowledge and ignorance, it will also witness rich and poor people, and it will suffer humiliation and enjoy dignity.[8]

Abdullah Khaleel[9] in his own analysis of the content of some Arab constitutions focuses on the freedom issue. He made a comparison between those constitutions and the rules mentioned in UN documents, particularly Article No.19 of the Universal Declaration of Human Rights, which reads:

> Everyone has the right to freedom of opinion and expression; this right includes freedom to hold opinions without interference and to seek, receive and impart information and ideas through any media and regardless of frontiers.

The second provision of Article 19 of the International Covenant on Civil and Political Rights also confirms:

> Everyone shall have the right to freedom of expression; this right shall include freedom to seek, receive, and impart information and ideas of all kinds, regardless of frontiers either orally, in writing or in print, in the form of art or through any other media of his choice.

The third provision of the same Article 19 declares as follows:

> The exercise of the rights [to freedom of expression] carries with it special duties and responsibilities. It may therefore be subject to some restrictions, but these shall only be such as are provided by law and are necessary (a)

[510]

for the respect of the rights or reputations of others (b) for the protection of national security or of public order, or of public health or morals.

This Covenant lays down a set of conditions to be observed while applying such restrictions so that the basic right cannot be endangered.

These conditions are:

- These restrictions should be mentioned in the text of law.
- These constraints should be imposed only for meeting the objectives mentioned in provision (a) which says: "The right to communications is connected to a huge number of issues which differ in nature and scope, and can be understood differently in different societies, and they are applied at many levels of the social system" and provision (b) which says: "This right is applicable to nations in their relationships with other nations and with the world in general, as well as their relationships with their own population. It is also applicable to social groups in their relationships with citizens, state and other groups. This right is also applicable to means of communications in their relationships with government, sources of communication and individuals; as well as individuals in their relationships within the group itself."
- These restraints should be justified and proved to be necessary for the relevant nation, in order to achieve one of these objectives.

The third provision of Article 21 of the Universal Declaration of Human Rights also stipulates:

> The will of the people shall be the basis of the authority of government; this will shall be expressed in periodic and genuine elections which shall be by universal and equal suffrage and shall be held by secret vote or by equivalent free voting procedures.

The second provision of Article 29 of the same Declaration also states:

> In the exercise of his rights and freedoms, everyone shall be subject only to such limitations as are determined by law solely for the purpose of securing due recognition and respect for the rights and freedoms of others and of meeting the just requirements of morality, public order and the general welfare in a democratic society.

In this context, Abdullah Khaleel says:

> Discussing the known rules "in the field of freedom of expression" and which "impose certain limitations" on the media and set the conditions which really affect the practice of this right, reveal the level of respect for this right in the relevant country. The interaction between the principle of freedom of expression and these limitations and restraints can clarify the real scope of individual freedom. Many attempts have been made by religious scholars and legal experts to clearly define some of the terminology pertinent to the challenges and limitations imposed on human rights and basic freedoms.

> There is no unified international definition of concepts and terminology such as: "respect for the freedoms and rights of others"; "ethics" "public order"; "national security" and "public welfare." However these concepts and terms express some vague ideas. The substance of those ideas can be gauged only through practical means and in the light of ongoing changes which occur under current circumstances and situations in the life of the international community. These concepts and terminology genuinely aim to maintain a fair balance between the rights and freedoms of the individual in a democratic society, and the public welfare of the society as a whole.

Types of Limitations

In attempting to categorize the various limitations imposed on the media in the Arab world, at least 20 types were identified. These include limitations relating to the following matters: publishing newspapers; financial insurance; ownership; prior censorship; bureaucratic barring and confiscation; censorship, prohibition and closure in exceptional emergency cases; administrative closure of newspapers; legal oversight on administrative resolutions to control and suspend newspapers; limitations imposed on the practice of journalism; confidentiality in journalism; the condition of "conscience"; the right to have access to information from original sources; the right to protection and ensuring the personal security of journalists; pre-trial detention for those who commit crimes relating to publications; the supervision imposed by government councils on journalism and journalists; legal limitations on the content of media missions; the nature of punishment; violation of the principle that "persons are generally presumed to be innocent"; expansion in the indictment policy stipulated in Arab regulations; and increasing restrictions on criticism.

The following are the details of such limitations in most Arab countries:[10]

1-Publishing Newspapers:

- *The United Arab Emirates*: Publishing a newspaper in the UAE can be done only after getting a license, which is generally issued by the Council of Ministers. The license application must be presented to the Council by the Minister of Information along with the recommendation of the Ministry of Information.[*]

- *Kuwait*: Getting a license to publish a newspaper is a mandatory process in Kuwait, and such a license is issued by the Head of the Publication and Printing Department.

- *Kingdom of Bahrain*: The license is issued by the Minister of Information after getting the approval of the Council of Ministers.

- *Qatar:* The license is issued by the Department of Publications at the Qatar General Authority for Radio & Television.

- *Sultanate of Oman*: The license is issued by the Department of Printing and Publications at the Ministry of Information and Culture.

- *Kingdom of Saudi Arabia*: The license for publishing a newspaper is issued by the Minister of Information. Magazines and bulletins published by institutions outside the professional media – such as government authorities, civil or private corporations – are licensed by the Minister of Information upon the approval of the Council of Ministers.

- *Syria*: The license is given through a decree which is issued by a decision of the Council of Ministers. The Prime Minister has the authority to refuse approval for granting the license to a periodical, and can reject the nomination of any person for the posts of owner,

---

[*] *Editorial Note*: With the formation of a new cabinet in February 2006, the UAE has abolished its Ministry of Information.

Managing Editor or Chief Editor of the periodical, if it is proved that any of them have supported unconstitutional situations in the country.

- *Lebanon*: The issue of new political publications is blocked in Lebanon. Buying concessions of old publications or issuing off-shoots of previously licensed publications is subject to the consent of the Minister of Information and the Journalists Association. However, issuing non-political publications requires a license from the Minister of Information as well as a recommendation by the Journalists Association. The law demands that the licensed publication – whether political or non-political – should be printed at least twice a year. The Minister of Information has the authority to revoke the license if this condition is not fulfilled. However, political power elites ignore the implementation of this aspect of the law as a courtesy to journalists in order to gain their support. It is worth mentioning that there are more than 50 licensed political publications in Lebanon (but less than a quarter are actually published) and there are more than 2000 non-political licenses (less than 15% of them are actually published). Political publications should be issued by joint-stock companies, the nominal shares of which are to be possessed by Lebanese only, and they should work in compliance with the Trade Law.
- *Jordan*: The license is issued by the Council of Ministers depending upon the recommendations of the Department of Printing and Publications.
- *Libya*: The Director of the Department of Publications is the person who is authorized to approve or reject the license of any publication, after consulting with the Minister of Information.
- *Tunisia*: The license application is submitted to the Interior Ministry, which transfers it to the Ministry of Information, after giving the applicant a receipt confirming the registration of the application. Without such a receipt, the applicant would not be allowed to publish a newspaper, magazine or a bulletin.
- *Algeria*: Issuing any publication is conditional upon registering the application in a prior declaration submitted 30 days before printing the

publication, to the State Minister who is in charge of the region where it is issued.

- *Morocco*: Provision V of Act No 587/58/1 says that prior to publishing every newspaper or periodical, a letter from the Director of Publications should be submitted to the Court of First Instance, and if such a court is not available the letter should be submitted to the Provincial Court in the area where the publication will be issued. The applicant is usually given a receipt of such letter.
- *Sudan*: A publication is licensed by the Council of Ministers after payment of the required fees. The license is to be renewed on an annual basis.
- *Egypt*: Publishing newspapers is an exclusive right of political parties and corporations in public and private sectors. Applications for publishing newspapers are submitted to the Supreme Council of Journalism which should take its decision within 40 days. Corporations should be either cooperatives or joint-stock companies, in which all shares should be nominal and exclusively owned by Egyptians. The foundation of these corporations should be upon the approval of the Council of Ministers, which in turn depends on the recommendation of the Minister of Economy.

Khaleel concludes: "There is not a single Arab regime which adopts the liberal system in issuing newspapers. Each of these regimes puts the condition of getting a license or a permit prior to publication."

2-Financial Insurance (Guarantee Money):

- *Kingdom of Bahrain*: During the licensing process the applicant is required to pay a guarantee money of 5,000 Bahraini Dinar (BD) for a daily publication; and BD3,000 for non-daily publication.
- *Qatar*: Fees are 3,000 Qatari Riyal (QR) for each journalistic publication if it is issued 3 times or more weekly. Fees for other publications are QR2,000.
- *Syria*: A guarantee money of 1,000 Syrian Pound (SP) is required for each daily publication and SP250 for other types of publications.

[515]

- *Lebanon*: The capital of a press corporation should be at least 30,000,000 Lebanese Lira (LL) The capital of a limited liability company should not be less than LL5,000,000. The owner of the printing house should deposit the guarantee money as determined by the Ministry of Information after consultation with the Journalists Association.
- *Jordan*: Licensing a daily publication is conditional upon prepayment of at least half a million Jordanian Dinar (JD); an amount of JD100,000 for non-daily publications; JD5,000 for specialized periodicals (non-political publications). However, newspapers issued by political parties are exempted from the minimum level of the pre-deposited capital. Also exempted from deposited capital are bulletins issued by government ministries, departments and official public corporations, universities and civil corporations which provide public services. The exemption will be valid only upon getting a notice from the Department of Publications.
- *Egypt*: A license is granted for corporations in public or private sectors, on condition that the relevant persons establish a form of cooperative or joint-stock company in which the nominal shares are exclusively owned by Egyptian citizens. The prepaid capital of the daily publication should be not less than one million Egyptian Pounds (EP); an amount of EP250,000 for weekly publications; EP100,000 for monthly publications; to be deposited at the bank before issuing the publication. The shares of any individual and his siblings – even those of the second degree – should not exceed 10% of the capital.
- *Kuwait*: The applicant seeking a publication license is required to deposit the following amounts at the Department of Publications: 1000 Kuwaiti Dinar (KD) for a monthly publication, KD2000 for a bi-monthly publication, KD3000 for a weekly publication, and KD4000 for any publication issued more than twice a week.
- *Yemen*: The insurance fund required for a daily publication is one million Yemeni Riyal (YR); an amount of YR700,000 for weekly publications; YR1,200,000 for weekly magazines; one million for monthly and quarterly magazines; YR100,000 for bulletins. Before

getting a license for a newspaper or a magazine, the applicant should deposit 5% of the insurance fund at the Ministry of Information.

- *Sudan*: The law requires that any applicant for a publication license must deposit a sum of money in a stipulated government-held account.

The above information indicates that 10 out of 16 Arab countries impose financial restrictions on issuing newspapers and publications. These restrictions are imposed by law and sometimes implemented arbitrarily.

3-Ownership

The general principle for newspaper ownership is based on the will of individuals to own a newspaper, and their freedom to choose the type of ownership. This freedom of ownership is one of the main standards to measure the level of democracy in a society. It may be noted that most Arab countries apply the authoritarian system in this regard.

- *Jordan*: Every Jordanian citizen, company owned by Jordanians and political party has the right to issue a publication. The Council of Ministers is the authorized institution to give a license for news agencies.
- *Lebanon*: A license is issued only for a journalist or a press organization, in accordance with the relevant law.
- *United Arab Emirates*: The owner of a newspaper must be a UAE citizen who ordinarily resides in the country.
- *Egypt*: A newspaper should be issued by cooperative institutions or joint stock companies, which usually belong to political parties and corporations in both public and private sectors.
- *Morocco*: Special procedures are laid down in Chapter V of the Basic Law.
- *Yemen*: According to the law, the right to issue publications is reserved exclusively for Yemeni citizens, political parties, corporations, public and creative organizations and government institutions.
- *Sultanate of Oman*: Newspapers are published by press organizations licensed by the Ministry of Information, in compliance with valid legal

procedures. Press organizations usually take the form of joint stock companies.

- *Algeria*: The right to publish newspapers is granted to the public sector, political associations, ordinary individuals and corporations that are in compliance with the law.
- *Sudan*: Newspapers are issued by companies or corporations in the form of registered companies in accordance with the law of companies.

It is worth noting that only Lebanon and Yemen allow individuals to own newspapers while two other Arab countries, Syria and Libya, restrict the ownership of newspapers to the public sector.

4-Transparency

Abdullah Khaleel observes that a reader has the right to know who owns a newspaper, the institution that publishes it, and the persons who set its guidelines. The reader also has the right to know the newspaper's economic and financial sources. In other words, the newspaper should be as transparent as a glass house, which allows everything inside to be viewed from the outside. In this way, the reader can be sure of knowing the real interests protected by the newspaper, and the influences shaping its content. Thus the reader can evaluate the news, ideas and opinions published in that newspaper, and ensure that it will not operate as a front for the owners so that they can fulfill their secret agenda, while the real identity of the newspaper remains hidden from public view. Khaleel also reveals that most Arab regulations impose restrictions for the sake of enforcing government censorship over newspapers, and whether the censorship relates to persons or funds, it ultimately does not serve the interest of the readers.

5-Prior Censorship

Censorship is considered one of the most dangerous and damaging restraints on the freedom of expression. It is a direct assault on the freedom of a journalist, a curb on the freedom of expression, a violation of the right to free media and flow of information. Furthermore, censorship reduces the freedom of a citizen to know the truth, and limits his right to oversee the way the affairs of his country are managed. It deprives him of effective participation in administration affairs with the aim to develop, improve and push for a better status.

- *The United Arab Emirates*: No publication can be printed without prior permission from the Ministry of Information and Culture. Also, the distribution of publications is not permitted without a specific license granted for this purpose.

- *Kingdom of Bahrain*: The Ministry of Information has the right to oversee the contents of any publication before or during the start of printing. Distribution of any publication is absolutely prohibited without prior permission.

- *Qatar*: Selling publications in Qatar is prohibited without prior permission from the Department of Publications. The head of this Department is authorized to delete any material from any publication if it contains anything prohibited by law. Deletion can be made by cutting, effacing with black ink, or any other proper way. If deletion is impossible, the circulation of that publication can be banned by a decision from the Head of the Department of Publications. No appeal or complaint can be filed against such decision to any legal authority.

- *Sultanate of Oman*: The printing house should obtain permission from the Ministry of Information before printing any publication.

- *Kingdom of Saudi Arabia*: The Ministry of Information is responsible for granting permission before the printing of any publication. Petitions can be submitted to the Minister of Information in case any publication is rejected and his decision is final.

- *Kuwait*: No publication can be sold or distributed without prior permission from the Department of Publications. The Minister of Information is authorized to impose prior censorship on all periodicals. Whatever censorship authorities declare as unacceptable would be prohibited from publication.

[519]

- *Yemen*: The law has cited the prohibited materials in Articles 138–151. One of those articles gives the government the authority to impose censorship before printing a publication, as well as prohibiting the circulation of those that are rejected.
- *Algeria*: The publisher should get permission to publish before printing any periodical.

Some would consider that being obliged to give prior notice to the authorities about publications is a kind of continuous censorship.

6-Bureaucratic Barring and Confiscation:

Preventing the circulation of a publication by bureaucratic barring or confiscation is one of the most common violations which curb the freedom to exchange information.

- *The United Arab Emirates*: The Minister of Information has the authority to prohibit the circulation of any publication. The Council of Ministers has the authority to close down any newspaper for a period not exceeding one year, or to cancel the license of any newspaper. This authority can be exercised if it publishes: any material that violates the law forbidding criticism of the President; assaults against Islam as a religion; provocations against the ruling regime; and material causing harm to the UAE's national interests; or publishes views which implicate violations of public norms and advocate vicious principles; reports falsifications about the sessions of the cabinet or the Federal National Council; or publishes fabricated news. Closure of the publication does not halt legal procedures and pursuit of criminal proceedings. In urgent cases, the Minister of Information has the authority to close down any publication for a period not exceeding two weeks, after sending a notice to the Council of Ministers.
- *Tunisia*: Any person who deliberately publishes, sells or distributes materials prohibited for publication under a different title, will be sentenced for 16 days to one year in prison, and will be fined between 60 and 600 dinar. The Ministry of Interior usually confiscates the published copies. The Ministry of Interior, after consultation with the

[520]

State Minister for Information Affairs, has the right to confiscate every issue of any periodical deemed to be harmful to public security.

- *Bahrain*: The Minister of Information has the authority to prohibit the circulation of any publication which contains material that may harm the ruling regime or the official religion of the nation, contain violation of public norms or criticism of religions as these violations may threaten civic peace. The Minister also has the power to stop the circulation of any publication if the publisher failed to notify the ministry of any content changes. The closure of any publication for a period not exceeding two years or the cancellation of its license can be done, based on a resolution from the Council of Ministers, if it is proved that the publication serves the interests of a foreign country or organization; if its policy contradicts the national interests of the Kingdom of Bahrain or if it appeared that the publication has received a grant, aid or benefit from a foreign country or entity, regardless of the benefit and whatever its reason, excuse or title, if it was received without prior permission from the Ministry of Information. In case of emergency, any publication can be closed down for a period not exceeding three months, based on a resolution issued by the Minister of Information.

- *Qatar*: Based on a decision by the Council of Ministers, it is possible to effect the closure of any publication for a period not exceeding one year, or the cancellation of its license, in case of contradiction between its policy and the national interests; or if it appeared that the publication served the interests of a foreign country; or if it appeared that the publication has received a grant, aid or any benefit whatsoever from a foreign country or entity, if it is without the permission of the Minister of Information. In exceptional cases, the head of the Department of Publications has the authority to issue a closure order in respect of any publication for a period not exceeding three months.

- *Oman*: The Minister of Information has the authority to issue orders prohibiting the circulation of any publications which contradict ethics and public norms, or criticize the ruling regime, or challenge Islamic

[521]

principles, traditions or social norms. The relevant authorities in the Ministry of Information have the power to confiscate any blacklisted publications and stop their circulation or prevent their entry to the country.

- *Saudi Arabia*: The Ministry of Information has the authority to confiscate or destroy any newspaper issue without paying the publisher any compensation, if that issue includes any reports tarnishing religious norms, causing any disturbance to the public security or violating public principles or public order. The violator is usually punished in compliance with the provisions of the law. The Minister of Information has the authority to stop the printing of any publication if it benefits national interests, for a maximum period of 30 days. If the closure period is more than 30 days, it requires the approval of the Council of Ministers.

- *Egypt*: The Minister of Information has the authority to prohibit any publication that might be of an erotic nature; and those that criticize religions in a way that might threaten public stability and peace.

- *Lebanon*: Closure or confiscation of newspapers can be implemented on the basis of a legal verdict – while it was done earlier by an executive order – and the same rule applies for the arrest of journalists. However, there is invisible censorship imposed daily by the General Security Department on newspapers and periodicals. No publication can be distributed or exported beyond the borders without a written permit from the General Security Department. There is a special form given to publishers for distribution and export. The export permission can be cancelled if the General Security Department finds that the newspaper issue contains news, opinions or photos that might harm Lebanon's reputation abroad.

- *Morocco*: The Interior Minister has the authority to issue an order to confiscate any periodical if it contains any material that may be harmful to national security. He also has the authority to close down any publication which contains material that might disturb political or religious status quo in the country, apart from the legal procedures that

[522]

can be taken against the publisher. The Prime Minister also has the authority to close down any publication and prohibit it from being issued.

- *Sudan*: The Council of Ministers has the authority to close down any publication for a maximum period of two months. It has also the authority to cancel the license of the printing house or the center of press services, in case of any violation of the terms of license.

7-Censorship and Prohibition

Freedom of opinion and expression is most affected during exceptional emergency situations.

- *Saudi Arabia*: Freedom of opinion is guaranteed in the Kingdom of Saudi Arabia within the framework of legal and religious rules, except in emergency situations when newspapers are usually subjected to censorship.
- *Qatar*: Any publication can be stopped based by a decision from the Head of the Publication Department for a period not exceeding three months. Newspapers are placed under censorship in exceptional emergency cases where the public interest necessitates such urgent procedures.
- *Lebanon*: In exceptional cases, when the country faces the dangers of an external war, an armed revolution, upheavals, situations or actions which threaten national security, order or public safety or when some catastrophic events occur, all publications and forms of media should be placed under censorship, based on a decree issued by the Council of Ministers (notably Decree No. 104, in 1977, as amended by Act No. 89/91 and Act No. 330/94). The Decree is designed to organize both the procedures for implementing censorship and the entity in charge of imposing it, which is usually the General Security Department. This decree does not allow any type of review to nullify it, including any parliamentary demand. This procedure is considered the most stringent and is sometimes preceded by what is known as "self-censorship" from the Journalists Association. This type of censorship is imposed by an

arrangement between the Journalists Association and the Ministry of Information and the General Security Department. A committee of journalists nominated by the Journalists Association would review materials gathered for publication in newspapers. I headed one such committee at *Al Nahar* newspaper at the time the Lebanese civil war broke out in 1975, before Syrian troops arrived to occupy the newspaper headquarters in 1976. These troops did not withdraw from that building until the ill-famed Decree No. 104 was issued and censorship was imposed by the General Security Department. I was also given charge of imposing this censorship at *Al-Nahar*. We were required to send the final lay-out of the pages ready for printing to the General Security Department. Blank spaces were strictly forbidden. Any deleted item was to be substituted by suitable material, or by an approved photo, to ensure that no traces of censorship were visible. Any publication could be confiscated if it violated censorship rules and could remain closed until a verdict was issued by the court of publications. The decisions of this court on the issue of censorship were beyond review or appeal.

- *Egypt*: The Press Law No. 96 issued in 1996, states that newspaper censorship is not generally permitted but can be imposed in exceptional cases such as emergency situations or times of war. An emergency was declared in Egypt after the assassination of President Sadat on October 6th, 1981. Under the emergency, the President or the official designated by the President, has the authority to impose censorship on mail, newspapers, bulletins, publications, written materials and all other means of expression, advertisement and publicity, prior to printing; and has the authority to confiscate the publication, stop its distribution or close it down. The Egyptian President has nominated the Minister of Interior to implement these procedures. The President or the official designated by him, has the authority to transfer the case of any newspaper from the jurisdiction of common law to the National Security courts. The Egyptian law has given the President or the designated official, the authority to transfer the case of any newspaper to the martial courts to judge issues that are not harmful to the military regime. This practice contradicts the principles of democracy, which separates civilian and military life.

8-Administrative Closure of Newspapers

Giving executive authorities the power to close down newspapers without a legal verdict is considered as a means of repression.

- *Yemen*: The license of a newspaper can be cancelled in the following cases: if the publication introduces content changes, which make them different from that mentioned in the license, without notifying the Ministry of Information within a maximum of ten days; if a daily ceases regular publication for three months; if a weekly stopped publication for three months; if a monthly stopped publication for six months; if a quarterly stopped publication for one year; if a newspaper was not published within six months of the date of issuing the license; or if the legal entity of the licensee ceased to exist; or if the owner of the publication died and his heirs were unable to issue the publication within one year of his death.
- *Egypt*: The license will be cancelled if the newspaper is not issued throughout three months starting from the date of granting the license; or if it is not issued regularly throughout nine months. The Higher Council of Journalists is responsible for verifying the difficulties involved in issuing the newspaper.
- *Kuwait*: The license will be canceled if its owner fails to pay financial liabilities, or if he fails to provide a bank guarantee during three months from the date of issuing the license; or if the publication was stopped for six consecutive months; or if the legal entity of the licensee whether a company, an association, a commission or a club ceased to exist; or if the owner of the publication died and his heirs were unable to issue the publication regularly even after one year.
- *Syria*: Publications can be shut down by an order issued by the Prime Minister, based on a proposal from the Minister of Information, in the

[525]

following cases: if the publication has not been issued for three months after the date of granting the license; or if within three successive months the publication failed to print two thirds of the number of normal issues published by similar publications; or if legal penal verdicts were issued against the publication within one year. The Syrian President has the authority to revoke the license of any publication, based on the decision of the Prime Minister, in the following cases: if it defamed the dignity of the President; published material which can harm Syrian relations with other countries; published material that may threaten the safety and security of the armed forces; published information that may be useful to the enemy; or if it published material which may destabilize or threaten the internal security of the country.

- *Jordan*: A license can be terminated in the following cases: if the publication has not been printed for six months from the date of issuing the license; if a daily stopped publication for three consecutive months; if a weekly failed to print 12 consecutive issues; if a non-daily publication with a printing frequency exceeding one week failed to publish four consecutive issues; or if the publication violated the terms mentioned in the license, including that of content changes without prior consent from the Department of Printing & Publications. However, in this case, cancellation can only be implemented after giving the publication two warning letters.

- *Libya*: A publication can be shut down if the owner had been a legal entity which ceased to exist; if it failed to print any issue for three months after getting the license; or if the daily failed to publish 7 consecutive issues, or 14 issues within one year without a reasonable justification. The cancellation decision is taken by the Minister of Information, after consultation with the Head of the Department of Printing & Publications.

- *Qatar*: Cancellation of the license of a publication can be decided in the following cases: upon the request of its owner; if it failed to be published regularly throughout six months; if it stopped for six consecutive months; if its owner did not pay the required financial guarantees in full; or if its owner died and his heirs were not able to issue the publication regularly within one year from the date of death.

- *United Arab Emirates*: The license of publications can be terminated in the following cases: if the publication failed to be issued throughout the six months following the date of the license; if it failed to be issued regularly within the six months following the grant of the license; or if its owner died and his heirs failed to issue the publication regularly within one year from the date of death.

- *Sultanate of Oman*: The license of a newspaper can be terminated if it failed to be issued throughout the six months following the date of the license; if it failed to be issued for six consecutive months without a reasonable justification. The Department of Printing & Publications is the authorized institution to cancel the license. A petition letter can be submitted to the Minister of Information.

- *Sudan*: The National Press Council is the institution with the authority to cancel the license of a publication, in case of violation of the terms of license.

9-Legal Supervision of Administrative Resolutions

- *Kuwait*: An appeal can be submitted to the court against the executive orders in case the license application is rejected. The Legal Supreme Council assumes the responsibility of legal supervision.

- *Bahrain*: In case the license is rejected, an appeal can be submitted to the Council of Ministers, and the decision of the Cabinet will be final.

- *Qatar*: An appeal can be submitted to the Council of Ministers against rejection, cancellation or blocking of the license. The decision of the Cabinet will be final.

- *Oman*: An appeal against the rejection of an application to establish a publishing house can be submitted to the Department of Printing and

Publications. The decision of the Department will be final after it is ratified by the Minister of Information.

- *Saudi Arabia*: Decisions on appeals should be taken by an ad hoc committee nominated by the Minister of Information, before which the applicant should appear and testify. Decisions by the Committee become valid only after being ratified by the Minister of Information. However, if the violation was an extraordinary one, the case should be referred to the Council of Ministers.

- *Syria*: The rejection of a license by the Council of Ministers is conclusive and cannot be refuted by any legal or administrative authority.

- *Libya*: An appeal regarding the rejection of a license should be submitted to the Council of Ministers.

- *Lebanon*: The authority to stop issuing any publication by an administrative decision was invalidated, after the amendment of Article 104 of the constitution as previously mentioned.

There are criminal grounds for closing down publications in Arab legislative systems such as: promoting racial incitement and resentment; provoking hatred and division; promoting matters that may influence the legal system; spreading false news that may destabilize civic peace; producing or possessing photos that may slander the reputation of the country; encouraging the violation of laws; falsifying legal proceedings; publishing closed court proceedings; publishing matters that were reviewed in closed parliamentary sessions, or falsifying the proceedings of public sessions; or broadcasting a covert or legal investigation.

Professional Restraints

One of the main criteria to assess the freedom of opinion and expression enjoyed by individuals in a certain society is the status of the rights and guarantees provided by that society to journalists in order to practice their job freely, particularly their right to gather information and their right to enjoy personal safety.

[528]

1-Prior License for Journalism

- *Yemen*: The Ministry of Information grants the journalist a Press Card to help him perform his tasks, and also grants him a professional card as a member of the Press Union. The Press Card usually gives its holder all facilities and advantages which are provided by the government based on the decision of the Council of Ministers.
- *Qatar*: To work in the press, one should get a license from the Department of Publications.
- *Bahrain*: No writer or editor is allowed to work in any newspaper, unless he gets a license from the Ministry of Information. The Minister of Information is responsible for setting the required conditions for granting a license.
- *United Arab Emirates*: A license is required to work as a writer or an editor in the press. Owners of publications are not allowed to employ any person who does not hold a permit from the Information Department at the Ministry of Information.
- *Sultanate of Oman*: The license is a requirement to work in press and it is issued by the Department of Printing and Publication.
- *Algeria*: The Press Supreme Council is responsible for setting the conditions for granting a Press Card for a professional journalist and its validity period. It is also responsible for the nomination of the issuing institution; how the card can be cancelled, and the ways of appealing against cancellation.
- *Morocco*: Holding a Professional Press Card is a mandatory condition for practicing journalism, and it is issued by Press Card Committee which consists of the following: a representative of the government department concerned with media affairs (head of the committee), four members representing the associations of professional journalists and individuals from the same category and an equal number of members representing media institutions.
- *Sudan*: A journalist should be listed in the register of journalists at the National Press Council.

[529]

2- Prior Registration at the Press Union

- *Lebanon*: A journalist should be enrolled at the register of Press Union at the Association of Editors. A journalist is usually granted a Press Card signed by both the Minister of Information, and the Head of Press Union; and the card is issued by the Press Supreme Council. In order to get a press card, one of the conditions requires that the holder should be a university graduate.

- *Egypt*: No one is allowed to work in press unless his name is enrolled in the Press Union list, after securing the approval of the Press Supreme Council. A journalist to be registered in the Press Union list should be: a professional journalist and not an owner, partner or shareholder of any newspaper or news agency. He also should be an Egyptian citizen of good conduct and clear record without any court conviction for dishonesty or any criminal act; Moreover, his name should not have been removed from the Press Union register for moral reasons or cases of dishonesty. He should also hold a higher studies qualification.

3-Professional Secrets

A journalist has the right to safeguard any confidential knowledge and to protect his sources before the courts and official organizations.

- *Egypt*: Egyptian Law stipulates that it is not permitted to force a journalist to reveal his sources of information. Thus, a journalist should not face any pressure from government authorities and should not be compelled to reveal the sources of his information.

- *Jordan*: A journalist has the right to maintain secrecy and he can claim confidentiality of sources as an excuse at the courts and official entities; he can keep his information and sources confidential, unless the court decides otherwise in criminal cases, with the objective of protecting national security, preventing crime or enforcing justice.

- *Algeria*: The Algerian law declares that professional confidentiality is a right of journalists. However, this professional right cannot be upheld by the legal authorities in the following cases: if it is going to reveal any military, economic and strategic secret; if the media clearly threatens national security in an unambiguous way; if media outlets are designed to address children or adolescents; if the media deals with any legal investigation and research. In case of investigating an article by an anonymous author or written under a pseudonym, the Editor-in-Chief may be exempted from the pledge of professional confidentiality at the request of the concerned authorities; and then he should reveal the identity of the real writer.

- *Yemen*: A journalist has the right to maintain the confidentiality of his information, and should not be forced to expose his sources.
- *Sudan*: The law protects the sources of information of any journalist.

4-Conscience Condition

The concept of respecting "freedom of conscience" is rooted in the Italian Press Professional Code issued in 1928. In compliance with that code, a journalist is required to resign from a newspaper individually and willingly and without notice to its owner, if the journalist's freedom and independency are influenced by his relations with the owner. In France, this "conscience" condition is applied to the professional journalist who is defined as: a person who regularly practices the profession of journalism, and works for a daily newspaper, a periodical or a news agency.

The scope for applying the "conscience condition" includes the following cases: the closure of the newspaper, a change in the newspaper ownership which may translate into a change in the relationship between the journalist and the owner, especially when both share a prior intellectual reasoning, and have a common understanding of the general line and approach of the newspaper. This case is applied in some Arab countries, namely in Algeria, Morocco and Egypt.

- *Algeria*: The Algerian Information Law views a change in the orientation or content of any media organization, the halt of its activities or concession of its ownership as a sufficient reason to cancel the work contract of a professional journalist. The cancellation of the contract is considered similar to lay-off which entails a payment of compensation.

- *Morocco*: The Moroccan Law No: 1/57/88 mentioned the cases for applying the "conscience condition" as follows: the concession of the ownership of the media organization; the halt or closure of its offices for whatever reason; or a major change in the newspaper which might damage the literary interests of the journalist or defame his honesty.
- *Egypt*: The conscience condition is applied if a policy change is introduced into the newspaper, or if the contractual terms are changed. In such a case, a journalist may cancel his contract with the institution he works for, willingly and individually; while he is required to notify the administration of the newspaper about his resignation, at least three months prior to the date of cessation of work. However, in this case, the journalist has the right to be compensated.

5-The Right to have Access to Information from Original Sources

- *Egypt*: The Egyptian Press Law says that a journalist has the right to have access to information, data and news legally permitted for publication, and which are not classified by the original sources, whether governmental or public. A journalist has the right to publish whatever information he gets. It is prohibited to impose any restraints which may obstruct the free flow of information, or undermine the right of different newspapers to have equal access to information; or which might terminate of the right of citizens to get information and knowledge. There only one condition to be fulfilled by the press—not violating the requirements of national security, national defense and major national interests.
- *Sudan*: Every public official or institution having information relating to the state or society should make this available to journalists, if it is not classified or categorized as non-publishable.
- *Yemen*: A journalist has the right to obtain information, news, data and statistics from their original sources.

[532]

- *Jordan*: Official institutions have to provide the opportunity for journalists to view their programs, projects and plans. This right includes the possibility to have access to information, news and statistics of public interest from their original sources, and the right to analyze, circulate and publish such information and comment on them.
- *Algeria*: The Algerian law gives professional journalists the right to have access to the sources of information, and to review the documents issued by the public department and related to the objectives of that department, if they are not classified information or protected by the law. This right of journalists is not unlimited, as the law has defined the information that cannot be published or manipulated as follows: information which may harm national security, national unity or state security, or which may pose a national threat; information which may reveal a secret relating to national defense or an economic, strategic or diplomatic secret; information that may hurt citizens' rights and their constitutional freedom; and information that may discredit an investigation or criminal research.
- *Lebanon*: The Lebanese law does not guarantee this right for journalists.

6- The Right of Personal Safety

- *Egypt*: Journalists enjoy independence in Egypt without any government control. Opinions and true information published by a journalist should not be made an excuse to harm his personal security. A journalist should not be dismissed from work unless and until the Press Union has been notified. Documents, data, information and papers in the possession of a journalist should not be used to indict him or as evidence against him in any criminal investigation, unless these documents and papers form the subject of investigations. A journalist should not be arrested as a suspect in a press-related crime, without a prior legal order by the prosecutor. A journalist should not be interrogated nor his office inspected by any authority except for the members of the prosecutor's office, and only after informing the Press Union. According to the Code of Ethics governing the Egyptian press,

[533]

a journalist should not be threatened or blackmailed in any way in order to force him to publish anything that may contradict his professional conscience or to secure personal gains to any individual or any institution. Also, a journalist should not be unjustly prevented from writing or practicing his job, and should not be transferred to a non-journalistic job, or to the back offices of the press agency which he works for, in a way that may hurt any of his material or intellectual rights. The Accord also stipulates that any insult to a journalist or any attack against him should not be tolerated, as it will be interpreted as an attack against the Freedom of Press. Furthermore, the security of a journalist should be guaranteed and he should be protected properly while working in the field. A journalist has the right to expose persons who provided him with false news and data. A journalist should not be pressurized by government authorities, nor be forced to reveal his sources of information.

- *Yemen*: A journalist should not be held liable for his opinion and true data published by him. A journalist should not be dismissed or transferred to a non-journalistic job, suspended or prevented from practicing his job or writing, nor should he be held accountable except within the minimum limits ratified by the Law.

- *Algeria*: If a professional journalist, while performing his task, has been exposed to violence, aggression, inducement, intimidation or direct pressure, the related legal authorities should be informed. The newspaper (which he works for) should be considered as a civil party in the case.

- *Morocco*: The government department that supervises media affairs has the right to withdraw the Press Card from a journalist after consultation with the Press Card Committee if the court indicts the journalist on the charge of violating Press Law.

- *Sudan*: A journalist in Sudan enjoys the following rights and immunities: a journalist should not be threatened with any illegal action with the purpose of influencing his job, integrity or professional commitments; a journalist can be arrested for any profession-related charges only after a notice is sent to the head of the General Press Association. However, the press law has introduced the following amendments: a journalist may receive a censure, warning letter and even be banned from publishing in newspapers for a period not exceeding two weeks.

7- Detention (Pending Investigation) for Publication Crimes

- *Lebanon*: Detention is not allowed for any kind of publication violation.
- *Egypt*: Detention pending investigation is not allowed in any kind of press violation, except those mentioned in criminal law, or those violations considered as an insult to the President of the republic.

Regulations in all other Arab countries have not included such basic guarantees to protect the freedom of journalists.

8-Guardianship over Press and Journalists by Government Councils

Some Arab countries have imposed official guardianship over press freedom by creating some government councils which control the media profession and its freedom. Among these countries are Egypt, Sudan, Lebanon and Algeria.

Legal Limitations on Press Content

Abdullah Khaleel says in his previously mentioned study: "Arab regulations are derived from a sole source which is the French Law, specifically, the provisions of the French Law promulgated on July 27,[th] 1848." He adds that Egyptian regulators took the terms constraining freedom of opinion and expression from French law. Arab regulations are ill-famed as being fiercely anti-press, and one of their notorious features is the expansion of the scope of the "crimes of opinion" in which it is considered a crime if a newspaper insults the President, or raises doubts about his personal credibility or actions; or if it contains any provocation against the ruling regime and questions the fairness of laws and decrees. Furthermore, any criticism of the government or the governing system is considered a crime, and the most severe punishments are applied against violators.

1-Expanding Indictment Policy

Arab regulations include greater expansion of the scope of indictment although criminal regulations are considered "the true mirror to assess individual freedom in a certain society." Khaleel explains that the "indictment policy in the Arab press regulations gives a clear indication about the oppressive tendency of the regulators...particularly the expansion of the acts considered as crimes of opinion and press." It is also an indication of the general obscurity and vagueness of some regulations, through using unclear terminology, such as "public order," "national security," "public interest," "higher interest," "national interest," "public peace," "ethics" and "public norms" without employing clear definitions of these terms.

In practice, the principle of individual punishment was overlooked, and the Editor-in-Chief of a publication would bear the criminal responsibility for any crimes committed by the publication, rather than the author if he were available or accessible, because the Editor-in-Chief is the one who controls the publication process.

Furthermore, regulations in all Arab countries agree to indict any person who attacked the President of the country. Some regulations prohibit even criticism or negative reporting of the President. Regulations prohibit the publishing of any insult to the President in countries such as Egypt, Tunisia, United Arab Emirates, Qatar, Bahrain, Jordan, Oman, Morocco, Kuwait, Lebanon and Yemen.

The UNDP's Arab Human Development Report, 2003 raises some important points:

> Yet the problem of freedom in the Arab world is not related to the implementation of laws as much as to the violation of these laws. Oppression, the arbitrary application of laws, selective censorship and

other politically motivated restrictions are widespread. They often take the form of legal constraints on publications, associations, general assemblies and electronic media, which prevent these from carrying out their communication and cultural roles. Such restrictions also obstruct the diffusion of knowledge and the education of public opinion.

The same Arab Human Development Report goes on to state:

> Yet the more dangerous restrictions are those imposed by security authorities when they confiscate publications or ban people from entering a country or prevent the sale of certain books during fairs while promoting other kinds of books. In committing these acts, these authorities reach above the constitutional institutions and the law, citing the pretext of 'national security' or public order. Other forms of restriction come from narrow-minded, self-appointed custodians of public morality, and from the censorship of books, articles and media events. Creativity, innovation and knowledge are the first victims of the suppression or denial of freedoms.[11]

2-Religious Fanaticism

Some Arab regulations combine religion with law, which may lead to a lot of dangers that threaten the freedom of press. While laws generally aim to regulate the conduct of individuals in society, Islam focuses on organizing social conduct. It structures the relation between individual and God, and the relation of the individual with himself. It also holds Man accountable for his intentions, even though punishment in law is different from punishment in religion.

Since laws with a religious background may impose the most serious and most effective restraints on personal freedom as they are applied in the United Arab Emirates, Kingdom of Saudi Arabia, Qatar, Bahrain and Oman, the actions prohibited by these laws should be defined very clearly, if freedom is to be guaranteed. Definitions of criminal acts should be crystal clear and regulators should avoid using ambiguous terminology when they set prohibitions and indictments related to religion, such as "mischief," "provocation," "dealing with," "violation of general norm," "criticism" and "damaging the sanctity of." In this context, Abdullah Khaleel says:

> The incessant differences in religious ways between one nation and another, and even within the same society, prevent the judge from applying fixed rules, which might lead sometimes to applying the religious jurisdiction and not the legal text of the law; and it may lead to creating a new crime which the regulator did not mean to establish in law.

Muhammad Al-Baalbaki, the head of Lebanese Press Association, who undertook higher studies in Islamic laws and Jurisdiction and intended to qualify as a prayer Imam, chose to be a journalist to serve both the people and God concurrently. He blames fanatical Muslims for the damage caused to the image of Islam and he quoted Jamal Al-Deen Al-Afghany who said more than one hundred years ago: "Islam has been distorted by Muslims."

In Baalbaki's opinion:

> ...the real dilemma is rooted in the mental imperfection which plagued the Islamic world and created a huge gap between Muslims in their real behavior and Islam as a theoretical ideology, particularly in the affairs of daily life and basic values, primarily the value of freedom.

He talked about 12 true facts in Islam:[12]

- The Prophet (PBUH) performs the role of a harbinger, reminds people and gives them advice, warnings, signs and notices and he acts as a witness.
- The final judgment in the Holy Quran is based on the freedom of opinion and freedom of choice, and the right to take part in the wider intellectual conflict, without using any type of violence.
- Having different opinions and different creeds is a part of human nature, or expressed simply: "God created people with different opinions and different creeds."
- The right to free choice is completely integrated with the individual responsibility which lies solely on the person making the choice himself. It is worth mentioning that: "God gives Man the freedom to choose between being a believer or a blasphemous person, while He warns them against evil consequences if they opted for the wrong choice."
- Reject blind imitation in adopting certain opinions without due thought, even if imitation is based on the heritage of parents and predecessors.

- Freedom is indivisible, being a gift for all human beings.
- Practicing freedom of thought can only be realized through judicious dialogue among people.
- Dialogue should be open without complexities or preconditions. It should not be limited to adopting inflexible ideas which cannot tolerate discussion, regardless of the loyalty of the individual to these ideas and his fixed belief that they are the only correct ones. The tools of dialogue include the mind, logic, science, proof and verification.
- The practice of free choice should not be conditional upon material gain or the balance of gains and losses, nor based on fear of terror.
- Abuse of freedom is not acceptable. Telling the truth is a precondition of freedom.
- The right to freedom cannot be attained without paying a high price. Every free choice can be guaranteed to its owner only through a great choice.
- Man's right to freedom necessitates the defense of such freedom by all means, even by fighting.

Journalism and Journalists vs. Money and Power

Needless to say, the violation of the right to freedom is not committed only by the ruling regime. It is also committed by influential people from both financial and political circles and even from the media sector. Violation of freedom is also committed by newspaper owners themselves. Therefore, it is useless to talk about the freedom of expression if there is not a level of independence which can protect journalism from the ruling authorities, money and influential parties and even from the owners of the papers themselves.

Professional Ethics and Responsibilities

In terms of professional ethics and responsibilities, Jean Claude Bertrand[13] a professor of *Professional Ethics and Norms* at the French Press Institute, says:

> Putting the press under the control of the state leads to misinformation and manipulation, and that is exactly what happened under Communism...While, on the other hand, giving full freedom to the media may lead journalists to practice media prostitution in their race for money and power.

In his view, the only way to force journalists to serve the public interest is to establish a "Code of Ethics" or a system that regulates the professional norms of journalism, along with a reliable system of accountability to and control by the owners of the media organization.

Bertrand lists the real obstacles which prevent the development of successful accountability systems to question the owners of media organs, as follows:

- *Thirst for influence:* The owners of media organizations, particularly the owners of newspapers and TV stations enjoy immense power to influence the public and they are not prepared to concede this power.
- *Haughtiness and superiority:* The owners of media organizations refuse to admit their mistakes.
- *Fragile arrogance and selfishness:* Owners of media organizations, who are used to criticizing others, whether in political or business sectors and attacking them ruthlessly, reject criticism against themselves, and they usually respond furiously to their critics.
- *The cost:* Accountability costs are often very high, whether material or moral.

Bertrand pointed out that accountability takes various forms: from establishing accountability councils within the newspapers to appointing "an investigator to review the complaints of readers" within the newspaper, and from assessing readers' opinions, to establishing local and regional accountability councils. Commitment to the Professional Accords of Honor should emphasize the honesty of reporters. Honesty of journalism is viewed by A. R. Mackenzie,[14] the former head of the UN Press and Information Department, to be manifested through truth, courage, balance and modesty. "Avoid arrogance and selfishness" he urges, as the media's ultimate goal is "to serve society and not the owner of the newspaper or the connected interest groups."

The Journalist is a Guardian of Society

The journalist remains a guardian of society and the nation. People would be surprised if a newspaper rejects an advertisement, which amounts to rejecting money for the sake of ethics and principles. It would be really astonishing if a newspaper accepts money to neglect its principles. Jibran Tuwainy, the founder of *Al-Nahar* newspaper about 65 years ago, said:

> The newspaper which concedes its principles for money, can easily concede its ideals....Therefore it loses its credibility – the most important of its assets – in the eyes of its readers.

Tuwainy emphasizes that the press is "one of the major powers of the state."

> It is free and does not need to wait for inspiration to be written, and does not have to ask anyone's permission to publish the truth. It provides its operational expenses and owners' expenses from its own incomes. It also maintains commitment to its own principles, resists despotism and defends the rights of the country...Therefore the press never misleads people, and never exploits the honesty of the reader. It is always honest in reporting the news, never lies, never conspires, nor contrives, nor changes loyalty."

Tuwainy also warns against turning the newspaper into a political tool because in doing so, it loses its credibility and honesty. In this regard he said: "Politics never knows credibility or honesty."[15]

Arabs today need to establish a free society; implement democratic reforms; widen the scope of liberties as real rights to be practiced and not merely theories for debates; establish good governance; enhance the role of civil society and public participation in decision-making processes; in accordance with the recommendations of the *Arab Human Development Reports, 2003 & 2004,* published by the UN Development Program. These reforms might help to avoid the escalating pressures by the United States on Arab countries, demanding actual democratic reforms in Arab societies and in political regimes. Such reforms might not be harmonious with Arab needs, culture, social or religious environment. The major guarantor of freedoms, particularly the freedom of press, should be a legal system of justice which is based on two pillars: an independent judicial system and independent lawyers. This is an institutional guarantor and inevitable component for the protection of human rights in a free democratic society. Therefore, international accords focused on the independence of the judicial system and independent lawyers, and on defining the standards and terms for this guarantee, as stated in the *Arab Human Development Report, 2004*.[16]

If Arabs really want change, they should start expanding freedom by expanding the base of democracy, and they should make media organizations – particularly the written ones – forums for dialogue. Furthermore, the citizen should restore his natural right to be as free as he was at birth. The citizen should enhance his right to choose, his right to know the truth, and establish a free public opinion capable of practicing criticism, accountability and responsibility.

It is quite certain that Arabs will never enjoy a good future or progress in any field, if freedom remains the exception and tyranny remains the general norm.

[542]

26

The Arab Press and Various Sources of Repression

Hazim Saghiya

Even if attempts were made to conceal flaws or present the best possible image, it cannot be truthfully claimed that all Arab governments love the media and seek the greater spread of knowledge via the media, or that they all have positive intentions to expand the freedom of the press. This is evidenced, among other things, by the fact that the ministries of information are still in position in most Arab countries although they have become redundant in many places outside the Arab world. The mere term "Ministry of Information" may be considered as a throwback to the age of totalitarian regimes which in the past often tried to obscure the truth and spread misinformation as widely as possible.

It is not without significance that the foremost Arab journalist in the twentieth century, Muhammad H. Haikal, attained this rank because of his relationship with the late Egyptian President, Gamal Abdul Nasser. Nasser was known for many controversial issues but promoting democracy and freedom of the press were definitely not among them. In comparison, there is no Arab journalist who has reached a distinguished position because he had made revelations of the kind that US journalist Bob Woodward made, for instance, when he informed the world of the Watergate scandal, which eventually toppled the President of his country.

[543]

Origins of Despotism in the Arab Press

In the current age, the status of the Arab press has roots and traditions that cannot be overlooked by any means. From relatively early times, despotic oriental regimes were quick to seek ownership of their media to repress popular social expression. In the Arab experience, this goes back to the press during the reign of Muhammad Ali Pasha in Egypt. Such experiences were embodied in the *Khedive Journal* which was issued in 1827, one year before it became the famous newspaper *Al Waqai' Al Misriyyah,* which continued as an official newspaper till the early twentieth century. Free market economies also have an appetite to gain a footing in the media arena, which is not a normal pursuit of regimes running controlled economies. This is true of wealthy states like Kuwait, Saudi Arabia and the United Arab Emirates, as well as less wealthy countries like Jordan. The relationship between the Palestinian Authority and the media attests to the fact that even "regimes" considered as alternatives to traditional regimes are no different in this regard.

It is clear that the effect of importing western modernization is restricted to discovering new technologies to extend control and expand the networks with the aim of seizing the core of society and controlling its movement. The origins of this strategy may go back to the initiative taken by the Ottoman government in 1863 to issue an Arabic language newspaper in Beirut called *Hadiqat al Akhbar.* One year later, the official newspapers of Tunisia and Morocco were issued, followed by *Al Ahram* in Egypt in 1875, with the latter enjoying the support of Khedive Ismail.

Nothing testified to this perception more than the actions of Khedive Ismail whose reign witnessed the beginning of modernity in Egypt, and the introduction of the Egyptian and Arabic pattern of dealing with the most prominent aspects of modernity—the institutional and constitutional aspect. Europeans did not pressurize him into establishing a constituent assembly or a parliament. When he did so in 1866, the motive was to give Egypt a western appearance to strengthen his position vis-à-vis the patron state—the Ottoman authority. His other objective was to confer a form of legitimacy and popular support on his rule, and to use both to support his financial policies, especially limitless borrowing. Moreover, the parliament, which was completely subjected to his authority, proved ineffectual. However, during the last year of his reign, Khedive Ismail exerted a notable effort to revive the parliament. In view of his accumulating debts, European powers applied pressure on him to entrust Egyptian public money to European auditors. This meant limiting Khedive Ismail's income and concessions and necessitated urging the parliament to object to the European plans which ran counter to the "interests of the Egyptian people." Hence the struggle was turned into one between a persecuted monarch and greedy foreign creditors.

Lord Cromer (British Commissioner and later Consul General in Egypt) was known for his direct knowledge of the country's circumstances during the last year of Khedive Ismail's rule. In his book *Modern Egypt* he devoted a chapter to describing with pointed sarcasm Ismail's awkward attempt to "conjure free institutions temporarily as a tool that enables him to regain by proxy his personal authority which was threatened by foreign intervention." Cromer wrote:

> The scene was curiosity-stirring to see Ismail, who was an embodiment of despotic rule in its most extreme form, masquerading as a ruler so enveloped in constitutionality as to be unable, because of his live conscience, to place himself in opposition to national interest.

In other words, a principle established itself. Its hallmark was that the political behavior of a despotic ruler was open to transformation in any form provided that it served the interests and continuity of despotism. Thus a prickly, unpredictable temperament combined with the severity and arbitrariness of despotism and the press was supposed to reflect the two dimensions and express its loyalty to both of them.

Given such a situation, it was not surprising that the first chapters in the life of Arab press in the nineteenth century coincided with emigration. Journalists from *Al Sham* countries (Lebanon and Syria) immigrated to Egypt under the British rule which had started in 1882. The newspaper *Al-'urwat Al-Wuthqā*, belonging to the two sheikhs Jamal-ud-Din Al-Afghani and

[545]

Muhammad 'Abduh, was moved to Paris to escape persecution. A similar move was undertaken by *Abu Nazara* magazine, published by the Egyptian theatre pioneer Y'agoub Sano,' to escape the Khedive's persecution. On a different temperamental note, the Khedive supported *Al Ahram.*

Experience of the Press in Egypt: The Quest for Freedom

The modernization of despotism in the twentieth century, via appeals to nationalist, socialist and other ideologies, empowered repressive practices and renewed such capabilities. The press in Egypt during the liberal era, which started after the 1919 revolution and formed the model training ground for the Arab press, was terminated by the Nasserite state by nationalizing private and independent newspapers in accordance with Act 156 issued in May 1960. However, the despotic tendencies of the officers of the July 1952 coup were publicly revealed years before, even when the new regime was being stabilized. Following the crisis between Gamal Abdel Nasser and General Mohammad Naguib in March 1954, Mahmoud Abu Al Fitooh, Chairman of the trade union of Egyptian journalists and Chief Editor of *Al Misri,* the largest newspaper in pre-revolution Egypt, was forced to immigrate to Switzerland together with his brothers. After 1960, this policy took a sharper and more rigid pattern, which led among other things, to the emigration of the famous journalist Ali Amin in the mid-1960s to Beirut where he worked under a pen name in the newspapers published by the Lebanese *Dar Al Sayad.* This happened after his brother, Mustafa Amin, was accused of carrying out "intelligence" services for the United States.

Having suffered from such heavy-handedness despotism, Egypt is still floundering in its efforts to deal with this inheritance. No sooner does it take a step forward, than it is forced to take a step backwards. Undoubtedly, some progress has been achieved. This has culminated in the current situation, which consists of a mix of national newspapers (governmental and semi-governmental), political party newspapers and private newspapers. Certainly, it is a media mix which enjoys a certain margin of freedom of opinion and expression. Yet it is less than what might be expected three decades after Nasser's death and the declared end of military dictatorship.

With the end of Nasser's era, direct censorship of the press was annulled. Since 1976, the ground was laid for a restricted and relative plurality. In this context, party newspapers were published which were beyond the reach of the state and outside its hold. Each political party has one or more platforms to speak on its behalf. However, this was not the sole route of development of the Egyptian media. As a result of the May 15, 1971 movement, which freed the late President Anwar Sadat from the power partnership with the Nasserites and the leftists, the two leftist magazines *Al Taliy'a and Al Katib* were closed down. The emigration of many Egyptian journalists started anew with many moving to Paris and London, as well as Tripoli, Baghdad, Beirut and other Arab capitals.

During the rule of President Hosni Mubarak, the *Al Da'wa* magazine, which expresses the view of the Muslim Brotherhood organization migrated to Vienna after it was closed down in Cairo. Also, the Nasserite newspaper *Sout al 'Arab* shifted to Paris and later London, after it was closed down in the summer of 1988.

The worst effect of the ideological phase that started with Nasserism but with some of its elements continuing even after that phase, is the state's insistence on maintaining a "national" press (either nationalized or semi-nationalized) though many economic and social sectors have been privatized in Egypt. Added to this reality is the state monopoly on the radio and television, all of which results in the creation of a despotic hold to be reckoned with.

For these reasons, the achievements realized by Egypt in the field of journalism seem like small steps on a long route. Moreover, these steps are not guaranteed against retreat, as there are no such assurances. Consider the events of March 1996 when the new Egyptian Press Act annulled the arrest of journalists by the administration, which had stirred a

[547]

wave of protests among journalists and human rights organizations, and reduced prison terms in publication cases. Generally, the Act was considered a triumph for liberties. On the other hand, however, it emphasized compensation and fines without eliminating the specter of government intervention in the press.

In early 1988, a new Act was issued in Egypt obliging those interested in publishing new newspapers to first obtain cabinet approval on the pretext of prohibiting foreigners from owning the press. Yet in a situation such as that of Egypt, which is economically so open that it is absolutely impossible and prohibitive to reject incoming foreign capital, the formality is maintained by publishing newspapers with licenses issued abroad. In this sense another type of emigration started by the end of 1980s. It took a different form compared to previous emigrations. Moreover, it had different motives, most importantly the desire of private and Arab investors to publish private publications. They could bypass licensing provisions by obtaining a license from outside Egypt, provided that the newspaper was edited and printed inside Egypt. This migrant press operating by foreign license was an indication of the deceptiveness and camouflage produced by a hybrid situation—by being democratic and semi-despotic at one and the same time.

Other forms of the "ideology of despotism" may be seen in more than one Arab country. If we overlook the complete lack of freedom under the Syrian and Libyan regimes and under the Iraqi regime during Saddam Hussein's rule, we can still cite the ideological camouflage in more confusing and complicated cases such as Lebanon. In this country, where the press has traditionally enjoyed a reasonable degree of freedom, the "Arabism of Lebanon" and the establishment of a "brotherly" regime that is strategically "congruent" with the Syrian regime had rendered the criticism of the Lebanese leader immeasurably easier than criticizing his Syrian "brother."

These forms have not stopped at physical liquidation. Lebanon, which has been more than once in its modern history become an "arena" for conflicting interests and ideologies, witnessed the killing of a relatively large number of journalists. On May 7, 1958, Naseeb Al-Matni, the Chief Editor of *Al Telegraf* newspaper, was killed. He was followed on May 16, 1966, by Kamil Muruwwa, the Editor of *Al Hayat* newspaper. Edward Saab, the Chief Editor of *L' Orient Le Jour*, was killed on May 16, 1976. On February 24, 1980, Salim El-Lawzi, the Chief Editor of *Al Hawadith* magazine, was abducted and killed whereas Riyad Taha, Chairman of the Lebanese journalists' trade union, was killed on July 23, 1980. In more recent times, in June 2005, Samir Kseir, the journalist and writer of *An Nahar* newspaper was killed.

These killings are linked to prevailing dictatorial and militia-like practices. This is evidenced by the fact that Abdel-Halim Qandil, the Editor of *Al-Arabi,* the Egyptian Nasserite newspaper, was abducted and subjected, to physical violence in early November 2004. The Egyptian Minister of Interior was accused of being behind the accident. Other cases attest to similar situations. In Yemen, a decree was issued on December 29, 2004, imposing a two-year term of imprisonment on Abdel Karim Sabra, the Chief Editor of *Al-Huriyya* newspaper and Abel Al Qawi al-Qbati, one of the newspaper's writers, and closing down the newspaper for one year.

Press Freedom: Political and Socio-cultural Determinants

In the presence of such closed cultural and political structures, press repression can take varying forms, but they are extremely effective in the domain of disseminating information, as well as the domain of the balance between society and the state. Suffice it to say that the despotic politician can inflict penalties on the press starting with the withholding of information and ending with closure, confiscation and imprisonment, in the absence of sufficient mandatory controls that limit the authority of the state. Almost all Arab constitutions lay down in several chapters, the freedom of the press and expression as well human rights guarantees, especially in matters pertinent to investigation, independent opinion and

[549]

expression in accordance with the articles (especially article 19) of the International Declaration of Human Rights, 1948. However, these same constitutions have legalized, and continue to legalize acts that usurp the very rights that the constitutions provide for.

In this case, the political issue will not be solved by technological progress or be overcome by globalization, the flow of information and the democratization of the media, as well all the iconic symbols over which discussion has flourished in the last three decades. It is not a mere coincidence that the beginning of this "modern" phase has been simultaneous, in the Arab World, with the new migration of the press, which was inaugurated by *Asharq Al Awsat* in London in 1978 before *Al Hayat* and *Al Quds Al Arabi* newspapers which were founded in London in 1989. At the same time, migration of newspapers to France, Cyprus and other places was taking place in earnest. In the same context, we can point to the consequences of the conjunction between the tearing up of the national fabric in the Arab states, a process initiated by the Lebanese Civil War in 1975, and the Arab oil boom which "modernized" among other things, the tools of coercion and confiscation.

In tackling with surprise and sometimes with denial, the attitude of Arab governments towards the freedom of the press, it is often assumed that governments spontaneously love the dissemination and exchange of information. However, this is a common mistake, since no authority surrenders this privilege voluntarily or automatically. The status quo will remain intact unless it is wrenched away from the authority. Hence any investigation into the attitudes of most Arab governments cannot be complete without posing the following question: Why have Arab societies not been able to assert their liberties? When such a question is posed, it will become impossible to consider the political sphere in isolation from the wider cultural and societal sphere.

Making this statement does not exonerate Arab governments from responsibility but it is an attempt to distribute responsibility with a greater measure of justice. We have to ponder the most important reasons which make the coercive role of governments possible and sometimes "desirable." In this regard it must be said that the governments concerned sometimes find that they are less inclined towards coercion than circumstances beyond their control dictate, and at times these circumstances might be against these governments. It is befitting here to cite a historical paradox which forms a distant background for much that is taking place in the Arab world. This stems from the fact that we employ western standards to measure what are non-western situations by definition. What I mean in this case is that the press has grown and developed in an atmosphere of defending public concerns. Its search for the truth and insistence on widening the margins of freedom often clash with despotic tendencies—nationalist, religious and militarist. The campaigning of the press for democracy, in this sense, is an expression of civil societies whose concern was to limit the power of authorities and their nationalist, religious or militarist ideologies. Thus it was possible to establish and develop a context and traditions characterized by continuity in its struggle to realize its demands. This context begins with the founding of the *Gazetta* newspaper in Venice in 1536 and the *Weekly News* newspaper in England in 1622.

Needless to say, this applies partially to Arab conditions. The majority in Arab press circles hold more extreme positions than their governments in nationalist, religious and militarist matters. This makes our call for democracy purely political, in the exclusive and narrow sense of the word "political," rather than a call for comprehensive freedom at all levels: private, public, political, social, religious, economic, cultural and sexual. Democratic countries are steeped in the practice of withholding information in wartime and sometimes there is exaggeration in making wars a pretext for holding back information—as found in several American practices during the never-ending war on terrorism. However, our situation as Arabs is different, because our continuous state of critical conflict makes the suppression of information a natural part of the scene. This suppression, in its turn, changes into a permanent pretext for the

[551]

authorities to maintain an atmosphere of ongoing repression, which constitutes a situation that is difficult to resist so long as "no sound is louder than that of battle."

This tendency is strengthened, on the one hand, by failure to follow the tradition of professional solidarity which places all journalists in confrontation with the machinery of the state, regardless of their political differences. Instead, some journalists have links that make them support the inclinations of the existing regime. On the other hand, we lack political and constitutional checks which can rectify cases of security excesses carried out at the expense of freedom. This brings us to the heart of another issue—a societal and cultural rather than political one. Without this issue no talk of freedoms can be correct, especially the freedom of the press.

The Arab Press and the Predicament of Legitimacy

The problems that Arabs faced with the issue of legitimacy came to the fore as colonialism made its exit and national independence was achieved. We have never succeeded, either in a populist or an elitist manner, in internalizing the concept of legitimacy with its modern temporal premises. We have also failed to sow this concept in our soil. Within a few years, legislative institutions that were founded in the colonialist era were dissolved. The dissolution was reinforced by a popularity that was impossible to underestimate. With the exception of Lebanon and Tunisia, the countries of the Arab world year after year have been diverted into two streams: first, the military order ensuing from a coup that has overthrown the previous authority and second, the royal order whose main prop is an ancient familial legitimacy. However, Lebanon and Tunisia themselves failed in preserving their share of modern legitimacy. The first was torn apart by the civil–regional war since 1975, whereas the second gravitated since the mid-1980s towards militarizing its order within the framework of continuing Bourguibism at its minimal level.

[552]

Hence it is not a mere coincidence that the coup – the purest political formula for hostility towards liberties – has been the most prominent form of so called "progressive" succession in authority between the Atlantic Ocean and the Arabian Gulf. Syria began this in 1949, followed by Egypt in 1952 and Iraq in 1958. It is to the discredit of the Middle East region and the Islamic world that the only popular revolution they had witnessed – the Iranian Revolution in 1979 – did not possess any progressive and contemporaneous concept of legitimacy. The new leaders of Iran replaced the ancient familial legitimacy of the Shah by a religious legitimacy, which proved to be neither less controversial nor more popular in terms of consensus.

All this boils down to the fact that the more charismatic and populist the ruler – in the sense that he addresses the public in isolation from state institutions – the more he is tempted to consolidate authority in his hands. Similarly, the more the country is burdened by "decisive" and "holy" causes that allow no accountability or skepticism, the more the division of powers is detestable. Can we conceive of subjecting the "historical leader" and the "historical cause" to the game of democratic balance between institutions? Is it conceivable, consequently, to recognize the permanence and continuity of institutions in a manner that exceeds the permanence of the "historical leader" and the "historical cause"?

In fact the gravity of our conflicts, or what is described as such, is the most prominent reason empowering governments to embark on repressing the freedom of the press and other freedoms. Hence no one can demand civil liberties and decisive battles at one and the same time, and with equal enthusiasm.

It requires little effort to recall the obstacles to the development of the press in countries that have witnessed events like the Yemeni War in the early 1960s, the Lebanese Civil War in the mid-1970s, the Islamic Revolution led by Ayatollah Khomeini at the end of 1970s, or the Arab–Israeli wars and their offshoots.

[553]

In this regard, what is of great significance here is the role of the Iran–Iraq War, followed by the invasion of Kuwait, in limiting the development of the Gulf press. For instance, Kuwait, whose press benefited from a distant decisive development like the Lebanese Civil War, paid much more than it benefited when these developments occurred. During the Iran–Iraq War, in the summer of 1986, the decree for modifying the Publications Act was issued to provide the cabinet with the right to "suspend a newspaper for a period not exceeding two years, or annulling its license altogether," if it becomes clear that "it serves the interest of a foreign state or authority, or if what it publishes contradicts national interest, or if it is proven that it has obtained any aid, assistance or benefit in any form from a foreign state or body, or if it has done so without the permission of the Ministry of Information." During the Iraqi invasion – less than four years after that date – the Kuwaiti press was squashed along with other institutions.

As critical issues generate domestic and civil conflicts giving rise to charges of apostasy and betrayal, they have a similar effect on other things. In 1995, under the burden of combating fundamentalist terrorism, the Press Act No. 93 was issued in Egypt. This Act was a setback for the press which lasted for more than a year. In Morocco, despite the relative progress in the field of liberties, the Casablanca bombings in May 2003 led to a tight state control on public liberties, as well as the freedom of the press and opinion. This is evidenced by the passing of administrative decrees closing down four newspapers and sentencing four journalists to jail, in addition to arresting other journalists for purposes of investigation. This was partially rectified later. In January 2004, King Mohammed VI issued a royal pardon setting free a number of prisoners including jailed journalists.

Societal Forces and the Freedom of Expression

Currently, radical forces, whether political or religious, push towards press restrictions as well as repressing expression in general. This is so because they adhere to sanctified ideologies which do not admit of any opposition or even criticism. This practice on their part might be in harmony with the powers that be. However, more often than not, they conflict with the wishes of the authority, which is forced to concede because of the holy character imposed on the issues at hand. The success of Kuwaiti fundamentalists in forcing the Minister of Information, Muhammad Abu Al-Hasan, to resign at the beginning of 2005 is a gentle reminder of this fact.

Yet this relationship often takes on more fierce and dangerous dimensions. On September 15, 1995, for instance, the Egyptian Human Rights Organization discussed in a report what could result from the actions of so called fundamentalist societal forces. The report pointed out that "political Islam groups in Egypt exercise increasing pressures on freedom of opinion and expression, especially in the judiciary." The organization did not fail to condemn the increasing deterioration of the freedom of opinion and expression, whether at the level of legislation or practice. It was reported that between October 1993 and August 1995, the Islamists submitted 26 notices and suits before the courts—amounting to a suit every month. The most famous of these led to a verdict in June 1995 separating university Professor Nasr Hamid Abu Zaid from his wife because he was accused of *riddah* (apostasy) on account of his writings about Islam.

The organization also said that the Islamists resort to apostasy campaigns "against writers, artists and journalists and misuse the right to sue." Also, "they use *fatwas* (legal opinions) and lawsuits of *hisba* (public accountability) against the freedom of opinion and expression." These lawsuits were annulled in Egypt except for cases of family law. They enable any Muslim to "sue on behalf of the whole society in pursuit of confirming what is right, negating what is false and public morality," against those who are accused of doing a disservice to Islam. The organization's report adds that this tendency has extended itself to publishers, books, the academic field and the cinemas. Naturally, the Islamists also attacked newspapers "when they filed lawsuits in August

1994 and May 1995 against *Sabah Al-Kheir* magazine for a cover photograph showing the bare shoulders and bosom of a woman and for publishing a caricature entitled 'Apostasy in Public Transports.' They filed other lawsuits against several newspapers protesting the use of terms such as "spell" and "exaltedness" and others insulting Islam. Also, they filed lawsuits against those who seek to "undermine the Islamic community" and "publish articles which "do Islamic morality a disservice." As the report adds, *Rose Al-Yousif* magazine was the most targeted magazine with eight lawsuits filed against it in the first seven months of the same year.

The organization also noted that the censorship role of *Al Azhar* has escalated as it has become "the major censorship authority, especially after the State Council has issued a *fatwa* in which it stated that *Al Azhar* is the sole authority whose opinion is the only binding one for the Ministry of Culture in matters pertinent to giving licenses to audio-visual works or withholding them." This *fatwa* is considered "a very significant indicator of the way fundamentalist thought has infiltrated the Egyptian judicial institutions." Attention has been drawn to the fact that the "Islamic Research Academy," which is affiliated to *Al Azhar*, is "abusing its authority in the process of censoring books thought to be connected with religions."

Things being as they are, one might recall the Catholic Church which is centered around the Vatican, and its prolonged negative effect on laws, ideas of political sovereignty and the institutional and intellectual structures of the societies concerned. The church derives its hegemonic role, as the Arab forces of apostasy do currently, from its rejection of any relativity, 'heretic' dissidence or free and independent thought. This wells up from the very term "Catholicism" itself—as in linguistic terms, "cosmic righteousness" is an absolutism which is indivisible.

One teaching of the German pioneer of the Reformation, Martin Luther, is that higher authorities might go wrong, and every Christian is a clergyman before God. On the other hand, according to him, the papacy contradicted Christ's teachings in the realm of beliefs. Luther thought that the conscience of man, his mind and the scripture taken collectively, form the frame of reference to which the believer refers. He developed the theory of the "two kingdoms" which is considered the most important approach to politics by the Protestants. The two kingdoms are the church and the state. The importance of the latter specifically derives from the lack of belief or its incomprehensiveness. In fact this theory differs from Catholicism which has admitted the need for political authority (*Potestas Coactiva*) as a result of original sin. However, it accepted the existence of the administrative state (*Potestas Directiva*) in separateness from sin. Luther's argument was that notwithstanding the type of the temporal (secular) ruler it is important not to confuse between the two kingdoms. Hence what is considered sacred should not be politicized and what is considered political should not be sanctified.

The painful reality of the Arab world is that all the major ideological currents which have dominated its consciousness – whether in this period or that – have all focused on the rights of groups as monolithic masses without categorization or divisions, and not on the rights of individual citizens. In additions, nationalists hold that the nation's right, and the right of the group in the case of Islamists, as well as that of industrious worker in the case of socialists, have all become pretexts for justifying violation of the right of citizenship when it contradicts the proponents of the aforementioned collectivist calls who divide people into "brothers," "infidels," or into "comrades" and "enemies." They never view the others as citizens with equal rights and duties irrespective of their thoughts. These ideologies grow in a soil that is barren of constitutional traditions and of liberal thoughts whose frame of reference derives from rights and laws. Our tradition is as far removed from an awareness of the rights of the state as it is far removed from an awareness of the rights of the citizen. It neither admits the rights of the former vis-à-vis the latter, nor does it require the state to carry out its duties towards the citizen. What governs the relationship between the two is the fear on the part of the ruled, of the state as symbolized by a particular person who occupies the rank of the highest patriarch—who is above the "fathers" of the family, the sect, the clan and the doctrine.

Movements that are radical and have a religious orientation are hostile to the west in organizational and cultural terms, as well as in political terms. In the same way, the press has been imported from the west—just as the party, the trade union and the parliament have been. For these two reasons, the pressure exercised by struggle-oriented radicalism is of necessity directed towards opposing the freedom of the press and progress. It goes without saying that the first press nucleus in the Arab World came with the French Campaign in Egypt in 1798—the first conflict with France. Other milestones followed such as Boulaq Press which was founded in the early 1920s till the first independent newspaper (*Al Jawaib* by Ahmed Faris Al Shidyaq, was issued in Astana in 1861. This was followed by *Wadi Al Neil* in 1866). It is a well-known fact that the British occupation authority in Egypt entered the political-media game more for the sake of competition than for repressive ends. It sought to find newspapers that would defend it like *Al Muqatam,* issued in 1889 in opposition to *Al-Moaiyd* nationalist newspaper which was edited by its owner Sheikh Ali Yosuf, the pioneer of the Egyptian press. This was the atmosphere in which the liberal era was sown.

As the nineteenth century drew to a close, the Arab press gained an expanding capacity to attract an audience, with a widening base of educated people who adopted new and western styles of living. When Gergi Zaiddan founded *Al Hilal* magazine in 1892, the door was thrown open for publishing newspapers and magazines in Cairo, Alexandria and Beirut. Ultimately, the number reached one hundred newspapers and magazines during the period 1899-1900. In other words, the hostile backlash against the West under the burden of aggressive political conflict – whether experienced simultaneously in politics and as a socio-cultural model, or first in politics and later as a socio-cultural model – is a backlash that opposes the flourishing of multiplicity whether in the press or otherwise.

[558]

Freedom of the Media and the Environment of Knowledge

The foregoing discussion reflects the objective expansion achieved by the climate of despotism at the expense of the climate of freedom. This is derived from the fact that one obstacle to the freedom of the media – and this is a joint responsibility between authority and society – is embodied in the shrinking of the environment of knowledge and letters under the combined pressures of poverty, illiteracy, tumultuous demographic change and unbridled population growth. In a state of population explosion and educational deterioration, the natural environment for the growth of freedom, including the freedom of the press, seems akin to an oasis surrounded by vast stretches of sand. If certain economic and developmental plans are causing these phenomena, then the function of the authority is clear. Such socio-cultural trends share responsibility with the authority, for these phenomena, by its tolerance of uncontrolled population explosion and dissemination of fanatical, radical and populist views which express this demographic mix and try to exploit it politically.

Modernity cannot grow amid widespread illiteracy. Moreover, development cannot be achieved, the economy cannot grow, the individual cannot be proud of his individuality and democracy cannot find stability and strike roots if education is not spread widely within the social milieu.

These are truisms that do not need repetition. Yet they remain difficult to achieve in many Arab countries. At the present time, according to the figures of the United Nations Educational, Scientific and Cultural Organization (UNESCO), which has declared its intention of eradicating illiteracy in 2015, the number of illiterates in the world was 875 million in 2000. This means that out of every seven persons in the world, there is one person who is illiterate. This statistic has terrible implications indeed, but it becomes worse when we assess the situation in the Arab World. The Arab League Educational, Cultural and Scientific Organization (ALECSO), announced in 2001 that there are 68 million illiterates in the

[559]

twenty two member states of the Arab League. This means that one out of every three Arabs is illiterate.

The difference between one-third and one-seventh is huge and glaring but it becomes more significant when we look into the details and scrutinize them. UNESCO's figures for 2000 say that two-thirds of the illiterates in the world are women. Yet the Arab percentage here too is immeasurably higher. Illiteracy among women over 25 years is more than 95% in Yemen and nearly 90% in Morocco and Sudan. It is 80% in Algeria and Egypt. When we translate these percentages into tens of millions of persons, the simultaneous humanitarian, economic and knowledge-related catastrophe becomes reaches a terrifying level.

Science has contributed to the democratization of life generally. For centuries after the fall of Rome, education in Christian Europe remained in the hands of the ecclesiastics. Educational materials were limited to the dogmatic beliefs of the church and only a few people received them. It is not insignificant that electoral rights in many western countries were obtained gradually—first by the learned, male property owners and later extended to all people.

Naturally, the present situation differs from the past. Equality in obtaining knowledge and information has become one of the conditions of democracy. This could not have happened if education had not spread, enabling people to assert theoretical and legal equality and to benefit from it. Democracy, in most cases, is the choice of educated nations exactly as despotism and dictatorship and allegiance to "sincere" leaders are the choices of poorly educated nations.

Attaining such an educational and democratic situation is a remote possibility unless the foundation is laid by deep religious and cultural transformations. Here the link with writing in general comes to the foreground, including the press. For instance, in European history we notice that through their opposition to the authority of the Catholic Church in the sixteenth century and their confirmation of the importance of returning to the scripture, the Protestants committed themselves to translating the Old and New Testaments into the spoken languages of northern and western Europe, subsequently committing themselves to spread its reading among nations. The most significant thing done by Martin Luther is that he had translated the Bible into his native language. In the process of integrating religious and educational imperatives, missionaries later spread out and went wherever European colonialism had reached so that the inhabitants of the colonies could easily read the scripture. After the Second World War and the rise of independent countries this grave concern over illiteracy appeared in the Third World and attained an unprecedented level of urgency. Indeed, eradicating illiteracy became the most important function of the United Nations via UNESCO, which is an affiliated agency. The latter provides member states with financial assistance in addition to coordinating programs, collecting data and research to provide the facts, statistics and professional expertise necessary for eradicating illiteracy.

Yet the problems in this field faced by the Third World, including the Arab world, are difficult to enumerate—shortages in resources and investment, civil wars that block children from attending schools or destroy existing schools, bureaucratic irresponsiveness, lack of basics such as official information about illiteracy, which are generally derived from population statistics and the tables of school registers or lists of volunteers for military service, most of which are not strictly compiled in our countries. Of course, there are always many dangerous cultural curbs. For instance, the Moroccan government announced "a plan for involving women in development" in March 1999. The plan consisted of several arrangements for improving the status quo of women, eradicating illiteracy amongst them and facilitating their involvement in work. However, what angered Islamists about the plan were the proposals relating to family law, such as increasing the age of consent from 15 to 18, division of properties in case of divorce, in addition to not making it obligatory for women to have a guardian to represent them during the wedding contract. They viewed this initiative as a movement to "shatter the Islamic fundamentals of society." In the end the whole project was abandoned.

In other words, we cannot conceive of the popularity of the press, or its move to gain larger margins of freedom, in the absence of an educated and reading-oriented environment. This weakness in learning results in the mounting power of despotism which capitalizes on the shortage in gender equality, receding tolerance and lack of religious renewal.

The Media and the Role of Arab Bourgeoisie

It difficult in this context not to pay attention to the absence of a certain Arab bourgeois class, which is concerned with broadening the margins of freedom by investing in the media. Such a bourgeois class views its interests and the effecting of structural and progressive transformation as one goal, or at least two intercepting and complementary goals by necessity.

However, such an achievement has many prerequisite conditions, at the head of which is freedom—the freedom of trade and the movement of goods and services. Additionally, what is indispensable is the freedom of expression, criticism and participation in making the political decision itself. If the confrontation against despotism in Europe began with raising the slogan "No taxation without representation," the activities of entrepreneurs and businessmen in our region are still weakly linked to the authority and are sometimes even non-existent. Despotism in the final analysis is nothing but the separation between the political entity and other entities in society— cultural, economic and demographic and others. This kind of separation allows the decision-maker to make his decision without recourse to the representatives of these societal activities. This is not to say the ruler ascends to power without consulting them or continues to rule in this way.

In contrast, historical facts in the West point to an element which has not been given due attention—the influence always exercised by businessmen and entrepreneurs. If it is true that the distribution of resources was constantly changing during the stages of growth, this class in particular guarded this process. Many economists in the past considered that the structure of the aforementioned entrepreneurial class and its performance help to explain the differences in the technological progress made from one country to the other. Since decisions made in the field of development relate to the ability to generate new products or new production processes, comparisons are often made between two countries that had benefited from equal amounts of investments but did not generate similar rates of technological development. The reason for this lies in the fact that businessmen in one of the countries depend on more advanced modes in the production process—those that lead to accelerating growth in productivity. By contrast, the same class in the other country is stagnant because of its hesitation or perceived sense of inferiority. Thus the activity of the latter group amounts to no more than slight changes in the production process, and the resulting growth in productivity and gross national product is negligible. Among the famous comparative examples is the perception after the Second World War about the assertive and aggressive nature of the German businessmen when compared with their British counterparts.

The focus on the role of the entrepreneurial class in economic growth stems from the research effort of the economist Joseph Schumpeter whose work later became a frame of reference for many books on economics. Schumpeter, for instance, maintained that this class is the driving force of progress and the intrusive element which imbalances existing economic equations and lays the foundation for new and finer ones. In the final analysis, what determines the beginning and end of economic cycles or what he called the "long waves," which extend from 40 to 50 years, is the role of the entrepreneurial class and its responsiveness. If Schumpeter has reviewed what he considered harmful effects of inherited wealth and some who favor the dynamism of self-made men have appeared in the scene, this does not rule out the fact that inherited wealth, just like the wealth of self-made men, plays individual roles which can be described as historic.

[563]

Here is embedded the historical mission of the bourgeoisie as a class which changes the world. Here we also find the difference between the bourgeoisie and the "rich men" who go through life without a historic mission which fulfills their interests and serves people in general.

These rich men constitute the great majority of the class of Arab entrepreneurs, who have not originally addressed the question of transforming themselves into a bourgeois class. The majority of them have been shaped by the state in contrast to the classic western scenario where social classes themselves shaped the state. This being so, these rich men have generally been attached to interests given to them by the ruler or the governing regime to the extent that challenging the status quo has become a threat to their interests.

The reality in the Arab world has been nurtured on the weakness of capitalist accumulation in our countries. Developments happened swiftly without being accompanied by notable thought and societal transformations. Or what happened was confined to importing influences without developing a local environment to accommodate them. Challenging and changing the status quo never featured on the agenda of rich Arabs whose interest in culture remained limited. This absence has allowed the spread of a vast populist culture which considers that the only "hero" is the military, political and religious leader and links wealth and trade to looting and theft.

True the merchants and rich men of the Arab world have sought roles to play in their countries. However, their efforts have generally dissipated due to being focused in the wrong place. In the field of media, these efforts have been restricted to a modest presence that is only matched by the limited ambition attached to these efforts. The Arab world has seen two waves of businessmen. The first wave was manifested in the Samsonite briefcase-carrying businessmen in the 1970s, who benefited from the four-fold oil price in that decade. The second wave was represented by those who capitalized on the new technological economics in the 1990s. Yet the two waves remained foreign: members of the first wave became a small segment in a wider global class, most of whose profits are employed abroad. What has made the situation more exasperating is the fact that the wealth of the members of this wave are derived from oil which does not provide many job opportunities despite its huge revenues, and the revenue from contracts and undertakings that do not continue for long after completion. In both cases, the integration of this activity into the core of society remains marginal as it neither affects this core nor changes it. The new technological economics is in its infancy in the Arab countries and there are still major obstacles to its spread. These relate to the nature of societies, the economies and the cultures themselves. In brief, the mission of change and reinforcing freedom is an issue of urgency for Arab societies.

The result of all this is that media investment is a field that is left to the regimes and those close to them who believe that preserving the status quo is a prerequisite for the continuity of their concessions and interests. Alternatively, it is left to the major political and ideological powers which feed on the ideas prevailing in society. This relegates journalists, writers and intellectuals to a position more akin to orphans who are only half fed. Since the work of Rifa'a Al-Tahtawi and Ahmed Faris Shidyaq in *Al Waqae Al Masriyyah* newspaper, the tragedy has been repeated and is likely to continue until writers and critics join state-owned newspapers.

In conclusion, it is hoped that the points raised in the foregoing discussion would serve to provide a wider and more accurate understanding of the kinds of repression to which the press is subjected from various sources.

New Challenges for the State's Influence on the Media

Abdullah Al-Olayan

When the Arab state was constituted and its authority and moral identity were established after the collapse of the Ottoman Caliphate in the first half of the twentieth century, the traditional pre-independence Arab state, and later the Arab nation-state which replaced it after independence, controlled the media and its different channels. The media was in the grasp of the state, which generally directed it in matters pertaining to the execution of its policies and political orientations.[1]

During that stage the Arab media was rather unsophisticated in its tools, instruments and effects on the public. It was also in an undeveloped state owing to the absence of freedom and the lack of a planned media mission. The official aim of the media was to enhance the authority of the state, justifying and defending its declared ideas, policies and plans to implement them. During that time the governments controlled the entire media and its relative impact on Arab public opinion.[2]

The Sole Means of Information

Some researchers maintain that dependence on a single, one-sided media channel throws doubt on its efficacy in influencing public opinion. This is so because it may promote impressionistic images, or sometimes distorted patterns or images biased in favor of a certain party. If the recipient fails to measure the accuracy of this image by comparing it with another specific standard other than media channels, the perception developed by the individual on the basis of such information also becomes distorted, stereotypical and biased.[3]

A media official and theoretician believes that building a state, with all its economic, social and political components, requires the help of various media channels. This could be done through information exchange between persons or between organized groups, or by mass media such as the press, publications, radio, television, cinema and other arts. In this regard, as with other affairs, achieving such media expectations depends on the determination, honesty and fairness of the people concerned. These things cannot be realized except through the media itself. There is nothing novel in this notion. The ancient Greek philosopher Aristotle maintained that friendly action is a necessary condition to achieve good communication between people. He also maintained that people cannot live together if they do not respect one another.[4]

Despite this, the Arab media remained weak in its institutions and the limited availability of qualified cadres to carry out its important multi-faceted role. There has been discussion for decades about the need to establish a new framework, which could create a new Arab media and communications system to combat the existing imbalance between the global media and the Arab media:

> [To] create a mutual channel for different aspects of intellectual production and information with the objective of creating opportunities for recognition and understanding, first within societies and then between nations in general. This system requires a group of choices and procedures at the international level. However, the desired change will not take place unless the steps taken abroad are accompanied by profound reformation efforts in the concerned societies in order to avoid shortcomings and discrepancies on the basis of new concepts of cooperation.

> The basics of this system at different levels and in different domains can be built only on the principle of the freedom of expression and publication and a wide and balanced flow of news and information of different kinds. At the national level, it advocates changing many situations at the level of existing relations between the ruled and the ruling, between the rural and urban populations, between men and women, and between different social classes within the territories of one country.[5]

[568]

Interaction with Developments

The interaction with the new media requirements in today's world has been legitimate and positive. This could have been achieved if Arab media officials had realized at an early stage its importance for the progress of the Arab media and its development in the light of major transformations in the media and other fields. As Mustafa Al Masmodi maintains, one problem was that the Arab media proved unequal to the mission entrusted to it. This mission may be described as follows:

> [To] deepen the consciousness of the Arab citizen and enhance his cultural identity, his integration and participation in society. Perhaps, at times, the Arab media was partly responsible for the confusion, inconstancy and contradictions of the Arab citizen. The media was assigned an unfamiliar task and it helped to consolidate conflict and divisiveness instead of supporting brotherly ties between the Arabs, enhancing vital relations between Arab people in different Arab countries, defending just Arab causes, and contributing to the programs of developing Arab societies.[6]

These policies have weakened the Arab media's role in influencing Arab citizens although the constant refrain of some Arab governments is about the constant concern for the Arab citizen, as well as his role and importance as the driving force at every crucial stage and turning point. However, the fact is that the Arab citizen is not involved in the steps taken towards these achieving these ends. Consequently, disasters have struck him from all sides.

This course of action in the Arab media system, which is controlled by the governments, has bred implications and objectives that lack sound planning. They focus merely on local affairs:

> Propaganda and consumption patterns prevail in comparison with the objectives of education and acculturation. Moreover, the dialects and lifestyles of Arab urban areas and capitals take the upper hand. Generally Arab media channels accommodate official viewpoints only; they are uni-directional with information flowing from the authority to the public. It is rare to produce and exchange any media or information content without subjecting it to a degree of censorship whose intensity varies from one country to the other.[7]

Some think that despite the potential of the official Arab media, some of its institutions have remained stagnant in terms of development and modernization of media facilities. There is also a lack of adequate care in maintaining and upgrading professional aspects. Certain media personnel are inefficient because professional standards are not observed in their selection. Sometimes, other standards such as nepotism and personal relationships are followed. Such personnel acquire experience merely through trial and error. Often their experience remains confined to narrow domains and exhibits a low level of professionalism. They move within a domain with limited horizons and lack moral and material incentives for improving their work. This fact does not encourage them to enhance their performance, especially in the absence of professional values and the spirit of competition. Often good and bad media output are treated equally. In other cases diligent people face difficulties (when their output is overlooked and they are denied opportunities) whereas incompetent and weak people are rewarded if they have personal and friendly relationships with the management.[8]

Lack of Technology

Developments in media and communications have occurred on a wide scale and this has resulted in the rise of satellite channels with certain technological capabilities and potential. This has enhanced the authority of the televised image and the influence of the visual media in particular. Consequently, there is a perception of danger and threat among weak nations because the modern media is capable of spreading patterns of life and behavior that are dominant in advanced countries. Perhaps what justifies this sense of danger is the awareness of the fragility of local media systems and their general lack of professionalism and perfection in making and broadcasting images, imbued with the ability to penetrate public opinion and influence it. These systems remain captive to content imported from abroad and are stifled by the burden of official censorship and self-censorship. On the other hand, the Arab media suffers from certain shortcomings and reveals an inability to project the image of the

[570]

Arab world. Other media channels do this in way which abuses and highly distorts the Arab image.[9]

With modern technological development and the emergence of a vast wealth of information, existing media balances and fundamentals have been overturned to such an extent that no government department, authority or institution can ban or neutralize this technological revolution or deny information access to others. Hence many governments have begun to lose control and influence over the flow of media information to the people in general. Communication technology has allowed the penetration of national borders and barriers and offers the chance to compete with other countries in broadcasting and coverage.

Thus "the global media community" and its influence have become a tangible, undeniable fact. Accordingly, some maintain that future developments will witness a notable decline in national sovereignty and national culture:

> The reason for this is that modern communication technology allows individuals access to multiple media and cultural domains without being subject to the will of the state and its media and cultural policies. This openness and its attendant information flow, which is intentionally directed towards the audience (recipients), must be so influential to the extent that the recipient becomes linked to a common stock of knowledge with the other source—a source which may affect this recipient's behavior and thought more than it affects his original identity.

> Perhaps the most dangerous transformations are represented in what the media does in shaping particular patterns of human behavior and in marginalizing others via the image and its symbols. According to these transformations, advanced countries realized the importance of these media roles as an alternative to democratic practices, especially since media channels have occupied the realm reserved for democratic practices. This realm has now become specific to the media. Therefore, the media no longer represents the fourth estate. Rather, it occupies the apparent realm between political and cultural action and the public reaction.[10]

Many of those concerned with the intellectual and cultural effects of globalization believe that these major developments in media and communication will change the world through greater interaction with other cultures by virtue of information and media channels. However,

[571]

according to them, the problems stem from the fact that traditional cultures will not survive in the face of cultures armed with the means of penetration.

> The culture of the Information Age does not recognize borders. Moreover, the individual culture that we seek to protect is not something clear and tangible like contemporary culture. It is rather unspecified and based on a verbal environment. It might be possible to criticize contemporary technological culture. However, this culture must be practiced before being criticized. Is it possible to adopt contemporary culture with its technologies without abandoning our traditional and inherited culture in accordance with the best solution? In other words, is it possible to reconcile traditions with technology or apply the principle of maintaining both originality and contemporaneity? Applying this principle means that our contemporary culture and identity will change and will not be as before and hence we will be in constant change because in the final analysis we must cope and coexist with changes in a manner that alters old concepts and behaviors.[11]

The Retreat of Sovereignty

The indications are that the world of informatics and the globalized media will expand to compete with the state in some areas of its authority, especially in the realm of the media, its effect on public opinion and its technological potential for global penetration and corresponding weakening of national sovereignty. Massive networks of powerful alliances and hegemony will operate via multinational companies and under cover of the World Trade Organization and other institutions that undermine sovereignty, especially through penetration by the media and information technology. Joseph Nye and William Owens, in an article published in the April 1996 issue of *Foreign Affairs* magazine, observe that it will be easy for the United States to control the world politically in the near future. This is so because of its unparalleled ability to integrate complex information systems. The authors of this American viewpoint clarify the extent to which national sovereignty has been eroded by information penetration via satellite televisions and the Internet. Countries with traditional systems of sovereignty are no longer capable of blocking their national spaces against the invasion of culture and information. This used to be achieved by traditional sovereign measures such as blocking geographical borders against foreign invasion. Some experts have described this global phenomenon as "soft power" which can achieve its colonial objectives on a large scale without provoking classical revolutionary reactions by the countries whose national dignity is abused, sovereignty violated and territories occupied.[12]

Some scholars maintain that effects on national sovereignty are not determined by the realms of media, information and economics. These effects extend to other more serious realms such as culture and national identity by creating new behavioral patterns and concepts which might contradict firm and established traditions.

> True, information technology has shortened the distances between different parts of the world and between its inhabitants by providing them with information and offering opportunities for learning and acculturation to all within the context of developing human society. To achieve this development, the culture spread by technology shapes the contours of human character and identity. Being a universal culture that is not identified with one particular region or country, it creates a individual with a more universal outlook, opposed to any form of particularity or originality. The basis of this is the multiplicity and differences in the cultures of various races and nations. By doing so it imposes its own thought pattern—which can be described as uni-directional.[13]

However, some people differ with this vision of dissemination. They believe that the new culture spread by technology will benefit other nations that do not possess many economic, or social or technological capabilities. Moreover, this development will help in erasing differences between nations and enhancing the rules of human solidarity.

> However, the positivity of this development stirs the fear of the death of the cultures that seem backward and incapable of satisfying the basic needs of man when compared with the universal culture. The efficacy of any new culture in substituting its values for prevalent values and making them a source of conduct depends on the ability of its economic system to satisfy basic needs and to provide individuals with compensation. Since the universal culture is a western culture because its source is rich countries that possess technology, the pervasiveness of its values in countries of the South seems inexorable if the cultures of the South do not try to confront it by developing their scientific and technological bases.[14]

The Free Flow of Information

No doubt the Information Revolution and free media exchange in today's world will in one form or another reduce considerably the influence of Arab states and governments on the media. This will help to crystallize new concepts of this free flowing media. Although some countries are presently capable of restricting – if only to a partial extent – the flow of media and information coming from abroad, this capability will recede and may disappear in the future, when confronted with tens of satellites competing in space.[15]

This flow of media and information will be clearly imbalanced because of the gap between the abilities of advanced countries and Arab nations in the fields of media and technology. It will leave its mark and have a huge impact on individuals. At the same time, the role of the Arab state will weaken owing to the information flowing in through new media technologies.

> [It is no longer] possible to speak today of information sovereignty within the political borders of the state or of controlling the flow of information within these borders and consequently forming the mindset of citizens single-handedly, in a manner that guarantees total loyalty to the state, as was the case before the collapse of the communist system under the domination of the former Soviet Union. This is particularly so because the influence of the Information Revolution has negatively encompassed all the constituents of the state—recognized political borders, people and government. The controlling of the flow of information has become almost impossible since information has been transformed into intangible and invisible elements which are easy to convey and can penetrate any geographical borders regardless of the quality, quantity and degree of protection against this modern media flow.[16]

Sabir Falhoot and Muhammad al Bukhari maintain that this free flow – despite some of its positive aspects – is nothing more than a uni-directional flow of information which serves the interests of the advanced industrial countries that control modern means of communication. They maintain that developing countries are very concerned about this painful reality, which is embodied in the control of advanced industrial countries over modern means of communication and news sources, and the fact that they employ these to further their own interests and propaganda at the expense of the national interests of the developing countries, which are economically, technologically and scientifically incapable of solving this dilemma. In their view, international information exchange is a vertical exchange in itself, which does not provide the conditions for horizontal exchange between all the countries of the world. For the most part, it is a uni-directional information flow and a one-sided viewpoint of the dominant party.

According to Professor Johan Galtung's model of the center and the margin, the world is divided into two unequal parts: the dominant "center" represented by advanced industrial countries which are few in number, and the "margin" which is less developed, backward and represents the subordinate in the model. The margin interacts with vertical, international information exchange from the top (advanced, industrial countries) to the bottom (less developed countries and developing ones).[17]

The End of Monopoly on Information

This media and information development, as well as the multiplicity of open space media in the Arab domain, such as satellite channels and the Internet, have erased the authorities' monopoly on news and information.

> The principle of hiding truths from the citizens has been annulled. In the past, the authorities, by means of monopolizing and controlling the means of local information and their vast influence on means of external information, especially the print media, had the ability to hide incidents from the Arab citizen, if only for a definite period and regardless of their sensational nature, or to provide half truths and summarized information.

> Under the influence of the revolution in satellite channels and the Internet, the authorities have been forced to take the initiative in informing citizens of the details of any event without delay. This is done, not out of respect for the citizen's right to know but for fear that other "competitive" and "hostile" sources might broadcast the news or information before the authorities concerned do so, and in a distorted or exaggerated form. This would do a disservice to the authority and embarrass it with respect to local and international public opinion. The rules governing the Arab media, which state that it is unnecessary to inform the Arab citizen the details of

happenings in his homeland immediately, have failed the test of Arab and international satellite channels and the Internet. Currently there is a race between the state media and its affiliated commercial agencies and other sources of external information, with the Arab citizen gaining the benefits arising from such competition as well as the struggle between political interests.[18]

This situation has led to the collapse of state monopoly on media channels and enabled some companies and individuals to found privately owned satellite channels and newspapers. This has happened because of the new global regimes in the world affecting the legislation involved in obtaining licenses to establish visual, audio and printed media institutions. This is especially true of the potential for Arab satellite broadcasting either from the western world or from certain Arab countries without restraints or difficulties which limit the independence and freedom of the institution in dealing with information.

Though the revolution in modern technology has brought down the traditional fetters which used to limit the freedom, independence and credibility of Arab media channels, it has created new problems which are not less complex and serious than the old ones. The core problem that needs to be addressed is how to deal with information under the free circumstances created by the technological revolution.[19]

Some disagree with the view that the age of globalization and informatics signals the end of the state. They argue that the weakness of the state and its declining influence do not mean the end of the state or the end of geography.

Rather, the concept of regional territories and their relationship with sovereignty have changed. Also, the nature of the state itself has profoundly changed after globalization has eroded the borders of their absolute function and reduced their political, economic and social role in the light of the flow of relationships that transcend these borders. These are represented by financial 'networks,' economic exchanges, media broadcasting, migration of individuals, religious, cultural and linguistic networks, as well networks of non-governmental organizations. The principle of territorial sovereignty is now confronting the world of networks. The former presupposes isolationism and exclusion whereas the latter is based on openness and profit.[20]

[576]

Merely stating this view, does not suggest a simple solution to deal with the new, rapid changes wrought by the globalized media. The issue is not only one of openness to the world. This new development is a cosmic reversal in which familiar concepts such as rationality, morality, human rights, democracy, the right of existence, and the right to be different have all changed. These concepts no longer preserve their original, conventional purity. They are now relative concepts full of impurities being subject to and driven simultaneously by competition and conflict between the forces of pressure, influence and interest.

Everything in the world has become open to the boundless ether. There is nothing to inhibit man from succumbing to the attraction of the voice and the image except his sense of commitment and entrenched rejection on the basis of civilization, culture and religion. However, all this depends on very complex mechanisms of conflict. Both the mighty and the weak must engage in an endless war—the former for hegemony and possession and the latter to preserve identity and the right to freedom.[21]

Imbalance in Media Systems

There can be no balance as long as there is a huge difference between what Arabs possess in terms of potential and experiences and the economic and technological capabilities of others. This stems from the lack of developed media systems accompanied by well planned modern methods and an expanded base of progress in various spheres. The process of achieving a balance between the Arab media and the media in advanced countries is not possible under present circumstances.

> [Arab media] must rely on scientific bases derived from media planning, which is capable of understanding the abilities of the present media channels, becoming aware of media potential and rectifying its old flaws. Successful media is based on understanding the permanent and the transient in the work of the media; in addition to an exceptional ability to calculate possibilities. At times of crises the media needs to plan a campaign targeting public opinion and achieving the desired effect.

> The media task goes beyond the mere communication of public opinion trends. It also involves forming public opinion; otherwise media channels will play the role of carrier pigeons whose task is confined to carrying messages from one party to the other.[22]

[577]

For these reasons, well-planned strategies for the Arab media need to be crystallized if it is to cope with the circumstances and changes associated with the globalized media and the age of informatics. This will reduce losses in the sphere of the written word, which can master the mind and thought of the reader and viewer in this age.

Escapism, isolation and seclusion will mean losing ground in the field of media influence as viewed from the perspective of openness and technological penetration. Arab governments have to accept the challenge and confront the reality of the new media by benefiting from communication technologies and informatics, devising a media strategy capable of dealing positively with developments, viewing these challenges with rationality, awareness and openness while exploiting the available opportunities arising from this accelerated information flow.[23]

In addition, the official Arab media will face challenges at an unprecedented level of competition. This may exceed expectations of what things will be like in the coming decades. This reality may lead to reviewing many theoretical fundamentals generally accepted by the global media, especially the impact caused by means of communication.

> The Bullet Theory, the Limited Effect Theory, the Moderate Effect Theory and the Powerful Effect Theory all do not respond to understanding the influence of communication on the recipient because they have originated in different contexts and concentrate on some changes and leave out others. Thus a vision of the effect of media channels on the recipient calls for a more comprehensive view to understand the impact of these media channels.[24]

Following this line of thought, previously established theories, ideas and realities will collapse because of the effect of these new developments and novelties.

Conclusions

The Information Revolution that has swept our age has made the world a global village, interconnected in terms of media and information. It is no longer possible to ban or block the imbalanced information flow between a capable global media and the Arab media. Hence, in the media sphere, the influence of some countries will be reduced in favor of countries with a stronger effect, which are capable of conveying information, spreading it and penetrating the open media space. This will limit the authority of the nation-state and its influence on the Arab world. Many actors in the Arab media system will play multiple roles in this free space, whether or not such functions are appreciated.

True, this development does not mean an end to the authority of the state, or reducing its major role in the legal, legislative and administrative domains. However, the new circumstances, variables and transformations will pose many challenges to these states, impelling them to interact with, and respond to, the wishes of the citizens in matters pertaining to the freedom of communication, flow of information and possessing media channels.

For this reason, I believe that the coming stage will favor media openness and free, accelerated – and sometimes uncontrolled – information flow. The task of governments is to facilitate this flow and organize its activities if possible, to emerge with the minimum losses incurred by this massive flow.

In this stage, I think that the positive contribution that Arab governments can make is to support and expand media choices and alternatives by allowing the establishment of strong and independent Arab media institutions that distance themselves from the direct influence of governments. These institutions should possess credibility, and hold a free and disciplined discourse which preserves professional ethics in order to win Arab and other audiences. These Arab media institutions will then be in a position to compete with other institutions and deal with the developments of the age in the realms of freedom, democracy, self-reform and the positive review of media policy. This is what is at stake and what we can rely on in the future.

28

The Imminent Collapse
of the Controlled Media

Abdullah Rasheed

At the outset, it should be noted that there are two types of media—the government-run (or controlled) media and the free media. As the first is subject to official scrutiny and censorship, it is no longer suited to the present era. Indeed, in the midst of the changes the world is witnessing, this type of media has become a legacy of the past when modern and sophisticated communication technologies were not yet available.

For many, such a reality might be annoying, or even irksome, but by refusing to perceive it, we will fail to cope with the rapid and successive transformations taking place in the world today. In order to realize the magnitude and power of the approaching hurricane, it is worthwhile to note that a new application in information and communication technology is introduced into the market every 15 days!

In order to comprehend the real meaning of the term "change." we will have to know the instruments that can bring about the required changes. The most important of such instruments is the deep-rooted convention that the transformation of a society into a modern, developed and civilized form will not occur in the absence of a free, balanced, open-minded and responsible media.

Despite the warnings of thinkers, intellectuals and all those concerned about the threat of "changes coming from abroad," "the Greater Middle East," "Western-style change," "imported Western democracy," or any

[581]

other concepts that have surfaced in the last few years, such changes are inevitable. At any rate, positive changes can only be realized through a free and alert media.

The effect of the developments and imperatives that accompany globalization is that change must begin with the mass media which is responsible for stimulating social progress and consolidating fundamental freedoms—particularly the freedom of communication and expression as well as freedom of publications and association. These freedoms cannot be obtained by the official, controlled media when the consequences of their failures are still being felt in Arab media circles.

Here the reference is not exclusively to the print media. The phenomenal progress achieved in the field of information technologies, has aligned all forms of mass media in a single bloc, so that it is incorrect to say that one particular medium can eclipse the role of other media. For example, when the radio stations appeared early 1930s, it was feared that this invention would put an end to the print media, or even jeopardize the whole journalism industry. Though these stations disseminate the news even before the printing machines start running, they failed to eliminate the print media. Indeed, the latter has maintained its status alongside other mass media even after the invention of the audio-visual medium of television (which marked the second revolution in the field of informatics).

The third qualitative stride came when the 1991 Gulf War broke out. Outer space has now effectively become the theater of conflict, and the whole world watched CNN broadcasting satellite war footage obtained through reporters deployed on the ground. Today, outer space is crowded with thousands of satellites that have ushered in the era of space channels along with the remarkable development of mobile phones as another vital communication technology. This was followed by the momentous invention which we call the Internet. The Internet era has witnessed the spread of electronic papers that are instantly communicated to their readers through this network.

This huge technological stride has highlighted two significant phenomena that the Arab controlled media has failed to perceive. The first is the ease by which the Arab recipient can gain access to the information suppressed by the censored state-owned media. The second is the threat that the Internet poses to the print media. The latter has not remained idle and has created its own websites through which the majority of international newspapers are reaching their readers, particularly those who are unable to obtain true information from the official media because of meaningless censorship.

The Essential Nature of Challenges

To comprehend the real nature of the challenges that the Arab media is confronting, we must understand the above mentioned realities and recognize that forthcoming changes will not be halted by backward mass media and obsolete legislation. Moreover, given the weakened conditions of the Arab mass media, there must be an extensive review of its role in determining our behavior towards major causes and in the development of our societies. This review should enable the Arab media to encounter imminent difficulties and obstacles and cope with the transformations wrought by globalization, especially in the wake of the Information Revolution and considerable changes taking place all over the world including the Arab region.

The bitter state of affairs of the Arab media can be illustrated by stating some of the facts highlighted in the annual reports of UN specialized agencies and the World Bank, as well as some western independent media outlets. For example, there are around 520 daily and weekly papers in the entire Arab world, almost equal to the number published in Pakistan, a poor developing country. It is worth noting that only sixty two children's magazines are published in the entire Arab world, of which only a dozen can be identified as "pan-Arab" while the rest are locally distributed. This number is less than half of the 180 children's magazines circulated in a small country like Denmark with a population of just 5 million.

Despite the existence of over 125 around-the-clock Arab satellite channels, surveys have shown that nearly 75% of their programming is devoted to light entertainment, whereas other countries are keen to launch specialized channels focusing on technological, scientific, educational and other purposes.

Has the official Arab media revealed the fact that all the Arab states spend less than 0.5% of their gross national product on providing education and health care to children? Or that the literacy percentage among children in poor, densely populated Arab societies could only reach 57%? Or that 62% of Arab children live below the poverty line, and around 32 million of them are suffering from malnutrition? Or that every year, 1.25 million Arab children die before reaching the age of 5 years? Or that 9 million Arab children do not attend school? Moreover, in one Arab country about 1 million children (7–11 year olds) are employed for ten weeks of every year (working 11 hours a day, every day of the week) to manually remove cotton worms from the crop.

The Totalitarian Ideology

The controlled media is the product of a totalitarian dictatorial ideology inspired initially by Fascism and Nazism, followed by socialism after the Second World War. Arab Nationalism has followed this ideology in the mistaken belief that it constitutes the perfect path that leads to the "Arab development stage," which proved to be a stage of retardation and defeats. In the meantime, the Arab media was dependent, restricted and government-run, whose only task was to draw a false, improved image of the prevailing misery and sufferings. Hence, the crisis in the Arab media stems from the Arab political system as a whole.

Such a totalitarian ideology does not create a free mass media, and its advocates tend to praise and defend it and defame opposing ideologies. Unfortunately, the two camps that have dominated the media during the so-called "nationalist wave" period and in the 1970s and 1980s are the Arab Nationalists and political Islam movements. Both have sought to mobilize all sorts of mass media to further bolster their ideologies. These attempts have resulted in retarding the media, the effects of which are still being felt today, including the almost total absence of all fundamental freedoms. For example, the Tunisian President endorsed a new law in 2004 (adopted during the October general elections that year) prohibiting opposition parties from making statements to satellite channels during their election campaigns! Obviously, the law reflects the Tunisian authorities' intention to curb the influence of media organizations, particularly Arab satellite channels, on the election process.

The US Freedom House organization, in its 2002 annual report on Freedom of the Press in the world (which rates each country's media as "Free," "Partly Free," or "Not Free"), stated that only two Arab states (Kuwait and Morocco) are "Partly Free," and that all other states are "Not Free," according to the criteria adopted by the organization.

The French organization "Reporters Without Borders" in its October 2004 report on the freedom of the press in the world has rated the Middle East region as "the worst in the world" (after East Asia) in terms of freedoms of the press, opinion and expression. Arab states occupied the tail-end of the Report's listing, which ranked 167 world states in terms of freedom of the press. None of the Arab countries figured within the first hundred states except for Lebanon which is rated 87th in the list.

The Guardian of the People!

Today, the government-run media no longer has any influence or role to play, or even a future. The world has become a global village where people communicate quickly and easily through highly developed information and communication technologies.

[585]

The government media's approach is based on the naive idea that the people are "not mature enough" to understand life and unable to identify either their goals or priorities. Hence, they have to comply with what is dictated to them by their governments. According to that backward notion, people need to be guided, and it is not surprising that Arab government-controlled media gives itself the status of the "guardian" of thought and attitudes, selectively and arbitrarily giving or depriving people of information.

As a result of these oppressive media policies, people have surrendered to the whims of the state-controlled media, acting according to its commands or bans. Not surprisingly the government departments in charge of official media were until recently given absurd and eccentric titles, like the "Ministry of Guidance"! Obviously, such a title harbors a symbolic connotation implying that the media's main task is guiding and instructing the people and even "thinking" on their behalf!

The general philosophy of the totalitarian media, as imitated by the Arab political regimes from the communist ideology of the Cold War era, is based on the narrow and limited understanding of the concept of "circulation of information." The mission designed for this type of media is to "fabricate" a stance identical to the official one, to "unify" all points of views, and create an environment where the individual must yield obediently to what they are told to do.

At the same time, the government media has sought to dismiss information coming from abroad by distorting established facts and twisting the original news wording with a view to tailoring the information in line with what is intended for the Arab recipient to receive.

Today, these outdated policies are no longer fruitful or effective enough to confront the massive revolution in information technologies which has swept the whole world.

To sum up, if the official state-controlled media has not already crumbled, its collapse is quite imminent!

29

Arab Governments and Intervention in the Media

Ahmad Abdul Aziz Al-Jarallah

When addressing the issue of the impact of Arab governments on the Arab media, it must be said at the outset that it was the Arab governments that created and supported the Arab media as an industry and a field of activity. At the same time, they enacted the unfair, restrictive laws that regulate media functions and prevent it from overstepping the limits set by governments. Not content with controlling their domestic media organizations, some of these governments also sought to interfere and influence the media organizations of other Arab countries through bribery and other corrupt practices.

By contrast, Western governments support the media only as part of a civil society structure and not as a propaganda agency working under their administrations. The media in many Western states is financed by the taxes paid by citizens who therefore have the right to freely express their demands and opinions through print, audio and visual media outlets.

In the past, the Arab world has witnessed two cases of advanced media developed by free civil societies—a media that represented different segments of society, spoke on behalf of all its political parties and propounded their political programs and social demands. The first case was the media experience in Lebanon before the outbreak of the civil war, and the second case was in Egypt before the Free Officers seized power in the Revolution of 1952. With the exception of these two cases, regimes

[587]

that may be considered revolutionary and authoritarian have reduced the media to a tool serving their political objectives, and substituted credible media reporting and dissemination of knowledge with what may be termed "cheerleading" and disinformation. As for other traditional regimes, the view expressed was that the setting up of media organizations was intended to counter the "threat" posed by the media outlets of the so-called revolutionary and authoritarian regimes and to protect the public.

This aspect became particularly apparent during my tenure as Editor-in-Chief when the decision was made to begin circulating the *As Siyassah* newspaper outside Kuwait. The paper was subjected to strict censorship. According to the Kuwaiti authorities, this censorship was necessary "in order to defend local public opinion." Such views are indicative of the reluctance of the authorities to allow their societies to know what is happening in other countries and their desire to control the information made available to the public. This version of journalism creates a press that avoids criticizing the leadership, the government or the state, and abides by the government's instructions even if they prove to be incorrect.

During the period preceding the 1967 War, when the *As Siyassah* newspaper published articles about the military strength of Israel in relation to that of Arab countries and the imbalance of power between them, its journalists were accused by the state-run press of being traitors, claiming that their reports were intended to glorify the enemy's power and demoralize the Arabs. However, in the wake of the Arab defeat (a "setback," according the state-run media) in the war, Arab governments removed the ban they had previously imposed on press reports about Israel, based on the principle of "Know Your enemy." This measure was seen at the time as a step towards expanding the margin of media freedom.

Since the Law No. 3 (1961) on Press and Publications was issued in Kuwait, there have been ongoing disputes between the government and newspaper organizations, as the former could not envisage the existence of a "Fourth Estate." However, press freedom was broader in Kuwait than in other Arab states, and thanks to the independence of the Kuwaiti judiciary, rulings issued in cases filed by the government against the media were fairly just. Indeed, with the passage of time, they have become basic articles and provisions of the law. Hence, media freedom has become a matter of concern even for governments, which have already permitted a certain margin of freedom.

Therefore, those who work in this field will have to keep up a sustained struggle to ensure complete freedom of the media, and to achieve greater progress in order to erase the dominance of governments over the Arab media, as democracy in the Arab world is still a matter for debate and discussion, and has yet to become a reality on the ground. However, despite this gloomy assessment of the Arab media scene, there are currently some "bright spots," where some Arab media entities are aware that they have no alternative but to associate themselves with civil society organizations. On the other hand, thanks to modern information and communications technologies, a climate of optimism is prevailing over the future of the Arab media, and I believe that the next few years will witness the growth of an impartial and powerful Arab media that will truly represent the "Fourth Estate."

H.H. SHEIKH MOHAMMED BIN RASHID AL MAKTOUM, the Vice President and Prime Minister of the UAE and Ruler of Dubai, is the third of four sons of the late H.H. Sheikh Rashid bin Sa'eed Al Maktoum. Born in 1949, H.H. Sheikh Mohammed grew up under the care and guardianship of the Al Maktoum family, the ruling family of the Emirate of Dubai. When he was four, his father H.H. Sheikh Rashid, taught him the basics of Arabic and Islamic teachings. In 1955, H.H. Sheikh Mohammed joined Al Ahmadiya School to complete his elementary education, and in 1965 received his secondary school diploma with distinction. In August 1966, H.H. Sheikh Mohammed joined the Bell School of Languages in Cambridge, UK. Thereafter, he completed his military studies at the Mons Officer Cadet School in the United Kingdom. After his graduation, H.H. Sheikh Rashid appointed H.H. Sheikh Mohammed in November 1968 to his first official post as Head of Dubai Police and General Security Department. In 1971, H.H. Sheikh Mohammed was appointed Minister of Defense in the first federal government. At that stage he was also assigned the task of administering several large projects in Dubai, the most important being the Dubai Drydocks, the biggest in the Middle East, and Dubai International Airport (1977). He was also in charge of handling oil-related issues in Dubai.

In 1995, H.H. Sheikh Maktoum bin Rashid Al Maktoum, in his capacity as Ruler of Dubai, appointed H.H. Sheikh Mohammed as Crown Prince of the Emirate of Dubai. Keen to transform Dubai into an international trade and tourist hub, H.H. Sheikh Mohammed in this capacity launched various pioneering initiatives that have consolidated his leading role in the development and modernization of the Emirate. Among these projects are the Dubai Shopping Festival (1995); Dubai Internet City (2000); Dubai Media City (2001); Dubai Electronic Government (October, 2001); the Palm Island Project (2001) the ultimate tourism project; the Dubai International Financial Centre and Dubai Healthcare City (2002); the Knowledge Village (2003); and the Dubai Land project

[591]

(2004). In the TIME/CNN Global Business Influentials survey conducted in December 2004, H.H. Sheikh Mohammed was chosen as one of the world's 10 most influential business leaders.

On January 4, 2006, H.H. Sheikh Mohammed bin Rashid Al Maktoum assumed the reins of government in the Emirate of Dubai, and became Vice President and Prime Minister of the UAE, succeeding his brother the late H.H. Sheikh Maktoum Bin Rashid Al Maktoum.

H.H. SHEIKH ABDULLAH BIN ZAYED AL NAHYAN was appointed the Foreign Minister of the UAE in February 2006. Prior to this, he was the Minister of Information and Culture of the UAE since March 1997. He has been Chairman of the Board of Directors of the Emirates Media Inc. (EMI) since January 1999.

H.H. Sheikh Abdullah was the Under Secretary of the UAE Ministry of Information and Culture from 1995 to 1997, the Chairman of the Annual Conference of Arab Ministers of Culture, the Chairman of the Annual Conference of the GCC Countries from 1998 to 1999. He is the Honorary President of the Abu Dhabi Committee for Classical Music.

H.H. Sheikh Abdullah was awarded a Bachelor of Arts degree in Political Science from the UAE University at Al Ain in 1995.

DR. MOHAMMED AL-SAYYED SAEED is the Deputy Director of the Al-Ahram Center for Political and Strategic Studies (CPSS), Egypt. In 2002 he was the head of *Al Ahram* newspaper's office in the United States. He worked as a Research Advisor at the Cairo Institute for Human Rights Studies from 1990 to 1994, and his experience also includes working in international academic institutions, such as the Center for International Development at the University of Maryland and the Department of Political Science at the University of North Carolina.

Dr. Saeed is the author and co-author of several books on political science and international relations. He has published a considerable number of monographs and papers on economic development and Arab affairs, such as "Arab League and National Security," "The Characterization of Religious Political Movements in the Arab World," and "Human Rights in the Arab World between Ideology and Universal Morality." Dr. Saeed received his BA and MA in Political Science from Cairo University in Egypt. In 1983 he was awarded a Ph.D in Political Science from the University of North Carolina after successfully completing his thesis on "Integration as a Mode of Ethnic Conflict Resolution in Sub-Saharan Africa."

DR. NAOMI SAKR is a Senior Lecturer in Communication in the School of Media, Arts and Design at the University of Westminster. Previously a journalist, editor and country analyst, Dr. Sakr specializes in the political economy of the media in the Arab Middle East, with a particular focus on media policy, media development and human rights. She has written reports for Amnesty International and Article 19 and contributed a background paper for the United Nations Development Program's global *Human Development Report 2002*.

Dr Sakr is the author of *Satellite Realms: Transnational Television, Globalization and the Middle East* (London: I B Tauris, 2002), winner of the Middle Eastern Studies Book Prize 2003 awarded by the British-Kuwait Friendship Society and administered by the British Society for Middle Eastern Studies. Her edited collection, *Women and Media in the Middle East: Power through Self-Expression*, was also published by I.B. Tauris in 2004. She has authored chapters in a number of recent books on subjects such as *Al Jazeera* satellite channel, the making of journalists, media reform, international news, the regionalization of transnational television, and governance in Gulf countries. Her recent academic articles have appeared in journals such as *Critique: Critical Middle Eastern Studies*, *Political Quarterly*, the *Journal of Human Development*, *Transnational Broadcasting Studies*, *Social Research*, *Javnost* and *Gazette*.

DR. KHALED AL-HROUB is the Director of the Cambridge Project for Arab Media, which was established in cooperation with Cambridge University's Center of Middle Eastern and Islamic Studies. He hosts the weekly book review program *The Book: The Best Companion* on *Al*

Jazeera satellite news channel. He also is a former Fellow of Cambridge University's Center of Middle Eastern and Islamic Studies and has participated in the Middle East Program of the London-based International Institute for Strategic Studies (1999–2000). Dr. Khaled Al-Hroub is a frequent commentator on Arab affairs in the British media and a regular contributor to a number of Arab dailies, such as the London-based *Al Hayat*, *Al Quds Al Arabi*, and *Ash Sharq Al Awsat*; the Abu Dhabi-based *Al-Ittihad*; the Doha-based *Ash Sharq*; the Amman-based *Al Ghad*; the Muscat-based *Oman*; and the Cairo-based *Al Qahira*.

Dr. Al-Hroub has authored a number of books and studies, including *Hamas: Political Thought and Practice* (2000), and a chapter in *Democracy and Citizenship in the Arab Countries* (2001). He is the editor of the forthcoming publication *New Media and Politics in the Arab World.* Some of his articles have been published by foreign journals, including the *British Journal of the Middle East, Critique: Critical Middle Eastern Studies, Journal of Palestine Studies, Outre Terre* and *Internationale Politik.*

DR. MUSA SHTEIWI is a lecturer in the Sociology Department and Women's Studies Program at the University of Jordan in Amman. He is the founder and Director of the Jordanian Center for Social Research. His main fields of research are growth, poverty, social policies, social inequality, women and civil society. Dr. Shteiwi gained his Ph.D in Sociology from Cincinnati University, USA in 1991.

Dr. Shteiwi's most important published studies include *Volunteering and Volunteers in the Arab World* (2000), *Gender Roles in School Curricula and Textbooks for the Foundation Stage in Jordan* (editor, 2001), *The Role of Small Projects in the Reduction of Poverty and Unemployment in Jordan* (editor, 2001), *A Report on Social Growth in Jordan* (for 2002 and 2003), *A Critical Review of Poverty Reduction Policies in Jordan* (ESCAW, 1999), and *Jordanian Women and Political Participation* (jointly with Dr. Amal Daghistani, 1995).

DR. ALI MOHAMMED FAKHRO is the Chairman of the Board of Trustees of the Bahrain Centre for Studies and Research. Previously, he held several governmental positions, including Minister of Health (1970–1982)

Minister of Education (1982–1995) and Bahrain's Ambassador to France (1995–2000). Dr. Fakhro was President of the Bahrain Red Crescent Society (1973–1981, 1988–1995); Chairman of the High Council of the Arab Board of Medical Specialties (1983–1987, 1990–1995), Chairman of the Board of Trustees of Bahrain University (1986–1995), Chairman of the Board of Directors of the Arabic *Encyclopedia Arabia* (1990–1991) and the elected President of the International Council for Education of Teachers (ICET) from 1994 to 1998. Dr. Fakhro has written many articles and given interviews on medical, educational, political and cultural aspects. He is a member of several organizations and institutions, including the Executive Board of the World Health Organization and the Executive Board of UNESCO. He is also a Board Member of the Written and Visual Arab Media Awards in Dubai; and a Trustee of the Arab Open University.

Dr. Fakhro received his B.Sc degree from the American University of Beirut (AUB) in 1954, and gained his M.D. from the School of Medicine at the AUB in 1958. He completed his internship from Baylor University Hospital, Dallas, Texas (1958–59), and his residency from the University Hospital, Alabama (1959–61). He is a Fellow in Gastroenterology and Cardiology at the Harvard School of Public Health and the American Board of Internal Medicine (1965).

MR. DAOOD AL-SHIRYAN is the creator and presenter of the "Al Maqal" (Essay) program on the Dubai satellite TV channel. He embarked on his career in journalism even as a student, serving as a freelance editor for the Riyadh-based *Al Yamama* weekly magazine. In 1977, Mr. Al-Shiryan obtained his Bachelor's degree in journalism from King Saud University in Riyadh and became the magazine's Editorial Secretary. In 1980, he became the correspondent for the Associated Press in the Kingdom of Saudi Arabia. In 1986, he left journalism and became a partner in a newly-established company in the field of information and documentation. He was the first publisher to introduce informational CDs in the Arab world.

In 1989, Mr. Al-Shiryan was appointed Editor-in-Chief of *Ad Da'wa* (The Call) magazine, and thereafter became Editor-in-Chief of *Al Muslmoon* international newspaper for two years. From 1987 to 1998 he

[595]

also gave lectures to students of journalism and the media on journalistic reports and articles. In 1993, he began to devote himself to his daily contributions in the Saudi press. He became well-known for his column entitled "Adhaf ul Iman" (The Weakest of Faiths). Mr. Al-Shiryan's writings were banned several times for criticizing the performance of government departments. Between 1998 and 2003 his articles also appeared in *Al Hayat* newspaper.

DR. ALI Q. AL-SHUAIBI is Director of the Security Awareness Department and Media Advisor of the Community Service Department at Dubai Police Headquarters. Between 1992 and 1998, he was Senior TV Director at the UAE TV in Abu Dhabi; Director (on deputation) at the Film Production Unit of the UAE Ministry of Information and Culture; and Director-General of the Dubai Center for Art Works. In 2001, he was appointed Director of the Mass Communication Department at Dubai Police Headquarters. Dr. Al-Shuaibi worked as a Teaching/Research Assistant at the UAE University's Media Department (1980), and became a lecturer (1990) and Chair of the Department (1991–1993). He was also an Adjunct Professor at the UAE University's Mass Communication Department (1993–2001).

Dr. Al-Shuaibi has prepared and presented many TV programs and directed a number of films and documentaries, such as *The Camera Tour*, *Pearls of the Gulf* and *TV Journal*. He is a lecturer at the Police Academies of Abu Dhabi, Dubai and Sharjah, Editor-in-Chief of *Al Shawati'* (Beaches) magazine and a regular contributor to *Al Ittihad* newspaper. Dr. Al-Shuaibi serves as a media advisor to a number of Arab and foreign corporations based in Rome, Prague, Abu Dhabi and Dubai. He chairs the Committee on Development of Educational Media and is a member of the Committee on the Development of Schoolteachers at the UAE Ministry of Education and Youth. He has authored two books: *The Guide to TV Production* and *The Arab Media*, in addition to other media-related studies. Dr. Al-Shuaibi received a Bachelor's degree (with distinction) in film direction from the Fine Arts Academy, Baghdad University. He attended a training course on Management of Television

Stations held in Tokyo in 1978. Dr. Al-Shuaibi holds a Master's Degree cum laude in Radio and Television Sciences from Butler University in the United States and he obtained his Ph.D (with distinction) in the same field from the Media Department of Cairo University.

MR. ABDUL RAHMAN AL-RASHID is Director General of the Dubai-based *Al Arabiya* satellite news channel. He writes a daily column in *Al Sharq Al Awsat* newspaper. In 1977, he became an editor of the Riyadh-based *Al Jazeera* newspaper. He also worked as a Correspondent and later as Director of its Washington bureau from 1981 to 1985. From 1987 to 1998 he was Editor-in-Chief of the London-based *Al Majala* magazine, and from 1998 to 2003 he was Editor-in-Chief of *Ash Sharq Al Awsat* newspaper, in which his contributions still appear.

Mr. Al-Rashid is a media expert with a Bachelor's degree in Visual Media from the American University in Washington. He created and produced a number of documentaries and TV programs, and presented the "Hour in Politics" program of the Lebanese Future TV channel. He has participated in several cultural forums.

MR. MOHAMMAD ABDUL-QADER AL-JASSEM has been Editor-in-Chief of the Kuwaiti-based *Al Watan* newspaper since 1997. He is also the Editor-in-Chief of *Samra* (a monthly social magazine) and the Arabic editions of *Newsweek, Foreign Policy* and *Arab Reform Bulletin*. Mr. Mohammed Al-Jassem is the author of two books, namely *Kuwait: The Triangle of Democracy* (1992); and (as a co-author with Sawsan Al Sha'air): *Bahrain: A Tale of Political Struggle* (2000).

Mr. Al-Jassem obtained his Bachelor of Law degree in 1977 from the Faculty of Law and Shari'a at the University of Kuwait. During the period 1978–1997, he worked as a lawyer and from 1988 to 1989 he was the Editor of the law section in *Al Watan* newspaper, becoming the Acting Editor of the newspaper in 1994. As a representative of Amnesty International, he was an observer at several political trials and also participated in many public forums. He has written many political articles and research papers.

MR. AHMAD ABDULKARIM JULFAR is a veteran of the UAE's telecommunications company, Etisalat with 17 years of experience to his credit. He took up the post of General Manager of Comtrust in November 2002. Subsequently, he was named General Manager of eCompany, which was formed in June 2004 by the merger of Etisalat's two business units—Comtrust and Emirates Internet and Multimedia. Prior to heading Comtrust, Julfar gained valuable experience working on some of Etisalat's high profile projects including the company's comprehensive e-business initiative, E4Me.

Having graduated from Gonzaga University, Washington State in 1985, with a Bachelor's Degree in Civil Engineering and Computer Science, Ahmad Julfar joined Etisalat soon after, in April 1986, as a Graduate Trainee in the Access Network Planning Section of the telecommunications giant. Since then, he has worked in various engineering sections and at different levels and has gained experience in diverse areas especially within the spheres of Telecommunication Network Planning as well as Installation and Operations activity. He also has wide-ranging experience in Customer Service Activities.

MR. FAHD AL-OTHMAN worked for nine years in the sphere of corporate lending at Burgan Bank (Kuwait), which was the starting point of his entrepreneurial career. As a financial and organizational development consultant, he revitalized a failing subsidiary of United Fisheries Company (Kuwait). In 1991, Mr. Al-Othman founded Al-Othman and Al-Sarraf Computer Services, which, in a relatively short period of time, became the main distributor of personal computers in Kuwait. Information technology and its strategic role in the development of the Middle East region was an important consideration in establishing this company. Mr. Al-Othman then established the US-based New Horizons Computer Learning Centers and began to realize his dream of facilitating the transfer of technology to the region. His New Horizons network achieved tremendous success due to these centers, through innovative product development and educative marketing. Their success earned them and Mr. Al-Othman several international awards and resulted in his election to the

[598]

worldwide Franchise Advisory Council of New Horizons in 1997, along with members from France and the United States.

Six years after establishing the first New Horizons Center in Kuwait, Mr. Al-Othman established HumanSoft; a US$120 million closed shareholding company, which is due to go public. It owns eight business units, including the New Horizons network, with specialized missions to achieve the objectives of the holding company. Mr. Al-Othman is a graduate of Drake University, Iowa, USA (1980). He is a member of the Institute of Directors, London and a member of Who's Who International.

DR. HUSSEIN IBISH is a Senior Fellow at the American Task Force on Palestine (ATFP) and Executive Director of the Hala Salaam Maksoud Foundation for Arab-American Leadership. From 1998–2004, he served as Communications Director for the American-Arab Anti-Discrimination Committee (ADC), the largest Arab-American membership organization in the United States. From 2001–2004, he was Vice President of the National Coalition to Protect Political Freedom. He holds a Ph.D. in Comparative Literature from the University of Massachusetts, Amherst.

Dr. Hussein Ibish has made frequent radio and television appearances, and has written for several newspapers, including the *Los Angeles Times*, the *Washington Post* and the *Chicago Tribune,* and was Washington Correspondent for the *Daily Star* (Beirut). He is editor and principal author of two major studies on *Hate Crimes and Discrimination against Arab Americans* 1998–2000 and Sept. 11, 2001–Oct. 11, 2002 (ADC, 2001& 2003). He is author of "At the Constitution's Edge: Arab Americans and Civil Liberties in the United States" in the collection *States of Confinement* (St. Martin's Press, 2000); "Anti-Arab Bias in American Policy and Discourse" in *Race in 21st Century America* (Michigan State University Press, 2001); and "Race and the War on Terror," in *Race and Human Rights* (Michigan State University Press, 2005). He is co-author, with Ali Abunimah, of "The Palestinian Right of Return" (ADC, 2001) and "The Media and the New Intifada" in *The New Intifada* (Verso, 2001).

DR. MICHAEL C. HUDSON is Director of the Center for Contemporary Arab Studies and Professor of International Relations and Seif Ghobash Professor of Arab Studies in the Edmund A. Walsh School of Foreign Service at Georgetown University. He completed his undergraduate studies at Swarthmore College and holds MA and Ph.D degrees in Political Science from Yale University. His research interests include political liberalization, politics in divided societies, Lebanese politics, US Middle East policy, Gulf security, the Arab-Israeli conflict, and the Information Revolution in the Arab world. He has held Guggenheim, Ford and Fulbright fellowships and is a past president of The Middle East Studies Association. He has lectured in universities and research institutes around the world and is regularly interviewed about Middle East issues in the news media.

Among Dr. Hudson's publications are *The Precarious Republic: Political Modernization in Lebanon*; *The World Handbook of Political and Social Indicators* (second edition, co-author); *Arab Politics: The Search for Legitimacy* and *The Palestinians: New Directions* (editor and contributor). His latest book is an edited volume, *Middle East Dilemma: The Politics and Economics of Arab Integration* (New York: Columbia University Press, 1999), and his latest articles are "Imperial Headaches: Managing Unruly Regions in an Age of Globalization," *Middle East Policy* IX: 4 (December 2002) [an Arabic version appears in *Al-Mustaqbil al-Arabi* (Beirut, November 2002)], and "Information Technology, International Politics, and Political Change in the Arab World," *Bulletin of the Royal Institute for Inter-Faith Studies* (Amman, Autumn/Winter 2002). His paper on "The Politics of Pax Americana in Iraq and the Middle East," presented to a conference in Beirut in March 2004, was reprinted as a series in *The Daily Star* (Beirut), April 6–8, 2004.

DR. JAMES J. ZOGBY is founder and President of the Arab American Institute (AAI) in Washington, DC, which serves as the political and policy research arm of the Arab-American community. He played a facilitating role in the Arab–Israeli peace process in 1991 by authoring a Middle East peace proposal that was endorsed by some Arab foreign ministers. In 1993 he became Co-President (with former US Congressman Mel Levine) of Builders for Peace, a private sector committee promoting US business investment in the West Bank and Gaza. He also chaired a forum on the Palestinian economy at the Casablanca Economic Summit in 1994.

Dr. Zogby hosts a weekly program entitled *Viewpoint* on Abu Dhabi Television. He has testified before US House and Senate committees and been a guest speaker at the US Department of State. He has addressed the United Nations and the Arab League and presented papers at research centers in the Arab world. He serves as a board member of Middle East Watch, the American Civil Liberties Union, the National Immigration Forum, and a Member of the Council on Foreign Relations. Since 1992, Dr. Zogby has written a weekly column on US politics for prominent Arab newspapers including *Ash Sharq Al Awsat* (London), *Arab News* (Saudi Arabia), *Al Ahram* (Egypt), *Al Qabas* (Kuwait), and *Al Quds* (Jerusalem). His columns and articles have also appeared in major US newspapers, including *The Washington Post*, *The Los Angeles Times*, *USA Today*, and the *Christian Science Monitor*.

MR. JIHAD B. AL-KHAZEN is a columnist for the London-based *Al Hayat* newspaper. He served as a reporter for the Reuters news agency (1963–1969). Later, he became Editor-in-Chief of the English newspaper *The Daily Star*, based in Beirut, Lebanon (1968–1976). He was Editor-in-Chief of the English-language *Arab News* daily, published in the Kingdom of Saudi Arabia (1976–1977). Mr. Al-Khazen was subsequently appointed as Editor-in-Chief and columnist for the London-based pan-Arab newspaper, *Ash Sharq Al Awsat* (1978 to 1986). Between 1988 and 1998, he served as Editor-in-Chief of the London-based *Al Hayat* newspaper. Thereafter, he resigned his position and devoted his time to daily writing. Mr. Al-Khazen is also the first Editor-in-Chief of *Newsroom Ink*, a joint venture between *Al Hayat* newspaper and the Lebanese Broadcasting Corporation (LBC). Mr. Al-Khazen is a Member of the Board of Directors of several institutions, including the Council for the Advancement of Arab–British Understanding, the Arab Thought Foundation and the Center for Contemporary Arab Studies of Georgetown University, Washington, DC. He is also a Member of the Board of Advisors of the World Bank, Middle East and North Africa (MENA).

Mr. Jihad Al-Khazen received his BA in Political Science and MA in Arabic Literature from the American University of Beirut (AUB). He has embarked on his Ph.D studies in Georgetown University, Washington DC. Two of Al-Khazen's books comprise collections of his articles published in different newspapers. The Beirut-based Arabic daily *An Nahar* has serialized three of his books.

MR. JEAN R. ABINADER is the Managing Director of IdeaCom, Inc and has spent more than 30 years in international marketing and communications as a trade association executive, public affairs advisor and public relations consultant. He has designed and managed public relations and information campaigns for US and foreign government agencies and corporations. He is also a lecturer, university adjunct professor, and specialist in US–Arab issues. As the Managing Director of the Arab American Institute (AAI), he directed federal and ethnic relations on issues such as immigration and civil liberties. He is the co-host of the weekly satellite television show entitled *Washington Insider* and has extensive media experience as a spokesperson for the Arab-American community on policy concerns.

Mr. Jean AbiNader has worked with Fortune 500 companies in marketing, training and promotions, and has provided his expertise to foreign governments and organizations. As the head of operations for the oldest private news service in the United States, he reshaped its business to utilize interactive media and telecommunications technologies. He completed his BA in Political Science from St. Vincent College and holds a Master of Public and International Affairs (MPIA) degree in Intercultural Communications from the University of Pittsburgh, where he also completed doctoral studies in organizational communications. He leads a graduate seminar at Georgetown University in international marketing.

MR. MOHAMMAD IBAHRINE is a lecturer in the Department for Media and Communication at the University of Erfurt (Germany). He is also the founding Director of the Arab Political Communication Network. He has served on a number of advisory panels, including *Deutsche Welle*, the German Public Broadcasting Service. He earned a BA in American Studies from the University of Casablanca (Morocco); MA in Political Science and Sociology; and Ph.D. in International Relations from the University of Hamburg (Germany). His Ph.D thesis, "The Political Use of the Internet by Islam-oriented Movements," examined the role of the Internet in the process of identity formation and its implications for the public sphere in Morocco. Mohammad Ibahrine's research focuses on International Communication, International Politics, Public Diplomacy and Science and Technology. Currently, he is working on a research project about Arab Satellite Broadcasting and Democratization in the Arab World under the directorship of Dr. Kai Hafez. He is also working on a project for the Arabic Program of *Deutsche Welle TV*.

Mr. Mohammad Ibahrine has authored several articles in German and English. Among his recent publications are "Towards a National Telecommunications Strategy in Morocco" (2004), "The Great Transformations of Arab Media" (2005), "US Public Diplomacy, The Iraq War and Al-Jazeera.Net" (2005), "Morocco: The Effect of the Internet on Democratization" (2005), "The Independent Media and Morocco's Democratization: The No-Go Areas" (2005) and "The Sunni Tendency in Morocco: From Dawa to Militancy" (2005). Papers he has presented include: "Democratization and the Media in the Maghreb: From an Authoritarian to a Democratic Media Model" (2004), "American Public Diplomacy: Between the Iraq War and Al-Jazeera.Net" (2005) and "The Image of Europe in the Arab Media" (2005).

DR. JACK G. SHAHEEN is Professor Emeritus of Mass Communications at Southern Illinois University. An acclaimed author and media critic, he is also a committed internationalist and humanist. A former CBS news consultant on Middle East Affairs, his lectures and writings illustrate the social impact of various racial and ethnic stereotypes. He has lectured in reputed universities across the United States and abroad and been consulted by the United Nations, the Los Angeles Commission on Human Relations, the Justice Department's Civil Rights Division, and New York City's Commission on Civil Rights. In cooperation with the United States Information Agency, he conducts communication seminars in the Middle East. He also serves as a consultant to film and television companies and discusses media stereotypes on national programs and networks in the United States.

Dr. Shaheen is the author of four books, the award-winning *Reel Bad Arabs: How Hollywood Vilifies a People*; *Arab and Muslim Stereotyping in American Popular Culture*; *Nuclear War Films*, and *The TV Arab*. His writings include essays in publications such as *Newsweek*, *The Wall Street Journal* and *The Washington Post* and chapters in college textbooks. Among the awards he has received are The University of Pennsylvania's Janet Lee Stevens Award; the American Arab Anti-Discrimination Committee's Lifetime Achievement Award and the Pancho Be Award for "the advancement of humanity." Dr. Shaheen is an Oxford Fellow and the recipient of two Fulbright teaching awards. He holds degrees from the Carnegie Institute of Technology, Pennsylvania State University and the University of Missouri.

MR. WADDAH KHANFAR has been the Director of *Al Jazeera* satellite channel since October 2003. He started his professional career as a Field Correspondent for *Al Jazeera* channel in Africa and later headed the channel's South Africa office.

He covered a number of troubled areas and important events such as the Afghanistan War, initially reporting from India (prior to the overthrow of the Taliban regime) and thereafter from Afghanistan. He also covered the Iraq War from the Kurdistan region in northern Iraq. After the fall of Baghdad in mid-April 2003, Mr. Khanfar was entrusted with the task of restructuring and running *Al Jazeera's* office in the Iraqi capital.

MR. GREG DYKE, former BBC Director-General, has been Chancellor of the University of York since November 2004, and Chairman of HIT, a production company specializing in programs for the under-fives, since May 2005. Appointed Director-General of the British Broadcasting Corporation (BBC) in January 2000, he served for four years in this capacity. During his tenure at the BBC, Greg Dyke started four new digital television channels, five new digital radio channels, opened two new BBC regions, launched the BBC's interactive television services and helped create Freeview, a new free to air digital platform. He also made major commitments to expand the BBC's education services and to improve the cultural diversity of the workforce. He left the BBC in January 2004 in controversial circumstances following the report of the Hutton Inquiry.

Educated at the Hayes Grammar School and later at York University where he read Politics, Greg Dyke embarked on an early career as a journalist. He started his broadcasting career in 1977 at London Weekend Television (LWT). He became Editor-in-Chief of TV-am in 1983 and the following year was appointed Director of Programs for Television South (TVS). He returned to LWT in 1987 as Director of Programs, and was made Group Chief Executive of LWT (Holdings) PLC from 1991 to 1994. After Granada Television's takeover of LWT, Greg Dyke joined Pearson Television as Chief Executive. Later, he guided the consortium which created Channel 5 and became its first Chairman.

DR. RICHARD CAPLAN is University Lecturer in International Relations and Official Fellow of Linacre College, Oxford University. He has also served as a Specialist-Advisor to the Select Committee on Foreign Affairs of the UK House of Commons; a Research Associate at the International Institute for Strategic Studies (IISS); Editor of *World Policy Journal*; and New York Director of the Institute for War and Peace Reporting (IWPR). Dr. Caplan holds degrees in Politics and International Relations from the University of London (Ph.D), the University of Cambridge (M.Phil), and McGill University (BA). He is a Fellow of the 21st Century Trust and a Trustee of the Institute for War and Peace Reporting.

Dr. Caplan has written widely on international organizations and conflict management, European security and defence policy, peacekeeping, and the crises in the former Yugoslavia, with articles and reviews appearing in *International Affairs, Survival, Global Governance, International Peacekeeping, Nations and Nationalism, Ethics & International Affairs, Diplomacy & Statecraft* and *The Journal of Strategic Studies*, as well as in various edited volumes. He has also written for the *New York Times*, the *International Herald Tribune*, the *Los Angeles Times*, *El Nacional* (Mexico) and *Utrechts Newsblad* (Netherlands). His most recent books include *International Governance of War-Torn Territories: Rule and Reconstruction* (Oxford University Press, 2005) and *Europe and the Recognition of New States in Yugoslavia* (Cambridge University Press, 2005).

MR. ROBERT HODIERNE is Senior Managing Editor of Army Times Publishing Co., the publisher of defense and military-related periodicals such as *Defense News, Army Times, Navy Times, Marine Corps Times, Air Force Times* and *Armed Forces Journal.* He began his 40-year career in journalism as a freelance photographer covering the Vietnam War and his photographs continue to appear in major newspapers and magazines. He later worked as an investigative reporter and editor for newspapers, wire services, magazines, television, radio and the Internet. In 1981 he was part of a team that won several American journalism awards, including the Pulitzer Prize. He has also served as a juror on the Pulitzer Prize panel.

Mr. Hodierne covered the first stage of the War in Iraq from Doha, Qatar, where he supervised 13 journalists embedded with US forces. In early 2004 he spent six weeks embedded with US forces in Fallujah and Mosul, visiting Iraq again in May–June 2005 to provide additional war coverage. He has lectured on journalism ethics to professional groups and taught journalism at the University of California at Berkeley. He makes frequent television appearances as an expert on military issues and also provides periodic essays on issues about American life for BBC Radio. He holds a Bachelor's degree in Political Science from Grinnell College.

MR. ABDUL WAHAB BADRAKHAN began his journalistic career in 1973 as an apprentice at the Beirut-based *An Nahar* daily, assigned to cover student activities. When the civil war erupted in Lebanon, the reporter on student affairs, although lacking military experience, covered the war while experiencing its most difficult circumstances and its gravest risks. Thereafter, during the years of relative stability, Mr. Badrakhan continued his studies at the Lebanese University, where he received two diplomas in history and media studies. In 1979, he went to Paris to pursue his higher studies in media affairs. However, when he was assigned by the *An Nahar Al Arabi Wal Duwali* magazine in 1980 to cover the Russian invasion of Afghanistan, he was lured back into journalism. He later moved to Pakistan to investigate the conditions of the Afghani Mujahideen in their forced exile.

During his extensive coverage of international news, Mr. Badrakhan sought to complete his studies at the Sorbonne University, working on a thesis on the migrant Arab press. At the end of 1988, he joined the London-based *Al Hayat* newspaper, which, in a few years, emerged as a remarkable phenomenon in the Arab press. Mr. Badrakhan was appointed as Director of *Al Hayat's* Arab political section, later as Managing Director, and became Deputy Editor-in-Chief in 1998. During that period, he was one of the newspaper's commentators and analysts. At present, Mr. Badrakhan is working on two books. The first focuses on the roots of the experiences that have motivated young Arab men to go to Afghanistan. The second book is devoted to Arab policies to counter terrorism, starting with the attacks of September 11, 2001 and covering the ensuing wars.

MR. HUSSEIN SINJARI is the Founder and President of the Iraq Institute for Democracy in Irbil and Editor-in-Chief of both the *Al Ahali* liberal weekly newspaper, and the *Iraq Today* daily newspaper. Mr. Sinjari served as Head of the Public Relations Department of the Kurdistan Democratic Party (1972–1974); Director of the Voice of Kurdistan radio station (1979–1981) and Director of the Media Department (1981–1984); and Advisor to the Kurdistan leadership (1988–1991). He was the

Founding Director of the Kurdistan TV channel Zakho (1991). Mr. Sinjari has held a number of senior positions, including Deputy Minister of the Ministry of Construction and Development (Irbil, 1992–1994); Deputy Minister of the Ministry of Communications (Irbil, 1995–1995); Deputy Representative of the Government of the Kurdistan region of Iraq to the United Kingdom, holding the rank of Deputy Minister (1995–1996); Minister of Municipalities and Tourism (Irbil, 1996–1999); and Professor of Sociology at Saladin University (Irbil, 1997-1998).

Mr. Sinjari has a good command of Kurdish, Arabic, English, German, Farsi and French and has authored several books, including *Bibliography of Kurds and Kurdistan*; *Sermon for the Kurds* (1996); *Culture of Liberation* (1997), and *Culture of Change* (2005). Many of his articles have appeared in Arabic, Kurdish and English newspapers. Mr. Sinjari completed his Bachelor's degree in English and French at the University of Baghdad (1972), and gained a diploma in German from Vienna University (1977). He obtained his MA degree in Cross-Cultural Studies from Essex University (UK) in 1988.

MR. EDMOND YOUSSEF SAAB has been the Executive Editor of *An-Nahar* newspaper since 1991. In this capacity he is involved in strategic planning (editorial column and advertising), serves as Head of the Economy Department, and writes a weekly political column.

Mr. Saab has more than 40 years of experience in journalism and the media, starting as a correspondent and reporter in 1961. From 1968 to 1975 he was the Managing Editor of weekly supplements at *An Nahar*. In 1975 he was appointed Assistant Managing Editor of *An Nahar* and from 1977 to 1978 he became Managing Editor of *An Nahar Al Arabi Wal Duwali* (Paris), the international weekly edition of *An Nahar*. From 1978 to 1991 he was the Editor-in-Chief of *Al Mukhtar*, the Arabic edition of Reader's Digest. Mr. Saab holds diplomas in Continental and Middle Eastern law from the University of Lyon in France and the Lebanese University.

MR. HAZIM SAGHIYA is a Lebanese writer and journalist who worked at the *As Safeer* daily newspaper from 1974 until 1988. Thereafter, he moved to the London-based *Al Hayat* newspaper, where he still works as a commentator and editor of *Currents*, the weekly political supplement issued by *Al Hayat*.

During this period, Mr. Saghiya wrote a number of books, including *Iraqi Baath: the Rise and Fall of Saddam's Power*; *The Nationalists of the Arab East*; *The Roots of Arab Nationalism*; *Farewell to Arabism*; *The Arabization of the Lebanese Phalangists*; and *The Cultures of Khomainism*. He is the co-author (with Saleh Bashier) of *The Division of the Arab East*. Mr. Saghiya has been working on a new book entitled *The Dilemma of the Individual in the Middle East*, due to be published in Arabic and English.

MR. ABDULLAH ALI AL-OLAYAN is a journalist at the Oman Establishment for Press, News, Publication and Advertisement. He is a regular contributor to the Opinions and Studies section of *Al Khaleej* daily, UAE. Many of his articles have appeared in several newspapers and magazines, including the London-based *Al Hayat* and *Ash Sharq Al Awsat* dailies; *Al Ma'rifa* magazine (Riyadh, London); *Al A'rabi* magazine (Kuwait); *The Diplomat Quarterly* (London); and *Strategic Issues Quarterly* (Damascus). He was awarded the Abdul Rahman Cano Prize at the Cultural Civil Forum on the Thinking of Dr. Mohammed Jabir Al Ansari, held in October 2000.

Mr. Al-Olayan has published several books, including *Dialogue of Civilizations: An Islamic Vision for Dialogue* (2004); *Orientalism: Between Justice and Prejudice* (2002); *On the Omani Modern Renaissance*; *Issues of Arab Reality*; and *Globalization and World Order* (2001). He is the co-author of two other books: *Al Ansari and the Crisis Sociology: Three Differing Studies* (2000) and *Gateways of Transition to Democracy in the Arab Countries* (2003). A new book by Mr. Al-Olayan entitled *We, the West and Conflicting Views* is currently under publication. He graduated in 1986 from the College of Law at Muscat University, Sultanate of Oman, and completed his higher studies at the same University.

MR. ABDULLAH RASHEED is a daily columnist for the Abu Dhabi-based *Al Ittihad* newspaper and an Executive Managing Editor of *Dunya Al Ittihad*, a supplement that has been issued by the same paper since 2003. He began his career in journalism in 1980, serving as Editor at the Foreign News Department of the *Al Ittihad* paper from 1980 to 1983. From 1983 to 1989, Mr. Rasheed was the head of the same department. He was appointed Deputy Managing Editor of International News and Foreign Correspondents from 1989 to 1995, and was the newspaper's Correspondent in Washington from 1995 to 2000. After his return from Washington, he served as the Head of the Department of Studies and Information and the Department of International News and Foreign Correspondents from 2000 to 2002.

Mr. Abdullah Rasheed received his Business Administration Diploma from Syria in 1980, a diploma in editing and writing news and analysis from Reuters News Agency in 1993, and a Diploma in Information Administration Systems from the United States in 2000.

MR. AHMAD ABDUL AZIZ AL-JARALLAH began his career in 1962 as a journalist with *Al Ra'i Al A'am* newspaper in Kuwait, eventually becoming Managing Editor and Deputy Editor-in-Chief. In 1965, he left *Al Ra'i Al A'am* to join *As Siyassah* weekly magazine as its Editor-in-Chief. During his tenure, the publication achieved remarkable success. In 1968, he became its owner, and upon his request, the authorities transferred its license from that of a weekly magazine to a daily newspaper. On April 8, 1968, the first issue of *As Siyassah* daily newspaper appeared, and the newspaper continues to be published today. Mr. Al-Jarallah has succeeded in consolidating *As Siyassah* into a major media group, which also publishes the English-language *Arab Times* newspaper and *Al Hadaf* weekly magazine.

As a prominent and distinguished Editor-in-Chief, Mr. Al-Jarallah has succeeded in making his publications an integral part of local and Arab political life, whether in terms of active participation or of shaping public opinion. Mr. Al-Jarallah maintains close relations with many local, regional and international political elites and decision-making centers.

[610]

Chapter 1

1. Khalil Sabat et al., "The Media," in *The Comprehensive Social Survey of Egyptian Society 1952–1980* (Cairo: Dar Al Ma'arif, 1985), 999.

2. Al Ahram Center for Political and Strategic Studies, *The Arab Strategic Report 1985* (Cairo: Al Ahram Foundation, 1986).

3. Khalil Sabat et al., op. cit.

4. Report by the Secretary-General of the Federation of Arab Journalists to the Federation 9th Conference, Amman (Amman: Publications of the Federation of Arab Journalists, 2004).

5. Marc Lynch, "Taking Arabs Seriously," *Foreign Affairs* (September–October 2003).

6. Arab Press Freedom Watch, Arab Media (http://www.al-bab.com/media).

7. New Media Consultants, "Media and Telecom Operators: Friends or Foes?" (http://www.un.org/news/press/docs/2003/pil1533).

8. Frank Koelsch, "Infomedia Revolution," translated by Husam Eddin Zakariya and reviewed by Abdul Salam Radhwan, *Alam Al M'rifa* series, no. 253 (Kuwait: The National Council for Culture, Arts and Literature, January 2000).

9. S. Abdullah Schleifer, "Media Explosion in the Arab World: The Pan-Arab Satellite Broadcasters," *Transnational Broadcasting Studies* no. 1, Fall 1998 (http://www.tbsjournal.com).

10. Augustus R. Norton, "The New Media: Civic Pluralism and the Slowly Retreating State," in Dale Eickelman and Jon W. Anderson (eds), *New Media in the Muslim World: The Emerging Public Sphere* (Bloomington, IN: Indiana University Press, 1999), 19–28.

11. Jon Anderson and Dale Eickelman, "Media Convergence and its Consequences in the Middle East," *Middle East Insights* vol. XIV, no. 2 (2000), 61.

12. Jon Anderson, "Globalizing Politics and Religion in the Muslim World," *Journal of Electronic Publishing* (http://www.press.umich.edu/jep/archive/anderson.html).

13. Susan Sachs, "In Arab Media, War is Shown as a Clash of Civilizations," *New York Times*, April 5, 2003.

14. James Dunnigan, "Fairytales versus Reality in Arab Media," *Strategy Papers,* May 7, 2003.

15. Mamoun Fandy, "To Reach Arabs, try Changing the Channel," *The Washington Post*, December 2, 2001.

16. "France May Sanction Al Manar," *The Daily Star*, December 11, 2004, 4.

17. Jon B. Alterman, *New Media New Politics? From Satellite Television to the Internet in the Arab World* (Washington, DC: The Washington Institute for Near East Policy, 1998).

18. James Zogby, "Don't Blame Arab Media" (http://www.reclaimthemedia.org/stories.php?story= 04/08/18/2570588).

19. Daoud Kuttab, "Making Arab Media Really Independent," *Media Monitors Network*, October 9, 2004 (http://middleast.mediamonitors.net/headlines/making_arab_media _really_ independent).

20. Report by the Secretary-General of the Federation of Arab Journalists, op. cit., 212.

21. Marwan Al Kabalan, "Arab Media is Spreading its Wings Far and Wide," *Gulf News*, October 10, 2003.

22. "Arab Media Slammed over War Coverage," *World Net Daily*, April 7, 2003 (http://www.worldnetdaily.com).

23. Jefferson Morley, "Arab Media Confront the 'New Rules of the Game,'" *Washington Post*, April 9, 2003 (http://www.washingtonpost.com/ac2/wp-dyn/A64349-2003Apr9).

[612]

24. Hussein Amin, "Two Different Wars: Comparing Arab and US coverage of the Iraq War" (http://www.pbs.newhour/extra/features/jan.june03/media_3-4.htm).

25. "Walking a Tightrope: New Media and Freedom of Expression in the Arab World," *Internews Open Media Watch*, July 13, 2004. (http://internews.org/openmedia/sept_11_media.htm).

26. Mohammad Fahd Al Harithy, "War and Media: Difference in Perception," *Arab News,* September 10, 2004.

27. Naomi Sakr, "Breaking Down Barriers in Arab Media," *Women International* (http://www.conference.org/magazine/features/Nieman_sakr01ppf).

28. World Electronic Media Forum Roundtable Discussion: Freedom and Media Landscape in Arab World (http://www.un.org/news/press/docs/2003).

29. "Arab Media: An Issue and Opinions," *Al Saha Al A'rabiya* (http://www.alsaha.fares.net/sahat?14%4070).

30. Walter Armbrust, "The Riddles of Ramadan: Media, Consumer Culture and the 'Christmas-ization' of a Muslim Holiday," paper delivered at the American Anthropological Association, November 2000 (http://nmit.georgetown.edu/papers/warmbrust.htm).

31. Alterman, op. cit.

32. Jon W. Anderson, "Technology, Media, and the Next Generation in the Middle East," paper delivered at the Middle East Institute, Columbia University, September 28, 1999 (http://nmit.georgetown.edu/papers/jwanderson.htm).

33. Ibid.

34. Will Taggart, "The Digital Revolt: Resistance and Agency on the Net," adapted from a paper delivered at a symposium on "Indigenous Cyber-Activism and Virtual Diasporas Over the World Wide Web,"

Guthenburg, Sweden, June 2001 (http://nmit.georgetown.edu/papers/wtaggert.htm).

35. Jacob Arback, "Unscripted Television Programs and Corporate/State Concerns: The View from Nilesat," Paper delivered at the Middle East Studies Association, November 1999 (http://nmit.georgetown.edu/papers/jarback.htm).

36. ICTDAR, "The Road to Tech Mecca," *Wired Magazine*, July 2004.

Chapter 2

1. The arguments set out in this paragraph and the next are drawn from Richard Collins, Nicholas Garnham and Gareth Locksley, *The Economics of Television: The UK Case* (London: Sage Publications, 1988), 7–19.

2. Collins, Garnham and Locksley, op. cit., 9.

3. For a recently published discussion on some of these issues, see David Hesmondhalgh, *The Cultural Industries* (London: Sage Publications, 2002), 17–22 and Gillian Doyle, *Understanding Media Economics* (London: Sage Publications, 2002).

4. Ben Bagdikian, *The Media Monopoly* (Boston, MA: Beacon Press, 2000), xxi.

5. Ipsos-Stat, "Satellite TV Study," *ArabAd* vol. 12, no. 8, September 2002, 9.

6. Dwayne Winseck, "Gulf War in the Global Village: CNN, Democracy and the Information Age," in Janet Wasko and Vincent Mosco (eds) *Democratic Communications in the Information Age* (Toronto: Garamond Press, 1992), 68–69.

7. Naomi Sakr, "Al Jazeera Satellite Channel: Global Newscasting in Arabic," in Chris Paterson and Annabelle Sreberny (eds), *International News in the Twenty-First Century* (London: John Libbey Publishing, 2004), 153–154.

8. Graham Murdock, "Citizens, Consumers and Public Culture," in Michael Skovmand and Kim Christian Schrøder (eds), *Media Cultures: Reappraising Transnational Media* (London: Routledge 1992), 18.

9. Ibid.

10. Communication to the author, London, December 10, 2004.

11. Walid Azzi, "It's About Time…," *ArabAd* vol. 12, no. 8 (September 2002), 7.

12. Information provided by Engineer Lutfi Saqr at MPC, November 22, 2004.

13. David Butter, "A Hint of Florida Comes to Cairo," *Middle East Economic Digest*, April 2, 1999, 8.

14. Eutelsat data put satellite penetration in Egypt at 7.2 per cent in 2002.

15. Heba Kandil, "ERTU, Investors at Odds over Media Privatization," *Transnational Broadcasting Studies* no. 4, Spring 2000 (http://www.tbsjournal.com).

16. Ahmed Bahgat explained this when he appeared on his own channel in November 2002 as the guest of a talk show hosted by Magdi Mehanna, Editor-in-Chief of the Egyptian opposition daily, *Al Wafd*.

17. Naila Hamdy, "A Dream TV Come True," *Transnational Broadcasting Studies* no. 8, Spring/Summer 2002 (http://www.tbsjournal.com).

18. Rasha Abdullah, "The Impact of Music Television (MTV) on Music Broadcasting in Egypt and the Region," paper delivered to Article 19 Conference on Satellite Broadcasting in the Middle East and North Africa (Cairo, February 1999).

19. Information collected by the author during a visit to Nilesat in November 2004.

20. A Pan-Arab Research Centre (PARC) finding reported by Eutelsat, Canal France International and others.

21. Shaden Shehab, "Dream's Wake-up Call?" *Al Ahram Weekly* no. 611, November 7–13, 2002.

22. Hamdy, op. cit.

23. Shehab, op. cit. Hala Sirhan confirmed the existence of a "little" government share when she was interviewed by Naila Hamdy ("A Dream TV Come True"). The ERTU also owns 50% of Media Production City and 40% of Nilesat.

24. Paul Schemm, "Outrage in Sinai," *Middle East International*, no. 736, October 22, 2004, 11.

25. Hamdy, op. cit.

26. Ibid.

27. Ahmad Osman, "Rude Awakening: Dream Drops Top Talkers," *Transnational Broadcasting Studies* no. 12, Spring/Summer 2004 (http://www.tbsjournal.com).

28. Hamdy, op. cit.

29. Ibid.

30. Shehab, op. cit.

31. *Middle East Online*, "Dream TV in Trouble over Program," November 1, 2002 (http://www.meo.tv).

32. Shehab, op. cit.

33. Osman, op. cit.

34. Brian Whitaker, "Battle Station," *The Guardian*, February 7, 2003; *The Economist*, "All that Jazeera," June 21, 2003, 74.

35. *Jordan Times*, "Al Jazeera TV Barred from Covering Hajj," February 11, 2003.

36. *Jordan Times*, "Al Jazeera closed down for 'hostile' stand against Kuwait," November 5, 2002.

37. News of *Al Arabiya's* launch was covered in the *International Herald Tribune, Washington Post, Los Angeles Times, Financial Times, BBC Online*, and BBC Radio 4, among others.

38. Ali Al Hedeithy, Chief Executive of *Al Arabiya*, acknowledged the role of Future TV in an interview with Abdullah Schleifer published in *Transnational Broadcasting Studies* no. 9, Fall/Winter 2002 (http://www.tbsjournal.com).

39. Muhammad Ayish, "Arab Television goes Commercial," *Gazette* 59 (December 1997) 490–91.

40. *Arab News*, "Al Arabiya: A Balanced Alternative to Al Jazeera?" February 17, 2003.

41. Naomi Sakr, *Satellite Realms: Transnational Television, Globalization and the Middle East* (London: I B Tauris, 2001), 120; *BBC News Online*, "Jordan carpets Qatar over TV," August 8, 2002 (http://news.bbc.co.uk).

42. See Note 38.

43. The author understands from *Al Arabiya* sources that Kuwait objected to the attack on Iraq being described as an "invasion," preferring the term "liberation."

44. *Washington Times*, "Al Arabiya seeks media niche," October 1, 2003.

45. S. Abdullah Schleifer, "Interview with Saleh Negm," *Transnational Broadcasting Studies* no. 10, Spring/Summer 2003 (http://www.tbsjournal.com).

46. Anthony Shadid, "Rivalry for Eyes of Arab World," *Washington Post*, February 11, 2003.

47. S. Abdullah Schleifer, "Interview with Salah Negm, Head of News, Al Arabiya" *Transnational Broadcasting Studies* no. 9, Fall/Winter 2002 (http://www. tbsjournal.com).

48. The author understands from *Al Arabiya* producers that this is a deliberate policy, not just a default position.

49. Peter Feuilherade, "Profile: Al Arabiya TV," November 25, 2003 (http://newsvote.bbc.co.uk).

50. Reuters, "Arab TV Offers job to ex-Iraq Information Minister," *Gulf News*, April 30, 2003.

51. Joe Khalil and Dareen Abu Ghaida, "Appealing to the Hearts and Minds: How Arab Channels Fought for the Gulf War Audience," *Transnational Broadcasting Studies* no. 12, Spring/Summer 2004 (http://www.tbsjournal.com).

52. Feuilherade, op. cit.

53. Agence France-Presse (AFP), "Al Arabiya to Resume Coverage from Iraq after Two-month Ban," *Middle East Times*, January 28, 2004.

54. Cecilia Zecchinelli, "News War Heats up between Rival Arab Satcasters," *Variety*, May 10–16, 2004.

55. *Gulf News*, "Dubai 2003, Al Arabiya Team up for TV Documentary," April 13, 2003.

56. Associated Press, "Arab Station: US Troops kill Cameraman," *The Atlanta Journal-Constitution*, March 18, 2004.

57. Associated Press, "Al Arabiya Lawyer Criticizes Military Report on Shooting of two Journalists," *Jordan Times*, March 31, 2004.

58. Committee to Protect Journalists, "Baghdad Car Bomb Kills Five Al Arabiya employees," *CPJ News Alert*, November 1, 2004.

59. According to PARC data up to end-2002.

60. PARC data reproduced in Jean-Marc Belchi, "Evolution of TV Viewing in the Middle East, 1996–2000." Paper presented to the conference on New Media and Change in the Arab World (Amman, February 27 to March 1, 2002).

61. For difficulties overcome by Solidère in evacuating property in downtown Beirut, see Human Rights Watch, *Lebanon: Restrictions on Broadcasting* (New York, NY: April 1997), 14, 51.

62. Bassam El Hachem, *Radio Orient: Intégration des musulmans en France et laïcité en question* (Paris: Publisud, 1998) 42–46.

63. Marwan M. Kraidy, "Broadcasting Regulation and Civil Society in Post-war Lebanon," *Journal of Broadcasting & Electronic Media*, vol. 42, no. 3 (Summer 1998), 390–391.

64. Kraidy op. cit., 394.

65. Sakr, *Satellite Realms*, op. cit., 51.

66. Dima Dabbous-Sensenig, *Ending the War? The Lebanese Broadcasting Act of 1994*, Ph.D thesis, Sheffield Hallam University, 2002, 189.

67. Dabbous-Sensenig, op. cit., 190–191.

68. Dabbous-Sensenig, op. cit., 188.

69. Nadim Munla, Future TV's president, told the author that Future TV was "well-received" and "watched heavily" in Syria. "We have no problems with Syria; we only get compliments from there," (Interview, Beirut, March 26, 1998).

70. Chantal Dagher, "FTV, MBC Merge Media Operations," *ArabAd*, vol. 11, no. 11, December 2001, 115.

71. Magda Abu Fadil, "Straddling Cultures: Arab Women journalists at Home and Abroad," in Naomi Sakr (ed.) *Women and Media in the Middle East: Power through Self-Expression* (London: I. B. Tauris, 2004) 192–195.

72. Maal Al Ghamri and Linda Ayashhia, "War Reporters Cross the Invisible Line for Arab Women," *Arab News*, August 7, 2003.

73. Anne Sebba, *Battling for News: The Rise of the Woman Reporter* (London: Hodder & Stoughton, 1994), 277, quoted in Margaret Gallagher, *An Unfinished Story: Gender Patterns in Media Employment* (Paris: UNESCO, 1995) 2.

74. Sana Kamal, "The Power of Satellite TV," *Middle East International* 673, April 19, 2002.

75. Hassan Fattah, "Zen Reaches out to Arab Youth," *Transnational Broadcasting Studies* no. 9, Fall/Winter 2002 (http://www.tbsjournal.com).

76. Ibid.

77. Author's interview with Nadim Munla, Beirut, March 26, 1998.

78. Samar Farah argued this in "Can Reality TV 'survive' in the Middle East?" *Christian Science Monitor*, March 26, 2004.

79. Dagher, op.cit.

80. According to Adam Boyd of FremantleMedia, addressing a seminar at the University of Westminster on February 26, 2003.

81. BBC News, "Jordanian wins Arab 'Idol,'" published online at news.bbc.co.uk, August 18, 2003; Adam Sherwin and Ian McKinnon, "Arafat and Gaddafi sing the praises of Arab Pop Idols," published online at *timesonline.co.uk*, August 23, 2004.

82. Rami G. Khouri, "Seeking Salvation among Libya, Lockerbie, and Future TV's Song Contest," *Jordan Times*, August 20, 2003.

83. Sakr, *Satellite Realms,* 53–54.

84. Nagib Khazzaka, "Row Grows in Lebanon over Government Bar on Saudi programme," *Middle East Times*, January 3, 2003; Jim Quilty, "The Politics of Television," *Middle East International*, January 10, 2003, 18.

85. Marwan M. Kraidy, "State Control of Television News in 1990s Lebanon," *Journalism and Mass Communication Quarterly* vol. 76, no. 3, 1999, 491.

Chapter 3

1. See Daniel Lerner, *The Passing of Traditional Society: Modernizing the Middle East* (Glencoe, IL: The Free Press, 1958).

2. For a guide we can refer here to the analysis in the UNDP *Arab Human Development Report 2002.* This report links the structural weakness of Arab societies to a shortage of freedom and good governance, as well as shortages in women's empowerment and knowledge. This means "social change" on the conciliatory level can be directed towards filling the gaps in these three domains, though there is no full consensus on the description of these shortages. What is deeper, however, is that conflict and contradiction arise as soon as we reach the threshold of an essential question—which direction do we want change to move towards?

3. Ilila Hariq, Al *Dimoqratiya wa Tahadiat Al Hadatha bain Al Sharq wa Al Gharb* (London: Dar Al Saqi, 2001), 244.

4. Halim Barakat says that speculating on the reality of the Arab society betrays two contradictory impressions. One reality seems to be "open to the changes that are sweeping the entire world to the extent that we think it is changing at an incredible pace which we are incapable of controlling, or keeping up with, it ... on the other hand the Arab society [seems] closed and withdrawn into itself, and persistently adhering to its culture and institutions that resist change and bold interaction with other civilizations." See Halim Barakat, Al *Mujtam'a Al Arabi fi Al Qarn Al 'Ishreen: bahath fi taqur Al Ahwal wa Al 'Alaqat* (Beirut: Markaz Dirasat Al Wihda Al 'Arabia, 2000), 917–918.

5. See majmo'at moalifeen, *Al 'Arab wa Al I'lam Al Fadaiy* (Beirut: Markaz Dirasat Al Wihda Al 'Arabia, 2000), 145–212.

6. See Sa'ad Al Faqiyh, "I'tradat Al Salafiyyn 'ala Al Dimoqratiya" in Ali Al Kawari (ed.) *Azmat Al Dimoqratiya fi Al Bildan Al 'Arabia:*

I'tradat wa Tahfuzat 'ala Al Dimoqratiya fi Al 'Alam Al 'Arabi (London: Dar Al Saqi, 2004), 67–92.

7. Azmi Bushara, *Torohat 'an Al Nahda Al Mu'aqa* (Beirut: Riyad Al Raiyys lil Al Kotob wa Al Nashr, 2003), 33. See also the vision of Abdullah Al Ghizami which confirms this trend in his book *Al Thaghafa Al Talifizonia: Soqot Al Nukhba wa Brooz Al Sha'abi* (Beirut wa Al Dar Al Baidaa: Al Markaz Al Thaghafi Al 'Arabi, 2004).

8. See, Jon B. Alterman, "Political Spectacle," *Middle East: Notes and Comment* vol. 2, no. 10 (Washington, DC: Center for Strategic and International Studies, October 1, 2004).

9. Quoted from Fatema Mernissi, *Les Sindbads Marocains: Voyage dans le Maroc Civique* (Rabat: Editions Marsam, 2004), 46.

10. See Sa'eda Kilani, *Freedom Fries: Fried Freedom, Arab Satellite Channels' Struggle between State Control and Western Pressure* (Amman: Arab Archives Institute, 2004), 28.

Chapter 4

1. See William A. Rugh, *The Arab Press: News Media and Political Process in the Arab World* (Syracuse, NY: Syracuse University Press, 1987).

2. See Abdullah Bilqzeez, "Arab Satellite Channels and Issues of the Nation," *Al Mustaqbal Al Arabi*, Year 27, no. 306 (Beirut, 2004), 124–178.

3. See Isam Sulaiman Musa, "Communications Revolution: Repercussions of the Stages of Development of Nationalist Arab Media," in *The Arabs and Satellite Media* (Beirut: Center for Arab Unity Studies, 2004), 46–47.

4. United Nations Development Program (UNDP), *Arab Human Development Report 2003*, "Building a Knowledge Society in the Arab States" (Amman: The National Press, 2003), 61.

5. Mohammed Shukri Salam, "The Communications Revolution and Media," *A'alam Al Fikr* vol. 32, no. 21 (Kuwait: 2003), 81–126.

6. See Hussein Y. Amin, "The Current Situation of Satellite Broadcasting in the Middle East." *Transnational Broadcasting Studies* no. 5, Fall/Winter 2001 (http://www.tbsjournal.com).

7. See Gregory Mendel Selber and Salma Ghanem, "Modernization and Media in the Arab World," *Global Media Journal* (Fall 2004).

8. See Nabil H. Dajani, "The Changing Scene of Lebanese Television," *Transnational Broadcasting Studies* no. 7, Fall 2001 (http://www.tbsjournal.com), 3–4.

9. See Musa Shteiwi, "New Social Spaces Created by Satellite TV and the Internet," paper presented to the conference on Women's Movement and Civil Society in the Arab World, The House of World Cultures, Berlin, Germany, April 25–26, 2003, 3–5.

10. See Ithiela da Sola Pool, *Technologies without Boundaries* (Cambridge, MA: Harvard University Press, 1990), 8.

11. Shteiwi, op. cit.

12. See: Ahmed Shukr Sbeihi, *Future of Civil Society in the Arab World*, (Beirut: Center for Arab Unity Studies, 2000), 32–37.

13. See Saad Eddin Ibrahim, "Thoughts on Arab Satellite Television, Pan-Arabism and Freedom of Expression," *Transnational Broadcasting Studies* no.13, Fall/Winter 2004 (http://www.tbsjournal.com) 1–6.

14. See: Jon W. Anderson, "Transnational Civil Society, Institution-Building, and IT: Reflections from the Middle East," paper delivered at SSRC Summer Institute on Information Technology and Social Research—Setting the Agenda, Columbia University, New York, June 5–8, 2002 (http://nmit.georgetown.edu/papers/ transnatcs.htm) 2, 12.

Chapter 9

1. See http://www.internetworldstats.com/stats5.htm#mereports.

2. Adeeb Murwa, Al *Sahafa Al Arabiya: Nasha'taha wa Tataworha* (Beirut: Dar Maktabat Al Hayat, 1961), 143.

3. Awatif Abdul Rahman, *Dirasat fi Al Sahafa Al Arabiya Al Mu'asira* (Beirut: Al Farabi, 1989), 47–48.

4. Awatif Abdul Rahman, op. cit., 51.

5. Awatif Abdul Rahman, op. cit., 52.

6. Awatif Abdul Rahman, op. cit., 53.

7. Awatif Abdul Rahman, op. cit., 61.

8. A group of authors, *Al 'Arab wa Al 'Ilaam Al Fada'iyi* (Beirut: Markaz Dirasat Al Wihda Al 'Arabiya, 2004), 35.

9. Awatif Abdul Rahman, op. cit., 42.

10. Jon Alterman, "Arab Satellite Television: Can it Rise Above Spectacle?" *Nashrat Al Islah Al 'Arabi*, mujalad 2, Al 'adad 11, December 2004 (the bulletin is published by Carnegie Endowment for International Peace, translated by Dar Al Watan lil Tiba'a wa Al Nashr, the State of Kuwait). See http://www.alwatan.comkw/arb/default.aspx?isu=2041200000211.

11. See http://www.internetworldstats.com/stats5.htm#mereports.

12. United Nations Development Program (UNDP), "Building a Knowledge Based Society," the *Arab Human Development Report, 2003* (Amman: Al Matba'a Al Watniya, 2003), 63.

13. The *Arab Human Development Report, 2003,* op. cit., 64.

14. See http://www.internetworldstats.com/stats5.htm#mereports

15. The *Arab Human Development Report, 2003*, op. cit, 48.

16. See, Hamoud Salhi, "The Political & Social Impact of Information Technology in the Gulf States" (http://nmit.georgetown.edu/papers /hsalhi.htm).

17. The *Arab Human Development Report, 2003*, op. cit, 48.

18. See the annual report of Human Rights Watch for 2003 (http://www.hrw.org/arabic/mena/wr2003/tunisia.htm).

19. See the Reporters sans Frontiers website (http://www.rsf.org).

Chapter 10

1. Natural Language Processing is an area of computational linguistics concerned with the processing of naturally occurring (human) language by computers.

2. For the automatic processing of written Arabic, certain core technologies have been developed with a set of products that use computational linguistic algorithms to transform language structure into binary systems. These components work on all language levels from the character level to the document level, passing through the word, sentence and paragraph levels.

3. In relation to computer technology, "on the fly" describes activities that develop or occur dynamically rather than as the result of something that is statically predefined. For example, the content of a page that is sent to the user from a Web site can be developed (and varied) "on the fly" based on dynamic factors such as the time of day, what pages the user has looked at previously, and specific user input.

Chapter 12

1. Colbert I. King, "Condoleezza Rice's Oddball Critic," *The Washington Post*, December 15, 2001, A-29.

2. Thomas L. Friedman, "Glasnost in the Gulf," *The New York Times*, February 27, 2001, 23.

3. John F. Burns, "Arab TV Gets a New Slant: Newscasts without Censorship," *The New York Times*, July 4, 1999, 1.

4. Jon B. Alterman, "An Evolving Arab Press," *The Washington Post*, March 28, 2001, A-23.

5. Zev Chafets, "Al Jazeera Unmasked: An Arab Propaganda Machine in the Guise of Real Journalism," *Daily News* (New York), October 14, 2001, 37.

6. Thomas L. Friedman, "The Sand Wall," *The New York Times*, April 13, 2003, 13.

7. Thomas L. Friedman, "Telling the Truth in Iraq," *The New York Times*, August 17, 2003, 9.

8. Thomas L. Friedman, "War of Ideas, Part 4," *The New York Times*, January 18, 2004, 11.

9. Tomlinson, Kenneth, "Al Hurra Disseminates Information to Arab-Speaking World," *Richmond Times Dispatch* (Virginia), September 20, 2004, A-11.

10. Mary O'Connell (Producer), "Spin Till You Win," radio documentary, Canadian Broadcasting Company, 2004.

11. Tariq Al Humayd, "Al Hurrah: Washington's Sin," *Al Sharq Al Awsat*, July 12, 2004.

12. "The Western media has lost its credibility," *Al Quds Al Arabi* editorial, translated and summarized in *Mideast Mirror*, April 1, 2003.

13. Jamil Matar, "A Deteriorating Media," *Al Hayat*, August 30, 2004.

14. Munir Shafiq, in the Jordanian daily *Al Ra'i,* cited in "How not to Mould Arab Opinion," *Mideast Mirror*, February 2, 2004.

15. Mohammad Qaju, "War under the Guise of 'Democracy,'" in the Syrian daily *Al Baath*, cited in *Mideast Mirror*, May 13, 2003.

16. Salaheddin Hafez, "Democracy Slaughtered by its Guardians," in the Egyptian daily *Al Ahram*, cited in *Mideast Mirror*, May 13, 2004.

17. Abdelkarim Abunasr, "No Exit from Iraq," in *Al Watan*, cited in *Mideast Mirror*, May 14, 2004.

18. Salameh Nematt, "Colleagues... and Colleagues!," *Al Hayat*, August 19, 2004.

19. "Arab Television Strongly Condemning Israel for Unleashing Fierce Attacks against Palestinian Targets," Mornings with Paula Zahn, CNN, December 5, 2001, Transcript # 120509CN.V74.

20. Bill O'Reilly, "Terror TV?," Monday, October 25, 2004 (http://www. foxnews.com/story/0,2933,136494,00.html). Accessed on October 26, 2004.

21. Samantha M. Shapiro, "The War inside the Arab Newsroom," *The New York Times Magazine*, January 2, 2005, 27.

Chapter 13

1. Mohammed El Nawawy and Adel Iskandar, *Al Jazeera: How the Free Arab News Network Scooped the World and Changed the Middle East* (Cambridge, MA: Westview, 2002), 20.

2. Thomas Friedman, "Glasnost in the Gulf," *The New York Times*, February 27, 2001.

3. Rami Khouri, "Uncovered: Arab Journalists Scrutinize Their Profession." Report from Georgetown University conference, October 7, 2004, with presentations by Thomas Gourguissian of *An-Nahar* (Beirut), Rami Khouri, Editor of *The Daily Star* (Beirut), Salama Nemaat of *Al Hayat* (London), and Hafez Al Mirazi, Bureau Chief of Al Jazeera (Washington), CCAS *Occasional Paper* (Washington, DC: Center for Contemporary Arab Studies, Georgetown University, January 2005).

4. Jon B. Alterman, *New Media, New Politics?* (Washington, DC: The Washington Institute for Near East Policy, 1998), 22.

5. Michael C. Hudson, "Information Technology, International Politics and Political Change in the Arab World," *Bulletin of the Royal Institute for Inter-Faith Studies* (Amman) vol. 4, no. 2 (Autumn/Winter 2002), 1–18.

6. Cameron W. Barr, "Top Arab TV Network Hits US Market," *The Christian Science Monitor*, December 26, 2002.

7. El Nawawy and Iskandar, op. cit., 95.

8. "Inside Al Jazeera." *60 Minutes,* CBS-TV, October 10, 2001. (http://www.cbsnews.com/stories/2001/10/10/60minutes/main314278.shtml).

9. David Dadge, "Al Jazeera: A Platform of Controversy," Ch. 2 in Dadge, *Casualty of War: The Bush Administration's Assault on a Free Press* (Amherst, NY: Prometheus Books, 2004), 63.

10. Dadge, op. cit., 66.

11. Fouad Ajami, "What the Muslim World is Watching," *The New York Times Magazine,* November 18, 2001. (http://www.allied-media.com/ARABTV/aljazeera/Nytimes%20article.htm).

12. Robert Fisk, "US Moves to Close Down Al Jazeera TV: Wolfowitz the Censor," *The Independent* (London), August 1, 2003.

13. Ibid.

14. Waddah Khanfar, "The Future of Al Jazeera," *Transnational Broadcasting Studies* no. 12, Spring/Summer 2004 (http://www.tbsjournal.com).

15. Associated Press report, November 26, 2003, to be found at http://www.newsmax.com/archives/articles/2003/11/25/173813.shtml. Rumsfeld's comments were made on the PBS televison program,

"The News Hour with Jim Lehrer." See also http://www.pbs.org/ newshour/media/media-watch/july-dec03/arab_networks.

16. Anthony Loewenstein, "Al Jazeera Awakens the Arab World." *Counterpunch,* June 13/14, 2004 (http://www.counterpunch.org/ loewenstein06132004.html).

17. Ibid.

18. "Colin Powell Registers US Complaints about Al Jazeera," *Los Angeles Times,* April 28, 2004 (http://www.showbizdata.com/contacts/ picknews.cfm/35316/COLIN_POWELL_REGISTERS_U.S._COMP LAINTS_ABOUT_AL-JAZEERA).

19. Donald Rumsfeld, Remarks at the Chicago Council on Foreign Relations, August 6, 2004 (http://usinfo.state.gov/mena/Archive/2004/ Aug/09-490718.html).

20. Samantha M. Shapiro, "The War Inside the Arab Newsroom," *The New York Times Magazine,* January 2, 2005.

21. Wendy Feliz Sefsaf, "US International Broadcasting Strategies for the Arab World: An Analysis of the Broadcasting Board of Governors' Strategy from a Public Communications Standpoint." *Transnational Broadcasting Studies* no. 13, Fall 2004 (http:// www.tbsjournal.com).

22. *Al Jazeera: Opportunity or Challenge for US Foreign Policy in the Middle East?* Congressional Research Service (CRS) Report to Congress by Jeremy M. Sharp, July 23, 2003 (http://fpc.state.gov/ documents/organization/23002.pdf).

23. Ibid.

24. Advisory Group on the Arab and Muslim World. "Changing Minds, Winning Peace: A New Strategic Direction for US Public Diplomacy in the Arab and Muslim World," October 1, 2003 (http://www. publicdiplomacy.org/23.htm).

25. Ibid.

26. Ibid.

[629]

27. Hafez Al Mirazi, "The 9/11 Commission Recommendations on Public Diplomacy: Defending Ideals and Defining the Message," Testimony before the House Committee on Government Reform Subcommittee on National Security, Emerging Threats and International Relations, August 23, 2004. (http://reform.house.gov/UploadedFiles/HafezAl MiraziTestimony.pdf).

28. Waddah Khanfar, "The Future of Al Jazeera," *Transnational Broadcasting Studies* no. 12, Spring/Summer 2004 (www. tbsjournal.com).

29. See for example, El Nawawy and Iskandar, op. cit.

30. Shapiro, op. cit.

31. Hafez Al Mirazi, "Uncovered: Arab Journalists Scrutinize Their Profession." Report from Georgetown University conference, October 7, 2004, CCAS *Occasional Paper* (Washington, DC: Center for Contemporary Arab Studies, Georgetown University, January 2005).

Chapter 16

1. See the following references: Ole Holsti, "Public Opinion and Foreign Policy: Challenges to the Almond-Lippman Consensus," *International Studies Quarterly* (1992). See also Ole Holsti, *Public Opinion and American Foreign Policy* (1996); Benjamin Page and Robert Y. Shapiro, *The Rational Public: Fifty Years of Trends in Americans' Policy Preferences* (1992); Warren Strobel, *Late Breaking Foreign Policy* (1997); E. Gilboa, "Mass Communication and Diplomacy: A Theoretical Framework," *Communication Theory* (2000); John Mueller, "Fifteen Propositions About American Foreign Policy and Public Opinion in an Era Free of Compelling Threats" (1996); and John Rielly (ed.) *American Public Opinion and US Foreign Policy* (1999).

2. See Marc Feustel, Olivier Germain, Lauren Matus, Philip Reuchlin and Belinda Ridley, "Free Press and Good Governance in Southern Africa: Media Assistance and Free Press Advocacy in Member States

of the Southern African Development Community: Mapping Roles and Relationships," Stanhope Centre for Communications Policy Research (2002) 16; Stuart Soroka, "Media, Public Opinion, and Foreign Policy" (2003); Shibley Telhami, "Finding the Right Media for the Message in the Middle East." Transcript of testimony before the Senate Foreign Relations Committee, April 29, 2004.

3. Personal interview with the Director of a prominent think tank in Washington, DC, December 2004.

4. As Rene Rodriguez noted in the review of *Control Room*. "That difference [between "true journalism" and catering to defined audiences] forms *Control Room*'s central theme, which is the elusive nature of objectivity, especially when processed through different cultures and ideologies. If one man's propaganda is another man's absolute truth, how will the two sides ever find common ground?" Rene Rodriguez, "TV News on the Other Side of the World," *Miami Herald*, July 11, 2004.

5. Mamoun Fandy complains, "The Arab world today swims in a sea of linguistic violence that justifies terrorism and makes it acceptable, especially to the young ... Articles like this [Buthaina Shaban in *Tishreen*], which glorify death and urge young people to be suicidal, are part of the steady diet that Arab youths are exposed to every day." Mamoun Fandy, "The Arab Media's Sense of Outrage?" *The Washington Post*, July 4, 2004.

6. Series of personal interviews conducted in Washington, DC, December 2004.

7. Among the many negative comments: Arthur Neslen quoting US Brigadier General Mark Kimmitt, "My solution is to change the channel (Al Jazeera) to a legitimate, authoritative, honest news station. The stations that are showing Americans intentionally killing women and children are not legitimate news sources." Neslen points out that "The targeting of Al Jazeera is all the more remarkable, given that it is the only Arab TV network to routinely offer Israeli, US and British officials a platform to argue their case." See Arthur Neslen,

[631]

"Reality Television: Al Jazeera has a track record of accurate reporting – which is why its journalists have been criminalized and its offices bombed." *The Guardian*, April 21, 2004. Susan Sachs in an earlier article in the *New York Times* mentioned how "As the Iraq war moved into its third week, the media in the region have increasingly fused images and enemies from this and other conflicts into a single bloodstained tableau. The Israeli flag is superimposed on the American flag. The Crusades and the 13[th]century Mongol sack of Baghdad, recalled as barbarian attacks on Arab civilization, are used as synonyms for the American-led invasion of Iraq." She quotes Abdel Moneim Said, director of the Al Ahram Center for Political and Strategic Studies in Cairo. "When you see the vocabulary and the images used [by some of the media], it is actually bringing everybody to the worst nightmare—the clash of civilizations." Susan Sachs, "A Nation at War: Mideast Coverage; Arab Media Portray War as Killing Field," *New York Times*, April 4, 2003, 1.

8. Jihad Fakhreddine comments: "In short, the way the West perceives the Arabs and Islam matters to Arabs and Muslims. The image issue has evolved into a situation where it is not clear to what extent the West is looking at the Arab and Muslim worlds through lenses that have the Osama bin Laden label on them." See Jihad Fakhreddine, "The US-Arab Cross-Communication Exchange: A Dialogue Among Mutes," *Transnational Broadcasting Studies* no. 8, Spring/Summer 2002 (http://www.tbsjournal.com).

9. Hussein Amin, *Watching the War in the Arab World* (2003).

10. R.S. Zaharna, "American Public Diplomacy in the Arab and Muslim World: A Strategic Communications Analysis," American University, 2001.

11. Marc Lynch, "Shattering the 'Politics of Silence;' Satellite Television Talk Shows and the Transformation of Arab Political Culture," in Amy Hawthorne (ed.) *Arab Reform Bulletin* vol. 2, no. 11, Carnegie Endowment for International Peace, December 2004.

12. William A. Rugh, "Washington and the Challenge of Arab Press Freedom," in Amy Hawthorne (ed.) *Arab Reform Bulletin* vol. 2, no. 11, Carnegie Endowment for International Peace, December, 2004.

13. Walter Armbrust, "Egypt: Political Films and the Politics of Filmmaking," in Amy Hawthorne (ed.) *Arab Reform Bulletin* vol. 2, no. 11, Carnegie Endowment for International Peace, December, 2004.

14. Jihad Fakhreddine, "The US-Arab Cross-Communication Exchange: A Dialogue among Mutes," *Transnational Broadcasting Studies* no. 8, Spring/Summer 2002 (http://www.tbsjournal.com).

15. Fakhreddine (2002) op. cit. "The Arabs have learned for decades that their marketing of the Arab cause, or more specifically the Palestinian cause, in the US has hardly made any headway. But the scale of the extent to which Arabs and Muslims are misperceived in the West has equally shocked them."

16. The September 11th attacks put the Arab and the Muslim worlds on the defensive with respect to how they are perceived in the West. The current media campaigns, particularly in the US press, against the Arab regimes and Islam have rung the alarm bells louder than ever before about how their image and reputation is being **remanufactured** [author's emphasis] by the US mainstream media.

17. Personal interview with news editor/reporter based in Washington, DC for an Arab satellite station.

18. Fakhreddine (2002), op. cit.

19. The observations that follow are from a personal interview with a senior US government policy analyst in December 2004.

20. All comments that follow are drawn from a personal interview with a leading media analyst at a Washington-based think tank.

21. All reported in the *Arab Reform Bulletin* vol. 2, no. 11, December 2004.

22. Stuart Soroka, *Media, Public Opinion, and Foreign Policy* (2003), 28.

23. Soroka (2003), op. cit., 44.

24. Paul Brewer, Kimberly Gross, Sean Aday and Lars Willnat, "International Trust and Public Opinion about World Affairs," *American Journal of Political Science* (2004), 1.

25. Brewer et al., ibid. 30.

26. Ibid., 26

27. Ibid., 8.

28. Ibid., 29.

29. "Restrictions on Civil Liberties, Views of Islam and Muslim Americans, US War on Terror, US Foreign Policy, and Anti-Americanism," Poll by Cornell University; report released December 17, 2004 (http://www.news.cornell.edu/releases/DecDu/DecDu/Muslim. poll.bpf.html).

Chapter 17

1. The term "soft power" was coined by Joseph S. Nye. For more details see J. Nye, "Soft Power," *Foreign Policy* 80 (1990), 153–171.

2. Wijk, R. "The Limits of Military Power," *The Washington Quarterly* vol. 25, no. 1 (2002), 75–92.

3. See J. Nye, 1990, op. cit.

4. A. Garfinkle, *A Practical Guide to Winning the War on Terrorism,* 2003 (http://www.hoover.stanford.edu/publications/books/practical. html).

5. W. Rugh, "Fixing Public Diplomacy for Arab and Muslim Audiences," 2004 (http://www.hoover.stanford.edu/publications/books/ fulltext/practical/145.pdf).

6. Hoffman, D. "Beyond Public Diplomacy," *Foreign Affairs* vol. 81, no. 2 (2002), 83.

7. D. Bollier, "The Rise of Netpolitik: How the Internet is Changing International Politics and Diplomacy." Report of the Eleventh Annual

Aspen Institute Roundtable on Information Technology, 2003, 6 (http://www.aspeninstitute.org/AspenInstitute/files/CCLIBRARYFILES/ FILENAME/0000000077/netpolitik.pdf).

8. K. Tomlinson, "American Public Diplomacy in the Islamic World," Testimony Before the Committee on Foreign Relations, 2003, 7 (http://www.iwar.org.uk/psyops/resources/public-diplomacy/Tomlinson Testimony030227.pdf).

9. Hoffman, 2002, op. cit., 83–95.

10. C. Beers, "American Public Diplomacy and Islam," Testimony before the Senate Foreign Relations Committee on February 27, 2003 (http://www.foreign.senate.gov/hearings/2003/hrg030227a.html).

11. J. Napoli and J. Fejeran, "Of Two Minds: US Public Diplomacy and the Middle East," 2004, 8 (http://lass.calumet.purdue.edu/cca/gmj/Submitted Documents/Fall2004/pdf_files/Napoli%20&%20Joshua-Refereed-GMJ -F04.pdf).

12. Beers, 2003, op. cit., 3.

13. A. Kohut, "American Public Diplomacy in the Islamic World," The Senate Foreign Relations Committee Hearing, 2003 (http://foreign. senate.gov/testimony/2003/Kohut Testimony030227.pdf).

14. It was reported that Charlotte Beers resigned for health reasons and her position remained vacant for many months. In December 2003, Margaret D. Tutwiler, a former American ambassador to Morocco, was appointed the new Under Secretary of State for Public Diplomacy and Public Affairs and remained only for five months. See Napoli and Fejeran, op. cit., 8.

15. S. Johnson and H. Dale, "How to Reinvigorate US Public Diplomacy," 2003 (http://www.heritage.org/Research/NationalSecurity/ bg1645.cfm).

16. USINFO, "US Image in the Islamic World: "Policy" is the Problem," 2002 (http://usinfo.state.gov/admin/005/wwwh21126.html).

[635]

17. J. Nye, "Soft Power: The Means to Success in World Politics," 2004, 10 (http://bcsia.ksg.harvard.edu/BCSIA_content/documents/Joe_Nye_Wielding_Soft_Power.pdf).

18. H. Finn, "The Case for Cultural Diplomacy: Engaging Foreign Audiences," *Foreign Affairs* vol. 82, no. 6 (2003), 15–20.

19. Tomlinson, 2003 op. cit., 8.

20. Nye, 2004, op. cit., 1.

21. M. Ayish, "Political Communication on Arab World Television: Evolving Patterns," *Political Communication* 19 (2002), 137–54.

22. Tomlinson, 2003, op. cit.

23. M. El Nawaway and A. Iskandar, *Al Jazeera: How the Free Arab News Network Scooped the World and Changed the Middle East* (Boulder, CO: Westview Press, 2002).

24. For further details, see Rugh, W. "How Washington Confronts Arab Media," *Global Media Journal* vol. 2, no. 4, 2004 [b] (http://lass.calumet.purdue.edu/cca/gmj/SubmittedDocuments/Fall2004/invited/rugh.htm).

25. Ibid.

26. A number of Arab regimes that carried out public relations functions for the United States in their respective countries cannot do it any longer. First, because they have become ineffective and second because their public relations energies and activities are concentrated on their own survival.

27. W. Rugh, "Fixing Public Diplomacy for Arab and Muslim Audiences," 2004 [a] (http://www.hoover.stanford.edu/publications/books/fulltext/practical /145.pdf).

28. W. Rugh, "How Washington Confronts Arab Media," *Global Media Journal,* vol. 2, no. 4, 2004 [b] (http://lass.calumet.purdue.edu/cca/gmj/SubmittedDocuments/Fall2004/ invited/rugh.htm).

29. For further details, see Rugh, 2004 [b] op. cit. For instance, on April 12, 2004, General John Abizaid, Commander of the US Central

Command, denounced the Arab media, particularly Al Jazeera and Al Arabiya for their false reports in Iraq.

30. Nisbet, E. et al., "Public Diplomacy, Television News, and Muslim Opinion," *Press/Politics* vol. 9, no. 2 (2004), 11–37.

31. Reporters without Borders, "Journalists Killed," 2003 (http://www.rsf.org/artkilled_2003.php3?id_article=5966).

32. The quotation was taken from the title of an article by William Rugh, published in the *Global Media Journal*. See W. Rugh, "How Washington Confronts Arab Media," *Global Media Journal* vol. 2, no. 4, 2004 (http://lass.calumet.purdue.edu/cca/gmj/SubmittedDocuments/Fall2004/invited/rugh.htm).

33. In 2002, the VOA Arabic service, which for decades had carried American material to Arab audiences, went off the air.

34. Rugh, 2004 [b], op. cit., 159.

35. Thatcher, G. "Interview about Middle East Radio Network," *PBS Online Newshour*, January 16, 2002 (http://www.pbs.org/newshour/media/public_diplomacy/thatcher.html).

36. Tomlinson, 2003 op. cit., 6.

37. Rugh, 2004 [b] op. cit.

38. Duncan, B. "Political discontent hinders US PR," 2004 (http://english.aljazeera.net/NR/exeres/05FAA6CA-6D62-4DCE-A779-1DBD0000C91F.htm).

39. Rugh, 2004 [b], op. cit., 159.

40. Marc Lynch, "Taking Arabs Seriously," *Foreign Affairs* vol. 82, no. 5, 2003 (http://www.foreignaffairs.org/20030901faessay82506/marc-lynch/taking-arabs-seriously.html).

41. Nye, 2004, op. cit., 10–11.

42. Fandy, M. "Interview about Middle East Radio Network," *PBS Online Newshour*, 16 January 2002 (http://www.pbs.org/newshour/media/public_diplomacy/fandy.html).

43. R. Keohane and J. Nye, "Power and Interdependence in the Information Age," *Foreign Affairs*, vol. 77 no. 5 (September/October 1998) (http://www.ksg.harvard.edu/prg/nye/power.pdf). See Nye 2004, op. cit.

44. M. Leonard and C. Smewing, *Public Diplomacy and the Middle East*, The British Council, 2003 (http://fpc.org.uk/reports/).

45. Potter, E. "Canada and the New Public Diplomacy," *Diplomacy Paper* Issue 81, July 2002 (http://www.clingendael.nl/publications/2002/20020700_cli_paper_dip_issue81.pdf).

46. Gunther Hellmann, "Der "deutsche Weg," Eine außenpolitische Gratwanderung." *Internationale Politik*, 9 (2002): 1–8.

47. Mulack, G. "Beim Dialog mit dem Islam zum Umdenken aufgefordert," *hib-Meldung of the German Bundestag*, 056/2003 (http://www.bundestag.de/bic/hib/2003/2003_056/01.html).

48. Gunter Mulack was German Ambassador to Kuwait and Bahrain from 1995 to 1999. He also served as Ambassador to Syria until 2002. He is fluent in Arabic.

49. In terms of expenditure, German public diplomacy is under-funded. Germany spent US$218 million on public diplomacy for the whole Islamic world last year. The US$218 million annual budget is but a small portion of what is being spent by the United States (see Table 10.1). The United States spends US$1.12 billion on its soft power. Despite its small budget on public diplomacy with comparison to the US, Germany is perceived by more and more people as a serious partner of dialogue.

50. Mulack, 2003, op. cit.

51. R. Schlageter, "Public Diplomacy," *Diplomatisches Magazin* no. 4 (2005), 28.

52. J. Fischer, "Rede von Bundesaußenminister Fischer vor der 56. Generalversammlung der VN in New York am 12. November 2001"

(http://www.auswaertiges-amt.de/www/de/ausgabe_archiv?archiv_id= 2908).

53. A recent example was the German University in Cairo, opened in 2003.

54. K. Hafez, *Auslandsrundfunk im "Dialog der Kulturen" Konzeptionelle Überlegungen zur Gestaltung der DW-Programme in der islamischen Welt,* 2002 (Unpublished Documentation).

55. K. Hafez, "The Iraq War 2003 in Western Media and Public Opinion: A Case Study of the Effects of Military (Non-) Involvement on Conflict Perception," *Global Media Journal* vol. 2, no. 4, 2004 (http://lass.calumet.purdue.edu/cca/gmj/SubmittedDocuments/archive dpapers/Fall2004/pdf_files/hafez.pdf)

56. The Institut fuer Auslandsbeziehungen (IFA).

57. IFA, "About IFA: Tasks, Purposes, Departments," IFA Website, 2004 (http://www.ifa.de/w/ewifa.htm).

58. IFA, 2004, op. cit.

59. Under the auspices of German President Johannes Rau, an international conference on "The Ethics of Journalism in the Islamic-Western Context" was held at the Bellevue Palace, Berlin in 2001. It was directed by Dr. Kai Hafez, Professor for International Communication at the University of Erfurt. In addition, the Stuttgart-based Institute for Foreign Affairs (IFA) has organized since 2000 a number of conferences in the Arab world and Germany respectively. The last German-Arab Media Dialogue was hosted in May 2004 in Abu Dhabi, UAE, under the title "Media Cultures and the Challenges of Globalization."

60. IFA, 2004, op. cit.

61. Most conferences organized by Germany declare both Arabic and German as official languages and always make translation services available.

62. It should be noted that the official Federal Foreign Office website has added information material in Arabic. Other European countries such as France and England offered no Arabic-language material on their respective websites.

63. J. Limbach, "10 Thesen zur Rolle des Goethe-Instituts," 2004 (http://www.goethe.de/uun/auz/ths/deindex.htm).

64. R. Keohane and J. Nye, 1998, op. cit. (http://www.ksg.harvard.edu/prg/nye/power.pdf).

65. E. Nisbet et al., "Public Diplomacy, Television News, and Muslim Opinion," *Press/Politics* vol. 9, no. 2 (2004), 11–37.

66. Radio programs such as the *VOA* and *RFE/RL* were important sources of unbiased information for audiences in Communist countries during the Cold War, when millions of Central and Eastern Europeans listened to news reports, commentary and analysis on current issues that provided alternatives to propaganda by their governments.

67. R. Zaharna, "Finding America's Voice in the Middle East," 2002 (http://www.fpif.org/commentary/2002/0204usmideast.html).

68. S. McEvoy-Levy, *American Exceptionalism and US Foreign Policy: Public Diplomacy at the End of the Cold War* (New York, NY: Palgrave, 2001).

Chapter 21

1. Cited in Bill Katovsky, "Introduction," in Bill Katovsky and Timothy Carlson (eds), *Embedded: The Media at War in Iraq* (Guilford, CT: Lyons Press, 2003), xii.

2. The British military had similar arrangements.

3. Kim Hume, "Birth of the Embed: How the Pentagon's Embedded Journalist Program Came to be," *The Daily Standard*, March 28, 2003.

4. See the comments of Capt. T. McCleary, Special Assistant for Public Affairs to the Joint Chiefs of Staff, in "Embedded Journalists: Is Truth

the First Casualty of War?" panel discussion at the School of Communication, American University, April 21, 2003 (see http://www.soc.american.edu/main.cfm?pageid=882).

5. Howard Fineman, "Political Lives: The Global War for Hearts and Minds," *Newsweek Web Exclusive*, March 19, 2003, accessed via Lexis-Nexis news archive.

6. "Public Affairs Guidance (PAG) on Embedding Media during Possible Future Operations/Deployments in the US Central Commands (CENTCOM) Area of Responsibility (AOR)," 101900z, Feb 03. Reprinted in the Appendix, Katovsky and Carlson, op. cit.

7. Ibid. This does not necessarily mean that the Al Jazeera correspondent enjoyed the same access to information as other correspondents. For an account of the experience, see Amr El Kakhy, "Trapped in the Media Crossfire," Katovsky and Carlson, op. cit., 179–92.

8. See comments of Capt. T. McCleary referred to in Note 4.

9. Comment of George C. Wilson aired on "The Media's War," *MacNeil/Lehrer News Hour*, April 21, 2003. Transcript accessed via Lexis-Nexis news archive.

10. Chris Hedges, "The Press and the Myths of War," *The Nation*, April 21, 2003 (available at http://www.thenation.com/doc.mhtml?i=2003 0421&s=hedges).

11. John Hendren, cited in Lieutenant Colonel Tammy L. Miracle, "The Army and Embedded Media," *Military Review*, September–October 2003, 44.

12. William Branigin, "The Checkpoint Killing," in Katovsky and Carlson, op. cit., 229–34.

13. "Open Letter to the Devil Dogs of 3.1," November 21, 2004 (available at http://www.kevinsites.net/2004_11_21_archive.html).

14. Bryan Whitman, "The Birth of Embedding as Pentagon War Policy," in Katovsky and Carlson, op. cit., 207.

15. Columbia University Journalism School, "Embedded Reporters: What are Americans Getting?" Report of the Project for Excellence in Journalism, April 2003 (http://www.journalism.org/resources/research/reports/war/embed/pejembedreport.pdf). See also Cardiff School of Journalism, "Too Close for Comfort? The Role of Embedded Reporting during the 2003 Iraq War," Report summary published 2004 (http://www.soc.surrey.ac.uk/warandmedia/documents/comfort_summary. doc).

16. "TV Combat Fatigue on the Rise, but 'Embeds' Viewed Favorably," Pew Research Center for the People and the Press, March 28, 2003 (http://people-press.org/reports/display.php3?ReportID=178).

17. The acknowledgment appeared in the May 26, 2004 edition of the paper as an "Editors' Note," A-10.

18. Michael Massing, "Unfit to Print?" *New York Review of Books*, June 24, 2004, 8.

19. Russell Smith, "The New Newspeak," *New York Review of Books*, May 29, 2003, 19.

20. "Too Close for Comfort?" report summary referred to in Note 15.

Chapter 22

1. Christopher Paul and James J. Kim, "Reporters on the Battlefield: The Embedded Press System in Historical Context" (Santa Monica, CA: RAND, National Security Research Division, 2004), 43.

2. Phillip Knightley, "The First Casualty: The War Correspondent as Hero and Myth-maker from the Crimea to Kosovo" (Baltimore and London: The Johns Hopkins University Press, 2000), iix.

3 Digital History, "War Fever and Antiwar Protests, 1820–1860" (http://www.digitalhistory.uh.edu/database/article_display.cfm?HHID =318).

4   Robert W. Johannsen, *To the Halls of the Montezumas: The Mexican War in the American Imagination* (Oxford and New York, NY: Oxford University Press, 1985), 16.

5   Johannsen, op. cit., 20.

6   Knightley, op. cit., 23.

7   Knightley, op. cit., 21.

8   Knightley, op. cit., 23.

9   Knightley, op. cit., 27.

10 Newseum, "The New History Gazette—The History of News" (Freedom Forum, 1997), 14.

11 Knightley, op. cit., 131.

12 Knightley, op. cit., 133.

13 Knightley, op. cit., 301.

14 Knightley, op. cit., 401.

15 Carol Morello, "Tight Control Marks Coverage of Afghan War; Curbs Exceed Those of Past; Broader Access is Promised," *Washington Post,* Dec. 7, 2001, A43.

16 Ibid.

17 Ibid.

18 Alicia C. Shepard, *Narrowing the Gap: Military, Media and the Iraq War* (Chicago, IL: Robert F. McCormick Tribune Foundation, 2003), 11.

19 Shepard, op. cit., 11–12.

20 Shepard, op. cit., 13.

21 Department of Defense, "Directive 5122.5: Principles of Information," December 2, 1993 (http://www.usmc.mil/directiv.nsf/0/2d60387a77a175a5852564970066850e/$FILE/MCO%205720.67.pdf).

22 Paul and Kim, op. cit., 112.

23 Shepard, op. cit., 23.

24 Paul and Kim, op. cit. 80.

25 Paul and Kim, op. cit., 82–83.

26 Shepard, op. cit., 58.

27 Victoria Clarke, panel member, "Assessing Media Coverage of the War in Iraq: Press Reports," Brookings Institution, June 17, 2003 (http://www.brookings.edu/dybdocroot/comm/events/20030617.pdf).

28 Peter Andrews, "The Media and the Military," *American Heritage* vol. 42, no. 4 (July 1991), 71.

29 David Lamb, "He Wages War—on Reality" (*Los Angeles Times,* April 8, 2003), 1.

30 Ibid.

31 Pew Research Center for the People and the Press, "TV Combat Fatigue on Rise," Pew Charitable Trust, March 28, 2003 (http://people-press.org/reports/display.php3?ReportID=178).

32 Paul and Kim, op. cit., 88.

33 The Gallup Organization, "Media Use and Evaluation," (www.gallup.com/poll/content/print.aspx?ci=1663).

34 Ibid.

35 Pew Research Center for the People and the Press, "Iraq Prison Scandal Hits Home, but Most Oppose Troop Pullout," Pew Charitable Trust, May 12, 2004 (http://people-pres.org/reports/print.pho3?PageID=824).

36 Josh Getlin, "All-News Channels Find Big Audience," *Los Angeles Times*, April 5, 2003, 4.

37 Ibid.

38 Pew Research Center for the People and the Press, op. cit.

39 Pew Research Center for the People and the Press, "Public Wants Neutrality *and* Pro-American Point of View," Pew Charitable Trust, July 13, 2003 (http://people-pres.org/reports/print.pho3?PageID=721).

40 The Project for Excellence in Journalism & the Committee of Concerned Journalists, "Embedded Journalists: What Are Americans Getting?" March 22, 2003 (http://www.journalism.org/resources/research/reports/war/embed/impressions.asp).

41 Ibid.

42 Greg Mitchell, "15 Stories They've Already Bungled," *Editor and Publisher* online, March 27, 2003 (http://www.editorandpublisher.com/eandp/news/article_display.jsp?vnu_content_id=1850208).

43 Noujaim, Jehane. *Control Room* documentary, Artisan Entertainment, DVD released October 26, 2004.

44 Rob Curtis, photo of mortally wounded soldier, *Army Times,* April 21, 2003, 6.

45 Ashley Gilbertson, photo of wounded Marine in Fallujah, *New York Times*, November 10, 2004,1.

46 Capt. David Connolly, "Media on the Battlefield: 'A Nonlethal Fire,'" US Army Infantry School, *Infantry Magazine* vol. 93, no. 3, May 1, 2004, 31.

47 Sherry Ricchiardi, "Close to the Action," *American Journalism Review*, May 2003, 28 (http://ajr.org/Article.asp?id=2991).

48 Bob Franken, panel member, "Assessing Media Coverage of the War in Iraq: Press Reports," Brookings Institution, June 17, 2003 (http://www.brookings.edu/dybdocroot/comm/events/20030617.pdf).

49 Liz Marlantes, "The Other Boots on the Ground: Embedded Press," *Christian Science Monitor*, April 23, 2003, 1.

50 House Armed Services Committee, November 17, 2004 (Transcript available at: http://www.house.gov/hasc/schedules/2004.html).

51 Connolly, op. cit., 31.

[645]

52 Ibid.

53 Stephen Hess, panel member, "Assessing Media Coverage of the War in Iraq: Press Reports," Brookings Institution, June 17, 2003 (http://www.brookings.edu/dybdocroot/comm/events/20030617.pdf).

54 Allan Johnson, "Cable News gets Huge Ratings Lift from War: Some Networks also see Gains," *Chicago Tribune*, March 27, 2003, 17.

Chapter 25

1 Salah Al Deen Al Hafiz, "Al Huriya: Ma'zaq Al'Ilam Al'Arabi," *Al Dirasat Al'Ilamiya* no. 95, Cairo, April-June, 1999, 7.

2 Al Hafiz, op. cit., 12.

3 Ghassan Tuwainy, "Sahafat Al Huriya wa Al Haqiqa," an article published in Al *Sahafa Al Siyasiya wa Al Iqtisadiya fi Libnan*, a special issue published by the Lebanese Consulate General in Dubai, 1994.

4 Quoted from Ghassan Tuwainy, "Jara'id Al Amas wa Al Yom," Beirut, August 4, 1971 (A special issue on the 35th anniversary of the founding of *An Nahar* newspaper).

5 Ibid.

6 See Abdullah Khaleel, "Tashri'at 'Ilam Al 'Arabia min Manzor Hiqoq Al Insan," in a debate titled *Dawra Wasail Al 'Ilam fi Nashr Thaghafat Hiqoq Al Insan*, Arab Institute for Human Rights and the Union of Arab Journalists, Cairo, September 30, 1999.

7 Egyptian Organization for Human Rights, "Halat Hiqoq Al Insan fi Misr," Annual Report for 2003, Chapter 6, Huriyat Al Rai wa Al T'abeer (www.eohr.org).

8 See UNDP, "Towards Establishing a Knowledge-based Society in Arab States," *Arab Human Development Report 2003* (Amman: Al Matba'a Al Wataniya, 2003), 146.

9   See Abdullah Khaleel, op. cit.

10 In using this survey of most Arab states, reliance was mainly placed on the study by Abdullah Khaleel, op. cit.

11 See *Arab Human Development Report 2003*, op. cit.

12 Muhammad Al Baalbaki, "al Huriyya fi Al Koran Al Kareem," lectures given at the Islamic Cultural Center, Beirut, May, 13, 1997, published in *An Nahar* newspaper, May 14, 1997.

13 Quoted from Media International Forum which held a debate on "Professional Ethics and Responsibilities," in Hungary. The summary of the debate was published in the Forum's bulletin in its March 29–April 1, 1996 issue.

14 Ibid.

15 Jibran Tuwainy, "al Sahafa wa kaif Akhdom biha Baladi," a lecture given in Al 'Orwatu Al Wothga Society, AUB, 1938. Quoted from Ghassan Tuwainy, *Sir Al Mihna wa Osolaha*, *Al Nahar* series, Kitabu Al Tis'iynyat (Beirut: Dar Al Nahar, 1990).

16 See UNDP, "Towards Freedom in the Arab World," *Arab Human Development Report 2004* (Amman: Al Matba'a Al Wataniya, 2005).

Chapter 27

1. In the era of the traditional Arab state, despite its flaws, there were many liberties and even media openness. There were multiple parties and a robust parliamentary life. However, the post-independence nation-state destroyed all existing structures on the pretext of corruption. However, the problem was that instead of carrying out the required purges, it ended all the existing positive aspects, and some of these states headed towards totalitarianism and autocracy in a style similar to some intellectual systems which dominated the West in the past two centuries. See, Abdullah Al Olayan, "Al 'Arab wa Al Sisiyasa: Munaqashat li Ishkaliyat Al Takween – Al Ta'azum – Al

Khalal" in *Al Ansari wa Sosologia Al Azma* (Beirut: Al Muassa Al 'Arabia lil Al Dirasat wa Al Nashr; Amman: Dar Al Faris, 2000), 201.

2. In the 1950s and 1960s our parents' generation used to follow breaking news and events via the radio as the only available means at that time – especially via the BBC. Exercising their critical sense, many tuned their radios to the BBC because news via some Arab radio stations lacked credibility and accuracy in reporting. I recall that in the late 1960s, as we became more conscious of world events, I and my friends did not appreciate what our parents used to say about our Arab radio stations until we realized the truth of their statements.

3. See Jihan Ahmed Rushti, Al *Ossos Al 'Almiya li Nazariyat Al 'Ilam* (Cairo: Dar Al Fikr Al 'Arabi, 1978), 559, 560.

4. See Muhammad Abdul Qadir Hatim, *Al Rai Al 'Aam wa Ta'thoraho bi Al 'Ilam wa Al Di'aya* (Beirut, Maktabat Libnan, 1973), 35. The media researcher Leo Bogart commented: "Media channels are a tool which can serve different ends. They are indispensable for any democratic society because they provide information to all social levels and reach all geographical locations. Media channels provide a forum for discussion and dialogue. They also create and determine the separate circles for different interest groups which are capable of bargaining for the sake of permission of democratic activity. At the same time, media channels – by creating expertise, common symbols and providing the public with a link to its leaders – consequently become a constant reminder of the national identity." See "Al 'Ilam wa Al Demqratiya," *Al Thaghafa Al 'Aalamiya* no. 83 (Kuwait: 1997), 55.

5. See Mustafa Al Masmodi, *Al Nizam Al I'alami Al Jadid, 'Aalam Al Ma'rifa* series, no. 94 (Kuwait: Kuwait National Council for Culture, Arts and Literature, 1985), 229. In his introduction to this book, Dr. Muhammad Al Rumaihi maintains that "though Arab media suffers from the weakness of its institutions and scarcity of specialized and trained human cadres, it also suffers from the censorship imposed on it and from the difficulties caused to those who work in this sector. If part of the solution may be found in training media personnel, upgrading the

level of their qualification and adhering to systematic methods, the other part certainly lies in giving freedom, both to the media organizations and to those who work in it. The freedom we call for is responsible freedom which rejects disorder and provides room for flexible, democratic dialogue whereby ideas gain maturity and decisions are made after lengthy reflection, assessment and deliberation to put the interests of the Arab nation and the preservation of its values and originality in the first place."

6. Al Masmodi, op. cit., 265.

7. Muhammad Shuman, "'Awlamat Al 'Ialam wa Mustaqbal Al A'lam Al 'Arabi," *'Aalam Al Fikr* vol. 82, no. 2 (Kuwait: October–December, 1999), 153. At one conference, Abdul Al Raouf Al Basti, Chairman of the Tunisian Radio and Television Corporation wondered, "Have those in charge of media channels in our countries understood that in the age of information and interactive media, their job no longer requires them to be leading and directing public opinion as much as it requires them to listen to others, especially since the level of awareness in their societies is expanding day by day? This knowledge base will rapidly expand, which will require developing greater interaction between the managers of media and communication channels and decision makers in their countries." See "Al 'Ialam Al 'Arabi fi Mowajahat Tahidiyat Al Marhala Al Rahina," First Arab Thought Conference (Cairo, October 27–29, 2002), 383.

8. 'Adnan Ahmed Ali, "Al 'Ialam wa Al Sulta fi Al Watan Al 'Arabi fi Dou Al Tataworat Al Qadima," *Shi'oun Al Awsat* no. 56 (Beirut: October, 1996), 70. It should be mentioned here that it is unfair for the writer to generalize such remarks with regard to the Arab media. Some Arab media institutions maintain high professional standards and have given competent nationals an opportunity to launch a career without recourse to nepotism, lip service and personal relationships.

9. Al Munji Al Zaidi, "Al Thaghafa wa Al Mal fi Mustaqbal Al Tanmiya Al Thaghafiya." See *Al Thaghafa Al 'Arabia: aselat Al Tatawor wa Al*

Mustagbal by a group of authors (Beirut: Markaz Dirasat Al Wihda
Al 'Arabia), 275.

10. Jab Allah Musa Hassan, "Mujtama'a Al 'Ialam Al 'Aalmi," *Sotour*
no. 37 (London: December 1999), 35. Dr. Abd Al Ilah Belqiziz
maintains that "the collapse of cultural sovereignty lies in the
increased exposure of the national cultural fabric to tearing caused by
intense external pressures, both cultural and normative. There are
successive self-failures internally inflicted on the institutions involved
in the production of symbols and values. This has occurred because of
the calcification of the structures of these institutions and their
inability to adjust positively to global cultural transformations. In
short, the traditional national cultural system has collapsed and Arab
society is incapable of producing an alternative from within its
existing structures. What is more poignant is that the collapse of
national culture – authority, frame of reference, sovereignty – lays the
foundations for eroding the conditions needed to resist the
mechanisms of an invading cultural globalization, which is growing
objectively with the ultimate goal of destroying borders and unifying
the world in consistency with a single system of values! Thus and
without considering any ontological priority, the expansion of cultural
globalization is accompanied by the ebbing and retreat of cultural
sovereignty in the societies of the South generally, and in Arab
societies particularly." see Abdul Ilah Belqaziz, 'Abdul Ilha Beqaziz,
"Al 'Awlam wa Al Al Hawiya Al Thaghafiya," in *Al Mustaqbal Al
Arabi* no. 229 (Beirut: March, 1998).

11. Jihan Saleem, "'Awlamat Al Thaghafa wa Istratigiyat Al Ta'amul
ma'ha fi Zil Al 'Awlama." See *Al Thaghafa Al Arabia: as'lat Al
Tatawor wa Al Mustagbal*, op. cit., 243.

12. Mahmoud Haider, "Moqawimat Al Sayadat Al Wataniya ba'ad Al
Harb Al Barida," *Al Tariq* no. 1, year 59 (Beirut: 2000), 139–140.
Bourhan Ghalioun maintains that many paradoxes have emerged from
the phenomenon of the Information Revolution. First, at the time
when the world is truly heading towards integration and a common
destiny more than in any previous epoch, such that an event occurring

anywhere in the world inevitably stirs reactions and affects people in other places, the world also seems more disintegrated and split asunder than at any past time. The second paradox is that while media channels and international officials ceaselessly remind people of the need to transcend political borders and become part of the huge global market, the borders between the North and the South have never been as completely closed against the movement of individuals as they are now. The third paradox is that while media channels freed by the telecommunications revolution have allowed all the people of the globe to communicate materially across borders and view what goes on in all countries and be familiar with the customs, working modes and lifestyles of other nations, human and spiritual communication is almost entirely non-existent, giving place to different forms of superiority and isolationism. The fourth paradox is that while the international community is undoubtedly witnessing the greatest leap in its technological progress, which has allowed and continues to allow it to increase average and total production, the areas stricken by poverty and threatened by famine is expanding. The fifth paradox is that although culture ranks as the first sector in economics, and the cultural industry sector, which includes media, information and communication industries, has become a pioneering sector with the highest profitability, the ideology of the market economy prevails. The sixth paradox is that while liberalism is becoming the religion of public life and the scripture of international relations, policies of protectionism continue to grow, as if the policy of openness is only required from weaker states vis-à-vis stronger ones. See Burhan Ghalyun, "Al 'Awlama wa Awham Al Mugtam'a Al M'alumati." *Shi'oun Al Awasat* no. 77 (Beirut: November 1998), 48, 49.

13. Suwaim Al 'Aazi, "Al 'Awlama wa Al Taba'iya wa dawor Al Thaghafa fi I'adat Al Ist'mar," *Shi'oun Al Awasat* no. 60 (Beirut: March 1997), 40.

14. Al 'Aazi, op.cit., 40–41.

15. Abdullah Al Olayan, "Hal Tataraj'a Sayadat Al Dawla fi Zil Al 'Awlama?" *Al Khaleej* newspaper (Sharjah: 5 January, 2004), 12.

16. Sabir Falhout and Muhammad Al Bukhari, *Al 'Awlama wa Al Tabadul Al 'lami Al Dawli* (Damascus: Manshurat Dar 'Ala ad-Din, 1999) 4–5. Jalal Amin says, "The beginning of globalization coincided five centuries ago with the dawn of the nation-state phenomenon, when technological progress and increasing productivity required expanding the domain of the market to include entire nations. Just as the state gradually replaced feudalism about five centuries ago, multinational companies are replacing the state today. In both cases, the reason is the same: technological progress, increasing productivity and the need for wider markets. The borders of the nation-state are no longer the borders of the new market. The whole world has become the domain of marketing, and thus the production company has leapt over the walls of the state … either by virtue of its ability to escape what the state imposes in terms of monetary and financial policies, or by its ability to impose whatever policies it likes on the state itself … not by armed invasion but by exerting conscious, deliberate efforts that help to destroy the old issue of loyalty – the homeland or the nation – and replacing it by new loyalties: ideas such as the end of ideology, the end of history, the global village, mutual interdependence … or of the Greater Middle East type." Jalal Amin, "Al 'Awlama wa a Dawla," a comment made in a debate organized by the Center for Arab Unity Studies in Beirut, 18–20 December, 1996, reviewed by Ali Ismail Nasar, *Shi'oun Al Awasat* no. 71 (Beirut: April, 1998), 84–85.

17. Jalal Amin, op. cit. 95.

18. Mustafa Al 'Ani, "Mulahazat Hawal Ta'amul Al I'alam Al Arabi Ma'a Qadaya Al Irhab wa Al O'nf Al Siyasi," *Araa Hawal Al Khaleej* no. 3 (Dubai: 2004), 33.

19. Al 'Ani, op. cit. The writer Jean Sutton believes that modern media channels that adopt offensive styles stir terror. When they hear a story, these channels act like demagogues and devote major resources to cover the news of a disclosed "scandal" and they convey this to the public in a dramatic way. Amid such a storm, the interest of media channels is confined to confirming the evidence supporting the existing orientation. Seldom do they consider whether the story in its

totality is "true." In many cases the evidence of the truth of such stories does not go beyond a few additions to previous press reports. This kind of behavior is not only the result of laziness or self-complacency but it is also the result of a more compelling feeling—fear. This includes the fear of missing a story which is being covered by all, fear of losing the opportunity of satisfying public thirst, fear of a fall in circulation figures and fear of losing job opportunities in a merciless, competitive market. See, "Al 'Aam wa Al Khas wa Wasail Al 'Ilam," trans. Safaa Romani, *Al Thaghafa Al 'Alamiya* no. 125 (Kuwait: July 2004), 25–26.

20. See Talal 'Itrisi, "Al Amn Al Qawmi wa Siyadat Al Dawlat fi 'Asr Al 'Awlama," by a group of authors, *Al 'Awlama wa Atharaha fi Al Mujtam'a Al Dawlii*, (Abu Dhabi: ECSSR, 2002), 63. Dr. Turki Al Hamad maintains that current developments in the age of globalization are a kind of "radical reversal in the relations between countries, in the traditional relations between the ruler and the ruled and what this entails in terms of possible changes in the form of the state and what is considered legitimate governing style. This is happening in a way that leads to the conclusion that such a reversal is not lesser in its future importance than that reversal in European history which eventually led to the end of an age and the beginning of another, and what this entails in the beginning of new political concepts, or new implications of old concepts." See Turki Al Hamad, "al Dawlat wa Siyasa fi 'Asr Al 'Awlama," a group of scholars, *Al Islam wa Al Gharb*, *Al 'Arabi* book series, no. 49 (Kuwait: 2002), 69.

21. See Mahmoud Haider, "Jadal Al 'Ilam wa Al Akhlaq fi Tahwolat Al Alf Al Thalitha," *Al Tariq* no. 1, Year 58 (Beirut: 1999), 68–69.

22. "Montalqat Al 'Ilam Al Gharbi," in Abdul Satar Jawad et. al., *Ishkaliyat Al 'Alaqa Al Thaghafiya ma'a Al Gharb*, (Beirut: Markaz Dirasat Al Wihda Al 'Arabia, 1997), 252.

23. See Abdullah Al Olayan, "Al Tahadi Al 'Ilami wa Kaifiyat Al Ta'amul Al Iyjabi ma'a Al Mutaghairat," *Araa Hawal Al Khaleej* no. 3 (Dubai: 2004), 41. Al Saiyd Yassin presents the issue of the new challenges of the information revolution from another angle: it can lead "to a cultural

and linguistic hegemony in the space of knowledge. Similarly, cultures and ways of life, a process which is unwelcome in some societies, will be an easy process via new technologies. For instance, consumption patterns, which are essential for the affluent economies in industrial societies, can be very harmful to the economies of developing countries. If the rich classes in society adopt these consumption patterns this may lead to greater impoverishment of the rest of the classes in society." See Al Saiyd Yassin, *Al Ma'lomatiya wa Hadarat Al 'Awlama: Ru'iya Naghadia 'Arabia* (Cairo: Nahdat Misr lil Al Tiba'a wa Al Nashr wa Al Tawzi'i, 2001), 39.

24. Salih Abu Osba,' *Tahadiyat Al 'Ilam Al 'Arabi* (Amman: Dar Al Shrough, 1999), 30.

2004 Report of the Advisory Commission on Public Diplomacy. September 28, 2004 (http://www.state.gov/r/adcompd/rls/36522.htm).

60 Minutes. "Inside Al Jazeera," CBS-TV, October 10, 2001 (http://www.cbsnews.com/stories/2001/10/10/60minutes/main314278.shtml).

Abdullah, Rasha. "The Impact of Music Television (MTV) on Music Broadcasting in Egypt and the Region." Paper delivered to Article 19 conference on Satellite Broadcasting in the Middle East and North Africa, Cairo, February 1999.

Abu Fadil, Magda. "Straddling Cultures: Arab Women Journalists at Home and Abroad," in Naomi Sakr (ed.) *Women and Media in the Middle East: Power through Self-Expression* (London: I.B. Tauris, 2004).

Abu Osba, Salih. *'Tahadiyat Al 'Ilam Al 'Arabi* (Amman: Dar Al Shrough, 1999).

Abunasr, Abdelkarim. "No Exit from Iraq," in *Al Watan*, cited in *Mideast Mirror*, May 14, 2004.

Advisory Group on the Arab and Muslim World. "Changing Minds, Winning Peace: A New Strategic Direction for US Public Diplomacy in the Arab and Muslim World." Oct. 1, 2003 (http://www.public diplomacy.org/23.htm).

Agence France-Presse (AFP). "Arab Station: US Troops kill Cameraman." *The Atlanta Journal-Constitution*, March 18, 2004.

Agence France-Presse (AFP). "Al Arabiya Lawyer Criticizes Military Report on Shooting of two Journalists." *Jordan Times*, March 31, 2004.

Agence France-Presse (AFP). "Al Arabiya to Resume Coverage from Iraq after Two-month Ban." *Middle East Times*, January 28, 2004.

Ajami, Fouad. "What the Muslim World is Watching." *The New York Times Magazine*, November 18, 2001 (http://www.allied-media.com/ARABTV/aljazeera/Nytimes%20article.htm).

Al 'Aazi, Suwaim. "Al 'Awlama wa Al Taba'iya wa dawor Al Thaghafa fi I'adat Al Ist'mar." *Shi'oun Al Awasat* no. 60 (Beirut: March 1997).

Al Ahram Center for Political and Strategic Studies. *The Arab Strategic Report 1985* (Cairo: Al Ahram Foundation, 1986).

Al 'Ani, Mustafa. "Mulahazat Hawal Ta'amul Al I'alam Al Arabi Ma'a Qadaya Al Irhab wa Al O'nf Al Siyasi." *Araa Hawal Al Khaleej* no. 3 (Dubai: 2004).

Al Faqiyh, Sa'ad. "I'tradat Al Salafiyyn 'ala Al Dimoqratiya," in Ali Al Kawari (ed.), *Azmat Al Dimoqratiya fi Al Bildan Al 'Arabia: I'tradat wa Tahfuzat 'ala Al Dimoqratiya fi Al 'Alam Al 'Arabi* (London: Dar Al Saqi, 2004).

Al Ghizami, Abdullah. Al *Thaghafa Al Talifizonia: Soqot Al Nukhba wa Brooz Al Sha'abi* (Beirut wa Al Dar Al Baidaa: Al Markaz Al Thaghafi Al 'Arabi, 2004).

Al Hamad, Turki. "al Dawlat wa Siyasa fi 'Asr Al 'Awlama," in *Al Islam wa Al Gharb*, by a group of authors. Al 'Arabi book series, no. 49 (Kuwait: 2002).

Al Harithy, Mohammad Fahd. "War and Media: Difference in Perception." *Arab News,* September 10, 2004.

Al Jazeera, Washington Bureau. *Fact Sheet*, 2004.

Al Kabalan, Marwan. "Arab Media is Spreading its Wings Far and Wide." *Gulf News*, October 10, 2003.

Al Masmodi, Mustafa. "Al Nizam Al I'alami Al Jadid." *'Aalam Al Ma'rifa* series, no. 94 (Kuwait: Kuwait National Council for Culture, Arts and Literature, 1985).

Al Olayan, Abdullah. "Al 'Arab wa Al Sisiyasa: Munaqashat li Ishkaliyat Al Takween - Al Ta'azum - Al Khalal," in *Al Ansari wa Sosologia Al Azma* (Beirut: Al Muassa Al 'Arabia lil Al Dirasat wa Al Nashr; Amman: Dar Al Faris, 2000).

Al Olayan, Abdullah. "Al Tahadi Al 'Ilami wa Kaifiyat Al Ta'amul Al Iyjabi ma'a Al Mutaghairat." *Araa Hawal Al Khaleej* no. 3 (Dubai: 2004).

Al Olayan, Abdullah. "Hal Tataraj'a Sayadat Al Dawla fi Zil Al 'Awlama?" *Al Khaleej* (Sharjah: January 5, 2004).

Al Saha Al A'rabiya. "Arab Media: An Issue and Opinions" (http://www.alsaha.fares.net/sahat?14%4070).

Al Thaghafa Al 'Aalamiya no. 83. "Al 'Ilam wa Al Demqratiya" (Kuwait: 1997).

Al Thaghafa Al 'Alamiya no. 125. "Al 'Aam wa Al Khas wa Wasail Al 'Ilam," translated by Safaa Romani (Kuwait: July 2004).

Al Zaidi, Al Munji. "Al Thaghafa wa Al Mal fi Mustaqbal Al Tanmiya Al Thaghafiya." *Al Thaghafa Al 'Arabia: aselat Al Tatawor wa Al Mustagbal,* by a group of authors (Beirut: Markaz Dirasat Al Wihda Al 'Arabia).

Al Baalbaki, Muhammad. "Al Huriyya fi Al Koran Al Kareem." Lectures given at the Islamic Cultural Center, Beirut, May, 13, 1997. Published in *An Nahar* newspaper, May 14, 1997.

Al Ghamri, Maal and Linda Ayashhia. "War Reporters cross the Invisible Line for Arab Women." *Arab News*, August 7, 2003.

Al Hafiz, Salah Al Deen. "Al Huriya: Ma'zaq Al 'Ilam Al 'Arabi." *Al Dirasat Al 'Ilamiya* no. 95, Cairo, April–June, 1999.

Al Humayd, Tariq. "Al Hurrah: Washington's Sin." *Al Sharq Al Awsat*, July 12, 2004.

Ali, 'Adnan Ahmed. "Al 'Ialam wa Al Sulta fi Al Watan Al 'Arabi fi Dou Al Tataworat Al Qadima." *Shi'oun Al Awsat* no. 56 (Beirut: October, 1996).

Alibhai-Brown, Yasmin. "What Perspectives for Islam and Muslims in Europe? An Overview Identifying Diversity—Muslim Demographics in Europe." The European Policy Centre, May 2004.

Allaf, Rime. "Qatar's Al Jazeera is not pro-Zionist enough for Fouad Ajami's taste." *The Daily Star,* Beirut, November 20, 2001 (http://www.medea.be/?page=lang=&doc=1101).

Alleyne, Mark D. *News Revolution: Political and Economic Decisions about Global Information* (1996).

Alleyne, Mark D. *International Power and International Communications* (Basingstoke: Macmillan, 1995).

Alloula, Malek. *The Colonial Harem* (Minneapolis, MN: University of Minnesota Press, 1986).

Al Mirazi, Hafez. "The 9/11 Commission Recommendations on Public Diplomacy: Defending Ideals and Defining the Message." Testimony before the House Committee on Government Reform Subcommittee on National Security, Emerging Threats and International Relations, August 23, 2004 (http://reform.house.gov/UploadedFiles/HafezAlMirazi Testimony.pdf).

Al Quds Al Arabi. "The Western media has lost its credibility." Editorial, translated and summarized in *Mideast Mirror*, April 1, 2003.

Alterman, Jon B. "Arab Satellite Television: Can it Rise above Spectacle?" *Nashrat Al Islah Al 'Arabi*, mujalad 2, Al 'adad 11, December 2004. Carnegie Endowment for International Peace, translated by Dar Al Watan lil Tiba'a wa Al Nashr, Kuwait (http://www.alwatan.comkw/arb/default.aspx?isu=2041200000211).

Alterman, Jon B. "An Evolving Arab Press." *The Washington Post*, March 28, 2001.

[658]

Alterman, Jon B. "Political Spectacle." *Middle East: Notes and Comment* vol. 2, no. 10, October 1, 2004 (Washington, DC: Center for Strategic and International Studies).

Alterman, Jon B. *New Media New Politics? From Satellite Television to the Internet in the Arab World* (Washington: The Washington Institute for Near East Policy, 1998).

Amin, Hussein. "The Current Situation of Satellite Broadcasting in the Middle East." *Transnational Broadcasting Studies* no. 5, Fall/Winter, 2001 (http://www.tbsjournal.com).

Amin, Hussein. "Two Different Wars: Comparing Arab and US coverage of the Iraq War" (http://www.pbs.newhour/extra/features/jan.june03/media_3-4.htm).

Amin, Hussein. "Watching the War in the Arab World." *Transnational Broadcasting Studies* no. 10, Spring/Summer 2003 (http://www.tbsjournal.com).

Amin, Jalal. "Al 'Awlama wa a Dawla." Comment in a debate organized by the Center for Arab Unity Studies in Beirut, 18–20 December, 1996, reviewed by Ali Ismail Nasar, *Shi'oun Al Awasat* no. 71 (Beirut: April, 1998).

Ammon, R. *Global Television and the Shaping of World Politics: CNN, Telediplomacy, and Foreign Policy* (Jefferson, NC: McFarland, 2001).

Anderson Jon W. "Technology, Media and the Next Generation in the Middle East." Paper delivered at the Middle East Institute, Columbia University, September 28, 1999 (http://nmit.georgetown.edu/papers/jwanderson.htm).

Anderson, Jon W. "Globalizing Politics and Religion in the Muslim World." *Journal of Electronic Publishing* (http://www.press.umich.edu/jep/archive/anderson.html).

Anderson, Jon W. "Transnational Civil Society, Institution-Building, and IT: Reflections from the Middle East." Paper delivered at SSRC

[659]

Summer Institute on Information Technology and Social Research—Setting the Agenda, Columbia University, New York, June 5–8, 2002 (http://nmit.georgetown.edu/papers/transnatcs.htm).

Anderson, Jon W. and Dale Eickelman. "Media Convergence and its Consequences in the Middle East." *Middle East Insights* vol. XIV, no. 2 (2000).

Andrews, Peter. "The Media and the Military." *American Heritage* vol. 42, no. 4 (July 1991).

Arab News. "Al Arabiya: A Balanced Alternative to Al Jazeera?" February 17, 2003.

Arab Press Freedom Watch. Arab Media (http://www.al-bab.com/media).

Arback, Jacob. "Unscripted Television Programs and Corporate/State Concerns: The View from Nilesat." Paper delivered at the Middle East Studies Association November 1999 (http://nmit.georgetown.edu/papers/jarback.htm).

Armbrust, Walter. "The Riddles of Ramadan: Media, Consumer Culture and the 'Christmas-ization' of a Muslim Holiday." Paper delivered at the American Anthropological Association, November 2000 (http://nmit.georgetown.edu/papers/warmbrust.htm).

Armbrust, Walter (ed.) *Mass Meditations: New Approaches to Popular Culture in the Middle East and Beyond* (University of California Press, 2000).

Arquilla, J. and D. Ronfeldt. *The Emergence of Noopolitik: Toward an American Information Strategy* (Santa Monica, CA: RAND, 1999).

Arquilla, J. and D. Ronfeldt. "Information, Power and Grand Strategy: In Athena's Camp," in Stuart J. D. Schwartzenstein (ed.) *The Information Revolution and National Security* (Washington, DC: Center for Strategic and International Studies, 1996).

Ayish, Muhammad. "Political Communication on Arab World Television: Evolving Patterns." *Political Communication* 19 (2002).

Ayish, Muhammad. "Arab Television goes Commercial." *Gazette* 59 (December 1997).

Azzi, Walid. "It's About Time ..." *ArabAd*, 12/8 (September, 2002).

Bagdikian, Ben. *The Media Monopoly* (Boston, MA: Beacon Press, 2000)

Barakat, Halim. Al *Mujtam'a Al Arabi fi Al Qarn Al 'Ishreen: bahath fi taqur Al Ahwal wa Al 'Alaqat* (Beirut: Markaz Dirasat Al Wihda Al 'Arabia, 2000).

Barr, Cameron W. "Top Arab TV Network Hits US Market." *The Christian Science Monitor*, December 26, 2002.

BBC News Online. "Jordan carpets Qatar over TV," August 8, 2002 (http://news.bbc.co.uk).

BBC News Online. "Jordanian wins Arab 'Idol.'" August 18, 2003 (http://news.bbc.co.uk).

Beers, Charlotte. "American Public Diplomacy and Islam." Testimony before the Senate Foreign Relations Committee, February 27, 2003 (http://www.foreign.senate.gov/hearings/2003/hrg030227a.html).

Belchi, Jean-Marc. "Evolution of TV Viewing in the Middle East, 1996–2000." Paper presented to the conference on New Media and Change in the Arab World (Amman, February 27 to March 1, 2002).

Belqaziz, Abdullah. "Al 'Awlam wa Al Al Hawiya Al Thaghafiya," in *Al Mustaqbal Al Arabi* no. 229 (Beirut: March, 1998).

Belqaziz, Abdullah. "Arab Satellite Channels and Issues of the Nation." *Al Mustaqbal Al Arabi* no. 306 (Beirut, 2004).

Blinken, Anthony J. "Winning the War of Ideas," in Alexander T.J. Lennon (ed.), *The Battle for Hearts and Minds: Using Soft Power to Undermine Terrorist Networks* (Cambridge, MA: MIT Press, 2003).

Bollier, D. "The Rise of Netpolitik: How the Internet is Changing International Politics and Diplomacy." Report of the Eleventh Annual Aspen Institute Roundtable on Information Technology, 2003

(http://www.aspeninstitute.org/AspenInstitute/files/CCLIBRARYFILE
S/FILENAME/0000000077/netpolitik.pdf).

Branigin, William. "The Checkpoint Killing," in Bill Katovsky and Timothy Carlson (eds), *Embedded: The Media at War in Iraq* (Guilford, CT: Lyons Press, 2003).

Brewer, Paul, Kimberly Gross, Sean Aday and Lars Willnat. "International Trust and Public Opinion about World Affairs." *American Journal of Political Science* (2004).

Brookings–Harvard Forum. "The CNN Effect: How 24-Hour News Coverage Affects Government Decisions and Public Opinion." Transcript, The Brookings Institution, January 23, 2002.

Brown, J. "The Purposes and Cross-Purposes of Public Diplomacy," *American Diplomacy,* 2002 (http://www.unc.edu/depts/diplomat/ archives_roll/2002_07-09/brown_pubdipl/brown_pubdipl.html).

Brown, Robin. "Clausewitz in the Age of Al Jazeera: Rethinking the Military-Media Relationship." Institute of Communications Studies, University of Leeds, 2002.

Buck, Pearl S. *What America Means To Me* (New York, NY: Arno Press, 1943).

Burns, John F. "Arab TV Gets a New Slant: Newscasts without Censorship." *The New York Times*, July 4, 1999.

Bushara, 'Azmi. *Torohat 'an Al Nahda Al Mu'aqa* (Beirut: Riyad Al Raiyys lil Al Kotob wa Al Nashr, 2003).

Butter, David. "A Hint of Florida Comes to Cairo." *Middle East Economic Digest*, April 2 (1999).

CAIR Action Alert. Poll on American Attitudes about Islam, July 2, 2004.

Cardiff School of Journalism. "Too Close for Comfort? The Role of Embedded Reporting during the 2003 Iraq War." Report summary, 2004 (www.soc.surrey.ac.uk/warandmedia/documents/comfort_summary.doc).

CCAS. "Uncovered: Arab Journalists Scrutinize Their Profession." Report from Georgetown University conference, CCAS *Occasional Paper,* October 7, 2004 (Washington, DC: Center for Contemporary Arab Studies, Georgetown University, January 2005).

CENTCOM. "Public Affairs Guidance (PAG) on Embedding Media during Possible Future Operations/Deployments in the US Central Command's Area of Responsibility (AOR)." 101900z Feb 03.

Clarke, Victoria (panel member). "Assessing Media Coverage of the War in Iraq: Press Reports." Brookings Institution, June 17, 2003 (http://www.brookings.edu/dybdocroot/comm/events/20030617.pdf).

Clinton, Hillary (Senator). Associated Press wire release, March 2, 1999.

Collins, Richard, Nicholas Garnham and Gareth Locksley. *The Economics of Television: The UK Case* (London: Sage Publications, 1988).

Columbia University Journalism School. "Embedded Reporters: What are Americans Getting?" Report of the Project for Excellence in Journalism, April 2003 (www.journalism.org/resources/research/reports/war/embed/pejembedreport.pdf).

Com, David. "Operation Stars and Stripes." *Alter Net*, August 2, 2002.

Committee to Protect Journalists (CPJ). "Baghdad Car Bomb kills Five Al Arabiya Employees." *CPJ News Alert*, November 1, 2004.

Congressional Research Service (CRS). *Al Jazeera: Opportunity or Challenge for US Foreign Policy in the Middle East?* CRS Report to Congress by Jeremy M. Sharp, July 23, 2003 (http://fpc.state.gov/documents/organization/23002.pdf).

Connolly, Capt. David. "Media on the Battlefield: A Nonlethal Fire." US Army Infantry School, *Infantry Magazine* no. 3, vol. 93, May 1, 2004.

Crowdus, Gary and Dan Georgakas. "Thinking about the Power of Images: An Interview with Spike Lee." *Cineaste* vol. XXVI, no. 2.

Curtis, Rob. Photo of mortally wounded soldier. *Army Times,* April 21, 2003.

[663]

Dabbous-Sensenig, Dima. *Ending the War? The Lebanese Broadcasting Act of 1994*. Ph.D thesis, Sheffield Hallam University, 2002.

Dadge, David. "Al Jazeera: A Platform of Controversy." Ch. 2 in Dadge, *Casualty of War: The Bush Administration's Assault on a Free Press* (Amherst, NY: Prometheus Books, 2004).

Dagher, Chantal. "FTV, MBC Merge Media Operations." *ArabAd* vol 11, no. 11, December 2001.

Dajani, Nabil H. "The Changing Scene of Lebanese Television." *Transnational Broadcasting Studies* no.7, Fall 2001 (http://www.tbsjournal.com).

Dean, Thalif. "Media: US Trying to Tighten the Screws on Al Jazeera." Inter-Press Service (IPS)/Global Information Network, October 12, 2004.

Deibert, R.J. *Parchment, Printing and Hypermedia: Communication in World Order Transformation* (Columbia University Press, 1997).

Department of Defense. "Directive 5122.5: Principles of Information." December 2, 1993 (http://www.usmc.mil/directiv.nsf/0/2d60387a77a175a 5852564970066850e/$FILE/MCO%205720.67.pdf).

Digital History. "War Fever and Antiwar Protests—Period: 1820–1860" (http://www.digitalhistory.uh.edu/database/article_display.cfm?HHID= 318).

Dizard, W. *Digital Diplomacy: US Foreign Policy in the Information Age* (Westport, CT: Praeger Publishers, 2001).

Dowd, Maureen. "Cuomos vs. Sopranos." *New York Times*, April 22, 2001.

Doyle, Gillian. *Understanding Media Economics* (London: Sage Publications, 2002).

Duncan, B. "Political Discontent hinders US PR," 2004 (http://english.aljazeera.net/NR/exeres/05FAA6CA-6D62-4DCE-A779-1DBD0000C91F.htm).

[664]

Dunnigan, James. "Fairytales versus Reality in Arab Media." *Strategy Papers,* May 7, 2003.

Egyptian Organization for Human Rights. "Halat Hiqoq Al Insan fi Misr." Annual Report for 2003. Chapter 6, Huriyat Al Rai wa Al T'abeer (www.eohr.org).

El Hachem, Bassam. *Radio Orient: Intégration des musulmans en France et laïcité en question* (Paris: Publisud, 1998).

El Kakhy, Amr. "Trapped in the Media Crossfire" in Bill Katovsky and Timothy Carlson (eds), *Embedded: The Media at War in Iraq* (Guilford, CT: Lyons Press, 2003).

El Nawaway, M. and A. Iskandar. *Al Jazeera: How the Free Arab News Network Scooped the World and Changed the Middle East* (Boulder, CO: Westview Press, 2002).

El Nawawy, M. and Gher, L. "Al Jazeera: Bridging the East-West Gap through Public Discourse and Media Diplomacy." *Transnational Broadcasting Studies* no. 10, Spring/Summer 2003 (http//:www.tbsjournal.com).

Entman, Robert. *Projections of Power: Framing News, Public Opinion and US Foreign Policy* (Studies in Communication, Media and Public Opinion, 2004).

Esposito, John. "American-Muslim Relations at a Crossroads." *Al Ahram* weekly, July 22, 2004.

Evers, Tré. "Success of and Challenges Facing US Public Diplomacy." Statement before the House Committee on Government Reform Subcommittee on National Security, Emerging Threats and International Relations, August 23, 2004 (http://www.state.gov/r/adcompd/rls/35707.htm).

Everts, Philip and Pierangelo Isernia (eds), *Public Opinion and the International Use of Force* (2001).

Fakhreddine, Jihad. "The US-Arab Cross-Communication Exchange: A Dialogue Among Mutes." *Transnational Broadcasting Studies* no. 8, Spring/Summer 2002 (http://www.tbsjournal.com).

Falhout, Sabir and Muhammad Al Bukhari. *Al 'Awlama wa Al Tabadul Al 'lami Al Dawli* (Damascus: Manshurat Dar 'Ala ad-Din, 1999).

Fandy, Mamoun. "Interview about Middle East Radio Network." *PBS Online Newshour*, 16 January 2002 (http://www.pbs.org/newshour/ media/ public_diplomacy/fandy.html).

Fandy, Mamoun. "The Arab Media's Sense of Outrage?" *The Washington Post*, July 4, 2004.

Fandy, Mamoun. "To Reach Arabs, try Changing the Channel." *The Washington Post*, December 2, 2001.

Farah, Samar. "Can Reality TV 'survive' in the Middle East?" *Christian Science Monitor*, March 26, 2004.

Fattah, Hassan M. "Zen Reaches out to Arab Youth." *Transnational Broadcasting Studies* no. 9, Fall/Winter 2002 (http://www. tbsjournal. com).

Feliz Sefsaf, Wendy. "US International Broadcasting Strategies for the Arab World: An Analysis of the Broadcasting Board of Governors' Strategy from a Public Communications Standpoint." *Transnational Broadcasting Studies* no. 13, Fall 2004 (http://www.tbsjournal. com).

Feuilherade, Peter. "Profile: Al Arabiya TV." November 25, 2003 (http://newsvote.bbc.co.uk).

Feustel, Marc et al. "Free Press and Good Governance in Southern Africa: Media Assistance and Free Press Advocacy in Member States of the Southern African Development Community: Mapping Roles and Relationships," Stanhope Centre for Communications Policy Research, 2002.

[666]

Fineman, Howard. "Political Lives: The Global War for Hearts and Minds." *Newsweek Web Exclusive*, March 19, 2003 (via Lexis-Nexis news archive).

Finn, H. "The Case for Cultural Diplomacy: Engaging Foreign Audiences." *Foreign Affairs* vol. 82, no. 6 (2003).

First Arab Thought Conference. "Al 'Ialam Al 'Arabi fi Mowajahat Tahidiyat Al Marhala Al Rahina" (Cairo, October 27–29, 2002).

Fischer, J. "Rede von Bundesaußenminister Fischer vor der 56. Generalversammlung der VN in New York am 12. November 2001" (http://www.auswaertiges-amt.de/www/de/ausgabe_archiv?archiv_id= 2908).

Fisk, Robert. "US Moves to Close Down Al Jazeera TV: Wolfowitz the Censor." *The Independent* (London), August 1, 2003.

Foyle, Douglas. *Counting the Public In: Presidents, Public Opinion and Foreign Policy* (1999).

Foyle, Douglas. "Foreign Policy Analysis and Globalization: Public Opinion, World Opinion, and the Individual." *International Studies Review* (2003).

Franken, Bob. "Assessing Media Coverage of the War in Iraq: Press Reports." Brookings Institution, June 17, 2003 (http://www. brookings.edu/dybdocroot/comm/events/20030617.pdf).

Frantzich, S. and J. Sullivan. *The C-Span Revolution* (1999).

Frederick, H. *Global Communications and International Relations* (New York, NY: Wadsworth, 1992).

Friedman, Thomas L. "Glasnost in the Gulf." *The New York Times*, February 27, 2001.

Friedman, Thomas L. "Telling the Truth in Iraq." *The New York Times*, August 17, 2003.

Friedman, Thomas L. "The Sand Wall." *The New York Times*, April 13, 2003.

[667]

Friedman, Thomas L. "War of Ideas, Part 4." *The New York Times*, January 18, 2004.

Gallagher, Margaret. *An Unfinished Story: Gender Patterns in Media Employment* (Paris: UNESCO, 1995).

Garfinkle, A. *A Practical Guide to Winning the War on Terrorism,* 2003 (http://www-hoover.stanford.edu/publications/books/practical.html).

Gerzon, Mark. Personal Interview, November 30, 2004.

Getlin, Josh. "All-News Channels Find Big Audience." *Los Angeles Times*, April 5, 2003.

Ghalioun, Bourhan. "Al 'Awlama wa Awham Al Mugtam'a Al M'alumati." *Shi'oun Al Awasat* no. 77 (Beirut: November 1998).

Gher, L.A., and H.Y. Amin. *Civic Discourse and Digital Age Communications in the Middle East* (2000).

Gilbertson, Ashley. Photo of wounded Marine in Fallujah. *New York Times*, November 10, 2004, 1.

Gilboa, E. (ed.) *Media and Conflict: Framing Issues, Making Policy, Shaping Opinions* (2002).

Goethe Institute. "About Us," 2004 (http://www.goethe-institut.de/uun/enindex.htm).

Greider, William. "Preface" in Jack Shaheen, *Reel Bad Arabs*.

Gulf News. "Dubai 2003, Al Arabiya Team up for TV Documentary." April 13, 2003.

Hafez, K. (ed.) *Islam and the West in the Mass Media: Fragmented Images in a Globalizing World* (2000).

Hafez, K. "Mass Media in the Middle East: Patterns of Political and Societal Change," in Kai Hafez (ed.) *Mass Media, Politics and Society in the Middle East* (Creskill, NJ: Hampton, 2001).

Hafez, K. "The Iraq War 2003 in Western Media and Public Opinion: A Case Study of the Effects of Military (Non-) Involvement on Conflict

[668]

Perception." *Global Media Journal* vol. 2, no. 4, 2004 (http://lass.calumet. purdue.edu/cca/gmj/SubmittedDocuments/archivedpapers/Fall2004/pdf_ files/hafez.pdf).

Hafez, K. "The West and Islam in the Mass Media: Cornerstones for a New International Culture of Communication in the 21st Century." (http://www.zei.de/download/zei_dp/dp_c61_hafez.pdf).

Hafez, K. *Auslandsrundfunk im "Dialog der Kulturen" Konzeptionelle Überlegungen zur Gestaltung der DW-Programme in der islamischen Welt* (Unpublished Documentation).

Hafez, Salaheddin. "Democracy Slaughtered by its Guardians," in *Al Ahram*, Cairo, cited in *Mideast Mirror*, May 13, 2004.

Haider, Mahmoud. "Moqawimat Al Sayadat Al Wataniya ba'ad Al Harb Al Barida." *Al Tariq* no. 1, year 59 (Beirut: 2000).

Haider, Mahmoud. "Jadal Al 'Ilam wa Al Akhlaq fi Tahwolat Al Alf Al Thalitha." *Al Tariq* no. 1, Year 58 (Beirut: 1999).

Hamdy, Naila. 'A Dream TV Come True.' *Transnational Broadcasting Studies* no. 8, Spring/Summer, 2002 (http://www.tbsjournal.com).

Hariq, Ilila. Al *Dimoqratiya wa Tahadiat Al Hadatha bain Al Sharq wa Al Gharb* (London: Dar Al Saqi, 2001).

Harmon, Matthew. "The Media, Technology and United States Foreign Policy: A Re-examination of the CNN Effect." *Swords and Ploughshares: A Journal of International Affairs* (1999).

Hassan, Jab Allah Musa. "Mujtama'a Al 'Ialam Al 'Aalmi." *Sotour* no. 37 (London: December 1999).

Hatim, Muhammad Abdul Qadir. *Al Rai Al 'Aam wa Ta'thoraho bi Al 'Ilam wa Al Di'aya* (Beirut: Maktabat Libnan, 1973).

Hawthorne, Amy (ed.) *Arab Reform Bulletin* vol. 2, no. 11, December 2004, various articles (Carnegie Endowment for International Peace).

[669]

Hedges, Chris. "The Press and the Myths of War." *The Nation*, April 21, 2003 (http://www.thenation.com/doc.mhtml?i=20030421&s=hedges).

Hellmann, G. "Der "deutsche Weg." Eine außenpolitische Gratwanderung." *Internationale Politik* 9 (2002).

Hesmondhalgh, David. *The Cultural Industries* (London: Sage Publications, 2002)

Hess, Stephen. "Assessing Media Coverage of the War in Iraq: Press Reports." Brookings Institution, June 17, 2003 (http://www.brookings.edu/dybdocroot/comm/events/20030617.pdf).

Hoffman, David. "Beyond Public Diplomacy." *Foreign Affairs* vol. 81, no. 2 (2002).

Hoffman, David. "Tune in to Democracy." *New York Times*, March 13, 2004.

Holsti, Ole. *Public Opinion and American Foreign Policy* (The university of Michigan Press, 1996).

House Armed Services Committee, November 17, 2004 (transcript available at http://www.house.gov/hasc/schedules/2004.html).

Hudson, Michael C. "Information Technology, International Politics and Political Change in the Arab World." *Bulletin of the Royal Institute for Inter-Faith Studies* (Amman) vol. 4, no. 2 (Autumn/Winter 2002).

Human Rights Watch. Annual Report 2003 (http://www.hrw.org/arabic/mena/wr2003/tunisia.htm).

Human Rights Watch. *Lebanon: Restrictions on Broadcasting* (New York, NY: April, 1997).

Hume, Kim. "Birth of the Embed: How the Pentagon's Embedded Journalist Program Came to be." *The Daily Standard*, March 28, 2003.

Ibrahim, Saad Eddin. "Thought on Arab Satellite Television, Pan-Arabism and Freedom of Expression." *Transnational Broadcasting Studies* no.13, Fall 2004 (http://www.tbsjournal.com).

[670]

ICTDAR. "The Road to Tech Mecca." *Wired Magazine*, July 2004.

IFA. "About IFA: Tasks, Purposes, Departments," IFA Website, 2004 (http://www.ifa.dc/w/cwifa.htm).

Independent Task Force. "Public Diplomacy: A Strategy for Reform," 2002 (http://www.cfr.org/pubs/Task-force_final2-19.pdf).

Institut Européen de recherche sur la coopération Mediterranéenne et Euro-Arabe, *Dossier Spéciale: Al Jazira, phénomene médiatique arabe,* 2004 (http://www.medea.be/index.html?page=0&lang=fr&idx=0&doc =717).

Internet World Stats (http://www.internetworldstats.com/stats5.htm# mereports).

Internews Open Media Watch. "Walking a Tightrope: New Media and Freedom of Expression in the Arab World," July 13, 2004 (http://internews. org/openmedia/sept_11_media.htm).

Ipsos-Stat. "Satellite TV Study." *ArabAd* vol. 12, no. 8, September 2002.

'Itrisi, Talal. "Al Amn Al Qawmi wa Siyadat Al Dawlat fi 'Asr Al 'Awlama," in *Al 'Awlama wa Atharaha fi Al Mujtam'a Al Dawlii*, by a group of authors (Abu Dhabi: ECSSR, 2002).

Jacobs, Lewis. *The Rise of the American Film* (New York, NY: Harcourt, 1961).

Johannsen, Robert W. *To the Halls of the Montezumas: The Mexican War in the American Imagination* (Oxford and New York, NY: Oxford University Press, 1985).

Johnson, Allan. "Cable News Gets Huge Ratings Lift from War: Some Networks also see Gains." *Chicago Tribune*, March 27, 2003.

Johnson, S. and H. Dale. "How to Reinvigorate US Public Diplomacy," 2003 (http://www.heritage.org/Research/NationalSecurity/bg1645.cfm).

Jordan Times. "Al Jazeera TV Barred from Covering Hajj," February 11, 2003.

Jordan Times. "Al Jazeera Closed Down for 'Hostile' Stand against Kuwait," November 5, 2002.

[671]

Jorgensen, Pernille Gylling. "The Media Situation in the Middle East." International Media Support, General Report (2004).

Kandil, H. "ERTU, Investors at Odds over Media Privatization." *Transnational Broadcasting Studies* no. 5, Spring 2000 (http:// www.tbsjournal.com).

Karim, H. K. *Islamic Peril: Media and Global Violence* (Montreal: Black Rose Books, 2000).

Katovsky, Bill and Timothy Carlson (eds). *Embedded: The Media at War in Iraq* (Guilford, CT: Lyons Press, 2003).

Kaufman, E. "A Broadcasting Strategy to Win Media Wars." *The Battle for Hearts and Minds* (Washington, DC: Center for Strategic and International Studies, 2003).

Kennedy, John F. Yale Commencement Address, 1962.

Keohane, R. and J. Nye. "Power and Interdependence in the Information Age." *Foreign Affairs* vol. 77, no. 5 September/October 1998 (http:// www.ksg.harvard.edu/prg/nye/power.pdf).

Khaleel, Abdullah. "Tashri'at 'Ilam Al 'Arabia min Manzor Hiqoq Al Insan," in *Dawra Wasail Al 'Ilam fi Nashr Thaghafat Hiqoq Al Insan*, Arab Institute for Human Rights and the Union of Arab Journalists debate, Cairo, September 30, 1999.

Khalil, Joe and Dareen Abu Ghaida. "Appealing to the Hearts and Minds: How Arab Channels fought for the Gulf War Audience." *Transnational Broadcasting Studies* no. 12, Spring/Summer 2004 (http:// www.tbsjournal.com).

Khanfar, Waddah. "The Future of Al Jazeera." *Transnational Broadcasting Studies* no. 12, Spring/Summer 2004 (http://www.tbsjournal.com).

Khanna, P. "America in the Age of Geodiplomacy." *Georgetown Journal of International Affairs* vol. 4, no. 1, Winter/Spring 2003 (http:// journal.georgetown.edu/Issues/ws03/khannalocked.pdf.).

Khazzaka, Nagib. "Row grows in Lebanon over Government Bar on Saudi Programme." *Middle East Times*, January 3, 2003.

[672]

Khouri, Rami G. "Seeking Salvation among Libya, Lockerbie and Future TV's Song Contest." *Jordan Times*, August 20, 2003.

Kilani, Sa'eda. *Freedom Fries: Fried Freedom, Arab Satellite Channels' Struggle between State Control and Western Pressure* (Amman: Arab Archives Institute, 2004).

King, Colbert I. "Condoleezza Rice's Oddball Critic." *The Washington Post*, December 15, 2001.

Knightley, Phillip. "The First Casualty: The War Correspondent as Hero and Myth-maker from the Crimea to Kosovo" (Baltimore and London: The Johns Hopkins University Press, 2000).

Koelsch, Frank. "Infomedia Revolution." Translation by Husam Eddin Zakariya, reviewed by Abdul Salam Radhwan, *Alam Al M'rifa* series no. 253 (Kuwait: The National Council for Culture, Arts and Literature, January 2000).

Kohut, A. "American Public Diplomacy in the Islamic World." The Senate Foreign Relations Committee Hearing, 2003 (http://foreign. senate.gov/ testimony/2003/KohutTestimony030227.pdf).

Kraidy, Marwan M. "Broadcasting Regulation and Civil Society in Postwar Lebanon." *Journal of Broadcasting & Electronic Media* vol. 42, no. 3 (Summer 1998).

Kraidy, Marwan M. "State Control of Television News in 1990s Lebanon." *Journalism and Mass Communication Quarterly* vol. 76, no. 3 (1999).

Kull, Steven (Principal Investigator). "Misperceptions, the Media and the Iraq War." Program on International Policy Attitudes/Knowledge Networks Poll, University of Maryland (study results released on October 2, 2003).

Kuttab, Daoud. "Making Arab Media Really Independent." *Media Monitors Network*, October 9, 2004 (http://middleast.mediamonitors. net/headlines/making_arab_media _really_ independent).

[673]

Lamb, David. "He Wages War—on Reality." *Los Angeles Times,* April 8, 2003.

Leonard, M. and C. Smewing. *Public Diplomacy and the Middle East*. The British Council, 2003 (http://fpc.org.uk/reports/).

Lerner, Daniel. *The Passing of Traditional Society: Modernizing the Middle East* (Glencoe, IL: The Free Press, 1958).

Limbach, J. "10 Thesen zur Rolle des Goethe-Instituts." 2004 (http://www.goethe.de/uun/auz/ths/deindex.htm).

Livingston, Steven. "Beyond the CNN Effect." George Washington University, 1998.

Loewenstein, Anthony. "Al Jazeera Awakens the Arab World." *Counterpunch,* June 13–14, 2004 (http://www.counterpunch.org/loewenstein06132004.html).

Los Angeles Times. "Colin Powell Register US Complaints about Al Jazeera," April 28, 2004 (http://www.showbizdata.com/contacts/picknews.cfm/35316/COLIN_POWELL_REGISTERS_U.S._COMPLAINTS_ABOUT_AL-JAZEERA).

Lynch, Marc. "Beyond the Arab Street: Iraq and the Arab Public Sphere." *Politics & Society* vol. 31, no. 1 (March 2003).

Lynch, Marc. "Taking Arabs Seriously." *Foreign Affairs* vol. 82, no. 5 (September–October, 2003).

Majmo'at moalifeen. *Al 'Arab wa Al I'lam Al Fadaiy* (Beirut: Markaz Dirasat Al Wihda Al 'Arabia, 2000).

Marlantes, Liz. "The Other Boots on the Ground: Embedded Press." *Christian Science Monitor,* April 23, 2003.

Marlowe, Ann. "Sex, Violence and the Arab Mind." *Salon.com*, June 8, 2004.

Mary O'Connell (Producer). "Spin Till You Win." Radio documentary, Canadian Broadcasting Company, 2004.

Massing, Michael. "Unfit to Print?" *New York Review of Books*, June 24, 2004.

Matar, Jamil. "A Deteriorating Media." *Al Hayat*, August 30, 2004.

McCleary, Capt. T. Special Assistant for Public Affairs to the Joint Chiefs of Staff. Comments in "Embedded Journalists: Is Truth the First Casualty of War?" Panel discussion at School of Communication, American University, April 21, 2003 (http://www.soc.american.edu/main.cfm?pageid=882.).

McEvoy-Levy, S. *American Exceptionalism and US Foreign Policy: Public Diplomacy at the End of the Cold War* (New York, NY: Palgrave, 2001).

Media International Forum. Summary of debate on "Professional Ethics and Responsibilities," in Hungary. Media International Forum bulletin, March 29–April 1, 1996.

Mernissi, Fatema. *Les Sindbads Marocains: Voyage dans le Maroc Civique* (Rabat: Editions Marsam, 2004).

Middle East Online. "Dream TV in Trouble over Program," November 1, 2002 (http://www.meo.tv).

Miracle, Lt. Col. Tammy L. "The Army and Embedded Media." *Military Review*, September–October 2003.

Mitchell, Greg. "15 Stories They've Already Bungled." *Editor and Publisher*, March 27, 2003 (http://www.editorandpublisher.com/eandp/news/ article_display.jsp?vnu_content_id=1850208).

Moran, Michael. "In Defense of Al Jazeera: Attacking the Messenger and our Message at the Same Time." MSNBC, October 18, 2001 (http://www.msnbc.com/news/643471.asp).

Morello, Carol. "Tight Control Marks Coverage of Afghan War; Curbs Exceed Those of Past; Broader Access Is Promised." *Washington Post,* December 7, 2001.

[675]

Moritz, Robert. "Natalie Portman: Every Bit of Good Helps." *Parade,* November 28, 2004.

Morley, Jefferson. "Arab Media Confront 'the New Rules of the Game.'" *Washington Post*, April 9, 2003 (http://www.washingtonpost.com/ ac2/wp-dyn/A64349-2003 Apr9).

Mornings with Paula Zahn. "Arab Television Strongly Condemning Israel for Unleashing Fierce Attacks against Palestinian Targets," CNN, December 5, 2001, Transcript # 120509CN.V74.

Mowlana, H. *Global Information and World Communication: New Frontiers in International Relations* (1997).

Mueller, J. E. *Policy and Opinion in the Gulf War* (1994).

Mulack, G. "Beim Dialog mit dem Islam zum Umdenken aufgefordert." *hib-Meldung of the German Bundestag*, 056/2003 (http://www. bundestag.de/bic/hib/2003/2003_056/01.html).

Murdock, Graham. "Citizens, Consumers and Public Culture," in Michael Skovmand and Kim Christian Schrøder (eds), *Media Cultures: Reappraising Transnational Media* (London: Routledge, 1992).

Murwa, Adeeb. Al *Sahafa Al Arabiya: Nasha'taha wa tataworha* (Beirut: Dar Maktabat Al Hayat, 1961).

Musa, Isam Sulaiman. "Communications Revolution: Repercussions of the Stages of Development of Nationalist Arab Media," in *The Arabs and Satellite Media* (Beirut: Center for Arab Unity Studies, 2004).

Mutz, D. *Impersonal Influence: How Perceptions of Mass Collectives Affect Political Attitudes* (1998).

Nacos, Brigitte, Robert Y. Shapiro and Peirangelo Isernia. *Decision-Making in a Glass House: Mass Media, Public Opinion, and American and European Foreign Policy in the 21st Century* (Rowman and Littlefield Publishers, 2000).

Naff, Alexia. *The Arab Americans* (New York, NY: Chelsea House, 1988).

Napoli, J. and J. Fejeran. "Of Two Minds: US Public Diplomacy and the Middle East," 2004 (http://lass.calumet.purdue.edu/cca/gmj/Submitted Documents/Fall2004/pdf_files/Napoli%20&%20Joshua-Refereed-GMJ-F04.pdf).

Nematt, Salameh. "Colleagues…and Colleagues!" *Al Hayat*, August 19, 2004.

Neslen, Arthur. "Reality Television: Al Jazeera has a Track Record of Accurate Reporting—which is why its Journalists have been Criminalized and its Offices Bombed." *The Guardian*, April 21, 2004.

New Media Consultants. "Media and Telecom Operators: Friends or Foes?" (http://www.un.org/news/press/docs/2003/pil1533).

New York Times. Editorial, July 14, 1993.

Newseum. "The New History Gazette—The History of News" (Freedom Forum, 1997).

Newsom, D. *The Public Dimension of Foreign Policy* (Indiana University Press, 1996).

Nisbet, E. et al. "Public Diplomacy, Television News, and Muslim Opinion." *Press/Politics* vol. 9, no. 2 (2004).

Norris, Pippa, Montague Kern and Marion R. Just. *Framing Terrorism: The News Media, the Government, and the Public* (2003).

Norton, Augustus R. "The New Media: Civic Pluralism and the Slowly Retreating State," in Dale Eickelman and Jon W. Anderson (eds), *New Media in the Muslim World: The Emerging Public Sphere* (Bloomington, IN: Indiana University Press, 1999).

Noujaim, Jehane. "Control Room." Documentary film about Al Jazeera (Artisan Entertainment, DVD released on October 26, 2004).

Nye, J. "Soft Power." *Foreign Policy* 80 (Fall 1990).

Nye, J. "Soft Power: The Means to Success in World Politics," 2004 (http://bcsia.ksg.harvard.edu/BCSIA_content/documents/Joe_Nye_Wielding_Soft_Power.pdf).

O'Reilly, Bill. "Terror TV?" Monday, October 25, 2004. Accessed on October 26, 2004 (http://www. foxnews.com/story/0,2933,136494,00.html).

Osman, Ahmad. "Rude Awakening: Dream Drops Top Talkers." *Transnational Broadcasting Studies* no. 12, Spring/Summer 2004 (http://www.tbsjournal.com).

Page, Benjamin and Robert Y. Shapiro. *The Rational Public: Fifty Years of Trends in Americans' Policy Preferences* (1992).

Paul, Christopher and James J. Kim. "Reporters on the Battlefield: The Embedded Press System in Historical Context" (Santa Monica, CA: RAND, National Security Research Division, 2004).

Peterson, P. "Finding America's Voice: A Strategy for Reinvigorating US Public Diplomacy," 2003 (http://www.cfr.org/pdf/public_diplomacy. pdf).

Peterson, P. "Public Diplomacy and the War on Terrorism." *Foreign Affairs* vol. 81, no. 5 (2002).

Pew Research Center for People and the Press. "Views of a Changing World: 2003 War with Iraq Further Divides Global Publics," 2003 (http://people-press.org/reports/display.php3?ReportID=185).

Pew Research Center for the People and the Press. "Iraq Prison Scandal Hits Home, but Most Oppose Troop Pullout," May 12, 2004 (http://people-pres.org/reports/print.pho3?PageID=824).

Pew Research Center for the People and the Press. "Public Wants Neutrality *and* Pro-American Point of View," July 13, 2003 (http://people-pres.org/reports/print.pho3?PageID=721).

Pew Research Center for the People and the Press. "TV Combat Fatigue on the Rise, but 'Embeds' Viewed Favorably," March 28, 2003 (http://people-press.org/reports/display.php3?ReportID=178).

Pool, Ithiela da Sola. *Technologies without Boundaries* (Cambridge, MA: Harvard University Press, 1990).

Potter, E. "Canada and the New Public Diplomacy." *Diplomacy Paper* Issue 81, July 2002 (http://www.clingendael.nl/publications/2002/20020700_cli_paper_dip_issue81.pdf).

Public Broadcasting Service (PBS). "A New Voice," 2004. (http://www.pbs.org/newshour/bb/media/jan-june04/voice_04-15.html#).

Qaju, Mohammad. "War under the Guise of 'Democracy,'" in *Al Baath*, cited in *Mideast Mirror*, May 13, 2003.

Quilty, Jim. "The Politics of Television." *Middle East International*, January 10, 2003, 18.

Rahman, Awatif Abdul. *Dirasat fi Al Sahafa Al Arabiya Al Mu'asira* (Beirut: Al Farabi, 1989).

Ramadan, Tariq. Op-ed essay, *New York Times*, September 1, 2004.

Report by the Secretary-General of the Federation of Arab Journalists to the Federation 9th Conference, Amman (Amman: Publications of the Federation of Arab Journalists, 2004).

Reporters Without Borders. "Journalists Killed," 2003 (http://www.rsf.org/artkilled_2003.php3?id_article=5966).

Reuters. "Arab TV Offers Job to ex-Iraq Information Minister." *Gulf News*, April 30 (2003).

Rodriguez, Rene. "TV News on the Other Side of the World." *Miami Herald*, July 11, 2004.

Rollins, Peter C. "C-SPAN: The White House in Film and TV," January 9, 2004.

Ross, C. "Public Diplomacy Comes of Age." *The Battle for Hearts and Minds* (Washington, D.C: Center for Strategic and International Studies, 2003).

Rotberg, R. I. *From Massacres to Genocide: The Media, Public Policy and Humanitarian Crises* (1996).

[679]

Rugh, William. "Fixing Public Diplomacy for Arab and Muslim Audiences," 2004 [a] (http://www-hoover.stanford.edu/publications/books/fulltext/ practical/ 145.pdf).

Rugh, William. "How Washington Confronts Arab Media." *Global Media Journal* vol. 2, no. 4, 2004 [b] (http://lass.calumet.purdue.edu/cca/gmj/ SubmittedDocuments/Fall2004/invited/rugh.htm).

Rugh, William. *Arab Mass Media: Newspapers, Radio and Television in Arab Politics*, 2004 [c].

Rugh, William. *The Arab Press: News Media and Political Process in the Arab World* (Syracuse, NY: Syracuse University Press, 1987).

Rumsfeld, Donald. Comments made during "The News Hour with Jim Lehrer." PBS Televison (http://www.pbs.org/newshour/media/media-watch/july-dec03/arab_networks). Associated Press report, November 26, 2003 (http://www.newsmax.com/archives/articles/2003/11/25/173813.shtml).

Rumsfeld, Donald. Remarks at the Chicago Council on Foreign Relations, August 6, 2004 (http://usinfo.state.gov/mena/Archive/2004/Aug/09-490718.html).

Rushti, Jihan Ahmed. Al *Ossos Al 'Almiya li Nazariyat Al 'Ilam* (Cairo: Dar Al Fikr Al 'Arabi, 1978).

Sabat, Khalil et al. "The Media," in *The Comprehensive Social Survey of Egyptian Society 1952–1980* (Cairo: Dar Al Ma'arif, 1985).

Sachs, Susan. "A Nation At War: Mideast Coverage; Arab Media Portray War as Killing Field." *New York Times*, April 4, 2003.

Sachs, Susan. "In Arab Media, War is Shown as a Clash of Civilizations." *New York Times*, April 5, 2003.

Safi, Omid. Professor of Religion, Cornell University. Personal interview, October 12, 2004

Said, Edward. *Orientalism* (New York, NY: Pantheon, 1978).

Sakr, Naomi. "Al Jazeera Satellite Channel: Global Newscasting in Arabic," in Chris Paterson and Annabelle Sreberny (eds) *International News in the Twenty-First Century* (London: John Libbey Publishing, 2004).

Sakr, Naomi. "Breaking Down Barriers in Arab Media." *Women International* (http://www.cmfmena.org/magazine/features/Nieman_Sakr_Winter01. pdf).

Sakr, Naomi. *Satellite Realms: Transnational Television, Globalization and the Middle East* (London: I B Tauris, 2001).

Salam, Mohammed Shukri. "The Communications Revolution and Media." *A'alam Al Fikr* vol. 32, no. 21 (Kuwait: 2003).

Saleem, Jihan. "'Awlamat Al Thaghafa wa Istratigiyat Al Ta'amul ma'ha fi Zil Al 'Awlama," in *Al Thaghafa Al Arabia: as'lat Al Tatawor wa Al Mustagbal*, by a group of authors (Beirut: Markaz Dirasat Al Wihda Al 'Arabia).

Salhi, Hamoud. "The Political & Social Impact of Information Technology in the Gulf States" (http://nmit.georgetown.edu/papers/hsalhi.htm).

Sbeihi, Ahmed Shukr. *Future of Civil Society in the Arab World* (Beirut, Center for Arab Unity Studies, 2000).

Schemm, Paul. "Outrage in Sinai." *Middle East International* no. 736, October 22, 2004.

Schlageter, R. "Public Diplomacy." *Diplomatisches Magazin* no. 4, 2005.

Schleifer, S. Abdullah. "Al Jazeera Update: More Datelines from Doha and a Code of Ethics." *Transnational Broadcasting Studies* no. 13, Fall 2004 (http://www.tbsjournal.com).

Schleifer, S. Abdullah. "Interview with Ali Al Hedeithy." *Transnational Broadcasting Studies* no. 9, Fall/Winter 2002 (http://www. tbsjournal.com).

Schleifer, S. Abdullah. "Interview with Salah Negm, Head of News Al Arabiya." *Transnational Broadcasting Studies* no. 9, Fall/Winter 2002 (http://www. tbsjournal.com).

[681]

Schleifer, S. Abdullah. "Interview with Saleh Negm." *Transnational Broadcasting Studies* no. 10, Spring/Summer 2003 (http://www.tbsjournal.com).

Schleifer, S. Abdullah. "Media Explosion in the Arab World: The Pan-Arab Satellite Broadcasters." *Transnational Broadcasting Studies* no. 1, Fall 1998 (http://www.tbsjournal.com).

Sebba, Anne. *Battling for News: The Rise of the Woman Reporter* (London: Hodder & Stoughton, 1994).

Selber, Gregory Mendel and Salma Ghanem. "Modernization and Media in the Arab World." *Global Media Journal* (Fall 2004).

Several co-authors. Al *'Arab wa Al 'Ilaam Al Fada'iyi* (Beirut: Markaz Dirasat Al Wihda Al 'Arabiya, 2004).

Shadid, Anthony. "Rivalry for Eyes of Arab World: New TV Station takes on Al Jazeera." *The Washington Post,* February 11, 2003.

Shafiq, Munir. Report in the Jordanian daily *Al Ra'I,* cited in "How not to Mould Arab Opinion." *Mideast Mirror*, February 2, 2004.

Shaheen, Jack G. *Reel Bad Arabs: How Hollywood Vilifies a People* (Northampton, MA: Interlink, 2001).

Shaheen, Jack G. "Arab Americans," in Peter C. Rollins, *The Columbia Companion To American Film and History (*Columbia University Press, 2004).

Shaheen, Jack G. "The Media's Image of Arabs." *Newsweek*, February 29, 1988.

Shaheen, Jack G. *The TV Arab* (Bowling Green, OH: Popular Press, 1984).

Shahid, Anthony. "Rivalry for Eyes of Arab World." *Washington Post*, February 11, 2003.

Shanker, Thom. "Pop Culture Alive and Well in Iraq." *International Herald Tribune*, April 13, 2004.

Shapiro, Samantha M. "The War Inside the Arab Newsroom." *The New York Times Magazine*, January 2, 2005.

[682]

Shehab, Shaden. "Dream's Wake-up Call?" *Al Ahram Weekly* no. 611, November 7–13, 2002.

Shepard, Alicia C. "Narrowing the Gap: Military, Media and the Iraq War." (Chicago, IL: Robert F. McCormick Tribune Foundation, 2003.

Sherry, Ricchiardi. "Close to the Action." *American Journalism Review*, May 2003 (http://ajr.org/Article.asp?id=2991).

Sherwin, Adam and Ian McKinnon. "Arafat and Gaddafi sing the praises of Arab Pop Idols." *The Times* (London) online, August 23, 2004 (http://www.timesonline.co.uk).

Shteiwi, Musa. "New Spaces Created by Satellite TV and the Internet." Paper presented at the conference on Women's Movement and Civil Society in the Arab World, House of World Cultures, Berlin, Germany, April 25–26, 2003.

Shuman, Muhammad. "'Awlamat Al 'Ialam wa Mustaqbal Al A'lam Al 'Arabi." *'Aalam Al Fikr* vol. 82, no. 2 (Kuwait: October–December, 1999).

Smith, Russell. "The New Newspeak." *New York Review of Books*, May 29, 2003.

Sobel, Richard. *The Impact of Public Opinion on US Foreign Policy Since Vietnam: Constraining the Colossus* (2001).

Soroka, Stuart. "Media, Public Opinion, and Foreign Policy" (2003).

Spitzer, Robert (ed.) *Media and Public Policy* (1992).

Strobel, Warren. *Late Breaking Foreign Policy* (1997).

Survey Research Institute, Cornell University. "Restrictions on Civil Liberties, Views of Islam and Muslim Americans, US War on Terror, US Foreign Policy, and Anti-Americanism." James Shanahan, principal investigator. Poll released on December 17, 2004 (http://www.news.cornell.edu/releases/Dec04/Muslim.Poll.bpf.html).

Taggart, Will. "The Digital Revolt: Resistance and Agency on the Net." Adapted from a paper delivered at a symposium on "Indigenous Cyber-Activism and Virtual Diasporas Over the World Wide Web," Guthenburg, Sweden, June 2001 (http://nmit.georgetown.edu/papers/wtaggert.htm).

Taylor, P. M. *Global Communication, International Affairs and the Media Since 1945* (1997).

Tehranian, M. *Global Communication and World Politics: Domination, Development, and Discourse* (1999).

Telhami, Shibley. "Finding the Right Media for the Message in the Middle East." Transcript of testimony before the Senate Foreign Relations Committee, April 29, 2004.

Thatcher, G. "Interview about Middle East Radio Network." *PBS Online Newshour*, January 16, 2002 (http://www.pbs.org/newshour/media/public_diplomacy/thatcher.html).

The Daily Star. "France May Sanction Al Manar," December 11, 2004.

The Economist. "All that Jazeera," June 21, 2003.

The Gallup Organization. "Media Use and Evaluation" (www.gallup.com/poll/content/print.aspx?ci=1663)

The Project for Excellence in Journalism & the Committee of Concerned Journalists. "Embedded Journalists: What Are Americans Getting?" March 22, 2003 (http://www.journalism.org/resources/research/reports/war/embed/impressions.asp).

Theoharis, Nathan. *Chasing Spies* (Chicago, IL: publisher Ivan R. Dee, 2002).

Thussu, D.K. *International Communication—Continuity and Change* (London: Arnold, 2000).

Tomlinson, Kenneth. "Al Hurra Disseminates Information to Arab-Speaking World." *Richmond Times Dispatch*, Virginia, September 20, 2004.

Tomlinson, Kenneth. "American Public Diplomacy in the Islamic World." Testimony Before the Committee on Foreign Relations, February 27, 2003 (http://www.iwar.org.uk/psyops/resources/public-diplomacy/Tomlinson Testimony030227.pdf).

Toplin, Robert Brent. "An Anatomy of the Genre." *Cineaste,* Spring 2004.

Tuch, H. *Communicating with the World: US Public Diplomacy Overseas* (New York, NY: St. Martin's Press, 1990).

Turan, Kenneth. "Who are you Going to Believe?" *The Los Angeles Times*, October 31, 2004.

Tuwainy, Ghassan. "Jara'id Al Amas wa Al Yom" (Beirut: Dar Al Nahar, August 4, 1971, special issue).

Tuwainy, Ghassan. "Sahafat Al Huriya wa Al Haqiqa," in Al *Sahafa Al Siyasiya wa Al Iqtisadiya fi Libnan* (Dubai: Lebanese Consulate General in Dubai, special issue, 1994).

Tuwainy, Jibran. "Al Sahafa wa kaif Akhdom biha Baladi." Lecture at Al 'Orwatu Al Wothga Society, American University of Beirut, 1938. Quoted in Ghassan Tuwainy, "Sir Al Mihna wa Osolaha." *Al Nahar* series, Kitabu Al Tis'iynyat (Beirut: Dar Al Nahar, 1990).

UNDP. "Towards Freedom in the Arab World," *Arab Human Development Report 2004* (Amman: Al Matba'a Al Wataniya, 2005).

UNDP. *Arab Human Development Report 2002.*

UNDP. "Towards Establishing a Knowledge-based Society in Arab States." *Arab Human Development Report 2003* (Amman: Al Matba'a Al Wataniya, 2003).

USINFO. "US Image in the Islamic World: "Policy" is the Problem." 2002 (http://usinfo.state.gov/admin/005/wwwh21126.html).

Washington Times. "Al Arabiya Seeks Media Niche," October 1, 2003.

Whitaker, Brian. "Battle Station." *The Guardian*, February 7, 2003.

[685]

Whitaker, Brian, "Another Rule for the Arabs." *The Guardian*, January 12, 2004.

Whitman, Bryan. "The Birth of Embedding as Pentagon War Policy," in Bill Katovsky and Timothy Carlson (eds), *Embedded: The Media at War in Iraq* (Guilford, CT: Lyons Press, 2003).

Wijk, R. "The Limits of Military Power." *The Washington Quarterly* vol. 25, no. 1 (2002).

Wilson, George C. Comment aired on "The Media's War." *MacNeil/Lehrer News Hour*, April 21, 2003 (via Lexis-Nexis news archive).

Winseck, Dwayne. "Gulf War in the Global Village: CNN, Democracy and the Information Age," in Janet Wasko and Vincent Mosco (eds) *Democratic Communications in the Information Age* (Toronto: Garamond Press, 1992).

Wittkopf, E. and James M. McCormick (eds). *The Domestic Sources of American Foreign Policy: Insights and Evidence* (Rowman and Littlefield Publishers, 1998).

World Electronic Media Forum Roundtable Discussion. *Freedom and Media Landscape in Arab World* (http://www.un.org/news/press/docs/2003).

World Net Daily. "Arab Media Slammed over War Coverage," April 7, 2003 (http://www worldnetdaily.com).

Yassin, Al Saiyd. *Al Ma'lomatiya wa Hadarat Al 'Awlama: Ru'iya Naghadia 'Arabia* (Cairo: Nahdat Misr lil Al Tiba'a wa Al Nashr wa Al Tawzi'i, 2001).

Zaharna, R. "American Public Diplomacy and Islam." Testimony before Senate Foreign Relations Committee, 2003 (http://foreign.senate.gov/hearings/ZaharnaTestimony030227.pdf).

Zaharna, R. "American Public Diplomacy and the Arab and Muslim Worlds: A Strategic Communication Analysis," 2001 (http://www.fpif.org/papers/communication.html).

Zaharna, R. "Finding America's Voice in the Middle East." 2002 (http://www.fpif.org/commentary/2002/0204usmideast.html).

Zakaria, Fareed. *The Future of Freedom* (W.W. Norton, 2003).

Zecchinelli, Cecilia. "News War Heats up between Rival Arab Satcasters." *Variety*, May 10–16 (2004).

Zelizer, Barbie and Stuart Allan (eds) *Journalism after September 11* (Routledge, 2003).

Zev, Chafets. "Al Jazeera Unmasked: An Arab Propaganda Machine in the Guise of Real Journalism." *Daily News,* New York, October 14, 2001.

Zinsser, William. "In Search of Lawrence of Arabia." *Esquire*, June 1961.

Zogby, James. "Don't blame Arab Media" (http://www.reclaimthemedia.org/stories.php?story= 04/08/18).

Zogby, James. "The Public Diplomacy Debate Again." Arab American Institute, February 2, 2004.

Zukor, Adolph. "Most Important Events of the Year." *Wid's Year Book*, 1918.

[694]

public domination motive 140,
174
state control of 34, 569, 586,
587, 588
traditional media as
"cheerleader" 126, 133, 155
US suppression demands 38, 42
military vs. royal orders 552
social discussion ban 90
see also authoritarian regimes
Grenada, US war in 390
Guantanamo Bay 350
The Guardian 266, 466
Gulf War (1990–91)
Arab media turning point 174
Arab public opposition 174
CNN dominance 42
and satellite development 36, 159,
582
United States
advertisers' stance 64
media credibility 415
media restrictions 389, 392,
395, 399, 408
Pentagon "spin" 392
wooing of US public 256–7

H
hajj 73
Hariri, Rafiq 77, 78, 79, 83, 84
Heritage Foundation 273
Hezbollah party 261
Hi magazine 158
Hollywood
Arab actors' blacklist 341
and Arab Americans 338–41
female executives 353
need for Arab presence 351–2, 355
non-Arab minority films 355, 356
vilification of Arabs 326, 328
Holy Month of Ramadan 46–7
Hudson Institute 272
human rights 190, 503

Human Rights Watch 451, 452–3
Hussein, Saddam 175, 268, 306
capture of 463
"hidden war" of 378
Oil-for-Food scandal 273–4, 276
tapes broadcast 76, 227
Hussein, Uday 457, 458, 459–60, 478

I
illiteracy
Arab numbers 559–60
and traditional media 126
and TV growth 484
vs newspaper growth 501, 559
Ina Television 444
The Independent 234
India, film production 156–7
Information Age 133, 183
Information Revolution
and "modern Arab media" 121
as transnational space 232–3
information technology (IT) 21, 32, 33
instant messaging 195
intelligentsia 30
Interim Iraqi Government (IIG)
Al Jazeera ban 456
media control 432, 469–70
Internet, Arab World
anonymity of 128–9, 181
and Arab diaspora 32
Arabization of 193–5, 196
broadband connection 187, 196
cost of access 177–8, 195–6
effect on women 127–30
"electronic freedom" 180–1, 182
first connections 175–6
and governments
censorship of 134, 178, 180,
196, 197
effect of 130, 179–80
propaganda websites 178
and media centralization 45
negative aspects 181